ENGAGING THE
DOCTRINE
OF THE HOLY SPIRIT

*Love and Gift
in the Trinity and the Church*

MATTHEW LEVERING

Baker Academic

a division of Baker Publishing Group
Grand Rapids, Michigan

Published by Baker Academic
a division of Baker Publishing Group
P.O. Box 6287, Grand Rapids, MI 49516-6287
www.bakeracademic.com

Printed in the United States of America

Library of Congress Cataloging-in-Publication Data
Names: Levering, Matthew, 1971– author.
Title: Engaging the doctrine of the Holy Spirit : love and gift in the Trinity and the church / Matthew Levering.
Description: Grand Rapids : Baker Academic, 2016. | Includes bibliographical references and index.
Identifiers: LCCN 2015051496 | ISBN 9780801049927 (cloth)
Subjects: LCSH: Holy Spirit—History of doctrines.
Classification: LCC BT119 .L48 2016 | DDC 231/.3—dc23
LC record available at http://lccn.loc.gov/2015051496

16 17 18 19 20 21 22   7 6 5 4 3 2 1

In keeping with biblical principles of creation stewardship, Baker Publishing Group advocates the responsible use of our natural resources. As a member of the Green Press Initiative, our company uses recycled paper when possible. The text paper of this book is composed in part of post-consumer waste.

To Gilles Emery, OP,
and Bruce Marshall

Contents

Acknowledgments

This book originated in thinking about two interrelated issues: first, the work of the Holy Spirit in guiding the church, an issue that came to the fore in my research on Mary's Assumption and on the church's mediation of divine revelation; and second, the holiness of the church, an issue that particularly took shape for me through Ephraim Radner's extraordinary book on the topic. It also originated in a powerful experience of the Holy Spirit during a moment of decision in the spring of 2010. I long for an intimate relationship with Jesus Christ through the Holy Spirit, both because I want to live a life of charity now and because I want to be prepared for passing from this life rather than dying in isolation and fear. I would like to know God intimately now, and not just be a student of a God whose presence I ward off.

In preparing this book, I was blessed to participate in two superb ecumenical conferences. Part of chapter 7, in an earlier version, was delivered at the invitation of Tal Howard and Mark Noll, at their conference "Protestantism? Reflections in Advance of the 500th Anniversary of the Protestant Reformation, 1517–2017," sponsored by the Center for Faith and Inquiry at Gordon College; my paper will appear in a forthcoming volume edited by Tal and Mark for Oxford University Press. An attendee at the conference, Ferde Rombola, saved me from a significant error in my paper. Part of chapter 3, in an earlier version, was delivered at Wheaton College's conference "The Spirit of God: Christian Renewal in the Community of Faith," at the invitation of Jeffrey Barbeau and Beth Felker Jones: see my "Rationalism or Revelation? St. Thomas Aquinas and the *Filioque*," in *Spirit of God: Christian Renewal in the Community of Faith*, ed. Jeffrey W. Barbeau and Beth Felker Jones (Downers Grove, IL: IVP Academic, 2015), 59–73. The palpable Christian faith at both Gordon and Wheaton was deeply inspiring. An earlier version of chapter 1 was published at the invitation of Daniel Castelo in a special issue of the *International Journal of Systematic Theology* (16 [2014]: 126–42) under the title "The Holy Spirit in the Trinitarian Communion: 'Love' and 'Gift'?"

This book would not have been written without the support of Dave Nelson, my editor at Baker Academic. Dave is both a master editor and a significant theological scholar in his own right. Similarly, I could not have written the book without Jim and Molly Perry, who, at the invitation of the now-Bishop Robert Barron, endowed the chair at Mundelein Seminary that I gratefully hold. My academic dean, Fr. Thomas Baima, made possible the appointment of David Augustine, a brilliant young theologian, as my research assistant. David helped me with obtaining books and articles, and he put together the bibliography and indexes. Even more important has been the wonderful friendship that he has given me. After I had drafted the book, I received superb corrections and criticisms on the whole manuscript from Alexander Pierce, who is currently completing a master's degree at Trinity Evangelical Divinity School. Comments on chapters 1–5 were given with typical grace, charm, and depth by Fr. Robert Imbelli, who first taught me the doctrine of the Holy Spirit in a doctoral course on that topic at Boston College. I owe him double thanks! Other expert theologians generously read the manuscript, in whole or in part, and made crucial corrections: Gilles Emery, OP, Bruce Marshall, Daniel Keating, Ken Loyer, and Dominic Langevin, OP. I am deeply grateful for their friendship and help. Let me also thank Brian Bolger and the editorial team at Baker Academic, who did an excellent job on the production of this book. I should note that throughout this book I employ the Revised Standard Version, Catholic Edition (Camden, NJ: Thomas Nelson & Sons, 1966; reprinted by Ignatius Press), unless noted otherwise.

To my beautiful wife, Joy: what a gift you are to me and to our beloved children, extended family, and friends. You exemplify the truth that "the fruit of the Spirit is love, joy, peace, patience, kindness, goodness, faithfulness, gentleness, self-control" (Gal. 5:22–23). May God the Father unite you ever closer to the love of Jesus Christ in the Holy Spirit, and may the work of your hands be blessed.

In the labor of theology, the study of what God has revealed for our salvation, we need masters who know well that we "have one master, the Christ" (Matt. 23:10). St. Thomas Aquinas is a master in Christ, and his insights have come to me through friends who are also master teachers. It is to two such learned and devout friends, Gilles Emery and Bruce Marshall, that I dedicate this book.

Introduction

Graham Tomlin has remarked that "today we need not just a theology *of* the Holy Spirit, but theology done *in* the Holy Spirit. Theology in the Spirit has to be theology done close to the community of the Spirit, the temple of God, the body of Christ in which the Spirit chooses to make Christ known."[1] This requires not only theology done by a Christian who shares in the life and worship of the church but also theology done with the great "cloud of witnesses" (Heb. 12:1) and with "all the saints" (1 Cor. 13:13), especially those whose teachings on the Holy Spirit, guided by the scriptural word, have informed the ways in which the church praises the Spirit.[2] Yet, Christians have disagreed and continue to disagree about the Holy Spirit's person and work. How then should a trinitarian theology of and in the Holy Spirit, whose aim is to contribute to understanding the Spirit found in "the body of Christ in which the Spirit chooses to make Christ known," proceed?[3]

1. Graham Tomlin, *The Prodigal Spirit: The Trinity, the Church and the Future of the World* (London: Alpha International, 2011), 11.

2. As David F. Ford states, "Much growth in wisdom in the Spirit comes through how we *re-read*, how we go back again and again to rich texts and slowly enter their depths" (Ford, "In the Spirit: Learning Wisdom, Giving Signs," in *The Holy Spirit in the World Today*, ed. Jane Williams [London: Alpha International, 2011], 42–63, at 49–50).

3. A theology of the Holy Spirit requires the full dimensions of trinitarian theology: as Kenneth Loyer states, "the proper basis of pneumatology is the doctrine of the Trinity" (Loyer, *God's Love through the Spirit: The Holy Spirit in Thomas Aquinas and John Wesley* [Washington, DC: Catholic University of America Press, 2014], 70). The present book is focused upon the person and work of the Spirit. For further Thomistic exploration of the doctrine of the Trinity, with respect to themes that are not the focus of this book, see my *Scripture and Metaphysics: Aquinas and the Renewal of Trinitarian Theology* (Oxford: Blackwell, 2004); Gilles Emery, OP, *La Trinité créatrice: Trinité et Création dans les commentaires aux Sentences de Thomas d'Aquin et de ses précurseurs Albert le Grand et Bonaventure* (Paris: Vrin, 1995); Hans Christian Schmidbaur,

I argue in this book that the Holy Spirit should be praised and contemplated under the proper names "Love" and "Gift," with respect both to his intra-trinitarian identity and to his historical work in Jesus Christ and the church.[4] These names of the Spirit, of course, find their first exponent in Augustine, influenced especially by Hilary of Poitiers. The names "Love" and "Gift" have for centuries been a linchpin of Western pneumatology, Catholic and Protestant, and they have also found their way, to a certain degree, into Greek Orthodox pneumatology. Thus the contemporary Orthodox theologian Boris Bobrinskoy describes the Holy Spirit as "the mutual love and the bond of love between the Father and the Son" and "the *common* gift of the Father and the Son," although Bobrinskoy distinguishes his position from that of Augustine by emphasizing that *each* person "gathers together and unites the others in himself" and that the Spirit gives himself (and gives the other persons) *to us*.[5]

Personarum Trinitas: Die trinitarische Gotteslehre des heiligen Thomas von Aquin (St. Ottilien: EOS Verlag, 1995); Paul Vanier, *Théologie trinitaire chez saint Thomas d'Aquin: Evolution du concept d'action notionnelle* (Paris: Vrin, 1953). See also Leo Scheffczyk, "Die Trinitätslehre des Thomas von Aquin im Spiegel gegenwärtiger Kritik," *Studi Tomistici* 59 (1995): 163–90.

4. See Bruce D. Marshall, "The Deep Things of God: Trinitarian Pneumatology," in *The Oxford Handbook of the Trinity*, ed. Gilles Emery, OP, and Matthew Levering (Oxford: Oxford University Press, 2011), 400–12, at 401. Indebted to Augustine, Marshall suggests that only the Spirit's "eternal origination as gift and love . . . is enough to ground his scripturally described temporal mission as gift of the Father and Son to creatures, and as their love for creatures" (ibid., 405). Since the names "Love" and "Gift" are analogical, not metaphorical, I differ from Elaine M. Wainwright, who in her consideration of trinitarian naming emphasizes "the *metaphoric nature of the task of naming or imagining the Divine*. All such attempts will be like a finger pointing toward the one who is beyond all our imagining but whose naming in our theologizing is limited to human language. G*d is always beyond our naming and imaging, hence the significance of the richness of our imagery as we strain toward divinity. Within the New Testament, the images of G*d and of Jesus are multiple. Focus on 'father,' 'son,' and 'spirit,' names or images which were drawn into later trinitarian theologizing, must be placed, therefore, within the context of this multitude of images and metaphors" (Wainwright, "Like a Finger Pointing to the Moon: Exploring the Trinity and/in the New Testament," in *The Cambridge Companion to the Trinity*, ed. Peter C. Phan [Cambridge: Cambridge University Press, 2011], 33–47, at 34). See also Nonna Verna Harrison's "The Trinity and Feminism," in Emery and Levering, *The Oxford Handbook of the Trinity*, 519–28.

5. Boris Bobrinskoy, "The *Filioque* Yesterday and Today," in *Spirit of God, Spirit of Christ: Ecumenical Reflections on the* Filioque *Controversy*, ed. Lukas Vischer (London: SPCK, 1981), 133–48, at 142. For the direct influence of Augustine's trinitarian theology upon Gregory Palamas, see Reinhard Flogaus, "Inspiration—Exploitation—Distortion: The Use of St. Augustine in the Hesychast Controversy," in *Orthodox Readings of Augustine*, ed. George Demacopoulos and Aristotle Papanikolaou (Crestwood, NY: St. Vladimir's Seminary Press, 2008), 63–80, esp. 77. Flogaus defends his previous research on this topic against the criticism of such scholars as Jeremy Wilkins and Joseph Lössl, SJ: see Wilkins, "'The Image of This Highest Love': The Trinitarian Analogy in Gregory Palamas' *Capita 150*," *St. Vladimir's Theological Quarterly* 47 (2003): 383–412; Lössl, "Augustine's 'On the Trinity' in Gregory Palamas' 'One Hundred and Fifty Chapters,'" *Augustinian Studies* 30 (1999): 69–81; Lössl, "Augustine in Byzantium," *Journal of Ecclesiastical History* 51 (2000): 267–95.

Today, however, many biblical scholars and theologians in the West have concerns about naming the Holy Spirit as "Love" and "Gift," concerns that go beyond the intrinsic mystery of trinitarian naming. For example, biblical scholars often deny that the "Spirit" was a distinct divine subject for the first Christians.[6] Going further, Paula Fredriksen underscores "the turbulence of Christianity's first four centuries" and argues that Christian doctrine in the fourth century is related only by the barest threads to the biblical testimony.[7] Theologians, while generally affirming the Spirit's divinity, often assume that names of the Spirit can be only metaphorical, rather than proper names. Thus Jürgen Moltmann holds that Christian experience of the Spirit makes it possible to name the Spirit metaphorically—he proposes the metaphors "lord," "mother," "judge," "energy," "space," "Gestalt," "tempest," "fire," "love," "light," "water," and "fertility"—but he does not think that the Spirit can be given a *proper* name (other than "Holy Spirit") in the way required by the specificity of "Love" and "Gift."[8] This is so even though Moltmann ends up at a definition of the Spirit's personhood that fits with the traditional emphasis

6. Larry W. Hurtado, although not opposed to later trinitarian developments, argues that the first Christians were "binitarian" in their devotional practice: see Hurtado, *Lord Jesus Christ: Devotion to Jesus Christ in Earliest Christianity* (Grand Rapids: Eerdmans, 2003), 651. Along similar lines—while disagreeing with Hurtado's view that the first Christians worshiped Jesus—James D. G. Dunn points out that "the Spirit was from the beginning a way of speaking of God's life-giving action in creating humankind (Gen. 2.7), of God's presence throughout the cosmos (Ps. 139.7). So the Spirit of God was, like Wisdom and Word, a way of speaking of the divine immanence" (Dunn, *Did the First Christians Worship Jesus? The New Testament Evidence* [Louisville: Westminster John Knox, 2010], 125–26).

7. Paula Fredriksen, *Sin: The Early History of an Idea* (Princeton, NJ: Princeton University Press, 2012), 1. For a much different view of doctrinal development, see Gilles Emery, OP, *The Trinity: An Introduction to Catholic Doctrine on the Triune God*, trans. Matthew Levering (Washington, DC: Catholic University of America, 2011), chap. 1. See also, for a christological emphasis, Kathryn Tanner, "The Trinity as Christian Teaching," in Emery and Levering, *The Oxford Handbook of the Trinity*, 349–57.

8. Jürgen Moltmann, *The Spirit of Life: A Universal Affirmation*, trans. Margaret Kohl (Minneapolis: Fortress, 1992), 269–85. Moltmann explains the limits and value of his metaphorical approach to the Spirit's personhood, whose reality he grounds in Christian experience:
> This is only a deductive knowing, derived from the operation experienced, not a direct knowing face to face. But neither is it a speculative intrusion into the depths of the triune Deity in an attempt to understand the primordial relationships of the Spirit who proceeds from the Father and radiates from the Son. In the primordial trinitarian relationships, the Spirit must appear simply as he is. There, it is of course true that only the Father knows the Spirit whom he breathes out, and only the Son knows the Spirit whom he receives. But in the efficacies experienced and in the energies perceived, this primal personhood of the Spirit is concealed from us, and we paraphrase the mystery of his life with many metaphors. And yet the operation of the Spirit is different from the acts in creation which we ascribe to the Father, and different from the reconciling sufferings which we ascribe to the Son; and from this difference in kind of his efficacy and his energies, the unique character of his personhood is revealed. (ibid., 285)

on love and gift: "The personhood of God the Holy Spirit is the loving, self-communicating, out-fanning and out-pouring presence of the eternal divine life of the triune God."[9]

Ephraim Radner criticizes the names "Love" and "Gift" more directly. Convinced that to name the Spirit "Love" is generally "a bad idea," he suggests that Augustine's "conceptualization of the Spirit as 'this' or 'that'—love, grace, copula, *vinculum*—establishes within the Western tradition a principle of pneumatic abstraction, capable in theory of being decoupled from Christian particularities."[10] This concern about "abstraction" appears in a different way in the work of Sinclair Ferguson. While conceding that in a "general sense" the Spirit is "the bond of love" between the Father and Son, Ferguson remarks approvingly that "contemporary Protestant Christianity tends to be impatient with subtle theological questions and distinctions such

---

In the first chapter of his book, Moltmann offers a lengthy defense of taking Christian experience as his starting point.

9. Ibid., 289.

10. Ephraim Radner, "The Holy Spirit and Unity: Getting Out of the Way of Christ," *International Journal of Systematic Theology* 16 (2014): 207–20, at 209. See also Louis Bouyer's largely historical study, in which he argues (much like Yves Congar) that the Baroque period ushered in a long-lasting eclipse of the Holy Spirit, so that Léon Bloy was right to argue that the church betrayed the Spirit: Bouyer, *Le Consolateur: Esprit-Saint et vie de grace* (Paris: Cerf, 1980). Bouyer offers a deeply critical reading of Thomistic presentations of the Spirit: see ibid., 421–24. Similarly, Bradford E. Hinze argues that "neoscholastic incarnational ecclesiologies and their variations in mystical body ecclesiologies could be alert to the supporting role of the Spirit, but only within the restrictive limits established by the institutional and hierarchical concerns that predominated in the late nineteenth and early twentieth centuries" (Hinze, "Releasing the Power of the Spirit in a Trinitarian Ecclesiology," in *Advents of the Spirit: An Introduction to the Current Study of Pneumatology*, ed. Bradford E. Hinze and D. Lyle Dabney [Milwaukee: Marquette University Press, 2001], 347–81). Hinze credits Yves Congar, Karl Rahner, and Heribert Mühlen for retrieving the doctrine of the Holy Spirit in the mid-twentieth century. As examples of earlier authors who restricted the doctrine of the Holy Spirit, he mentions Johann Adam Möhler (in his later work), Cardinal Henry Edward Manning, Pope Leo XIII's encyclical *Divinum illud* (1897), Sebastian Tromp, Emile Mersch, and Charles Journet. In my view, these authors and earlier post-Tridentine figures merit a reassessment, now that the battles of the 1940s and 1950s are no longer fresh. For Hinze, the ecclesiologies of Henri de Lubac, Hans Urs von Balthasar, and Joseph Ratzinger represent a step back to a christocentric and incarnational vision of the church. Without agreeing with his critique of their ecclesiologies, I agree with his judgment "that neither christomonist nor pneumatomonist ecclesiologies suffice" (ibid., 367). See also Hinze's "The Holy Spirit and the Catholic Tradition: The Legacy of Johann Adam Möhler," in *The Legacy of the Tübingen School: The Relevance of Nineteenth Century Theology for the Twentieth Century*, ed. Donald J. Dietrich and Michael J. Himes (New York: Crossroad, 1997), 75–94. For cogent doubts regarding whether the twentieth century actually witnessed a trinitarian renewal or renaissance vis-à-vis earlier centuries, as Bouyer and many others think, see Bruce D. Marshall, "Trinity," in *The Blackwell Companion to Modern Theology*, ed. Gareth Jones (Oxford: Blackwell, 2004), 183–203 (esp. his quotations from the neoscholastic manualists Johann Baptist Franzelin and Riccardo Tabarelli).

as this [the *filioque*]."[11] Instead, Ferguson approaches the Spirit biblically as the Paraclete, the Spirit of Christ, the Spirit of truth, the eschatological Spirit, the Spirit of new creation and renewal, the life-giving Spirit, the Spirit of order and unity, the Spirit as bestowing divine gifts (such as faith), and the Spirit of holiness, and the Spirit of intercession and communion. Ferguson finds these biblical depictions of the Spirit to suffice on their own. To give a final example, Steven Studebaker considers that "the result of relying on the processions of the divine persons as the source of their personal identities is to conceive of the Spirit in derivative and passive terms."[12] For Studebaker, to name the Holy Spirit "Love" and "Gift" is to consign the Spirit to the status of a passive, less-than-personal fruit of the activity of the Father and Son, so that the Spirit is fatally subordinated to the Father and Son.

By contrast, I argue in this book that, without compromising the divine incomprehensibility, the names "Love" and "Gift" instruct us about the distinct divine personality of the Spirit and shed light upon the biblical, liturgical, and experiential testimonies to the Spirit's missions. In his 1986 encyclical on the Holy Spirit, *Dominum et vivificantem*, Pope John Paul II emphasizes that the Holy Spirit is "he who is the love of the Father and of the Son, he who is gift."[13]

11. Sinclair B. Ferguson, *The Holy Spirit* (Downers Grove, IL: InterVarsity, 1996), 74, 77.

12. Steven M. Studebaker, *From Pentecost to the Triune God: A Pentecostal Trinitarian Theology* (Grand Rapids: Eerdmans, 2012), 116. Studebaker bemoans the fact that "christological emphases still dominate Trinitarian theology," and he argues that "the doctrine of the *filioque* overlooks the biblical data that portrays the Holy Spirit involved as much in constituting the Son as the Son is in sending the Spirit: e.g., conception, baptism, empowerment in temptation and ministry, and raising Christ from the dead" (ibid., 120). I take up this basic concern later in this introduction in relation to the work of Thomas Weinandy and Sarah Coakley. For Studebaker, as for others whose approaches we will examine, "the Spirit brings to completion the fellowship of the trinitarian God. The Father and the Son are not in communion until the Holy Spirit brings them into loving communion. That is, the identities of the Father and the Son described in John 17 are not realized in the immanent *taxis* 'until' the third stage of the *taxis*—the subsistence of the Holy Spirit" (ibid., 121). He explains, "The unavoidable temporal sound of this description—that is, 'until'—reflects the limitation of human language and does not introduce a temporal sequence into the Godhead any more than does the traditional discussion of the immanent order of the processions of the divine persons" (ibid.). This position undermines the Father's full begetting of the Son; the Father (or quasi-Father) would beget a quasi-Son, who would be completed and made "Son" by the Spirit. Studebaker embraces the implications of his position: "Rather than halting the formation of the identities of the divine persons at the moment of the double procession of the Holy Spirit, I want to expand the dynamic development of the divine persons' identities beyond the processions. . . . More specifically, the activity of the Holy Spirit in the immanent Godhead contributes to the personal identity of not only the Father and the Son, but also of the Holy Spirit" (ibid., 122). He thereby anthropomorphizes the divine persons.

13. Pope John Paul II, *Dominum et vivificantem*, in *The Encyclicals of John Paul II*, ed. J. Michael Miller, CSB (Huntington, IN: Our Sunday Visitor, 2001), 244–302, at §35, p. 268. See also Pope Leo XIII's encyclical *Divinum illud munus*, §9 (www.vatican.va).

Among contemporary theologians, Gilles Emery and Bruce Marshall have prominently defended these names. Drawing upon the biblical and liturgical portraits of the Holy Spirit, Emery states, "The Spirit is, in person, the 'Gift of God Most High,' as the church chants in the hymn *Veni Creator Spiritus*. The Holy Spirit is the Gift of the Father and of the Son in the same manner that he is the Love of the Father and of the Son. The first Gift of God is Love himself."[14] Similarly, Marshall has highlighted the way in which the Holy Spirit "is perfect gift from perfect giver" and possesses "love as a property marking his personal distinction from the Father and the Son."[15]

Should the Father and Son Also Be Named "Love" and "Gift"?

Why, however, should not the other persons of the Trinity also be named Love and Gift? Certainly each of the persons must be fully love, because "God is love" (1 John 4:8).[16] Since this is so, how can we reserve the names "Love" and "Gift" for the Holy Spirit? Indeed, writing from within what John Milbank calls "a voluntarist line of descent which seeks to comprehend the Trinity entirely in terms of the categories of 'will,' 'love,' and 'freedom,'" Hans Urs von Balthasar has argued that kenotic love and gift define the core of each of the divine persons.[17] Thus, regarding the Father's "generation" of the Son,

14. Emery, *Trinity*, 156.

15. Marshall, "Deep Things of God," 404. Graham Tomlin puts it in more popular terms: "There is no other way to know the love of the Father for the Son, the love that lies at the heart of God, the love that lies at the very centre of the universe, that alone can change and transform human hearts, affections and behaviour, than through the Holy Spirit" (Tomlin, *Prodigal Spirit*, 34).

16. R. W. L. Moberly urges theologians not to ignore the christological and epistemological context of 1 John 4. For Moberly, 1 John's point is simply that "one can know that one knows God only if the loving reality of God in Jesus is appropriated and demonstrated"—or, in other words, "the way to know that one knows God is to display that love for the brethren which is not only embodied by Jesus but also mandated by Jesus as the form that the knowledge of God must take" (Moberly, "'Test the Spirits': God, Love, and Critical Discernment in 1 John 4," in *The Holy Spirit and Christian Origins: Essays in Honor of James D. G. Dunn*, ed. Graham N. Stanton, Bruce W. Longenecker, and Stephen C. Barton [Grand Rapids: Eerdmans, 2004], 296–307, at 304–5). Moberly warns against the theological tendency to treat 1 John 4:8, "God is love," as "a freestanding axiom" or "a theoretical definition of deity in terms of a supreme human quality" (ibid., 305). But in my view, Moberly is restricting the range of meanings too narrowly, as though stating that the God of Israel is "love" (in the sense of an infinite, analogous attribute) need be in competition with the revelation of this God in Jesus Christ or with the requirements of discipleship.

17. John Milbank, "The Second Difference," in *The Word Made Strange: Theology, Language, Culture* (Oxford: Blackwell, 1997), 171–93, at 174–75. For important background, see Michele M. Schumacher, *A Trinitarian Anthropology: Adrienne von Speyr and Hans Urs von Balthasar in Dialogue with Thomas Aquinas* (Washington, DC: Catholic University of America Press, 2014),

Balthasar prefers to speak of "the self-giving of the Father to the Son," or of the Father's self-dispossession "in favor of the Son," or of the Son's genera-tion as an "expression" or "act of the Father's love."[18] In begetting the Son, the Father shows himself to be Gift-Love. Although Balthasar identifies the Holy Spirit as "the 'gift' par excellence, the gift of the Father and of the Son and of their reciprocity," in his view the Son too is best construed in terms of gift (and love).[19] Along these lines, Balthasar remarks that the Son "represents the

---

46–63, 323–44, 357–66; Pascal Ide, *Une théologie du don: Le don dans la 'Trilogie' de Hans Urs von Balthasar* (Leuven: Peeters, 2013). Schumacher's work addresses and often bridges gaps between Balthasar's theology (and Adrienne von Speyr's) and Aquinas's, but gaps remain, and at times one must choose between the two perspectives.

18. Hans Urs von Balthasar, *Theo-Logic*, vol. 2, *Truth of God*, trans. Adrian J. Walker (San Francisco: Ignatius, 2004), 136–37, 167. Balthasar appeals to Bonaventure's description of the Son as a "similitudo expressa," as well as to Bonaventure's refusal "to abstract from the love of the Father when considering the procession of the Son" (ibid., 164). For Balthasar, as for Bonaventure, the revelation that God is love requires that God be Trinity, since real love requires "transcendental plurality" (Balthasar, *Theo-Logic*, vol. 3, *The Spirit of Truth*, trans. Graham Harrison [San Francisco: Ignatius, 2005], 217). Indebted to Balthasar, Anne Hunt argues that it is especially the paschal mystery—the mystery of Christ's cross, descent into hell, and resurrection—that displays this "inextricably interconnected" relationship of the missions of the Son and the Spirit (Hunt, "The Trinity through Paschal Eyes," in *Rethinking Trinitarian Theology: Disputed Questions and Contemporary Issues in Trinitarian Theology*, ed. Giulio Maspero and Robert J. Woźniak [London: T&T Clark, 2012], 472–89, at 486). In her view, the paschal mystery shows the error of explicating the Father's begetting of the Son "by way of intelligence. . . . Both processions, from the vantage point of the paschal mystery, are proces-sions of love" (ibid., 488). I would add that surely both processions, from this vantage point, are also wisdom and truth. For the movement from the economy of salvation to the doctrine of the Trinity and back again, see especially Emery, *Trinity*.

19. Balthasar, *Theo-Logic*, vol. 2, *Truth of God*, 156; cf. Balthasar, *Theo-Drama*, vol. 5, *The Last Act*, trans. Graham Harrison (San Francisco: Ignatius, 1998), 83–85 and elsewhere. As Michael Schulz comments (with an eye to Hegel's personalist development of the notion of "substance"):

> Starting with the idea of essential "being-love" Balthasar emphasizes that the productive recognition of the Father is to be understood as love, wherein the selflessness of the recogni-tion and its productivity stand as the centre point, and not the self-reference (*Selbstbezug*) of the Father, who would only find himself through the generation (*Zeugung*) as the knower (*Erkenner*). . . . Balthasar famously defines that loving, productive knowing of the Father as the *ur-kenosis*, as a radical self-emptying, which becomes apparent in the historical gift of self (*Dahingabe*) of the Son through the Father. The Son reveals his identity in his kenosis and self-giving; it is the answer to the Father. The essential recognition and loving is immanent to the Spirit. (Schulz, "The Trinitarian Concept of Essence and Substance," in Maspero and Woźniak, *Rethinking Trinitarian Theology*, 146–76, at 165, 172)

Criticizing scholastic trinitarian theology, Balthasar states,

> If we look from the Scriptures to Scholasticism, we can only wonder at the complete change of intellectual atmosphere. The general Scholastic procedure is to lay down an initial thesis about the impenetrability of the trinitarian mystery but then, in spite of that, to attempt to get to the bottom of the relationships between the unity of the divine essence and the trinity of the hypostases using ever more hairsplitting distinctions. . . .

entire trinitarian love in the form of expression," namely the expression of the Father's self-dispossession or absolute kenosis.[20] From this perspective, "Gift" and "Love" can hardly be *proper* names of the Holy Spirit, since both Father and Son are also best understood as sheer Gift-Love. Or even if they are proper names of the Holy Spirit, they are such insofar as they indicate that the Gift-Love characteristic of the Father and Son finds its "epitome and fruit" in the Spirit.[21]

For his part, Thomas Aquinas gladly affirms that in the economy of salvation at least, "the Son is given . . . from the Father's love."[22] The Trinity is

---

Also astonishing is the fascination exercised by the Augustinian analogue drawn from the human mind, which attains to an explicit self-consciousness (*memoria*) only through projection of itself (*intellectus*) and through affirmation of its self-identity in its image (*voluntas, amor*). (Balthasar, *Theo-Logic*, vol. 2, *Truth of God*, 161)

20. Balthasar, *Theo-Logic*, vol. 2, *Truth of God*, 154. Along similar lines, see also Antonio López, *Gift and the Unity of Being* (Eugene, OR: Cascade, 2014), esp. chaps. 4–6; López, "Eternal Happening: God as an Event of Love," *Communio* 32 (2005): 214–45; Margaret Turek, *Towards a Theology of God the Father: Hans Urs von Balthasar's Theodramatic Approach* (New York: Peter Lang, 2001), 97–154; Gisbert Greshake, "Trinity as 'Communio,'" in Maspero and Woźniak, *Rethinking Trinitarian Theology*, 331–45, at 343–44; David Bentley Hart, *The Beauty of the Infinite: The Aesthetics of Christian Truth* (Grand Rapids: Eerdmans, 2003), 168–87, 260–68. For background to Georg W. F. Hegel's "generalizing of kenosis" and his "speculative chain of kenosis" (166–67) as an influence on Balthasar's perspective, which seeks to invert Hegel's position along lines suggested by Sergius Bulgakov, see Cyril O'Regan, *The Anatomy of Misremembering: Von Balthasar's Response to Philosophical Modernity*, vol. 1, *Hegel* (New York: Crossroad, 2014), 165–69. O'Regan provides a helpful insight into Balthasar's approach:

"Ur-kenosis," which refers to the trinitarian event in which the Father empties himself to give space to the Son, is understood as the ground of the radical kenosis of the incarnation and cross that is the subject of Philippians 2:5–11. Balthasar does not draw attention to Hegelian anticipations. Yet, given his knowledge of Hegel's texts, it is unlikely that he is unaware of Hegel's appeal to kenosis at the level of the Trinity either in the *Phenomenology* (#770), where the Word uttered by the Father represents his emptying, or in the *Lectures on the Philosophy of Religion* (1821 MS, 83), in which Hegel speaks with somewhat of a greater distance from Christianity about the 'self-emptying' (*Selbstablassen*) of the universal and abstract divine. Yet, whatever the degree of anticipation, Hegel fails to grasp that intra-divine kenosis is a relation that is as much constituted by the paternity and filiality as explaining them. (ibid., 229–30)

For Balthasar's strong critique of Hegel in the context of pneumatology, see his *Theo-Logic*, vol. 3, *The Spirit of Truth*, 41–51.

21. Balthasar, *Theo-Logic*, vol. 3, *The Spirit of Truth*, 218. López points out that for Balthasar, unlike Sergius Bulgakov, "there is no kenosis of the Holy Spirit" (López, *Gift and the Unity of Being*, 201n25). López explains, "If the Son is the *reddition* (reciprocation) of the gift, the Holy Spirit is the confirmation of the Father's gift. The third person thus discloses the gratuitous nature of divine *agape*. Because the Holy Spirit is given by the Father, with and through the Son, as the overabundant confirmation of the gift that God is, no other person proceeds from him, nor does he need to 'empty' himself" (ibid., 213). It would seem, however, that "the gratuitous nature of divine *agape*" is also disclosed by the Father (and the Son).

22. Thomas Aquinas, *Summa theologiae* I, q. 38, a. 2, ad 1 (trans. Fathers of the English Dominican Province [Westminster, MD: Christian Classics, 1981]). Note also, in a similar vein,

indeed always a mystery of inexhaustible self-giving love, as revealed in Jesus Christ. But although each person is love, and although the incarnate Son's self-giving love manifests the Father (John 14:9), Aquinas nonetheless holds that the names "Love" and "Gift" *properly* apply in the Trinity only to the Holy Spirit. Likewise, although each person is wise, and although the Spirit expresses the truth of the Father and Son in the economy (John 16:13), only the Son is properly "Word" in the Trinity.[23] As I will discuss in more detail in the chapters that follow, I find Aquinas's approach to biblically and analogously naming the Spirit to be persuasive. The Holy Spirit's names Love and Gift, in conjunction with the Son's name Word, well express the biblical witness to what the Orthodox theologian David Bentley Hart calls "the 'intellect' and 'will'—the Logos and Spirit—of the Father."[24] When Jesus "returned in the power of the Spirit into Galilee" (Luke 4:14), this "power" (the Spirit) was distinctively Love and Gift.

The Plan of the Work

The present book begins with three chapters whose integration will be evident: a chapter on the exegetical path by which Augustine names the Holy Spirit "Love" and "Gift"; a chapter on whether these names are sufficiently cautious

---

Lewis Ayres's remark that "Augustine's trinitarian vision suggests ways of understanding the Father's role as *principium* that penetrates to the heart of what it means to speak of God as love; from eternity the Father gives fully of himself to establish a communion in the Spirit of love" (Ayres, "*Sempiterne Spiritus Donum*: Augustine's Pneumatology and the Metaphysics of Spirit," in Demacopoulos and Papanikolaou, *Orthodox Readings of Augustine*, 127–52, at 150).

23. For Balthasar's exegesis of "Word," "wisdom," and "Spirit" in the Old and New Testaments (as well as in Irenaeus), see his succinct survey in Balthasar, *Theo-Logic*, vol. 2, *Truth of God*, 158–61.

24. Hart, *Beauty of the Infinite*, 270. Gilles Emery helpfully points out that
the idea of the Word and Love cannot be boiled down to the extension of a "psychological analogy," one which leaves the Trinity shut in on itself. To contrast this psychological analogy with the biblical economy is to forget one of its major strengths. The analogy of word and love enables one to disclose the eternal distinctions of the persons, but it also allows us to put the profound personalism of the divine action in the world in the picture. The Father acts through his Word and his Love. The divine persons act in virtue of who they are, to the power of their characteristic properties. Created to the image of God, human beings are inspired by grace to return to the Triune God through faith and charity: through the gift of Son and Holy Spirit, they are conformed to the inmost properties of Word and Love, that is, to the relations which the Word and Love have with the Father. (Emery, *The Trinitarian Theology of Saint Thomas Aquinas*, trans. Francesca Aran Murphy [Oxford: Oxford University Press, 2011], 413–14) (Cf. 416 on the importance of "Love" and "Gift" for displaying the way in which the doctrine of the Trinity in the economy of salvation is bound to the doctrine of the Trinity in itself.)

in their analogical usage; and a chapter on whether the *filioque* implies rationalism. These three chapters focus largely on the Holy Spirit in the eternal
trinitarian communion. The final four chapters address the Holy Spirit as Love
and Gift in the economy of salvation. I examine the Holy Spirit's missions to
Jesus Christ and the church: specifically, the Spirit's indwelling of Jesus and
the manifestation of the Spirit at Jesus's baptism and transfiguration (chap.
4), and the Spirit's missions to and manifestations in the church (chap. 5).[25]
Chapters 4 and 5 do not explicitly address the names "Love" and "Gift," but
they do indicate the accordance of these names with what the Holy Spirit does
for Christ and the church. I then take up two contested areas, among the many
that could be addressed,[26] with respect to the Spirit's gifting to the people of
God: the Spirit as the giver of a visible, institutional unity to the church through
the bond of love (chap. 6); and the Spirit as the giver of true holiness to the
church (chap. 7). In my four chapters on the Spirit's work, I emphasize that
if we accept the New Testament's testimony to Jesus's inauguration of the
messianic kingdom of God, we need a correspondingly rich theology of the
Spirit's outpouring, both upon Jesus himself and upon the community of his

25. Drawing upon John Zizioulas, Reinhard Hütter makes a point that also serves to illumine my approach in this book: "The specific emphasis on pneumatology in Eastern Orthodox
ecclesiology has christological roots. An emphatically pneumatological understanding of Christology avoids the false alternative between a christological and a pneumatological grounding
of ecclesiology. This view develops God's economy of salvation from a strictly trinitarian perspective; that is, it does not separate the salvific-economic mission of the Son from that of the
Holy Spirit" (Hütter, *Suffering Divine Things: Theology as Church Practice*, trans. Doug Stott
[Grand Rapids: Eerdmans, 2000], 118). Writing as a Lutheran, Hütter already has a high view
of the church, a view that I share and seems to me to be necessitated by Jesus's eschatological
prophecies of the kingdom of God and by his outpouring of the eschatological Spirit. Hütter
states, "'In the Spirit' the church becomes an image (εἰκών) of the Trinity itself; it becomes
'communion' of the triune love. . . . As an eschatological new creation, it [the church] can be
described both as 'being' and as 'act.' Its being always remains dependent on the presence and
activity of the Holy Spirit, and remains a being in invocation of the Holy Spirit—*epicletic
being*, being that is completely the *work* of the *Spiritus Creator*. At the same time, as the work
of the Holy Spirit it is also characterized by duration, concreteness, and visibility, and as such
is identical with distinct practices or activities, institutions, offices, and doctrines" (ibid., 119).
Hütter's perspective here deeply informs my own.
26. The Catholic charismatic movement, the global spread of Pentecostalism and the development of a significant Pentecostal theology, and the issues raised therein (e.g., the nature
of Spirit baptism, Oneness Pentecostalism, etc.) compose a major contested area that I do not
treat in this book; here one should see such works as Amos Yong, *The Spirit Poured Out on All
Flesh: Pentecostalism and the Possibility of Global Theology* (Grand Rapids: Baker Academic,
2005); Frank D. Macchia, *Baptized in the Spirit: A Global Pentecostal Theology* (Grand Rapids:
Zondervan, 2006); Heribert Mühlen, *A Charismatic Theology: Initiation in the Spirit*, trans.
Edward Quinn and Thomas Linton (New York: Paulist Press, 1978); Ralph Del Colle, "Oneness
and Trinity: A Preliminary Proposal for Dialogue with Oneness Pentecostalism," *Journal of
Pentecostal Theology* 10 (1997): 85–110.

disciples. As we would expect from Love and Gift, this outpouring configures humans to self-giving love and unites and sanctifies believers.

Let me describe the chapters in a bit more detail. The first chapter focuses on Augustine's naming of the Spirit but is also a defense of a particular mode of biblical exegesis, one that anticipates the presence of God the Teacher in the biblical texts and that reads them accordingly. The second chapter engages with an array of contemporary theologians, including Hans Urs von Balthasar, Robert Jenson, and especially Dumitru Stăniloae, and also treats at length the views of John Damascene, Gregory of Nazianzus, and Basil the Great. In this second chapter, the pattern for the remainder of the book emerges: I devote the most space to exposition of Thomas Aquinas's teaching about the Holy Spirit in his *Summa theologiae*.[27] Although I could have chosen

27. Lewis Ayres warns that during the period of Leonine neo-Thomism, and even afterward, Catholic historical narratives of the development of trinitarian doctrine "tended . . . to present Latin theology as moving by stages toward a Thomist synthesis" (Ayres, "Into the Cloud of Witnesses: Catholic Trinitarian Theology Beyond and Before Its Modern 'Revivals,'" in Maspero and Woźniak, *Rethinking Trinitarian Theology*, 4–25, at 10). Ayres goes on to point out that contemporary trinitarian revivalists have often been fueled by a sharp critique of Latin trinitarian theology as a "fall" from true trinitarianism, and that Hegelian and post-Hegelian philosophy (including Schelling's personalist approach) stand behind many revivalist trinitarian theologies. Here Ayres draws upon the work of Cyril O'Regan, especially his *Gnostic Apocalypse: Jacob Boehme's Haunted Narrative* (New York: State University of New York Press, 2002). Ayres's purpose is to show that Latin trinitarianism itself has resources for internal critique and revival, once one rejects the "assumption of linear and cumulative progress in Latin theology" ("Into the Cloud of Witnesses," 11). He emphasizes that "we should be wary of treating [Augustine] as an inchoate Thomas waiting only for the latter to define with clarity the *relatio subsistens*" (ibid., 14). For Ayres, indeed, Augustine "makes little use of the relationship between love and knowledge to explore the relationship between Son and Spirit," and therefore "the emergence of Thomas' account of the interrelationship between intellect and will is a story to be traced through attention to post-Augustinian developments, and through attention to developments away from (even if in the wake of) Augustine's own project" (ibid., 15). My view is that Aquinas's pneumatology, broadly rooted in certain insights of Augustine, offers valuable truth about the person and work of the Holy Spirit, and so it is important to employ and exposit Aquinas's pneumatology in dialogue with contemporary theologians—without pretending that Aquinas's contributions, profound though they are, are the "last word" (an attitude that would be a distortion of the theological enterprise). In distinction from my emphasis on the *Summa theologiae*, more historically focused presentations of Aquinas's pneumatology have explored the perspectives offered by his *Commentary on the Sentences*, his *Summa contra gentiles*, his *Quaestiones disputatae de potentia Dei*, and his biblical commentaries. See, e.g., Gilles Emery's *Trinitarian Theology of Saint Thomas Aquinas*. For the relationship between Aquinas's pneumatology and Augustine's, see Emery, "Trinitarian Theology as Spiritual Exercise in Augustine and Aquinas," in *Aquinas the Augustinian*, ed. Michael Dauphinais, Barry A. David, and Matthew Levering (Washington, DC: Catholic University of America Press, 2007), 1–40; Bruce D. Marshall, "Aquinas the Augustinian? On the Uses of Augustine in Aquinas's Trinitarian Theology," in Dauphinais, David, and Levering, *Aquinas the Augustinian*, 41–61; Loyer, *God's Love through the Spirit*, 64–69. See also André Malet's *Personne et amour dans la théologie trinitaire de saint Thomas d'Aquin* (Paris: Vrin, 1956), whose insights have been absorbed by Emery.

a number of other theologians, I selected Aquinas as my touchstone for a vigorous presentation of the Holy Spirit as Love and Gift, in part because Aquinas's theology of the person and work of the Spirit is so richly developed, and in part because its influence in the West has made Aquinas's theology of the Spirit a magnet for critical attention and dialogue.[28] Jeremy Wilkins has rightly noted that "the commonplace that the Latin tradition neglected pneumatology, or displaced the concerns of pneumatology into other areas, is not true about Thomas Aquinas."[29]

Chapter 3, which explores the *filioque*, ends with an extensive discussion of Aquinas's treatment of this theme in the *Summa theologiae*. I set up this discussion by first engaging contemporary ecumenical statements, especially the Pontifical Council for Promoting Christian Unity's "The Greek and Latin Traditions regarding the Procession of the Holy Spirit," and then turning to

28. Aquinas's closeness to the patristic vision of the Spirit becomes apparent in the valuable synthesis of patristic thought on the Holy Spirit edited by Joel C. Elowsky: *We Believe in the Holy Spirit* (Downers Grove, IL: IVP Academic, 2009). For another medieval approach to the Spirit, affirming with Augustine (and Aquinas) that the Holy Spirit is Love but offering a different understanding of this reality, see Richard of St. Victor, *On the Trinity*, trans. Christopher P. Evans, in *Trinity and Creation: A Selection of Works of Hugh, Richard and Adam of St. Victor*, ed. Boyd Taylor Coolman and Dale M. Coulter (Hyde Park, NY: New City Press, 2011), 209–382. See also Anselm's approach in his *Monologion*, trans. Simon Harrison, in Anselm of Canterbury, *The Major Works*, ed. Brian Davies, OP, and G. R. Evans (Oxford: Oxford University Press, 1998), 3–81. For discussion of Anselm, Richard of St. Victor, and their influence upon later medieval theologians (especially Bonaventure and Aquinas), see Yves Congar, OP, *I Believe in the Holy Spirit*, trans. David Smith (New York: Crossroad, 1997), 3:96–127; Brian Gaybba, *The Spirit of Love: Theology of the Holy Spirit* (London: Geoffrey Chapman, 1987), 78–88; Dominique Poirel, "Scholastic Reasons, Monastic Meditations and Victorine Conciliations: The Question of the Unity and Plurality of God in the Twelfth Century," in Emery and Levering, *The Oxford Handbook of the Trinity*, 168–80, at 176–80. As Poirel observes, Hugh of St. Victor and Richard of St. Victor elaborated the medieval doctrine of trinitarian appropriation. Gilles Emery emphasizes that for Aquinas, "The Holy Spirit is personally the Gift (*ST* I, q. 38) because he is Love in person (q. 37). . . . The Holy Spirit is given by the Father and the Son in as far as he is *Love proceeding from the Father and the Son*" (Emery, "The Holy Spirit in Aquinas's Commentary on Romans," in *Reading Romans with St. Thomas Aquinas*, ed. Matthew Levering and Michael Dauphinais [Washington, DC: Catholic University of America Press, 2012], 127–62, at 161n148). For an extensive study of Richard of St. Victor in relation to social trinitarianism, see Nico den Bok, *Communicating the Most High: A Systematic Study of Person and Trinity in the Theology of Richard of St. Victor († 1173)* (Paris: Brepols, 1996). See also Joseph P. Wawrykow, "Franciscan and Dominican Trinitarian Theology (Thirteenth Century): Bonaventure and Aquinas," in Emery and Levering, *The Oxford Handbook of the Trinity*, 182–94; Russell L. Friedman, *Medieval Trinitarian Thought from Aquinas to Ockham* (Cambridge: Cambridge University Press, 2010); and Friedman's "Medieval Trinitarian Theology from the Late Thirteenth to the Fifteenth Centuries," in Emery and Levering, *The Oxford Handbook of the Trinity*, 197–208.

29. Jeremy D. Wilkins, "Trinitarian Missions and the Order of Grace according to Thomas Aquinas," in *Philosophy and Theology in the Long Middle Ages: A Tribute to Stephen F. Brown*, ed. Kent Emery Jr., Russell L. Friedman, and Andreas Speer (Leiden: Brill, 2011), 689–708, at 708.

the vigorous criticisms of Aquinas's pneumatology offered by Sergius Bulgakov and Vladimir Lossky. In chapter 4, on the Holy Spirit's work in Jesus himself, I begin with the way in which the biblical scholar James D. G. Dunn foregrounds the Gospels' testimony to the Spirit's impelling of Jesus and to Jesus's unique experience of the Spirit. Through this exegetical lens, I examine Aquinas's theology of the Spirit's "missions" to Jesus, who supremely embodies the Gift of Love for our salvation.[30] In chapter 5, which treats the Holy Spirit's work in the church, I start with the ongoing exegetical debate regarding Jesus's eschatological prophecies about the imminent arrival of the kingdom of God.[31] After setting forth the positions of N. T. Wright, James Dunn, and Dale Allison, I argue that scholarship regarding this topic crucially presumes a judgment about the Spirit's eschatological outpouring among the earliest Christians, to which Paul and the book of Acts testify.[32] If the Spirit was indeed poured out, through the risen and exalted Jesus, then the kingdom that Jesus proclaimed has indeed been inaugurated.[33] And if the Spirit

30. As Alasdair I. C. Heron observes, "According to the New Testament, Jesus is not only the giver but also the *receiver* of the Spirit. If that is not kept in view, it is all too easy to absorb pneumatology in christology, and so to reduce the very name 'Holy Spirit' to a mere cipher. . . . Christology itself requires pneumatology, not in order to be 'less christocentric,' but precisely in order to be *christo*logy, the doctrine of Jesus as the Christ, the one anointed with the Spirit" (Heron, *The Holy Spirit* [Philadelphia: Westminster, 1983], 127). Note also Ian A. McFarland's correct insistence that "Jesus fulfills his specifically human vocation from conception to glory through the power of the Spirit. In this Jesus shows his likeness to us, since for every human being it is the gift of the Spirit that both constitutes (in creation) and completes (in glory) a person's human nature" (McFarland, "Spirit and Incarnation: Toward a Pneumatic Chalcedonianism," *International Journal of Systematic Theology* 16 [2014]: 143–58, at 158). McFarland adds that as the divine Son, "Jesus has the Spirit in a manner that no one else does," since "the Holy Spirit is *his* Spirit" and so "it is impossible for Jesus to lose the Spirit" (ibid.).

31. For the argument that the early church profoundly distorted Jesus's proclamation of universal grace and earthly liberation (a liberation not least from religion), see Thomas Sheehan, *The First Coming: How the Kingdom of God Became Christianity* (New York: Random House, 1986). Joseph Ratzinger takes up this topic in various writings; see, e.g., his "The Origin and Essence of the Church," in *Called to Communion: Understanding the Church Today*, trans. Adrian Walker (San Francisco: Ignatius, 1996), 13–45, at 21–29; *Jesus of Nazareth: From the Baptism in the Jordan to the Transfiguration*, trans. Adrian Walker (New York: Doubleday, 2007), 46–63.

32. C. K. Barrett rightly remarks, "No more certain statement can be made about the Christians of the first generation than this: they believed themselves to be living under the immediate government of the Spirit of God. . . . The Church of the first century believed that the Holy Spirit had been poured out upon it in a quite exceptional manner" (Barrett, *The Holy Spirit and the Gospel Tradition*, 2nd ed. [London: SPCK, 1966], 1–2).

33. Ola Tjørhom suggests that the inauguration here should be understood in terms of sacrament: the church is "an anticipatory sign of God's kingdom. To be sure, a total identification of *signum* and *res* (the sign and the reality it signifies) must be avoided. Yet it remains clear that the church is to be an effective and most real representation of the kingdom" (Tjørhom, *Visible Church—Visible Unity: Ecumenical Ecclesiology and "The Great Tradition of the Church"*

has been poured out, then the Spirit is even now powerfully at work in the ongoing church, "God's own people" (1 Pet. 2:9). Aquinas's presentation of the Holy Spirit's missions makes theologically manifest the all-encompassing character of the Spirit's work, as Love and Gift, in configuring the church to the image of Christ's self-giving love.

Chapter 6 examines the Holy Spirit's role in uniting the church.[34] I begin with the views of Michael Welker and Kendall Soulen, both of whom emphasize the Spirit's fruitfulness in human multiplicity and diversity. Aquinas recognizes that the Holy Spirit meets us in our diversity, but he shows that the Spirit's characteristic work in the church is the strengthening of unity, just as in the Trinity itself the Spirit is associated with unity. The church's unity does not squelch believers' diversity, although unity in truth and love does overcome certain kinds of diversity. Chapter 7 takes up the question of whether the church is holy. Again I find Aquinas's insights helpful, but I note first the ways in which contemporary Reformed theologians and John Calvin seek to affirm the holiness of the church while accounting at the same time for the ways in which the church falls short of holiness. I also discuss the positions of Cyprian and Augustine, who emphasize that the church's faithful mediation of divine teaching and divine sacraments requires that the church be holy, despite its sinful members.

My point in these final two chapters is that the eschatological outpouring of the Spirit, if it means anything, must mean the establishment and sustaining of a visibly united messianic people of God, possessed of an ecclesial holiness that manifests itself in the faithful mediation of the truth of the gospel and the holy sacraments by which, in faith, we are joined to Jesus Christ. The eschatological outpouring of Love and Gift could mean no less. While real, the unity and holiness of the church remain imperfect on earth, and our configuration to Christ by the Holy Spirit does not override our diversity, but instead enables us to work together in self-giving love as members of Christ's body.

[Collegeville, MN: Liturgical Press, 2004], 63). Certainly the church, as the inaugurated kingdom, is not yet the consummated kingdom, and indeed the difference between the two can be described in sacramental terms so long as one does not separate the church (as a *mere* sign) from the kingdom. Gerald O'Collins, SJ, comes too close to just such a separation when, as part of an argument regarding the salvation of non-Christians, he argues (indebted especially to Jacques Dupuis, SJ) that "the reign of God is the decisive point of reference. The Church exists for the kingdom and at its service, and not vice versa" (O'Collins, *The Second Vatican Council on Other Religions* [Oxford: Oxford University Press, 2013], 195). This disjunctive language, which presents the church as a servant of the kingdom and thus as something that will not be needed when the kingdom fully arrives, construes the church in a merely juridical fashion.

34. As Brian Gaybba says with respect to Augustine's theology of the Holy Spirit, "One could say that this theology is but the detailed and consistent application of the idea that love unites and, by uniting, transform all it unites" (Gaybba, *Spirit of Love*, 66).

In short, with regard to the person (chaps. 1–3) and work (chaps. 4–7) of the Holy Spirit, the present book aims to show the value of the names "Love" and "Gift" for illumining the Spirit in his eternal procession and temporal mission to Jesus Christ and the church. Guided especially by Thomas Aquinas, whose theology retains its power to inspire and instruct, I seek to respect the profound mystery of the Spirit—who, as Martin Sabathé remarks, "proceeds from an infinitely mysterious source: the Father and the Son . . . [who] 'dwell in unapproachable light' [1 Tim. 6:16]"[35]—while at the same time proclaiming and praising the Spirit in ways warranted by divine revelation. The impetus for this study is well summed up by Jürgen Moltmann: "The gift and the presence of the Holy Spirit is the greatest and most wonderful thing which we can experience."[36]

There are many other important dimensions of the Spirit's work that I am unable to address in this book, but for which I hope this book provides some foundational insights and which I hope to treat in the future. These dimensions include the Spirit as Creator, the Spirit's presence in the natural world, the Spirit's activity in other religions, the presence of the Holy Spirit among the people of Israel, and the Spirit and prophecy, to name but a few.[37]

35. Martin Sabathé, *La Trinité rédemptrice dans la* Commentaire de l'Évangile de saint Jean *par Thomas d'Aquin* (Paris: Vrin, 2011), 255.

36. Jürgen Moltmann, *The Source of Life: The Holy Spirit and the Theology of Life*, trans. Margaret Kohl (Minneapolis: Fortress, 1997), 10.

37. See, e.g., Colin Gunton, "'The Spirit Moved over the Face of the Waters': The Holy Spirit and the Created Order," in *Spirit of Truth and Power: Studies in Christian Doctrine and Experience*, ed. D. F. Wright (Edinburgh: Rutherford House, 2007), 56–72; Michael Welker, ed., *The Spirit in Creation and New Creation: Science and Theology in Western and Orthodox Realms* (Grand Rapids: Eerdmans, 2012); Robert L. Hubbard Jr., "The Spirit and Creation," in *Presence, Power and Promise: The Role of the Spirit of God in the Old Testament*, ed. David G. Firth and Paul D. Wegner (Downers Grove, IL: IVP Academic, 2011), 71–91. Hubbard notes that Gerhard "von Rad overstated his case against the relationship of the spirit and creation in the OT. Granted, only two texts (Gen. 1:2; Ps. 104:30) expressly link *rûaḥ* with creation (*bārā'*), but they are telling" (Hubbard, "Spirit and Creation," 91). As Christian theologians since Justin Martyr have taught, "seeds of the Word" have been present in all cultures throughout history, and the Creator Spirit too has been actively present everywhere (inseparably from the Word). God offers his saving grace to all humans; on this point, see Congar, *I Believe in the Holy Spirit*, 2:118; cf. 2:218–28. But I do not agree with Gerald O'Collins, SJ's claim that since "revelation" primarily means God's self-disclosure and since God offers grace (thereby in a certain sense disclosing himself) to everyone, "all divine self-revelation, wherever and whenever it occurs, must accordingly be deemed supernatural in its purpose and nature" and "all events of God's self-disclosure are supernatural or aimed to gift human beings with unmerited grace here and with glory hereafter" (O'Collins, *Second Vatican Council on Other Religions*, xi). O'Collins rejects any "distinction between 'super-nature' and 'nature'—in this case between a supernatural revelation granted by God and a merely natural knowledge of God resulting from a human search" (ibid.). See also the discussion of Jacques Dupuis's theology, in light of the Congregation of the Doctrine of the Faith's *Dominus Iesus* (2000), in Edward T. Oakes, SJ,

Pneumatological Paths Not Taken: Weinandy, Coakley, Hasker

Before I proceed, some further sense of recent trinitarian theology and pneumatology will be helpful, so as to show more clearly the differentiating characteristics of the path I take in this book. In this section, therefore, I survey and critically evaluate three works, each from influential streams of contemporary thought: trinitarian theology that seeks to retrieve and accentuate the role of the Spirit; postmodern or contextualized trinitarian theology; and social trinitarianism. From the first stream of thought, I focus on Thomas Weinandy's *The Father's Spirit of Sonship*; from the second, Sarah Coakley's *God, Sexuality, and the Self*; and from the third, William Hasker's *Metaphysics and the Tri-Personal God.*[38]

Thomas Weinandy

Weinandy's *The Father's Spirit of Sonship*, published two decades ago, remains significant for its creative extension of a thesis that gained wide adherence in the twentieth century and continues to be highly influential today, namely that the Holy Spirit is involved in the Son's procession from the Father.[39] Among the Catholic, Orthodox, and Protestant theologians

---

Infinity Dwindled to Infancy: A Catholic and Evangelical Christology (Grand Rapids: Eerdmans, 2011), 408–17. For the Trinity/Holy Spirit and religious pluralism, see Gavin D'Costa, "The Trinity in Interreligious Dialogues," in Emery and Levering, *The Oxford Handbook of the Trinity*, 573–84; D'Costa, *Christianity and World Religions: Disputed Questions in the Theology of Religions* (Oxford: Blackwell, 2009); D'Costa, *The Meeting of Religions and the Trinity* (Maryknoll, NY: Orbis, 2000); D'Costa, "Christ, the Trinity, and Religious Plurality," in *Christian Uniqueness Reconsidered: The Myth of a Pluralistic Theology of Religions*, ed. Gavin D'Costa (Maryknoll, NY: Orbis, 1990), 16–29; Studebaker, *From Pentecost to the Triune God*, 208–39; Veli-Matti Kärkkäinen, *Trinity and Religious Pluralism: The Doctrine of the Trinity in Christian Theology of Religions* (Burlington, VT: Ashgate, 2004); Kärkkäinen, "'How to Speak of the Spirit among the Religions': Trinitarian Prolegomena for a Pneumatological Theology of Religions," in *The Work of the Spirit: Pneumatology and Pentecostalism*, ed. Michael Welker (Grand Rapids: Eerdmans, 2006), 47–70; Amos Yong, *Discerning the Spirit(s): A Pentecostal-Charismatic Contribution to Christian Theology of Religions* (Sheffield: Sheffield Academic Press, 2000). D'Costa's work stands out in this regard.

38. The historical study by Anthony C. Thiselton also deserves mention here: Thiselton, *The Holy Spirit—In Biblical Teaching, through the Centuries, and Today* (Grand Rapids: Eerdmans, 2013). Recent pneumatological studies include Veli-Matti Kärkkäinen, *Pneumatology: The Holy Spirit in Ecumenical, International, and Contextual Perspective* (Grand Rapids: Baker Academic, 2002); Eugene F. Rogers Jr., *After the Spirit: A Constructive Pneumatology from Resources outside the Modern West* (Grand Rapids: Eerdmans, 2005). Rogers's book, which emphasizes the Spirit's resting on the Son, is marred by lack of sustained attention to the wide array of classical theologians whom he cites, and also by misplaced references to male homosexual erotics.

39. For discussion of Weinandy's book, see Brian E. Daley, SJ, "Revisiting the 'Filioque': Part Two, Contemporary Catholic Approaches," *Pro Ecclesia* 10 (2001): 195–212, at 205–6; Studebaker, *From Pentecost to the Triune God*, 138–46; David Coffey, "Spirit Christology and the Trinity,"

whom Weinandy cites in favor of some version of the view that "the Father begets the Son in the Spirit" are François-Xavier Durrwell, Jürgen Moltmann, Olivier Clément, Paul Evdokimov, and Edward Yarnold.[40] Weinandy does not deny that the Father is the primary principle of the Son. He argues, however, that the Holy Spirit cannot be fully a divine person if the Spirit has solely a passive role as the Father and Son's Love and Gift. He also raises the concern that Greek and Latin trinitarian theologies were overly influenced

in Hinze and Dabney, *Advents of the Spirit*, 315–38, at 334–35. Daley notes with concern that Weinandy "effectively abandons the traditional supposition of a τάξις or sequential order in the divine persons," but he appreciates Weinandy's biblical emphasis on the Spirit's active role and Weinandy's characterization of the Spirit "in terms of the relationships implied by personal love rather than in terms of causality" (Daley, "Revisiting the 'Filioque': Part Two," 206). He holds with Weinandy that "perhaps one may . . . conjecture that it is the Spirit's role even within the triune mystery of God to bring the relationship of Father and Son to its perfection of form" (ibid.). For his part, Studebaker values Weinandy's critique of "the Western tradition for portraying the Spirit in passive terms," and he also approves Weinandy's challenge to "the traditional order of processions among the divine persons—Father, Son, Spirit" (Studebaker, *From Pentecost to the Triune God*, 139). Nonetheless, Studebaker concludes that Weinandy, like those whom Weinandy criticizes, gives the Spirit only an instrumental role: the Father and the Son relate to each other through the Spirit, but they do not relate to the Spirit. For Studebaker too, "Weinandy does not succeed in transcending an immanent order of processions, although he does reconfigure them" (ibid., 145). Studebaker argues that Weinandy's position requires that "the Spirit, in the first mode of his subsistence, is prior to the subsistence of the Son because the Spirit is the instrument that proceeds from the Father and in whom the Father begets the Son" (ibid.). Studebaker notes that his concern regarding the Spirit's instrumental role is also expressed by Thomas R. Thompson, review of *The Father's Spirit of Sonship* by Thomas G. Weinandy, *Calvin Theological Journal* 32 (1997): 195–200. See also Gilles Emery's critical review of *The Father's Spirit of Sonship* in *Revue Thomiste* 96 (1996): 152–54. Emery argues that the Rahnerian principle of the identity between the economic Trinity and the immanent Trinity leads Weinandy to transpose to the Son, in his divine nature, the action of the Holy Spirit toward the humanity of Christ. Emery also suggests that Weinandy's approach produces a certain "pneumatomonism," since for Weinandy it is the Spirit who enables the Father to be Father and the Son to be Son. I would add that emphasis on whether an equal amount of active roles are played by all the persons indicates a misunderstanding of the goal of identifying opposed relations in the order of origin. See also the highly positive appropriations of Weinandy's position in Myk Habets, *The Anointed Son: A Trinitarian Spirit Christology* (Eugene, OR: Pickwick, 2010); Tomlin, *Prodigal Spirit*, 22–23, 29, 35.

40. Sergius Bulgakov, who influenced Evodokimov and Clément on the Trinitarian *ordo*, could also be named. For criticism see Luis F. Ladaria, *La Trinità, mistero di comunione*, trans. Marco Zapella (Milan: Paoline, 2004), 272–319; as well as Gilles Emery's trenchant review of Durrwell's *Jésus, Fils de Dieu dans l'Esprit Saint* (Paris: Desclée, 1997) in *Revue Thomiste* 98 (1998): 471–73. Emery comments, "The trinitarian structure elaborated by F.-X. Durrwell recalls in certain respects the theory proposed earlier by Bulgakov. One does not hesitate to follow Durrwell when he criticizes the idea of a Father-Son relation from which the Spirit would be absent, and when he emphasizes the intimate connection between spiration and generation as well as the eternal presence of the Spirit in the Son. But the conception of a kind of 'priority' of the Spirit to the Son (and to the Father) undermines, it seems to us, the *order* of the divine persons who dwell in the total simultaneity of the processions and in the Trinitarian perichoresis" (ibid., 471 [my translation]).

by the options available in Neoplatonic emanationism and in Aristotelian epistemology (according to which one must know something in order to love it).[41] The key mistake, Weinandy thinks, consists in imagining the Godhead to be simply the Father, out of whom come the Son and the Spirit, rather than recognizing that the Godhead itself is trinitarian. Weinandy holds that all "sequentialism" must be rejected. Instead, "A proper understanding of the Trinity can only be obtained if all three persons, logically and ontologically, spring forth in one simultaneous, nonsequential, eternal act in which each person of the Trinity subsistently defines, and equally is subsistently defined by, the other persons."[42]

41. From a different perspective, F. LeRon Shults and Andrea Hollingsworth raise similarly serious concerns about Plato and Aristotle in their *The Holy Spirit* (Grand Rapids: Eerdmans, 2008). They state that "both Platonism and Aristotelianism tended to privilege the concept of *logos* (rational order) over the concept of *pneuma* (dynamic movement), which partly explains why christology (the enfleshment of the divine *Logos*) received more attention during this period than pneumatology (the indwelling of the divine *Spirit*). This privileging was less explicit in the third strand of Middle Platonism, but even the Stoics sometimes seemed to conflate *pneuma* and *logos*, a habit taken over by some early Christian theologians. . . . Interpretations of the Holy Spirit throughout history have certainly not been *controlled* by philosophical approaches, but they have no doubt been *conditioned* by critical engagement with them" (ibid., 12).

42. Thomas G. Weinandy, OFMCap, *The Father's Spirit of Sonship: Reconceiving the Trinity* (Edinburgh: T&T Clark, 1995), 14–15. By contrast, as Christopher A. Beeley states, Gregory of Nazianzus would

> reject any notion of Trinitarian *perichoresis* that conceives of the divine life as being purely reciprocal and not eternally based in the monarchy of the Father—as if, once the Father establishes the consubstantial Trinity, the hierarchical structure of the divine generations gives way to a purely reciprocal exchange of Divinity. Gregory is insistent that the three persons do not mingle with one another in such a way that their identities relative to one another change . . . and he is equally clear that the Father is always the source of Divinity in the Son and the Spirit. . . . Even though the Father, Son, and Holy Spirit continually pour out and return the divine being and so can be said mutually to inhere in one another, it is always, in an eternally prior sense, the *Father's* divine being that they share. The entire process of divine generation and reception is caused by and originates with God the Father. (Beeley, *Gregory of Nazianzus on the Trinity and the Knowledge of God: In Your Light We Shall See Light* [Oxford: Oxford University Press, 2008], 212–13)

> Note also the protest lodged by Photius against (as he thought) the logic of the *filioque*: For if the Son and the Spirit came forth from the same cause, that is to say, the Father, and if—as this blasphemy cries out—the Spirit also proceeds from the Son, then why not simply tear up the Word and propagate the fable that the Spirit also produces the Son, thereby according the same dignity to each person by allowing each person to produce the other person? For if each person is in the other, then of necessity each is the cause and completion of the other. And not according to any different manner—by no means!—even if you say that the Spirit proceeds and the Son is begotten! For reason demands equality for each person so that each person exchanges the grace of causality indistinguishably. (Saint Photios, *The Mystagogy of the Holy Spirit*, trans. Joseph P. Farrell [Brookline, MA: Holy Cross Orthodox Press, 1987], §3, p. 60)

According to Weinandy, overcoming sequentialism allows for a proper understanding of the eternal coequality and coactivity of the divine persons. It also enables theologians to read biblical texts more insightfully. For example, he interprets John 4:24, "God is spirit," to mean that without the Spirit, God cannot be God. The Jewish people already knew that God is spirit. But they did not know God's trinitarian nature. To know the Father correctly requires knowing the Spirit, in whom the Father is Father. Weinandy observes, "Love (the Spirit) is what makes the Father the Father for it is in love that he begets the Son and it is love (the Spirit) that makes the Son the Son for it is in the Spirit, in whom he is begotten, that he loves the Father."[43] Once we attain a

43. Weinandy, *The Father's Spirit of Sonship*, 50. Note also the comment of François-Xavier Durrwell, *The Holy Spirit of God: An Essay in Biblical Theology*, trans. Benedict Davies, OSB (London: Geoffrey Chapman, 1986), 139: "it is in the Spirit that there is a Father and a Son; by reason of the third person, there exists a first and a second . . . . In the Spirit God leaves himself and is carried towards the Son and himself becomes what he is: the Father." Boris Bobrinskoy too insists that "if it is true that the Son is not extraneous to the procession of the Holy Spirit (without bringing in the idea of causality), on the other hand neither is the Holy Spirit extraneous, exterior to the generation of the Son" (Bobrinskoy, "The *Filioque* Yesterday and Today," 145) (cf. Bobrinskoy, *The Mystery of the Trinity: Trinitarian Experience and Vision in the Biblical and Patristic Tradition*, trans. Anthony P. Gythiel [Crestwood, NY: St. Vladimir's Seminary Press, 1999], 71: "the Son and the Spirit come *simultaneously* from the Father, without it being possible to establish a gap between a first moment and a second moment, the Spirit being present and participating in the eternal generation"). More recently, David Bentley Hart has advocated the same case: "the Son is begotten in and by the agency of the Spirit as much as the Spirit proceeds through the Son, inasmuch as the incarnation, unction, and even mission (Mark 1:12) of the Son are works of the Spirit, which must enter into our understanding of the Trinitarian *taxis*" (Hart, "The Mirror of the Infinite: Gregory of Nyssa on the *Vestigia Trinitatis*," in *Re-thinking Gregory of Nyssa*, ed. Sarah Coakley [Oxford: Blackwell, 2003], 111–31, at 129n11). Although I disagree with Weinandy et al. here, I can agree with the more limited claim of Emmanuel Durand, OP, that "the understanding of generation would be incomplete without taking into account the love that accompanies it in every father worthy of the name. . . . Connected to the very act of generation that eternally places the Son as the Beloved of the Father, the Spirit proceeds as precisely this love of the Father for the Son" (Durand, "Perichoresis: A Key Concept for Balancing Trinitarian Theology," in Maspero and Woźniak, *Rethinking Trinitarian Theology*, 177–92, at 185). Durand adds, "Without being principle of the Son in any way, the Holy Spirit is nevertheless eternally present in the very 'place' of his eternal birth (*in sinu Patris*), as the paternal Love that eternally 'hypostates' itself in its reposing on the Son. The Son is himself fully Son in the very fact that He returns this same Love to the Father in eternal thanksgiving" (ibid.). What both Durand and Weinandy wish to emphasize is that (in Durand's words) "the paternal-filial relation cannot completely express the Persons of the Father and the Son in their Trinitarian perfection without the implication of the proper relativity of the Spirit" (ibid., 187). This is true, but it cannot be taken to mean that the Father's generation of the Son is imperfect in itself, as though the Son were not "fully Son" as generated by the Father. Durand credits the patristic and medieval theologians with eliminating "any connotation of anteriority-posteriority or superiority-inferiority from the concept of order, to keep from origin only the relationship of that which has a principle to its principle" (ibid.). Durand's position on these matters echoes that of his mentor Jean-Miguel Garrigues's *Le Saint-Esprit sceau de*

full appreciation of the eternal perichoretic relations of the three persons, we can recognize that the Holy Spirit must be actively present in the relation of the Father and the Son.[44] The alternative would be to imagine the Spirit as absent at first, as though there were originally just a Father, and then just a Father and Son, from whom the Spirit proceeds.

Does Weinandy therefore reject the Father's "monarchy"? He does not, but rather he argues that the "monarchy of the Father as well as the unity of the Trinity will only be rightly understood if an appropriate active role is given to the Holy Spirit."[45] This is because the Father begets the Son in love. The Father is never without a fatherly love for his Son. Indeed, this fatherly love is present in the Father's monarchy as the source of the Son. Weinandy states that "the Spirit proceeds from the Father as the fatherly Love in whom or by whom the Son is begotten."[46] If there were no fatherly Love, no Spirit, there would be no begetting and no Son. The Father's monarchy is not challenged by this because knowing and loving, begetting and spirating are utterly simultaneous in God. In Weinandy's view, however, not even a *logical* priority holds with respect to the Trinity, since such priority is merely the philosophical fruit of Aristotelian epistemology.[47] The Father's monarchy requires that the Spirit be

la Trinité: Le Filioque *et l'originalité trinitaire de l'Esprit dans sa personne et dans sa mission* (Paris: Cerf, 2011), 43, 226–29 and elsewhere.

44. On trinitarian perichoresis, see Durand, "Perichoresis"; Durand, *La périchorèse des personnes divines: Immanence mutuelle, réciprocité et communion* (Paris: Cerf, 2005). For Durand, following Bonaventure, "perichoresis is a concept that integrates unity of essence and personal distinction" ("Perichoresis," 178). Durand argues that in Aquinas we nonetheless find "a certain subordination of the relation of the Father and Son to the Spirit in relationship to the relation of the Father to the Son" (ibid.). I do not think that this is the case. Durand later observes, correctly, that "divine generation cannot be fully understood without its intrinsic connection to the procession of the Spirit as the Love of the Father for the Son. Thus even if an order between generation and procession exists, it is free of all posteriority or subordina-tion, and in no way represents a juxtaposition of two independent acts in the divine life" (ibid., 183). For an approach to the relationship of divine essence and persons via *redoublement* and subsisting relation, see Gilles Emery, OP, "Essentialism or Personalism in the Treatise on God in St. Thomas Aquinas?," in *Trinity in Aquinas*, trans. Teresa Bede et al., 2nd ed. (Ann Arbor, MI: Sapientia Press of Ave Maria University, 2006), 165–208.

45. Weinandy, *Father's Spirit of Sonship*, 65. Weinandy, I expect, would fully agree with John Milbank's point (with which I also concur) that Thomas Aquinas rightly holds that "the non-reversibility of spiration from the Father through the Son indicates precisely *not* an 'order of power,' but only an 'order of *supposita*'" (Milbank, "Second Difference," 176).

46. Weinandy, *Father's Spirit of Sonship*, 69.

47. By contrast, John Zizioulas argues, "The generating is first, for it cannot be logically placed after the generated one, albeit not in the sense of a 'given' entity, since it is established in relationship with the generated (and the spirated) one, but only because of the difference of their hypostatic properties (generator, generated, spirated). Trinitarian hierarchy (first-second-third) is therefore not to be understood as an order of individuals ontologically established in that particular *taxis*, but as an order implied in their distinct hypostatic properties: *agennētos*,

fully active and present in the begetting of the Son, because the Father begets with love. As Weinandy explains, "The Father is the Father because, in the one act by which he is eternally constituted as the Father, the Spirit proceeds as the Love (Life and Truth) in whom the Son is begotten of the Father."[48] The Father retains his "monarchy" as the paternal fount of divinity, but the Son and Spirit possess active roles too in accord with a nonsequentialist approach. Thus Weinandy can say, without in his view removing the Father's monarchy, that "it is by the Spirit that the Father substantiates or 'persons' himself as Father because it is by the Spirit that he begets the Son."[49]

Yet, if the Father becomes the Father "by the Spirit," why does this formulation not give (atemporal) precedence to the Spirit? Even if the Father remains the monarchical fount, it seems that the Father does so only because of the Spirit, who thereby seems to be the fount of the fount, or at least a co-fount. Weinandy responds by underscoring that the trinitarian order cannot be envisioned in terms of a linear Neoplatonic emanationism. No logical priority or sequence accords with the perichoretic, eternal mystery of the Trinity. The Father's monarchy is sustained because the Son and Spirit proceed from the Father. But this does not mean that the Son and Spirit themselves lack an active role. The Spirit plays this active role even in the begetting of the Son, so that the Spirit "'persons' the Father as Father" even while being "'personed' by the Father and Son."[50]

---

gennētos, ekporeutos" (Zizioulas, "Trinitarian Freedom: Is God Free in Trinitarian Life?," in Maspero and Woźniak, *Rethinking Trinitarian Theology*, 193–207, at 203). Boris Bobrinskoy shares Weinandy's position here, though only with regard to the Son and Spirit: "Any introduction, even purely conceptual and speculative, of anteriority in the generation of the Son relative to the procession of the Spirit, contributes to the rationalization and unbalancing of the trinitarian mystery, to the great hurt of the Church" (Bobrinskoy, "*Filioque* Yesterday and Today," 145).

48. Weinandy, *Father's Spirit of Sonship*, 72.

49. Ibid., 73.

50. Ibid., 74. Aristotle Papanikolaou argues along the same lines, though even more strongly: "the Son *causes* the Father and the Spirit to be, . . . the Spirit *causes* the Father and the Son to be; as much as the Father *causes* the Son and the Spirit to be. The identity of each person is dependent on the other persons. On the level of freedom, each person being the *cause* of the existence of the other persons means that each person freely confirms their free will to exist in communion with other persons, and by so doing, *causes* the existence of the other as person" (Papanikolaou, *Being with God: Trinity, Apophaticism, and Divine-Human Communion* [Notre Dame, IN: University of Notre Dame Press, 2006], 151). For concerns about the contemporary "emphasis on perfectly reciprocal relations among the members of the Trinity and severe downplaying of any idea of their fixed positions in an order (e.g., the persons are often now said to be all equally origins of one another, even if they are always properly named in the order Father, Son, and Holy Spirit)," see Kathryn Tanner, "Social Trinitarianism and Its Critics," in Maspero and Woźniak, *Rethinking Trinitarian Theology*, 368–86, at 376–77. Tanner has in view Leonardo Boff's *Trinity and Society*, trans. Paul Burns (Maryknoll, NY: Orbis, 1988). For concerns similar to Tanner's (and my own), see Bruce D. Marshall, "The

Weinandy employs the name "Word" to make the same point. To speak a word requires breath. In God, the Son is the Word and the Spirit is the "breath." The Father cannot speak the Word unless the Father "already" has breath.[51] As Weinandy notes, Clément, Boff, and Moltmann make this same point. Weinandy sums up his position as advocating a *"perichoresis* of *action* within the Trinity,"* so that the Father is the source of all, and yet the other two have their own active role.[52] He recognizes that this meaning of *perichōrēsis* transforms the traditional meanings of *perichōrēsis/circumcessio* in the East and West, which were predicated respectively upon Neoplatonic and Aristotelian doctrines. In his view, the active role of the Holy Spirit is necessary for affirming the full divine personhood of the Spirit.[53]

Filioque as Theology and Doctrine: In Reply to Bernd Oberdorfer," *Kerygma und Dogma* 50 (2004): 271–88. For Oberdorfer, as Marshall observes, "While the Spirit originates from the Father, he also acts upon the Father so as to open up the Father for the Son, or make the Son accessible to the Father. This action is the service (*Leistung*) which the Spirit eternally renders to the Father, and the significance of the Spirit's action for the Father goes all the way down. The Father is eternally constituted as a person, and has his identity, at least in part as a result of this action by the Spirit. Without this action of the Spirit, in other words, there would be no trinitarian Father, but some other person, or no person at all. In a different way the Spirit also opens up the Son for the Father, and so has an indispensable role in constituting the Son's personal identity" (Marshall, "Filioque as Theology and Doctrine," 278). In response, Marshall identifies the problem with, and correct response to, Oberdorfer's approach and others like it (including, Marshall notes, Wolfhart Pannenberg's *Systematische Theologie*, vol. 1 [Göttingen: Vandenhoeck & Ruprecht, 1988], 283–364): "How can a Father who is (for example) eternally closed to his own Son bring forth a Spirit who is open to the Son, and capable of opening the Father to the Son? If the Father is closed to the Son, and the Spirit originates from—owes his being to—the Father, then the Spirit will also be closed to the Son. . . . No person who comes forth from the Father can bring it about that the Father has some attribute or characteristic he would otherwise lack. Since the Father is the unoriginate origin of both the Son and the Spirit, he cannot get anything it takes for him to be God, or to be the Father, from them. If he did, they would not originate from him, but he from them" (Marshall, "Filioque as Theology and Doctrine," 280). As Marshall goes on to point out, "Modern trinitarian theology has been widely shaped by the (Hegelian) idea that the Father brings forth the Son and the Spirit out of a primordial lack or need, which these two who originate from him make good" (ibid., 281). Marshall concludes by stating a fundamental principle: "However we seek to account for the unity and equality of the three divine persons, we will have to do without the thought that the Father somehow gets being from the Son or the Holy Spirit" (ibid.).

51. See Weinandy, *Father's Spirit of Sonship*, 75.

52. Ibid., 78.

53. See also Weinandy's "Clarifying the *Filioque*," which appears on pages 355–67 of Thomas G. Weinandy, OFMCap, Paul McPartlan, and Stratford Caldecott, "Clarifying the *Filioque*: The Catholic-Orthodox Dialogue," *Communio* 23 (1996): 354–73. In this essay, which is a response to the Pontifical Council for Promoting Christian Unity's 1995 document "The Greek and Latin Traditions regarding the Procession of the Holy Spirit," Weinandy argues that "the Orthodox and the Catholic Churches need to formulate a new common Creed, one that embodies the past, but equally one that transcends or goes beyond the past. Thus together, the East and the West must achieve a true development of the doctrine of the Trinity, comparable

Sarah Coakley

Sarah Coakley's *God, Sexuality and the Self: An Essay "On the Trinity"* provides another contemporary creative reading of the Holy Spirit, from a self-consciously postmodern/feminist Anglican perspective. Her emphasis is on desire, divine and human.[54] She develops "a vision of God's trinitarian nature as both the source and goal of human desires," and she seeks to show "how God the 'Father,' in and through the Spirit, both stirs up, and progressively chastens and purges, the frailer and often misdirected desires of humans, and so forges them, by stages of sometimes painful growth, into the likeness of his Son."[55] Her work stands broadly in the line of Christian

---

to the doctrinal development obtained at Nicaea and Constantinople. . . . I conclude by making bold to offer what the new Creed might contain: 'We believe in the Holy Spirit, the Lord the Giver of Life, who comes forth (*ekporeuetai*) from and through the Son as the one in whom the Son is begotten and who proceeds (*proēsi*) from and through the Son in communion with the Father, and together with the Father and the Son is worshiped and glorified'" (ibid., 367). Weinandy restates the position of his book as follows:

> While there is an order of origin and derivation among the Persons of the Trinity, there is not an order of priority, precedence and sequence. . . . A proper understanding of the Trinity can be obtained only if all three Persons, logically and ontologically, spring forth in one simultaneous, nonsequential, eternal act in which each Person of the Trinity subsistently defines, and equally is subsistently defined by, the other Persons. . . . I would argue that the Father begets the Son in or by the Holy Spirit, that is, that the Spirit proceeds (*ekporeuetai*) simultaneously from the Father as the one in whom the Son is begotten. The Spirit, then, who proceeds from the Father as the one in whom the Father begets the Son, both conforms or defines (persons) the Father to be the Father. The Holy Spirit, in proceeding from the Father as the one in whom the Father begets the Son, conforms the Father to be Father for the Son and conforms the Son to be Son for (of) the Father and is equally conformed, defined (personed) by the Father (*principaliter*) and the Son to be the Spirit of both. (ibid., 363–64)

In his contribution to the symposium, "Concluding Comments" (370–73), Caldecott defends Weinandy's position against criticisms made by McPartlan. Caldecott offers a diagram of a circle with a line through it and explains that the line (the generation of the Son) is analogously "the gulf between Self and Other" (ibid., 371). He then argues that "the Father 'breathes forth' the Holy Spirit as a circular movement that by definition returns to him. The Spirit traverses the same 'distance' as the Son (the distance from Self to Other, thus constituting a third, distinct Person), but in a different way, the way of *spiration*. In a sense it is the Spirit who brings the Son back to the Father, overcoming otherness in the communion of love. It might equally be said that the Spirit leads the Son away from the Father 'before' leading him back" (ibid., 372). This analogy from Self and Other, construed psychologically and spatially, strikes me as unhelpful, not least in its construal of trinitarian "otherness."

54. For postmodern/feminist philosophical texts on desire, see, e.g., Julia Kristeva, *Desire in Language: A Semiotic Approach to Literature and Art*, trans. Thomas Gora, ed. Leon S. Roudiez (New York: Columbia University Press, 1980); as well as the collection *Philosophy and Desire*, ed. Hugh J. Silverman (London: Routledge, 2000). See also John Milbank's emphasis on "desire" in connection with the Holy Spirit: Milbank, "Second Difference," 187–88.

55. Sarah Coakley, *God, Sexuality and the Self: An Essay "On the Trinity"* (Cambridge: Cambridge University Press, 2013), 6. For discussion of Coakley's contributions to (feminist)

Platonism, insofar as she sees desire as drawing us constantly toward God; an analysis of desire will lead us to ascend beyond embodied sexual desire (without thereby negating its goodness) and to recognize that when we desire, we desire union with the Good, with Beauty itself. She argues that desire, *eros*, "is an ontological category belonging primarily to God," although as a divine attribute, desire does not indicate any lack.[56] As a divine attribute, desire "connotes that plenitude of longing love that God has for God's own creation and for its full and ecstatic participation in the divine, trinitarian, life."[57] The incarnation makes clear that in this movement of God's desire for us, and our desire for God, we do not need to jettison bodiliness. We must simply learn—as Christ exemplifies for us—to place desire for God at the center of everything we are and do.

In this context, Coakley conceives of the Holy Spirit's work as consisting in inflaming us with desire for God and purifying our desires. She describes the Holy Spirit as "the vibrant point of contact and entry into the flow of this divine desire, the irreplaceable mode of invitation for the cracking open of the crooked human heart."[58] She speaks of the Spirit consistently in terms of desire: the Spirit is the one whose work consists in "alluring, delighting,

---

theology of the Trinity, emphasizing her prioritizing of the Holy Spirit, see Patricia A. Fox, "Feminist Theologies and the Trinity," in Phan, *The Cambridge Companion to the Trinity*, 274–90, at 279–81. Fox's own interests center around feminine images of the divine, as opposed to an all-masculine symbol of God. She seeks to make "connections between the neglect of nature, women, and the Spirit, and between trinitarian theology and ecofeminism and ecotheology" (Fox, "Feminist Theologies and the Trinity," 287). See also Elizabeth A. Johnson, CSJ, *Women, Earth, and Creator Spirit* (New York: Paulist Press, 1993). I approach the theologies of Catholic women from a different angle, arguing implicitly that the best such theologies are radically transformative because radically orthodox, in my *The Feminine Genius of Catholic Theology* (London: T&T Clark, 2012).

56. Coakley, *God, Sexuality, and the Self*, 10.

57. Ibid. See also David Hart's remarks, in critical dialogue with Gilles Deleuze, in his *Beauty of the Infinite*. Hart states that "for Christian thought, the true creativity of desire must be inseparable from charity" (Hart, *Beauty of the Infinite*, 269). Drawing upon Maximus the Confessor (and exhibiting his own speculative and rhetorical gifts), Hart explains further, "In God desire both evokes and is evoked; it is one act that for us can be grasped only by analogy to that constant dynamism within our being that comprises the distinct but inseparable moments of interior energy and exterior splendor. In the life of the Trinity, the other is given by desire and also calls forth desire; God is both address and response, gift and appealing radiance. And it is of this love that both ventures forth and is drawn out that creation is a rephrasing, an 'object' of divine delight precisely in being a gift of divine love, shining within the infinitely accomplished joy—the *apatheia*—of the Trinity" (ibid., 270). For a similarly fruitful emphasis on "our desire-love," as well as the claim that "a *full* Trinitarian theology should be a mystical theology of union," see David Tracy, "Trinitarian Theology and Spirituality: Retrieving William of St. Thierry for Contemporary Theology," in Maspero and Woźniak, *Rethinking Trinitarian Theology*, 387–420, here quoted at 406–7.

58. Coakley, *God, Sexuality, and the Self*, 24.

inflaming, in its propulsion of divine desire."[59] This movement of desire, of course, is unitive, but the unity that it establishes does not do away with distinction. Coakley states that "the Spirit is no less also a means of distinguishing hiatus: both within God, and in God's relations to creation. It is what makes God irreducibly *three*, simultaneously distinguishing and binding Father and Son, and so refusing also—by analogous outreach—the mutual narcissism of even the most delighted of human lovers."[60] Union and distinction are both the work of the Holy Spirit. It is important to note here that Coakley envisions the Spirit's work in us to be inseparable from Christ's saving work: thus "the Spirit progressively 'breaks' sinful desires, *in and through* the passion of Christ," so that the Spirit both propels us toward divine union and corrects our fallen desires "to possess, abuse, and control."[61]

Coakley goes on to compare two biblical models of the Holy Spirit. In the first model, found in John's Gospel and in Acts, the Holy Spirit shares with the church the relationship of the Father and the Son; the Holy Spirit's role here is secondary. In the second model, the Holy Spirit incorporates believers into the trinitarian life and has a much more central role. Coakley explains that in this Pauline model "the Holy Spirit is construed not simply as extending the revelation of Christ, nor even merely as enabling Christ's recognition, but as actually catching up the created realm into the life of God."[62] Coakley calls this Pauline model "incorporative," and she judges it to be more adequate to the Spirit than the Johannine and Lukan model, which she terms "linear." Paul's incorporative model of the Spirit, found paradigmatically in Romans 8, gives the Spirit a central activity of his own in salvation history, one that is in a certain sense distinct from the "linear" economy of salvation. This model of the Spirit (and thus of the Spirit's personal distinctiveness) comes to the fore, Coakley argues, particularly in the experience of prayer, as Romans 8 suggests. In Coakley's view, the incorporative model of the Spirit, which gives "experiential priority to the Spirit in prayer" and which allows for "a

59. Ibid. Note also Rowan Williams's insight that "to speak of the Spirit's presence in the church is to speak of that dimension of the life of Christ's body that is consumed with longing. At the heart of the church, there is a yearning to be what God designs us to be, a yearning to receive the full gifts that God wants us to receive—and that carries with it the implication that there is indeed something that we are for. . . . The Spirit in us is desire, not any old desire, but the desire towards the unreachable God, who is also the God who has himself reached out to us and put the Spirit of his Son into our hearts" (Williams, "Holy Spirit in the Bible," in J. Williams, *Holy Spirit in the World Today*, 64–71, at 65–66). Williams connects this desire or passion with Christ's passion: the Holy Spirit leads us to share in Christ's radical self-offering. This "self-emptying means being filled with the energy of gift and being fully alive" (ibid., 68).

60. Coakley, *God, Sexuality, and the Self*, 24.

61. Ibid., 14–15.

62. Ibid., 111.

simultaneous [rather than linear] experience of 'Father,' 'Son,' and 'Spirit,'"
has tended to stimulate pneumatologically rich, ascetically rigorous, prophetic
movements that find themselves at the margins of the established and/or hierarchical church (and that encourage women's leadership).[63] Examining the
views of the early fathers of the church, Coakley focuses on the connections
between the priority of ecstatic experience of the Spirit, erotic desire for
incorporation into the Trinity, and an ambiguous "renegotiation of gender"
vis-à-vis sexuality and leadership.[64]

Coakley credits the monastic movement for keeping alive the priority of the
ecstatic experience of the Holy Spirit, and for energizing Athanasius's mature
commitment to the coequality of the Spirit and his corresponding interest in
Romans 8's incorporative pneumatology.[65] Gregory of Nyssa and Augustine
both evince at least moments of incorporative pneumatological logic, as do,
of course, many medieval mystical theologians. She devotes a full chapter to
a comparative study of Gregory and Augustine on gender, prayer, and the
Trinity. She finds that Gregory's mystical writings allow for the priority of
"the Spirit's lure into the life of the Godhead," whereas his earlier doctrinal
treatises "are more infected by a safe 'linear' and hierarchical ordering of
the persons than is suggested by Paul's vision in Romans 8 of the 'reflexive'
answering of Spirit to Father in and through the pray-er."[66] By contrast, she
finds Augustine's view of gender to underwrite the subordination of women
more than does Gregory. Yet in book 15 of Augustine's *De Trinitate*, she identifies the incorporative pneumatology with its emphasis on inflaming desire
and trinitarian indwelling. She connects the incorporative pneumatological

63. Ibid., 116. From a different angle, Gary Tyra seeks to stimulate prophetic Christian
movements and to equip them to reevangelize Europe and North America, building upon Lesslie
Newbigin's famous observation that Europe and North America are now mission fields. He
argues that "the remarkable spread of Pentecostal and charismatic Christianity around the
world in recent years can be attributed, at least in part, to the dynamic of prophetic activity
taking place in the lives of rank-and-file church members. This realization offers hope that a
similar missional faithfulness can be experienced in Western, industrialized nations should the
dynamic of prophetic activity be rediscovered by the evangelicals living within them" (Tyra,
The Holy Spirit in Mission: Prophetic Speech and Action in Christian Witness [Downers Grove,
IL: IVP Academic, 2011], 34–35). Although in the present book I discuss the Holy Spirit's guidance of the church's teachings, I have left a fuller discussion of individual proclamation and
preaching—a central engine of practical evangelization, and what Tyra has in view when he
uses the phrase "prophetic speech"—for a future book.

64. Coakley, *God, Sexuality, and the Self*, 132.

65. Coakley is less positive about Basil the Great, who seems to "redistinguish" the Son and
Spirit in a linear movement of the economy (see ibid., 138).

66. Ibid., 287. For reflection on Gregory of Nyssa's pneumatology, see Khaled Anatolios,
Retrieving Nicaea: The Development and Meaning of Trinitarian Doctrine (Grand Rapids:
Baker Academic, 2011), 204–12.

dimensions of Gregory and Augustine with Pseudo-Dionysius's depiction "of a *divine* ecstatic yearning meeting and incorporating a responsive human, ecstatic yearning."[67]

The passage from Pseudo-Dionysius's *The Divine Names* that Coakley examines in some detail is found in 4.12–17. There Dionysius notes that "some of our writers on sacred matters have thought the title 'yearning' to be more divine than 'love.'"[68] He quotes Ignatius of Antioch as well as Wisdom of Solomon 8:2: "I loved her and sought her from my youth, and I desired to take her for my bride, and I became enamored of [or: yearned for] her beauty."[69] Dionysius holds that "yearning" (*eros*) and "love" (*agapē*) are synonymous. He recognizes, of course, that some theologians reject the name "yearning" as inapplicable to God, a fact that he attributes to their inability "to grasp the simplicity of the one divine yearning," because they think of erotic desire solely in bodily, divided terms.[70] For Dionysius, yearning, when applied to God, signifies "a capacity to effect a unity, an alliance, and a particular commingling in the Beautiful and the Good."[71] He goes on to explain the standing of *eros* in God: "It is a capacity which preexists through the Beautiful and the Good. It is dealt out from the Beautiful and the Good through the Beautiful and the Good. It binds the things of the same order in a mutually regarding union."[72] Love involves yearning or desire, because love goes out to the beloved ecstatically, so that the lover belongs to the beloved. Our yearning or desire is a participation in the divine yearning or desire. Thus theologians should name God "Yearning and Love," *Eros* and *Agapē*, because God himself "is yearning on the move, simple, self-moved, self-acting, preexistent in the Good, flowing out from the Good onto all that is and returning once again to the Good."[73] The divine yearning moves in a circular fashion, "always proceeding, always remaining, always being restored to itself."[74]

Coakley points out that in making this argument, Dionysius is relying on Proclus as well as seeking to connect this view of *eros* with Paul. She also

67. Coakley, *God, Sexuality, and the Self*, 295.

68. Pseudo-Dionysius, *The Divine Names* 4.12, in *The Complete Works*, trans. Colm Luibheid with Paul Rorem (New York: Paulist Press, 1987), 81.

69. For background to Ignatius of Antioch's "tendency of assimilating Son and spirit, for 'spirit' conveys the status of being an inhabitant of the heavenly court and an emissary of God," see John Anthony McGuckin, "The Trinity in the Greek Fathers," in Phan, *The Cambridge Companion to the Trinity*, 49–68, at 53.

70. Pseudo-Dionysius, *The Divine Names* 4.12, p. 81.

71. Pseudo-Dionysius, *The Divine Names* 4.12, p. 81.

72. Pseudo-Dionysius, *The Divine Names* 4.12, p. 81.

73. Pseudo-Dionysius, *The Divine Names* 4.13–14, pp. 82–83.

74. Pseudo-Dionysius, *The Divine Names* 4.14, p. 83.

underscores that, *pace* Sigmund Freud, it turns out here that sexual desire is, ultimately, sublimated desire for God rather than the converse. Yet as she notes, Dionysius does not make a connection to the Trinity, let alone to gender (or, of specific interest to Coakley, to the issue of gendered naming of the Trinity).

The question of the *filioque* provides Coakley, at the end of her book, with a way of drawing out the trinitarian significance of envisioning God in terms of the attribute of desire. Insisting upon the Spirit's primary role against linear subordinationism, she suggests that understanding the divine persons in terms of processions causes problems unless one recognizes that processions "are about the perfect mutual ontological desire that only the Godhead instantiates."[75] The Father alone cannot be the source of the Trinity, since otherwise the linear model would be unavoidable. Rather, since divine desire is ecstatic, the Father must be a "source" whose status depends upon the activity of the other two persons, activity that Coakley describes as "the Spirit's reflexive propulsion and the Son's creative effulgence."[76] The point is that each person must be the "source," in some way, of the other two. This fits with divine desire, which is ecstatic: each person enacts both "active plenitude and longing love" vis-à-vis the other two persons.[77] The Spirit's role must be accentuated if this fully mutual, ecstatic sourcing is to be appreciated; otherwise the linear Father-Son model, with the Spirit as an extrinsic and subordinated add-on, will predominate. The Father is "source" only in the Son and through the Spirit; the Son has his source in the Father through the Spirit; the Spirit too is "sourced" by the Father and the Son. The mutual ecstasis of desire, rather than linear processions, characterizes the trinitarian persons. We come to know this when our own desires have been rightly purified by the Holy Spirit, so that we can participate in the reflexive, vulnerable movements of divine ecstasis.

William Hasker

My third representative contemporary approach to the Holy Spirit is the social trinitarianism of William Hasker. Hasker draws upon Carl Mosser (who himself is critical of social trinitarianism) to provide a fourfold definition of the constituent elements of social trinitarianism: "1. Inter-personal unity is irreducibly social in nature; 2. The members of the Trinity are persons in the full, modern sense; 3. Therefore, the unity of the Trinity is genuinely social in

---

75. Coakley, *God, Sexuality, and the Self*, 333.
76. Ibid. For patristic and medieval concerns regarding this kind of approach, see Marshall, "Filioque as Theology and Doctrine," 281–82.
77. Coakley, *God, Sexuality, and the Self*, 333.

nature; 4. The divine persons interpenetrate, co-inhere, and mutually indwell one another in *perichoresis*."[78] For Hasker, it is particularly important to insist that the divine persons have "personhood" in the modern sense of the term. He largely grants the need for analogy rather than strict univocity in speaking of divine realities, but not so as to make the personhood of the divine persons less than that connoted by the modern sense of "personhood." In this regard, he returns frequently and with approval to Cornelius Plantinga's contention that the Father, Son, and Holy Spirit must be distinct centers of consciousness with distinct knowledge, will, and action.

Like Coakley, Hasker devotes sustained attention to Gregory of Nyssa and Augustine. Regarding Gregory of Nyssa, Hasker's main interest consists in inquiring whether *On "Not Three Gods," to Ablabius* supports social trinitarianism. He emphasizes that in this work, Gregory argues that when Peter, James, and John are referred to as "three men," this is a mistake, since it implies that there are three human natures.[79] The same, then, holds for the Father, Son, and Spirit: they too share one nature and should be called one God. Further, Gregory contends that the Father himself does not judge humans because the Father has committed all judgment to the Son. In *Contra Eunomium* too Gregory attributes to the Son a number of actions not possessed by the Father. Thus for Gregory, the Father, Son, and Holy Spirit share a nature in a manner similar to (though not identical with) the way that three men do, and the Son performs distinct actions that the Father does not do. Although he is well aware of arguments to the contrary, Hasker concludes that Gregory supports the basic contentions of social trinitarianism. Indebted to Andrew Radde-Gallwitz, Hasker notes that even Gregory's version of divine simplicity differs from the strict version adopted by Augustine and others. Here Hasker employs an essay by Richard Cross, in which Cross argues that

---

78. William Hasker, *Metaphysics and the Tri-Personal God* (Oxford: Oxford University Press, 2013), 20. See Carl Mosser, "Fully Social Trinitarianism," in *Philosophical and Theological Essays on the Trinity*, ed. Thomas McCall and Michael C. Rea (Oxford: Oxford University Press, 2009), 131–50. For a critique of privileging social trinitarianism on practical-political grounds, see Tanner, "Social Trinitarianism and Its Critics." See also Sarah Coakley's helpful "'Persons' in the 'Social' Doctrine of the Trinity: A Critique of Current Analytic Discussion," in *The Trinity: An Interdisciplinary Symposium on the Trinity*, ed. Stephen T. Davis, Daniel Kendall, SJ, and Gerald O'Collins, SJ (Oxford: Oxford University Press, 1999), 123–44.

79. For an explanation and defense of Gregory's understanding of "nature" (*physis*) here, and his distinction between the ordinary and the strictly technical meaning of the term, see Lewis Ayres, *Nicaea and Its Legacy: An Approach to Fourth-Century Trinitarian Theology* (Oxford: Oxford University Press, 2004), 349; Thomas Cattoi, "The Relevance of Gregory of Nyssa's *Ad Ablabium* for Catholic-Orthodox Ecumenical Dialogue on the Trinity and the Church," in *The Holy Trinity in the Life of the Church*, ed. Khaled Anatolios (Grand Rapids: Baker Academic, 2014), 183–98, at 190–91.

classical trinitarian theology holds both that the divine person is the same as
the divine essence and that relations are mental rather than real, as evidence
that divine simplicity in its stronger forms logically negates trinitarian doctrine of any kind.[80]

Hasker takes as confirmation of Augustine's support for the basic contention of social trinitarianism the fact that Augustine holds that not only the
Holy Spirit loves in the Trinity but rather the Father loves, the Son loves, and
the Holy Spirit loves. If each person loves, this must mean—so Hasker concludes—that each person is a distinct center of consciousness. Further, if the
Father and Son have mutual love, as Augustine says they do, it again follows
that each person must be a distinct center of consciousness.[81] Hasker argues

80. See Richard Cross, "Latin Trinitarianism: Some Conceptual and Historical Considerations," in McCall and Rea, *Philosophical and Theological Essays on the Trinity*, 201–13.
For a more recent proposal by Cross, promoting the approach of John Duns Scotus among
others, see his "Medieval Trinitarianism and Modern Theology," in Maspero and Woźniak,
Rethinking Trinitarian Theology, 26–43. Comparing "social trinitarianism" with "Latin trinitarianism," Cross argues that "if Latin views are construed as entailing that the only feature
that one person can possess uniquely is a relation (to the other persons), then Latin trinitarianism must be false. My reason for holding this is that the only obvious rationale for accepting
trinitarianism is the Christian doctrine of the Incarnation, and this doctrine seems to entail
that at least one person possesses a set of properties—i.e., human properties—that the other
persons do not possess" (Cross, "Medieval Trinitarianism and Modern Theology," 43). In
my view, the incarnate Son's contingent properties—those that he possesses in virtue of the
incarnation, such as being born of the Virgin Mary—must be carefully distinguished from the
eternal relational properties that distinguish the Son in the Trinity. The properties that the Son
obtains in virtue of the incarnation pertain to his humanity and neither change the eternal
Son nor distinguish the Son, as Son, from the Father or the Holy Spirit. In the strict sense,
whose full meaning remains beyond our reach due to the divine incomprehensibility (which
pertains as much to the divine persons as to the divine essence), the property that eternally
distinguishes the Son is only his opposed relation to the Father in the order of origin. See also
Cross's controversial *The Metaphysics of the Incarnation: Thomas Aquinas to Duns Scotus*
(Oxford: Oxford University Press, 2002).

81. Hasker is frequently in dialogue here with the work of Lewis Ayres, and he argues that
Ayres (like Augustine) runs into trouble regarding the doctrine of the persons' unity of will/
operation and the doctrine of divine simplicity; see Hasker, *Metaphysics and the Tri-Personal
God*, 48–49 and 58–59, citing Ayres, *Nicaea and Its Legacy*, 292–301, 319, 378–80; and Ayres,
Augustine and the Trinity (Cambridge: Cambridge University Press, 2010), 320–25. For his
part, Ayres points out that "Augustine's pattern of 'redoublement' does not proceed via an
examination of the language of persons and essence, but via the interweaving of two strands
of exegesis and philosophical reflection. The first strand focuses on the divine three as active
agents, and here Augustine seems to have moved cautiously towards an account of the three as
existing dynamically *ad aliquid*. . . . The second strand of discourse focuses on the divine three
as each being the one fullness of the Godhead and as also the fullness of the indivisible Godhead
inseparably with the others" (Ayres, *Augustine and the Trinity*, 260–61). Note also Gilles Emery's
explanation of the necessity of "*redoublement*" in trinitarian theology according to Aquinas,
for whom the mysteries of the Triune God require two distinct approaches: "The complexity
of our knowledge of the mystery, faced with the impossibility of extracting the persons from

that Augustine's strong doctrine of divine simplicity necessarily implies unitarianism and must be rejected. He also points out that the patristic rejection of patripassianism means that the Father and the Son have distinct actions. Indeed, Scripture's testimony to the Father and Son would otherwise make no sense. In Scripture, we find the Father and Son acting vis-à-vis each other with distinct, conscious intentionality, a point that Hasker considers to be validated in Khaled Anatolios's interpretation of Athanasius.[82]

In the New Testament, Hasker finds that the Holy Spirit receives significantly less attention, at least as an explicitly personal agent, than do the Father and the Son. He notes that although the Spirit is depicted in personal terms in Romans 8:26–27, Ephesians 4:30, and John 14:26, nonetheless "the Spirit was not made the center of attention, reflection, and worship as was Jesus Christ. Rather, the Spirit was the energizing power that made faith in Christ, and the new life in Christ, possible."[83] Even the fourth-century Niceno-Constantinopolitan Creed does not explicitly affirm the coequal divinity of the Holy Spirit. Yet Hasker, of course, affirms the Spirit's coequal divinity. The divine nature ("God") does not exist on its own, but rather exists solely as the Father, Son, and Holy Spirit. Further, the Spirit is never independent of the Father and Son in the sense of autonomy; rather, all three persons are intimately and supremely united. They are distinct in will, but they are also united in will by perfect love.[84] Even so, the Holy Spirit (like the Father and

---

the essence as if they were an emanation or an effusion of it, obliges us to approach subsistence by a double knowledge," with the integration taking place in the person as subsisting relation (see Emery, "Essentialism or Personalism in the Treatise on God in St. Thomas Aquinas?," 202). For further reflections on the value of conceiving personhood metaphysically in terms of the dignity of subsistence in a rational nature, see Emery, "The Dignity of Being a Substance: Person, Subsistence, and Nature," *Nova et Vetera* 9 (2011): 991–1001, esp. 1000–1001.

82. See Hasker, *Metaphysics and the Tri-Personal God*, 201, citing Anatolios, *Retrieving Nicaea*, 153.

83. Hasker, *Metaphysics and the Tri-Personal God*, 183.

84. Here Hasker notes that Michel René Barnes, in an essay titled "Divine Unity and the Divided Self: Gregory of Nyssa's Trinitarian Theology in Its Psychological Context," holds that (in Hasker's words) "for Gregory, each of Father, Son, and Spirit is a real individual, possessing will (*boulē*) and a faculty of moral choice (*proairetikēn*)" (Hasker, *Metaphysics and the Tri-Personal God*, 207). Hasker adds that Barnes considers the will in the three persons to be one will (common to the divine persons) possessed by the persons according to the order of origin. Hasker states that Barnes "fails to attend to the distinction between the content of will, the act of will, and the faculty of willing. Once we notice this distinction, we can see immediately that even if the content of will is the same for the Father, Son, and Spirit, we simply cannot make sense of the biblical data if we refuse to attribute to them distinct acts of will and faculties of willing. . . . The Son, and only the Son, willed *to become incarnate*" (ibid.). See Barnes, "Divine Unity and the Divided Self: Gregory of Nyssa's Trinitarian Theology in Its Psychological Context," *Modern Theology* 18 (2002): 475–96, at 489. For a position that emphasizes the distinct agency and intentionality of the divine persons while noting that such

the Son) can and does will things that the other two persons do not will. The Holy Spirit has free will, so that his will is not governed by the will of the Father or the Son. The trinitarian persons, in other words, enjoy real and fully personal relationships with one another, but they do so without the conflict that mars the human relationships that we see around us.

Hasker insists that the persons share "a singular concrete divine nature," but how could they do so if they have distinct consciousness?[85] How can they be of one *concrete* nature if they relate to one another in I-thou relationships? Seeking to understand how this could be so, Hasker examines the case of commissurotomy (surgically split brains), in which at least in some instances a person seems to develop two centers of consciousness. He also examines evidence for psychiatric cases of multiple personality. His suggestion is that if one human mind can support multiple consciousnesses, so too, analogously, can God. A human mind here is the "constituting" element, while the multiple consciousnesses are what is constituted. In the case of God, the constituting element is the one concrete divine nature, and what are constituted are the three divine persons. The divine nature could conceivably not have sustained three persons, but in fact it does sustain three persons. Hasker concludes that "the one concrete divine nature sustains eternally the three distinct life-streams of Father, Son, and Holy Spirit, and that in virtue of this nature *constitutes* each of the persons although it *is not identical* with the persons."[86] In his view, this "constitution relation" saves Augustine's claim, based on a strong doctrine of divine simplicity, that the persons and the essence do not really differ in God, since each person is fully God.[87]

Critique of the Three Approaches

Each of the three paths described above represents a significant stream of contemporary trinitarian thought in general and pneumatological thought in particular. Why, then, do I not follow any of these paths in this book? Let me begin with Hasker's analytic social trinitarianism. He and I part ways when it comes to thinking about the divine nature. He suggests that divine nature can be defined in terms of a set of properties that, when added together, provide all the necessary properties for a divine entity. It seems to me that a better way is to begin with God's instruction to Moses, "Say this to the people of

terms apply only analogously, not univocally, to the divine persons, see Khaled Anatolios, "Personhood, Communion, and the Trinity in Some Patristic Texts," in Anatolios, *Holy Trinity in the Life of the Church*, 147–64.

85. Hasker, *Metaphysics and the Tri-Personal God*, 227.
86. Ibid., 244.
87. Ibid., 245.

Israel, 'I AM has sent me to you'" (Exod. 3:14). What would it take for God to be in an absolutely unbounded way, so that he can name himself simply in terms of the verb "to be"? The notion that the act of being is merely one property among others is not sufficient here. Rather than existing in a limited or dependent mode, God must exist in an infinite, utterly unlimited mode, and thus be describable as pure actuality with no potentiality (no limitation of act) whatsoever. I thus do not think that Hasker's "constitution" model of the divine nature works. The three persons that he describes have a finite mode of being; their distinct consciousness, knowledge, will, and activity delimit their being from the being of the other two divine persons. They are not infinite, unrestricted act, since their act comes up against a boundary, namely the differentiation of their actuality from the actuality of the other two persons. What Hasker has described are, metaphysically speaking, three finite entities, no matter if each one is eternal, omnipotent, omniscient, and so forth. These can only be three gods—powerful and divinelike, no doubt, but not the transcendent, infinite, uncreated, pure actuality whose existence is utterly self-sufficient in every way.[88]

Hasker arrives at this view of the three persons in part because of his failure to seriously explore classical metaphysics. However, he also finds this conclusion to be necessary because of his frequently reiterated view that otherwise one will be forced into unitarianism. For Hasker, the patristic doctrine of divine simplicity is, for the trinitarian, incoherent and unthinkable. If the persons are literally the same as the essence, so that the divine essence in one person literally differs in no way from the divine essence in another person, then the persons are likewise identical. As I noted above, he bases this conclusion upon a statement from Richard Cross to the effect that relations are solely in the mind. But he does not address the point made by a number of theologians that, if there are real relations in God, these relations not only are God, but also subsist distinctly. They are not mere mental constructs. Rather, they are in God (and thus are God) but are toward the other person in the relation of origin. Hasker leaves the theory of subsisting relations entirely uninvestigated.

The reasons for Hasker's neglect of the theory of subsisting relations, and for his failure to understand cognate proposals prior to the full medieval development of this theory, are no doubt complex. It is clear, however, that one of the reasons is that he does not think that a subsisting relation can

88. See the important concerns raised with respect to analytic philosophical theology by David Bentley Hart, *The Experience of God: Being, Consciousness, Bliss* (New Haven: Yale University Press, 2013), 123–42. In the same section, Hart explains why God must be simple, infinite actuality. For further discussion see my *Proofs of God: Classical Arguments from Tertullian to Barth* (Grand Rapids: Baker Academic, 2016).

sustain the thick description of the distinctive activity of divine persons that we find in the New Testament. Hasker repeatedly cites the Son's suffering on the cross as an example, since the church fathers denied that the Father suffered. Yet he strangely does not seem to notice that many of the fathers placed a heavy emphasis on the fact that the Son suffered *as man*. Many of the acts that Hasker identifies as evidence for three distinct divine personalities flow from the theology of the incarnation: these acts belong to the Son, but they belong to him by virtue of his humanity. Hasker seems unaware that the fathers did not attribute a simple convergence between the human acts of the incarnate Son and the Son's acts. When Jesus wept, this does not mean that the divine person of the Son became sad, except precisely insofar as the Son became sad in his humanity. When Jesus willed to go to the cross, this does not mean that the divine person of the Son demonstrated a volition distinct from that of the Father, except insofar as the Son's humanity is not the Father's. What is needed is a way of accounting for the creature-Creator relation in the incarnation itself. The fact that the change is on the side of the creature does not take away from the intimacy of the incarnation. The Son must remain pure act, after all, if there is to be an incarnation at all—as Thomas Weinandy has rightly emphasized in various works.[89]

The biblical testimony to distinct divine personalities—Father, Son, Spirit—thus need not mean all that Hasker takes it to mean. The New Testament can describe the Son's incarnate suffering, or the Father's voice speaking, or the Spirit's descending like a dove without us thereby assuming that these economic manifestations must translate into three persons in the sense of three distinct centers of consciousness. John Zizioulas articulates the alternative, with which I agree: "The Trinitarian persons are not to be understood as subjects of consciousness, since they possess but one will, mind etc. both *ad intra* and *ad extra*."[90] What this means is not that the divine persons lack subjectivity, but rather that the persons, who are one God, possess this in a manner that is beyond our comprehension and that would be undermined

89. See Thomas G. Weinandy, OFMCap, *Does God Change? The Word's Becoming in the Incarnation* (Still River, MA: St. Bede's Publications, 1985); Weinandy, *Does God Suffer?* (Notre Dame, IN: University of Notre Dame Press, 2000); Weinandy, "God IS Man: The Marvel of the Incarnation," in *Aquinas on Doctrine: A Critical Introduction*, ed. Thomas G. Weinandy, OFMCap, Daniel A. Keating, and John P. Yocum (London: T&T Clark, 2004), 67–89.

90. Zizioulas, "Trinitarian Freedom," 206. Likewise, Brian Daley, SJ, remarks that "the Holy Trinity is not a committee, or even a community, of three persons with three consciousnesses, three minds, and three wills" (Daley, "Conclusion: A God in Whom We Live: Ministering the Trinitarian God," in Anatolios, *Holy Trinity in the Life of the Church*, 217–31, at 226).

(not aided) by any denial of the unity and simplicity of the divine mind, will, and so forth.[91]

Yet Hasker's point goes deeper. Who, after all, would suppose that Jesus came to reveal three subsisting relations in God? If all we can say about the distinction between Father, Son, and Holy Spirit is that they are distinct in their relation of origin, then Christian worship of the Trinity seems to have been gutted of content from the outset.

When we do not conceive of the Holy Spirit as a distinct center of consciousness in a discursively I-thou relationship with the Father and the Son, we appear to have taken the vital dramatic texture out of pneumatology.

In response to this concern, I note the importance of affirming that the names "Love" and "Gift" are descriptive of the Spirit's personal properties in the Trinity. Dramatically, these names are hardly worthless, once they have been rightly understood. Contemporary thinkers such as Jean-Luc Marion have shown that these two names may serve to set forth an ontology and indeed an entire understanding of creation and redemption.[92] If the action of the Holy Spirit in the economy is that of hypostatized "Love" and "Gift," this opens up plenty of theo-drama, as indeed we find in Scripture. The eschatological Spirit pours himself out upon us and configures the church to the radical Love and Gift that characterize the Spirit-filled Messiah. Thus Thérèse of Lisieux can beg Jesus, with allusions to our participation in Christ's passion and to the sacrificial offerings of Israel, "let me be this happy victim; consume Your holocaust with the fire of Your Divine Love!"; and she discovers that "*love comprised all vocations.*"[93] Toward the very end of her life, she affirms that "everything is a grace" and that, in her life, "everyone will see that everything comes from God" as "a gratuitous gift from God."[94] To name the Spirit personal "Love" and "Gift" in the Trinity is to invite entry into a highly personal, dramatic mystery of inexhaustible communion.

Yet, at the same time, these names retain a spareness that I find salutary. While we know that the persons of the Trinity are distinct, and while this is made clear by the very fact of personal names, nonetheless what individual personhood means in the Trinity is utterly beyond our ken. It is a mystery

91. This point could assist Khaled Anatolios's insights in his "Personhood, Communion, and the Trinity in Some Patristic Texts."

92. See Jean-Luc Marion, *In Excess: Studies of Saturated Phenomena*, trans. Robyn Horner and Vincent Berraud (New York: Fordham University Press, 2002); Marion, *Being Given: Toward a Phenomenology of Givenness*, trans. Jeffrey L. Kosky (Stanford, CA: Stanford University Press, 2002).

93. Thérèse of Lisieux, *Story of a Soul: The Autobiography of St. Thérèse of Lisieux*, trans. John Clarke, OCD, 3rd ed. (Washington, DC: ICS Publications, 1996), 181, 194.

94. Ibid., 266–67.

that is caught up in the revealed order of origin, and that is recognizable, very partially, through meditation on personal properties that befit the order of origin. The persons are unique and individual. But they are not distinct from one another in any easily understandable way, or else they would be three gods. Although surely they do not lack subjectivity, they are distinguished via a mystery above that of knowledge, will, being, and suchlike; their distinction flows from relations of origin in the communication of the divine essence that do not render the essence distinct in the persons. Their distinction flows from a relationality that goes deeper than any relationality that we can imagine or conceive. But how can they have true relationality if they cannot be conceived as distinct centers of consciousness? The answer to this question is found in the answer to precisely how they can be transcendentally one in the fullest and most simple way, yet utterly (and nonquantitatively) three. In short, the answer eludes us. We must be content with glimpsing this revealed relationality; and as I hope to show in the chapters that follow, we can do this with respect to the Holy Spirit by meditating upon the names "Holy Spirit," "Love," and "Gift." Surely this trinitarian relationality somehow includes, in a supereminent form, all that we find valuable in human relationality. But depicting the Father, Son, and Holy Spirit as three centers of being and consciousness lacks the necessary apophaticism and metaphysical caution due to "the blessed and only Sovereign" who "dwells in unapproachable light" (1 Tim. 6:15–16).

My appreciation for the names "Love" and "Gift" also helps to explain why I do not follow Coakley's approach. Recall that Coakley, indebted to Pseudo-Dionysius and reading Christian Platonism through her own distinctive feminist lens, emphasizes "desire" as the path into trinitarian naming, both through the prayerful purgation of desire by the Spirit, and through the Spirit's incorporation of desiring humans into the divine "desire." Coakley wishes to undercut the linear procession models in which the Spirit seems an overly passive and rather third-rate addition to the work that the Father and Son have already done. In the linear models, it seems that the Spirit comes on the scene after the real, or at least the main, salvific work has been done.

For my part, I affirm the value of the linear models (John and Luke), even while appreciating the attention that Coakley gives to what she terms the Pauline incorporative model of the Spirit's work. The linear models reveal the eternal order of origin, which is a central aspect of the mystery of the Trinity. Among the coequal persons, there is an order of origin, and indeed they are distinguished by relative opposition in this order of origin. The fact that there is a nontemporal order in the communication of the divine essence—Father-Son-Spirit—is one of the main things that the New Testament teaches us about the Trinity.[95] Even though God is supremely one, there is relationality in God constituted by an order of origin in the communication of the divine essence. The primacy of the Father is seen in John 1, where we learn that the Word "was in the beginning with God; all things were made through him, and without him was not anything made that was made" (John 1:2–3). God makes all things through the Word; this indicates the primacy of the Father, a primacy that does not undercut the divinity of the Word ("the Word was God" [John 1:1]). The relationship Father-Son likewise indicates the Father's primacy, since a son is begotten by a father. Hasker makes this point well, drawing upon Hebrews 1:5 and other texts from John's Gospel.

It seems to me that the linear model fits quite well with the incorporative model. As Coakley notes, an emphasis on the Holy Spirit's incorporative work characterizes Romans 8: "When we cry, 'Abba! Father!' it is the Spirit himself bearing witness with our spirit that we are children of God, and if children, then heirs, heirs of God and fellow heirs with Christ" (Rom. 8:15–17). The Spirit enables us to cry out for the Father and thereby shows that we have been made sons and daughters in the Son. The Spirit incorporates us into the Son and enables us to approach the Father as his children. This does not seem so different from the linear model, in which the Spirit comes to dwell in us with the result that the Father and Son also indwell us (John 14:17, 23). Although I can see the difference between the two models, they appear complementary to me. The emphasis on the order of origin—on the Father begetting the Son and the Father (and Son) spirating the Spirit[96]—enhances the incorporative

95. Jean-Miguel Garrigues argues that the trinitarian order is "a *pure order of origin without anteriority and posteriority*, whether of nature, of time or even of reason" (Garrigues, *Le Saint-Esprit sceau de la Trinité*, 228). Garrigues excludes logical anteriority and posteriority on the grounds that the "Father" always, even logically, requires a "Son." It seems to me, however, that *some* kind of logical anteriority and posteriority is required; otherwise, it hardly seems possible to maintain (as Garrigues very much wishes to do) the monarchy and fontality of the Father.

96. Emmanuel Durand emphasizes in this regard that the Father "is relative to the Son *and* to the Spirit. Even if the name of Father does not formally and directly consignify more than the Son, the hypostasis of the Father is no less relative to the Spirit than to the Son" (Durand, "Perichoresis," 185–86). For Durand, "considering the Father-Son relation as completed in itself leads to a subordination of the Spirit in reference to the Father-Son pair" (ibid., 186–87). I would say that the Father-Son relation is complete in itself, but not in the sense of being separable from the Father/Son-Holy Spirit relation. As Aquinas remarks, following Augustine, "the Son is the Word, not any sort of word, but one who breathes forth Love" (*Summa theologiae* I, q. 43, a. 5, ad 2). Gilles Emery, OP, comments in this regard, "One cannot fully grasp the begetting if one thinks only in terms of the relation of Father and Son, for the begetting of the Son cannot be detached from the procession of the Holy Spirit" (Emery, *Trinitarian Theology of Saint Thomas Aquinas*, 390).

model by showing us that our unexpected entrance into the divine life means not pure relationality but an ordered relationality.

In my view, the ordered relationality that the linear model shows us does not require (even if the New Testament may have originally allowed for, as Hurtado claims) a subordination of Son and Spirit. Coming second or third in an atemporal order does not lessen the place of the Son or Holy Spirit, not least because of the evident centrality of the Spirit's coming in the economy of salvation as lived out by believers: "When the Spirit of truth comes, he will guide you into all the truth" (John 16:13).[97] Put another way, ordered relationality does not necessitate subordination in the Trinity, because of the perfection of the communication of all that God is: "All that the Father has is mine [the Son's]" and the Spirit "will take what is mine and declare it to you" (John 16:14–15). The perfection of the processions means that all that the Father has, the Son and the Holy Spirit also have. We are incorporated into the trinitarian life when we come to share in this life in a manner that befits its pattern of ordered relationality.

Coakley's emphasis on desire will not be rejected by an admirer of Dionysius, as I certainly am. Dionysius refuses to name God "agapē" without also naming God "eros." Recall how Dionysius describes God as "yearning on the move, simple, self-moved, self-acting, preexistent in the Good, flowing out from the Good onto all that is and returning once again to the Good."[98] Even so, another admirer of Dionysius, Thomas Aquinas, offers some helpful qualifications. Discussing love as a passion, though without referring explicitly to *eros* and *agapē*, Aquinas states in the *prima-secundae pars* of the *Summa theologiae* that the term "love" (*amor*) possesses "a wider signification" than the terms "dilection" (*dilectio*) and "charity" (*caritas*).[99] He explains that "every dilection or charity is love, but not vice versa."[100] This is so because "dilection implies, in addition to love, a choice [*electionem*] made beforehand," which means that *dilectio*, unlike *amor*, can be only in the will, not in the

97. Commenting on the way in which the revelation of the Spirit differs from the revelation of the Son in the New Testament, Robert Sokolowski observes, "This anonymity of the Spirit is somehow necessary; there must be someone with the authority to reveal the Son and, through the Son, the Father, but that person must remain hidden and ought not to declare himself. . . . He is, after all, the Spirit and not the Word; he is an agent of truth in a manner different from the Son. The Son has said everything that needs to be said, but the Spirit brings it to life" (Sokolowski, "The Revelation of the Holy Trinity: A Study in Personal Pronouns," in *Christian Faith and Human Understanding: Studies on the Eucharist, Trinity, and the Human Person* [Washington, DC: Catholic University of America Press, 2006], 131–48, at 147).

98. Pseudo-Dionysius, *The Divine Names*, 4.14, pp. 82–83.

99. I-II, q. 26, a. 3.

100. I-II, q. 26, a. 3.

concupiscible passion.[101] For its part, *caritas* involves a perfection of *amor*, rather than *amor* per se.

In question 20 of the *prima pars* of the *Summa*, Aquinas asks whether "amor" is in God. Answering in the affirmative, he distinguishes love from "desire," which regards "good as not yet possessed."[102] But he also makes clear that love in a certain sense encompasses desire, since love "regards good universally, whether possessed or not," so that "love is naturally the first act of the will and appetite."[103] Love is the root of desire to possess a good, and love is the root of joy in possessing a good. Since desire implies lack of a good, however, desire can be attributed to God only metaphorically: God's love embraces the Good (God himself) in which nothing is lacking. If there were any lack in God, then God could not be supremely actual love and the center of all desire.[104]

Yet the divine *eros* that Dionysius has in view—"yearning on the move, simple, self-moved, self-acting, preexistent in the Good, flowing out from the Good"—is not rejected by Aquinas. Citing book 4 of *The Divine Names*, Aquinas shows in question 6 of the *prima pars* that God is supremely good because supremely desirable.[105] And in the first question of the *tertia pars*, Aquinas again cites book 4 of *The Divine Names* so as to indicate the fittingness of the incarnation: "it belongs to the essence of goodness to communicate itself to others," and it is therefore fitting that God share himself "in the highest manner" with his rational creatures.[106] This is indeed the "yearning on the move, simple, self-moved, self-acting, preexistent in the Good, flowing out from the Good" that Dionysius envisions. Even if "desire" can be applied to God only metaphorically, the divine goodness and love encompass the ecstatic gifting and selfless outpouring that Dionysius names by means of "desire." As Pope Benedict XVI puts it in his encyclical *Deus caritas est*, "God's *eros* for man is also totally *agape*."[107]

This is a roundabout way of getting to my point, which is that "Love" and "Gift," as names of the Spirit, provide a richer and clearer way of describing the incorporative work of the Spirit than does "desire." Without rejecting

---

101. I-II, q. 26, a. 3.

102. I, q. 20, a. 1.

103. I, q. 20, a. 1.

104. See I, q. 20, a. 2. In relation to creatures, God's love is causal: God gives a finite participation in his goodness and thereby enables the creature to be.

105. I, q. 6, a. 1.

106. III, q. 1, a. 1. For discussion, see Andrew Hofer, OP, "Dionysian Elements in Thomas Aquinas's Christology: A Case of the Authority and Ambiguity of Pseudo-Dionysius," *The Thomist* 72 (2008): 409–42, at 423–24, 442.

107. Pope Benedict XVI, *Deus caritas est* (Vatican City: Libreria Editrice Vaticana, 2006), §10.

Coakley's emphasis on desire, I think that we can say much the same thing—and say it more precisely and within a fuller context—by attending to the names "Love" and "Gift." Coakley, of course, is attempting what she terms a "théologie totale" in which her reading of the Trinity in terms of desire seeks to underscore that "no trinitarian language is innocent of sexual, political, and ecclesiastical overtones and implications."[108] My book is not this kind of "théologie totale," but I seek to name the Holy Spirit in a manner whose "overtones and implications" befit the Gift of Love I have experienced within the body of Christ, in which we are called to "know the love of Christ which surpasses knowledge" and to "be filled with all the fullness of God" (Eph. 3:19).

If neither social trinitarianism (not least in its analytic-theology mode) nor the dynamics of *eros* alone seems suited to unfolding the theology of the Holy Spirit, what about the third popular contemporary approach, set forth by Weinandy? Here the goal is to give the Spirit an active work within the Trinity and thereby to be more faithful to our experience of the Spirit as an active, fully personal agent in the world. Insisting upon "the Spirit's mutual infusion *in* Son and Father," Coakley agrees with Weinandy's point that (in her words) "there can be in God's trinitarian ontology no Sonship which is eternally 'sourced' by 'Father' *in the Spirit*."[109] She disagrees, however, with Weinandy's blaming Neoplatonic emanationism and Aristotelian epistemology for the inability of theologians prior to the twentieth century to think outside the traditional order of origin. In a formulation that I expect

108. Coakley, *God, Sexuality, and the Self*, 308. From a liberationist perspective, Miguel H. Díaz argues that "a theology of God that does not attend to issues of human liberation, a trinitarian theology unable to challenge oppressive human experiences that cause death, does not reveal the life-giving mystery of God. . . . God who is for us (Father), from us (Son), and permanently among us (Holy Spirit) is *mysterium liberationis*" (Díaz, "The Life-Giving Reality of God from Black, Latin American, and US Hispanic Theological Perspectives," in Phan, *The Cambridge Companion to the Trinity*, 259–72, at 269). Díaz's theology of the Trinity is a theology of history: "The doctrine of the Trinity is a signpost that points to God's mystery as a life-giving triune presence in history. . . . This one history neither 'hyper-inflates' human realities nor focuses on the 'immanent' reality of God to the detriment of God's historical mediations. History, especially the history of liberation from racial, socio-economic, and cultural oppressive human experiences, is the exterior manifestation of the triune life of grace, just as conversely this triune life is the intrinsic presupposition and perfection of that history (that for the sake of which history exists)" (ibid., 259, 261–62). What would it take to produce a trinitarian theology able "to challenge oppressive human experiences that cause death"? Oppressive human experiences and death stem from a lack of unity in love, and from a lack of holiness (sin). Thus a trinitarian theology that challenges oppressive experiences should have a central place for love, unity, and the gift of holiness. Love also prompts the desire to know the life-giving God who reveals himself, and Díaz's way of naming this God—"for us (Father), from us (Son), and permanently among us (Holy Spirit)"—is inadequate.

109. Coakley, *God, Sexuality, and the Self*, 332.

Weinandy would find to his liking, she states, "The deeper problem lies in rightly locating the *intrinsic* role of the Spirit in the Father-Son relationship."[110]

Recall that Weinandy considers that just as the Father and Son have active roles in the Trinity, so must the Spirit, in order to be fully a coequal divine person. The Father begets and spirates; the Son spirates; but the Spirit (as traditionally understood) has no active role in the production of another divine person. Weinandy states, "The Spirit is merely the Love or Gift shared by the Father and the Son. It is therefore difficult to see why, in the Western conception of the Trinity, the Holy Spirit is a distinct person or subject—a who."[111] Given the conditions that Weinandy sets here, it would be difficult to see why, in the traditional Eastern conception of the Trinity, either the Son or the Spirit is a distinct person. Only the Father would be such, since in the traditional Eastern view only the Father is responsible for the production of another divine person. To prevent misunderstanding, it is worth reiterating here that contemporary Orthodox theologians such as Paul Evdokimov and Olivier Clément have advocated trinitarian theologies similar to Weinandy's.

When Weinandy turns to the trinitarian theology that I profess, then, he thinks that the Spirit's names of "Love" and "Gift" are too passive for full personhood. He appreciates the emphasis on relationality and agrees that the divine persons are distinguished by their mutual relations. In his view, however, "the persons subsist not only in opposition to one another, but also in complementarity to one another. They consummate one another."[112] He underscores this point with respect to his own view of the Trinity: "Because each of the persons now actively plays a role in determining the subjectivity of the others, they complement one another."[113] He credits the complementarity of the persons, in fact, to the activity of the Holy Spirit. The Spirit is involved in making the Son "Son" and the Father "Father." Weinandy affirms, "By being the one in whom the Father begets the Son and so is Father for the Son, and by being the one in whom the Son is begotten and so is Son for the Father, the Holy Spirit subsists as the source of their complementarity."[114] The relations of opposition that constitute the Father and Son are made complementary relations by the Spirit's activity.[115]

110. Ibid., 333n34.

111. Weinandy, *Father's Spirit of Sonship*, 8.

112. Ibid., 82.

113. Ibid.

114. Ibid., 83.

115. In its 1995 document "The Greek and Latin Traditions regarding the Procession of the Holy Spirit," the Pontifical Council for Promoting Christian Unity makes an argument that, in certain ways, is similar to Weinandy's perspective: "It is in the Spirit that this relationship between

As Weinandy points out, indeed, "Love" and "Gift" are "less than subjective or personal names," especially by comparison with "Father" and "Son."[116] Weinandy nonetheless accepts the fact that the name "Holy Spirit" is less personal than "Father" or "Son," on the grounds that the Spirit gains his distinct subsistence via the activity of being the one in whom the Father and the Son are related. While the Holy Spirit is not merely passive, the Holy Spirit does

---

the Father and the Son itself attains its Trinitarian perfection. Just as the Father is characterized as Father by the Son he generates, so does the Spirit, by taking his origin from the Father, characterize the Father in the manner of the Trinity in relation to the Son and characterizes the Son in the manner of the Trinity in his relation to the Father: in the fullness of the Trinitarian mystery they are Father and Son in the Holy Spirit." For this text, see http://www.ewtn.com /library/curia/pccufilq.htm. I can agree with the Pontifical Council insofar as its aim is to affirm the ineffable richness and perfection of trinitarian perichoresis. David Coffey argues in light of this text that "the Son draws his being entirely and exclusively from the Father and not at all from the Holy Spirit. Any and all suggestion of a Spirituque must be resolutely rejected as antithetical to authentic Christian doctrine. But at the same time the fullness of the relationship between the Father and the Son cannot be understood or appreciated without an affirmation of the Holy Spirit who, as their mutual love, exists *between* them" (Coffey, *"Did You Receive the Holy Spirit When You Believed?" Some Basic Questions for Pneumatology* [Milwaukee: Marquette University Press, 2005], 66). I agree in rejecting "all suggestion of a Spirituque," and it is also true that the Son cannot be understood fully without the Spirit, since the Son is a Word who breathes forth Love. But I think that Coffey's way of describing "the relationship between the Father and Son" and his conception of the Spirit as existing *"between"* them" fall into anthropomorphism. The relationship of the Spirit to the Father and the Son needs to be approached more cautiously. Coffey contrasts the "procession model" (Father-Son-Spirit) with the "return model" (Father-Spirit-Son) and argues that the latter "deals with the fullness of life and relationships that obtains among the three persons" (ibid., 67; cf. 79). In my view, the latter oversteps the bounds of what we can know. For Coffey, "if the Son is the self-communication of the Father *simpliciter*, the Holy Spirit is the self-communication of the Father to the Son. . . . The Holy Spirit is the divine person who mediates the Father and the Son to each other in mediated immediacy" (ibid., 98, 102). Commenting on Coffey's earlier distinction between a "procession model" and a "bestowal model" (an earlier version of the "return model"), Ralph Del Colle argues in favor of Coffey's position:

> Incarnation and anointing are the appropriate terms for the procession and bestowal models, respectively. In the traditional procession model the Holy Spirit is offered (only to believers, this being exclusive of Jesus, on whom it is simply bestowed); in the bestowal model the Spirit is in reality "bestowed." In the procession model no significant role is assigned to the Holy Spirit in the incarnation. In the bestowal model Jesus is anointed to divine sonship with the Holy Spirit. In the procession model the Son is co-principle of the Holy Spirit, while in the bestowal model the bestowing of the Holy Spirit is alternatively carried out by the Father upon the Son and then by the Son upon the Father. . . . In sum, in the anointing theology of Coffey, the Father anoints Jesus with the Holy Spirit to divine sonship, this being identical with the incarnation. (Del Colle, *Christ and the Spirit: Spirit-Christology in Trinitarian Perspective* [Oxford: Oxford University Press, 1994], 124)

The problem here is anthropomorphism, which the procession model avoids; once the missions are factored in, the procession model is hardly as deficient as Coffey and Del Colle suggest.

116. Weinandy, *Father's Spirit of Sonship*, 83.

remain somewhat "hidden" or translucent within the Trinity, because his role is relationally oriented toward the Father and Son: his role is "to substantiate or person the Father and the Son for one another."[117] In the Trinity, the Spirit seeks to make the Father and Son manifest, just as the Spirit does in the economy of salvation.

I question, however, whether the Spirit needs an active role in the communication of the divine essence in order to be a coequal divine person. If every divine person needed an active role, then the divine person who is most active would be the greatest. Assuming Weinandy to be correct, the Father would be active in producing the Son and Spirit; the Spirit would be active in making the Father to be "Father" and the Son to be "Son"; and the Son would be active in producing the Spirit. Unless I have missed an active role of the Son, it would seem as though the Spirit is now the most active—or perhaps the Father is still most active. The Son now appears to be the least active. The point is that productive activity is not what makes a coequal divine person.

In addition, I do not see why the Spirit need be active in begetting the Son, as though the Father-Son relation were not sufficient. The rejection of a nontemporal order of origin seems a heavy price to pay for attempting to equalize the productive activity of all the divine persons. The Father's unbegotten paternity, his personal property to which Scripture repeatedly testifies, seems to be rendered meaningless once we suppose that the Holy Spirit, who proceeds from the Father and Son, is present "already" in the begetting of the Son. Why talk as though the Spirit proceeds from the Father and Son, if the Spirit is there in the begetting of the Son? If the Spirit is present in the Son's eternal begetting, how can we also posit that the Spirit proceeds from the Father and the begotten Son—proceeds from the begotten one in whose begetting he *already* acts?

Puzzles such as this would force us to abandon utterly the order of origin, and would render nonsensical any talk about the processions. It will not do to say that the Spirit proceeds from a divine person whom that same Spirit helps to beget; this puts an end to any intelligible talk about an order in the processions, and indeed to any intelligible talk about the processions themselves as constitutive of divine persons. Instead, one is left with a purely circular Trinity in which no one person is productive of any other person, since production requires at least some kind of intelligible (atemporal) priority. It also renders obsolete the notion of relative opposition as constitutive of persons, because (as Weinandy recognizes) the Spirit's "complementary" role now makes the

117. Ibid., 84.

Father to be "Father," in a way that the Father-Son relative opposition apparently cannot do.

Ultimately, the usefulness of the order-of-origins model, rooted in processions and relations, is evacuated by Weinandy's additions to that model. The fundamental mistake consists in supposing that each person needs an active productive role in order to be a coequal person. This might be the case if the divine persons were like human persons, although even here it seems to me that human dignity and coequality do not depend upon a certain level of activity. But the divine persons are not coequal by reason of what they do in the order of origin. They are coequal persons because they are distinct relations in God, and therefore are *subsisting* relations, fully divine. To describe the Father, Son, and Holy Spirit as subsisting relations makes them sound quite different from anything that we encounter in our productive lives; and so they are. The persons are relations that do not impair perfect transcendental unity. They are a divine communion that is the one God. Their relationality is ordered to one another, in the order of origin that involves no temporal priority but is an order nonetheless.

The Eschatological Spirit

Examining the biblical depiction of the Spirit's work, Rodrigo Morales observes, "Although the Spirit of God plays various roles in the prophetic literature of the OT, perhaps the most dominant theme taken up by the early Christian movement is the eschatological outpouring of the Spirit."[118] This Old Testament theme of the Spirit's eschatological outpouring appears, for example, in Ezekiel. Ezekiel's prophecies unite two senses of "restoration":

---

118. Rodrigo J. Morales, *The Spirit and the Restoration of Israel: New Exodus and New Creation Motifs in Galatians* (Tübingen: Mohr Siebeck, 2010), 13. Indebted to E. P. Sanders, Morales defines "restoration eschatology" and "restoration of Israel" as follows:

> With regard to the OT Prophets and later Second Temple Jewish literature, the terms refer to the expectation that God would finally act to bring the tribes of Israel back to the land, sometimes under a Davidic ruler—in other words, he would *restore* Israel to its former glory. With respect to Paul, the terms describe the apostle's conviction that God had begun to fulfill his promises to redeem Israel through the death and resurrection of Jesus. . . . Unlike the authors of texts such as the *Psalms of Solomon*, Paul did not expect a nationalistic return of the tribes of Israel to the land under an earthly Davidic ruler. Nevertheless, he did believe that through the cross and the outpouring of the Spirit God had begun to fulfill the promises spoken through the prophets. Indeed, though Paul's message of the cross was not at all clear from the writings of the OT (as though Jesus's death on the cross were the obvious solution that all first-century Jews would have expected), Paul's emphasis on the phenomenon of the Spirit makes the most sense in light of eschatological expectations that frequently appear in the context of a hope for the restoration of Israel. (ibid., 10–11)

the people will be restored to the land of Israel, and they will be spiritually restored and renewed. It is the latter sense that most clearly involves the Spirit. Thus the Lord promises, "I will take you from the nations, and gather you from the all the countries, and bring you into your own land. I will sprinkle clean water upon you, and you shall be clean from all your uncleannesses, and from all your idols I will cleanse you. A new heart I will give you, and a new spirit I will put within you" (Ezek. 36:24–26).[119] Through the prophetic image of the valley of dry human bones, Ezekiel goes on to show that the people will be created anew by God's breath, just as the breath of God created the first man (Gen. 2:7). This vision of restoration combines a return to the land and a return from spiritual death: "I will bring you home into the land of Israel. And you shall know that I am the LORD, when I open your graves, and raise you from your graves, O my people. And I will put my Spirit within you, and you shall live" (Ezek. 37:12–14). Furthermore, at the same time that the people receive God's Spirit, they will be ruled by one Davidic king and no longer be separated into two kingdoms. The Lord explains, "I will make a covenant of peace with them; it shall be an everlasting covenant with them; and I will bless them and multiply them, and will set my sanctuary in the midst of them for evermore" (Ezek. 37:26).[120]

This restoration of Israel through the coming of God's Spirit and a Davidic king is presented in different ways elsewhere in the prophets. Its roots are found in the covenantal relationship of God with Abraham, and in the renewal and deepening of this covenant at Mount Sinai. Moses tells the Israelites that the Lord "loved your fathers and chose their descendants after them, and brought you out of Egypt with his own presence" (Deut. 4:37). God did this for no reason other than his love; his covenant and his saving acts are gifts of his love. Moses

119. See James Robson, *Word and Spirit in Ezekiel* (London: T&T Clark, 2006), as well as (engaging a variety of prophetic texts, including Ezek. 36) Robin Routledge, "The Spirit and the Future in the Old Testament: Restoration and Renewal," in Firth and Wegner, *Presence, Power and Promise*, 346–67. With respect to Pauline pneumatology, Gordon D. Fee shows the importance of Ezekiel 36–37 for "the eschatological implications of Paul's understanding of the Spirit—as fulfillment of God's promised gift of Spirit at the end of the ages" (Fee, *God's Empowering Presence: The Holy Spirit in the Letters of Paul* [Peabody, MA: Hendrickson, 1994], 304).

120. Joseph Blenkinsopp comments, "While the major prophetic books have little to say about the spirit, for Ezekiel, as for primitive prophecy, it is the decisive agent, being not only the principle of movement and renewal but the dynamic factor in prophetic possession" (Blenkinsopp, *A History of Prophecy in Israel: From the Settlement in the Land to the Hellenistic Period* [Philadelphia: Westminster, 1983], 204). Yet Blenkinsopp's reading of Ezekiel 37 is rather dull, seeing in it only a portrait of a community that "has lost its will to survive" and "is vivified by the spirit activated through the word of God addressed to the community" (ibid.). See also the relevant passages in Blenkinsopp, *Ezekiel* (Louisville: John Knox, 1990). On the apocalyptic eschatology of Ezekiel 38–39, see Stephen L. Cook, *Prophecy and Apocalypticism: The Post-Exilic Social Setting* (Minneapolis: Fortress, 1995), 85–121.

reminds the people of Israel, "For you are a people holy to the LORD your God; the LORD your God has chosen you to be a people for his own possession, out of all the peoples that are on the face of the earth. It was not because you were more in number than any other people that the LORD set his love upon you and chose you . . . but it is because the LORD loves you" (Deut. 7:6–8). Because God has established this covenantal relationship of love with Israel, the people are called to know and love God, and to love one another. Through Moses, God commands Israel, "You shall be holy; for I the LORD your God am holy. . . . You shall love your neighbor as yourself" (Lev. 19:2, 18), and "Hear, O Israel: the LORD our God is one LORD, and you shall love the LORD your God with all your heart, and with all your soul, and with all your might" (Deut. 6:4–5). God loves Israel, and each Israelite must love God and neighbor.

The context of covenantal love explains why a "restoration" is needed and sought.[121] In fact, a "restoration" is sought almost from the outset of Israel's Scriptures. Consider Genesis 6, which reports that at the same time that "men began to multiply on the face of the ground" (Gen. 6:1), sin multiplied too, so that "the earth was corrupt in God's sight, and the earth was filled with violence. And God saw the earth, and behold, it was corrupt; for all flesh had corrupted their way upon the earth" (Gen. 6:11–12). The time before Noah was marked by the fact that "every imagination of the thoughts of his [man's] heart was only evil continually" (Gen. 6:5). After the flood, the same alienation persisted: Noah got drunk and his son Ham "saw the nakedness of his father" (Gen. 9:22). The men of Babel sought to "make a name" for themselves by building "a tower with its top in the heavens" (Gen. 11:4), repeating the desire of Adam and Eve to seize divinity for themselves, in response to the serpent's temptation, "your eyes will be opened, and you will be like God, knowing good and evil" (Gen. 3:5).

Yet, despite human wickedness and alienation from God, God does not give up on humans—as is shown first by God's clothing Adam and Eve after their fall (Gen. 3:21), notwithstanding the pain, hardship, and death to which they have made themselves subject. After the flood, the rainbow stands as God's covenant with all creation (Gen. 9). But it is especially through his covenantal relationship with Abraham and his descendents that God works to restore

---

121. For the range of meanings (both communal and individual) associated with the hoped-for "restoration" in Second Temple Judaism, see Jon D. Levenson, *Resurrection and the Restoration of Israel: The Ultimate Victory of the God of Life* (New Haven: Yale University Press, 2006); N. T. Wright, *The New Testament and the People of God* (Minneapolis: Fortress, 1992), 280–338. See also, in support of Wright's work, Craig A. Evans, "Jesus and the Continuing Exile of Israel," in *Jesus and the Restoration of Israel: A Critical Assessment of N. T. Wright's Jesus and the Victory of God*, ed. Carey C. Newman (Downers Grove, IL: InterVarsity, 1999), 77–100.

humans from the state of sinful alienation. The law given to Moses, in this light, was not a mere legal code; rather, it was an act of love and a path of life. As the psalmist implores God, "Lead me in the path of your commandments, for I delight in it. Incline my heart to your testimonies, and not to gain! Turn my eyes from looking at vanities; and give me life in your ways" (Ps. 119:35–37). Since it remains the case that sinfulness overcomes humans, however, the psalmist laments, "The LORD looks down from heaven upon the children of men, to see if there are any that act wisely, that seek after God. They have all gone astray, they are all alike corrupt; there is none that does good, no, not one" (Ps. 14:2–3); and Isaiah echoes, "Behold, the LORD's hand is not shortened, that it cannot save, or his ear dull, that it cannot hear; but your iniquities have made a separation between you and your God, and your sins have hid his face from you. . . . The LORD saw it, and it displeased him that there was no justice" (Isa. 59:1–2, 15). Given this situation of alienation, Isaiah prophesies restoration. The Lord promises through Isaiah, "I will pour my Spirit upon your descendants, and my blessing on your offspring" (Isa. 44:3). Isaiah says of God's Servant, "I have put my Spirit upon him, he will bring forth justice to the nations. . . . He will not fail or be discouraged till he has established justice in the earth; and the coastlands wait for his law" (Isa. 42:1, 4).[122] The result will be the restoration and redemption of Israel and indeed of all the nations.

The eschatological outpouring of the Spirit foretold by the prophets will overcome idolatry and injustice. This can be accomplished interiorly only by an infusion of love, so that the people of God truly become able to "love the LORD your God with all your heart" and to "love your neighbor as yourself." It is no wonder that Jesus identifies these as the two greatest commandments

---

122. Walter Brueggemann cautions with regard to Christian interpretations of Isaiah 42:1–4 such as my own: "It is a difficult question about how to interpret the 'universal outreach' of this imagery. It is asserted in verse 4 that the 'coastlands' wait for the new ordering of social reality to be accomplished by the servant. It is a characteristic propensity of Christian interpretation . . . that Israel's work is to transform the Gentile world and to make a welcoming place for the vulnerable. Such a reading, however, must be done with extreme caution. It is equally possible (probable?) that this scenario concerns *Jewish* people scattered around the Mediterranean basin who wait for Jewish rehabilitation" (Brueggemann, *Isaiah 40–66* [Louisville: Westminster John Knox, 1998], 42–43). The centrality of the restoration of Israel, however, need not be set in opposition to Israel's mission for the world. See Christopher T. Begg, "The Peoples and the Worship of Yahweh in the Book of Isaiah," in *Worship and the Hebrew Bible*, ed. M. P. Graham, R. R. Marrs, and S. L. McKenzie (Sheffield: Sheffield Academic Press, 1999), 35–55; Joseph Blenkinsopp, "Second Isaiah—Prophet of Universalism," *Journal for the Study of the Old Testament* 41 (1988): 83–103; G. I. Davies, "The Destiny of the Nations in the Book of Isaiah," in *Le livre d'Isaïe*, ed. J. Vermeylen (Leuven: Leuven University Press, 1989), 93–120. See also J. Ross Wagner, *Heralds of the Good News: Isaiah and Paul in Concert in the Letter to the Romans* (Leiden: Brill, 2002).

(see Mark 12:29–31), and that the scribe, with whom Jesus is in conversation, agrees with him. The letters of Paul, which testify joyfully to the eschatological outpouring of the Spirit, depict the Spirit's outpouring as a gift of love. Rejoicing that "we have peace with God through our Lord Jesus Christ," Paul proclaims that "God's love has been poured into our hearts through the Holy Spirit who has been given to us" (Rom. 5:1, 5).[123] Through this gift of love, the Spirit unites us to God in such a way that nothing "will be able to separate us from the love of God in Christ Jesus" (Rom. 8:39). Paul makes clear that the eschatological outpouring of the Spirit enables us to fulfill the law—to avoid idolatry and injustice—precisely by enabling us interiorly to love God and neighbor: "Love does no wrong to a neighbor; therefore love is the fulfilling of the law" (Rom. 13:10).[124] As Graham Tomlin points out, the eschatological kingdom "is the kingdom of the love of God," and it is "what happens when the Spirit comes."[125]

Elsewhere Paul states that "the fruit of the Spirit is love, joy, peace, patience, kindness, goodness, faithfulness, gentleness, self-control" (Gal. 5:22–23). It is because God loves us that he has given us the Spirit: "He destined us in love to be his sons through Jesus Christ" (Eph. 1:5), and he did so "out of the great love with which he loved us, even when we were dead through our trespasses" (Eph. 2:4–5). Hearing and believing in the gospel, we have been "sealed with the promised Holy Spirit, who is the guarantee of our inheritance until we acquire possession of it" (Eph. 1:13–14). Strengthened by the indwelling Spirit and by faith in Christ, we are "rooted and grounded in love" and come to "know the love of Christ which surpasses knowledge, that you may be filled with all the fulness of God" (Eph. 3:17, 19). Paul prays for his flock that "your love may abound more and more, with knowledge and discernment" (Phil. 1:9). The Spirit's gift of love is profoundly unitive: "So if there is any encouragement in Christ, any incentive of love, any participation in the Spirit, any affection

123. See Fee, *God's Empowering Presence*, 493–98.

124. Fee comments on Romans 13:8–10, "There is no direct reference or allusion to the Spirit in this paragraph. I include it here because it is another of many texts that presuppose the Spirit without mentioning him. The connections are obvious: In 8:4 Paul has argued that those who 'walk in the Spirit' thus 'fulfill' the 'righteous requirement of the Law.' Having begun the general paraenesis dealing with relationships with the word that 'love must be sincere' (12:9), Paul now tells them that the love-command, which 'sums up' all other commands, is precisely how the 'righteous requirement of Torah' is 'fulfilled.' Thus in 14:15 the one who disregards a brother or sister on the issue of food is 'not *walking* in *love*.' Not only so, but in Gal. 5:22 this love that 'fulfills' Torah is expressly designated as the 'fruit of the Spirit' (cf. Rom. 15:30), whose very existence puts one in a sphere where Law no longer pertains. Even though not mentioned in this passage, what is said here about love 'fulfilling' the Law is in Pauline understanding a direct outworking of the Holy Spirit in the life of the believer" (ibid., 613).

125. Tomlin, *Prodigal Spirit*, 52–53.

and sympathy, complete my joy by being of the same mind, having the same love, being in full accord and of one mind" (Phil. 2:1–2).[126] Paul praises the Colossians for their "love in the Spirit" (Col. 1:8), which is evidence of the Spirit's eschatological work in the Colossian church; they and other Christian churches are "knit together in love" (Col. 2:2).

I have focused here on the Old Testament and Paul in order to emphasize that the root of the naming of the Spirit "Love" and "Gift" is what Jacob Neusner calls the "urgent love between God and Israel, the holy people."[127] As we saw in the prophets, the Holy Spirit's characteristics begin to come to light within this covenantal context, which was Paul's own context within which he encountered the Lord on the road to Damascus. I am persuaded that these characteristics from the salvific economy identify the eternal distinctiveness of the Holy Spirit as the communion of Love of the Father and Son.[128]

The church, of course, is a mixed body whose members often look little like a people who are indwelt by the Holy Spirit. And yet, by the redemptive power of Jesus's cross and resurrection, the church is being "prepared as a bride adorned for her husband" (Rev. 21:2) by means of Spirit-filled teaching and sacraments. James Dunn observes with regard to the earliest church that alongside the conviction that Jesus had been raised from the dead and exalted to the right hand of God, "The other most striking feature of the earliest days was the vitality of the spiritual experience of the first believers, attributed to the outpouring of the God's Spirit upon them."[129] Indeed, the Holy Spirit,

126. For emphasis on joy in the Christian life, a note frequently sounded by Paul, see Aquinas's treatment of joy as an effect of charity in *Summa theologiae* II-II, q. 28. See also the recent popular book, filled with folksy stories, by James Martin, SJ, *Between Heaven and Mirth: Why Joy, Humor, and Laughter Are at the Heart of the Spiritual Life* (New York: HarperCollins, 2011).

127. Jacob Neusner, *Israel's Love Affair with God: Song of Songs* (Valley Forge, PA: Trinity Press International, 1993), 1. Scot McKnight suggests that the "new covenant" hermeneutic must have arisen, sometime after Pentecost, from "the conviction that the pneumatic experience of Pentecost was in fact what was expected by Jeremiah and Ezekiel" (McKnight, "Covenant and Spirit: The Origins of the New Covenant Hermeneutic," in Stanton, Longenecker, and Barton, *Holy Spirit and Christian Origins*, 41–54, at 54).

128. As Anne Hunt says, "In terms of our actual experience of the Trinity in salvation history, the Trinity *ad extra*, it is the Spirit whom we first encounter, the Spirit who is given to us: 'God's love has been poured into our hearts through the Holy Spirit who has been given to us' (Rom. 5:5). It is the Holy Spirit who leads us to recognize, and incorporates us into, the mystery of Christ, in and through whom we are made sons and daughters of the Father" (Hunt, "Trinity, Christology, and Pneumatology," in Phan, *The Cambridge Companion to the Trinity*, 365–80, at 370).

129. James D. G. Dunn, *Christianity in the Making*, vol. 2, *Beginning from Jerusalem* (Grand Rapids: Eerdmans, 2009), 1169. Similarly, Craig S. Keener comments that "the experience of and dependence on the Spirit was pervasive in early Christianity, which was thoroughly charismatic in the general sense of the term. Further, although some Jewish contemporaries sought revelatory experiences, the early Christians were more consistently charismatic than most of

promised by Israel's God and given by Israel's crucified, risen, and exalted Messiah, is now poured forth so that we might be made children of God, "a dwelling place of God in the Spirit" (Eph. 2:22) and "knit together in love" (Col. 2:2). This occurs when we are united to Jesus Christ and, in Christ, to the Father; as Yves Congar says, "Although all this is accomplished by the Spirit, it constitutes not the Body of the Spirit, but that of Christ."[130] "If we live by the Spirit, let us also walk by the Spirit. Let us have no self-conceit, no provoking of one another, no envy of one another. . . . Bear one another's burdens, and so fulfil the law of Christ" (Gal. 5:25–26; 6:2). "I will be glad and exult in thee, I will sing praise to thy name, O Most High" (Ps. 9:2).[131]

---

mainstream Judaism; although NT Spirit-language may fail to strike us today due to its familiarity, it radically defined early Christians as the community of the new age" (Keener, *The Spirit in the Gospels and Acts: Divine Purity and Power* [Peabody, MA: Hendrickson, 1997], 4). As Keener points out, in Second Temple Judaism the Spirit was linked with purification and inspiration, and these same emphases (along with others) are found in the New Testament. Keener observes that the most distinctive Christian teaching on the Spirit is, not surprisingly, the Spirit's inseparability from Christ.

130. Yves Congar, OP, *The Word and the Spirit*, trans. David Smith (London: Geoffrey Chapman, 1986), 60.

131. The present book on the Holy Spirit should be read as a part of an ongoing effort, spiritual as well as intellectual, to overcome what David Tracy calls "the disastrous separation of theology and spirituality along with the modern separation of philosophy and a way of life" (Tracy, "Trinitarian Theology and Spirituality," 410). On these separations, see also Matthew L. Lamb's *Eternity, Time, and the Life of Wisdom* (Naples, FL: Sapientia Press of Ave Maria University, 2007). For a study of spiritual theology that is also, necessarily, a study of the work of the Holy Spirit, see Edith M. Humphrey, *Ecstasy and Intimacy: When the Holy Spirit Meets the Human Spirit* (Grand Rapids: Eerdmans, 2006).

1

THE HOLY SPIRIT AS LOVE AND GIFT

Hans Urs von Balthasar's essay "The Holy Spirit as Love," written two decades prior to his full-fledged exposition of the Holy Spirit in the final volume of his *Theo-Logic*, begins with a challenge to Latin theology of the Spirit. Balthasar remarks, "Since Augustine, speculation about the Trinity of God has so accustomed us to see the Second Divine person, whom John called the Logos, in the same perspective as 'truth' and 'knowledge,' while seeing the Third person in the same perspective as 'will' and 'love,' that we are astonished and confused when we are asked what is the basis for these statements in Sacred Scripture."[1] Pressing the issue, Balthasar asks whether the name "Love" should in fact be properly associated with the Holy Spirit. He finds numerous passages that describe the Father's love for the Son, for the world, and for Jesus's followers. In the Gospel of John, for example, either John the Baptist or the evangelist states that "the Father loves the Son, and has given all things into his hand" (John 3:35).[2] The evangelist John famously proclaims that "God so loved the world that he gave his only Son, that whoever believes in him should not perish but have eternal life" (John 3:16). In 1 John 4:8 we read that "God is love,"

1. Hans Urs von Balthasar, "The Holy Spirit as Love," in *Explorations in Theology*, vol. 3, *Creator Spirit*, trans. Brian McNeil, CRV (San Francisco: Ignatius, 1993), 117–34, at 117.
2. The verse prior to this states, "For he whom God has sent utters the words of God, for it is not by measure that he gives the Spirit" (John 3:34). For commentary, see Marianne Meye Thompson, *The God of the Gospel of John* (Grand Rapids: Eerdmans, 2001), 170–71, 175.

and Balthasar takes this to refer to God the Father. Balthasar shows that the Son too is associated with love in the Gospel of John, for instance in John 11:5; 13:1; 14:31.

In the Johannine literature, moreover, the Holy Spirit is rather overwhelmingly associated with truth. In three places—John 14:17; 15:26; 16:13—Jesus names the Spirit "the Spirit of truth" and 1 John 5:7 states that "the Spirit is the truth." The Spirit's task in the Gospel of John, as Balthasar says, is "to 'teach' and to 'recall' (14:26), 'to lead into all the truth' (16:13), to 'proclaim' (16:13, 14), 'to give testimony' (15:26)."[3] All of these are tasks associated with the intellect, just as the Son, as "Word/Logos," is associated with the intellect by the Gospel of John.

The Gospel of John also describes the Spirit as a lawyer or (in Balthasar's words) an "'advocate' in a trial who works for the clients who are referred to him (John 14:26; 15:26; 16:7) and attacks the opposite party by 'convincing' it 'that there exists a sin, a righteousness and a judgment' (16:8)."[4] Surely a lawyer is not to be described as personal "Love"; it would rather seem that the lawyer's work strictly involves the intellect's tools. The major Pauline text that is often cited in support of the Spirit's proper name of "Love" (comparable to the Son's proper name of "Word") is Romans 5:5: "God's love has been poured into our hearts through the Holy Spirit who has been given to us." But Balthasar shows that in fact in Paul's letters "the overwhelming majority of texts link to the Pneuma the concept of power (*dynamis*), of a possession and ability given by God (*charisma*) and not infrequently of the knowledge of God's salvific thoughts (1 Cor. 2:10–15)."[5] It hardly seems that the Holy Spirit should be connected to "Love" any more than should the Father and Son, and indeed one might conclude that the Holy Spirit may be *less* connected to "Love" than are the Father and Son.

Although Balthasar goes on to creatively defend the connection of the Holy Spirit with love—in a fashion that raises its own difficulties—his central

3. Balthasar, "Holy Spirit as Love," 117. On the Spirit of truth, see also Raniero Cantalamessa, *The Mystery of Pentecost*, trans. Glen S. Davis (Collegeville, MN: Liturgical Press, 2001), 42–43. Cantalamessa states, "The action of the Spirit of truth . . . is not limited only to a few rare and solemn moments of the life of the Church. There exists an institutional action, exercised through the institutions (councils, bishops, popes) of the Church, and there exists an inner action, daily and uninterrupted, in the heart of every believer" (ibid., 42).

4. Balthasar, "Holy Spirit as Love," 117. Cantalamessa proposes a more sympathetic view of the Spirit as "Advocate": "The Holy Spirit defends the faithful and 'intercedes' ceaselessly for them before God with 'inexpressible groanings' (Rom. 8:26ff.)" (Cantalamessa, *Mystery of Pentecost*, 44). For the importance of the name "Advocate" or "Paraclete," see also Wolfhart Pannenberg, *Systematic Theology*, vol. 1, trans. Geoffrey W. Bromiley (Grand Rapids: Eerdmans, 1991).

5. Balthasar, "Holy Spirit as Love," 117.

contribution for my purposes here consists in identifying the problem.[6] Was Augustine, in his *De Trinitate*, correct in claiming that the Holy Spirit should be properly named "Love" and "Gift"? This question, which is fundamental for my theology of the Holy Spirit, requires for its answer a careful investigation of the biblical paths by which Augustine arrives at the names "Love" and "Gift."[7] Like Luigi Gioia, I consider that Augustine's biblical exegesis plays the decisive role in his naming of the Holy Spirit, even if it is not enough to say, with Gioia, that Augustine's naming of the Holy Spirit is "rigorously regulated by Scripture and the dynamic of salvation."[8] At issue is what it

6. Indebted to Heribert Mühlen, Jean Galot, Otto Kuss, and others, Balthasar resolves the problem to his satisfaction by arguing that "the Pneuma is fundamentally the fact that the sphere of the love of the Father is opened up for men, the love that has borne witness to itself through the Son, and men are called to this sphere in the future and invited to exist in it" (ibid., 131). Balthasar puts the same point in various ways, drawing upon Paul and the Gospels: "The only way in which we come to know the 'Spirit' of God is from the unfathomable self-revelation of the love of the Father in the crucified Son: it is this that the Spirit attests, he gives a share in this, he continually defends the 'truth' of this" (ibid., 134); "The Personal Being that is authentically his cannot be described in any other way than this: both the Father and the Son, as those who send him, are distinguished from him, yet he is the fruit of the common work of Father and Son (since the Father gives the Son out of love for the world, and the Son gives himself in order to reveal the Father's love): both leave it to this 'fruit' to give himself with divine sovereign freedom and to permit men to share in him" (ibid., 126); "Thus the Spirit appears (first) essentially as the common *fruit* of the Father and the Son, which (secondly) can become autonomous in relation to them (the result is 'sent'), and, further (thirdly), as the gift of God to the world, once again permits the whole sovereign freedom of God to be known in the manner in which it holds sway in creation, in the covenant, and in the Church" (ibid., 125). Balthasar adds that the Spirit can be conceived of as the "We" arising from the "I-Thou" of the Father and Son.

7. For background in Augustine's early writings, see Lewis Ayres, "*Spiritus Amborum*: Augustine and Pro-Nicene Theology," *Augustinian Studies* 39 (2008): 207–21; Chad Tyler Gerber, *The Spirit of Augustine's Early Theology: Contextualizing Augustine's Pneumatology* (Burlington, VT: Ashgate, 2012). See also the fourth-century background provided by Ayres, "Innovation and *Ressourcement* in Pro-Nicene Pneumatology," *Augustinian Studies* 39 (2008): 187–206. In "*Spiritus Amborum*" Ayres helps us to envision the path to the pneumatology of the *De Trinitate*:

> Even before the *De fide* [*et symbolo*], Augustine already had developed the idea (in part adopted from Hilary) that the Spirit is called the Gift because the Spirit enables us to return in love to God. In the *De moribus ecclesiae Catholicae* he insists that the Spirit was able to be such a gift because of his perfection: here Augustine is moving hesitantly toward the position that the Spirit as love is the substance of the gifts he gives. This position will appear fully developed only in his mature work. Augustine also seems to have linked that which he learnt from Ambrose and/or Hilary to language probably encountered in Victorinus's *Hymns*, describing the Spirit as the *copula*, *conexio*, and *complexio* of Father and Son. These same *Hymns* also speak of the Trinity as a communion of mutually entailing *caritas*, *gratia*, and *communicatio*. (Ayres, "*Spiritus Amborum*," 211–12)

8. Luigi Gioia, OSB, *The Theological Epistemology of Augustine's* De Trinitate (Oxford: Oxford University Press, 2008), 138. Gioia's emphasis provides a helpful corrective to the view, frequently found in Orthodox theology, that Augustine is rationalistically "reducing the mystery of the Godhead to human categories" (Andrew Louth, "Love and the Trinity: Saint Augustine and the Greek Fathers," *Augustinian Studies* 33 [2002]: 1–16, at 14). Yet, as Gilles Emery points

means for naming of the Holy Spirit to be "rigorously regulated by Scripture," especially since some of Augustine's exegetical moves would not be accepted by contemporary exegetes.[9]

Augustine's arguments are most persuasive if one accepts, as I think we should, his assumptions about what Scripture is and does—above all his view that the Triune God wills to teach us about himself through Scripture, so that we might come to know and love the living God. The faith-based expectation that God in Scripture is teaching us about his triunity leads Augustine to be alert for clues to the identity of the Holy Spirit, clues that Augustine employs to build his case that the Spirit is properly (i.e., distinctively among the three persons) named not only "Holy Spirit" but also "Love" and "Gift."[10] Let us

out in his review of Gioia's book (*Revue Thomiste* 109 [2009]: 321–23), Gioia's interpretation of Augustine is in certain places overly influenced by the perspective of Karl Barth and dialectical theology. See also Lewis Ayres and Michel René Barnes's helpful attention to "the importance of rethinking early Christian doctrinal development as a series of developments in the exegesis of key scriptural texts" (Ayres and Barnes, "Introduction and Acknowledgments," *Augustinian Studies* 39 [2008]: 165–67, at 165). Joseph Ratzinger also examines Augustine's exegetical development of these names: see his "The Holy Spirit as Communio: Concerning the Relationship of Pneumatology and Spirituality in Augustine," trans. Peter Casarella, *Communio* 25 (1998): 324–37, at 327–31. Ratzinger's focus, however, is on ecclesiological issues. For further background, see also Roland Kany, *Augustins Trinitätsdenken* (Tübingen: Mohr, 2007); Gerald Bonner, "St. Augustine's Doctrine of the Holy Spirit," *Sobornost* 4 (1960): 51–66; Basil Studer, OSB, "Zur Pneumatologie des Augustinus von Hippo (*De Trinitate* 15.17.27–27.50)," in *Mysterium Caritatis: Studien zur Exegese und zur Trinitätslehre in der Alten Kirche* (Roma: Pontificio Ateneo S. Anselmo, 1999), 311–27.

9. For background to the connection between the fathers' biblical exegesis and trinitarian doctrine, see Khaled Anatolios, "The Canonization of Scripture in the Context of Trinitarian Doctrine," in *The Oxford Handbook of the Trinity*, ed. Gilles Emery, OP, and Matthew Levering (Oxford: Oxford University Press, 2011), 15–26; Frances Young, *Biblical Exegesis and the Formation of Christian Culture* (Cambridge: Cambridge University Press, 1997); Young, "The Trinity and the New Testament," in *The Nature of New Testament Theology: Essays in Honour of Robert Morgan*, ed. Christopher Rowland and Christopher Tuckett (Oxford: Blackwell, 2006), 286–305; Lewis Ayres, "'There's Fire in That Rain': On Reading the Letter and Reading Allegorically," in *Heaven on Earth? Theological Interpretation in Ecumenical Dialogue*, ed. Hans Boersma and Matthew Levering (Oxford: Wiley-Blackwell, 2013), 33–51.

10. In book 6 Augustine observes that Hilary of Poitiers describes the Holy Spirit as "gift." Maarten Wisse has noted that this context is crucial for the way in which Augustine engages the name "gift." As Wisse says, "Hilary's language is . . . rather functionalized language," whereas Augustine's theology of the Trinity emphasizes the full equality of the Father, Son, and Holy Spirit (Wisse, *Trinitarian Theology beyond Participation: Augustine's* De Trinitate *and Contemporary Theology* [London: T&T Clark, 2011], 294). Since Hilary was a recognized authority on the Trinity, Augustine sets himself the task of reconceptualizing Hilary's language so as to strip it of any "functionalizing" tendency. Wisse remarks that Augustine therefore "seems to be eager to keep the Gift-language entirely scriptural. He keeps its meaning as closely as possible to the concept of the Spirit as giver of love, and he proves at length that in that sense the Spirit is indeed 'Gift'" (ibid.). See also the comparison of Hilary and Augustine (on the topic of Gift) in Ayres's "*Spiritus Amborum*," 219–20. Ayres suggests that Augustine's approach to

now turn to Augustine's exegetical arguments for his influential naming of the Spirit.[11]

Augustine on the Holy Spirit as "Love" and "Gift"

In book 15 of the *De Trinitate* Augustine develops his argument for the view that "the Spirit is distinctively called by the term charity" by first appealing to 1 John 4:7–8.[12] This passage reads, "Beloved, let us love one another; for love is of God, and he who loves is born of God and knows God. He who does not love does not know God; for God is love." In his commentary on this passage from 1 John, Rudolf Schnackenburg observes, "The author is concerned to differentiate between the Christians and the false prophets, in order to establish that the real Christian is one who loves."[13] Schnackenburg interprets the phrase "love is of God" (1 John 4:7) to mean that love is God's nature: "God is love" (1 John 4:8).[14]

Gift was influenced both by his broader theology of the reformation of desire/love, and by his anti-Donatist focus on the unity of the church.

11. Here I pass over Augustine's discussion, earlier in book 15, of the Spirit's procession from the Father and Son—a discussion in which Augustine relies upon Galatians 4:6; Luke 6:19; John 5:26, 14:26, 15:26. See Ayres, "*Spiritus Amborum*," 214–18. Ayres observes that for Augustine,

In the double procession all remains the Father's: there is no act of the Father limited by a separate and subsequent causal act of the Son. As Spirit of both Father and Son, the Spirit comes from both but he does so in a way that is intended to secure the Father's status at the head of a causal order that is not subject to any temporal or material condition. . . . The Son does not join the Father in begetting the Spirit as their Son: apart from the material and sexual connotations against which Augustine has already railed, such a picture would fail to preserve the Father's role as the cause of the Spirit. But, Augustine continues, the Spirit is rather said to proceed so that we might have a term other than "unbegotten" or "begotten." Once again we are back to Gregory Nazianzen: "procession" is a comprehensible technical term only in being different from generation. (ibid., 217)

See also Ayres's more extensive discussion of the "double procession" in his "*Sempiterne Spiritus Donum*: Augustine's Pneumatology and the Metaphysics of Spirit," in *Orthodox Readings of Augustine*, ed. George E. Demacopoulos and Aristotle Papanikolaou (Crestwood, NY: St. Vladimir's Seminary Press, 2008), 127–52.

12. Citing passages from books 6–7 with an eye to Augustine's discussion in book 15 of the Holy Spirit as Love, Gioia remarks that "a closer look at the passages where Augustine links the Holy Spirit with charity, reveals that Augustine *constantly nuances his assertions concerning the identification between the two*. . . . How should we interpret this caution? The main explanation for it is not the lack of clarity of Scripture on this matter but that, even though love is a property of the Holy Spirit in particular, it constitutes the life of the Trinity as a whole and belongs to the Father and the Son as well" (Gioia, *Theological Epistemology of Augustine's* De Trinitate, 135).

13. Rudolf Schnackenburg, *The Johannine Epistles: Introduction and Commentary*, trans. Reginald and Ilse Fuller (New York: Crossroad, 1992), 207.

14. R. W. L. Moberly criticizes this interpretation of 1 John 4:8 as insufficiently attentive to the christological and epistemological context of the verse (see Moberly, "'Test the Spirits': God, Love, and Critical Discernment in 1 John 4," in *The Holy Spirit and Christian Origins*:

Augustine, by contrast, sees a meaning in 1 John 4:7–8 about God the Trinity. On the one hand, love is "of God" (*ex deo*); on the other hand, love "is" God. The same love that is "of God" *is* "God." Putting the two verses together, then, Augustine arrives at the following insight: 1 John 4:7–8 teaches that "love" is not only "God," but is "God *of* God." This is crucial because, as Augustine points out, the condition of being "God of God" in fact pertains to two persons, the Son and the Holy Spirit, who are fully divine but not unoriginate.[15] For Augustine, therefore, the question is whether 1 John 4:7–8 is referring to the Son or to the Spirit.

To answer this question, Augustine appeals to what follows in 1 John 4. In verses 9 and 10 John explains that God manifested his love by sending "his Son to be the expiation for our sins" (1 John 4:10). In verse 11 John adds that since God has shown his love for us by sending his Son, "we also ought to love one another." Indeed, "if we love one another, God abides in us" (1 John 4:12). How is it that we can love in this way? The crucial answer comes in verse 13: "By this we know that we abide in him and he in us, because he has given us of his own Spirit." We know that God abides in us when we love; and we love when God gives us his Spirit. Augustine concludes that the "God of God" about whom John speaks when he say "love is of God" (1 John 4:7) is none other than the Holy Spirit, and God "has given us" the Spirit (1 John 4:13). Augustine sums up: "He [the Holy Spirit] then is the gift of God who is love."[16] The two names "Love" and "Gift" imply each other.

In Augustine's view, this conclusion that 1 John 4:7–13 is speaking about the Holy Spirit as "Love" receives further confirmation from 1 John 4:16: "God is love, and he who abides in love abides in God, and God abides in him." Augustine points out that verse 13 assures us that we know that we abide in God because God gives us the Holy Spirit. Now, in verse 16, John tells us that when we abide in love, we abide in God. It follows that the Holy Spirit abiding in us, and "love" abiding in us, are the same. The person who abides in the Holy Spirit ("love") abides in God. Thus for Augustine, when verse 16 says "God is love, and he who abides in love abides in God," the reference to the Holy Spirit is clear.[17] When God gives us his Spirit, we can be sure that we

---

Essays in Honor of James D. G. Dunn, ed. Graham N. Stanton, Bruce W. Longenecker, and Stephen C. Barton [Grand Rapids: Eerdmans, 2004], 296–307).

15. He has already shown this on the basis of other scriptural texts. The church affirmed that the Son and Spirit are "God of God" at the Council of Constantinople.

16. Augustine, *The Trinity*, trans. Edmund Hill, OP (Hyde Park, NY: New City Press, 1991), 15.31, p. 421.

17. Gioia underscores the centrality of verses 13 and 16 for Augustine's theology of the Holy Spirit as Love: "Everything we have seen above concerning the role of love and of the Holy Spirit under the heading of unity, comes together here in the assertion that God dwells in us and we

abide in God, which would not be possible if God's Spirit were not the "love" that ensures we abide in God. On this basis, Augustine again concludes that the Holy Spirit "is the one meant when we read, *Love is God* (1 John 4:8)."[18]

Augustine holds that this conclusion refers both to the Holy Spirit in his eternal procession (he proceeds as Love), and to the Holy Spirit in his temporal mission (he "fires man to the love of God and neighbor when he has been given to him").[19] None of this means, of course, that the Father and the Son are not *also* love. But the Holy Spirit is *uniquely* the "love" that is "of God" the Father (1 John 4:7), distinct from the Son of God. Augustine concludes that the Holy Spirit uniquely proceeds from God the Father as Love (or as the Gift of Love), because we know that we abide in God the Father when we abide in love and, equally, we know that we abide in God the Father when God the Father gives us "his own Spirit" (1 John 4:13).

To this exegesis of 1 John 4:7–16 Augustine adds the point that sinners can love God only when God makes this possible. For us to love God, God must transform our hearts, and 1 John 4:19 speaks about God doing just that: "We love, because he first loved us." Schnackenburg connects verse 19 with verse 10, which reads in full, "In this is love, not that we loved God but that he loved us and sent his Son to be the expiation for our sins."[20] Augustine certainly would not deny this connection, but he makes a different one. He connects 1 John 4:19's insistence on God loving us first with Paul's understanding of the gift of the Holy Spirit. Thus after quoting 1 John 4:19, Augustine

---

in God. *John's First Epistle ascribes this mutual indwelling identically to love and to the Holy Spirit, thus implying that love is indeed the property of the Holy Spirit*" (Gioia, *Theological Epistemology of Augustine's* De Trinitate, 136). Along the same lines, see Ratzinger, "Holy Spirit as Communio," 328.

18. Augustine, *The Trinity* 15.31, p. 421. In his ecclesiologically focused *Homilies on the First Epistle of John*, Augustine makes the same connection:

> How, then, could it be a short while ago, *Love is* from *God*, and now, *Love is God*? For God is Father and Son and Holy Spirit. The Son is God from God, the Holy Spirit is God from God, and these three are one God, not three gods. If the Son is God and the Holy Spirit is God, and he loves him in whom the Holy Spirit dwells, then love is God, but it is God because it is from God. For you have each one in the epistle—both *Love is* from *God* and *Love is God*. Of the Father alone scripture cannot say that he is from God. But when you hear *from God*, either the Son or the Holy Spirit is understood. But, because the Apostle says, *The charity of God has been poured out in our hearts through the Holy Spirit, who has been given to us* (Rom. 5:5), we should understand that in love there is the Holy Spirit. For the Holy Spirit is he whom the wicked cannot receive. (Augustine, *Homilies on the First Epistle of John*, trans. Boniface Ramsey [Hyde Park, NY: New City Press, 2008], 7.6, p. 108)

See also Basil Studer, OSB, "Spiritualità Giovannea in Agostino: Osservazioni sul commento Agostiniano alla Prima Ioannis," in Studer, *Mysterium Caritatis*, 143–58, at 148.

19. Augustine, *The Trinity* 15.31, p. 421.

20. See Schnackenburg, *Johannine Epistles*, 225.

immediately quotes Romans 5:5, "[the love of God] has been poured into our hearts through the Holy Spirit who has been given to us."[21] The gift of the Holy Spirit is "the love of God," the very point that Augustine has been making on the basis of 1 John 4. At the same time, Augustine affirms that Romans 5:5 describes the love of God transforming our hearts.[22] Such transformation is possible, he argues, only because the Holy Spirit *is* the love of God. He therefore considers 1 John 4:19's statement that we love because God loved us first to be further confirmation that the Holy Spirit, given by God to change our hearts, is distinctively Love in the Trinity.[23]

21. As indicated by the brackets, I am adjusting the RSV here in accord with Augustine's (and the standard patristic) way of translating this text. Wisse notes that this discussion "is intimately related to the question of grace because Augustine claims that the love that is poured out into our hearts towards God and neighbour is not merely a gift of the Holy Spirit but the Holy Spirit itself, so that, in and through love, God the Holy Spirit dwells in us and we dwell in him" (Wisse, *Trinitarian Theology beyond Participation*, 291). For discussion of Romans 5:5, see Robert Louis Wilken, "*Fides Caritate Formata*: Faith Formed by Love," *Nova et Vetera* 9 (2011): 1089–1100. Citing Joseph Fitzmyer, SJ's *Romans: A New Translation with Introduction and Commentary* (New York: Doubleday, 1993), 398, Wilken notes that "the conventional modern interpretation" of Romans 5:5 is "that the 'love of God' refers to God's love for us. In grammatical terms, the phrase is a subjective genitive" (Wilken, "*Fides Caritate Formata*," 1090). By contrast, as Wilken says, "For Augustine the phrase 'love of God' in Romans 5:5 was *always* taken as an objective genitive, that is our love for God" (ibid.). Wilken goes on to point out that although in *Summa theologiae* II-II, q. 23, a. 2 Thomas Aquinas interprets Romans 5:5 as our love for God, in his *Commentary on Romans* Aquinas "observes that the phrase 'love of God' can be taken either as God's love for us or as our love for God, citing appropriate biblical passages to support each understanding. For the first, God's love for us, he cites Jeremiah, 'He loved you with an everlasting love' (31:3), and for the second, our love for God, Romans 8: 'I am sure that nothing in all creation will be able to separate us from the love of God' (8:39). It is telling that he cites this passage from Romans—a verse that modern interpreters also take as referring to God's love for us" (ibid., 1094). Furthermore, Origen, who unlike Augustine and Aquinas read Romans in Greek, also interpreted Romans 5:5 as being about our love for God. The key point is that the two meanings imply each other: "For Origen the two possible interpretations of the passage merge into one. Even if the second meaning is adopted, that the love is God's love for us, the purpose of the outpouring of the Holy Spirit is that we might love God" (ibid., 1099).

22. Brendan Byrne's commentary on Romans 5:5 suggests that Paul thinks of the outpouring of the Holy Spirit simply as God's transformation of our hearts: "The apocalyptic tradition saw the Spirit as the eschatological gift *par excellence*—the creative force of the new creation. . . . Through the Spirit the eschatological people of God was to be purified, cleansed and readied for the life of the new age" (Byrne, SJ, *Romans* [Collegeville, MN: Liturgical Press, 1996], 167). Similarly, at the conclusion of his discussion of Romans 5:1–11 (and related Pauline texts), Michael J. Gorman states that for Paul the "divine love is the love of the Father who sends in love, the Son who dies in love, and the Spirit who produces the fruit of love in those hearts he inhabits" (Gorman, *Cruciformity: Paul's Narrative Spirituality of the Cross* [Grand Rapids: Eerdmans, 2001], 73).

23. On Augustine's use of 1 John and Romans 5:5 in book 15, see also Studer, "Zur Pneumatologie des Augustinus von Hippo (*De Trinitate* 15.17.27–27.50)," 314–16, 321–22, as well as bibliographical materials cited by Studer.

Indeed, without this "gift of God"—without this "love"—our faith is "nothing" (1 Cor. 13:2). Augustine remarks, "Why is the Spirit distinctively called gift? Only because of the love without which the man who has not got it, though he speak with the tongues of men and of angels, is booming bronze and a clashing cymbal [cf. 1 Cor. 13:1]."[24] In Augustine's view, this same point is suggested by Paul in Galatians 5:6 (to which I add Gal. 5:5): "For through the Spirit, by faith, we wait for the hope of righteousness. For in Christ Jesus neither circumcision nor uncircumcision is of any avail, but faith working through love." The connection here between faith, on the one hand, and love *and the Holy Spirit*, on the other, helps Augustine to conclude that "the love which is from God and is God is distinctively the Holy Spirit; through him the charity of God is poured out in our hearts, and through it the whole triad dwells in us."[25]

Having shown that the Spirit is biblically named "Love," Augustine proclaims that "nothing is more excellent than this gift of God."[26] To demonstrate more fully that the Holy Spirit is not only "Love" but also "Gift," Augustine turns first to the Gospel of John. In this Gospel Jesus compares the Holy Spirit to living water. Jesus proclaims on the last day of the Feast of Booths, "If any one thirst, let him come to me and drink. He who believes in me, as the scripture has said, 'Out of his heart shall flow rivers of living water'" (John 7:37–38). The evangelist John comments that the "living water" to which Jesus is referring is in fact "the Spirit, which those who believed in him were to receive" (John 7:39). As Augustine points out, Paul likewise uses the

---

24. Augustine, *The Trinity* 15.32, p. 421. Note Gioia's emphasis that Augustine's "notion of the Holy Spirit as gift [*donum*]" depends upon Augustine's scriptural exposition of 1 John 4:13, 16 (Gioia, *Theological Epistemology of Augustine's* De Trinitate, 136) rather than upon Augustine's conceptual work (in book 5) "where Augustine tries to determine how the Holy Spirit is a relation (*ad aliquid*) as compared with the relation between the Father and the Son" (ibid., 136–37).

25. Augustine, *The Trinity* 15.32, p. 421.

26. Augustine, *The Trinity* 15.32, p. 421. Gioia notes here the context of the Pelagian controversy: "'Gift of God' means here the gift which only God can give. . . . *The fact that charity-Holy Spirit is a gift from God means that we are saved by grace*; it means that salvation is truly divine, that only God's very self-giving can save us" (Gioia, *Theological Epistemology of Augustine's* De Trinitate, 138). For Gioia, it is this sheer grace that constitutes Augustine's attraction to the book of Acts's references to the "gift of God." Similarly Wisse comments, "One wonders why Augustine brings in so many proofs from Scripture for the use of 'Gift' as a name for the Holy Spirit. Primarily, this is again the question of grace, because 'Gift' as something that comes from God might suggest that God's grace is not the immediate divine activity itself but a gift or activity that remains different from God, and thus it would not be Godself who acts in believers. In this context, Augustine stresses that Gift-language in Scripture does not imply that the gift is not the Holy Spirit itself" (Wisse, *Trinitarian Theology beyond Participation*, 293).

imagery of water to describe the gift of the Spirit, when Paul says of baptized believers that "all were made to drink of one Spirit" (1 Cor. 12:13).[27]

Augustine also notes that earlier in the Gospel of John, Jesus employs the same image of living water when he tells the Samaritan woman at the well, "If you knew the gift of God, and who it is that is saying to you, 'Give me a drink,' you would have asked him and he would have given you living water" (John 4:10). In Augustine's view, this "living water" is the Holy Spirit; otherwise Jesus could not say that "whoever drinks of the water that I shall give him will never thirst; the water that I shall give him will become in him a spring of water welling up to eternal life" (John 4:14). In light of John 7:39, Augustine argues that the "gift of God" to which Jesus refers in John 4:10 is the "living water," the Holy Spirit. As the "gift of God," the Holy Spirit is thus rightly named "Gift" in the Trinity.[28]

Augustine finds that a similar connection of the Holy Spirit to "Gift" appears in Paul's Letter to the Ephesians. Just as Paul compares the Holy Spirit with water in 1 Corinthians, so also Paul depicts the Holy Spirit as a gift when he writes that "grace was given to each of us according to the measure of Christ's gift" (Eph. 4:7).[29] That Christ's gift to us is the Holy Spirit becomes even clearer in the next verse, where Paul quotes (and adapts to his purposes) Psalm 68:18: "When he ascended on high he led a host of

27. See Ratzinger, "Holy Spirit as Communio," 330. Commenting on Romans 5:5, with its image of God's love being "poured into our hearts through the Holy Spirit," Brendan Byrne remarks, "Since water is the dominant symbol of cleansing and new life, the idea of 'pouring' (*ekkechytai*) is a natural association (cf. already Joel 2:28 [Heb. 3:1]; cf. Acts 2:17; 1 Cor. 12:13)" (Byrne, *Romans*, 167).

28. See Ratzinger, "Holy Spirit as Communio," 330. Francis J. Moloney, SDB's commentary on John 4:10 argues that "the genitive in *tēn dorean theou* is objective, indicating that Jesus promises a gift that has its origins in God. . . . The gift of God that the one speaking to her would give is the lifegiving revelation of the heavenly, which only Jesus makes known" (Moloney, *The Gospel of John* [Collegeville, MN: Liturgical Press, 1998], 117). But it seems to me that Moloney is missing not only the connection to John 7:39, but also the emphasis on an interior "spring of water welling up to eternal life" (John 4:14), an interior "spring of water" whose work is clearly that of the Holy Spirit.

29. The connections that Augustine makes between Ephesians 4:7–8 and the ascended Christ's sending of the Holy Spirit at Pentecost are not made by contemporary biblical exegetes, who instead interpret Christ's "gift" here to be "grace" in a broad sense. Margaret Y. MacDonald comments that "Eph. 4:7 contains the specific word 'gift' (*dōrea*; cf. Acts 2:38; 8:20; 10:45; 11:17). This word is functionally the equivalent of the word for 'gift' (*charisma*) that occurs in 1 Cor. 12:4 and Rom. 12:6. In the NT both *dōrea* and *charisma* are associated with gifts of the Spirit. Here *dōrea* refers to Christ's gift, but the notion of the Spirit's agency is not necessarily excluded" (MacDonald, *Colossians and Ephesians* [Collegeville, MN: Liturgical Press, 2008], 289). MacDonald adds that "the main theme of Eph. 4:1–16 is the unity of the church in one Spirit" (ibid., 297), which perhaps makes more plausible the link that Augustine makes.

captives, and he gave gifts to men" (Eph. 4:8).[30] It is undeniable, Augustine points out, that the ascended Jesus, who "gave gifts to men," sent the Holy Spirit upon the apostles on the day of Pentecost. In Augustine's view, the psalmist's use of the plural "gifts" befits the fact that (in Paul's words) "there are varieties of gifts, but the same Spirit" (1 Cor. 12:4)—the same Spirit "who apportions to each one individually as he wills" (1 Cor. 12:11).[31] The plurality of the Spirit's gifts can also be seen in Hebrews 2:4's reference to the "gifts of the Holy Spirit" and in Paul's statement that Christ's "gifts were that some should be apostles, some prophets, some evangelists, some pastors and teachers" (Eph. 4:11).[32] The Holy Spirit is the "Gift" that the ascended Jesus gives, and the Spirit manifests his interior presence through the diverse gifts of believers.

Augustine next turns to Peter's references in the book of Acts to the Spirit as "Gift." At Pentecost, Peter urges his hearers, "Repent, and be baptized every one of you in the name of Jesus Christ for the forgiveness of your sins; and you shall receive the gift of the Holy Spirit" (Acts 2:38). The Holy Spirit, or the power to bestow the Holy Spirit, is similarly described as the "gift of God" (Acts 8:20) by Peter in his response to Simon Magus, who attempted to purchase the power to bestow the Holy Spirit. In his interpretation of Acts 8:18–20, Joseph Fitzmyer similarly suggests that the "gift of God" is the

30. In the RSV the full text of Psalm 68:18 reads, "Thou didst ascend the high mount, leading captives in thy train, and receiving gifts among men, even among the rebellious, that the LORD God may dwell there."

31. Raniero Cantalamessa observes that for Paul, advancing beyond earlier understandings of the Spirit, "the Holy Spirit is not only an *action* but also an *actor*, that is, a principle endowed with will and intelligence who acts consciously and freely. We say of him that he teaches, bears witness, laments, intercedes, grieves, that he knows, that he has desires" (Cantalamessa, *Mystery of Pentecost*, 52 [cf. 55]).

32. Regarding the pneumatology of Hebrews, the insights of C. Kavin Rowe are helpful: Hebrews mentions the Holy Spirit only seven times (Heb. 2:4; 3:7; 6:4; 9:8; 14; 10:15, 29). Yet it does so in a way that makes clear the relational determination of the Spirit's identity. Speaking of the nature of salvation, the author of Hebrews says, "It was declared at first by the Lord, and it was attested to us by those who heard him, while God also bore witness by signs and wonders and various miracles and by gifts of the Holy Spirit distributed according to his own will" (Heb. 2:3–4). Here the Spirit is explicitly described as God's Spirit—the Spirit's gifts are distributed according to God's will—and tied to the salvific life of Jesus (the Lord). To speak of the Holy Spirit, therefore, is also to speak of God and of the Lord Jesus (cf. the context in Heb. 6:4 and 10:29). Moreover, the Holy Spirit cannot be reduced to a simple metaphorical way to speak about God's presence, as if using Spirit language were but another way to speak of God's immanence. The Spirit in Hebrews is rather the one through whom Christ offered himself to God. (Rowe, "The Trinity in the Letters of St. Paul and Hebrews," in Emery and Levering, *The Oxford Handbook of the Trinity*, 41–53, at 48)

See also Rowe's discussion of 1 Corinthians 12:4–6 and Ephesians 4 (ibid., 49–52).

Holy Spirit. For Fitzmyer, the meaning of the passage is that "no outsider can acquire the power to bestow the Spirit. . . . The Spirit is not for sale and is not available at the beck and call of a magician."[33] Even if the "gift of God" is the *power to bestow* the Holy Spirit, this gift must also be the Holy Spirit himself, because it is by the Holy Spirit that the apostles bestow the Spirit upon others. We find the "gift of the Holy Spirit" again in Acts 10:45, when the gentile Cornelius and his family receive the Holy Spirit. Recounting this event later, Peter remarks that "God gave the same gift to them as he gave to us" (Acts 11:17). Augustine explains that "the gift of the Holy Spirit is nothing but the Holy Spirit."[34]

Peter's repeated testimony in the book of Acts to the Holy Spirit as "Gift," when connected with the testimonies of Paul and of Jesus in the Gospel of John, seems to Augustine to show that being given, in a certain sense at least, must belong to the Spirit not only in the Spirit's temporal mission but also in his eternal procession: the Spirit is always the "gift of God." But is being given *to creatures* constitutive of who the Holy Spirit eternally is, so that he would lose something of himself if he were not given to creatures? In other words, is the Spirit's identity determined fundamentally by a *temporal* relation? Augustine replies that "in himself he [the Spirit] is God even if he is not given to anyone, because he was God, co-eternal with the Father and the Son, even before he was given to anyone."[35] Another question that Augustine addresses is whether the name "Gift" subordinates the Spirit to the Father and the Son. Are the Father and the Son "givers" vis-à-vis creatures, whereas the Holy Spirit is not a giver but solely what is given? Augustine's answer is that the Holy Spirit "is given as God's gift in such a way that as God he also gives himself."[36] The Spirit is not, then, a merely passive gift; along with the Father and the Son, he is the "giver" in relation to us, notwithstanding that he is also the "gift."[37] Here Augustine quotes two texts that express the Holy Spirit's agency—again one from the Gospel of John and one from Paul: "The wind [spirit] blows where it wills" (John 3:8) and "All these are inspired by one and the same Spirit, who apportions to each one individually as he wills" (1 Cor. 12:11). Augustine concludes that it is particularly fitting that the Holy

33. Joseph A. Fitzmyer, SJ, *The Acts of the Apostles: A New Translation with Introduction and Commentary* (New York: Doubleday, 1998), 401.

34. Augustine, *The Trinity* 15.36, p. 424.

35. Augustine, *The Trinity* 15.36, p. 424.

36. Augustine, *The Trinity* 15.36, p. 424.

37. Gioia comments that "not only is the Holy Spirit given, but also he is freely given, he freely gives himself and he remains free in his self-gift. . . . This implies, of course, that gift means presence of the giver, i.e., of the Holy Spirit" (Gioia, *Theological Epistemology of Augustine's* De Trinitate, 139).

Spirit be named "Love" and "Gift" in the New Testament, because "there is nothing greater than charity among God's gifts, and . . . there is no greater gift of God's than the Holy Spirit."[38] This greatest Gift, who "is God" and who is "of God," is Love.

In sum, in book 15 Augustine sets forth the biblical witness to a "Love" who is God and who is "of/from God," and who is the Holy Spirit. Augustine also shows the recurrent biblical references to the Holy Spirit as "gift of God," and he shows that the greatest "Gift" is love. He thereby makes clear that although "the Holy Spirit is not alone in that triad in being charity" (just as he is not alone in being "holy" and "spirit"), "there is a good reason for distinctively calling him charity."[39] In this vein Augustine asks rhetorically, "If the charity by which the Father loves the Son and the Son loves the Father inexpressibly shows forth the communion of them both, what more suitable than he who is the common Spirit of them both should be distinctively called charity?"[40]

---

38. Augustine, *The Trinity* 15.37, p. 424. Lewis Ayres's succinct analysis of book 15 on the Holy Spirit as Love and Gift is worth quoting:

> While "gift" itself is used by Scripture of that which is given to Christians for their salvation, Augustine contends that the Spirit is *eternally* gift on the basis of further links that he suggests Scripture invites us to draw. The term "gift" is used, Augustine tells us, *because* the Spirit is also love. That which the Father gives us is the Spirit of his Son (Gal. 4.6), but the gift *of* the Spirit *is* the Spirit, and the Spirit is love (Rom. 5:5). "Love" like "Spirit" is a term which may be predicated of all three persons, but, Augustine argues, Scripture uses it so that when we grasp that the love which the Spirit gives is the Spirit, we will understand that the love which we receive is the love with which Father and Son love each other. Augustine then emphasizes the Spirit as an active giver of himself. . . . The Spirit gives himself as the Father's gift and as the Son's gift. Father and Son are one because the Spirit gives himself in the begetting of the Son and gives himself as the Son's love for the Father. (Ayres, *Augustine and the Trinity*, 254)

It seems to me that the Spirit is "giver," however, vis-à-vis creatures rather than in his eternal procession. Ayres cites Rowan D. Williams's view that for Augustine "the Spirit is 'common' to Father and Son not as a quality characterizing them equally, an impersonal attribute, but as that active divine giving, not simply identical with the person of the Father, which the Father communicates to the Son to give in his turn. . . . The Father, in eternally giving (divine) life to the Son, gives that life as itself a 'giving' agency, for there is no pre-personal or sub-personal divinity; he gives the Son the capacity to give that same giving life" (Williams, "*Sapientia* and the Trinity: Reflections on the *De trinitate*," in *Collectanea Augustiniana: Mélanges T. J. van Bavel*, ed. B. Bruning et al. [Leuven: Leuven University Press, 1990], 1:317–32, at 327–28).

39. Augustine, *The Trinity* 15.37, p. 424.

40. Augustine, *The Trinity* 15.37, p. 424. See also Gioia, *Theological Epistemology of Augustine's* De Trinitate, 140–41, on the Holy Spirit as the common love and gift of the Father and Son. In Gioia's view, "the use of the notions of 'procession' and 'generation' leads to a very abstract description of this mystery. Only when inner-Trinitarian life is seen under its proper light, i.e., as life of love, and the Holy Spirit is seen in his property of love, do these very abstract explanations reveal their real theological meaning" (ibid., 141). But Augustine describes "the generation of the Son" and "the procession of the Holy Spirit" in other contexts (see, e.g., Augustine, *The Trinity* 15.47). I think that Gioia's formulation exaggerates matters, but I grant

In the eternal Trinity, the Holy Spirit is the Love of the Father and Son, the bond of their communion.[41]

Book 5 of *De Trinitate* sheds further light on Augustine's view that names drawn from the temporal economy should be applied to the Holy Spirit in his eternal procession. Here Augustine begins with the general question of whether all names apply to God "substantially," that is, with respect to what is common in God. If they do, then it would make no sense to say that the Father and the Son are the same God, since the Father is "unbegotten" and the Son is "begotten." Augustine answers that some names, including "unbegotten" and "begotten," describe relation rather than substance. He observes that "unbegotten and begotten need not be said substance-wise," and that "what is stated relationship-wise does not designate substance."[42] Applying this to God, we can say that "whatever that supreme and divine majesty is called with reference to itself is said substance-wise; whatever it is called with reference to another is said not substance- but relationship-wise."[43] Nothing that has to do with substance differentiates Father, Son, and Holy Spirit, for they are one God.

Augustine then remarks that each of the three divine persons has names that "are proper or peculiar to himself."[44] These names describe a real differentiation in God, and thus a real relation in God. Seeking to answer why "Holy Spirit" is a proper name in God, Augustine explains that it is fitting that, as the common "Gift" of the Father and Son, the Holy Spirit "is properly called what they are called in common, seeing that both Father and Son are holy and both Father and Son are spirit."[45] He cites John 4:10 and Acts 8:20 for their description of the Holy Spirit as "the gift of God." For Augustine, the Spirit is the Father's gift, since we read that "the Spirit of truth . . . proceeds from the Father" (John 15:26); the Spirit is also the

---

that, as Lewis Ayres says, "'Procession' and 'generation' are not used here [book 5] as technical terms" (Ayres, "*Spiritus Amborum*," 215).

41. Gioia argues that "the foundation of Augustine's Trinitarian theology" is "the identification between the *form and content* of revelation and the *identity* of the revealer developed through the theology of missions. . . . *The form of the mission and the role the Holy Spirit plays in it corresponds to his identity in the highest possible degree, owing to the divine nature of salvation*" (Gioia, *Theological Epistemology of Augustine's* De Trinitate, 142). Although this identification is likely present, I think that Augustine argues something more: he considers that the biblical formulations themselves (the God who is love and who is "of God," the "gift of God") make clear that the eternal procession, and not simply the temporal mission, is under discussion.

42. Augustine, *The Trinity* 5.4, p. 191; 5.8, p. 194.
43. Augustine, *The Trinity* 5.9, p. 195.
44. Augustine, *The Trinity* 5.12, p. 197.
45. Augustine, *The Trinity* 5.12, p. 197.

Son's gift, since Paul calls the Spirit both the "Spirit of God" and the "Spirit of Christ" (Rom. 8:9). As the eternal Gift of the Father and Son, the Holy Spirit "is a kind of inexpressible communion or fellowship of Father and Son."[46] The name "Gift," then, helps Augustine in book 5 to account for why the name "Holy Spirit" distinctively applies to the third person, when in fact all three persons are equally "holy" and "spirit." It befits the third person to be expressed by a name that involves what is shared by the other two persons, since it is in their "inexpressible communion or fellowship" that we find their mutual "Gift" who is the Holy Spirit.[47] This mutual "Gift" is their Love.

At the same time, Augustine asks whether it is a problem that the name "Holy Spirit" does not convey a particular relation, unlike the pair of names "Father" and "Son" which clearly signify a relation. The person of the Father is "Father" only of his Son. He is not Father of the Holy Spirit, for then the Holy Spirit would be merely another Son, another instance of the Father-Son relation. Similarly, the Son is not the Son of the Holy Spirit. The solution for Augustine is found in the name "Gift," which conveys a particular relation. He remarks that in conceiving the distinct procession of the Holy Spirit, "we cannot say Father of the gift or Son of the gift, but . . . we say gift of the giver and giver of the gift."[48] The Spirit is related to the Father and Son as their shared Gift. The Spirit proceeds by way of "being given" rather than by way of being begotten.[49]

46. Augustine, *The Trinity* 5.12, p. 197. For discussion, see Ayres, *Augustine and the Trinity*, 251–52. On the one hand, Ayres connects this affirmation also with certain passages in Augustine's *The Trinity* 6.7. On the other hand, Ayres notes that "if we look forward a few years to *De trinitate* 15, not surprisingly we see much greater clarity in Augustine's discussion of the Spirit's agency" (ibid., 254).

47. Ayres points out, "Even when the unique title Gift provides the key (and Augustine does not always turn to this title), it does so because it reveals dimensions of the appropriated titles Holy, Spirit, and Love. These titles must take centre stage because only meditation on them helps us to understand that all of the Spirit's actions are founded in and reveal the Spirit's status as the (co-equal) Spirit of Father and Son. Only by learning that this is so do we grasp what it means for the Spirit to be eternally gift and fully 'personal'" (ibid., 255). Augustine leaves plenty of mystery, as Ayres would surely agree, with respect to "what it means for the Spirit to be eternally gift." Ayres's distinction between a "unique" and an "appropriated" title has to do with whether the title can be applied to all three persons; if so, then the titles are "appropriated." "Gift" is a "unique" title because the Father and Son cannot be described as "gift," whereas the Father and Son can be described as holy, spirit, and love. Ayres argues that for Augustine, "Scripture's appropriation of common titles" to the Holy Spirit observes the following rule: "Scripture appropriates to the Spirit terms common to each of the divine three in order to show the character of the Spirit's derivation from and consubstantiality with the Father" (ibid.).

48. Augustine, *The Trinity* 5.13, p. 198.

49. Augustine, *The Trinity* 5.15, p. 199.

To be a "gift," however, is to be passive by contrast to the active giver. Is the Spirit then merely passive and thereby less than divine? In response, Augustine notes in book 5 that the Spirit is for us an active origin or divine giver of gifts. Otherwise it would have been impossible for Paul to speak of "one and the same Spirit, who apportions to each one individually as he wills" (1 Cor. 12:11). As God, the Spirit gives to us the "varieties of gifts" that Paul describes in 1 Corinthians 12. The point is that the Spirit's identity as the Gift of the Father and Son does not render him inherently passive, since the economy of salvation displays him as fully active.

Augustine employs 1 Corinthians 12:6–11 to show both that the Holy Spirit is connected uniquely with "gift" and that the Holy Spirit is fully the divine giver. He also emphasizes that this connection with "gift" helps us to understand why affirming that the "Spirit of truth . . . proceeds from the Father" (John 15:26) does not make the Spirit into another Son. In the eternal Trinity, the Spirit is "given" by the Father and the Son, even though in the economy of salvation he is an active giver as well as being gift.

What does it mean for the Holy Spirit to be a gift for us? Augustine notes that we receive two life-giving gifts: first, our created spirits, by which we are human, and second, the gift of the Holy Spirit that makes us a new creation in Christ. Here he cites Paul's statement "What have you that you did not receive?" (1 Cor. 4:7). Augustine then differentiates the two gifts by noting that "what we received in order to be is one thing, what we received in order to be holy is another."[50] When we read of a "spirit" possessed by humans that is distinct from our shared spiritual nature, Augustine thinks that we should interpret such passages as having to do with the Holy Spirit. In this way, he interprets the coming of John the Baptist in "the spirit and power of Elijah" (Luke 1:17) and YHWH's statement to Moses that "I will take some of the spirit which is upon you and put it upon them [the seventy elders]" (Num. 11:17).[51] In both cases, the gift of the power of holiness—the Holy Spirit—is the distinguishing element.

Augustine also investigates how it is that in God, the Holy Spirit is the Gift of the Father and Son. Prior to the creation of rational creatures, there was no one to whom the Holy Spirit could be given. How then can the Spirit be eternal "Gift"? Augustine notes that it would seem that if the Holy Spirit "only proceeds when he is given, he would surely not proceed before there

---

50. Augustine, *The Trinity* 5.15, p. 199.
51. John R. Levison shows that the conception of the spirit found in Numbers 11:17 is also importantly present in 1 John 4:13 (Levison, *Filled with the Spirit* [Grand Rapids: Eerdmans, 2009], 414). For Levison, however, 1 John is a deeply disconcerting text due to its way of claiming authority.

was anyone for him to be given to," which, if true, would negate the divinity of the Holy Spirit.[52] In reply, Augustine says that something can be a "gift" without yet having been given to someone. The Holy Spirit "so proceeds as to be giveable," and, therefore, "he was already a gift even before there was anyone to give him to."[53]

Conclusion

We began with Hans Urs von Balthasar's question about whether "Love" can be justified biblically as a proper name for identifying the distinctiveness of the Holy Spirit in the trinitarian communion. Balthasar is aware that Latin trinitarian theology takes this name from Augustine's *De Trinitate*. But in the New Testament, as Balthasar reminds us, *truth* is arguably more closely associated with the Spirit than either "love" (or "gift"). Our task, then, was to inquire into how Augustine derives these names from Scripture, and, at the same time, to consider whether contemporary theology should affirm his naming of the Spirit as "Love" and "Gift."

For the name "Love," the central biblical texts are 1 John 4 and Romans 5:5, read in light (at least implicitly) of such texts as John 1:1 and 1 Corinthians 1:24. In 1 John 4 it is proclaimed that God is love, and that love is of God, from which Augustine deduces that 1 John 4 is speaking of "God of/from God." Augustine identifies this "God of God," who is "love," as the Holy Spirit. He does so on the basis of further clues in 1 John 4, as well as on the basis of the Latin text of Romans 5:5, which reads that the "love of God" is given to us through the Holy Spirit. For the name "Gift," the central biblical passages are John 4, John 7, 1 Corinthians 12, Ephesians 4, Acts 2, Acts 8, and Acts 10. The passages from John's Gospel emphasize the image of life-giving water, which Jesus describes as "the gift of God" and connects explicitly with the Holy Spirit. The passages from 1 Corinthians 12 and Ephesians 4 have to do with the ascended Jesus's gifts to his church and with the measure of Christ's gift; in both cases there is a fairly clear link to the Holy Spirit. The passages from Acts describe the Holy Spirit as the "gift of God" received by believers.

As we noted, the fact that the Holy Spirit is frequently depicted as the "gift of God" seems to Augustine to be evidence for the name "Love" as well. As Brian Daley puts it, "It is precisely as *God the Gift*, God given away, that

---

52. Augustine, *The Trinity* 5.16, p. 200.
53. Augustine, *The Trinity* 5.16, p. 200.

the Spirit can be thought of primarily in terms of love."[54] Love, after all, is the greatest gift. The Father begets the Word and gives the Spirit, a giving in which the Son shares, since the Spirit is both the "Spirit of God" and the "Spirit of Christ" (Rom. 8:9). The Spirit can be eternally "Gift" as eternally "giveable," without thereby requiring that he be a gift *to us*—although the Spirit is indeed gift to us. The Spirit is no passive gift to us, but instead, as Love and Gift, he divinely gives us supernatural gifts, not least by imparting to us the Truth that is the Word incarnate (see John 16:13–15).

The above summary of Augustine's use of Scripture in his naming of the Holy Spirit returns us to our fundamental concern, instigated by Balthasar: Does Augustine's naming of the Spirit as "Love" and "Gift" have adequate biblical warrant to be followed by contemporary theology of the Holy Spirit? In other words, is there really a biblical basis for naming the Holy Spirit by any names other than "Holy Spirit" and "Paraclete," specifically by the names "Love" and "Gift"? Or has Augustine—and the Western tradition that follows him—overreached, in seeking to do for the Spirit what the Gospel of John does for the Son through the name "Word"?

There is no doubt that Augustine's exegetical arguments about the Spirit's names "Love" and "Gift" often go beyond what contemporary exegetes find in the New Testament. For example, 1 John 4:13 seems to say that God's gift of his Spirit *teaches* us that we abide in God, rather than *giving* us the love by which we abide in God. Similarly, Augustine's view that the phrase "love is of God" (1 John 4:7) describes the eternal procession of a divine person ("God of God") is hardly a reading that contemporary exegetes would share. Indeed, the biblical scholar Walter Moberly criticizes theologians who, by adducing a divine attribute from 1 John 4:8, violate "the time-honored principle that one should not take words out of context, a principle sometimes easier to acknowledge than to observe."[55] In the context of 1 John, Moberly determines that 1 John 4:7–8 is about how we can recognize the true God, namely by discipleship to Jesus.

---

54. Brian E. Daley, SJ, "Revisiting the 'Filioque': Part One, Roots and Branches of an Old Debate," *Pro Ecclesia* 10 (2001): 31–62, at 40. Michael Reeves arrives at a similar conclusion by drawing our attention to Matthew 3:16–17, which reads, "And when Jesus was baptized, he went up immediately from the water, and behold, the heavens were opened and he saw the Spirit of God descending like a dove, and alighting on him; and lo, a voice from heaven, saying, 'This is my beloved Son, with whom I am well pleased.'" Reeves comments, "Here, the Father declares his love for his Son, and his pleasure in him, and he does so *as the Spirit rests on Jesus*. For the way the Father makes known his love is precisely through giving his Spirit. In Romans 5:5, for instance, Paul writes of how God pours his love into our hearts *by the Holy Spirit*. It is, then, through giving him the Spirit that the Father declares his love for his Son" (Reeves, *Delighting in the Trinity: An Introduction to the Christian Faith* [Downers Grove, IL: IVP Academic, 2012], 29).

55. Moberly, "Test the Spirits," 296.

For Augustine, however, the proper context of 1 John 4:7–8 includes not only 1 John 4 but also the Gospel of John and indeed the whole of Scripture, since the Triune God inspired the whole of canonical Scripture in order to teach us about himself.[56] In Scripture, our Creator and Redeemer desires to teach us about the unity and distinctiveness of the Father, Son, and Holy Spirit. Thus John's statement that "love is of God" and "God is love" (1 John 4:7–8) should be read with the expectation of learning something about "God of God," since John (the evangelist) instructs us along similar lines about the Son as the Word who "was with God" and "was God" (John 1:1). Given God's intention to teach about himself in Scripture, it is also fitting to probe 1 John 4 in the light of other canonical texts, such as Romans 5:5, with its conjunction of the "love of God" and the Holy Spirit. Although 1 John 4 and Romans 5:5 are about the Holy Spirit in the economy of salvation, I think that Augustine is right to anticipate a divine intention to acquaint us not only with the Holy Spirit in the salvific economy but also, in the process, with the mystery of the eternal distinctiveness of the Spirit.

The same expectations hold for the Holy Spirit as "Gift," although here Augustine is able to be less bold than is his reading of 1 John. As we have seen, in the New Testament the Spirit is quite frequently identified as the "gift of God" or is otherwise associated with "gift" in the economy of salvation. From Augustine's perspective, it makes sense that God wills in this way to teach us about the Holy Spirit as uniquely "Gift" of the Father and Son, in a manner parallel to the way in which the Son is uniquely the "Word" of the Father. This view also helps to explain why the Holy Spirit has a name whose two terms ("holy" and "spirit") are shared by the Father and Son and do not express a relation (unlike Father-Son). The Holy Spirit is "the gift of both."[57]

In sum, the web of scriptural texts that insistently associate the coming forth of the Spirit with "love" and "gift" suggests that in these two terms we have found a scriptural parallel with the Son's name "Word." "Love"

56. See Matthew Levering, *Participatory Biblical Exegesis: A Theology of Biblical Interpretation* (Notre Dame, IN: University of Notre Dame Press, 2008). For similar perspectives on Scripture, see, for example, Angus Paddison, *Scripture: A Very Theological Proposal* (London: T&T Clark, 2009); Gilles Emery, OP, "*Theologia* and *Dispensatio*: The Centrality of the Divine Missions in St. Thomas's Trinitarian Theology," *The Thomist* 74 (2010): 515–61, at 543–46. I should add that Moberly is generally superb at appreciating canonical context, as in his *The Bible, Theology, and Faith: A Study of Abraham and Jesus* (Cambridge: Cambridge University Press, 2000), 31–37 and elsewhere. In fact, his essay "Test the Spirits" appears under the title "John: God's Incarnate Love as the Key to Discernment" as chap. 5 of his *Prophecy and Discernment* (Cambridge: Cambridge University Press, 2006), in a manner that shows his essay to be shaped by fully canonical concerns.

57. Augustine, *The Trinity* 5.12, p. 197.

and "Gift" offer a limited, but precious, instruction from God the Teacher regarding the distinctiveness of the Holy Spirit in the Trinity. Through the economic manifestations of and inspired scriptural witness to the Spirit, we gain insight into the eternal identity of the Spirit. Augustine's interpretation of the New Testament's characteristic ways of speaking about the Spirit, therefore, should continue to guide contemporary theology of the Spirit: the Holy Spirit is the Gift of Love. It is possible to appreciate the insights of historical-critical biblical interpretation without denying the validity of Augustine's participatory mode of reading the New Testament texts about the Spirit. As Amy Plantinga Pauw reminds us: "To be a reader of Scripture is to be bound in love by the Spirit to the ancient writers and redactors of Scripture and to an enormous community of fellow readers, both past and present."[58] Within this community of readers, "holy scripture requires to be read and interpreted in the light of the same Spirit through whom it was written."[59] Augustine's exegetical principle—that the Spirit wills to teach us scripturally about his distinctiveness in the Trinity—is what we should expect from the "Spirit of truth" (John 16:13) who enables us in Christ Jesus to "receive the gift of the Holy Spirit" (Acts 2:38) and to receive the love of God that "has been poured into our hearts through the Holy Spirit who has been given to us" (Rom. 5:5).

---

58. Amy Plantinga Pauw, "The Holy Spirit and Scripture," in *The Lord and Giver of Life: Perspectives on Constructive Pneumatology*, ed. David H. Jensen (Louisville: Westminster John Knox, 2008), 25–39, at 29. Admittedly, Pauw also speaks of the need to exorcise our "inherited readings of Scripture," as well as to cultivate "a hermeneutic of suspicion toward our contemporary readings of Scripture" (ibid., 38). Her warnings seem geared to supporting contemporary liberationist and/or ecological readings of Scripture, but she leaves this somewhat unclear.

59. *Dei Verbum* §12, in *Decrees of the Ecumenical Councils*, vol. 2, *Trent to Vatican II*, ed. Norman P. Tanner, SJ (Washington, DC: Georgetown University Press, 1990), 976.

2

NAMING THE HOLY SPIRIT:
EAST AND WEST

In his influential essay on Augustine's pneumatology, Joseph Ratzinger cautions, "There is a certain difficulty in speaking about the Holy Spirit, even a certain danger. . . . It is quite possible that this topic has sparked only idle speculation and that human life is being based upon self-made fantasies rather than reality."[1] Similarly, Boris Bobrinskoy comments that although "we are witnessing in our time a notable deepening of pneumatology," nonetheless "too *direct* and scrutinizing an approach to the mystery of the procession of the Holy Spirit runs the risk of hardening and emptying out what is inexpressible."[2] Another Orthodox theologian, Andrew Louth, insists in his own essay on Augustine's pneumatology that "the mystery of God overwhelms any human categories; all one can do is stutter the precise distinctions that belong to the doctrine of the Trinity, which do not so much reveal the divine mystery, as prevent one's reducing it in one's conception to a bare philosophical unity

1. Joseph Ratzinger, "The Holy Spirit as Communio: Concerning the Relationship of Pneumatology and Spirituality in Augustine," trans. Peter Casarella, *Communio* 25 (1998): 324–37, at 324–25.
2. Boris Bobrinskoy, "The *Filioque* Yesterday and Today," in *Spirit of God, Spirit of Christ: Ecumenical Reflections on the* Filioque *Controversy*, ed. Lukas Vischer (London: SPCK, 1981), 133–48, at 146. Bobrinskoy adds that "today, as before, it is only the patristic synthesis, renewed in Palamism and realized today in modern Orthodox 'neo-patristic' theology which will be capable of reinserting theological speculation in its living and creative context" (ibid.).

or a pagan pantheon or any other misconception."[3] Louth warns that theologians in the wake of Augustine "begin to *imagine* the Trinity as a community of loving individuals. The Trinity then becomes an object of human speculation in itself: we are well on the way to a kind of mythological notion of the Trinity."[4] For Louth, Augustine's "doctrine of the Trinity has its own apophaticism; but his use of the doctrine of love . . . advances along a road ruled out altogether by the Greek Fathers."[5]

After Augustine, then, how should we Christians guard our speech about the Holy Spirit, so that we do not fall into a rationalistic fantasy about, in Brian Daley's words, "the impenetrable mystery of God's interior life"?[6] Bobrinskoy considers Augustine's pneumatology to be acceptable as "the expression of a personal and hence provisional theological investigation," so long as one does not follow Augustine's bolder claims, such as the *filioque*.[7] But for many contemporary theologians, Augustine's naming of the Spirit, far from being too bold, is much too tame. For instance, while stating that "it must be firmly borne in mind that the Trinity is and remains an absolute mystery," Hans Urs von Balthasar argues that the Holy Spirit's freedom "arises from the renunciation of both Father and Son: both refuse to be understood except in terms of self-emptying."[8] Similarly, he explains that the Holy Spirit, as "the

---

3. Andrew Louth, "Love and the Trinity: Saint Augustine and the Greek Fathers," *Augustinian Studies* 33 (2002): 1–16, at 13.

4. Ibid., 15.

5. Ibid., 16. On Augustine's apophaticism, Louth cites Vladimir Lossky, "Les elements de 'théologie negative' dans la pensée de saint Augustin," in Congrès International Augustinien, *Augustinus Magister* (Paris: Études Augustiniennes, 1954), 1:575–81.

6. Brian E. Daley, SJ, "Revisiting the 'Filioque': Part One, Roots and Branches of an Old Debate," *Pro Ecclesia* 10 (2001): 31–62, at 32.

7. Bobrinskoy, "*Filioque* Yesterday and Today," 138. In addition to these Catholic and Orthodox voices, note also the Protestant theologian Alister McGrath's warning "against the dangers of inflationary trinitarian language and speculation, which has lost its moorings in the language of Scripture" (McGrath, "The Doctrine of the Trinity: An Evangelical Reflection," in *God the Holy Trinity: Reflections on Christian Faith and Practice*, ed. Timothy George [Grand Rapids: Baker Academic, 2006], 17–35, at 30). As a model for the kind of trinitarian theology that he wishes to see, McGrath holds up Robert W. Jenson's insistence that Christians know not merely an abstract God, but the God who has the proper name "Father, Son, and Holy Spirit." See Jenson, *The Triune Identity: God according to the Gospel* (Philadelphia: Fortress, 1982).

8. Hans Urs von Balthasar, *Theo-Logic*, vol. 3, *The Spirit of Truth*, trans. Graham Harrison (San Francisco: Ignatius, 2005), 157, 241. Balthasar remarks, "Those who are reluctant to import such concepts into God (preferring to stay at the level of the equation *relatio = persona*) ought to remove these imperfect likenesses from the world. Hegel insisted on the inner connection between generation and death. . . . The child awakes to genuine freedom only through his parents' sacrificial self-denial" (ibid., 241–42). For discussion of Balthasar's trinitarian theology, arguing that Balthasar claims to know more than can be known about the trinitarian life, see Karen Kilby, "Hans Urs von Balthasar on the Trinity," in *The Cambridge Companion to the Trinity*, ed. Peter C. Phan (Cambridge: Cambridge University Press, 2011), 208–22. For an appreciative

excess of love that is 'always more,' is the incomprehensible and unsurpassable peak [unüberschreitbare Gipfel] of absolute love" in the Trinity.[9] Balthasar affirms that the Spirit is Gift and Love, but he adds that the Spirit "realizes himself in ways that are always new (*tropos tēs hyparxeōs*), incomparable, and personal."[10] Although Balthasar is drawing upon the scriptural portrait of Christ and the Spirit and is making theological use of metaphorical language, what does it mean to call the Holy Spirit the "unsurpassable peak" of love in the Trinity? Does not this imagery necessarily imply that the Father and Son are less fully love than is the Spirit, who is the high point? And what are the Spirit's ever-new self-realizations? Does this mean that the Spirit is not yet perfect, but instead is still developing? These formulations add excitement to trinitarian theology, but, despite the cautions that Balthasar insists upon, at the cost of saying too much.[11]

---

overview, see Rowan Williams, "Balthasar and the Trinity," in *The Cambridge Companion to Hans Urs von Balthasar*, ed. Edward T. Oakes, SJ, and David Moss (Cambridge: Cambridge University Press, 2004), 37–50.

9. Balthasar, *Theo-Logic*, vol. 3, *The Spirit of Truth*, 159–60. Note also Adrienne von Speyr's statement that "Father and Son see their reciprocal love surpassed as it proceeds from them as a Third Person" (von Speyr, *The World of Prayer* [San Francisco: Ignatius, 1985], 23, quoted in Balthasar, *Theo-Drama*, vol. 5, *The Last Act*, trans. Graham Harrison [San Francisco: Ignatius, 1998], 79). In a more muted manner, Emmanuel Durand, OP, affirms that we should "consider the Spirit, following Cyril of Alexandria, as the 'culmination of the Trinity' (*sumplèrôma*), in the sense that the perfection of communion of the Father-Son relation is expressed in it" (Durand, "Perichoresis: A Key Concept for Balancing Trinitarian Theology," in *Rethinking Trinitarian Theology: Disputed Questions and Contemporary Issues in Trinitarian Theology*, ed. Giulio Maspero and Robert J. Woźniak [London: T&T Clark, 2012], 177–92, at 188). Durand cites M.-O. Boulnois, *Le paradoxe trinitaire chez Cyrille d'Alexandrie* (Paris: Études Augustiniennes, 1994), 437–42. Note also J.-Y. Brachet and Emmanuel Durand's comment: "For our part, we think that the formula: 'the Spirit proceeds from the Father who is only Father in relation to the Son' well expresses the possible unity at the level of dogmatic content [with regard to the *filioque*]" (Brachet and Durand, "La réception de la 'Clarification' de 1995 sur le '*Filioque*,'" *Irénikon* 78 [2005]: 47–109, at 108). This formulation, like the view that the Spirit is the "culmination of the Trinity," immediately requires further logical clarification in order for one to be sure what precisely is being expressed.

10. Balthasar, *Theo-Logic*, vol. 3, *The Spirit of Truth*, 161. Balthasar also criticizes Augustine's trinitarian theology as an essentialist reduction of the Persons to "three functions in the one Spirit" (ibid., 157). On the other hand, he rightly warns that in trinitarian theologies "where there is genuine communication and hence fruitfulness, in the interpersonal realm, what is lacking is the unity of the concrete essence; a doctrine of the Trinity that proceeds from *purely* 'economic' diastasis is always in danger of putting forward a tritheism, where the unity of essence emerges at best, if at all, from the *circuminsessio*" (ibid.).

11. Thus, with regard to the Father and Son, Balthasar states, "As Adrienne von Speyr has shown, this results in the interplay of reciprocal wonder and worship, of infinite reciprocal gratitude (on the Father's part, because the Son eternally allows himself to be begotten; and on the Son's part, because the Father eternally gives himself) and reciprocal entreaty (on the Father's part, that the Son will carry out all the Father's wishes; and, on the Son's part, that the Father will permit the Son to fulfill his uttermost wishes)" (ibid., 159); Balthasar cites von Speyr's

The Lutheran theologian Robert Jenson shares or even exceeds Balthasar's boldness about the inner life of the Trinity. Jenson finds that the Holy Spirit is the one who "in his own intention," through his own active work, "liberates Father and Son to love each other."[12] Furthermore, the Holy Spirit is no merely passive recipient of spiration; rather, "the Spirit so proceeds from the Father as himself to be the possibility of such processions, his own and the Son's."[13] The Spirit's procession thus works backward in the Trinity, so that he can be the possibility of his own procession. His procession also, according to Jenson, works forward in the Trinity: "To say that the Holy Spirit is without qualification 'one of the Trinity' is to say that the dynamism of God's life is a narrative causation in and so of God. It is in that the Spirit is God as the Power of God's *own* and our future and, that is to say, the Power of a future that also for God is not bound by the predictabilities, that the Spirit is a distinct identity of and in God."[14]

The World of Prayer. See also Michele M. Schumacher, *A Trinitarian Anthropology: Adrienne von Speyr and Hans Urs von Balthasar in Dialogue with Thomas Aquinas* (Washington, DC: Catholic University of America Press, 2014).

12. Robert W. Jenson, *Systematic Theology*, vol. 1, *The Triune God* (Oxford: Oxford University Press, 1997), 156. For extended critiques of Jenson's theology of the Trinity, see David Bentley Hart, *The Beauty of the Infinite: The Aesthetics of Christian Truth* (Grand Rapids: Eerdmans, 2003), 157–67; Scott R. Swain, *The God of the Gospel: Robert Jenson's Trinitarian Theology* (Downers Grove, IL: IVP Academic, 2013); Francesca Aran Murphy, *God Is Not a Story: Realism Revisited* (Oxford: Oxford University Press, 2007).

13. Jenson, *Systematic Theology*, vol. 1, *The Triune God*, 158.

14. Ibid., 160. Paul S. Fiddes voices the common critique that Latin trinitarian theology, especially as represented by those who hold that Holy Spirit is the Father's and Son's bond of love, obscures the Spirit's distinct identity in the Trinity. He states that "the obvious problem with this Western approach is that the Spirit does not appear to have a distinct identity, being either the common factor between Father and Son, or simply the divine nature" (Fiddes, *Participating in God: A Pastoral Doctrine of the Trinity* [Louisville: Westminster John Knox, 2000], 265). However, this is a misunderstanding not only of what it means for the Spirit to be the bond of love, but also of what Augustinian trinitarian theology sets out to do. The Spirit's distinct identity in the Trinity is "Love proceeding" and "Gift," just as the Son's distinct identity is "Word." We cannot expect trinitarian naming to deliver more than a glimpse into the inexhaustible divine mystery of triunity. We can, of course, expect these names to deliver insight into the economy of salvation from which they arise. Fiddes is even harder on the Cappadocians: "Having worked out the model of the Fatherly begetter and the Filial begotten, the theologians of the fourth century thus portrayed the Spirit as a pale shadow of the Son. While progressing beyond the tendency of earlier theologians to subordinate the Spirit to the Son 'in third rank' or as 'the prophetic spirit' or as 'the grace of God,' the Spirit now duplicates the Son in fainter outline" (ibid., 254). Fiddes's solution is much like Jenson's: "It would correspond to our *experience* of Spirit that Holy Spirit should be the movement within God that is constantly opening up the relationship of Father and Son to new depths of personality and to new fulfilment in the future. *All* the relations in God are movements of being, but we may discern a distinct movement that is always opening up the others, so that another image for the Spirit might be 'the disturber'" (ibid., 264).

Jenson's position, if true, would significantly add to what we know about the Spirit. If the Spirit is the one who liberates the Father and Son to love each other and who is the Power of God's future, however, are the Father and Son deficient in their own love and power? To name the Spirit in these ways may sound exciting, but such naming dramatizes the Spirit, and historicizes the Trinity, in a manner that goes far beyond what Scripture tells us (not least in its use of Hellenistic philosophical insights) about God and the Spirit.

By contrast, most Orthodox theologians would accept Louth's firm warnings against Augustine's naming the Spirit "Love" and "Gift."[15] Since I agree with the emphasis on the need for caution in naming the Spirit, I devote the first section of this chapter to sketching the approaches to the Holy Spirit found in John of Damascus, Gregory of Nazianzus, and Basil the Great, as well as in the eminent twentieth-century Orthodox theologian Dumitru Stăniloae. I then turn to Thomas Aquinas's reception of Augustine's naming of the Spirit. In this regard, the Benedictine scholar Luigi Gioia cautions that "the use of the notions of 'procession' and 'generation' leads to a very abstract description of this mystery."[16] Lewis Ayres similarly suggests that Augustine's trinitarian theology is more biblical than Aquinas's: "Augustine's pattern of 'redoublement' does not proceed via an examination of the language of persons and essence, but via the interweaving of two strands of exegesis and philosophical reflection."[17] Yet Ayres grants that "there is a deep consonance between Augustine's account of persons as constituted by their eternal intradivine acts, which are in turn identical with their eternally being generated and spirated, and Thomas's account of subsisting relations."[18]

I hope to show that Aquinas appropriates Augustine's theology of the Spirit in a manner that accords with the Eastern concern for caution in naming the

15. Lewis Ayres points out in this regard, "It is sometimes asserted that the 'Cappadocians' (or even Greek pro-Nicenes in general) spoke of the Spirit proceeding 'from the Father through the Son.' De Régnon himself remarks to his own surprise that the phrase is very rare: he identifies only two passages that qualify as direct statements of the formula. In fact, 'Cappadocian' texts show a great reluctance to define the Spirit's mode of procession. At the same time we should notice that statements which could be (and have been) extracted to build up an account of what one or other figure says about the Spirit's procession, are frequently *en passant* statements in arguments concerned with different or wider problems" (Ayres, "Innovation and *Ressourcement* in Pro-Nicene Pneumatology," *Augustinian Studies* 39 [2008]: 187–206, at 200–201).

16. Luigi Gioia, OSB, *The Theological Epistemology of Augustine's De Trinitate* (Oxford: Oxford University Press, 2008), 141.

17. Lewis Ayres, *Augustine and the Trinity* (Cambridge: Cambridge University Press, 2010), 260–61.

18. Ibid., 271.

Spirit.[19] As Brian Daley says, "Thomas approached the mystery of the Trinity and its persons and processions with a modesty that sometimes escapes notice in the thicket of his tightly-wound argument, but which resembles more the apophatic austerity of the Cappadocians than the bold personalist speculations of Richard of St. Victor."[20] Questions 37 and 38 of the *prima pars* of the *Summa theologiae* focus respectively on the Spirit's names "Love" and "Gift." Here Aquinas addresses speculative issues that arise from Augustine's position, and does so, in my view, without overreaching with regard to what theologians can hope to know about the Spirit's eternal procession. By examining questions 37 and 38, I hope to show that Daley is right to conclude that "Thomas succeeds to an unusual degree in striking a balance between an overly abstract or essentialist, and an overly concrete or interpersonal approach to speaking of the three persons in God."[21]

19. I do not mean to overemphasize this caution, which characterizes the Creed's intentional refusal to state that the Spirit is "God" or "consubstantial" with the Father and Son. As Brian Daley remarks, "Epiphanius of Salamis, for instance, a contemporary of the Cappadocians, likes to combine John 16.14–15 (which says the Spirit 'receives from' the Son) with John 15.26 (he 'proceeds from' the Father) when speaking about the Spirit's origin; so he speaks of the Spirit several times as 'being from' the Father and the Son, without further explication, and explicitly takes these two Johannine texts, in two passages, to mean the Spirit 'is from the two.' Gregory of Nyssa himself, who generally insists that the only αἰτία or 'cause' of the divine being is the Father, in whom the substantial unity of God is entirely grounded, still suggests, in a few passages, that the Son also plays a part in the 'causation' of the Spirit, in a way that does not derogate from the primary role of the Father in that causation" (Daley, "Revisiting the 'Filioque': Part One," 43). Daley points out that Cyril of Alexandria goes even further: Cyril repeatedly teaches that the Spirit comes through the Son and comes forth (πρόεισι) from both. Citing Jean-Miguel Garrigues's *L'Esprit qui dit 'Père!' et le problème du filioque* (Paris: Téqui, 1981), 77–80, Daley emphasizes that "the credal formula of Constantinople was intended to affirm—albeit in indirect terms—the divine status and activity of the Holy Spirit, alongside the Father and the Son; it was not intended precisely as a definition of the mode of the Spirit's origin, or of the exact character of his relationship to Father and Son. On these matters, two distinct and—Garrigues argues—complementary 'sister-traditions' of terminology and conceptual modeling already existed in East and West, as we have seen, which were to continue to develop along generally parallel rather than intersecting lines" (Daley, "Revisiting the 'Filioque': Part One," 46).

20. Daley, "Revisiting the 'Filioque': Part One," 58–59. Among the bolder, less apophatic approaches, Daley also includes Anselm's approach. Daley continues, "The result of this conviction, obvious as it may seem, is that Thomas is in fact quite reluctant to say more about the persons of the Trinity and their mutual relations than what their names, invoked in baptism, reveal, and what the handful of New Testament passages alluding to their distinctive roles in history suggest" (ibid., 59).

21. Ibid., 60. As Daley remarks, Aquinas uses the term "person" with appropriate analogical caution, but does not go too far in an impersonal direction along the lines of Anselm, who elaborates his trinitarian theology largely from the consideration of the divine essence. In this regard, Daley approvingly cites André Malet, OSB, *Personne et amour dans la théologie trinitaire de saint Thomas d'Aquin* (Paris: Vrin, 1956), 159. Daley's position contrasts, as he recognizes, with that of Jean-Miguel Garrigues, who finds Aquinas to veer too frequently toward conceiving of the Holy Spirit as a "property" of the Father and Son rather than as a distinct person.

Orthodox Caution in Naming the Holy Spirit

John of Damascus

The master synthesizer of the Greek patristic tradition, John of Damascus, affirms in his *An Exact Exposition of the Orthodox Faith* that it is "necessary that the Word have a Spirit," since even our words are breathed forth.[22] He notes that revelation teaches that "there is a Spirit of God," and that this Spirit should be conceived of "as associated with the Word and making the operation of the Word manifest."[23] The Spirit is "a substantial power found in its own individuating personality, proceeding from the Father, coming to rest in the Word and declaring Him."[24] The Spirit is therefore "distinctly subsistent like the Word."[25]

How then should we differentiate the Holy Spirit's procession from the Word's generation, since both come forth perfectly from the Father? Damascene exhibits great caution here. He affirms that "only the Son is begotten, for He is begotten of the substance of the Father without beginning and independently of time. And only the Holy Spirit proceeds: not begotten, but proceeding from the substance of the Father."[26] But when it comes to distinguishing these two in any further way, Damascene observes solely that the distinction between generation and procession "is the teaching of sacred Scripture, but as to the manner of the begetting and the procession, this is beyond understanding."[27] He emphasizes that he did not invent the terms "paternity," "sonship," and "procession," but received them from Scripture. At the conclusion of his discussion of the distinctiveness of the Holy Spirit in the Trinity, he repeats that since both the Son and Holy Spirit come forth from the Father, "there is a difference between begetting and procession, but what the manner of this difference is we have not learned at all."[28] He comments

---

See Garrigues, "À la suite de la clarification romaine: Le *Filioque* affranchi du 'filioquisme,'" *Irénikon* 69 (1996): 189–212, at 200–207.

22. John of Damascus, *An Exact Exposition of the Orthodox Faith* 1.6, in John of Damascus, *Writings*, trans. Frederic H. Chase Jr. (Washington, DC: Catholic University of America Press, 1958), 174. For a helpful succinct discussion of Damascene on the Holy Spirit, see Andrew Louth, *St. John Damascene: Tradition and Originality in Byzantine Theology* (Oxford: Oxford University Press, 2002), 98, 107–10.

23. John of Damascus, *An Exact Exposition of the Orthodox Faith* 1.7, p. 175.

24. John of Damascus, *An Exact Exposition of the Orthodox Faith* 1.7, p. 175.

25. John of Damascus, *An Exact Exposition of the Orthodox Faith* 1.7, p. 175.

26. John of Damascus, *An Exact Exposition of the Orthodox Faith* 1.8, p. 182.

27. John of Damascus, *An Exact Exposition of the Orthodox Faith* 1.8, p. 182.

28. John of Damascus, *An Exact Exposition of the Orthodox Faith* 1.8, p. 184. He holds that the Spirit "proceeds from the Father and is communicated through the Son and is participated in by all creation" (ibid.), but he does not hinge the difference between begetting and

only that the difference is certainly not a temporal one, as though the Son were prior in time to the Spirit; although the Son and Spirit come forth in a certain order, they come forth simultaneously and eternally.

It would seem, then, that Damascene carefully says nothing more than that the Father, Son, and Holy Spirit are distinct only in "the being unbegotten, the begetting, and the procession. For it is only in these personal properties that the three divine persons differ from one another, being indivisibly divided by the distinctive note of each individual person."[29] Nonetheless, occasionally Damascene seems to set aside this caution, at least to some degree. Seeking to name the Father, Son, and Holy Spirit more extensively, he proposes that "the Father is a supersubstantial sun, a well-spring of goodness, an abyss of essence, reason, wisdom, power, light, and divinity, a begetting and emitting well-spring of the good hidden in Himself."[30] Using terms drawn from Scripture (e.g., John 1:1; 1 Cor. 1:24; Col. 1:15; Heb. 1:3), he goes on to say that the Son is "son, word, wisdom, power, image, radiance, and type of the Father."[31] Building upon this, he then argues that "whatsoever pertains to the Son as caused, begotten son, word, primordial force, will, and wisdom must be attributed to the Son alone."[32] This does indeed seem to be moving in the direction of seeking to understand the mystery of eternal "generation" by means of other biblical names for the Son.[33] The same holds, broadly speaking,

---

procession on the point that the Spirit "is communicated through the Son," not least because this communication occurs in the temporal economy. As he states more fully,

> One should know that we do not say that the Father is of anyone, but that we do say that He is the Father of the Son. We do not say that the Son is a cause or a father, but we do say that He is from the Father and is the Son of the Father. And we do say that the Holy Spirit is of the Father and we call Him the Spirit of the Father. Neither do we say that the Spirit is from the Son, but we call Him the Spirit of the Son—"Now if any man have not the Spirit of Christ," says the divine Apostle, "he is none of his" [Rom. 8:9]. We also confess that He was manifested and communicated to us through the Son, for "He breathed," it says, "and he said to his disciples: Receive ye the Holy Spirit" [John 20:22]. It is just like the rays and brightness coming from the sun, for the sun is the source of its rays and brightness and the brightness is communicated to us through the rays, and that it is which lights us and is enjoyed by us. Neither do we say that the Son is of the Father, nor, most certainly, from the Spirit. (John of Damascus, *An Exact Exposition of the Orthodox Faith* 1.12, p. 188)

He likewise observes a bit later that the Holy Spirit is "a power of the Father revealing the hidden things of the Godhead and proceeding from the Father through the Son, not by begetting, but in a manner which He also knows. . . . He is the Spirit of the Son, not as being from Him, but as proceeding through Him from the Father—for the Father alone is Cause" (John of Damascus, *An Exact Exposition of the Orthodox Faith* 1.12, p. 196).

29. John of Damascus, *An Exact Exposition of the Orthodox Faith* 1.12, p. 184.
30. John of Damascus, *An Exact Exposition of the Orthodox Faith* 1.12, p. 96.
31. John of Damascus, *An Exact Exposition of the Orthodox Faith* 1.12, p. 96.
32. John of Damascus, *An Exact Exposition of the Orthodox Faith* 1.12, p. 96.
33. See also John of Damascus, *An Exact Exposition of the Orthodox Faith* 1.13, pp. 200–201.

for his treatment of the Holy Spirit. He remarks that "whatsoever pertains to the caused, proceeding, revealing, and perfecting power must be attributed to the Holy Spirit," and he adds that the Spirit is the Spirit precisely as "proceeding from the Father" because "without the Spirit, there is no impulsion."[34] These terms appear to illumine not only the temporal economy but also, in a fashion that Damascene does not develop or defend, the eternal procession itself. Indeed, Damascene goes on to describe the Holy Spirit as "the median of the Unbegotten and the Begotten" and as the one who "proceeds unceasingly from the Father and abides in the Son."[35] This language too seems to describe in more detail how procession differs from generation.

In addition, Damascene occasionally and very cautiously uses analogies to illumine unity and distinction in the one God. For example, he compares the divine unity of the Father, Son, and Spirit to the unity of "three suns joined together without any intervening interval," which would of course make one sun.[36] The weakness of this analogy is obvious to him. It provides simply a way of thinking about the three-and-one in terms of light, without being otherwise taken too seriously. In the same way, he compares the relationship of the Father and Son to that of "the fire with its light."[37] Although the analogy would (if pressed) lead to inability truly to distinguish the persons, a very cautious use of the analogy provides some insight, insofar as "the light is ever being begotten of the fire, is always in it, and is in no way separated from it."[38]

Gregory of Nazianzus

Perhaps an even more cautious approach to the Holy Spirit's eternal procession is taken by Gregory of Nazianzus, whose theology Damascene followed closely. Like Damascene, Gregory displays philosophical resources of the kind that undermine simplistic divisions between "patristic" and "scholastic" theological styles.[39] Regarding the question of the divinity of the Holy Spirit, for example, Gregory notes, "The Holy Spirit must be presumed to be either a being existing in its own right or an inherent property of something else—what

---

34. John of Damascus, *An Exact Exposition of the Orthodox Faith* 1.12, p. 196.
35. John of Damascus, *An Exact Exposition of the Orthodox Faith* 1.13, pp. 200–201.
36. John of Damascus, *An Exact Exposition of the Orthodox Faith* 1.8, p. 187.
37. John of Damascus, *An Exact Exposition of the Orthodox Faith* 1.8, p. 180.
38. John of Damascus, *An Exact Exposition of the Orthodox Faith* 1.8, p. 180.
39. Both styles include spiritual practice and spiritual exegesis. Christopher A. Beeley observes that "the soteriological heart of Gregory's Pneumatology" is the fact that "the knowledge of the Holy Spirit derives directly from the Spirit's saving work of divinization" (Beeley, *Gregory of Nazianzus on the Trinity and the Knowledge of God: In Your Light We Shall See Light* [Oxford: Oxford University Press, 2008], 176).

the subtle here call a 'substance' or an 'accident' respectively."[40] He goes on
to deny that the Holy Spirit is an "accident" or "an activity of God," because
Scripture clearly presents the Holy Spirit as a distinctive agent, not a mere
activity that ceases at a certain point and that is activated by another.[41] But,
given that the Holy Spirit is God, a number of questions arise, most pressingly
the issue that if the Spirit is begotten from the Father rather than unoriginate,
then it would seem that "there will be two sons who are brothers."[42]

In reply, Gregory first charges that proponents of such views are relying
upon implicitly corporeal notions of the coming forth of the Son and Spirit
from the Father. Along these lines, he says mockingly, "Make them twins if
you like, or one older than the other, since you have a penchant for corporeal ideas."[43] Far from describing a corporeal coming forth, the name "Son"
describes "his consubstantial derivation from God."[44] The seeming problem
of the Son and Spirit as "two sons who are brothers" is also solved, Gregory
thinks, by simply accepting that Jesus Christ, in revealing the Holy Spirit,
means what he says. Jesus tells us that the Spirit "proceeds from the Father"
(John 15:26). Gregory grounds his theology of the Holy Spirit on this teaching: "Insofar as he [the Spirit] proceeds from the Father, he is no creature;
inasmuch as he is not begotten, he is no Son; and to the extent that procession is the mean between ingeneracy and generacy, he is God."[45] The Spirit
comes forth from the Father in a particular way: he "proceeds." Since this is
so, there is obviously no need to imagine two (begotten) Sons.

Gregory recognizes, however, that his opponents may wish to challenge
him to explain further what it means for the Spirit to proceed from the Father.
Is it intelligible merely to claim that "procession" differs from "generation"?
In response, Gregory raises the question of what "proceeding" is, in order to
show the question's absurdity. After all, if procession is anything, then it is
a divine mystery; to probe further into it, as if God were an object that we
can understand, would be pure pride. Gregory informs his opponents, "You
explain the ingeneracy of the Father and I will give you a biological account
of the Son's begetting and the Spirit's proceeding."[46] In case his opponents
have not gotten the message, he adds that after such (absurd) explanations

40. Gregory of Nazianzus, *On God and Christ: The Five Theological Orations and Two
Letters to Cledonius*, trans. Lionel Wickham (Crestwood, NY: St. Vladimir's Seminary Press,
2002), Oration 31.6, p. 120.
    41. Gregory of Nazianzus, Oration 31.6, p. 120.
    42. Gregory of Nazianzus, Oration 31.7, p. 121.
    43. Gregory of Nazianzus, Oration 31.7, p. 121.
    44. Gregory of Nazianzus, Oration 31.7, p. 121.
    45. Gregory of Nazianzus, Oration 31.8, p. 122.
    46. Gregory of Nazianzus, Oration 31.8, p. 122.

have been exchanged, "Let us go mad the pair of us for prying into God's secrets."[47]

The point is not that God's secrets are utterly hidden; after all, Jesus Christ has freely revealed to us that the Spirit "proceeds from the Father." The point is that this revelation of what was previously hidden should suffice for us. As Gregory observes, "What competence have we here? We cannot understand what lies under our feet, cannot count the sand in the sea, 'the drops of rain or the days of this world,' much less enter into the 'depths of God' and render a verbal account of a nature so mysterious, so much beyond words."[48] Further reflection on the Spirit's procession goes beyond the bounds of our limited intellect, although mystical experience of the Holy Spirit might be able to ascend to some form of intimate knowledge "beyond words." It is enough to know that the divine "Spirit is not Son," since the Son comes forth by generation, whereas the Spirit comes forth by procession.[49]

Is there then no way to understand the difference between generation and procession? For Gregory, divine revelation does not give us further information, and the transcendence and uniqueness of God prevent us from finding analogies in creatures that would guide us into more insight. As Gregory remarks, "It is a singularly graceless, and not just graceless but a pretty well futile, notion to get a picture of things heavenly from things of earth, of things fixed immutably from this transitory element."[50] Nonetheless, in order to show that the distinction between generation and procession is not unintelligible, Gregory provides a simple analogy, whose limits he emphasizes. He notes that Eve and Seth came forth from Adam, and yet only Seth was an offspring. All three shared human nature. It is possible, then, that three entities can share a nature, that two can come forth from an original one, and that only one of these two who come forth can be rightly termed "begotten." Those who think that the Spirit must be simply another Son are mistaken.

Regarding the economy of salvation, of course, Gregory is willing to say much more about the Spirit, since the Spirit's agency and role in the economy of salvation is relatively clear in Scripture. In this regard, Gregory's main goal

47. Gregory of Nazianzus, Oration 31.8, p. 122.

48. Gregory of Nazianzus, Oration 31.8, p. 122.

49. Gregory of Nazianzus, Oration 31.9, p. 123. Brian Daley points out that the debate with the Eunomians shapes Gregory's theology here: "In contrast to the exuberant and confident rationalism of the Eunomians, the Cappadocians generally prefer to remain within the barest framework of biblical language in describing what distinguishes each 'person' in the divine mystery from the others" (Daley, "Revisiting the 'Filioque': Part One," 42). See also Bernd Oberdorfer, *Filioque: Geschichte und Theologie eines ökumenischen Problems* (Göttingen: Vandenhoeck & Ruprecht, 2001), 83–88.

50. Gregory of Nazianzus, Oration 31.10, p. 124.

is to defend the Spirit's full divinity. Gregory's opponents argue, for example, that when the Gospel of John teaches that the Word "was in the beginning with God" and that "all things were made through him," this reference to "all things" must include the Holy Spirit, since only God and the Word are mentioned prior to the "all things" that are made. In arguing against these "ditheists," Gregory takes pains to defend his position against those who would accuse him of tritheism. Here he uses the analogy of three suns and one light: "It is as if there were a single intermingling of light, which existed in three mutually connected Suns."[51] But he cautions against such examples on the grounds that they contain "a hint of those very things which are inconceivable in the case of God—composition, dispersion, and the lack of a fixed, natural stability."[52] Gregory emphasizes that Scripture attributes divine titles and divine functions to the Holy Spirit, and so the Spirit must be divine. For Gregory, Scripture frequently uses the language of gift with respect to the Spirit not in order to subordinate the Spirit to the divine Giver, but in order to make clear that the Spirit proceeds from the Father: "All the less exalted expressions which talk of his being given, sent, divided, or his being a grace, a gift, an inspiration, a promise, a means of intercession or anything else of the same character—all these are to be referred back to the Primal Cause, as indicating the Spirit's source and preventing a polytheistic belief in three separate causes."[53]

Basil the Great

For Gregory, it is best to "rest content with some few words," rather than seeking to develop "images and shadows, deceptive and utterly inadequate as

---

51. Gregory of Nazianzus, Oration 31.14, p. 127. Insofar as the image of "light" comes from John 1:9, Gregory is happy to use it: "For our part we have such confidence in the Godhead of the Spirit, that, rash though some may find it, we shall begin our theological exposition by applying identical expressions to the Three. 'He was the true light that enlightens every man coming into the world'—yes, the Father. 'He was the true light that enlightens every man coming into the world'—yes, the Son. 'He was the true light that enlightens every man coming into the world'—yes, the Comforter. These are three subjects and three verbs—he was and he was and he was. But a single reality *was*. There are three predicates—light and light and light. But the light is one, God is one. This is the meaning of David's prophetic vision: 'In your light we shall see light' [Ps. 36:9]. We receive the Son's light from the Father's light in the light of the Spirit" (Gregory of Nazianzus, Oration 31.3, p. 118).

52. Gregory of Nazianzus, Oration 31.33, p. 142. He remarks, "Another illustration I pondered over was that of Sun, beam, and light. But here again there was the danger, first of imagining in the incomposite nature the sort of composition which belongs to the Sun and its inherent properties, and second, of making the Father a substance but the others potentialities of God inherent in him, not actual beings. Beam and light are not extra Suns, but emanations from the Sun, substantial qualities" (Gregory of Nazianzus, Oration 31.32, p. 142).

53. Gregory of Nazianzus, Oration 31.30, p. 141. See Beeley, *Gregory of Nazianzus on the Trinity and the Knowledge of God*, 206–10.

they are to express the reality."[54] By comparison, Gregory's fellow Cappadocian Basil the Great uses more analogies and titles when treating the Holy Spirit. Basil begins by praising the appropriateness of the name "Holy Spirit," since it evokes the uncircumscribed, all-holy, life-giving divinity.[55] Basil mixes references to the Spirit's role in the economy with descriptions of divine attributes: "He [the Holy Spirit] fills all things with power, but only those who are worthy participate in him. He is not participated in all at once but shares his energy in 'proportion to faith' (Rom. 12.6). He is simple in substance, but manifold in powers. He is present as a whole to each and wholly present everywhere."[56] Basil compares the Holy Spirit to "a sunbeam whose grace is present to the one who enjoys him as if he were present to such a one alone, and still he illuminates land and sea and is mixed with the air."[57] Similarly, in conceiving of creation, Basil proposes that we should "consider . . . the initial cause of their existence (the Father), the Maker (the Son), the Perfecter (the Spirit)."[58] The distinctive characteristic of the Holy Spirit is to be the "Perfecter," and yet, as Basil emphasizes, the power of the Father and Son is not deficient. Basil states that "the Father, who creates by his will alone, would not need the Son, but nevertheless he wills through the Son. The Son, who works according to the likeness of the Father, would not need a co-worker, but the Son wills that perfection should come about through the Spirit."[59] Basil connects the Spirit with the gift of holiness; thus the angels, for example, "have acquired holiness as a gift given to them by the Holy Spirit."[60]

When it comes to distinguishing generation and procession, Basil's approach is quite similar to that of Gregory. Basil observes that "the Spirit is said to be from God, not as all things are from God, but insofar as he comes

---

54. Gregory of Nazianzus, Oration 31.33, p. 143.

55. See Basil the Great, *On the Holy Spirit*, trans. Stephen Hildebrand (Yonkers, NY: St. Vladimir's Seminary Press, 2011), 9.22, p. 53. Later in his book Basil reflects further on the name "Holy Spirit": "The Spirit has been given the following names. 'God is Spirit' (John 4:24). 'The Spirit of our face, Christ the Lord' (Lam. 4:20). 'Holy,' as the Father is holy and the Son is holy (for holiness is supplied to creation from the outside, while for the Spirit, holiness is an essential part of his nature, so that he is not made holy but makes holy). 'Good,' as the Father is good and the One begotten from the good is good. He has goodness as his substance" (Basil the Great, *On the Holy Spirit* 19.48, p. 84). For discussion of Basil's theology of the Holy Spirit, see Stephen M. Hildebrand, *The Trinitarian Theology of Basil of Caesarea: A Synthesis of Greek Thought and Biblical Faith* (Washington, DC: Catholic University of America Press, 2007), chap. 6; Bernard Sesboüé, *Saint Basile et la Trinité: Un acte théologique au IVe siècle* (Paris: Desclée, 1998).

56. Basil the Great, *On the Holy Spirit* 9.22, p. 53.

57. Basil the Great, *On the Holy Spirit* 9.22, p. 53. Later in the book, Basil states that "no gift at all comes to creation without the Holy Spirit" (Basil the Great, *On the Holy Spirit* 24.55, p. 94).

58. Basil the Great, *On the Holy Spirit* 16.38, pp. 70–71.

59. Basil the Great, *On the Holy Spirit* 16.38, p. 71.

60. Basil the Great, *On the Holy Spirit* 16.38, p. 70.

forth from God, not begottenly as the Son does, but as the breath of his mouth."[61] Basil proposes that the Spirit's intimacy with the Father is shown by his being breathed forth from the Father, and he is also the Spirit of the Son by being related naturally to the Son.[62] The Spirit reveals and reflects the glory of the Father, from whom he proceeds. Basil also includes the Son in the relationship of shared glory: "the Spirit is glorified through the communion that he has with the Father and the Son."[63] The intimacy of the Spirit with the Father and the Son appears in the economy, which reveals that "the way to knowledge of God is from the one Spirit, through the one Son, to the one Father. And conversely the goodness and holiness by nature and the royal dignity reach from the Father, through the Only-Begotten, to the Spirit."[64] In addition to the name "Holy Spirit," Basil points out that there are other titles of the Holy Spirit that indicate the Spirit's unity with the Father and Son. Most important is the name "Paraclete," which the Spirit shares with the Son, as we learn in the Gospel of John when Jesus says that the Father will send "another Paraclete" (John 14:16) to be with the disciples. Other shared titles noted by Basil include "'director,' 'Spirit of truth,' and 'Spirit of wisdom.'"[65] As can be seen, Basil's central goal is to combat subordinationist views of the Spirit, which becomes especially clear in his treatment of the name "gift." His opponents teach that "the Spirit . . . is in us as a gift from God, and surely the gift is not exalted by the same honors as the giver."[66] He replies that the Spirit is a gift of life and power, in a way that only God can be; and besides, did not God "give the Son also to men?"[67]

Even if it is in certain ways less refined than Gregory's Oration—for example, in its treatment of the Holy Spirit as "Perfecter"—Basil's work stands as a masterful scriptural and liturgical defense of the coequal, ordered communion

---

61. Basil the Great, *On the Holy Spirit* 18.46, p. 81. For discussion see Lucas Francisco Mateo-Seco, "The Paternity of the Father and the Procession of the Holy Spirit: Some Historical Remarks on the Ecumenical Problem," in Maspero and Woźniak, *Rethinking Trinitarian Theology*, 69–102, at 86–88.

62. See Basil the Great, *On the Holy Spirit* 18.46, pp. 81–82.

63. Basil the Great, *On the Holy Spirit* 18.46, p. 82. For discussion of this text, see Boris Bobrinskoy, *The Mystery of the Trinity: Trinitarian Experience and Vision in the Biblical and Patristic Tradition*, trans. Anthony P. Gythiel (Crestwood, NY: St. Vladimir's Seminary Press, 1999), 240; for a broader discussion of Basil's *On the Holy Spirit*, see 237–45.

64. Basil the Great, *On the Holy Spirit* 18.47, p. 83. For discussion of this text, see Bobrinskoy, *The Mystery of the Trinity*, 237; Ayres, "Innovation and *Ressourcement* in Pro-Nicene Pneumatology," 198.

65. Basil the Great, *On the Holy Spirit* 19.48, p. 84.

66. Basil the Great, *On the Holy Spirit* 24.57, p. 95.

67. Basil the Great, *On the Holy Spirit* 24.57, p. 95. See Stephen M. Hildebrand, *Basil of Caesarea* (Grand Rapids: Baker Academic, 2014), 66–67.

of the Holy Spirit with the Father and the Son. He does not speculate much on the Spirit's characteristics within the Trinity. He is content simply to distinguish begetting (generation) and procession. In this way, his work belongs firmly within the cautious path that we saw in Gregory and, generally, also in Damascene.

Dumitru Stăniloae

The Romanian Orthodox theologian Dumitru Stăniloae has Augustinian trinitarian theology in mind when he promises to "refrain from explaining the generation of the Son and the procession of the Holy Spirit, that is, the mode of being of the three persons."[68] He affirms, of course, that "God is essence subsisting in three persons," but he warns against probing much further into this ineffable mystery.[69] He also insists—against "essentialist" views of the origination of the divine persons, and presumably also against the notion that the Father and Son's love is the Holy Spirit—that love in the Trinity "does not produce the divine persons, as Catholic theology affirms, but presupposes them."[70] He explains that he seeks "to avoid the psychologizing explanations of Catholic theology which has recourse to these only from its desire to find human arguments in favor of the *Filioque*."[71] Instead, he prefers the analogy of three suns of one infinite light. He states, "The Father—the sun in the sense of the paternal subsistence of infinite light—causes the Son to appear in him in the sense of a reflection of the whole of that infinite light which subsists in the Father. . . . Moreover, the Father also projects within himself as another sun, as Holy Spirit."[72] The Father thereby reveals "himself even more luminously as paternal sun" and also luminously reveals the Son to be "filial sun."[73]

It should be noted that this analogy of a sun and its perfect reflection and perfect projection—three suns that indwell one another and bear one undivided light—has biblical roots in John 1:9's statement about the Son that "the true light that enlightens every man was coming into the world" and Colossians 1:15's statement that the Son "is the image of the invisible God." As a way of providing some understanding of the Trinity, however, this analogy hardly seems less speculative than Augustine's analogy from memory, understanding,

---

68. Dumitru Stăniloae, *The Experience of God*, trans. and ed. Ioan Ionita and Robert Barringer (Brookline, MA: Holy Cross Orthodox Press, 1994), 247.
69. Ibid., 245.
70. Ibid.
71. Ibid., 247–48.
72. Ibid., 255.
73. Ibid.

and will, which is biblically rooted in John 1:1's identification of the Son as the Word. Indeed, Stăniloae does not refrain from trinitarian speculation. He holds, for example, that "the begetting of the Son by the Father is the premise for the knowledge which the Father has of himself, a knowledge brought about in common with the Son."[74] But it is true that Stăniloae does not seek to adduce from Scripture further proper names of the Holy Spirit, as Augustine does. Other than in his analogy of the suns, an analogy that does not produce further speculative conclusions, Stăniloae is content simply to observe that "the divine nature is hypostatized in the second hypostasis through his generation from the first, and in the third hypostasis through his procession from the first."[75]

Despite the modesty of this formulation, however, Stăniloae adds certain clarifications that make his final position less cautious. For example, he specifies that "procession" does not render the Holy Spirit merely passive. Both Father and Holy Spirit are active in the procession, so that "the procession of the Spirit from the Father is itself an act of pure intersubjectivity of Father and Spirit, without there being any confusion between them."[76] Indeed, he argues that the Spirit is intersubjectively and joyfully present in the Son's generation and the Son is intersubjectively and joyfully present in the Spirit's procession, although he does not clarify what this means for the trinitarian order of origin.[77] In his view, the value of the term "intersubjectivity" is that it personalizes, in a tripersonal communion, what otherwise might be the impersonal "relations of opposition" that Thomas Aquinas speaks about.

Toward the end of his argument, furthermore, Stăniloae appears to come quite close to Augustine's position regarding "love" as a proper name of the Holy Spirit, even though he does not go so far as to argue that the name "love" indicates something about the eternal procession. He grants that the name "Holy Spirit" is "closely associated with love," because "that name is the sign of perfect love in God."[78] It is so because three persons are required for the fullness of interpersonal communion. He comments, "Only the third implies complete deliverance of love from selfishness. . . . Only because a third exists can the two become simultaneously one, not merely through the reciprocity

74. Ibid., 259.
75. Ibid., 260.
76. Ibid., 261.
77. Elsewhere Stăniloae states that "each Person of the Holy Trinity is a Person not only insofar as he has a relation with the other, but insofar as he has a different relation with the other two" (Stăniloae, "The Procession of the Holy Spirit from the Father and His Relation to the Son, as the Basis of Our Deification and Adoption," in Vischer, *Spirit of God, Spirit of Christ*, 174–86, at 185).
78. Stăniloae, *Experience of God*, 267.

of their love alone, but also through their common self-forgetfulness in favor of the third."[79] Does this "common self-forgetfulness" of the Father and Son produce the eternal procession of the Spirit? In fact, Stăniloae's remarks about love and self-forgetfulness have to do not with the procession of the Holy Spirit but with the existential requirements of love per se. Love, like goodness, requires generous self-dispossession or self-diffusion beyond what two persons alone, were they not to share their love further, can provide. The Holy Spirit is thus a "sign" of a fundamental rule about love, but for Stăniloae, the Holy Spirit's eternal procession in the Trinity is not thereby distinctively "love."[80]

79. Ibid. For the same point, see Stăniloae, "Procession of the Holy Spirit from the Father," 185–86. Note also Antonio López's view that

in an analogical sense to the Son's "perfecting" of the Father, the Holy Spirit also "completes" the Son because it is the Holy Spirit who unites and distinguishes the source (Father) and its perfect expression (Son). The Spirit, *donum doni*, binds together the Father and the Son while preserving their difference. . . . Because it is the Spirit in whom Father and Son are united and distinguished, the Holy Spirit also "perfects" the Father and not only the Son. In this sense, as in Hegel's Trinitarian doctrine, the Holy Spirit, by confirming the gift, also contributes to the Father's being a person, but not because the Holy Spirit is another Son; the contribution is as Spirit. The Father is a person because he is his relation with the Son, yet it is only because this relation is confirmed by the Holy Spirit that there is a difference and a unity between the first two hypostases. (López, *Gift and the Unity of Being* [Eugene, OR: Cascade, 2014], 213)

In a number of essays over the past decade Bruce Marshall has expressed grave concerns about this Christian Hegelian view of the Trinity, and I share his concerns.

80. Bruce Marshall suggests that the difference between Stăniloae's position and that of Thomas Aquinas may be "merely verbal," since Stăniloae insists that the Holy Spirit "shines forth" from the Son; it may be that Stăniloae agrees with Aquinas on the *filioque* without knowing it. See Marshall, "*Ex Occidente Lux? Aquinas and Eastern Orthodox Theology*," in *Aquinas in Dialogue: Thomas for the Twenty-First Century*, ed. Jim Fodor and Frederick Christian Bauerschmidt (Oxford: Blackwell, 2004), 19–46, at 34; Stăniloae, *Theology and the Church*, trans. Robert Barringer (Crestwood, NY: St. Vladimir's Seminary Press, 1980), 98. For Marshall, the key point is the need "to save both the scriptural data regarding the sending of the divine persons and the principle that these data, rightly read, disclose to us their eternal origin and identity" (Marshall, "*Ex Occidente Lux?*," 36). As Marshall observes, one of Aquinas's central aims is to bring "into sharper relief the bond of mission to personal identity, the necessity that any possible economy of salvation take shape in conformity to the non-contingent identities of the divine persons" (ibid., 39). See also Michael D. Torre, "St. John Damascene and St. Thomas Aquinas on the Eternal Procession of the Holy Spirit," *St. Vladimir's Theological Quarterly* 38 (1994): 303–27, at 324–26. For Torre, Stăniloae's

theology is just what we might expect from someone combining Damascene with the idea that the Spirit is Love. Thus, what we see today are Orthodox theologians, working out of their *own* tradition, articulating a doctrine in perfect accord with Catholics. For they assert *with Damascene* that the Spirit eternally proceeds from the Father *to abide* in the Son and that He *eternally radiates from* the Son to the Father. This is to express, even more richly than the Latin tradition, its own doctrine. For it manages to express the way in which the Father is the *unoriginate* cause of the Spirit, and the Son is His *mediating* principle or "condition." This is to *express* the teaching of the West *according to the mind of the East*. And, when so many great Orthodox theologians also say that

Stăniloae employs his fundamental rule about love to explain the association of the Holy Spirit with love in the economy of salvation. Because the Spirit (as the third divine person) "represents the possibility of extending the love between Father and Son to other subjects," the Spirit also "represents the right which a third has to a part in the loving dialogue of the two, a right with which the Spirit invests created subjects."[81] Stăniloae makes a similar point with regard to the "objectivity" of the tripersonal communion. He argues that on the human level, it takes three persons to ensure the "objectivity" of communion. Existentially speaking, the Holy Spirit ensures that the divine communion is not locked in itself: "The third fulfills the role of 'object' or horizon, assuring the sense of objectivity for the two by the fact that he keeps the two from becoming confused within an indistinct unity because of the exclusiveness of their love, an exclusiveness which can flow from the conviction of each that nothing worthy of love exists outside the other."[82] Again, this is a philosophical or existential point that illumines the significance of the fact that there are three persons and that validates a broad association of the Spirit with love, without claiming that "love" names something proper to the eternal procession.

Stăniloae also uses this philosophical insight to shed light on why the Holy Spirit is called the "Spirit of truth" (John 15:26; 16:13). The fact that there is a third person confirms the "truth" of God's existence as love. If there were only one or two persons, this truth "would be confirmed only in part" or "would remain uncertain."[83] Since the Holy Spirit attests in this way to God's existence as love, Stăniloae notes that the Spirit also "receives the further

---

the Spirit abides in the Son as the Father's *Love* and that He radiates to the Father as the Son's *Spirit* returned, they manifest their *perfect unity* with Catholics. (ibid., 325–26)

Torre's proposal has evident strengths, but it also envisions the distinction of the Father and Son in such a way as to make the Son not truly involved in the Spirit's procession. The Father and Son are envisioned as eternally passing love (the Spirit) back and forth, with the Son not really a source of the procession and the Spirit linking the Father and Son. There are numerous problems here.

81. Stăniloae, *Experience of God*, 268.

82. Ibid., 268–69. For an insightful critique of a similar position (in Walter Kasper), see John Milbank, "The Second Difference," in *The Word Made Strange: Theology, Language, Culture* (Oxford: Blackwell, 1997), 171–93. Milbank states, "When he [Kasper] tries to think of the Spirit as personal, and not simply as 'ground of possibility,' then he resorts to the need for a 'we' experience, to indicate why a twofold relation would be insufficient. But this is a weak argument: first it is not clear that the 'we' experience—the basis for mass collectivity and politics—is ultimately desirable; second, while it is true that *given* the reality of a plurality of persons any single human relationship risks an *egoisme à deux*, it is not equally clear that this is an inevitable outcome for the relationship in itself, such that there is something self-evidently deficient about the notion of an eternal binity" (ibid., 178).

83. Stăniloae, *Experience of God*, 269.

name of the 'Spirit of love,' and for creatures this signifies 'the giver of life' and 'the comforter,' or 'the Holy Spirit' and 'the sanctifier' (John 17.17, 19)."[84]

Stăniloae is willing to associate the Spirit in the Trinity with the role of ensuring the Father's and Son's distinctiveness, by ensuring their "sense of objectivity" or openness to a third.[85] The Spirit does so precisely through his presence as a third. Assuming that it takes openness to a third to have a real communion, Stăniloae analogously applies this conclusion to the threeness of God. He is not thereby making a claim about the Spirit's procession per se, however. The claim that the Spirit proceeds as the love of the Father and the Son seems to Stăniloae, as to other Orthodox theologians, to turn the Father and Son into one blended person, that is to say into one principle that could not in fact manifest interpersonal love. If the Father and the Son are "drowned within some indistinct whole," the Spirit who proceeds from this impersonal whole would be unable to be a person.[86]

Thomas Aquinas on the Holy Spirit's Procession as "Love" and "Gift"

What are we to make of this pneumatological caution, which either limits the distinction between Son and Spirit to a not further explicable distinction between "generation" and "procession" or else links love and intersubjectivity to the Spirit, but without holding that the Spirit proceeds eternally as "Love"?[87] I applaud and wish to imitate the Greek fathers' emphasis on the revealed order of origin and their cautious refusal to say more about the Holy Spirit in the intratrinitarian life than can be warranted by divine revelation. Stăniloae's preference for the analogy from the sun is understandable, given

84. Ibid.

85. Ibid., 268. Stăniloae goes on to say, "In God the 'we-thou' or 'I-you' relations all obtain simultaneously with the 'I-thou' relation. Each divine subject is capable of this simultaneous attentiveness to the others, whether seen as distinct or in pairs. To make the fullness of existence something actual and to confirm the two in existence, a 'fourth' is not a further necessity. The third represents all that can exist over and above the two, the entire reality in which the two can be confirmed. A fourth in God would disperse and limit the third and diminish his importance. The existence of a fourth would mean that the whole of the objective horizon in which the two are found is no longer concentrated within one person" (ibid., 270).

86. Ibid., 271–72.

87. Gilles Emery, OP, rightly points out that even "if one sets aside the word *ekporeusis* for the Holy Spirit, a problem remains, for we have hardly any analogy *within this world* which enables us to distinguish an '*ekporeusis*' from another spiritual origin. And, in order to *disclose* the faith to our minds, it is precisely such an analogy that Thomas is looking for, so that we can grasp something of the content of the profession of faith, by putting it in the light of the knowledge of something whose object is proportioned to what we can know through our own human experience" (Emery, *The Trinitarian Theology of Saint Thomas Aquinas*, trans. Francesca Aran Murphy [Oxford: Oxford University Press, 2011], 222n13).

his concern that the Augustinian analogy depersonalizes Father and Son by making them into one principle (a concern to which I respond in the next chapter). In my view, where Stăniloae's expressions are boldest—with respect to the existential exigencies of divine interpersonal love—we can be less bold. But we should be bolder with respect to the Spirit's personal property as the Love (and Gift) of the Father and Son. As we have seen, Stăniloae conceives of the Spirit in terms of filling up what would otherwise be lacking in the divine interpersonal communion.[88] Guided by a philosophical understanding of love, he contends that the Holy Spirit is the person in whom the unselfishness of the love of the Father and Son is demonstrated, so that the Spirit ensures a "sense of objectivity." Yet Stăniloae also makes clear that he does not mean to connect the Spirit with love in a way that properly distinguishes the Holy Spirit's procession. His existential language about the interactions of the persons does not in fact touch the true triune mystery, because this mystery has to do with what is relationally proper to each divine person.

At issue, then, is whether more can and should be said of the love that is central to Stăniloae's theology of the Holy Spirit. Is there a way, as Augustine puts it at the outset of *De Trinitate*, to "set out along Charity Street together, making for him of whom it is said, 'Seek his face always' (Ps. 105:4)"?[89] Can we know the Holy Spirit as the Gift/Love of the Father and Son? And can we do so in a way that, as the Eastern fathers rightly require, does not claim to know more about the Spirit's procession than divine revelation tells us? Much depends here upon what we consider to be appropriate with regard to apprehending to divine revelation. For Augustine, as we saw in chapter 1, the divine revelation of the Word, and of two fully divine (and distinct) modes of coming forth from the Father, should alert us to the implications of the New Testament's connecting the Holy Spirit with love and gift. At the same time, the fear of rationalism should be at its highest here: "For nowhere else [than in trinitarian theology] is a mistake more dangerous."[90]

---

88. For his part, Thomas Aquinas holds that we cannot know philosophically what is required for the infinite divine love to be perfect. In response to Richard of St. Victor, Aquinas observes that "when it is said that joyous possession of good requires partnership, this holds in the case of one not having perfect goodness" (*Summa theologiae* I, q. 32, a. 1, ad 2). For discussion of Richard's position that on the basis of the exigencies of infinite goodness we can demonstrate that God must be Trinity, see William J. Hill, OP, *The Three-Personed God: The Trinity as a Mystery of Salvation* (Washington, DC: Catholic University of America Press, 1982), 226–30. Hill argues that Richard's arguments, while not demonstrative, can be useful for shedding light upon the revealed mystery of the Trinity. The same could be said for Stăniloae's arguments, although they tend to picture the Trinity as three interacting figures.

89. Augustine, *The Trinity* 1.1.5, trans. Edmund Hill, OP (Brooklyn, NY: New City Press, 1991), 68.

90. Augustine, *The Trinity* 1.1.5.

Focusing on questions 37 and 38 of the *Summa theologiae*, I inquire in this section of chapter 2 into whether Thomas Aquinas, in defending Augustine's naming of the Spirit as "Love" and "Gift," shows a lack of pneumatological caution and falls into a rationalistic pneumatology. Aquinas's treatment of the Holy Spirit as "Love" identifies the Spirit as "Love proceeding"—not merely the love that is common to the divine persons, but Love coming forth from the Father and Son as their communion or "mutual Love."[91] This distinction between essential love and proper Love (the Holy Spirit) appears also in Augustine, but Aquinas delves more deeply into what it means.

In order to make sense of the distinction between essential love and proper Love in God, let me first turn to Aquinas's discussion of how to conceive spiritual procession in God.[92] When he takes up this topic in *Summa theologiae* I, q. 27, a. 1, he structures his exposition around John 8:42, where Jesus says, "I proceeded [ἐξῆλθον] and came forth from God." Aquinas reads John 8:42 in light of 1 John 5:20, "we are in him who is true, in his Son Jesus Christ. This is the true God."[93] Since the one who "proceeded and came forth from God" is "the true God," it is biblically revealed that there is a procession in God—a procession that gives rise to a divine Son or Word.

The nature of this procession was the contested point during the Sabellian and Arian controversies of the third and fourth centuries, the decisive period for the development of the church's trinitarian doctrine. Aquinas shows, however, that both the Sabellians and the Arians conceived of this divine procession in outward or material terms. An outward procession occurs in an act that tends toward external realities. When the procession is understood as a "cause proceeding to the effect, as moving it, or impressing its own likeness on it,"

91. I, q. 37, a. 1, ad 3. For an account of the mid-twentieth-century debate over the interpretation of Aquinas on the Holy Spirit as "mutual love," with Maurílio T.-L. Penido on the one side and François Bourassa, SJ, on the other, see Kenneth M. Loyer, *God's Love through the Spirit: The Holy Spirit in Thomas Aquinas and John Wesley* (Washington, DC: Catholic University of America Press, 2014), 103–13, 134–36. Loyer's constructive approach to this topic (ibid., 113–40) follows Emery, *Trinitarian Theology of Saint Thomas Aquinas*, 233–42, and Jean-Pierre Torrell, OP, *Saint Thomas Aquinas*, vol. 2, *Spiritual Master*, trans. Robert Royal (Washington, DC: Catholic University of America Press, 2003), 183–88. See also Bourassa's "'Dans la communion de l'Esprit Saint': Étude théologique," parts I–III, *Science et Esprit* 34 (1982): 31–56, 135–49, 239–68, which studies this topic in the fathers, medievals, and Thomistic commentators through Réginald Garrigou-Lagrange, OP (with a focus on Augustine and Aquinas); also Bourassa's "Le Saint-Esprit unite d'amour du Père et du Fils," *Sciences ecclésiastiques* 14 (1962): 375–416.

92. For a similar emphasis upon "considering procession in God in an interior sense" (75), see Loyer, *God's Love through the Spirit*, 73–80. Like me, Loyer is indebted in his reading of Aquinas to the work of Gilles Emery and Bruce Marshall (who directed the dissertation that became Loyer's book).

93. See I, q. 27, a. 1, *sed contra* and *respondeo*.

then the procession is nothing other than the cause.[94] The Sabellians imagined the Father as a cause proceeding to various temporal effects, and so they supposed that the Father does some works under the name "Son" and some works under the name "Spirit," without in fact ever being other than the Father. By contrast, the Arians understood the procession as an outward "effect proceeding from its cause."[95] On this view, the procession is less than the cause. The Arians imagined the Son as an effect proceeding from the Father, and so they conceived of the Son as less than the Father, indeed as an elevated creature.

According to Aquinas, the way to avoid these errors is to recall that no procession in God can be an outward procession. Instead, a procession that is truly in God will be an act that remains within the divine agent, a spiritual procession. Here a bit more background is needed. In I, q. 3, a. 1, Aquinas takes as his *sed contra* Jesus's words to the Samaritan woman, "God is spirit" (John 4:24), and argues that this implies not only that God is not a body (immaterial), but also that God, as the uncreated source of all finite being, has nothing of what Aristotle terms "potentiality." Like Gregory of Nazianzus, Aquinas therefore interprets certain biblical texts about God as metaphorical. Gregory states, "In the Bible, God 'sleeps,' 'wakes up,' 'is angered,' 'walks,' and has a 'throne of cherubim.' . . . This is a nonfactual, mental picture. We have used names derived from human experience and applied them, so far as we could, to aspects of God."[96] Aquinas makes the same point in reflecting upon biblical texts that describe God as having dimension and corporeal parts, including Job 11:8–9; 40:4; Psalms 34:15; 118:16; Isaiah 6:1; 3:13. He affirms, "Corporeal parts are attributed to God in Scripture on account of His actions, and this is owing to a certain parallel. For instance the act of the eye is to see; hence the eye attributed to God signifies His power of seeing intellectually, not sensibly."[97] Since God is infinitely actual, God possesses all perfections of being in his simple "I am." Aquinas observes, "Since therefore God is subsisting being itself, nothing of the perfection of being can be wanting to Him."[98] For our purposes, the central conclusion here has to do with God's knowledge and will. In the simplicity of his infinite act, God understands himself and loves himself. Each of the divine persons, then, has in common infinite wisdom and infinite love.

---

94. I, q. 27, a. 1.
95. I, q. 27, a. 1.
96. Gregory of Nazianzus, Oration 31.22, pp. 133–34. For discussion of God as utterly simple, infinite act, see Hart, *The Beauty of the Infinite*, 211–49; Hart, *The Experience of God: Being, Consciousness, Bliss* (New Haven: Yale University Press, 2013), chap. 3.
97. I, q. 3, a. 1, ad 3.
98. I, q. 4, a. 2.

Returning now to question 27 on procession in God, we recognize that God possesses the perfections of intelligence and will (love) in an infinite mode. With regard to interior procession in God, then, Aquinas takes up Augustine's appeal to the perfection of rationality. It is not that we have rationality (intellect and will) and God simply has the same thing to a much greater degree. On the contrary, as Aquinas points out, "Although it may be admitted that creatures are in some sort like God, it must nowise be admitted that God is like creatures."[99] God's infinite rationality is not like creatures' finite rationality. How then can an analogy between creatures and God be properly made? Aquinas shows that a finite perfection in humans is not simply equivocal to that perfection as it exists infinitely in God. Instead, "every creature represents Him, and is like Him so far as it possesses some perfection: yet it represents Him not as something of the same species or genus, but as the excelling principle of whose form the effects fall short, although they derive some kind of likeness thereto."[100] The movement of analogy is from a created perfection to the perfect Creator, stripping away the finite "mode of signification" by which we name the created perfection. God's wisdom and love are not like ours, because the infinite infinitely surpasses the finite, but our wisdom and love are nonetheless a finite reflection (image) of his. Rationality, like the other perfections, "pre-exists in Him in a more eminent way than can be understood or signified."[101]

99. I, q. 4, a. 3, ad 4.
100. I, q. 13, a. 2. Note David Bentley Hart, "The Destiny of Christian Metaphysics: Reflections on the *Analogia Entis*," in *The Analogy of Being: Invention of the Antichrist or the Wisdom of God?*, ed. Thomas Joseph White, OP (Grand Rapids: Eerdmans, 2011), 395–410, at 398–99:

> The proportion of likeness within the analogy subsists simply in the recognition that God alone is the source of all things, while we are contingent manifestations of his glory, destined for a union with him that will perfect rather than destroy our natures; entirely dependent as it is upon his being—receiving even its most proper potentiality from him as a gift—our being declares the glory of He Who Is. The proportion of unlikeness, however, which is the proportion of infinite transcendence, subsists in the far more vertiginous recognition that God is his own being, that he depends upon no other for his existence, that he does not become what he is not, that he possesses no unrealized potential, that he is not a thing set off against a prior nothingness, that he is not an essence joined to existence, and that he is not a being among other beings.

101. I, q. 13, a. 2, ad 2. See Steven A. Long, *Analogia Entis: On the Analogy of Being, Metaphysics, and the Act of Faith* (Notre Dame, IN: University of Notre Dame Press, 2011). Retrieving Cajetan's position, and in critical dialogue especially with the work of George Klubertanz, SJ, Ralph McInerny, and Bernard Montagnes, OP, Long defends "the intrinsic analogicity of being as divided by act and potency, an analogical division that is the foundation both for the doctrine of participation and for the causal demonstrations proving the truth of the proposition that God exists" (Long, *Analogia Entis*, 1). As he explains against the view of Montagnes, "Relation to God—the relation of createdness, the causal relation of participation—presupposes the being of the creature inasmuch as nonexistent beings have no real relations (and God is not really

Any inquiry into procession in God, then, must take into account that God is spirit and that God is rational (indeed, suprarational). Not acts of outward procession, but acts of *interior* procession—procession within infinite simple spirit—are what must be conceived if we are to gain some appreciation of divine procession. Aquinas observes in this regard, "As God is above all things, we should understand what is said of God, not according to the mode of the lowest creatures, namely bodies, but from the similitude of the highest creatures, the intellectual substances."[102] It is fitting, therefore, to approach procession in God through the similitude of the intellectual processions of understanding and will. By means of this path, Aquinas can respond to the Sabellian and Arian objections to the real existence of procession in God, including the objections that "procession signifies outward movement," that "everything which proceeds differs from that whence it proceeds," and that "to proceed from another seems to be against the nature of the first principle."[103]

In adopting this path, of course, Aquinas is guided especially by the fact that the Gospel of John names the Son "Word" (John 1:1), a Word that "proceeded and came forth from God." With respect to the similitude of an interior spiritual procession in the human mind, Aquinas notes that our interior act of understanding generates an interior word or concept.[104] Analogously,

---

related to the creature). Hence the analogy of being is necessarily ontologically prior to participation and the relation to God. Attributive analogies of created effect to God as first cause, and of proportion of one to another, always presuppose, and must be finally retranslated into, the analogy of being as an analogy of proper proportionality regarding the likeness of diverse *rationes* of act as limited by potency" (ibid., 4 [cf. 26]). To underscore that he is not attributing autonomy to the creature, Long adds that "only *pari passu* with God's bestowal of being to the creature—and only because of that being—is the creature really related to God. It may sound good to say that the creature is constituted by its relation to God, but this is not true: the creature is not constituted by its relation to God, but by God; and for God to constitute or cause is not for God to change or be really related, but for the creature to be" (ibid., 9–10). Does analogy of proper proportionality negate God's transcendence? No, because, as Long remarks, it "is fitted to express the variegated *rationes* of potency and act in the creature whereby the creature's determined relation to God is articulated, and which is the source both of its real likeness and real unlikeness to God; whereas, it is also fitted to affirm God as pure act with no limitation of potency whatsoever . . . which infinitely transcends proportionate being" (ibid., 93, 99). See also, for approaches that differ from Long's but that share many of his insights, Joshua M. Hochschild, "Proportionality and Divine Naming: Did St. Thomas Change His Mind about Analogy?," *The Thomist* 77 (2013): 531–58; Hart, *Experience of God*, 131–32. For the view that the creature is "*constituted* by . . . an immediate relation with the founding agency of God," see Kathryn Tanner, *God and Creation in Christian Theology* (Oxford: Blackwell, 1988), 84.

102. I, q. 27, a. 1.

103. I, q. 27, a. 1, obj. 1–3.

104. See Emery, *Trinitarian Theology of Saint Thomas Aquinas*, 58–61, 180–95; Bernard Lonergan, SJ, *Verbum: Word and Idea in Aquinas*, ed. Frederick Crowe, SJ, and Robert M. Doran, SJ (Toronto: University of Toronto Press, 1997). Emery explains, "The conception we form is the *concept* or *word* of the known thing which our intellect *expresses* within itself and which *proceeds*

then, God's speaking of himself in the Word does not produce a different God; rather, since God is infinite spirit, his speaking of himself in his Word is the same as himself. There is no difference in nature between God and the Word, but only a difference rooted in the procession or coming forth. This difference does not subordinate the Word to God the Father, since the Word is perfectly the same God, distinct from the Father solely in the nontemporal order of origin. Procession from a principle involves subordination only when the procession is outward and temporal.

Although the Gospel of John reveals this coming forth of a coequal Word, the Son of the Father, Aquinas considers the generation of the Word to have already been prefigured in the Old Testament, for instance in Psalm 2:7, "You are my son, today I have begotten you," which is quoted by various New Testament authors, and in Proverbs 8:24, "When there were no depths I was brought forth."[105] The coming forth of the Word consists in a "begetting" or "generation," because the Word that comes forth is perfectly like its divine source and "exists in the same nature."[106]

Even granting (as the Eastern fathers would) the value of this analogy from rational procession for appreciating the begetting or generation of the Word, however, why should we use this analogy to illumine the distinctive procession of the Holy Spirit? One reason, clearly, is that if the analogy of the mind's interior processions helps to elucidate the mystery of the generation of the "Word"—if Scripture itself employs this similitude for describing the distinction of the divine Son from the Father—then it stands to reason that the same analogy will be useful for the procession of the Holy Spirit. Biblically, Aquinas cites two texts that show that there is in fact a second procession in God, namely that of the Holy Spirit: "The Spirit of truth, who proceeds [ἐκπορεύεται] from the Father" (John 15:26), and "I will pray the Father, and he will give you another Counselor [παράκλητον], to be with you for ever, even the Spirit of truth" (John 14:16).[107] Given that there is a second procession from the Father,

---

internally within our mind. . . . The word is not that *through which* the mind knows (which is the *species*) but is, rather, the *fruit* of an internal making or conceiving, the expression of the reality known within our mind: the word is that 'in which' (*in quo*) our mind knows realities. The word is thus relative through and through" (Emery, *Trinitarian Theology of Saint Thomas Aquinas*, 184).

105. I, q. 27, a. 2, *sed contra*. For historical-critical discussion of the New Testament use of Psalm 2:7, see, for example, N. T. Wright, *Paul and the Faithfulness of God* (Minneapolis: Fortress, 2013), 692–701.

106. I, q. 27, a. 2.

107. I, q. 27, a. 3, *sed contra*. Regarding John 15:25, Francis J. Moloney, SDB insists that "this passage is not to be read in the light of fourth-century trinitarian debates" (Moloney, *The Gospel of John* [Collegeville, MN: Liturgical Press, 1998], 434). In a manner that reflects these fourth-century debates (and later debates), however, Moloney also states that the fact that "the Paraclete comes from the Father (cf. 14:16, 26), even though Jesus [the divine Word: see John 1]

Aquinas points out that in humans there are in fact only two processions that remain interior rather than extending outward. These two processions consist in that of the intellect (the generation of a "word") and that of the will (the procession of "love" for the thing known). In fact, then, the only way for us to conceive of two *nonexternal* processions is to follow this path of interior procession: intellect/word and will/love. Aquinas adds that in God, "the divine nature is communicated by every procession which is not outward."[108]

Perhaps, however, the similitude fails for lack of a distinct "intellect" and "will" in God, since God is perfectly simple? Aquinas states that although the powers of intellect and will are not distinct in God, nonetheless God possesses in his infinite and ineffable mode the perfections of rationality. Since these perfections are present in God, furthermore, they are present in a certain "order," although not an order that involves temporal priority. This is so because love always has an "order" vis-à-vis knowledge, an order that is necessarily part of the similitude. Namely, in interior procession, the procession of love relies upon the existence of an interior word or concept. Aquinas explains, "Though will and intellect are not diverse in God, nevertheless the nature of will and intellect requires the processions belonging to each of them to exist in a certain order. For the procession of love occurs in due order as regards the procession of the Word; since nothing can be loved by the will unless it is conceived in the intellect."[109]

---

now involves himself in the sending of the Spirit of truth (cf. 14:17), points to the identity of the origin of the former Paraclete (Jesus) and that of the other Paraclete (cf. 14:16)" (ibid.). The insistence on separating fourth-century trinitarian debates from historical-critical exegetical debates is a mistake, as Wesley Hill has conclusively shown in his *Paul and the Trinity: Persons, Relations, and the Pauline Letters* (Grand Rapids: Eerdmans, 2015).

108. I, q. 27, a. 3, ad 2. Quoting I, q. 32, a. 1, ad 2, Gilles Emery asks, "Has one then fallen for the rational temptation to *prove* an article of the Creed and *demonstrated* the personal being of a Word in God? St. Thomas' answer to this would be 'No,' because 'the analogy with our minds does not constitute a sufficient proof to demonstrate something about God, because reason does not exist univocally in God and in us.' It is a matter of an 'argument from congruity,' a 'persuasive reason' which enables one to grasp only what has been received from revelation. . . . This analogy preserves a profound respect for God's spiritual nature, since it draws on the word's spiritual procession. It attempts to illuminate believers' minds by starting from what is closest to them, the word in our own human mind, to open the door a little way onto the mystery of the divine generation of the Word" (Emery, *Trinitarian Theology of Saint Thomas Aquinas*, 185).

109. I, q. 27, a. 3, ad 3. This view is challenged by Hans Urs von Balthasar: "Might not this ranking of knowledge before love be an importation from the created order into the divine world? And may not the only reason for maintaining this priority in trinitarian doctrine be to guarantee the ability to distinguish between the processions of the Son and of the Spirit? Would it not be possible, however, to differentiate God's all-embracing love (which includes all his other divine properties: knowledge, omniscience, wisdom, and so forth) so as to evidence, after all, something like a foundation for the distinction of the two processions within the one divine love?" (Balthasar, *Theo-Logic*, vol. 2, *Truth of God*, trans. Adrian J. Walker [San Francisco:

In question 27 Aquinas investigates two further issues: whether the procession of love (the Holy Spirit) is another "begetting" or "generation"; and whether there should logically be more than two interior processions in God. With respect to the first issue, he points out that generation is so called because it proceeds by way of likeness. An interior "word" is like that of which it is a concept. By contrast, the interior procession of love does not proceed by way of likeness. Rather, love proceeds "by way of impulse and movement towards an object."[110] It is appropriate, therefore, that the second interior procession in God be named "Holy Spirit," because "spirit," unlike "word," "expresses a certain vital movement and impulse, accordingly as anyone is described as moved or impelled by love to perform an action."[111] One could turn this around and note that the revealed name "Holy Spirit" helps us to appreciate why the name "Love," as a way of understanding the second procession in God, especially befits the Holy Spirit. The main point is that recognizing that rational procession in humans occurs either as knowledge or as love helps us to gain some analogous understanding of why in God there is only one "begetting" or "generation," only one Son, despite the fact that there are two processions (or interior coming forths) from the Father.

With respect to the second issue—whether there is any intelligibility to the revealed datum that limits the divine processions to two—Aquinas alerts us to some significant objections. The first objection has to do with intellect and will: certainly these are perfections in God, but so is power. If there were a procession of power, however, this third procession would negate the analogy's accordance with the revealed data, and would render us entirely speechless before the mystery of the Word and Spirit. The second objection proposes a procession of goodness, since goodness is self-diffusive and thus a natural source of procession. The third objection notes that we generate, in fact, not just one but many interior words or concepts, and the same holds true for

---

Ignatius, 2004], 162–63). See also, indebted to Balthasar, D. C. Schindler's "Does Love Trump Reason? Toward a Non-Possessive Concept of Knowledge," in *The Catholicity of Reason* (Grand Rapids: Eerdmans, 2013), 85–115. Balthasar's position, in my view, misunderstands the analogy. There is no "ranking" in the sense of subordination (of the Spirit to the Son). Aquinas is simply arguing that there is an order in the mind's processions, and this order (certainly not a "ranking") seems to me to be on solid ground; love for a good depends upon apprehending that good in some way, however limited. Balthasar's proposal is to employ "love" analogously and find "the two processions" within "love." But this goes beyond what can be done via the path of analogy, because the analogy is from our experience of rationality and its processions (knowing and loving). If we are speaking of love as a divine attribute common to the persons, it is important to note again that Aquinas's position implies no "ranking" (in the sense of the subordination of one attribute to another) between love and understanding.

110. I, q. 27, a. 4.
111. I, q. 27, a. 4.

our loves. Therefore, since God is far more fruitful than we are, God should contain multiple processions rather than only two.

In answer, Aquinas returns to the purpose and structure of the analogy, rooted as it is in the Johannine identification of the Son as the divine Word. The Sabellians and Arians could not comprehend the Word's full divinity because they imagined the procession of the Word in terms of an outward procession. The analogy helps to correct this mistake, by recalling that in humans there are only two rational processions that remain within the mind. Power has to do with one thing acting upon another, and thus power tends outward; goodness is not itself a procession but instead pertains to the object of the will. Given that procession remains interior to God, who is infinite spirit, we can analogously conceive of only two such processions: the procession by which God expresses himself perfectly (intellect) and the procession by which God loves himself as expressed (will). This is not a rationalistic claim, as though our mode of conceiving of interior procession restricts what is possible in God. Rather, it manifests the intelligibility of the data of revelation, which attest to two processions, and it displays the appropriateness of John's use of the name "Word." In God there is "only one perfect Word, and one perfect Love; thereby being manifested His perfect fecundity."[112]

Let us now turn to Aquinas's discussion in *Summa theologiae* I, question 37 of "Love" as a name of the Holy Spirit. If "God is love" (1 John 4:8), how can the Holy Spirit alone be distinctively "Love" in the Trinity? Rather than reprising the biblical exposition that Augustine gives in *De Trinitate*, Aquinas raises a concern about the analogy from the mind: it does not seem to provide a ground for distinguishing what is common to the persons from what is proper to each of them. After all, the perfections of understanding and will belong to the divine nature, to what it means to be God. The Son, as Word, does not possess more understanding than does the Father or the Holy Spirit, and it is not as though the Father gains his understanding by generating the Word. The *same* divine understanding is the Father, Son, and Holy Spirit. The perfections of intellect and will do not in fact distinguish the divine persons.

Aquinas makes this quandary into the first objection of the first article of his question 37 on "Love" as a proper name of the Holy Spirit. Citing Augustine—and thereby signaling that Augustine too recognized and responded to the quandary—the objection states, "It would seem that *Love* is not the proper name of the Holy Spirit. For Augustine says (*De Trin.* xv.17): 'As the Father, Son, and Holy Spirit are called Wisdom, and are not three Wisdoms,

112. I, q. 27, a. 5, ad 3.

but one; I know not why the Father, Son, and Holy Spirit should not be called Charity, and all together one Charity.'"[113] If each one is named "Charity," then it hardly seems possible to give to the Holy Spirit the name "Love" as a *proper* name, as a name descriptive of the Spirit's distinctive mode in the Trinity.

In response, Aquinas reflects further on how to distinguish common names and proper names in God. He first defends the biblical name "Word" as a *proper* name of the Son. Having observed that "understanding" pertains to what is common in God, Aquinas notes that the interior path that leads to understanding has various stages in the human mind. The intellect conceives or generates an interior word, a conceptual judgment of truth. Aquinas describes this production of an interior "word" as an interior "speaking." It differs from "understanding," because understanding *possesses* the interior word, whereas "speaking" *generates* the interior word. The key to the analogy, then, is the differentiation between understanding (which pertains to what is common in God) and the act of conceiving an inner word (which pertains to the person of the Father).[114]

Why, however, should we imagine that such distinctions have any application (however analogous) to God? Not least in light of contemporary biblical scholarship, the evangelist John hardly can be imagined to have had these distinctions in view when he named the Son "Word"—although as Andrew Lincoln observes, "the basic force of 'the Word' is God's self-expression," the expression of God's wisdom (cf. Wis. 1:1; 9:1–2; 18:15–16).[115] Aquinas's argument is that given the revealed reality of procession in God, including the procession of the Word, the distinctions have value. Our conception of procession in God determines whether we can intelligibly affirm both unity and distinction in God, without falling into Sabellianism, Arianism, or a mere silence that would be unable to defend Christian faith against the charge of polytheism.

The Holy Spirit, however, cannot be simply named "love"; because God is love, each person is love. For this reason, Aquinas distinguishes between "love" and "Love proceeding," which corresponds in the realm of pneumatology to the distinction between "understanding" and "speaking an interior word."[116]

113. I, q. 37, a. 1, obj. 1. Here we might recall the concerns of William Hasker (see my introduction to this book), as well as chap. 1 on Augustine's naming of the Spirit.

114. On this topic, see the seminal essay by Gilles Emery, OP, "Essentialism or Personalism in the Treatise on God in St. Thomas Aquinas?," in *Trinity in Aquinas*, trans. Teresa Bede et al., 2nd ed. (Ann Arbor, MI: Sapientia Press of Ave Maria University, 2006), 165–208.

115. Andrew T. Lincoln, *The Gospel according to Saint John* (London: Continuum, 2005), 95; see his helpful discussion on 94–98. See also Francis J. Moloney, SDB, *Belief in the Word: Reading John 1–4* (Minneapolis: Fortress, 1992).

116. I, q. 37, a. 1.

The name "Love proceeding" makes clear that "Love" here does not describe what Aquinas calls "the relation of the lover to the object loved [the divine goodness]."[117] In terms of the relation of the lover to the object loved, each of the divine persons is love in the unity of the divine essence. But the Holy Spirit is properly "Love" in the sense of "the relation to its principle."[118] In the relation of "to spirate love" and "love spirated," we find the basis for speaking analogously of the Holy Spirit as "Love proceeding"—as the impulsion or imprint of love in the will of the lover, and as the "mutual Love" of the Father and Son.[119] As Gilles Emery remarks, the Holy Spirit is "the radiance of the divine communion, the Love of the Father and the Son, the Charity that is God's greatest gift."[120]

Yet, it might seem as though the name "Love proceeding" makes the Holy Spirit into a passive effusion, rather than an active person in his own right. Does the name "Love proceeding" paradoxically make the Holy Spirit seem *impersonal*?[121] Aquinas considers that the answer is no. His full reasoning depends upon his account of the relation of the Spirit to the Father and Son. Reserving my discussion of the *filioque* for the next chapter, here let me observe that in question 37 Aquinas addresses Augustine's depictions of the Spirit as the "bond of the Father and the Son," as the "mutual Love" of the Father and Son, and as the Love by which the Father and Son love each other.[122] Does this language turn the Holy Spirit into a mere link, rather than a truly distinct and active person in himself?[123]

Here we need to return once more to the structure of the analogy. In the analogy, the key point is that "to will" or "to love" is an action (an interior procession) that, by producing an interior term ("love spirated"), constitutes a relation. Aquinas explains that "although to understand, and to will, and to

117. I, q. 37, a. 1.
118. I, q. 37, a. 1.
119. See I, q. 37, a. 1, ad 3. For discussion, see Loyer, *God's Love through the Spirit*, 134–37; Emery, *Trinitarian Theology of Saint Thomas Aquinas*, 236.
120. Gilles Emery, OP, *The Trinity: An Introduction to Catholic Doctrine on the Triune God*, trans. Matthew Levering (Washington, DC: Catholic University of America Press, 2011), 139.
121. For this question, and a helpful response, see Loyer, *God's Love through the Spirit*, 221–24.
122. I, q. 37, a. 1, ad 2–3; I, q. 37, a. 2. Lucas Francisco Mateo-Seco shows that for Athanasius too "the relation between the Father and the Son . . . is a relation of mutual love" (Mateo-Seco, "The Paternity of the Father and the Procession of the Holy Spirit," at 80). For Aquinas, see especially Emery, *Trinitarian Theology of Saint Thomas Aquinas*, 233–42. See also Anthony Keaty, "The Holy Spirit Proceeding as Mutual Love: An Interpretation of Aquinas' *Summa Theologiae* I.37," *Angelicum* 77 (2000): 533–57.
123. See also Loyer, *God's Love through the Spirit*, 114–18. For a brief articulation of the problem, see Milbank, "Second Difference," 172–73.

love signify actions passing on to their objects, nevertheless they are actions that remain in the agents" and that "import a certain relation to their object."[124] In God, these relations are distinct and subsist. Given that the Holy Spirit has been revealed in Scripture and tradition as fully divine and distinct from but intimately related to the Father and the Son, the identification of the Spirit as "Love proceeding" affirms the Spirit's relational personhood in the Trinity, just as the identification of the Son as "Word" affirms the Son's relational personhood. As Love proceeding, the Spirit is the bond or communion of the Father and the Son. Since this procession constitutes a distinct subsisting relation, the Spirit is not a mere bond, but Love in person. As Emery comments, "This does not imply any 'passivity' in the Holy Spirit, any more than generation implies 'passivity' in the Son who is begotten. *To proceed is an act.*"[125] Lest the Spirit's proceeding as Love still seems somewhat passive and less than fully personal, Emery goes on to explain that "it is by one operation that the Father and the Son 'breathe' ('spirate') the Holy Spirit and that the Holy Spirit proceeds; but this operation is in the Father and the Son, and in the Holy Spirit, under *distinct relations*. In the Father and the Son, this action possesses the relative mode of 'spiration'; while in the Holy Spirit, this action possesses the relative mode of 'procession.'"[126]

When the Father loves the Son, however, does he have to call upon the Holy Spirit to accomplish this, as might seem implied by Augustine's claim that "the Father loves the Son by the Holy Spirit"?[127] In the second article

124. I, q. 37, a. 1, ad 2.
125. Emery, *Trinity*, 149–50.
126. Ibid., 150.
127. I, q. 37, a. 2. Lewis Ayres interprets Augustine's doctrine of the Spirit as the bond of love to mean that Father and Son maintain their "unity by their acts of giving and loving; the Father giving and loving the one who begets, the Son giving and loving the one who begot him. The mutual love of which Augustine speaks is thus a love identical with the eternally constitutive acts that are what it is to be Father and Son; their love is their essence because in God there is nothing accidental. When Father and Son give this love, what they give is what it is to be Father and Son; it is their own gift and (being God) necessarily a gift of themselves. And so, if the Spirit is love, that love must be the fulness of God, fully wisdom and truth and life and power; that love must, hence, be an active giving gift, it must be an irreducible divine 'person'" (Ayres, "*Sempiterne Spiritus Donum*: Augustine's Pneumatology and the Metaphysics of Spirit," in *Orthodox Readings of Augustine*, ed. George E. Demacopoulos and Aristotle Papanikolaou [Crestwood, NY: St. Vladimir's Seminary Press, 2008], 127–52, at 143–44). Going further, Ayres adds both that "Father and Son are one because the Spirit gives himself in the begetting of the Son and gives himself as the Son's love for the Father," and that "the Son is the Son because the Spirit is the essence of the Father and Son as active giving love" (ibid., 144–45). Among other texts, Ayres here draws upon tractate 39 of Augustine's *Tractates on the Gospel of John*, in which Augustine teaches, "Si ergo caritas dei diffusa in cordibus nostris per spiritum sanctum qui datus est nobis, multas animas facit unam animam, et multa corda facit unum cor, quanto magis pater et filius et spiritus sanctus, deus unus, lumen unum, unumque principium?"—the

of question 37 Aquinas reviews five common ways—with all of which he disagrees—of interpreting Augustine's language so as to remove its sting. In his own answer, which I will discuss in more detail in chapter 6, Aquinas emphasizes that the Father and the Son love each other because as God they *are* infinite love, just as the Father and the Son understand each other because as God they *are* infinite understanding. But when we say that the Father and the Son love each other in the sense of "to spirate love," then it is true that "the Father and the Son love each other and us, by the Holy Spirit, or by Love proceeding."[128] When the Father and Son love each other by the Spirit, they also love us, because "the Holy Spirit proceeds as the love of the primal goodness whereby the Father loves himself and every creature," each of which is expressed in the Word.[129]

In short, much of Aquinas's labor consists in distinguishing the two meanings of "love"—essential love versus notional love ("to spirate love")—so as to show how the name "Love" signifies the Spirit's relational personhood, insofar as it can be analogously illuminated.[130] Pope John Paul II expresses the two meanings of love in his encyclical on the Holy Spirit, *Dominum et vivificantem*: "In his intimate life, God 'is love,' the essential love shared by the three divine persons: personal love is the Holy Spirit as the Spirit of the Father and the Son. Therefore he 'searches even the depths of God' [cf. 1 Cor. 2:10], as *uncreated Love-Gift*."[131] Aware of the danger of rationalism, Aquinas thinks that the

---

last clause of which Ayres translates, "how much more does [the Spirit] make the Father and the Son and the Holy Spirit one God, one light, one *principium*?" (ibid., 144, citing Augustine, *In Evangelium Johannis tractatus* 39.5 [CCSL 36.348]). In its context, Augustine's meaning is difficult to apprehend with certainty, since he is playing on the identity of the Spirit and the love that pertains to God's essence (and the latter may be what is being described by "one God, one light, one *principium*"). Ayres cautiously links his interpretation of Augustine with Thomas Weinandy's *The Father's Spirit of Sonship: Reconceiving the Trinity* (Edinburgh: T&T Clark, 1995), 50, 69. In my view, this interpretation is mistaken. Even so, Ayres's central point is surely accurate: "The Father's begetting of the Son is identical with the establishment of the communion of Father, Son, and Spirit because in the begetting of the Son the Father gives his love (or substance), thus eternally establishing the Son as lover of the Father and the Spirit as the personal giving love of Father and Son" (Ayres, *"Sempiterne Spiritus Donum,"* 147; see also Ayres, *Augustine and the Trinity*, 256–58; Ayres, "Augustine on the Trinity," in *The Oxford Handbook of the Trinity*, ed. Gilles Emery, OP, and Matthew Levering [Oxford: Oxford University Press, 2011], 123–36, at 129–31). Like Ayres, Brian Daley holds that for Augustine, the Holy Spirit "personally brings to perfection the relationship of Father and Son as distinct yet united persons" (Daley, "Revisiting the 'Filioque': Part One," 40).

128. I, q. 37, a. 2.

129. I, q. 37, a. 2, ad 3. See also Loyer, *God's Love through the Spirit*, 125, 139.

130. See Loyer, *God's Love through the Spirit*, 118–23; Emery, *Trinitarian Theology of Saint Thomas Aquinas*, 225–43, esp. 225–33.

131. Pope John Paul II, *Dominum et vivificantem*, in *The Encyclicals of John Paul II*, ed. J. Michael Miller, CSB (Huntington, IN: Our Sunday Visitor, 2001), 244–302, at §10, p. 250.

revelation of the two intradivine processions and of the Son's name "Word" warrants naming the Holy Spirit "Love," in accordance with the reality that "God's love [the love of God] has been poured into our hearts through the Holy Spirit who has been given to us" (Rom. 5:5).[132] The name "Love" instructs us about the personal property of the Holy Spirit in the Trinity by giving us an experientially rich conception of the Spirit's procession as Love in person, the communion or bond of the Father and the Son. At the same time, this name describes the Holy Spirit analogously, within a strictly delimited framework, and in a manner that does not justify further imaginative speculation about the interactions of the three persons—speculation that arises when the weakness of the analogy and the limits of the biblical testimony have been forgotten.

What about Augustine's second name for the Holy Spirit, "Gift"? As in the first article of question 37 on the name "Love," the first article of question 38

See also David Coffey's short speculative treatise, *"Did You Receive the Holy Spirit When You Believed?" Some Basic Questions for Pneumatology* (Milwaukee: Marquette University Press, 2005), 52–58. As confirmation that "Love" properly names the person of the Holy Spirit, Coffey cites Pope John Paul II's encyclical. Coffey observes, "The Pope does not attempt to dilute the strangeness of identifying the Holy Spirit with the operation of divine love by resorting to more 'personal' categories. Instead, in calling the Holy Spirit 'Person-Love,' he embraces with zest the paradox and mystery of the mutual-love theology" (*"Did You Receive the Holy Spirit When You Believed?,"* 57–58). Coffey goes further and contrasts this "mutual-love theology," which he considers to require that the Holy Spirit be the one in whom the Son is begotten (the "model of return"), with the "procession model," in which the Spirit comes forth "after" the Son. For Coffey, both these models—the former being synoptic, the latter Johannine—are true. Here Coffey cites Hans Urs von Balthasar's theory of "trinitarian inversion" in the economic order (Father-Spirit-Son); see Balthasar's *Theo-Drama*, vol. 3, *The Dramatis Personae: Persons in Christ*, trans. Graham Harrison (San Francisco: Ignatius, 1988), 183–91. Balthasar holds that the economic priority of the Spirit belongs to the Son's *kenōsis*, as well as to the Spirit's role as bond between Father and Son. For Aquinas (and for Thomas Weinandy as well [see Coffey, *"Did You Receive the Holy Spirit When You Believed?,"* 105–6]), the mission of the Spirit in the incarnation comes "after" the hypostatic union of the Son, who is the "principle of the union" (*Summa theologiae* III, q. 7, a. 13). To my mind, the claim that the Spirit, not the Son, is determinative for Jesus Christ prior to the resurrection sets up a false opposition. For further examples of "Spirit Christology," see Myk Habets, *The Anointed Son: A Trinitarian Spirit Christology* (Eugene, OR: Pickwick, 2010); Steven M. Studebaker, *From Pentecost to the Triune God: A Pentecostal Trinitarian Theology* (Grand Rapids: Eerdmans, 2012).

132. In his commentary on Romans 5:5 Aquinas states, "For the Holy Spirit, who is the love of the Father and of the Son, to be given to us is our being brought to participate in the love who is the Holy Spirit, and by this participation we are made lovers of God" (Thomas Aquinas, *Commentary on the Letter of Saint Paul to the Romans*, trans. Fabian Larcher, OP, et al. [Lander, WY: Aquinas Institute for the Study of Sacred Doctrine, 2012], 5.1.392, p. 132). For discussion of Aquinas's commentary on Romans 5:5, see Gilles Emery, OP, "The Holy Spirit in Aquinas's Commentary on Romans," in *Reading Romans with St. Thomas Aquinas*, ed. Matthew Levering and Michael Dauphinais (Washington, DC: Catholic University of America Press, 2012), 127–62, at 150–51; Robert Louis Wilken, *"Fides Caritate Formata*: Faith Formed by Love," *Nova et Vetera* 9 (2011): 1089–1100.

on the name "Gift" contains in the first objection a passage from book 15 of *De Trinitate*, thereby signaling that Aquinas's own discussion stands as a speculative commentary upon Augustine's biblical and theological exposition of the name. In both cases Aquinas cites a passage from *De Trinitate* in which Augustine suggests that the name applies equally well to the other persons and therefore is not a distinctive name of the Holy Spirit. In both cases too the first article assumes (instead of reprising) Augustine's extensive biblical exposition of the name.[133]

Aquinas's question is whether the name "Gift" belongs among the personal names of the Holy Spirit, that is to say whether it belongs among the names that properly signify "a distinction in God."[134] The objections provide various reasons to suppose that "Gift" does not belong among such names. For example, to be given—to be a gift—seems to involve subordination. Similarly, even if in God the Holy Spirit is given, he is not given to the Father or Son as "gift"; the name "Gift" comes about in the economy of salvation, as the New Testament makes clear, when believers receive the gift of the Holy Spirit. If the name solely pertains to the temporal economy, then it does not describe an eternal distinction in God and cannot be a personal name of the Holy Spirit.[135]

In his *sed contra*, Aquinas highlights Augustine's remark—behind which stands Augustine's exegesis of various New Testament texts—that "the gift of the Holy Spirit is nothing but the Holy Spirit."[136] If the "Holy Spirit" is synonymous with "the gift of the Holy Spirit," then "gift" here means "Holy Spirit." But if so, do we dare to say that we have received the Holy Spirit as a gift? And is the Word also a gift? Whatever we receive as a gift, we possess, and "we are said to possess what we can freely use or enjoy as we please."[137]

---

133. By contrast, in *Summa contra gentiles* 4.21–22 Aquinas adduces a number of biblical texts—including Psalm 103:30; Romans 5:5; 8:15; 1 John 4:10, 13, 16; 1 Corinthians 2:9–10; 3:16; 12:8, 11—with regard to the Spirit's dwelling as Love and Gift in us. See Thomas Aquinas, *Summa contra gentiles*, book 4, *Salvation*, trans. Charles J. O'Neil (Notre Dame, IN: University of Notre Dame Press, 1975). For discussion, see Loyer, *God's Love through the Spirit*, 158–62.

134. I, q. 38, a. 1, obj. 1. For discussion of Aquinas on the Holy Spirit's name "Gift," see Emery, *Trinitarian Theology of Saint Thomas Aquinas*, 249–58; Loyer, *God's Love through the Spirit*, 142–46. As Emery observes, for Aquinas, "The Spirit is personally the Gift because he is the person of Love, in the precise meaning given to *Love* when it designates the personal character of the Holy Spirit, as the fruit of the love of the Father and Son proceeding as an impulse or affection. Otherwise put, even though the names *Gift* and *Love* are not synonyms, they refer to the same personal property of the Holy Spirit, the Gift overtaking our spirits as the immediate result of Love" (Emery, *Trinitarian Theology of Saint Thomas Aquinas*, 257).

135. On creaturely being as gift, see López, *Gift and the Unity of Being*, esp. chap. 2. See also Kenneth L. Schmitz, *The Gift: Creation* (Milwaukee: Marquette University Press, 1982), esp. chap. 4.

136. I, q. 38, a. 1, *sed contra*. See Augustine, *The Trinity* 15.36, p. 424.

137. I, q. 38, a. 1.

Should we really dare to say that we "can freely use or enjoy as we please" the Holy Spirit (or the Word)?

Aquinas does not hesitate to say yes to this question. Unlike nonrational creatures that can be moved by the Son and Holy Spirit but cannot enjoy them, humans are indeed "able to enjoy the divine person, and to use the effect thereof."[138] The just are really related to the distinct divine persons. In this condition, a human being "is made partaker of the divine Word and of the Love proceeding, so as freely to know God truly and to love God rightly."[139] With Augustine, Aquinas emphasizes that such a relationship with God is sheer grace. When it comes to possessing a divine person as "gift," our "own power avails nothing."[140] We can see, then, that Aquinas's understanding of the deifying work of the Word and Holy Spirit drives his interpretation of the name "Gift," because naming the Holy Spirit as Gift formally implies that we can receive the divine person of the Holy Spirit himself (and not just his created gifts) indwelling in us. Therefore, prior to investigating whether the Holy Spirit alone should receive the name "Gift" in the Trinity, Aquinas wishes to affirm as strongly as possible that a divine person can be "given" to us, so that we possess and enjoy him as "gift."[141] The contemplative desire to name the Holy Spirit must keep at the forefront this truth that it is the Holy Spirit himself who wills to enable us to know and enjoy him as he is.

Aquinas points out that "gift" can have various meanings. Thus when the Father gives the divine essence, "gift" indicates an identity with the giver. Can the Holy Spirit be "Gift" in the Trinity, however, if he is given (as Scripture reveals) not to another divine person but to creatures? Answering in the affirmative, Aquinas explains, "Gift is not so called from being actually given, but

---

138. I, q. 38, a. 1.

139. I, q. 38, a. 1.

140. I, q. 38, a. 1. See Joseph P. Wawrykow, *God's Grace and Human Action: "Merit" in the Theology of Thomas Aquinas* (Notre Dame, IN: University of Notre Dame Press, 1995).

141. Although Aquinas does not quote Basil here, one is reminded of Basil's reflection on "Spirit-bearing souls that are illuminated by the Holy Spirit" (prophets, apostles, saints), who receive and enjoy "foreknowledge of the future, understanding of mysteries, apprehension of secrets, distributions of graces, heavenly citizenship, the chorus with angels, unending joy, remaining in God, kinship with God, and the highest object of desire, becoming God" (Basil, *On the Holy Spirit* 9.23, p. 54). Aquinas's approach shows the unfortunate misunderstanding present in Stăniloae's contention that "in the West the relations between the divine Persons are seen almost exclusively as an inner-trinitarian question, and thus as a question of speculative theology without consequences in practical life, or in the salvation of man understood as his transformation" (Stăniloae, "Procession of the Holy Spirit from the Father," 178). Stăniloae imagines that "in the West . . . one avoids drawing from the eternal relation of the Spirit to the Son, the conclusion that the Spirit is sent to men for a work which consists essentially in the deification and adoption of man" (ibid.).

from its aptitude to be given."[142] The same point holds for the Son. When we call the Son the Father's gift, or the Spirit the gift of the Father and Son, "gift" here refers to origin and to the fact that the gift "is personally distinguished from the giver" so as to be actively able to "use or rather enjoy Himself."[143] This kind of gift, Aquinas observes, "does not imply subjection, but only origin as regards the giver."[144] Here is the decisive explanation (as the next article will make explicit): the distinction between the "Giver" (Father and Son) and the "Gift" (Holy Spirit) involves an eternal relation of origin, which accounts for a *personal* distinction within the Trinity.[145] Lastly, there are also "gifts" that are "essentially distinct from the giver."[146] The created gifts of the Spirit in us—gifts of grace—are "gifts" that are essentially distinct from the Spirit.

In affirming that the Son and Spirit can both be "gift," Aquinas may seem to have deprived the Spirit of the proper name "Gift." In a passage quoted by Aquinas, Isaiah prophesies that "to us a son is given" (Isa. 9:6).[147] If the Son and the Spirit are both "gifts," then the name "Gift" does not distinctively name the Holy Spirit, and cannot be a proper name of the Spirit. Are we then left solely with the name "Love" (along with the name "Holy Spirit") for characterizing the Spirit's distinctiveness in the Trinity? As we noted, Aquinas's insistence on the necessity of conceiving the divine processions as interior rather than external leads him to accept without much difficulty the Holy Spirit's name "Love" or (as he prefers) "Love proceeding," given that the Son is named "Word" and that the second interior procession (in humans) is that of will. But in his recognition that the Son too is given, has Aquinas undermined the ability of "Gift" to be a proper name of the Holy Spirit? Since love is the greatest gift, this would seem also to undermine the Spirit's personal property as "Love proceeding"—and to make it more difficult for believers, seeking to praise the eternal Trinity, to contemplate the distinctive personhood of the Holy Spirit.

Aquinas takes up this issue in the second article of question 38. After quoting the authority of Augustine in the *sed contra*, Aquinas draws from Aristotle a definition of "gift" as an "unreturnable giving," something that "is not given with the intention of a return."[148] He then asks why one would

---

142. I, q. 38, a. 1, ad 4.
143. I, q. 38, a. 1, ad 1.
144. I, q. 38, a. 1, ad 3.
145. For further elaboration, see the master's thesis of Pauline Friche, "L'Esprit Saint comme Don: Étude dans le *De Trinitate* d'Augustin et la *Somme de théologie* de Thomas d'Aquin" (University of Fribourg, 2014), a thesis directed by Gilles Emery.
146. I, q. 38, a. 1, ad 1.
147. I, q. 38, a. 2, obj. 1.
148. I, q. 38, a. 2.

give something freely without seeking a return, and he answers that the reason must be love. Before we give someone a gift, we give that same person love. Love, then, "has the nature of a first gift, through which all free gifts are given."[149] Aquinas thus arrives at the same conclusion as Augustine, but from a somewhat different angle. He reasons that because the Holy Spirit proceeds uniquely as "Love," he must therefore proceed uniquely as primal "Gift." It is because the Holy Spirit is eternal Gift, the first gift, that the Holy Spirit is the source of the gifts that believers receive.[150] Aquinas concludes his reasoning by quoting a passage from book 15 of *De Trinitate*, in which Augustine links the "gift" that is the Holy Spirit, with the gifts that the members of Christ's body receive from the Holy Spirit.

What then about the apparent problem that the Son also can receive the name "gift"? Aquinas answers that the Son cannot receive this name properly, whereas the Spirit can. He points to the begetting of the Son as a parallel: the Son is begotten by way of similitude or likeness ("Word"), and the Holy Spirit too receives the likeness of the divine Father. But the Holy Spirit is not named Word or Image. Certainly it would be a mistake to deny that the Son is the Father's gift, given "from the Father's love."[151] In this regard Aquinas quotes John 3:16, "For God so loved the world that he gave his only[-begotten] Son."[152] Certainly the Son too is given. But the Son's proper mode of procession is as "Word" and thus as "Image" (by way of likeness), whereas the Spirit's proper mode of procession is as "Love" and thus as "Gift" (by way of imprint). The fact that the Spirit too is an image, and the Son too is a gift, shows that we do not know much about the inner life of the Trinity.

"Word/Image" and "Love/Gift" give us a glimpse into the trinitarian mystery, rooted in the testimony of Scripture and illuminated by the analogy of interior processions that bring about distinct relations of origin without impairing the divine simplicity. In this glimpse, as Augustine emphasizes, we must "note how great the dissimilarity is in whatever similarity there may be."[153] For Aquinas, we can rightly name the Spirit "Love" and "Gift" in the eternal Trinity. Yet for Aquinas as much as for Augustine, it remains the case that none of our words "is worthy of this unimaginable mystery," the triunity of God.[154]

---

149. I, q. 38, a. 2.

150. As Gilles Emery says, indebted to Aquinas's *Commentary on Peter Lombard's Sentences*, the Holy Spirit is "the divine person 'closest to us,' so to speak, the one who is most intimate with us, because he is given to us. It is through him that we receive the Father and the Son, and it is through him that we receive all gifts" (Emery, *Trinitarian Theology of Saint Thomas Aquinas*, 258).

151. I, q. 38, a. 2, ad 1.

152. I, q. 38, a. 2, ad 1.

153. Augustine, *The Trinity* 15.5.39, p. 426.

154. Augustine, *The Trinity* 15.Epilogue.50, p. 434.

Conclusion

In his book *The Trinity*, Gilles Emery observes that "the union of angels and of humans with God is accomplished by an 'assimilation' to the personal relation that the Son and the Holy Spirit have with the Father."[155] Thus there is no manifestation of the Holy Spirit in the economy of salvation that does not exhibit to us in some way the eternal procession of the Spirit. Yet, Emery points out that "like the Greek tradition, the Latin tradition insists upon the incomprehensible character of the origin of the Holy Spirit."[156] If the procession of the Holy Spirit is ultimately incomprehensible, how is it that Aquinas feels free (with Augustine) to name the Spirit, with respect to his eternal procession, "Love" and "Gift"?

Emery observes, as I also have, that the answer begins with the Son's revealed name "Word" (John 1:1). The name "Word" directs our attention to the fact that divine generation and procession cannot be compared to outward processions, but solely to the interior processions of the mind and their relative opposition in the order of origin. But even here, it would be a mistake to claim too much: the analogy does not enable us to narrate the mysterious inner life of the tripersonal God. That the analogy nonetheless gives us real insight, Emery goes on to say, has to do with the fact that we are made in God's image, which God enlightens, and also with the fact that God created the world and inspired Scripture with the aim of leading us to himself. The analogy from the human mind is pertinent because God intends for creation itself to point toward God. But it is the biblically attested work of the Holy Spirit, not the analogy, that is the *fundamental* ground for naming the Spirit. Citing Romans 5:5, Emery remarks, "The Holy Spirit manifests himself in the communion of love that is poured out when he dwells in the heart of believers. Through what he does, the Holy Spirit reveals who he is."[157] Along similar lines, Brian Daley emphasizes with appreciation that for Aquinas, the "work of the Spirit, this manifestation of divine love, is not simply something superadded to his existence as a distinct person within the life of God; it is a living out, in temporal, created terms, of what the Holy Spirit is as a divine person."[158]

---

155. Emery, *Trinity*, 187.
156. Ibid., 136.
157. Ibid., 139.
158. Daley, "Revisiting the 'Filioque': Part One," 62. Daley continues by noting that the Spirit is "a flowing out from the other two, whose very act of breathing him forth brings their own union to perfection, creating unity by way of gift, giving personal reality to the self-spending action of love. . . . The Spirit by which God loves us and makes us his friends, by which he enlightens and cleanses us and communicates his very life to us, is the divine Spirit whose very origin lies in God's delighted affirmation of his own ideas—ideas of Christ and of ourselves; it

I began this chapter by surveying Greek patristic caution, as well as a similar caution among contemporary Orthodox theologians, with respect to the meaning of the Spirit's "procession." By contrast to some contemporary theologies that seem to know more than revelation teaches about the procession of the Holy Spirit, such caution about naming the Spirit is right and salutary. Nonetheless, even in John of Damascus we found numerous names for the Father and Son, and we found the claim that "whatsoever pertains to the caused, proceeding, revealing, and perfecting power must be attributed to the Holy Spirit."[159] In Basil the Great, we found the image of the Spirit proceeding "from God . . . as the breath of his mouth."[160] And in Stăniloae, we found a number of philosophical or existential arguments about the Holy Spirit, including the view that "only because a third exists can the two become simultaneously one, not merely through the reciprocity of their love alone, but also through their common self-forgetfulness in favor of the third."[161]

While sharply critical of positions like Stăniloae's, namely those of Walter Kasper and Bertrand de Margerie,[162] John Milbank argues that some explicitly dynamic account of the Spirit in the Trinity is necessary. Grounding his position in Marius Victorinus, he advocates a viewpoint that resonates with the perspectives of Weinandy and Coakley that I treated in the introduction to this book, as well as with the perspective of Balthasar. Milbank states that the Holy Spirit "renews the fundamental being which characterizes the Father. Somehow, because the divine *actus* is *infinite*, and therefore 'interminably terminated' it comprises a non-temporal dynamic or mutual 'play' between an infinite 'conclusion' of expression in the Son, and an endless 're-opening' of that conclusion by the desire of the Spirit which re-inspires the paternal *arche*."[163] For Milbank, this emphasis on the Spirit's renewing, reopening, and reinspiring the Father is necessary not least in order to ensure a trinitarian theology that affirms "a constant passage beyond the given," a truly dynamic

---

is God's joyous eternal commitment to all that is contained in that Word who would someday become flesh and dwell among us" (ibid.).

159. John of Damascus, *An Exact Exposition of the Orthodox Faith* 1.12, p. 196.

160. Basil the Great, *On the Holy Spirit* 18.46, p. 81.

161. Stăniloae, *Experience of God*, 267.

162. See Milbank, "Second Difference," 174–80; see also Walter Kasper, *The God of Jesus Christ*, trans. Matthew J. O'Connell (New York: Crossroad, 1997), 289, 308–9; Bertrand de Margerie, SJ, *La Trinité chrétienne dans l'histoire* (Paris: Beauchesne, 1975), 4–6. Milbank's critique of Kasper's overall theology of the Trinity is superb.

163. Milbank, "Second Difference," 187. See also Milbank, "Can a Gift Be Given? Prolegomena to a Future Trinitarian Metaphysic," *Modern Theology* 11 (1995): 119–61, at 150, 153–54. For important concerns, with which I agree, see Guy Mansini, OSB, "Balthasar and the Theodramatic Enrichment of the Trinity," *The Thomist* 64 (2000): 499–519.

Trinity.[164] Milbank's portrait of the Spirit enriching the Father by interpreting the Son seems to me to be anthropomorphic. But even if it were not, the lineaments of a truly dynamic Trinity are already and sufficiently present in the relational distinction of Father, Word/Image (Son), and Love/Gift (Holy Spirit). Once these names have been rightly understood, we do not need to go further, nor can we do so. These revealed names themselves illumine the wondrously dynamic *communio* of the Trinity.

Recall Andrew Louth's insistence that "the mystery of God overwhelms any human categories; all one can do is stutter the precise distinctions that belong to the doctrine of the Trinity, which do not so much reveal the divine mystery, as prevent one's reducing it in one's conception to a bare philosophical unity or a pagan pantheon or any other misconception."[165] Louth is right to warn us against imagining the Trinity "as a community of loving individuals" and to emphasize the task of warding off errors (above all, the ever-recurring Sabellian and Arian errors).[166] As Louth makes clear, we are certainly not called upon to develop a narrative of the inner life or the existential enrichment of the Trinity, as much trinitarian theology today strives to do.[167] Yet the name "Word," even if it is still a stuttering, offers fruitful insight into the

---

164. Milbank, "Second Difference," 189 (cf. 183). Bernd Jochen Hilberath advances a broadly similar position, although in psychological (and spatial) terms rather than in terms of literary theory: the Holy Spirit "is not only the *condilectus*, the co-loved third person, in whom the duality of the mutual love of Father and Son transcends and offers itself, and precisely in this is bound together again (*vinculum amoris* = bond of love); rather he is the one who perfectly grants room for being-in-each-other, the perichoresis of Father and Son, he is the one whose own being is realized in selflessly making possible this being-in-each-other. Thus the Spirit proceeds not in supplementary fashion as a third from the first and second self-constituting or rather mutually constitutive persons; rather, he reveals himself as the always already opened space for interpersonal encounter in person" (Hilberath, "Identity through Self-Transcendence: The Holy Spirit and the Fellowship of Free Persons," in *Advents of the Spirit: An Introduction to the Current Study of Pneumatology*, ed. Bradford E. Hinze and D. Lyle Dabney [Milwaukee: Marquette University Press, 2001], 265–94, at 284).

165. Louth, "Love and the Trinity," 13.

166. Ibid., 15.

167. See especially Bruce Marshall's "The Absolute and the Trinity," *Pro Ecclesia* 23 (2014): 147–64. See also Marshall, "The Dereliction of Christ and the Impassibility of God," in *Divine Impassibility and the Mystery of Human Suffering*, ed. James F. Keating and Thomas Joseph White, OP (Grand Rapids: Eerdmans, 2009), 246–98; Marshall, "Trinity," in *The Blackwell Companion to Modern Theology*, ed. Gareth Jones (Oxford: Blackwell, 2004), 183–203. For his part, Milbank offers a trenchant critique of Kantian and Hegelian theologies of the Trinity, including those of Walter Kasper, Jürgen Moltmann, Wolfhart Pannenberg, and Eberhard Jüngel. Milbank shows their thoroughgoing voluntarism (neglecting the Son's procession as Word) and their mythological portraits of the Spirit as the final agent in a narrative of thesis-anthithesis-synthesis. See Milbank, "Second Difference," 174–83. Yet Milbank also identifies Hegel as "the most profound modern meditator upon the identity of the Holy Spirit" (ibid., 183), and he incorporates a large amount of Hegelian "becoming" into his own constructive proposal, as I noted above.

distinctiveness of the Son in the Trinity. Likewise, we are justified in asking whether the Holy Spirit can be named in a manner that corresponds to the Son's name "Word" and that befits the Spirit's association with love and gift in the economy of salvation.

Aquinas approaches the topic of naming the Holy Spirit from within an Augustinian framework, according to which the names "Love" and "Gift" pertain properly to the Spirit in a manner that corresponds to the Son's name Word, and that makes intelligible what Milbank calls "the second difference."[168] The Spirit is the Love who proceeds as the inexhaustible communion of the Father and Son, as their coequal Gift. Aquinas's main concern in questions 37 and 38 consists in ensuring that these names are affirmed within fitting bounds. He devotes his energy to making clear that the Spirit's proper name "Love" does not take away from the fact that the divine essence is love; to showing that the Spirit is not the Love of the Father and Son in the sense that they would otherwise lack love; to showing that the Spirit's name "Gift" does not imply subordination and that the Son is also a gift; and to explaining that the Spirit properly receives the name "Gift" because he proceeds as Love. In offering these clarifications, Aquinas assumes the biblical exposition that Augustine provides in *De Trinitate* and also draws upon his own doctrine of interior processions and relations, grounded in the Gospel of John's naming of the Son as "Word." Aquinas shows that by following this biblical path, we can name the Spirit "Love" and "Gift" in a manner that illumines the eternal procession of the Holy Spirit, in the trinitarian order of origin that excludes temporal priority.

In contemplating and praising the Spirit as eternal Love and Gift, our minds and hearts are inflamed and empowered to enter into the communion of the Spirit, and through the Spirit with the Father and Son. Here we enter into the heart of the theo-drama. Rejoicing that the Holy Spirit eternally "proceeds as the love of the primal goodness whereby the Father loves Himself and every creature," let us, as Saint Paul urges, "be aglow with the Spirit" and "serve the Lord" (Rom. 12:11).[169]

---

168. See Milbank, "Second Difference."
169. I, q. 37, a. 2, ad 3.

THE HOLY SPIRIT AND THE *FILIOQUE*

Does it matter whether the Holy Spirit proceeds not only from the Father but also from the Son? In his *Orthodox Readings of Aquinas*, the Orthodox scholar Marcus Plested piles up case after case of Orthodox theologians who criticize Aquinas for the doctrine of the *filioque*, even while they often admire Aquinas's theology in other respects.[1] For example, Plested observes that Theophanes III, Metropolitan of Nicaea, shows ample and appreciative

---

1. Gregory Palamas firmly rejected the *filioque*, even if, influenced by Augustine, Plested reads him (rather controversially) as allowing "for an 'Orthodox *filioque*' [or 'co-procession'] both in respect of the eternal divine life and the manifestation of the divine *energeia* among creatures" (Plested, *Orthodox Readings of Aquinas* [Oxford: Oxford University Press, 2012], 39). For a similar reading of Palamas, see Michael D. Torre, "St. John Damascene and St. Thomas Aquinas on the Eternal Procession of the Holy Spirit," *St. Vladimir's Theological Quarterly* 38 (1994): 303–27, at 322–23. See also John Breck, "'The Two Hands of God': Christ and the Spirit in Orthodox Theology," *St. Vladimir's Theological Quarterly* 40 (1996): 231–46. Breck carefully distinguishes between what in Palamas's statement pertains to the divine essence and what pertains to the energies. For Breck, "Both East and West . . . should be able to agree on the affirmation that the Spirit 'proceeds' from the Father (alone), yet, with regard to the ἐνέργεια, he is communicated reciprocally between Father and Son, and by the Father and the Son to the world, as the effulgence of divine love. Accordingly, it may be affirmed that while the Spirit '*proceeds*' from the Father alone, he is *communicated* by the Father and the Son together, both within the immanent Trinity itself as the expression of their mutual love, and from the Trinity to creation in the divine *economia*" (ibid., 241–42). For a helpful analysis of the trinitarian analogy from word and love in chaps. 34–38 of *Capita 150*, see Jeremy D. Wilkins, "'The Image of This Highest Love': The Trinitarian Analogy in Gregory Palamas' *Capita 150*," *St. Vladimir's Theological Quarterly* 47 (2003): 383–412, esp. 394–410.

knowledge of Aquinas's theology, but "in the matter of the *filioque* any positive appreciation of Aquinas is, naturally, out of the question."[2] The same
thing was true for Neilos Kabasilas (d. 1363), Nicholas Kabasilas (d. 1397),
Joseph Bryennios (d. 1431), Mark of Ephesus (d. 1445), Gennadios Schol-
arios (d. 1472), Maximos Margounios (d. 1602), Gabriel Severos (d. 1616),
Nicholas Koursoulas (d. 1652), George Koressios (d. 1660), and many others.
Indeed, in his book *The Filioque*, Edward Siecienski counts Aquinas among
the significant "post-schism figures on both sides whose writings contributed
to the increasingly divergent views on the procession of the Holy Spirit."[3]

Reading this sad history of real appreciation for Aquinas's theology combined with strong rejection of the *filioque*, one understands why many Catholic
theologians have wondered whether insistence upon the truth of the *filioque*
is worth the ecumenical cost. While supportive of at least some version of
the *filioque*,[4] Hans Urs von Balthasar points out that Pope Pius XI celebrated
Mass in 1925 according to the Greek rite and omitted the *filioque*, and that
Pope John Paul II likewise omitted the *filioque* at a Mass celebrating the

2. Plested, *Orthodox Readings of Aquinas*, 94.

3. A. Edward Siecienski, *The Filioque: History of a Doctrinal Controversy* (Oxford: Oxford
University Press, 2010), 14. Among other figures who could have been engaged in this chapter,
Karl Barth stands out for his vigorous deployment of the *filioque*. For discussion, both appreciative and critical, see David Guretzki, *Karl Barth on the Filioque* (Burlington, VT: Ashgate,
2009); Bruce McCormack, "The Lord and Giver of Life: A 'Barthian' Defence of the *Filioque*,"
in *Rethinking Trinitarian Theology: Disputed Questions and Contemporary Issues in Trinitarian
Theology*, ed. Giulio Maspero and Robert J. Woźniak (London: T&T Clark, 2012), 230–53,
esp. 250–52. McCormack's essay is largely a defense of his view that Barth holds the election
of Jesus Christ to be constitutive of the eternal Son. See also, for contrasting evaluations of
Barth's theology of the Holy Spirit, Philip J. Rosato, *The Spirit as Lord: The Pneumatology of
Karl Barth* (Edinburgh: T&T Clark, 1981); John Thompson, *The Holy Spirit in the Theology
of Karl Barth* (Allison Park, PA: Pickwick, 1991).

4. Thus Balthasar remarks that "the Logos has a 'toward' together with his 'from': the
groundlessly loving production of the one whom we call, for want of a clearer term, the Holy
Spirit. At this point, it becomes an idle debate whether we say that the Father produces the
Spirit *with* the Son (*filioque*) or *through* the Son (*dia hyiou*), but it is also idle to attempt to
define this joint action [*Miteinander*] once again (restrictively) as a single 'principle of spiration'" (Balthasar, *Theo-Logic*, vol. 2, *Truth of God*, trans. Adrian J. Walker [San Francisco:
Ignatius, 2004], 152–53). See also his more extensive discussion of the *filioque* in his *Theo-
Logic*, vol. 3, *The Spirit of Truth*, trans. Graham Harrison (San Francisco: Ignatius, 2005),
207–18. Indebted to Karl Barth's defense of the *filioque*, Balthasar argues that "as for the
Spirit being both epitome and fruit of eternal love, the New Testament is full of it. It is this
induction from the unity of Son and Spirit, in the *oikonomia*, and specifically in terms of
love, that causes Karl Barth to insist convincingly that this unity must be anchored in the immanent Trinity" (ibid., 218). Yet Balthasar also finds that the notion that the Father and the
Son are one principle of the Spirit is "the Achilles' heel of the Western model" and shows the
"impossibility . . . of using the concept 'person' univocally for the divine Hypostases" (ibid.,
217). See also, from a similar perspective, Claude Bruaire, *L'être et l'esprit* (Paris: Presses
Universitaires de France, 1983), 187.

fifteen-hundredth anniversary of the Council of Constantinople. Balthasar cites Jean-Miguel Garrigues, Louis Bouyer, and Yves Congar as examples of leading Catholic theologians who, with regard to the Latin version of the creed, call for the *filioque* "to be dropped for the sake of peace in the Church."[5] Congar nonetheless affirms that the doctrine of the *filioque* has been taught by the magisterium of the Catholic Church, and therefore he concludes that the Catholic Church "cannot be asked to deny its teaching about the part played by the Son in the eternal procession of the Spirit."[6]

5. Balthasar, *Theo-Logic*, vol. 3, *The Spirit of Truth*, 208–9. See Jean-Miguel Garrigues, *L'Esprit qui dit 'Père!' et le problème du filioque* (Paris: Téqui, 1981), 94; Yves Congar, OP, "Should the *Filioque* Be Suppressed in the Creed?," in *I Believe in the Holy Spirit*, trans. David Smith (New York: Crossroad, 1997), 3:204–7; Congar, *The Word and the Spirit*, trans. David Smith (London: Geoffrey Chapman, 1986), 101–21; Louis Bouyer, *Le Consolateur* (Paris: Cerf, 1980), 299–307. Congar sets two necessary conditions for the suppression of the *filioque* in the Latin version of the Creed: "(1) Together with recognized and authoritative representatives of the Orthodox Churches, the non-heretical character of the *Filioque*, properly understood, should be made clear and recognized, as should the equivalence and complementarity of the two dogmatic expressions, 'from the Father as the absolute Source and from the Son' and 'from the Father through the Son'"; and "(2) The Christian people on both sides should be prepared for this so that it may be done in the light, in patience, with respect for each other's legitimate sensibilities, and in love" ("Should the *Filioque* Be Suppressed in the Creed?," 206). Along the same lines, see also André de Halleux, "Toward an Ecumenical Agreement on the Procession of the Holy Spirit and the Addition of the Filioque to the Creed," in *Spirit of God, Spirit of Christ: Ecumenical Reflections on the* Filioque *Controversy*, ed. Lukas Vischer (London: SPCK, 1981), 69–84. For a revisionist Catholic advocate of dropping the *filioque* from the creed (in connection with the Klingenthal Memorandum), see Francine Cardman, "The Holy Spirit and the Apostolic Faith, A Roman Catholic Response," in *Spirit of Truth: Ecumenical Perspectives on the Holy Spirit*, ed. Theodore Stylianopoulos and S. Mark Heim (Brookline, MA: Holy Cross Orthodox Press, 1986), 59–80. Cardman is sympathetic with the view that "in subordinating the Spirit to the Son, the *filioque* leads to a subordination of Church to Pope as vicar of Christ, or of charism/ Spirit to office" (ibid., 67); and she argues that masculine names for the Triune God (Father, Son) need to be superseded. For his part, Garrigues proposes that Orthodox in the West who liturgically employ Latin-based languages should avoid using words drawn from *"procedere"* (see Garrigues, "A Roman Catholic View of the Position Now Reached in the Question of the *Filioque*," in Vischer, *Spirit of God, Spirit of Christ*, 149–63, at 158–59). In response to this proposal, however, Theodore Stylianopoulos observes, "The Orthodox can accept the use of 'proceeds' in its etymological meaning (thus literally, 'the Holy Spirit . . . who goes forward from the Father and the Son') because such use implies no *filioquism*, but they cannot by any means accept a precise alternative based on *exportare* or another such verb because that would heighten *filioquism* by emphasizing the Spirit's eternal origin from the Father and the Son as from a joint cause" (Stylianopoulos, "The Filioque: Dogma, Theologoumenon or Error?," in *The Good News of Christ: Essays on the Gospel, Sacraments and Spirit* [Brookline, MA: Holy Cross Orthodox Press, 1991], 196–232, at 230n56). Stylianopoulos holds that by ignoring the Cappadocian matrix of the creed and changing the meaning of "proceeds," the Augustinian doctrine of the *filioque* goes against the Council of Constantinople's affirmation of the Father's monarchy, no matter what the intention of Augustine himself or later Catholics might be.

6. Congar, "Dogmatic Definitions in Pneumatology: A Need for Hermeneutics," in *I Believe in the Holy Spirit*, 3:128–32, at 131. Congar refers specifically to the "ordinary" magisterium,

A negative determination regarding the *filioque*'s place in the Latin version of the creed was also reached by a group of Orthodox, Catholic, and Protestant theologians who convened in 1978 and 1979 at Schloss Klingenthal, France, under the auspices of the Faith and Order Commission of the World Council of Churches. Siecienski describes this as "the single most significant dialogue on the *filioque*."[7] The resulting "Klingenthal Memorandum" argues for removing the *filioque* from the creed not merely as an ecumenical concession, but on the grounds that the notion that the Father and Son are one principle of the Spirit fails to appreciate that the Spirit has a different

---

manifested for instance in the centuries of communal recitation of the Latin version of the Creed. He adds that the Catholic Church "can, however, reasonably be expected to recognize that the Western formulae do not express everything that the Catholic Church believes, that certain points of doctrine are a matter, not absolutely of faith as such, but of theological explanation, and that it is possible for other expressions of the same faith to exist, taking different insights as their point of departure and using other instruments of thought" (ibid.). Commenting on Congar's view that the *filioque* is a defined teaching of the magisterium, Brian E. Daley, SJ, proposes that since the Council of Florence (an exercise of the "extraordinary" magisterium), the Catholic Church has taught that "and the Son" and "through the Son" mean fundamentally the same thing, so that "the normative interpretation of the *Filioque* for the Catholic . . . has been, since Florence, a theological position that is also generally accepted in the Eastern tradition" (Daley, "Revisiting the 'Filioque': Part Two, Contemporary Catholic Approaches," *Pro Ecclesia* 10 [2001]: 195–212, at 210). Most Orthodox theologians today, however, deny that the Son shares in any way in the Father's spirating of the Spirit. In my view, Daley's interpretation of the Council of Florence is ingenious but difficult to square fully with the conciliar text. The Council of Florence teaches that the Greeks have mistakenly thought that the Spirit's procession "from" the Son requires "two principles and two spirations"; because the Latins affirm that the Father is "the source and principle of all deity" and that the Father and Son are "one principle" in the "single spiration of the Holy Spirit," the Council of Florence concludes (perhaps rather hastily) that the Greeks and Latins fundamentally agree about "from" the Son, and therefore the council defines "that the following truth of faith shall be believed and accepted by all Christians and thus shall all profess it: that the Holy Spirit is eternally from the Father and the Son, and has his essence and his subsistent being from the Father together with the Son, and proceeds from both eternally as from one principle and a single spiration" (Norman P. Tanner, SJ, ed., *Decrees of the Ecumenical Councils* [Washington, DC: Georgetown University Press, 1990], 1:526).

7. See Siecienski, *Filioque*, 208–9. For treatments of the *filioque* in contemporary theology, in addition to Daley's "Revisiting the 'Filioque': Part Two," see Ralph Del Colle, "Reflections on the *Filioque*," *Journal of Ecumenical Studies* 34 (1997): 202–17; Bernd Oberdorfer, *Filioque: Geschichte und Theologie eines ökumenischen Problems* (Göttingen: Vandenhoeck & Ruprecht, 2001); Oberdorfer, "Brauchen wir das Filioque? Aspekte des Filioque-Problems in der heutigen Diskussion," *Kerygma und Dogma* 49 (2003): 278–92; and Bruce D. Marshall's trenchant response to Oberdorfer's article, "The Filioque as Theology and Doctrine: In Reply to Bernd Oberdorfer," *Kerygma und Dogma* 50 (2004): 271–88. Oberdorfer, like the Klingenthal Memorandum, holds that arguments in favor of the *filioque* are unpersuasive and therefore the *filioque* should be removed from the Creed. See also Marshall's brief critique of the Klingenthal Memorandum in his "The Defense of the *Filioque* in Classical Lutheran Theology: An Ecumenical Appreciation," *Neue Zeitschrift für systematische Theologie und Religionsphilosophie* 44 (2002): 154–73, an essay that is largely devoted to examining classical Lutheran arguments for deriving the *filioque* from Scripture.

relationship to the Father than the Spirit does to the Son. Granting that the Spirit's procession from the Father presupposes the Son's coming forth from the Father, the Klingenthal Memorandum suggests that the *filioque* be replaced with one of the following formulae: "The Spirit proceeds from the Father of the Son; the Spirit proceeds from the Father through the Son; the Spirit proceeds from the Father and receives from the Son; the Spirit proceeds from the Father and rests on the Son; the Spirit proceeds from the Father and shines out through the Son."[8]

Against this trend, the Pontifical Council for Promoting Christian Unity published in 1995 a document titled "The Greek and Latin Traditions regarding the Procession of the Holy Spirit." The Pontifical Council first underscores the high regard in which the Catholic Church holds the creed proclaimed at Constantinople. As the Pontifical Council states, "The Catholic Church acknowledges the conciliar, ecumenical, normative and irrevocable

8. Klingenthal Memorandum, "The Filioque Clause in Ecumenical Perspective," in Vischer, *Spirit of God, Spirit of Christ*, 3–18, at 16. Note Jürgen Moltmann's view that "the Holy Spirit does not 'proceed from the Father and the Son,' as the Western church's Nicene Creed maintains. The Spirit proceeds from the Father, rests on the Son, and from the Son radiates into the world" (Moltmann, *The Source of Life: The Holy Spirit and the Theology of Life*, trans. Margaret Kohl [Minneapolis: Fortress, 1997], 17); cf. Moltmann's "Theological Proposals towards the Resolution of the *Filioque* Controversy," in Vischer, *Spirit of God, Spirit of Christ*, 164–73. Similarly, Dumitru Stăniloae holds that the Spirit "proceeds from the Father with a view to his 'repose' in the Son" (Stăniloae, "The Procession of the Holy Spirit from the Father and His Relation to the Son, as the Basis of Our Deification and Adoption," in Vischer, *Spirit of God, Spirit of Christ*, 174–86, at 181). Stăniloae considers it "preferable not to use the word 'proceed' for the relation of the Spirit to the Son, since it can give the impression of a confusion of this relation with the procession of the Spirit from the Father. It would be preferable to use the word 'procession' for the relation of the Spirit to the Father, and for his relation to the Son, the term 'goes out from' doubled with other terms like 'shines out from' or 'is manifested by,' terms which have been used by the eastern Fathers" (ibid., 177). Boris Bobrinskoy too recognizes that the New Testament includes a "Father-Spirit-Christ" schema, according to which "the Spirit proceeds from the Father and rests on Christ" (Bobrinskoy, *The Mystery of the Trinity: Trinitarian Experience and Vision in the Biblical and Patristic Tradition*, trans. Anthony P. Gythiel [Crestwood, NY: St. Vladimir's Seminary Press, 1999], 66); cf. 99, where Bobrinskoy states that the Spirit eternally rests upon the Son. Bobrinskoy adds irenically, "If Christ truly sends the Spirit who proceeds from the Father, the Son is not only the One on whom the Spirit rests, but the One who gives the Spirit. However, this view which I would call filioquist in the positive sense, acceptable to Orthodoxy, must be balanced by the vision of Christ as the One on whom the Spirit rests, the One who is obedient to the Spirit, the One who is sent by the Spirit. . . . In this view, *filioquism* is balanced by a complementary schema which would be, one might say, that of a '*Spirituque*,'" some kind of presence and "participation of the Spirit in the relation Father-Son" (ibid., 70–71). Bobrinskoy concludes that "the Spirit and the Son come, on the one hand, from the Father, each in a direct, unique manner, and, on the other, originate in the presence, the transparency, and the full participation of the Third, of the Spirit for the Son as of the Son for the Spirit" (ibid., 71). In favor of this "*Spirituque*," see also Paul Evdokimov, *L'Esprit-Saint dans la tradition orthodoxe* (Paris: Cerf, 1969).

value, as expression of the one common faith of the church and of all Christians, of the Symbol professed in Greek at Constantinople in 381 by the Second Ecumenical Council."[9] This acknowledgment puts in some question the status of the Latin version of the creed, especially when the Pontifical Council goes on to say that "no profession of faith peculiar to a particular liturgical tradition can contradict this expression of the faith taught and professed by the undivided Church." Rather than criticizing the Latin version of the creed, however, the Pontifical Council is affirming the binding truth of the Creed of Constantinople and insisting that no later creed can be interpreted in a manner that contradicts the Greek creed professed at Constantinople.

The Pontifical Council then undertakes the task of interpreting both the Greek creed and the later Latin version in relation to the Greek creed. It notes firstly that "Gregory of Nazianzus . . . characterizes the Spirit's relationship of origin from the Father by the proper term ἐκπόρευσις, distinguishing it from that of procession (τὸ προϊέναι) which the Spirit has in common with the Son."[10] For the Cappadocians, basing themselves on John 15:26's "τὸ πνεῦμα . . . τοῦ πατρὸς ἐκπορεύεται," the term ἐκπορευόμενον (as the verb appears in the creed) can only characterize the Spirit's relation *to the Father*. On this basis, the Pontifical Council emphasizes that the Greek creed must not be tampered with in contemporary Greek liturgical proclamation. Thus the Catholic Church today rejects the addition of "and the Son" to the creed's Greek form "even in its liturgical use by Latins."[11]

After discussing the Greek fathers' general approval of the formula "through [διά] the Son," the Pontifical Council emphasizes that the *filioque* belongs to "a theological and linguistic context different from that of the affirmation of

9. Pontifical Council for Promoting Christian Unity, "The Greek and Latin Traditions regarding the Procession of the Holy Spirit," http://www.ewtn.com/library/curia/pccufilq.htm. All my quotations from the document are taken from this online version, which unfortunately does not specify paragraph numbers.

10. In Oration 25.15–18, quoted by Christopher A. Beeley, Gregory of Nazianzus confesses "one Holy Spirit, who proceeds (προελθόν) or goes forth (προϊόν) from the Father" (Beeley, *Gregory of Nazianzus on the Trinity and the Knowledge of God: In Your Light We Shall See Light* [Oxford: Oxford University Press, 2008], 202).

11. It is worth noting that due to the lack of any Latin bishops at the Council of Constantinople, it is possible that when Latin bishops later formally affirmed the Creed of Constantinople (at the Council of Chalcedon), "they simply assumed that its characterization of the origin of the Spirit was to be understood within the framework of their own Latin tradition of a procession *ab utroque*. In the later fifth and sixth century, such an interpretation of the Spirit's origin continued to be taken for granted by mainstream Latin theologians, who accepted the faith of Chalcedon and the earlier formulas Chalcedon had affirmed—Fulgentius of Ruspe, Eucharius of Lyon, Avitus of Vienne" (Brian E. Daley, SJ, "Revisiting the 'Filioque': Part One, Roots and Branches of an Old Debate," *Pro Ecclesia* 10 [2001]: 31–62, at 46).

the sole monarchy of the Father."[12] Namely, the Latin verb "procedere" signifies "the communication of the consubstantial divinity from the Father to the Son and from the Father, through and with the Son, to the Holy Spirit."[13] It follows that the Latin "procedit" corresponds to the meaning of the Greek "προϊέναι," which is applicable to both the Son and the Spirit. This crucial point for harmonizing the Greek creed with the later Latin version was originally articulated by Maximus the Confessor in his *Letter to Marinus of Cyprus*, which was written from Rome.[14]

On this basis, the Pontifical Council suggests that the *filioque*, in the Latin version of the creed, can be squared with the teaching of the Greek fathers.

12. Daley emphasizes that for Augustine, "the Father is the origin of the Spirit *principaliter*— 'by way of first principle,' ἀρχικῶς as the Greeks would say—while the Son's role must be understood in terms of his second place in the biblically warranted 'order' of persons in God. . . . The language of the Spirit's 'proceeding' from both Father and Son, as Latin Christians understood *procedere* and (after Augustine) with all the necessary qualifications assuring the Father's primacy as ultimate source, was well established in the West by the mid-fifth century" (ibid., 41).

13. In his discussion Daley states, "The familiar phrase of the Latin version of the Constantinopolitan Creed, however, *qui ex Patre Filioque procedit*, uses a word—*procedere*—that in the Vulgate translates not just the Greek word ἐκπορεύεται in John 15.26, referring to the Spirit, but also ἐξῆλθον in John 8.42 (Jesus's saying, 'I came forth . . . from the Father')" (ibid., 35). Daley provides valuable historical background in Tertullian: "The rhythm and ordered flow of the divine 'substance,' from Father to Son and through Son to Spirit, is for Tertullian the only way to express the common deity of all three" (ibid., 37). As Daley shows, Hilary of Poitiers cautiously proposes that the Spirit's proceeding from the Father is the same as the Spirit's receiving from the Son (in accord with John 16:14–15). Daley points out that Ambrose, whose sources included Basil the Great and Didymus the Blind, "was apparently the first to make explicit use of the phrase *Spiritus procedit a Patre et Filio*" (ibid., 39), although Ambrose was speaking of the economy of salvation.

14. On this point, see ibid., 46–47. See also Andrew Louth, "Late Patristic Developments on the Trinity in the East," in *The Oxford Handbook of the Trinity*, ed. Gilles Emery, OP, and Matthew Levering (Oxford: Oxford University Press, 2011), 138–49. Louth remarks that "Maximos understands the Spirit to proceed from the Father, but to come forth through the Son: the position of Cyril of Alexandria, though it is clear in Maximos that this is eternally true, and belongs to the realm of *theologia*" (ibid., 146). As Louth goes on to explain, in his *Letter to Marinus of Cyprus* "Maximos defends the Roman Church against accusations from Constantinople that the Romans were heretical in asserting that the Spirit also proceeded from the Son. . . . Maximos does not defend the precise accusation—that the Spirit proceeds (ἐκπορεύεσθαι) from (ἐκ) the Son; he seems to set that aside (as a misinterpretation?) and affirms that the Romans agree with Cyril of Alexandria in asserting that there is one cause within the Godhead, the Father, and that the Spirit goes forth (προϊέναι) through (δία) the Son" (ibid., 146–47). See also A. Alexakis, "The *Epistula ad Marinum Cypri Presbyterum* of Maximus the Confessor (*CPG* 7697.10) Revisited: A Few Remarks on Its Meaning and Its History," *Byzantinische Zeitschrift* 94 (2001): 545–54; Carlo dell'Osso, "*Filioque* in Massimo il Confessore," in *Il Filioque. A mille anni dal suo inserimento nel Credo a Roma (1014–2014)*, ed. Mauro Gagliardi (Vatican City: Libreria Editrice Vaticana, 2015), 147–64; Brian Daley, SJ, "The Fullness of the Saving God: Cyril of Alexandria on the Holy Spirit," in *The Theology of St. Cyril of Alexandria*, ed. Thomas G. Weinandy, OFMCap, and Daniel A. Keating (London: T&T Clark, 2003), 113–48; Bobrinskoy, *Mystery of the Trinity*, 254.

The *Catechism of the Catholic Church* similarly affirms that the *filioque* controversy involves "legitimate complementarity," since the Catholic Church by no means aims to deny that the Father is the "first origin of the Spirit," although "as Father of the only Son, he is, with the Son, the single principle from which the Holy Spirit proceeds."[15] Commenting on the *Catechism*'s formulation, the Pontifical Council explains, "Even if the Catholic doctrine affirms that the Holy Spirit proceeds [in the sense of πρόεισι] from the Father and the Son in the communication of their consubstantial communion, it nonetheless recognizes the reality of the original relationship of the Holy Spirit as person with the Father, a relationship that the Greek Fathers express by the term ἐκπόρευσις."[16] The basic point here is that so long as the procession of the Spirit from the Son is understood in the sense of πρόεισι, the *filioque*

15. *Catechism of the Catholic Church*, 2nd ed. (Vatican City: Libreria Editrice Vaticana, 1997), §248. The *Catechism* is here following the Second Council of Lyons (1274). For discussion, see David Coffey, "The Roman 'Clarification' of the Doctrine of the Filioque," *International Journal of Systematic Theology* 5 (2003): 3–21, at 8–9, 15. Regarding the reception of this Second Council of Lyons today, Bobrinskoy states, "The promulgation of the *filioque* as a truth of faith at the Council of Lyons in 1274 must first of all be freed from the anathemas which accompany it. If the Latin dogma of the *filioque* loses, in the eyes of the Orthodox, its constraining character, if the Niceno-Constantinopolitan Creed recovers its common primitive form and becomes again a true 'Symbol' of unity and love, then the *filioque* will cease to be seen as a sin against unity and love. It will then be possible for the Orthodox to consider it as a particular theological investigation belonging to a certain region, to a certain period of Christianity, seeking to express a particular aspect of the Catholic faith" ("*Filioque* Yesterday and Today," 147–48). But the removal of the anathemas would still leave the question of the status of the dogmatic teaching of church councils since the first seven ecumenical councils.

16. Jean-Miguel Garrigues argues, in what seems to me to be an exaggeration, that the Catholic Church holds dogmatically only that the Father (precisely as the Father of the Son) is the source of the Spirit, so that further doctrinal elucidation of the *filioque* has the status simply of venerable theological opinion (see Garrigues, *L'Esprit qui dit 'Père!' et le problème du filioque*, 95–100). In his recent *Le Saint-Esprit sceau de la Trinité: Le Filioque et l'originalité trinitaire de l'Esprit dans sa personne et dans sa mission* (Paris: Cerf, 2011), Garrigues defends the doctrine of the *filioque* in the following terms: "In the Trinitarian order, the origin of the Spirit implies the distinction-communion of the Father and the Son. This is where the revealed basis of the *Filioque* is to be found. The patristic tradition would therefore say that the Holy Spirit *comes forth* (ἐκπορεύεται) from the Father through the Son, if one considers first his relation to the Father as fontal principle, or that the Holy Spirit *proceeds* (*procedit*, προεῖσι) from the Father and Son (*Filioque*), if one considers first the consubstantial communication that he receives from their communion. . . . It is in giving himself totally to the Son in this communion of love that the Father, the unique fontal principle of the Trinity, is *himself* in the Son, through him and with him, the unique principle of the Holy Spirit" (Garrigues, *Le Saint-Esprit sceau de la Trinité*, 228). Garrigues distinguishes his position sharply from "filioquism," which he associates especially with (essentialist) scholasticism, and which disconnects the consideration of the pair Father-Son (or Son-Father) from the pair Father/Son-Holy Spirit (or Holy Spirit-Father/Son) (see ibid., 42–43, 51). While agreeing with Garrigues that the pair Father-Son is unthinkable without the Holy Spirit (since the Son is no mere Word, but a Word that breathes forth Love), I would underline that the Father's begetting of the Son, in itself, is full and complete.

in the Latin version of the creed expresses something that the Orthodox can also uphold.[17]

The Pontifical Council lastly reflects upon the Spirit as "Gift of Love," in light of the *filioque*. The Gift of Love "characterizes the relation between the Father, as source of love, and his beloved Son," as is manifested in the Spirit's work in Jesus Christ. Here, in addition to adducing numerous biblical citations, the Pontifical Council argues that Gregory Palamas's teaching about the Spirit is broadly in accord with the view of Augustine (and of Thomas Aquinas): "This doctrine of the Holy Spirit as love has been harmoniously assumed by St. Gregory Palamas into the Greek theology of the ἐκπόρευσις from the Father alone: 'The Spirit of the most high Word is like an ineffable love of the Father for this Word ineffably generated. A love which this same Word and beloved Son of the Father entertains (χρῆται) towards the Father: but insofar as he has the Spirit coming with him (συνπροελθόντα) from the Father and reposing connaturally in him.'"[18] This way of drawing the Word into the Father's spiration

17. Thus Bobrinskoy affirms that "the eternal Son is not extraneous to the procession of the Holy Spirit," while noting the following qualifications: "(i) in an ineffable manner, (ii) without bringing in the idea of causality, (iii) without calling into question the untransmissable character of the Father's hypostatic property of being the one Source and Principle of the Divinity of the Son and of the Spirit" (Bobrinskoy, "*Filioque* Yesterday and Today," 143). However, Bobrinskoy also states, "I do not . . . believe that the compromise formula *per filium* can of itself offer a satisfactory solution to the conflict, on account of the ambiguities it can contain" (ibid., 146).

18. See Gregory Palamas, *Capita physica* 36, in *PG* 150, 1144, D-1145A. See *Saint Gregory Palamas: The One Hundred and Fifty Chapters; A Critical Edition, Translation, and Study*, ed. Robert E. Sinkewicz (Toronto: Pontifical Institute of Medieval Studies, 1988). Reinhard Flogaus points out that "it was likely [Jacques] Lison's dissertation that caused the Pontifical Council for Promoting Christian Unity in 1995 to refer to Gregory Palamas as an eastern witness for the Augustinian interpretation of the Holy Spirit as mutual bond of love between the Father and the Son" (Flogaus, "Inspiration—Exploitation—Distortion: The Use of St. Augustine in the Hesychast Controversy," in *Orthodox Readings of Augustine*, ed. George Demacopoulos and Aristotle Papanikolaou [Crestwood, NY: St. Vladimir's Seminary Press, 2008], 63–80, at 74). See Jacques Lison, *L'Esprit répandu: La pneumatologie de Grégoire Palamas* (Paris: Cerf, 1994). See also Lison's "L'Esprit comme amour selon Grégoire Palamas: Une influence augustinienne?," *Studia Patristica* 32 (1997): 325–32. Focusing on the Holy Spirit's personal indwelling and deifying action (adoptive sonship), on the one operation of the Trinity *ad extra* vis-à-vis the distinction of persons, and on the question of whether disagreement over the *filioque* entails disagreement over the Spirit's identity (i.e., the reference of the name "Holy Spirit"), Bruce D. Marshall argues that Palamas and Aquinas are in basic agreement about the Holy Spirit; see Marshall, "Action and Person: Do Palamas and Aquinas Agree about the Spirit?," *St. Vladimir's Theological Quarterly* 39 (1995): 379–409; cf. the broadly similar concerns of Marshall's "*Ex Occidente Lux*? Aquinas and Eastern Orthodox Theology," in *Aquinas in Dialogue: Thomas for the Twenty-First Century*, ed. Jim Fodor and Frederick Christian Bauerschmidt (Oxford: Blackwell, 2004), 19–46, esp. n55, where he expresses less optimism about whether Aquinas and Palamas can be brought into agreement on the *filioque*. See also A. N. Williams, *The Ground of Union: Deification in Aquinas and Palamas* (Oxford: Oxford University Press, 1999); Robert E. Sinkewicz, *La théologie byzantine et sa tradition*, vol. 2 (Brussels: Brepols, 2002), 131–89. In

of the Spirit, with the Spirit as like the Father's love for his Word and indeed in a certain sense (without denying the Father's primacy) as the mutual love of the Father and his Word, helps to confirm for the Pontifical Council that the Latin version of the creed is not *opposed* to the normative Greek meaning.

The Pontifical Council's document has generally been well received, including by such eminent Orthodox theologians as Olivier Clément and Metropolitan John Zizioulas, although Zizioulas considers that the document should have gone further and denied that the Son is in any way a "cause" (αἰτία) in the Spirit's procession.[19] Similarly, in remarks at the Centre for Faith and Culture at Westminster College of Oxford University, Metropolitan Kallistos Ware responded to the document (according to the published summary of his remarks provided by Stratford Caldecott) by granting that "the *filioque* is not necessarily heretical in the way it is understood" by the document, but also by asking why the document does not address Orthodox objections to the unilateral insertion of the *filioque* into the creed and by strongly rejecting the view that the Spirit proceeds from the Father and the Son as "one principle."[20] The most critical response from an Orthodox theologian has come from Jean-Claude Larchet, who argues that the document greatly misinterprets Maximus.[21] Catholic theologians such as David Coffey and Jean Galot have also raised concerns, not least about whether the status of the Father and Son as "one principle" of the Spirit in the one spiration (as taught by the Council of Florence) has been adequately upheld by the document.[22]

---

his commentary on the *Capita 150*, Sinkewicz argues at length, but unpersuasively, against any influence of Augustine upon Palamas.

19. To my mind, this could be said only if "cause" were a technical term that signified the monarchy of the Father; otherwise, this position would rule out a real sharing of the Son in the Father's spirating of the Holy Spirit. On the responses to the Pontifical Commission's document, see Siecienski, *Filioque*, 210–11; J.-Y. Brachet and Emmanuel Durand, "La réception de la 'Clarification' de 1995 sur le '*Filioque*,'" *Irénikon* 78 (2005): 47–109. Siecienski cites John Zizioulas, "One Single Source: An Orthodox Response to the Clarification on the Filioque," http://agrino.org/cyberdesert/zizioulas.htm. See also Thomas G. Weinandy, OFMCap, Paul McPartlan, and Stratford Caldecott, "Clarifying the *Filioque*: The Catholic-Orthodox Dialogue," *Communio* 23 (1996): 354–73; George H. Tavard, "A Clarification on the 'Filioque'?," *Anglican Theological Review* 83 (2001): 507–14; Del Colle, "Reflections on the *Filioque*," 202–17; Lucas Francisco Mateo-Seco, *Teología Trinitaria: Dios Espíritu Santo* (Madrid: Rialp, 2005), 146–203. See also the Agreed Statement of the North American Orthodox-Catholic Theological Consultation, "The *Filioque*: A Church-Dividing Issue?," *St. Vladimir's Theological Quarterly* 48 (2004): 93–123.

20. See Stratford Caldecott, introduction to Weinandy, McPartlan, and Caldecott, "Clarifying the *Filioque*," 354–55.

21. Jean-Claude Larchet, "À propos de la récente Clarification du Conseil Pontifical pour la Promotion de l'Unité des Chrétiens," *Le Messager orthodoxe* 129 (1997): 3–58.

22. See Jean Galot, SJ, "L'origine éternelle de l'Esprit Saint," *Gregorianum* 78 (1997): 501–22; Coffey, "Roman 'Clarification' of the Doctrine of the Filioque." See also Carl Krauthauser, "The

Although the document could certainly have been clearer in certain respects, and does indeed elide some important differences, the basic position that the document sets forth strikes me as a promising path to follow: the Son's sharing in the spiration of the Spirit does not do away with the Spirit's relation to the Father as the primal fount, but rather serves to distinguish the Spirit from the Son in a manner that can be compared to the Greek distinction between ἐκπόρευσις and πρόεισι. In my view, however, the document's progress makes it especially necessary to return to the powerful criticisms of the *filioque* offered by Sergius Bulgakov and Vladimir Lossky. Bulgakov and Lossky identify the key underlying question that continues to trouble Orthodox theologians such as Metropolitan Kallistos: Is the doctrine of the *filioque*, especially as formulated by Aquinas and taught (in Thomistic terms) by the Second Council of Lyons and by the Council of Florence, the full flowering of a trinitarian rationalism initiated by Augustine?[23]

Council of Florence Revisited: The Union Decree in Light of the Clarification," *Diakonia* 29 (1996): 95–107; Jean-Miguel Garrigues, "La Clarification sur la procession du Saint-Esprit," *Irénikon* 68 (1995): 501–6; Garrigues, "À la suite de la clarification romaine: Le *Filioque* affranchi du filioquisme," *Irénikon* 69 (1996): 188–212 (chaps. 1 and 2 of his *Le Saint-Esprit sceau de la Trinité*).

23. For Augustine on the "*filioque*," defined as "the doctrine that, within the triune Godhead, the Holy Spirit proceeds from both the Father and the Son as from one principle," see Joseph T. Lienhard, SJ, "Augustine and the *Filioque*," in *Tolle Lege: Essays on Augustine and on Medieval Philosophy in Honor of Roland J. Teske, SJ*, ed. Richard C. Taylor, David Twetten, and Michael Wreen (Milwaukee: Marquette University Press, 2011), 137–54, here quoted at 139. See also Émile Bailleux, "L'Esprit du Père et du Fils selon saint Augustin," *Revue Thomiste* 77 (1977): 5–29. Robert W. Jenson complains with regard to the *filioque* that "in Western teaching as brought to perfection by Thomas the trinitarian relations' capacity to distinguish triune identities depends in large part on sheer geometry. Nor is this sort of thinking Thomas's innovation; looking back at Augustine's use of the *filioque* to show how the Spirit can be another identity than the equally spiritual Father and Son, we recognize the same conceptual style" (Jenson, *Systematic Theology*, vol. 1, *The Triune God* [Oxford: Oxford University Press, 1997], 151). Jenson, however, finds Lossky's position to be equally disastrous, because Lossky rules out conceiving the trinitarian processions as in any way marked by "becoming." After describing Lossky's position, Jenson states,

> This is a vision of God as frozen as any we have encountered, and a new evacuation of trinitarianism. The trinitarian propositions in their Eastern use fail to describe the Father's subordinating of the Son and the Spirit, we discover, only because they do not describe any action at all; in which case, given their semantic foundation and content, they can mean nothing whatever, also not as items of negative, "apophatic" theology. And trinitarian teaching's undeniable starting point in revelation, on which Lossky so insists, turns out to be *not* the biblical narrative, but rather some other revelation of God, whatever that may be. This static vision of God is not Lossky's personal aberration. He derives it from the representative theologian of Byzantine Orthodoxy, Gregory Palamas. (ibid., 152)

For Jenson, Greek metaphysics (as distinct from Hegelian metaphysics, which plays a significant role in Jenson's theology) is antithetical to Scripture and must be uprooted from

In what follows, I investigate this question by first surveying Sergius Bulgakov's view that the real problem with the doctrine of the *filioque* is its reliance on Aquinas's understanding of causality. I then take up Vladimir Lossky's critique of the *filioque*, which Lossky published in critical response to Bulgakov's pneumatology. Whereas Bulgakov absolutely rejects the applicability of causality and the order of origin, Lossky retains causality and the order of origin (at least for the uncreated divine energies). Yet Lossky rejects both the Augustinian analogy from the mind and Aquinas's account of distinct relations of opposition in the order of origin, by which Aquinas seeks to do more than simply enumerate the Son's filiation and the Spirit's procession.[24]

In light of Bulgakov's and Lossky's concerns, I explore Aquinas's theology of the Holy Spirit in *Summa theologiae* I, question 36, a question largely devoted to the issue of the *filioque*. For Brian Daley, Aquinas's approach should be appreciated as a fruitful and "genuine attempt to present the Eastern and Western positions on the origin of the Holy Spirit as complementary, even substantially identical."[25] Is Daley correct, or are Bulgakov and Lossky right that Aquinas's position on the *filioque*—and thus also his naming of the Spirit as "Gift" and "Love" of the Father and the Son—is the product of an

theology. For the opposite view, see Matthew Levering, *Engaging the Doctrine of Revelation: The Mediation of the Gospel through Church and Scripture* (Grand Rapids: Baker Academic, 2014), chap. 8.

24. For discussion of Bulgakov and Lossky on the *filioque*, see Andrea Pacini, "La processione dello Spirito Santo nella teologia ortodossa contemporanea: alcune prospettive," in *Il Filioque*, 287–308; Gregory Collins, OSB, "Three Modern 'Fathers' on the *Filioque*: Good, Bad, or Indifferent?," in *The Holy Spirit in the Fathers of the Church*, ed. D. Vincent Twomey, SVD, and Janet E. Rutherford (Dublin: Four Courts, 2010), 164–84, at 176–82; Bobrinskoy, "*Filioque* Yesterday and Today," 136–37. Pacini's article covers much of the same expository ground that I do in this chapter, although I focus more on Bulgakov's and Lossky's criticisms of Aquinas. Pacini shows Bulgakov's influence upon Paul Evdokimov and Olivier Clément. See also the background provided by Aristotle Papanikolaou, "Contemporary Orthodox Currents on the Trinity," in Emery and Levering, *The Oxford Handbook of the Trinity*, 328–37. For a detailed study focused on Bulgakov, see Pacini's *Lo Spirito Santo nella Trinità. Il Filioque nella prospettiva teologica di S. Bulgakov* (Rome: Città Nuova, 2004).

25. Daley, "Revisiting the 'Filioque': Part One," 34. Later in his essay, Daley describes Aquinas's position on the *filioque* as "both a luminous synthesis and a subtle reshaping of the Western tradition" (ibid., 50). See also Jaroslav Pelikan, "The Doctrine of Filioque in Thomas Aquinas and Its Patristic Antecedents: An Analysis of *Summa Theologiae*, Part I, Question 36," in *St. Thomas Aquinas (1274–1974): Commemorative Studies*, ed. Armand Maurer, CSB (Toronto: Pontifical Institute of Mediaeval Studies, 1974), 1:315–36. Daley comments at some length, and generally quite positively, on Aquinas's treatment of the procession of the Holy Spirit in Aquinas's *Liber contra errores Graecorum*, ed. H.-F. Dondaine, in vol. 40 of the Leonine Commission's *Sancti Thomae de Aquino opera omnia* (Rome: Ad Sanctae Sabinae, 1969); his *Summa contra gentiles* 4.24–25, trans. Charles J. O'Neil (Notre Dame, IN: University of Notre Dame Press, 1975); his *Quaestiones disputatae de Potentia Dei*, q. 10, art. 1–5, trans. the English Dominican Fathers (Eugene, OR: Wipf & Stock, 2004); and his *Summa theologiae* I, q. 36.

Augustinian theological rationalism that Aquinas inherits and intensifies? Would it be better, as Paul McPartlan argues, for the West to finally "give up the whole enterprise of reading the data from the economy directly back into the immanent Trinity and appreciate the gulf of unknowability that in fact separates the two"?[26]

Sergius Bulgakov and Vladimir Lossky on the *Filioque*

Sergius Bulgakov

Sergius Bulgakov warns against understanding either generation (of the Son) or procession (of the Spirit) "in the anthropomorphic sense of origination or production, for this aspect of generation [or procession] belongs only to temporal being, to being that has an origin."[27] For Bulgakov, instead of conceiving the Trinity in a manner that emphasizes causality, we must find images that emphasize love, relationship, and revelation, without thereby falling into ontological subordinationism between the three persons. Bulgakov is willing to use the term "principle" to describe the Father, but he purifies it of causal associations. As "principle," the Father "is the source hypostasis, for *He* reveals himself in the other hypostases, is their subject, in relation to which they are predicate and copula. He is the ontological and logical center of the union that forms the three hypostatic centers of the Divine triunity."[28] From this perspective, Bulgakov incorporates Augustine's view that the Holy Spirit is hypostatic Love. He explains,

> The Father, revealed in the Son, goes out of Himself in His love; and this love is for Him the hypostatic Spirit. The *Spirator*, the One Who breathes out the

26. Paul McPartlan, "Response," in Weinandy, McPartlan, and Caldecott, "Clarifying the *Filioque*," 367–70, at 369. Indebted to John Zizioulas, McPartlan suggests that this apophatic divide is bridged in the (eschatological) eucharistic liturgy, which is "a truly communional image of the primordial gathering of the Son and the Spirit *with* the Father in the immanent Trinity" (ibid., 370); see also McPartlan's *The Eucharist Makes the Church: Henri de Lubac and John Zizioulas in Dialogue* (Edinburgh: T&T Clark, 1993). I do not see why this position should preclude the view that Scripture, proclaimed in the liturgy, gives us treasured insight into the distinctiveness of the Father, Son, and Holy Spirit. As Lienhard says approvingly with respect to Augustine, "His explication makes no distinction between what later theologians call the immanent Trinity and the economic Trinity," because "how God acts corresponds precisely to what God is, and what God is determines how God is" (Lienhard, "Augustine and the *Filioque*," 152)—an observation that differs in its import from Rahner's rule that the economic Trinity is the immanent Trinity and vice versa. For insightful criticism of Rahner's rule, see Congar, *Word and the Spirit*, 104–5.

27. Sergius Bulgakov, *The Comforter*, trans. Boris Jakim (Grand Rapids: Eerdmans, 2004), 136.

28. Ibid., 137.

Spirit, loves the Spirit by the Spirit Himself; whereas the Spirit proceeds *Himself*, giving Himself, His hypostasis, for the service of Love, in order to be Love itself. The hypostasis does not arise in the procession; rather, the mutual service of love and the images of supra-eternal love are realized in the procession by the fact that the Father loves, whereas the Spirit is the hypostatic love of the Father.[29]

It should be clear that Bulgakov's perspective goes beyond both East and West on this topic, as is frequently the case in his theology.[30] He does so on the grounds that the fathers themselves, like the ecumenical councils, did not dogmatically define either generation or procession. On this view, both the Latin *filioque* and the Greek διά were mere "theologoumena," tolerable on both sides, at least prior to the medieval period. They were mere "dogmatic hypotheses, attempts to descriptively express an idea that had not received or, at that point, had not even sought for itself a precise dogmatic definition."[31] After all, the fathers all affirmed the monarchy of the Father and the ontological coequality of the three persons. In the patristic period, Bulgakov says, "the question of the *origination* of one hypostasis from another, in particular the question of the procession of the Holy Spirit from the Father alone or from the Father and the Son, and whether He proceeds from one cause or from

29. Ibid. For discussion, see Aristotle Papanikolaou, "Sophia, Apophasis, and Communion: The Trinity in Contemporary Orthodox Theology," in *The Cambridge Companion to the Trinity*, ed. Peter C. Phan (Cambridge: Cambridge University Press, 2011), 243–57, at 244.

30. Bulgakov comments, "Each side in this dogmatic dispute attacked and anathematized the other for distorting the most important dogma concerning the Holy Spirit. Therefore, it would have been natural to expect that the existence of such a grave heresy, of such a fundamental dogmatic divergence, would permeate the entire life of the two churches and their entire doctrine. Over the course of many years, I have sought traces of this influence, and I have attempted to comprehend the *life*-significance of this divergence and to find out *where* and *in what* it is manifested *in practice*. And I must admit that I have not been able to find this practical life-significance; and, more than that, I deny that there is any such significance" (Bulgakov, *Comforter*, 131). For Bulgakov, nonetheless, the *filioque* is the fruit of a serious dogmatic imbalance, rooted in "*christocentrism*," that "provides the religio-psychological basis for the possibility of the dogma of the pope as the vicar of Christ, with the idea of the Church clearly centered here on the Second hypostasis (and this is equally, or perhaps even more so, the case in Protestantism)" (ibid., 131–32). Without referring to Bulgakov, Michael Fahey, SJ, argues, rightly in my view, that "the idea that somehow the West is exclusively Christomonist in its faith and practice is a flight of fancy. As far as functional or 'economical' pneumatology is concerned, there exists a shared faith [between East and West] even to our day" (Fahey, "Son and Spirit: Divergent Theologies between Constantinople and the West," in *Conflicts about the Holy Spirit*, ed. Hans Küng and Jürgen Moltmann [New York: Seabury, 1979], 15–22, at 15, 22). Fahey warns against forming "caricatures of theologies: The West's is philosophic, the East's is mystical, one is kataphatic, the other apophatic, one is liturgical, the other juridical. These sorts of assessments that are still found in manuals of theology simply perpetuate the appalling ignorance of one another's traditions" (ibid., 22).

31. Bulgakov, *Comforter*, 143.

two causes, had not yet been placed at the center of attention (though it had been adumbrated)."[32]

In rejecting the use of causal concepts to depict the procession of the Spirit, Bulgakov admits that some such concepts were in fact employed by the fathers, even in the East. But such concepts, he argues, are not present in the Bible. He remarks rather forcefully, "If we ask if the application of the concept of *cause* and *causality* to Divinity has a justification in the Bible, in the Gospel, in revelation, we must answer: Absolutely not! We find in the Bible only concrete definitions of the hypostases and their interrelations."[33] It might seem that "begetting" and "sending," as well as creating, are causal terms. Given his understanding of causality as inextricably linked to a mechanistic worldview, however, Bulgakov holds that in fact causal terms cannot be applied even analogously to God, since God is eternal and is not within any causal framework, as the Bible makes clear. As Bulgakov remarks, "What can *causal origination in eternity* signify? Can one in general speak here about cause, *aitia* (with the group of derivative concepts, *anaitios, aitiatos*)? This is a rationalistic category that is valid only with reference to this empirical world, but is not applicable to the *Ding an sich*, to Divinity."[34]

Of course, the application of causality to God appears in the fathers, including "the Cappadocians and St. John of Damascus," and indeed "in individual passages of these Fathers this concept received a rather extreme expression as the doctrine of the acquisition of being itself from the Father as cause."[35] But the saving grace, Bulgakov thinks, was that the fathers did

32. Ibid.

33. Ibid., 134. By contrast, John Zizioulas argues that causal origination is necessary, on the ground that the divine freedom is a primary biblical datum: "The reason why the Cappadocian Fathers introduced the idea of causation into Trinitarian theology was precisely in order to safeguard freedom in the emergence of the Trinitarian persons. As Gregory of Nazianzen argued, Trinitarian life must not be understood as the natural overflowing of a crater; it should be attributed to personal freedom. Only if personal existence is due to a person—and not some impersonal natural factor—can it be free. We cannot, therefore, drop the idea of causality in Trinitarian life without risking the loss of freedom in Trinitarian existence" (Zizioulas, "Trinitarian Freedom: Is God Free in Trinitarian Life?," in Maspero and Woźniak, *Rethinking Trinitarian Theology*, 200). Zizioulas rejects the view that "all three divine persons cause each other's personal existence," and he strongly defends the Father's monarchy (ibid.). He adds, "The debate about the *Filioque* demonstrated the personalistic approach to monotheism, which characterized the Trinitarian theology of the Greek theologians. Two 'causes' would mean two Gods" (ibid., 201); cf. his essays "The Father as Cause: Personhood Generating Otherness" and "Pneumatology and the Importance of the Person: A Commentary on the Second Ecumenical Council," in *Communion and Otherness: Further Studies in Personhood and the Church*, ed. Paul McPartlan (London: T&T Clark, 2006), 113–54 and 178–205).

34. Bulgakov, *Comforter*, 134.

35. Ibid. In "Trinitarian Freedom," Zizioulas is responding to Aristotle Papanikolaou's engagement with his work in Papanikolaou, *Being with God: Trinity, Apophaticism, and*

not try to specify the concept further. In Bulgakov's view, the application of causality to generation and procession "was never logically polished by them, but was used descriptively for the most part, alongside other expressions, which refer to the Father as root (*rhiza*), source (*pēgē*), principle (*archē*), and cause (*aitia*)."[36] What Bulgakov has in mind when he speaks of causality seems to be largely the modern, Newtonian conception of cause (through which lens he reads Aristotle), since otherwise it would be difficult to explain his claim that, generally speaking, "antiquity did not put any emphasis on the category of causality."[37] Yet even with this clarification, the weakness of his case is demonstrated by his repeated appeal to the fathers' "imprecision" of language whenever he faces the fact that the fathers describe "the interrelations of the hypostases by the concept of causality."[38]

When did the concept of causality become a real problem? Bulgakov blames scholasticism, whose roots he finds in the patristic period, especially John Damascene. Arguing that the problem consists in understanding procession (and generation) "in the sense of the causal origination (or '*productio*') of one hypostasis from another as from its cause (*aitia, causa*) or principle (*archē, principium*)," Bulgakov observes that "in the East, this conception of the

---

Divine-Human Communion (Notre Dame: University of Notre Dame Press, 2006), 148–54. Papanikolaou himself is drawing upon, and partly agreeing with, a criticism originally lodged by T. F. Torrance (and seconded by Alan Torrance): see T. F. Torrance, *The Christian Doctrine of God: One Being Three Persons* (Edinburgh: T&T Clark, 1996), 180–93; Alan J. Torrance, *Persons in Communion: An Essay on Trinitarian Descriptions and Human Participation, with Special Reference to Volume One of Karl Barth's Church Dogmatics* (Edinburgh: T&T Clark, 1996). For T. F. Torrance, the Cappadocians' theology of the Father's monarchy destroys the equality and unity of the persons, by subordinating the Son and Spirit and attributing freedom (in its deepest sense) only to the Father. For discussion of T. F. Torrance's and Alan Torrance's debate with Zizioulas, see Ralph Del Colle, "'Person' and 'Being' in John Zizioulas' Trinitarian Theology: Conversations with Thomas Torrance and Thomas Aquinas," *Scottish Journal of Theology* 54 (2001): 70–86. Like Bulgakov, the Torrances propose eliminating causality from the doctrine of the Trinity. (T. F. Torrance also holds that the being of the Father, not the person, is the source of the processions of the Son and Spirit.) For his part, Papanikolaou argues for the equal causality of all three persons: "if the Son and the Spirit are to be on an equal footing with the Father in terms of freedom, then they must 'cause' the Father's existence as much as the Father is the cause of their existence. . . . By extending the notion of causality to the three persons, the act of freedom to affirm God's existence as trinitarian is one attributable to all three persons rather than simply one person" (Papanikolaou, *Being with God*, 151).

36. Bulgakov, *Comforter*, 134.

37. Ibid.

38. Ibid., 135. Michel René Barnes points out that the term "homoousios" was originally bound up with causal origination: "For Athanasius and the Greeks he influenced, *homoousios* was a unique and one-way predicate statement: one could and should say 'the Son is *homoousios* with the Father' but one could not meaningfully or piously say 'the Father is *homoousios* with the Son'" (Barnes, "Latin Trinitarian Theology," in Phan, *The Cambridge Companion to the Trinity*, 70–83, at 77).

Holy Trinity as bound by causal origination from the Father received the right of citizenship thanks to a doctrine that considers the Father to be *anaitiatos* (uncaused) while being the *aitia* (cause) of the other hypostases, who are *aitiatoi* (caused)."[39] Basil the Great was responsible for introducing this notion of *aitia*, and John Damascene popularized it more widely, to the degree that it came to seem a "clear and self-evident" concept.[40]

Under the influence of Damascene, we find (according to Bulgakov) the spread of a mechanistic numeration of the two processions or "originations," which are in fact divine and thus beyond numeration. The consequence is that "the First hypostasis is thus understood not as the concrete image of the Father, the Engenderer of the Son and the Spirator of the Holy Spirit, but as the 'Principle, Source, and Cause' (St. John of Damascus), from which the Second and Third hypostases get Their very being (*auto to einai*), Their existence (*huparxin*)."[41] In Bulgakov's view, this misunderstanding plagues both pro- and anti-*filioque* controversialists from Photius onward, with the result that "this millennium-and-a-half logomachy pertaining to the procession of the Holy Spirit was totally fruitless."[42] Both East and West separated

39. Bulgakov, *Comforter*, 132–33. Lucas Francisco Mateo-Seco observes regarding causality and the order of origin in Basil, "Basil deduces the necessity for the generation of the Word to be eternal, and consequently, that order in the Trinity is not to be taken as a before and after, but as an order that comes from 'causality': the Father and the Son are co-eternal, but the Father is the first Person, because He truly engenders the Son, and the Son is the second Person, because He is truly engendered by the Father" (Mateo-Seco, "The Paternity of the Father and the Procession of the Holy Spirit: Some Historical Remarks on the Ecumenical Problem," in Maspero and Woźniak, *Rethinking Trinitarian Theology*, 69–102, at 84). As John Zizioulas says, causality cannot here mean that "the Father exists as Father prior to his relationship with the Son (and the Spirit). There is no such an entity as a person prior—and therefore given—to the Son and the Spirit, since the Father himself emerges in and through his relationship (communion) with them" (Zizioulas, "Trinitarian Freedom," 203).

40. Bulgakov, *Comforter*, 133.

41. Ibid., 134.

42. Ibid., 129. For the decisive work of Photius, Patriarch of Constantinople in the years 858–867 and 877–886, see Saint Photios, *The Mystagogy of the Holy Spirit*, trans. Joseph P. Farrell (Brookline, MA: Holy Cross Orthodox Press, 1987). For historical background to the controversy, see Karl Christian Felmy, "The Development of the Trinity Doctrine in Byzantium (Ninth to Fifteenth Centuries)," in Emery and Levering, *The Oxford Handbook of the Trinity*, 210–22, at 212–18; Richard Haugh, *Photius and the Carolingians: The Trinitarian Controversy* (Belmont, MA: Nordland, 1975); John Meyendorff, *Byzantine Theology: Historical Trends and Doctrinal Themes* (New York: Fordham University Press, 1974), 91–94; Oberdorfer, *Filioque*, 151–64. See also Farrell's anti-Augustinian introduction to his translation of Photius's work: Farrell, "A Theological Introduction to the Mystagogy of Saint Photios," in *The Mystagogy of the Holy Spirit*, 17–56. Farrell concludes, "This is the bottom line: there are two opposing and mutually contradictory views of God at work in the controversy. The *filioque* would have it that God is perfectly capable of definition, that there is some degree of logical necessity in Him" (ibid., 47). For more balanced analysis, see Andrew Louth, "Photios as a Theologian," in

themselves from what Bulgakov considers to be the fundamental principle of trinitarian (rather than causality-centered) theology, namely that "fatherhood, sonship, and procession are not modes of origination. In general, they refer not to origination but to the concrete interrelations of the equi-eternal hypostases."[43] Bulgakov sums up his constructive position: "The fact of the matter is that the hypostases, supra-eternal and equi-eternal, do not have any *origin*. For their being they do not need relations of origination, and in particular those according to opposition. They are subjects of relations, as related to each other, but they are in no wise these relations themselves."[44]

For Bulgakov, it is Athanasius and the Cappadocians who display the salutary patristic desire to provide "not a dyadic theology, which divides the Holy Trinity into two dyads, but a triadic theology, which establishes concrete trinitarian interrelationships, even if on the basis of the monarchy of the Father."[45] Bulgakov determines that unlike the subordinationist theologies of Origen and Tertullian, Athanasius rejects "the doctrine of the two-stage origination of the hypostases," so that "the problem of the *origination* of the Holy Spirit as such remains totally *outside* the field of vision of St. Athanasius and his problematic."[46] Basil admittedly considers the Father to be "cause," but Bulgakov is able to conclude that the Cappadocians "never divided the

---

Byzantine Style, Religion, and Civilization, ed. Elizabeth M. Jeffreys (Cambridge: Cambridge University Press, 2006), 206–23; Andreas Andreopoulos, "The Holy Spirit in the Ecclesiology of Photios of Constantinople," in Twomey and Rutherford, *Holy Spirit in the Fathers of the Church*, 151–63. See also the concerns raised about Photios's approach in Olivier Clément, *L'essor du christianisme oriental* (Paris: Presses Universitaires de France, 1964), 5–22. John Anthony McGuckin approves of Photios's criticism of Augustine for undermining the Father's monarchy in communicating his being to the Son and Spirit; see McGuckin, "The Holy Trinity as the Dynamic of the World's Salvation in the Greek Fathers," in *The Holy Trinity in the Life of the Church*, ed. Khaled Anatolios (Grand Rapids: Baker Academic, 2014), 65–77, at 73.

43. Bulgakov, *Comforter*, 128.

44. Ibid., 127. Bulgakov argues that we must "emancipate the dogmatic doctrine from the imaginary problematic of *procession as origination*" (ibid., 146).

45. Ibid., 77.

46. Ibid., 78. Michel Barnes points out that

    Montanism leads Tertullian to stress the continuing role of the Holy Spirit as the source of prophecy, inspiration, and ecstatic revelation, but unlike Athenagoras, Theophilus, and Irenaeus, Tertullian does not describe the Holy Spirit as co-creator, which is a very important omission. A second omission, inherited from Irenaeus, is a weak account of the generation of the Holy Spirit. From the late second century onward aetiological accounts play a fundamental role in Christian trinitarian theology, and the lack of a causal model for describing the Spirit's origin translates into a weak sense of the Holy Spirit's relationship to God the Father. (Conversely, the "high" pneumatologies of the late fourth century all articulate accounts of the Holy Spirit's origin.) A third reason for Tertullian's weak pneumatology is that in his account of the incarnation, "Spirit" names the second person who is joined with human flesh in Mary's womb. The exegetical result of this judgment is that any Old Testament "high" description of God's Spirit is

Holy Trinity into two dyads on the basis of origination, the dyads of the Father and the Son and the Father and the Holy Spirit. On the contrary, they understood this interrelation in a trinitarian manner."[47] Despite their imprecise language, then, the Cappadocians and Athanasius are on the right side, the side of a fully trinitarian account of the hypostases.[48]

By contrast, Augustine represents "a wholly different direction in the doctrine of the procession of the Holy Spirit."[49] Bulgakov follows Théodore de Régnon in interpreting Augustine's trinitarian theology as beginning with the divine essence or nature, with the persons then arising "in the one nature by an interrelationship."[50] By equating the divine nature with the Father, Augustine gains something comparable to, but not equivalent with, the Eastern emphasis on the Father's monarchy. Augustine works out the Holy Spirit's procession from the Father and the Son in terms of Love and Gift: as the love that unites the Father and Son, and as their common gift, the Holy Spirit proceeds from both. In begetting the Son, the Father gives the Son all that he (the Father) is except paternity; thus if the Spirit proceeds from the Father, the Spirit also proceeds from the Son, even if it is from the Father that the Spirit *principally* proceeds. Having summarized this position, Bulgakov notes that "it is hard to reduce Augustine's doctrine of the procession of the Holy Spirit to a totally coherent theologeme."[51] As the "progenitor of the *entire* Western theory of the procession of the Holy Spirit," Augustine changed the entire course of trinitarian theology by focusing it on the *filioque* and thus, necessarily, on causal relations of origin.[52]

---

taken to refer to the Son, and not, as we would expect, to the third person of the Trinity. (Barnes, "Latin Trinitarian Theology," 75–76)

See also Barnes's "Irenaeus's Trinitarian Theology," *Nova et Vetera* 7 (2009): 67–106; Anthony Briggman, *Irenaeus of Lyons and the Theology of the Holy Spirit* (Oxford: Oxford University Press, 2012); Brian Gaybba, *The Spirit of Love: Theology of the Holy Spirit* (London: Geoffrey Chapman, 1987), 36–50.

47. Bulgakov, *Comforter*, 80.

48. Here Lewis Ayres's cautionary remark is apropos, even though he has Bulgakov's opponent Georges Florovsky in view: "I do not think that a dialogue between Latin theology and Greek (or Russian) theology can any longer be understood as one between two distinct traditions known in their essences by particular and secure tokens. If we are to think about the engagement between Greek and Latin theology, we must always ask ourselves about the origins of any particular unitary vision of Greek tradition, and we must be careful to offer precision about which text or theologian or particular part of Greek tradition we seek to bring into dialogue" (Ayres, "Into the Cloud of Witnesses: Catholic Trinitarian Theology Beyond and Before Its Modern 'Revivals,'" in Maspero and Woźniak, *Rethinking Trinitarian Theology*, 4–25, at 20).

49. Bulgakov, *Comforter*, 87.

50. Ibid., 88.

51. Ibid., 90.

52. Ibid. For Bobrinskoy, Augustine is somewhat excused because in his theology "the *filioque* remains the expression of a personal and hence provisional theological investigation; his

Although Bulgakov is not enthusiastic about Augustine, he does not blame the emergence of theological rationalism on Augustine's effort (in the words of Theodore Stylianopolous) to "explain the matter of the generation of the Son and the manner of the procession of the Spirit in rational terms."[53] For Bulgakov, theological rationalism instead takes its full shape in the early scholastic period and has a distortive effect both in the West and in the East. The full flowering of rationalism awaits Thomas Aquinas, since Bulgakov finds Aquinas to be the theologian par excellence of mechanistic causality.[54]

---

psychological analogies have only an illustrative character" (Bobrinskoy, "*Filioque* Yesterday and Today," 138). He warns more strongly against Anselm and Aquinas: "What, in Augustine, only had an illustrative character, became a systematic criterion of later theological thought, with Anselm and in Thomism. This view reflects a profound knowledge of the psychological domains, and thereby tries to have access to the divine Mystery. It is an essentialist vision which, from the outset, moves from the vision of the One God to elaborate a doctrine of the Trinity" (Bobrinskoy, *Mystery of the Trinity*, 284).

53. Stylianopoulos, "Filioque," 200. Stylianopoulos states, "The crucial difference seems to be that, despite his own repeated reservations, Augustine seems to try to explain the Trinity as a metaphysical problem; he thinks that he could possibly explain the matter of the generation of the Son and the manner of the procession of the Spirit in rational terms" (ibid.). The key point for Stylianopoulos is that the Cappadocians rightly did not dare to try to explain how it is that the Son and Spirit differ. They simply asserted it and employed a word to describe it, namely ἐκπόρευσις. Stylianopoulos finds that Augustine "committed an unsuspecting but fateful error by Cappadocian criteria, i.e., confusing in a modalistic way the persons of the Father and the Son, an error which stands in its specificity in irreducible conflict with the conciliar principle of the 'monarchy' of the Father and therefore should be removed from the Nicene Creed on theological as well as canonical grounds" (ibid., 216). In Stylianopoulos's view, had Augustine understood the council's use of ἐκπορευόμενον, then "Augustine, without violating his own presuppositions, could have speculated, theoretically speaking, that the Spirit 'is' from the Father and is 'eternally breathed' by the Father 'through' the Son" (ibid., 231n70). See also Stylianopoulos's suggestion in his "The Orthodox Position" that theologians in the West "must reflect on whether the Augustinian premise of rationally explaining the data of faith has not in part led western theology, either in its scholastic or modern liberal forms, to subtle but deep shifts away from the spirit and authority of Scripture and the Catholic tradition" (Stylianopoulos, "The Orthodox Position," in Küng and Moltmann, *Conflicts about the Holy Spirit*, 23–30, at 30).

54. See also Sergius Bulgakov, *The Bride of the Lamb*, trans. Boris Jakim (Grand Rapids: Eerdmans, 2002), 204–31, where he seeks the intellectual roots of the Augustinian-Thomistic doctrine of predestination and finds these roots in the application to God of the doctrine of causality. For Bulgakov, "God is not the cause of the world, but its Creator. Causal connection is valid only within the *limits* of the creaturely world, as its particular, concrete determination. It cannot be applied outside the creaturely world for determining this world's origin and correlation with the Creator (the causal connection encounters here the barbed-wire barriers of Kant's cosmological antinomy). Moreover, even when applied to the world, the category of causality has a limit, since human freedom and creative activity operate there, interacting with causality. The world does not have a cause, since it is created; and *God is not the cause of the world and not a cause in the world, but its Creator and Provider*. God's creative act is not the mechanical causation through Himself of the world's being" (ibid., 221–22). See also his discussion of Aquinas on the doctrine of creation (ibid., 19–79). Bulgakov's interpretation of

In spelling out his concerns, Bulgakov centers his attention upon a relatively lengthy quotation from Aquinas's *Summa theologiae* I, question 36, article 2. In this passage, Aquinas argues that if the relation of the Son were to the Father alone, and the relation of the Spirit to the Father alone, then these two relations would not be distinct: there would be no way of distinguishing the Son from the Spirit. Bulgakov finds this to be a rather brazen rationalizing of an ineffable mystery. The rationalism follows from the *filioque*'s distortive reduction of trinitarian theology to dyadic processions based on causal origination. Bulgakov comments on Aquinas's text, "Here, with full certainty, the doctrine of the Filioque is a logical consequence postulated from the doctrine of the hypostases as relations of origination; and the source of this doctrine is not revelation but scholastic theology with its erroneous conclusions, so that one wishes to say to it: hands off!"[55]

Bulgakov adds two more quotations from Aquinas, from question 36, article 4, and question 29, article 4, respectively. These quotations assure Bulgakov that Aquinas grounds his doctrine of the Holy Spirit upon a philosophical theory of opposed relations of origin; this confirms the point made in question 36, article 2, and shows that Aquinas seeks to understand the divine persons by means of Aristotle rather than by means of the content of divine revelation. Secondly, unlike the relations with which Aristotle was concerned, a relation in God cannot be a mere "accident" in a subject, but must be none other than the divine essence itself, since whatever is in God, is God. Bulgakov finds here a summation of the consequences of Augustinian essentialism mingled with Aristotelian rationalism. For Aquinas, Bulgakov supposes, "In the impersonal and pre-personal *Divinitas*, persons originate from relations in the capacity of substantial accidents, the ontological priority belonging to this *Divinitas*, whereas the persons appear in the capacity of accidents, although substantial ones."[56] Drawing out the implications of his critique of Aquinas and scholasticism, Bulgakov concludes, "The Filioque attempts to connect the Second and Third hypostases by a relation of causal origination, but this attempt is unsuccessful, for the two dyads, the dyad of the Father and the Son and the dyad of Father-Son and the Holy Spirit, remain separate. In other words, the *causal* interpretation inevitably destroys the triunity of the Holy Trinity."[57]

Aquinas is consistently governed by the view that "as his point of departure, Thomas Aquinas takes not the Christian dogma of the personal, trihypostatic God, but Aristotle's impersonal divinity" (ibid., 19).

55. Bulgakov, *Comforter*, 122. In my view, it is through the mistake of reading only the *respondeo* that the charge of rationalism gains traction, since in the *respondeo* Aquinas simply assumes the scriptural and conciliar points that he makes in his answers to the objections.

56. Ibid., 123.

57. Ibid., 138.

Having rejected causality and subsisting relation, what does Bulgakov advocate positively? In his view, "All the hypostases supra-eternally posit themselves in defining themselves; and the self-definition of each of them includes and presupposes not only a distinct and personal but also a trihypostatic self-definition."[58] Bulgakov recognizes that this means positing a Son who is begotten precisely in giving "Himself for this revelation of the Father."[59] As he goes on to explain, "None of the hypostases is *produced* by any other, such as the Father, the Son, or the Holy Spirit; but each defines, qualifies, or 'produces' Itself: the Father is the image of Paternal sacrificial love, the Son is sacrificial Filial love, the Holy Spirit is the exultant love of the Holy Spirit."[60] This "aseity," which cuts against the grain of the traditional ways of understanding generation and procession, does not mean, of course, that the hypostases are self-sufficient or autonomous. On the contrary, says Bulgakov, "The Holy Trinity is the *trinitarian* act of the self-definition of the hypostases; and each of the elements of this trinitarity, despite the aseity and equi-divinity of the three hypostases, is *correlative* to the other two hypostases and in this sense is conditioned by them."[61]

Bulgakov adds that those who follow the *filioque* doctrine, perfected systematically by Aquinas, inevitably import a "hypostatic subordinationism of the ontological type."[62] This is found even in the *filioque* itself, where the Son is the "principle" in a lesser way than the Father, since the Father is unbegotten whereas the Son is begotten. According to Bulgakov, the relation of the Holy Spirit to the Father/Son is also profoundly problematic, because the Holy Spirit is not related either to the Father or to the Son, but to a supposed "Father-Son bi-unity."[63]

Bulgakov concludes his reflections on the Thomistic synthesis by noting, "The fundamental defect of the whole of the Catholic triadology, and of the Filioque doctrine in particular, is that it considers the hypostases as relations, and in particular relations of origination by opposition."[64] By putting it this way, Bulgakov seeks to undermine the notion that trinitarian theology should begin with the Father who shares himself entirely in begetting the Son and spirating the Spirit. Bulgakov's critique of Aquinas (and the Augustinian tradition) aims ultimately at changing the way in which the East has traditionally

58. Ibid., 138.
59. Ibid., 136.
60. Ibid., 138.
61. Ibid., 141.
62. Ibid.
63. Ibid., 125.
64. Ibid., 127.

understood generation and procession as the causal origination of the Son and Spirit from the Father.

Vladimir Lossky

Vladimir Lossky shares Bulgakov's negative evaluation of Aquinas's theology of the Holy Spirit.[65] In Lossky's view, the Thomistic *filioque* is grounded in three claims, each of which is faulty: "(1) That relations are the basis of the hypostases, which define themselves by their mutual opposition, the first to the second, and these two together to the third. (2) That two persons represent a non-personal unity, in that they give rise to a further relation of opposition. (3) That in general the origin of the persons of the Trinity therefore is impersonal, having its real basis in the one essence."[66] Lossky deplores this impersonal essentialism, which in his view characterizes Aquinas's approach. He argues that by insisting upon the unity of Father and Son as the principle of spiration, Aquinas undermines the personal distinctiveness of each of the divine persons, especially the Holy Spirit who proceeds from an impersonal unity. Further, Aquinas's Aristotelian emphasis on "relations of opposition" leads him away from the true path of trinitarian theology, namely "relations of origin."

Unlike Bulgakov, Lossky considers that relations of origin are acceptable and indeed necessary for trinitarian theology because they signify only an ineffably diverse "mode of origin": the Father generates the Son and

65. For further discussion of Lossky on the *filioque*, see Papanikolaou, *Being with God*, 65–70; Olivier Clément, *Orient-Occident: Deux passeurs, Vladimir Lossky et Paul Evdokimov* (Geneva: Labor et Fides, 1989), 76–89; Rowan Williams, "The Theology of Vladimir Nikolaievich Lossky: An Exposition and Critique" (PhD diss., Oxford University, 1975), esp. 129–56 for his critique of Lossky's treatment of Aquinas. For Lossky's successful effort to bring Bulgakov's theology under ecclesiastical condemnation, see Paul Valliere, *Modern Russian Theology: Bukharev, Soloviev, Bulgakov; Orthodox Theology in a New Key* (Grand Rapids: Eerdmans, 2000).

66. Vladimir Lossky, "The Procession of the Holy Spirit in Orthodox Trinitarian Doctrine," in *In the Image and Likeness of God*, trans. Edward Every, ed. John H. Erickson and Thomas E. Bird (Crestwood, NY: St. Vladimir's Seminary Press, 1974), 71–96, at 76–77. Gilles Emery, OP, cautions against using the phrase "relation of opposition," which was not used by Aquinas: "In contemporary theology textbooks, one often comes across the phrase 'relation of opposition,' but this formula—which St. Thomas never uses—is inapt. For Thomas, the relations of origin, which by definition include opposition, specify a kind of opposition. These relations involve a special mode of distinction, the kind which the doctrine of the Trinity recognizes in God. So it is preferable to speak of 'relative opposition,' and, when one wants to refer to a pair of relations (such as paternity and filiation), of 'opposed relations'" (Emery, *The Trinitarian Theology of Saint Thomas Aquinas*, trans. Francesca Aran Murphy [Oxford: Oxford University Press, 2011], 99).

spirates the Spirit.[67] In accepting the trinitarian application of the notions of origination and causality, Lossky carefully strips those notions of any sense of temporal priority. He states, "Not only the image of 'cause,' but also such terms as 'production,' 'procession,' and 'origin' ought to be seen as inadequate expressions of a reality which is foreign to all becoming, to all process, to all beginning."[68] He also defends the dyadic model of generation and procession from the Father alone, on the grounds that via the monarchy of the Father, this model preserves the three persons.[69] By comparison,

67. Lossky, "Procession of the Holy Spirit in Orthodox Trinitarian Doctrine," 79. Lossky further observes, "If the Holy Spirit proceeds from the Father alone, this ineffable procession confronts us with the absolute diversity of the three hypostases, excluding all relations of opposition. If He proceeds from the Father and the Son, the relations of origin, instead of being signs of absolute diversity, become determinants of the persons, which emanate from an impersonal principle" (ibid., 87).

68. Ibid., 82. Note also Papanikolaou's observation, influenced by Lossky, that "causality within divine existence does not lead to separation and division that inevitably results within the limits of space and time; divine causality results in distinctions in communion, and eternal event of love and freedom" (Papanikolaou, *Being with God*, 152). In his essay, Lossky goes on to explain (against Bulgakov's position),

> Just as relations of origin mean something different from relations of opposition, so causality is nothing but a somewhat defective image, which tries to express the personal unity which determines the origins of the Son and the Holy Spirit. This unique cause is not prior to his effects, for in the Trinity there is no priority and posteriority. He is not superior to his effects, for the perfect cause cannot produce inferior effects. He is thus the cause of their equality with himself. . . . What the image of causality wishes to express is the idea that the Father, being not merely an essence but a person, is by that very fact the cause of the other consubstantial Persons, who have the same essence as He has. With reference to the Father, causality expresses the idea that He is God-Person, in that He is the cause of other divine persons—the idea that He could not be fully and absolutely Person unless the Son and the Holy Spirit are equal to Him in possession of the same nature and *are* that same nature. (Lossky, "Procession of the Holy Spirit in Orthodox Trinitarian Doctrine," 82–83)

Lossky references Bulgakov's *Le Paraclet* (Paris: Aubier, 1946)—translated as *The Comforter*—only on page 91, where his critique of Bulgakov becomes more direct and clear: "It is not possible to replace the conventional term 'causality' by that of 'manifestation' of the Father—as Fr. Bulgakov has tried to do—without confounding the two planes of thought: that of the existence of the Trinity in itself, and that of existence *ad extra*, in the radiance of the essential glory of God. If the Father is the personal cause of the hypostases, He is also, for that very reason, the principle of their common possession of one and the same nature; and in that sense, He is the 'source' of the common divinity of the Three" (ibid., 91). For Lossky, "manifestation" has to do with the divine energies and thus with the economic plane.

69. Dumitru Stăniloae comments that "the word *alone* (from the Father alone) is not a mere theologoumenon, but a point of faith, since it does no more than express, in another form, the monarchy of the Father which is based on the scriptures and affirmed by all the Fathers of the first Christian centuries. Furthermore, the easterners were forced to make use of the word *alone* in order to reaffirm the monarchy of the Father, as a consequence of the fact that the westerners had begun to use the *filioque* which contradicted this monarchy as it was expressed in the Creed itself" (Stăniloae, "Procession of the Holy Spirit," 175). Like Lossky (and Gregory Palamas),

in his view the *filioque* posits two nonintegrated dyads that confine the Trinity within "the laws of quantitative number."[70] He concludes that the *filioque* makes sense only within an essentialist, monadic understanding of the Trinity.

Not surprisingly, Lossky firmly rejects the conceptual place of "notional acts" and of two processions distinguished *"per modum intellectus* and *per modum voluntatis."*[71] He considers all this to be a gross "philosophical anthropomorphism" that seeks rationalistically to name the hidden Trinity by means of the external acts or energies.[72] He emphasizes that the trinitarian persons are utterly beyond our human philosophical concepts, including knowledge, love, relation, and so forth.[73] This stricture includes such names as "Word" and "Paraclete," as well as "Image," "Love," and "Gift"; such names pertain solely to the "manifesting and energetic aspect of the Trinity" in the divine economy.[74] Regarding the eternal Trinity, Scripture teaches us solely that the Father begets

---

Stăniloae is vigorously opposed to the *filioque*: "Since the *filioque* destroys both the doctrine of the Fathers concerning the monarchy of the Father, and the expression of our common faith in the Creed, we consider it to be placed beyond the border of theologoumena and in the realm of error" (ibid.). In Stăniloae's view, the *filioque* turns the Son into a Father.

70. Lossky, "Procession of the Holy Spirit in Orthodox Trinitarian Doctrine," 87 (cf. 85).

71. Ibid., 86.

72. Ibid. For discussion of Lossky's doctrine of the essence/energies distinction, see Duncan Reid, *Energies of the Spirit: Trinitarian Models in Eastern Orthodox and Western Theology* (Atlanta: Scholars Press, 1997), esp. 46–54, 80–81, 94. See also Lossky's *The Mystical Theology of the Eastern Church*, trans. the members of the Fellowship of St. Alban and St. Sergius (Crestwood, NY: St. Vladimir's Seminary Press, 1976), chap. 4.

73. Thus Lossky remarks, "By the dogma of the *Filioque*, the God of the philosophers and savants is introduced into the heart of the Living God, taking the place of the *Deus absconditus, qui posuit tenebras latibulum suum*. The unknowable essence of the Father, Son, and Holy Spirit receives positive qualifications. It becomes the object of natural theology" (Lossky, "Procession of the Holy Spirit in Orthodox Trinitarian Doctrine," 88). This dimension of Lossky's thought is highlighted by Papanikolaou, *Being with God*, 69–70. Thus Papanikolaou observes, "For Lossky, the rationalization of theology precludes an ascent toward union with God insofar as the truth of God is defined in terms of concepts and propositions and not in terms of union with the living God. . . . For Lossky, apophaticism is the precondition for trinitarian theology, since it alone can secure the antinomy of the unity-in-distinction of God's trinitarian life. A non-apophatic approach, as represented in Aquinas and Bulgakov, collapses the antinomy either in favor of the unity or the diversity" (ibid., 69–70). Yet Papanikolaou cautions, "The problem with Lossky's critique of the *filioque* . . . is that he rejects any speculation on the 'how' of the relations in the Trinity for fear of making hypostatic diversity depend on some thing. Ironically, this rejection runs the risk of depersonalization, the one thing Lossky sought to avoid. The Father as the source of the Trinity implies a rich concept of person as freedom and love, one which Lossky himself attempted to clarify later in his career. But such a notion of person is only possible if ontological status is given to this 'how' of the relations in the Trinity. This notion of person becomes empty when Lossky continues to affirm that the 'relations of origin' only serve to indicate diversity and not explain it" (ibid., 70).

74. Lossky, "Procession of the Holy Spirit in Orthodox Trinitarian Doctrine," 92.

the Son and the Father spirates the Spirit. As Lossky says, emphasizing the need for a strict apophaticism, "Every name except those of Father, Son, and Holy Spirit . . . is inappropriate for designating the special characteristics of the hypostases in the inaccessible existence of the Trinity, and refers rather to the external aspect of God, to His manifestation, or even to His economy."[75]

In sharply critiquing Aquinas, Lossky also criticizes Bulgakov. He argues that a fundamental imbalance appears not only in Aquinas's model but also in Bulgakov's view that the Trinity is the "internal revelation of the hypostases or of the 'Tri-hypostatic subject.'"[76] For Lossky, both Aquinas and Bulgakov break "the equilibrium between essence and hypostases," with Aquinas favoring the essence and Bulgakov favoring the hypostases.[77] Both approaches, then, must be relinquished in favor of a return to the fundamental Cappadocian model of two ineffable modes of origin from the Father.

75. Ibid., 89–90. Here Lossky observes, "Apart from the names denoting the three hypostases and the common name of the Trinity, the innumerable names which we apply to God—the 'divine names' which textbook theology calls his attributes—denote God not in his inaccessible Being but in 'that which surrounds the essence,'" namely the divine energies (ibid., 90). David Guretzki comments that Lossky applies "the concepts of 'procession' and 'generation' to the divine energies only" (Guretzki, *Karl Barth on the Filioque*, 114). For important concerns in this regard, see Marshall, "*Ex Occidente Lux?*," 31–34.

76. Lossky, "Procession of the Holy Spirit in Orthodox Trinitarian Doctrine," 93.

77. Ibid. Lossky adds, "The distinction between the unknowable essence of the Trinity and its energetic processions, clearly defined by the great councils of the fourteenth century, allows Orthodox theology to maintain firmly the difference between tri-hypostatic existence in itself and tri-hypostatic existence in the common manifestation outside the essence. In His hypostatic existence, the Holy Spirit proceeds from the Father alone; and this ineffable procession enables us to confess the absolute diversity of the Three Persons, *i.e.,* our faith in the Tri-Unity. In the order of natural manifestation, the Holy Spirit proceeds from the Father through the Son" (ibid.). He argues that there is doctrinal continuity but not doctrinal development here: "Defense of the doctrine of the procession of the Holy Spirit from the Father alone necessitates a decision as to the import of the phrase διά Υἱοῦ; this in turn opens the way for the distinction between essence and energies. . . .ʹ. One and the same tradition is defended, at different points, by the Orthodox from St. Photius to George of Cyprus to St. Gregory Palamas" (ibid., 94). The Latin thinkers from the early medieval period onward, by contrast, either were ignorant of or rejected the key "distinction between hypostatic existence of the Holy Spirit and eternal manifestation of the divine nature in His person" (ibid., 95). The solution, Lossky thinks, is for Western theologians and laypeople to turn eastward and recognize the fidelity of Byzantine theology to the tradition of the fathers. It is worth noting that Photius, for his part, sought to distance the *filioque* from the Latin fathers: "You call Ambrose, Augustine and other good men your fathers. But does this make it any more tolerable, since you suppose them to be armed against the Master's teaching, to draw the condemnation on yourselves and also on these men? For you certainly assign your own evil reward to the fathers. But it is only the offspring of this novelty which is evil. Your anathema will not pass through you into those blessed men, because not one of your godless and senseless sophisms will be found with them" (Photios, *Mystagogy of the Holy Spirit*, §68, p. 92). Photius grants that Augustine taught the *filioque* in a moment of weakness, but Photius points out that "no one composed of dust and ephemeral nature can avoid some step of defilement" (ibid., §69, p. 93), and so this error should be covered up by filial piety.

Thomas Aquinas on the Holy Spirit's Procession from the Father and the Son

After all this, is Aquinas's theology of the *filioque* worth saving? To compound matters, in writing against the Greek rejection of the *filioque*, Aquinas presumed a faulty understanding of the Greek word ἐκπόρευσις and its cognates. He thought that "processio" adequately translated these words, whereas in fact ἐκπόρευσις pertains solely to the Spirit's relation to the Father as monarchical principle. Furthermore, through his extensive use of Aristotle's doctrine of relation (present, of course, also in Augustine), Aquinas opened up the Latin West more acutely to the charge of philosophizing about an ineffable and inaccessible divine mystery. The criticisms that we found in Bulgakov include the view that emphasis on "opposed relations of origin" is rationalistic and the view that attention to causality and origination is a mistaken use of temporal categories to describe the eternal *perichoresis*. To my mind, Lossky effectively answers these criticisms; his main point is that the Greek fathers used causality and origination to good effect. Lossky's own criticisms of Aquinas's theology of the *filioque* amount to the following:

- the unity of the Father and the Son as one "principle" in spirating the Holy Spirit undermines the ability of theology to affirm the distinctiveness of each person;
- the association of love (and the movement of the will) with the Holy Spirit confuses the energies and the essence, and employs terms from the economy to depict the hidden and utterly ineffable mystery of the person who proceeds from the Father;
- the *filioque* is not biblically attested.

With such criticisms in mind, let us try to understand how Aquinas approaches the name "Holy Spirit" and the *filioque* in question 36 of the *Summa theologiae*. Much depends upon what portrait of the Holy Spirit, and of the spiration of the Spirit, emerges from question 36. Although it will not be possible to address every concern (e.g., Lossky considers the distinction between the essence and energies to be of the utmost importance, but I cannot directly address the essence-energies distinction here[78]), I hope to show that the basic critique put forward both by Lossky and by Bulgakov—namely that the *filioque* is rationalistic—does not do justice to Aquinas's account of this doctrine about the Holy Spirit. The result should be a greater appreciation

---

78. For discussion of the essence-energies distinction, see my *Engaging the Doctrine of Creation: The Wise and Good Creator and His Theophanic, Fallen, and Redeemed Creatures* (Grand Rapids: Baker Academic, forthcoming), chaps. 1 and 2.

for the foundations of Aquinas's theology of the Holy Spirit, and thus of the Spirit's fully personal procession as Love and Gift.

The Name "Holy Spirit"

The first article of *Summa theologiae* I, question 36 inquires into why the Holy Spirit is named "Holy Spirit." In other words, does this name give us any help in understanding the distinctiveness of the third person of the Trinity? Why did God will that the third person be revealed under the name "Holy Spirit"?[79] The objections at the outset of the article suggest that there is in fact no reason. The first objection emphasizes that biblical usage shows that "spirit" names not only the Holy Spirit, but also the Son and the Father. After all, each of the three persons in the one God is holy, and each is spirit (rather than matter). Citing Hilary of Poitiers, the first objection interprets Isaiah 61:1, "The Spirit of the Lord GOD is upon me," as referring to the Father who is spirit. Hilary takes the same approach to Matthew 12:28, where Jesus says, "But if it is by the Spirit of God that I cast out demons, then the kingdom of God has come upon you." Hilary interprets this to be referring to the Son's own power as Son, and thus to the Son as "spirit."[80]

The second objection identifies a further problem: the divine persons cannot be distinguished by substance, and so we understand their distinction in terms of opposed relations of origin, as the relation "Father-Son" (or "Father-Word") teaches us to do. But while the name "Son" obviously implies a relation to the Father who begot him, the name "Holy Spirit" does not evoke any particular relation. Finally, the third objection raises another biblical (or anthropological) problem: the word "spirit" lends itself to misunderstanding because humans possess their own proper spirit. The objector cites Numbers 11:17, where the Lord, preparing to commission the seventy elders, tells Moses, "I will take some of the spirit which is upon you and put it upon them." Moses has a special spirit or charism, and the Lord is going to share this with certain others so that they too can participate in the governance of the people of Israel. Along the same lines, the objector cites 2 Kings 2:15, where certain "sons of the prophets" at Jericho observe that "the spirit of Elijah rests on Elisha." The point here is that just as the Son "cannot be called the Son of this or of that," because he is the Son of the Father, so also the Holy Spirit should have a name that ensures that no one imagines the spirit of Moses or the spirit of Elijah to be the same thing as the Holy Spirit.

---

79. For discussion, see Emery, *Trinitarian Theology of Saint Thomas Aquinas*, 220–25.
80. On Aquinas's use of Hilary in discussing the *filioque*, see Pelikan, "Doctrine of Filioque in Thomas Aquinas and Its Patristic Antecedents," 323–26, 329.

Against these strong objections to the biblical naming of the Holy Spirit, does the *sed contra* of article one offer any help? Aquinas, of course, intends to affirm that the "Holy Spirit" is a good name for the third person of the Trinity—that is, not merely an arbitrary name but a name that helps us to have some understanding of the Spirit's distinctiveness in the Trinity. The *sed contra* quotes one of Augustine's favorite biblical texts, 1 John 5:7, which in Aquinas's version reads "Tres sunt qui testimonium dant in caelo, Pater, Verbum et Spiritus Sanctus [There are three who give testimony in heaven, the Father, the Word, and the Holy Spirit]."[81] This trinitarian formula, known as the "Three Heavenly Witnesses," first appeared in Latin Bibles in the fourth century, although it appears in no Greek Bibles until the fifteenth century. Among modern critical translations, the RSV is typical in adopting the following translation of 1 John 5:7: "And the Spirit is the witness, because the Spirit is the truth." In short, unfortunately, the trinitarian formula found in the *sed contra* cannot now help us much. In the *sed contra* Aquinas also quotes from book 7 of Augustine's *De Trinitate*, where Augustine asks what we should call the three in God. Augustine answers that in order to be able to call them something, the Latins call them three "persons (*personae*)," despite this not being a biblical term.[82]

The *sed contra*, then, defends the usefulness of the name "Holy Spirit" simply on the grounds that Scripture and the theological tradition use it to name the third person. Indeed, the *sed contra* has a salutary spareness: the name "Holy Spirit" is a good one because it has been used in authoritative scriptural and theological texts. Is this approach betrayed, however, by Aquinas's more philosophically minded reflection in his *respondeo* upon the fittingness of the name "Holy Spirit"?

In his *respondeo* Aquinas first notes that, unlike the pairing Father-Son, the name "Holy Spirit" does not evoke a relational image: the second procession in God "has no proper name of its own." Despite this deficiency, the name

81. Presumably he employed the Parisian version of the Vulgate, a version indebted to the editorial work of Alcuin, but scholars have not been able to pin down the precise biblical text used by Aquinas. For background to the history of the Vulgate, see "Preface to the First Edition (1969)," in *Biblia Sacra: Iuxta Vulgatam Versionem*, ed. Robert Weber et al. (Stuttgart: Deutsche Bibelgesellschaft, 1994), xxix–xxxiii.

82. For Aquinas's use of Augustine in discussing the *filioque*, see Pelikan, "Doctrine of Filioque in Thomas Aquinas and Its Patristic Antecedents," 327–31. Pelikan observes that "the identification of the third person of the Trinity with 'amor' was, to put it mildly, far less explicit in the biblical text than was the identification of the second person with 'verbum'; the latter identification was the achievement of the Gospel of John, the former the achievement largely of Augustine. Yet Thomas, together with most of the Western tradition, simply took for granted the validity of this piece of Augustinian trinitarianism" (ibid., 331).

"Holy Spirit" succeeds in showing that the Spirit shares the same nature as the Father and Son, both of whom are holy and spirit. Even more important in Aquinas's view, the name sheds light on the third person by helping us to see that just as the Word's generation can be understood in terms of intellectual similitude, so also the Spirit's procession can be understood in terms of the outward impulse of the rational appetite (love).

Aquinas explains that "the name spirit in things corporeal seems to signify impulse and motion; for we call the breath and the wind by the term spirit." Spirit is the life-force that propels us outward, toward the good that attracts us. As Aquinas remarks, love does the same thing: "It is a property of love to move and impel the will of the lover towards the object loved." Just as "Word" is suitable for generation, then, "Spirit" is particularly suitable for procession, in a manner that links the second procession in God with the rational impulse of love—as befits the first procession's connection with the rational generation of a word.

What about the term "holy"? Why "Holy Spirit" rather than simply "Spirit," since, after all, we do not say "Holy Word" or "Holy Son"? Aquinas states that the good toward which the divine Spirit "moves" is none other than the entire reality of God, just as the Word expresses the entire Godhead. To be ordered to (or in "motion" toward) God is what it means to be "holy." In this way, Aquinas suggests that the analogy from the interior processions of the mind suitably arises not only from the name "Word" but also from the name "Spirit." He concludes that "because the [third] divine person proceeds by way of the love whereby God is loved, that person is most properly named the *Holy Spirit*." In his reply to the second objection, furthermore, Aquinas remarks that the name "Holy Spirit," even if at first glance it does not seem to express a relation (by contrast to "Son" or "Word"), does express a relation if one thinks in terms of breath. In this sense, we breathe forth our "spirit." Where there is "spirit" or "breath," there must be a "spirator," or one who breathes the spirit forth. In Latin the connection is even clearer than it is in English, since the verb for "to breathe" is "spirare." For Aquinas, then, the name "Holy Spirit," like the name "Son," instructs us about the distinctive procession of the divine person.

A Rule of Holy Scripture: The Son Has All the Father Has

Aquinas turns to the issue of the *filioque* in the second article of question 36. It is necessary first to review the seven objections that Aquinas sets forth, so as to see fully what he considers to be at stake here. As we will see, Aquinas considers that his task is not simply to show that without the *filioque* there would be no way of distinguishing between the Son and the Holy Spirit. More important, his task involves asking how Scripture and tradition are authoritative with respect to trinitarian doctrine. The central authority for Aquinas is neither the analogy of the mind nor the philosophical doctrine of substance and relation, but rather is Scripture as interpreted in the tradition.

The first objection gets to the nub of the matter. Aquinas here grants that the procession of the Holy Spirit from the Son is not explicitly taught in Scripture. He also accepts Pseudo-Dionysius's principle, articulated in *The Divine Names*, that we should say nothing about God except what divine revelation, given in Scripture, has expressed about God. In this light, it seems that to adopt the *filioque* would be to fall into rationalism. The objection quotes John 15:26 as evidence that the Spirit proceeds from the Father, since Jesus here says that "when the Counselor [παράκλητος] comes, whom I shall send to you from the Father, even the Spirit of truth, who proceeds from the Father, he will bear witness to me." Aquinas does not challenge the objector by appealing to Jesus's economic sending of the Spirit "from the Father." As he admits in his response to the first objection, "we do not find it verbally [*per verba*] expressed in Holy Scripture that the Holy Spirit proceeds from the Son."

What then is his avenue for defending the *filioque*, since he has accepted that it is not found verbally in Scripture and since (against rationalism) he affirms Pseudo-Dionysius's principle for a scriptural dogmatics? Aquinas's path is to argue that Pseudo-Dionysius's principle does not limit speech about God solely to what Scripture explicitly says. Rather, the principle also allows for what Scripture implicitly says. As Aquinas puts it, the *filioque* is present in Scripture not *per verba* but *per sensum*.

In defense of this view, Aquinas turns to John 16:14, where Jesus says of the Spirit, "He will glorify me, for he will take what is mine and declare it to you." (Aquinas's Latin text reads "Ille me clarificabit, quia de meo accipiet," and the Greek word λήμψεται can mean "take" or "receive.") What is included in Jesus's reference to "what is mine"? The answer, as Aquinas knows, comes in the very next verse, where Jesus adds, "All that the Father has is mine; therefore I said that he will take what is mine and declare it to you." In short, the Son has all that the Father has, with the obvious exception of the Father's paternity.[83]

---

83. For discussion of the use of this passage by Martin Luther and classical Lutheran theologians to validate the *filioque*, see Marshall, "Defense of the *Filioque* in Classical Lutheran Theology," 169–72. For a further biblical argument, see Aquinas's *Commentary on the Gospel of John*, where he notes that Jesus, while stating that the Spirit "proceeds from

On this basis, Aquinas identifies as a "rule of Holy Scripture" the principle that the Son has all that the Father has. In this regard, he also quotes Matthew 11:27: "All things have been delivered to me by my Father; and no one knows the Son except the Father, and no one knows the Father except the Son and any one to whom the Son chooses to reveal him." Aquinas draws the conclusion that other than what is contained in the relational distinction (Father-Son, begetting-begotten), the Son fully has all that the Father has, so that the Son expresses the Father fully. The fullness of the Son's expression of the Father includes even the Father's spiration of the Holy Spirit, so that the Son shares in the Father's spiration of the Spirit. Given that the Son can truly affirm that "all that the Father has is mine," it follows for Aquinas that "when we say that the Holy Spirit proceeds from the Father, even though it be added that He proceeds from the Father alone, the Son would not thereby be at all excluded."[84]

All of this is found in Aquinas's response to the crucial first objection, which makes clear that what is at stake is not a philosophical analogy or philosophical categories (such as opposed relations of origin), but a point of exegetical engagement with what the living God has revealed about himself and has communicated to us in Scripture.[85]

---

the Father" (John 15:26), calls the Spirit "the Spirit of truth" (15:26). Since in John 14:6 Jesus proclaims himself to be the "truth," and since Galatians 4:6 identifies God's Spirit as "the Spirit of his Son," Aquinas reasons that the Spirit, in his eternal procession, "is related both to the Father and the Son." See Thomas Aquinas, *Commentary on the Gospel of John: Chapters 13–21*, trans. Fabian Larcher, OP, and James A. Weisheipl, OP, ed. Daniel Keating and Matthew Levering (Washington, DC: Catholic University of America Press, 2010), no. 2062, p. 127. For discussion of Aquinas's commentary on John 14:6, 15:26, and related texts, with reference to the *filioque*, see Denis-Dominique le Pivain, FSSP, *L'action du saint-Esprit dans le Commentaire de l'Évangile de saint Jean par saint Thomas d'Aquin* (Paris: Téqui, 2006), 69–79.

84. Thus, in view of the Pontifical Council's "Greek and Latin Traditions regarding the Procession of the Holy Spirit," Emmanuel Durand, OP notes that "the Father is not Father except as Father of his Son, and as loving Him. Because of their communion, the Son is inseparable from the Father, even in so far as the Father is principle of the procession of the Holy Spirit, since it unfailingly belongs to the very Person of the Father to love his Son as the proper object of his good pleasure" (Durand, "Perichoresis: A Key Concept for Balancing Trinitarian Theology," in Maspero and Woźniak, *Rethinking Trinitarian Theology*, 177–92, at 188. The same point is made by Jean-Pierre Torrell, OP: "If we suppress in our minds this communion of the Father and the Son, we also suppress the procession of the Holy Spirit, for these two realities are interdependent" (Torrell, *Saint Thomas Aquinas*, vol. 2, *Spiritual Master*, trans. Robert Royal [Washington, DC: Catholic University of America Press, 2003], 187–88).

85. It is also the case, as George Sabra emphasizes, that in arguing for the *filioque* in his *Commentary on the Gospel of John* and his *Summa contra gentiles*, "Thomas introduces certain arguments which infer the eternal procession of the Spirit from the Son from the economic relationship of Christ and the Spirit. Thus, from the notion that the Son *sends* the Spirit, that

In the same response to the first objection Aquinas also employs the philosophical point about opposed relations (*oppositas relationes*), but in a way that makes clear that this philosophical tool, while helpful, is secondary. Specifically, in interpreting Jesus's claim that he has all that the Father has, Aquinas draws upon the philosophical (and patristic) doctrine of relation, since Jesus is describing the relation Father-Son.[86] Aquinas states that "as regards being the principle of the Holy Spirit, the Father and the Son are not opposed to each other, but only as regards the fact that one is the Father, and the other is the Son." It should be clear here that the Father and the Son are not one "principle" as an undifferentiated amalgam: the "one principle" of the Holy Spirit is not just the Father and the Son in their consubstantial unity (the Father and the Son as *one in essence*), but this "one principle" of the Holy Spirit is the Father and the Son in their mutual communion of love (that is, *as one in "spiration,"* a quasi-property common

---

the Son *operates* through the Spirit, that the Father and the Son *give* the Spirit, and that the Son is *manifested* through the Spirit, Thomas concludes that the Spirit proceeds from the Son eternally. . . . This correspondence of the immanent and economic Trinity as far as the procession of the Spirit is concerned means that, for Thomas, the Holy Spirit must always be seen as the Spirit of the Son, eternally as well as temporally" (Sabra, *Thomas Aquinas' Vision of the Church* [Mainz: Matthias Grünewald Verlag, 1987], 80).

86. Gilles Emery points out that far from being original to Aquinas (or even to Augustine), relation was brought into Trinitarian theology right at the start of the Arian crisis. Before the Council of Nicaea, in his Profession of Faith to Alexander of Alexandria, Arius maintained that the Son is not co-eternal with the Father, explaining that: "He did not exist at the same time as the Father, as some have said in speaking of 'relatives' (*ta pros ti*)." Arius' remark is a good indication that, already at the beginning of the fourth century, some Alexandrian Catholics (whose identity remains a tricky question) were using the Aristotelian category of relation to show the co-eternity of the Father and the Son: relative beings are simultaneous; if "Father" and "Son" are indeed mutually related names, then whenever there was a Father, there must have been a Son. But it was left to the Cappadocians to exploit the theory of relation more systematically; the first of them to do so was Basil of Caesarea. In his *Contra Eunomius*, St. Basil made relation a central feature of his argument against radical Arianism. . . . The idea of "opposition" was not discovered in the Middle Ages; it does not even come from the Latin West. As early as Basil of Caesarea, one finds the comment that, under the aspect of the divine substance, there is no opposition between the Father and the Son, but "in so far as one engenders and the other is engendered, one must consider them under the aspect of their opposition (*antithesis*)." (Emery, *Trinitarian Theology of Saint Thomas Aquinas*, 79–80, 98)

This point is significant for responding to Lossky's and (especially) Bulgakov's concerns about Aquinas's use of the doctrine of relation. Emery references Bernard Sesboüé's *Saint Basile et la Trinité: Un acte théologique au IVe siècle* (Paris: Desclée, 1998), 19–53. As Emery goes on to show, Gregory of Nazianzus, Augustine, and Boethius also make use of relation in trinitarian theology. He explains that "Augustine's view that the persons are formally characterized by their mutual relations is an extension of the Cappadocians' theory" (Emery, *Trinitarian Theology of Saint Thomas Aquinas*, 82).

to the Father and the Son, and which the Son receives from the Father in the act of generation).

Changing the Creed: A Theology of Church Councils

The first objection pertains to Scripture; the second pertains to the creed and to conciliar decrees. Although Aquinas is unaware of the Spirit-specific signification of ἐκπόρευσις, he knows of course that the Latin church changed the Creed of Constantinople. He observes in the second objection, therefore, that adding something to the creed—like inventing things about the Spirit with no scriptural basis—seems surely to be anathema. The question then is whether and by whom the creed can be changed.[87]

How are we to interpret past councils, and who is to interpret them? What is the means of arriving at a definitive interpretation of a past council? For Aquinas, the answer is found in Constantinople itself, which provided a definitive interpretation of Nicea. Constantinople shows that one means of interpreting a past council is, under the guidance of the Holy Spirit, a further council. This is not a vicious circle, but instead it simply indicates that the church is alive; a living church cannot help but continually interpret its past, and a primary way of doing that is through councils.[88] The East, of course, privileges the seven ecumenical councils, after which it does not recognize any further ecumenical councils.[89] But the East continues to have

87. In Theodore Stylianopoulos's view, those who change the creed can rightly do so only from the perspective of the specific theology that informed the creed, in this case the theology of the Cappadocians; see Stylianopoulos, "Filioque." Aquinas would grant that we need to know Cappadocian theology. But in his view, the fundamental issue is the church's ability to teach over the centuries, given that new controversies are continually arising. If each new church council had to wait for the most up-to-date and consensual historical research regarding all the earlier councils, then the church would be sorely pressed ever to teach anything.

88. As Michael Fahey says, "The West reasoned that since the Church is a living society it can never renounce its mission to preserve intact the treasury of divine revelation. So that if it decided that it was pastorally expedient to add some words that did not distort the faith, indeed words that preserved the true faith, then this was not innovating but simply continuing a process begun at earlier councils. It is true that this reasoning remained at first implicit and became the subject of explicit reflection only after Byzantine objections to the addition of *Filioque*" (Fahey, "Son and Spirit," 20).

89. For discussion of the enumeration and nature of "ecumenical councils" from an Eastern Catholic perspective, see Petro B. T. Bilaniuk, *Theology and Economy of the Holy Spirit: An Eastern Approach* (Bangalore: Dharmaram, 1980), chap. 7: "The Holy Spirit and the Ecumenical Councils." Note, however, the strong concerns of Boris Bobrinskoy, building upon A. S. Khomiakov: "It is perhaps the slavophile theologian A. Khomiakov who has uncompromisingly formulated this consciousness of the Orthodox Church of having been subjected to a real *moral fratricide* through the dogmatic constraint exercised down the centuries. Only the whole and unanimous Church has the right to define new dogmas or to

local councils of various kinds at which important matters of interpretation are decided.[90] And the West, for its part, does not fail to give a privileged position to the first seven councils; they remain at the heart of the most important elements of Christian faith, namely the identity of Jesus Christ and of the Triune God.

The key point for Aquinas is that since under the Spirit's guidance council interprets council, subsequent councils can and should interpret Constantinople and its creed. Indeed, subsequent councils have done so and have determined that the affirmation of the Spirit proceeding from the Father and the Son does not undermine what Constantinople was affirming regarding the person of the Spirit. The additions made by subsequent councils do not negate the original creed, let alone change the apostolic deposit of faith. Rather, they belong to the process by which the church professes the faith of the original creed in light of new challenges and concerns.[91] The best example of this process, Aquinas suggests, is Constantinople itself. As he states, "Hence in the decision of the council of Chalcedon it is declared that those who were congregated together in the council of Constantinople, handed down the doctrine about the Holy Spirit, not implying that there was anything wanting in the doctrine of their predecessors who had gathered together at Nicaea, but explaining what those fathers had understood of the matter."[92]

---

modify the symbol of faith. By arrogating this right to itself, one part of the Church 'was destroying the equality of rights between the various communities, and the central importance of unity of spirit and love, on which were based all the concepts of the primitive Christian community.' 'This pride of the separated Churches, who have had the effrontery to alter the Creed of the whole Church without the consent of their brethren, was not inspired by love: it was a crime before God and before Holy Church. And how can the faith, the truth, survive intact, where love has been impoverished?'" (Bobrinskoy, "The *Filioque* Yesterday and Today," 139, citing texts found in A. Gratieux, *A. S. Khomiakov et le movement slavophile*, vol. 2 [Paris: Cerf, 1939], 83, 86). Yet, I cannot imagine that the church has been left at any stage without dogmatic teaching authority, at least in the Catholic sense of "dogma." In addition, despite the sins (on all sides) that have produced scandalous divisions, it remains necessary to defend the church's unity, as I do in chap. 6, without denying that this unity urgently needs to be increased and perfected.

90. See, for example, Hyacinthe Destivelle, OP, *The Moscow Council (1917–1918): The Creation of the Conciliar Institutions of the Russian Orthodox Church*, ed. Michael Plekon and Vitaly Permiakov, trans. Jerry Ryan (Notre Dame, IN: University of Notre Dame Press, 2014).

91. See John Henry Newman, *An Essay on the Development of Christian Doctrine*, 6th ed. (Notre Dame, IN: University of Notre Dame Press, 1989); Jaroslav Pelikan, *The Christian Tradition: A History of the Development of Doctrine*, 5 vols. (Chicago: University of Chicago Press, 1971–1989). See also chap. 6 of Levering, *Engaging the Doctrine of Revelation*.

92. I, q. 36, a. 2, ad 2. See Christopher Kaczor, "Thomas Aquinas on the Development of Doctrine," *Theological Studies* 62 (2001): 283–302.

We do not here have an instance of refusal to take Constantinople seriously as a historical phenomenon, nor do we have a rationalistic procedure whereby certain claims about relation and causality dictate the interpretation of Constantinople.[93] On the contrary, Aquinas argues on the basis of the history of the councils, in which he finds Chalcedon commenting upon Constantinople, and Constantinople commenting upon and augmenting Nicaea. Assuming the operation of the Holy Spirit, we need not imagine the Nicene fathers themselves being able to spell out all that the later Council of Constantinople said; we need simply imagine the Nicene fathers as being able to arrive at these conclusions (such as the Spirit's divinity) had the Nicene fathers been present at the Council of Constantinople.

Admittedly, Aquinas is only vaguely aware of the historical circumstances that prompted the church in the West, in response to "Arian" views, to affirm the *filioque*. He comments solely that "because at the time of the ancient councils the error of those who said that the Holy Spirit did not proceed from the Son had not arisen," the fathers of the first few ecumenical councils did not address the issue; whereas "later on, when certain errors rose up, in another council assembled in the west, the matter was explicitly defined by the authority of the Roman Pontiff, by whose authority also the ancient councils were summoned and confirmed."[94] He does not state which specific council addressed the problem, perhaps because he was unsure.[95] For his part, Siecienski points to the late fourth-century creed of Pope Damasus, which affirmed that the Holy Spirit proceeds "from the Father and the Son," and whose aim was simply to affirm the Holy Spirit's full divinity.[96] Siecienski explains that "the *Decretum Gelasianum* (*Explanatio fidei*), or at least the first three chapters, is thought by some to be the work of the Roman Synod of 382 also held under Damasus," although the section of the *Decretum Gelasianum* that defends the *filioque* is often thought to be a later interpolation.[97] The *Decretum Gelasianum* contains the two crucial biblical texts cited by Aquinas in question 36, article 2, objection (and reply) 1: John 15:26 and John 16:14. Siecienski observes that the relevant section from the *Decretum Gelasianum* "became an important prooftext

93. This is especially so in light of the fact, demonstrated by Emery, that the Cappadocians (whose theology was influential at Constantinople) used relation in their trinitarian theology.

94. I, q. 36, a. 2, ad 2.

95. See Gilles Emery, OP, "The Procession of the Holy Spirit *a Filio* according to St. Thomas Aquinas," in *Trinity in Aquinas*, trans. Teresa Bede et al., 2nd ed. (Ann Arbor, MI: Sapientia Press of Ave Maria University, 2006), 209–69, at 247–48.

96. Siecienski, *Filioque*, 56.

97. Ibid., 57.

in later pro-*filioque florilegia*, especially given its (alleged) acceptance by a Roman synod."[98]

Aquinas's claim that "in another council assembled in the west, the matter was explicitly defined by the authority of the Roman Pontiff," introduces another principle regarding the interpretation of a past council, namely the role of the bishop of Rome. This papal role, however, does not take away from the fact that Aquinas's emphasis here remains focused upon later councils authoritatively interpreting earlier councils. His interpretation of what later councils were doing, and of whether later councils (let alone popes) possessed authority to make decisions for the whole church, is obviously contestable.[99] But far from following a rationalistic path, it is Scripture as interpreted by church councils that is determinative for Aquinas.

The Perfection of the Holy Spirit's Procession

Of the remaining objections in article 2 of question 36, the most significant are the fourth, sixth, and seventh. Before turning my attention to these

98. Ibid. Siecienski concludes, "Authentic or not, it provides evidence that Latin theology already by the later fourth century was moving toward a particular way of understanding the biblical truth that the Holy Spirit was 'Spirit of the Son'" (ibid.).

99. For his part, Karl Barth observes, "Some in the older Protestant theology (e.g., J. Cocceius, *S. theol.*, 1662, 12, 8) might occasionally judge that it had been a mistake for the Roman Church to alter the creed when Leo III had solemnly endorsed it in its ancient form—the business is not in fact a shining testimonial to the Roman Catholic theory of the certainty of the Church's teaching authority as concentrated in the hands of the pope. . . . Both Lutheran and Reformed, however, were almost completely unanimous that materially we should accept this decision even though it was reached in so unusual a way, apart from either council or pope" (Barth, *Church Dogmatics* I/1, 2nd ed., trans. G. W. Bromiley, ed. G. W. Bromiley and T. F. Torrance [Edinburgh: T&T Clark, 1975], 478). For Barth the key point is that

> statements about the divine modes of being antecedently in themselves cannot be different in content from those that are to be made about their reality in revelation. . . . In connexion with the specific doctrine of the Holy Spirit this means that He is the Spirit of both the Father and the Son not just in His work *ad extra* and upon us, but that to all eternity—no limit or reservation is possible here—He is none other than the Spirit of both the Father and the Son. "And the Son" means that not merely for us, but in God Himself, there is no possibility of an opening and readiness and capacity for God in man—for this is the work of the Holy Ghost in revelation—unless it comes from Him, the Father, who has revealed Himself in His Word, in Jesus Christ, and also, and no less necessarily, from Him who is His Word, from His Son, from Jesus Christ, who reveals the Father. Jesus Christ as the Giver of the Holy Spirit is not without the Father from whom He, Jesus Christ, is. But the Father as the Giver of the Holy Spirit is also not without Jesus Christ to whom He Himself is the Father. The Eastern doctrine does not contest the fact that this is so in revelation. (ibid., 479–80)

Barth goes on to say quite strongly, "If the Spirit is also the Spirit of the Son only in revelation and for faith, if He is only the Spirit of the Father in eternity, i.e., in His true and original reality, then the fellowship of the Spirit between God and man is without objective ground or content" (ibid., 481).

objections, however, let me briefly review the third and fifth objections. The third is a quotation from John of Damascus in which Damascene affirms that the Holy Spirit is from the Father and denies that the Holy Spirit is from the Son. The authority of Damascene is obviously a respected one for Aquinas, but in this case Aquinas suggests that Damascene's opinion—if it is true (Aquinas adds) that Damascene was intending to deny the *filioque*—derives from a Nestorian creed that, among other things, denied the *filioque* and was condemned at the Council of Ephesus. Aquinas is working with faulty historical information here: Siecienski observes that "the council of Ephesus had approved certain portions of the Nestorian creed presented by the priest Charisius, including the statement that 'the Holy Spirit is not the Son, neither does he take his existence through the Son.'"[100] Whether or not Damascene's views are indebted to the approved portions of this Nestorian creed, the story is clearly far more complicated, to say the least, than Aquinas supposes.[101]

The fifth objection seems to have its origin, probably not known to Aquinas, in Gregory of Nyssa's theology.[102] The objection states that "our breath (*spiritus*) does not seem to proceed in ourselves from our word," and so it would appear to follow that the Holy Spirit does not proceed from the Son/Word. Aquinas's answer here is to distinguish between an exterior word and an interior word; it is the latter that supports the procession of the Holy Spirit from the Father and his Word.

The fourth and sixth objections are significant because they help to illumine how the *filioque* impacts our understanding of the Holy Spirit, beyond the mere affirmation that the Holy Spirit proceeds not only from the Father but also from the Son. In other words, why does the *filioque* matter? In the fourth objection, citing a formulation taken from the legend of St. Andrew, Aquinas affirms that the Holy Spirit "rests" (*quiescit*) in the Son. But how could the Holy Spirit "rest" or abide in the Son if the Holy Spirit proceeds from the Son? Answering the objection, Aquinas points out that the Son himself rests or abides (*manere*) in the Father (cf. John 1:18). Proceeding from the Father does not mean that the Son cannot rest in the Father; likewise proceeding from the Father and the Son does not mean that the Spirit cannot rest in the Son. The abiding of the Son "in the bosom of the Father," an image of supreme

100. Siecienski, *Filioque*, 159.

101. For criticism of Aquinas on this score, see Pelikan, "Doctrine of Filioque in Thomas Aquinas and Its Patristic Antecedents," 333–34. For the argument that Damascene and Aquinas nonetheless hold complementary views of the Spirit's procession, see Torre, "St. John Damascene and St. Thomas Aquinas on the Eternal Procession of the Holy Spirit," 303–13.

102. For Gregory of Nyssa's use of the analogy of breath, see Gaybba, *Spirit of Love*, 56–57.

intimacy, fits with the abiding of the Spirit in the Son, an abiding that procession from the Father and Son supports.

The sixth objection is a marvelously simple one: "The Holy Spirit proceeds perfectly from the Father. Therefore it is superfluous to say that He proceeds from the Son." In other words, why complicate matters? What is gained by the affirmation "and the Son," even if it happened to be true?

In reply, Aquinas remarks that if one affirms that the Holy Spirit proceeds perfectly from the Father, one should equally insist that the Son proceeds perfectly from the Father. This means that the Son perfectly receives all that the Father is, except, of course, paternity.[103] And if the Son perfectly receives *all* that the Father is, this can hardly exclude a share in the spiration of the Spirit, so long as the Father's monarchy as the fount of the Godhead remains intact (as it does, since the Son's spirative power comes from the Father).[104] The *filioque*, in other words, helps to emphasize that the Father is truly able to communicate himself perfectly. His perfect communication of himself is what entails that the Holy Spirit, in proceeding perfectly from the Father, proceed also from the Son. At stake, then, is the *perfection* of the Holy Spirit's procession.[105] In this reply Aquinas again shows that the unity of the Father and Son as the principle of the Spirit follows precisely from the specific character of their personal differentiation, which is always present: "Whatever is from the Father must be from the Son unless it be opposed to the property of filiation; for the Son is not from Himself, although He is from the Father."

Having emphasized, as fruits not least of the *filioque*, the intimacy of the Son and Spirit and the perfection of their coming forth, Aquinas in the seventh objection takes up Anselm's point that the difference between generation and procession, by itself, would suffice to differentiate the Son and Spirit, whether or not the Spirit is also differentiated by proceeding from the Father *and* the

103. As Lucas Francisco Mateo-Seco states with regard to Basil's trinitarian theology, "The Son cannot be father of anyone, because his entire being is essentially and completely filiation" (Mateo-Seco, "Paternity of the Father and the Procession of the Holy Spirit," 82).

104. See also I, q. 33, aa. 1, 4, on the person of the Father. For discussion see John Baptist Ku, OP, *God the Father in the Theology of St. Thomas Aquinas* (New York: Peter Lang, 2012); Emery, *Trinitarian Theology of Saint Thomas Aquinas*, 156–60.

105. One finds a similar concern for the perfection of the generation of the Son and of the procession of the Spirit in Gregory of Nazianzus's insistence (in Christopher Beeley's words) that "the priority of the Father within the Trinity does not conflict with the divine unity and equality, but is rather what causes and enables them. . . . Gregory is firmly rejecting the notion that the monarchy of the Father in any way conflicts with the equality of the three persons—on the grounds that it is precisely what brings about that equality!" (Beeley, *Gregory of Nazianzus on the Trinity and the Knowledge of God*, 210). See also Beeley's "Divine Causality and the Monarchy of God the Father in Gregory of Nazianzus," *Harvard Theological Review* 100 (2007): 199–214.

Son. This view of Anselm's mirrors that of the Greek fathers and the East in general, although Anselm, of course, accepts the *filioque*.[106] The significance of this objection consists primarily in its leading Aquinas into the major themes of his *respondeo*. In his reply to the objection Aquinas states that the personal distinction of the Son and Spirit requires a distinction of origin. If the Son and the Spirit both had the exact same origin, then they would not be distinct persons. This is the argument that so concerned Bulgakov and Lossky (and that has been unpersuasive to generations of Orthodox theologians), on the grounds that it seems to know too much about the second procession and to view the Trinity too much in terms of philosophical categories such as causality, origin, and relation.

To undermine the position of his adversaries, or at least to soften their opposition, Aquinas cites (or tries to cite) Athanasius in the pivotal *sed contra* of article 2. The Athanasian Creed or *Quicunque vult* is now known, however, to have been composed in the Latin West around the year 500.[107] Its

---

106. For a succinct presentation of Anselm's theology of the Trinity, including his views on the *filioque*, see Lauge O. Nielsen, "Trinitarian Theology from Alcuin to Anselm," in Emery and Levering, *The Oxford Handbook of the Trinity*, 155–66, at 162–65. Nielsen notes, "In the late autumn of 1098 Anselm participated in the council at Bari where he debated the procession of the Holy Spirit with the Greek representatives" (ibid., 165). For Anselm, "Because the Son is born from the Father as God from God and the Son is the very same divine nature as the Father it follows that the Father and the Son must be the very same principle of the procession of the Holy Spirit" (ibid.). John Milbank blames Anselm, along with Photius, for the division between East and West on the matter of the *filioque*. For Milbank, Anselm "inaugurated a tendency to subordinate the persons to the substance" and thereby set forth "on the road to modalism" (Milbank, "The Second Difference," in *The Word Made Strange: Theology, Language, Culture* [Oxford: Blackwell, 1997], 171–93, at 172). See also the concerns of Oberdorfer, *Filioque*, 171–82; as well as Dennis Ngien, *Apologetic for* Filioque *in Medieval Theology* (Milton Keynes: Paternoster, 2005), 23–50. Ngien treats Anselm in dialogue with a variety of contemporary theologians, such as Colin Gunton, Jürgen Moltmann, and Karl Barth. Ngien defends the *filioque* but deplores the fact that Anselm's "thinking is still under the grip of Aristotelian philosophy, especially its idea of divine *apatheia*. . . . Anselm denies God any real feelings of love and compassion" (Ngien, *Apologetic for* Filioque *in Medieval Theology*, 47). On this latter point, see Paul L. Gavrilyuk, *The Suffering of the Impassible God: The Dialectics of Patristic Thought* (Oxford: Oxford University Press, 2004); Thomas G. Weinandy, OFMCap, *Does God Suffer?* (Notre Dame, IN: University of Notre Dame Press, 2000); James F. Keating and Thomas Joseph White, OP, eds., *Divine Impassibility and the Mystery of Human Suffering* (Grand Rapids: Eerdmans, 2009).

107. For background, see Pelikan, "Doctrine of Filioque in Thomas Aquinas and Its Patristic Antecedents," 321–22; Siecienski, *Filioque*, 8, 68. Siecienski adds, "Most of the quotations used by Thomas Aquinas in the *Contra Errores Graecorum*, which had been taken from the *Libellus de fide ss. Trinitatis* of Nicholas of Cotrone, have since proven to be spurious, and the version of Basil's *Contra Eunomium* employed by the Latins at Florence is now known to include sections of Eunomius's own work, added later by an ancient editor" (Siecienski, *Filioque*, 8). Siecienski complains that "despite the hundreds of texts collected over the centuries either proving or disproving the orthodoxy of the *filioque*, there were few efforts made to understand the fathers or their writings on their own terms. . . . It would not be until the twentieth century, when Catholic

testimony in favor of the *filioque* is therefore not relevant to addressing the concerns of the East, other than perhaps exacerbating those concerns due to its history as a forged prooftext. From this inauspicious beginning, Aquinas opens his *respondeo* with the claim that if the Holy Spirit were not from the Father and the Son, then the Holy Spirit could not be distinguished from the Son.[108] The persons cannot be distinguished by substance, and so (as Basil and Augustine also recognized) Aquinas considers that they must be distinguished by relation, since relation is the only accident that does not import finitude/materiality.[109] In God, relations are constituted by the two processions in the communication of the divine essence. For one relation to be really distinct from another in God, the two relations must be relatively opposed to each other in the order of origin, since a distinct relation in God comes about solely in the communication of the immaterial divine essence.[110]

---

and Orthodox scholars in Europe began to study the sources together, that serious dialogue on the meaning of these patristic texts finally started" (ibid., 9).

108. See John Milbank's insistence, in agreement with Aquinas, that "without the *Filioque* there is absolutely no way nor reason to think of the Spirit's personhood" (Milbank, "Second Difference," 173). Milbank adds that "preservation of the *per Filium* is merely the minimal condition for comprehending the identity of the Spirit" (ibid.).

109. It should be noted that a different way of accounting for the distinction of persons is developed by Bonaventure and later medieval theologians (especially Franciscans). Without denying the role of relation, Bonaventure highlights emanation: the Father is unemanated, the Son emanates as generated by the Father ("by way of nature"), and the Holy Spirit emanates as freely spirated by the Father and the Son ("by way of will"). For Bonaventure, the Father's "primitas" (the fact that he is unemanated) contains a positive disposition or fontal plenitude to bring forth another person. Thus the persons can be distinguished by their emanational properties: only the Son possesses "filiation" and only the Spirit possesses "passive spiration." For discussion, see Russell L. Friedman, *Medieval Trinitarian Thought from Aquinas to Ockham* (Cambridge: Cambridge University Press, 2010); Emery, *Trinitarian Theology of Saint Thomas Aquinas*, chap. 11; Bruce D. Marshall, "The Deep Things of God: Trinitarian Pneumatology," in Emery and Levering, *The Oxford Handbook of the Trinity*, 400–412, at 406–8. On this basis, John Duns Scotus concludes that the Greeks' denial of the *filioque* is not as ecumenically grave as Aquinas supposes it to be (a conclusion with which I am glad to concur). I am not persuaded, however, that emanational properties are not in fact undergirded by opposed relations of origin or that "primitas" can be logically prior to "paternitas" in the Father. The Father's "fontal plenitude" is precisely that *of the Father*.

110. For a detailed discussion of "relation" in Aquinas's trinitarian theology, see Emery, *Trinitarian Theology of Saint Thomas Aquinas*, 84–102. It is necessary to keep in view that "relation" does not mean what we mean by "relationship." Emery explains, "A relation needs two legs to be real: a connection to another thing, but also a 'foundation' in reality, that is, a 'cause' giving rise to the relation. . . . Relations of origin prove to contain the two elements: they involve a connection to someone else within the same order, and they are founded on the 'communication of the divine nature' (generation and spiration). With the second factor, Thomas takes further care to emphasize that it is not about a relationship of knowledge and love with a known and loved being . . . but concerns, rather, the procession of the Word engendered by its Principle, and the procession of the *impression* or *affection of Love*, in which one can see a real distinction" (ibid., 89). Emery goes on to specify the importance of "opposed"

It follows that the Father is Father because he has a Son, since "Father" is opposed relationally to "Son." But in spirating the Holy Spirit, is not the Father thereby related in the order of origin to the Spirit? Aquinas certainly recognizes this to be the case, but he observes that the Father's relations to the Son and Spirit "are not opposite relations": it is the same Father.[111] The two relations therefore "do not make two persons, but belong only to the one person of the Father." Given that the Spirit comes forth from the Father, then, the question is whether the Spirit's relation to the Father is the same as the Son's relation to the Father. If the Son and Spirit were relationally opposed to the Father *in the same way*, the Holy Spirit would be the same subsisting relation (or person) in God as is the Son, and indeed would be no different at all from the Son.[112] For this reason, the Son and Holy Spirit must be "related to each other by opposite relations" of origin, which can be the case only if the Holy Spirit is from the Father and the Son. It is not enough, then, to say simply that the nature of their origin (filiation and procession) is distinct; one must explain why such a distinction is not irrational. Earlier, Aquinas had noted that "spiration belongs to the person of the Father, and to the person of the Son, forasmuch as it has no relative opposition either to paternity or to filiation."[113]

Does this approach to illumining the revealed mystery of the Holy Spirit in the Trinity—an approach rooted in the recognition, already present *in nuce* in Basil of Caesarea, that the persons must be constituted by relative opposition in the order of origin—turn the Son into another Father with regard to the Holy Spirit? I think that the answer is no. The distinction of the Father and Son is due to their relative opposition in the act of begetting,

---

relations: "The word 'opposition' obviously does not indicate competition, but must be taken in its formal meaning: opposition is the *principle of a distinction*. This opposition is required because the distinction of the divine persons is not 'material.' No opposition, no distinction: to reject such 'opposition' comes down to an acceptance of Sabellianism. . . . The only relation which can be attributed to the Trinity is that founded on immanent action, the relation of origin. Here we have the principle of the intra-Trinitarian distinction: 'relative opposition as to origin'" (ibid., 98–99).

111. See ibid., 101.

112. For discussion of the persons as "subsisting relations," see ibid., 114–27. See also Anselm Kyongsuk Min, "God as the Mystery of Sharing and Shared Love: Thomas Aquinas on the Trinity," in Phan, *The Cambridge Companion to the Trinity*, 87–106, at 89–94. Note also Ángel Cordovilla Pérez's comment that "Thomas' great contribution is the definition of the Trinitarian persons as subsisting relations, thus placing the foundations for what will henceforth be called a relational ontology centred in the person" (Pérez, "The Trinitarian Concept of Person," in Maspero and Woźniak, *Rethinking Trinitarian Theology*, 105–45, at 122). Yet in Pérez's view, "the Trinitarian doctrine in the Summa of Theology turns around the concept of substance" (ibid.). This is a grave misunderstanding, as Emery makes clear.

113. I, q. 30, a. 2.

and this relative opposition (and thereby the Father-Son distinction) fully remains in the act of spiration: "The Holy Spirit proceeds from the Father immediately, as from him, and mediately, as from the Son."[114] Because the act of spiration does not itself relatively distinguish the Father and the Son, the only person produced via spiration is the Holy Spirit who proceeds.[115] The monarchy of the Father remains firm, since the Son spirates precisely as the one begotten by the Father. The unity of one principle is not an impersonal amalgam, because the principle is the Father and Son.[116] The Holy Spirit and the Son are distinguished by different relations of origin because the Spirit does not come forth only from the Father; yet the Son does not become the Father.[117]

This approach via distinct relations or origin also fits with the analogy of the mind, which relies upon knowing and loving. In his *respondeo* of article 2 Aquinas moves directly from his argument that only relations can truly distinguish persons without dividing the divine "substance," to an argument based upon the analogy of the mind, rooted in John 1:1 and in the fact that

114. I, q. 36, a. 3, ad 1.

115. David Coffey points out that "the Father and the Son cannot be 'partial causes' (*Teilursachen*) of the Holy Spirit, as Heribert Mühlen has opined, since this would be incompatible with the divine perfection. In any case the power to breathe forth the Holy Spirit is identical (not just similar or equal) in the Father and the Son, because it is communicated by the Father to the Son in the act of generation. Therefore each of them is the *total* cause of the Holy Spirit" (Coffey, *"Did You Receive the Holy Spirit When You Believed?" Some Basic Questions for Pneumatology* [Milwaukee: Marquette University Press, 2005], 72). See Heribert Mühlen, *Der Heilige Geist als Person: In der Trinität, bei der Inkarnation, und im Gnadenbund: Ich—Du—Wir* (Münster: Aschendorff, 1963), 78–80. For background, see Coffey's *Deus Trinitas: The Doctrine of the Triune God* (Oxford: Oxford University Press, 1999).

116. *Pace* the Klingenthal Memorandum, *"Filioque* Clause in Ecumenical Perspective," 15. Emmanuel Durand, OP, explains in an irenic way, "The Father is certainly the only 'fontal' principle on which depends the full communication of the divine nature to the Spirit. . . . Without making the Son a principle that is extrinsic to the Father in the procession of the Spirit, the paternal origin of the Spirit will only be honoured in its fullness if one does not abstract the Father-Son relation from this origin" (Durand, "Perichoresis," 186–87).

117. In his *Commentary on the Gospel of John*, when treating John 15:26, Aquinas points out that if "the Son and the Holy Spirit are distinct persons proceeding from the Father, they have to be distinguished by some properties that are opposed. These properties cannot be opposed like affirmation and negation or privation and possessing are opposed, because then the Son and the Holy Spirit would be related to one another like being and non-being and as the complete to the deprived, and this is repugnant to their equality. Nor can these properties be opposed like contraries are opposed, one of which is more perfect than another" (Aquinas, *Commentary on the Gospel of John*, no. 2063, p. 127). He concludes that if there are properties that distinguish the Son and Holy Spirit, then these properties can only involve "relative opposition" (ibid.). Aquinas reasons that the two processions "are distinguished only by the order of origin," and if this is so, then the Spirit's origin cannot be the same as the Son's (ibid., no. 2064, p. 128). The Spirit must proceed from the Father and the Son or else there would be no real difference between the Spirit and the Son in the order of origin.

the processions must be conceived as *interior* rather than as directed outward. He states that "the Son proceeds by way of the intellect as Word, and the Holy Spirit by way of the will as Love." Here he takes up Augustine's oft-repeated point that only if we know something in some way, can we love it. Aquinas states, "Now love must proceed from a word. For we do not love anything unless we apprehend it by a mental conception." To this argument, Aquinas adds a third, based on the "order of nature." He observes that while a craftsman may make many knives without these knives having an order to one another, in things that differ on more than a material basis there is always an order. The Son and the Holy Spirit both proceed from the Father, and so for there to be a relational order of origin between the Son and the Holy Spirit, one of them must be the principle of the other. Aquinas considers this argument to be the strongest one for persuading the East, since the Greek fathers also describe some order between the Son and the procession of the Holy Spirit. As he says, albeit without a sufficient understanding of the theology of the East on this point, "they grant that the Holy Spirit is the Spirit *of the Son*; and that He is from the Father *through the Son*. Some of them are said also to concede that *He is from the Son*; or that He *flows from the Son*, but not that He proceeds."[118]

All three of these arguments in Aquinas's *respondeo* should be seen in light of the scriptural and conciliar testimony that governs the first two objections and their replies. If we reach to the heart of the arguments in the *respondeo*, we can see that each of them promotes two aspects of the trinitarian mystery: the extraordinary intimacy between the Son and the Holy Spirit, and the personal distinction of the two. This is accomplished by the relational model (relations of origin) through showing that the Son and Spirit must be intimately related to each other in a way that distinguishes them. It is accomplished by the analogy from the mind through showing that loving arises from knowing, and thus by examining the mystery via the revelation of the Word.[119] Lastly, it is accomplished by the "order of nature" through pointing out that when two things (differentiated by more than matter) proceed from the same source, they possess an order to each other. Both the kinship and the distinction of the Son and Spirit are thereby underscored. In each case, it

118. Lewis Ayres points out that instances of "through the Son" are extremely rare in Greek pro-Nicenes; see Ayres, "Innovation and *Ressourcement* in Pro-Nicene Pneumatology," *Augustinian Studies* 39 (2008): 187–206, at 200–201. On this topic, see also André de Halleux, "La profession de l'Esprit Saint dans le Symbole de Constantinople," in *Patrologie et oecuménisme: Recueil d'études* (Leuven: Peeters, 1990), 303–37, at 334–35. On Aquinas's understanding of "through the Son," see, for example, Ngien, *Apologetic for* Filioque *in Medieval Theology*, 96–97.

119. For further discussion, see Ku, *God the Father in the Theology of St. Thomas Aquinas*, 260–61.

can be seen how closely the argument follows the scriptural teachings, which certainly display, in the economy of salvation, both the inseparable intimacy and the relational differentiation of the Son and Holy Spirit.[120]

Articles 3 and 4 of I, Question 36: Further Refining the Filioque

The third and fourth articles communicate similar points to those found in the *respondeo* of article 2. Aquinas recognizes that the East would prefer "through" the Son rather than "and" the Son. For this reason, having explained in the second article that the Spirit proceeds from the Father and the Son, he devotes the third article to the Spirit's procession "from the Father through the Son."[121] He finds this formula in the Latin West, specifically in book 12 of Hilary of Poitiers's *De Trinitate*. He quotes Hilary in the *sed contra*, in

---

120. Siecienski notes that "most biblical scholars today doubt that the New Testament authors even thought in trinitarian terms (i.e., with Father, Son, and Spirit each understood as distinct 'persons' within God). While post-Nicene writers would find the Scriptures littered with texts describing Jesus's divine origin, modern exegetes question whether the New Testament ever explicitly refers to Jesus as 'God' or whether Jesus thought of himself as such. There are many verses that might be references to the persons or activity of the Trinity (Luke 1:35, 3:22, 4:1–14; Matt. 1:18–23, 3:16–17, 28:19; Acts 1:1–6, 2:33, 38–39), but one must be careful about imposing later categories upon the biblical witness. Even Paul's frequent allusions to the activity of Father, Son, and Spirit (Eph. 4:4–6, Gal. 4:4–6, Titus 3:4–6, 1 Cor. 12:4–6) do not necessarily prove an explicit understanding of God's triune nature" (Siecienski, *Filioque*, 17–18). It is clear that the New Testament authors did not teach Niceno-Constantinopolitan doctrine in the manner that the Council of Constantinople taught it, but it still seems to me that their formulations are intelligible, as a whole, only in light of the doctrine taught by the Council of Constantinople. Following Raymond Brown's interpretation of John 15:26, Siecienski argues that the meaning of this text (and others like it in John 14–16) is simply to coordinate the coming of Christ with the coming of the Spirit: "Inasmuch as the death and glorification of Christ is a precondition for the coming of the Spirit, he is sent by the Son, but he is also sent by the Father, whose emissary he ultimately is. It is this reality that verse 15:26 tries to convey, as the Comforter 'whom I will send you from the Father' becomes also 'the Spirit of Truth who proceeds from the Father'" (ibid., 22). In my view, the divinity of the Son and the Spirit is more clearly attested in Scripture than many exegetes allow. For exegesis that helps to illumine the divinity of the Son and Spirit according to the New Testament, see, for example, Richard Bauckham, *Jesus and the God of Israel: God Crucified and Other Studies on the New Testament's Christology of Divine Identity* (Grand Rapids: Eerdmans, 2008); Gordon D. Fee, *God's Empowering Presence: The Holy Spirit in the Letters of Paul* (Peabody, MA: Hendrickson, 1994); Fee, "Paul and the Trinity: The Experience of Christ and the Spirit for Paul's Understanding of God," in *The Trinity: An Interdisciplinary Symposium on the Trinity*, ed. Stephen T. Davis, Daniel Kendall, SJ, and Gerald O'Collins, SJ (Oxford: Oxford University Press, 1999), 49–72; Simon J. Gathercole, *The Pre-Existent Son: Recovering the Christologies of Matthew, Mark, and Luke* (Grand Rapids: Eerdmans, 2006); C. Kavin Rowe, *Early Narrative Christology: The Lord in the Gospel of Luke* (Berlin: de Gruyter, 2006); Sean M. McDonough, *Christ as Creator: Origins of a New Testament Doctrine* (Oxford: Oxford University Press, 2009); Wesley Hill, *Paul and the Trinity: Persons, Relations, and the Pauline Letters* (Grand Rapids: Eerdmans, 2015).

121. I, q. 36, a. 3, obj. 1.

what can be seen as an effort to draw together East and West, having quoted Scripture and Augustine in the *sed contra* of article 1 and (what he thought to be) Athanasius in the *sed contra* of article 2. The key question in Aquinas's mind is whether "through" means that the Spirit does not proceed "immediately" from the Father: Is the Son here a mediator of the Spirit, in such a way as to undermine the Father's role as the immediate principle of the Spirit? A second question is whether the "through" implies that the Father is a greater principle of the Spirit than is the Son. A third question is whether "through" indicates that the Son's generation occurs temporally prior to the procession of the Spirit, in which case the divinity of the Spirit would be denied. Lastly, a fourth question is whether the Father's acting "through" the Son requires that the obverse be true, so that the Son acts through (or on behalf of) the Father. In short, the central concerns of article 3 consist in the fear that "through" subordinates the Son and Holy Spirit or undermines the Father's monarchy as the fount of the Godhead.

In his *respondeo* Aquinas seeks to remove this fear by clarifying how "through" operates here. "Through" can be used in various ways. For example, it can signify the reason why someone does something, or the art through which one works, or the fact that one acts through the authority of another, or the tool (e.g., a hammer) through which one accomplishes a task. When applied to the Son's role in the procession of the Spirit, Aquinas says, "through" means simply that "the Son receives from the Father that the Holy Spirit proceeds from Him." Along these lines, Aquinas notes in his response to the first objection that the Son is not the power or instrument through which the Father acts. That would be to subordinate the Son in an unacceptable manner. Instead, since the Father gives to the Son all that the Father is, which includes the power of spiration, "through" indicates the order of origin that characterizes the eternal act of spirating. The Father alone is the "immediate" source of the Spirit; the Son is source in a "mediate" way because the Son's spirative power comes from the Father.[122] Aquinas also grants, in response to

---

122. I, q. 36, a. 3, ad 1. Emmanuel Durand remarks, "The common spirative *virtus* is important in the perspective of the *Filioque*, since it avoids conceiving of the implication of the Son in the procession of the Spirit as simply an instrumental role, something that would lead to an unacceptable subordination of the Son" (Durand, "Perichoresis," 189). See also, along the same lines, Min, "God as the Mystery of Sharing and Shared Love," 98; as well as Ku's remark that "spiration is intrinsically bound to generation which formally includes spiration. The Father, *as Father*, gives the power to spirate to the Son, *as Son*. Spiration formally belongs to the Father *as Father*. His constitution by paternity, through his relation to the Son, formally includes the power to breathe forth the Spirit. Thus, while the relation itself of common spiration cannot be said to constitute the Father or the Son, it is included in paternity and filiation insofar as the spirative power is included in generation" (Ku, *God the Father in the Theology of St. Thomas*

the second objection, that we can say that the Spirit proceeds "principally or properly from the Father," so long as by this we mean simply to defend the Father's monarchy (without turning the "through" into a subordinationatist instrumentalizing of the Son). In his response to the third objection, Aquinas adds that it is important to keep in mind that not merely the Son and Spirit, but also the begetting of the Son and procession of the Spirit, are coeternal with the Father; in this sense, "the Son was not begotten before the Holy Spirit proceeded."

If the third article's emphasis on "through" seems more amenable to Eastern views—even though the East does not accept that the Father shares his spirative power with the Son—the fourth article puts things in a manner far from the East's sensibilities, by arguing that the Father and Son are "one principle" of the Holy Spirit.[123] Both articles, of course, simply clarify article 2's affirmation that the Spirit proceeds from the Son, rather than adding anything substantive. The clarification in the third article underscores the Father's monarchy and rejects any subordinationist implication, while at the same time interpreting "through" in terms of a communicated spirative power, on the grounds that otherwise the Father would not have shared all that he is (except paternity) with the Son. This shared spirative power, however, might

---

Aquinas, 257). Ku points out that since the spirative power itself belongs to the divine essence, even though it is the Father and Son who spirate, "the Holy Spirit too must possess the power to spirate. Analogous to the Son's possession of the power to generate, the Holy Spirit 'has the power to spirate not as one who spirates but as the one who is spirated' [I *Sent.*, d. 11, q. un., a. 1, ad 2]" (ibid., 256–57).

123. For further discussion, see Ku, *God the Father in the Theology of St. Thomas Aquinas*, 257–59. Indebted to André Malet, Gilles Emery, and Emmanuel Durand, Ku observes that "there are two spirating as one single principle by the unique notion of spiration," and therefore Aquinas in the *Summa theologiae* (as opposed to in the *Commentary on the Sentences*) does not speak of "two spirators" even though there are two persons spirating. Ku further explains,

> Durand points out that these two angels of consideration (supposit versus power) according to the hypostatic principle *what* (*quod*) and the formal principle *that by which* (*quo*), complete each other mutually. The first gives place to an articulation of the principle of the procession of the Holy Spirit in terms of loving inter-personality; the second ends in the affirmation of one single principle in terms of essential unity. . . . Acts belong to supposits, and supposits that share one divine nature act by one same divine power. Since spiration is a personal action in God, spiration necessitates the distinction of supposits; but the two spirating act as a single principle. Spiration presupposes simultaneously the distinction of the Father and the Son in paternity and filiation, and their union in the common spiration of love. (ibid., 259)

See also Malet, *Personne et amour dans la théologie trinitaire de saint Thomas d'Aquin* (Paris: Vrin, 1956), 144–55; Durand, *La périchorèse des personnes divines: Immanence mutuelle, réciprocité et communion* (Paris: Cerf, 2005), 266; Emery, "Procession of the Holy Spirit *a Filio* According to St. Thomas Aquinas," 219–21.

seem to depersonalize the spiration of the Spirit by attributing the spiration to a shared power, even if the Father and Son are the ones spirating. This fear might appear to be confirmed by the view, highlighted in article 4, that the Father and Son are "one principle."

The first objection of article 4 shows this fear. It rejects the notion of "one principle" on the grounds that the Father and Son are not the source of the Holy Spirit insofar as they are one, either in nature or in any characteristic proper to one or the other of them. The objection concludes that rather than thinking of the spiration as being from "one principle," supporters of the *filioque* must resolutely think of the spiritation as being from the Father and Son distinctly. This objection suggests that the notion of "one principle" depersonalizes the spiration. The second objection makes clear both that an amalgam of Father and Son cannot be considered, and that the Father and Son are not united by one personal spirative property. The latter condition would split the Father by turning him into two distinct principles of the Son and Spirit. The fourth, fifth, sixth, and seventh objections rule out an amalgam by arguing that the term "principle" must apply to one person, which cannot be the case if it here applies to two. For its part, the third objection takes up another possible fear arising from Aquinas's interpretation of the Spirit proceeding from or "through" the Son: it might seem that the Son is more privileged than the Spirit. The Son's relation to the Father should not make the Son any closer to the Father than is the Spirit, but the Spirit does not form "one principle" with the Father, which seems to denote a lack of equality.[124]

How does Aquinas address these concerns? The *sed contra* of article 4 cites book 5 of Augustine's *De Trinitate* as evidence for the validity of the "one principle" view; the implied point is that Augustine would not have been so foolish as to amalgamate or subordinate any of the divine persons. In the *respondeo* Aquinas repeats the point that he has made above (in the

---

124. Bruce Marshall, in his examination of classical Lutheran defenses of the *filioque*, responds to a similar objection. The objection and Marshall's response (drawing upon classical Lutheran theologians, who read Aquinas on this topic) are as follows: "Inferring the procession of the Spirit from the Son on the basis of the Spirit's being 'of' the Son undercuts the independence and equality of the Spirit; it threatens to deny that he is a hypostasis distinct from, and equal to, the Son. To the theologians of classical Lutheranism this has the matter backwards. The teaching that the Spirit proceeds from the Son as well as from the Father is designed precisely to account for the distinction of the Spirit from both Father and Son, and thereby the equality of the Spirit with both" (Marshall, "Defense of the *Filioque* in Classical Lutheran Theology," 160) (cf. 164–65 on the "power to send"). Note also André de Halleux's observation: "The *taxis* of the spiration of the Spirit by the Son no more implies the subjection of the Spirit to the Son than the generation of the Son by the Father implies any inferiority of the Son in relation to the Father" (de Halleux, "Toward an Ecumenical Agreement on the Procession of the Holy Spirit," 73).

second article) regarding the Father and the Son's unity in everything other than their opposite relation, namely paternity-filiation. This opposite relation does not distinguish them vis-à-vis spiration. Therefore, in spiration, they are not opposed to each other, and so it is correct to term them "one principle." Does this mean then that there is only one spirator—in other words, that we are dealing here with an amalgam? Aquinas offers his fullest response to this concern in the reply to the seventh objection, by which he brings his treatment of the *filioque* to an end. He makes a rather fine distinction: "we can say that the Father and the Son are two spirating, by reason of the plurality of the *supposita*, but not two spirators by reason of the one spiration." There are two spirating persons, the Father and the Son. But there are not two spirators, because otherwise there would be two spirations, one coming from the Father and one coming from the Son. The spiration is in fact a unity, because the Father and the Son do it through their perfect sharing of the spirative power. The value of this distinction between "two persons spirating" and "two spirators" consists in its ability to resist amalgamating the persons while at the same time insisting that the spiration is one act that the Father and Son truly share, due to the Father's communication of spirative power to the Son.

What about the other central problem, namely the Holy Spirit's seeming subordination to the Son because the Son is united to the Father in a way not enjoyed by the Spirit? Again insisting upon the value of the relational model for understanding personal distinction in God, Aquinas points out that the opposed relations of the persons—their personal properties of paternity, filiation, and procession—do not make the persons more or less like one another. Likeness among the persons has to do solely with the fact that they are the one divine "substance." They differ only in relation of origin; they cannot be said to be more or less like each other, since their likeness is utterly perfect and not affected whatsoever by their personal distinction. They are truly one God. In his reply to the third objection, Aquinas explains, "Hence, as the Father is not more like to Himself than He is to the Son; so likewise neither is the Son more like to the Father than is the Holy Spirit."

The purpose of articles 3 and 4, then, is to illumine the Holy Spirit as described in the first article. This Holy Spirit is utterly one with the Father and Son, as is indicated by the terms "holy" and "spirit." This Holy Spirit, as the *respondeo* of the first article says, "proceeds by way of the love whereby God is loved"—a mode of procession indicated by "Spirit" (which signifies "impulse and motion") and by "Holy" (which signifies movement ordered to God and his goodness). The distinctiveness of the Holy Spirit is illumined not simply by the analogy from the mind and its central interpersonal acts of knowing and loving, but also by the opposed relations of origin constitutive of personal distinction in God. The Son is the one who can say "all that the Father has is mine" (John 16:15). The Father and the Son communicate this to the Spirit, who will "take what is mine [the Son's] and declare it to you" (John 16:14). The Spirit receives all that is the Father's and all that is the Son's, except their personal properties.

Where do we learn to read Scripture in this way, since other modes of scriptural interpretation—for example, historical-critical modes—might not arrive at the same conclusions? For Aquinas, the answer is primarily the councils of the church, guided by the Holy Spirit, since in these councils the authority of the successors of the apostles (including the distinctive authority of the successor of Peter) is exercised. It is these councils that instruct the Christian community, and these councils, along with the bishop of Rome, have the power to interpret definitively the doctrinal import and implications of earlier councils in order to respond to new challenges in the interpretation, proclamation, and defense of the gospel.[125]

The Holy Spirit's procession from the Father "through" or "and" the Son does not mean either that the Son is instrumentalized or that the Son and Father are amalgamated, let alone that the Spirit is subordinated. The Father's nontemporal primacy remains, as does the distinction of persons spirating in the one spiration. The Son's reception of all that the Father possesses is definitive of the Son, just as the Spirit's intimate relation not only to the Father ("immediately") but also to the Son ("mediately") is definitive of the Spirit. It

---

125. For discussion of Aquinas's theology of the episcopacy and papacy, in light of various contemporary theological perspectives, see Matthew Levering, *Christ and the Catholic Priesthood: Ecclesial Hierarchy and the Pattern of the Trinity* (Chicago: Hillenbrand, 2010). See also, for insight into the challenge to ecclesial authority in the years directly after the Second Vatican Council, Clarence Gallagher, SJ, "Authority and the Spirit," in *The Spirit in Action: Papers Read at the Second Catholic Dogma Course Roehampton 1967*, ed. Robert Butterworth, SJ (Langley, UK: St. Paul Publications, 1968), 79–91. In the same volume John Ashton, SJ describes the charge, with which he clearly has some sympathy, that "from being the servant, the handmaid of the Lord, who is King, Prophet and Priest, the Church has taken on the mantle of the Master himself, and demands the same total and unswerving allegiance of will, mind and conscience" (Ashton, "Spirit and the Church," in Butterworth, *The Spirit in Action*, 11–30, at 16). Ashton points out, however, that "the new covenant which establishes the Church demands some form of ecclesiastical structure or hierarchy precisely *because* of the new way in which God, through the Spirit of his Son, is present. Re-presentation, in the area of the transmission of revelation, demands representation. If the Lordship of Christ is to be acknowledged, not just by an inner group of disciples, however large, but by an ever expanding circle, which, starting from a room in Jerusalem, will extend to Judaea, Samaria and the ends of the earth (cf. Acts I, 8), then this group must have the power, the authority, to transmit the message they have themselves received" (ibid., 28). Ashton concludes that the determinative question is whether the Holy Spirit is guiding the church, as Christ promised would be the case—a question whose answer requires the eyes of faith, though evidences of credibility also play a role. See also Levering, *Engaging the Doctrine of Revelation*.

is the personal, relational distinctiveness of each divine person that Aquinas's approach seeks to preserve and affirm.[126] In seeking insight into the revealed tripersonal God, he employs two philosophical tools: opposed relations as constitutive of real distinction in the utterly simple God, and the analogy of the mind. These tools help to make manifest the intelligibility of divine revelation, by showing that Christians do not worship three gods, and that the real distinction of three persons in one God is not irrational. But Aquinas employs these tools only to illumine what he already finds to be present in scriptural and conciliar teaching.

In his response to the first objection of article 4 Aquinas notes that "if we consider the *supposita* of the spiration, then we may say that the Holy Spirit proceeds from the Father and the Son, as distinct; for He proceeds from them as the unitive love of both." Does the claim that the Spirit is the "unitive love" of the Father and the Son exceed what we can know on the basis of revelation? As we saw in the previous chapter, Aquinas addresses this issue in question 37, and he devotes question 38 to asking whether the Holy Spirit can also be properly named Gift, presuming in both cases Augustine's biblical exposition. These names, "Love" and "Gift," depend in certain ways upon the *filioque*. That Aquinas's use of the model of relations and the analogy of the mind supports such names for the Spirit, in accord with Scripture's association of the Spirit with love and gift in the economy of salvation, suggests once more to me that Aquinas's approach is fundamentally rooted in Scripture rather than arising from a rationalistic desire to philosophically master the divine mysteries.

Conclusion

As Edward Siecienski remarks, Aquinas's writings "presume the Augustinian understanding of the Trinity (i.e., the Holy Spirit as the bond of love between Father and Son)."[127] Siecienski also observes that, after Aquinas's death, "the writings of the 'Angelic Doctor' achieved a level of authority in the West unknown since Augustine, and his arguments in favor of the *filioque* became an important part of the Latin theological tradition. Thomas's position on

126. Thus Emmanuel Durand remarks that the doctrine of perichoresis's "help in specifying the immanence and reciprocity between the Father and the Son disposes one for a better understanding of the procession of the Holy Spirit. . . . The manner in which the Spirit is understood needs to be verified through the mutual immanence of the Father and the Holy Spirit, as well as by the reciprocity of their relation. A conception of the Spirit as that of the Love that comes forth from the Father satisfies these criteria" (Durand, "Perichoresis," 183).

127. Siecienski, *Filioque*, 128.

the *filioque*, like his opinion on so many subjects, became the position of the Church itself."[128] However, Siecienski considers that Aquinas's position locked the Catholic Church into a deeply unfortunate Augustinian framework. Siecienski argues that the solution is to return to Maximus the Confessor's *Letter to Marinus*, with its insistence that the Father is the "sole cause" (μία αἰτία) in the Trinity and its distinction between ἐκπόρευσις (reserved for the Spirit's procession from the Father) and προϊέναι. In order "to account for both the essential unity and eternal relationship shared between the Son and the Spirit," Maximus follows Gregory of Nyssa (and Cyril of Alexandria) in distinguishing between ἐκπόρευσις and προϊέναι and "speaking not only of the Spirit's procession from the Father, but also of his eternal progression [προϊέναι] through the Son with whom the Father is in eternal relationship."[129] Siecienski sums up Maximus's reading of Latin theology, which he finds to be much superior to Aquinas's later rendition of the Latin theological tradition on the Holy Spirit: "According to Maximus, Latins and Greeks together affirmed both the monarchy of the Father (as sole cause of the Son and the Spirit) and the Spirit's comprehension of the Father's unique relationship to the Son, as he flows from the begetter through the begotten, manifesting the common nature of both."[130]

128. Ibid., 131. See also Oberdorfer, *Filioque*, 186–202; note also the remark of Andreas Andreopoulos: "Aquinas' writings are surprising for two reasons: firstly because he seems to have a very good understanding overall of Greek objections to the *filioque*; and secondly because, despite his apparent understanding and support of these objections, he does an about-face intellectually and supports the *filioque* anyway, on very weak grounds proportionately to the objections he lists. . . . One suspects that the good Doctor responded to one strand of theology in citing and analyzing Dionysios the Areopagite, the second ecumenical council and John of Damascus and several arguments against the *filioque*, and then to a different strand of ecclesiology, which compelled him to adhere to the polemics of the Latin Church of the previous few centuries" (Andreopoulos, "Holy Spirit in the Ecclesiology of Photios of Constantinople," 156).

129. Siecienski, *Filioque*, 81. On Cyril of Alexandria's contribution (in light of his dialogue with Theodoret of Cyrus), see Evdokimov, *L'Esprit-Saint dans la tradition orthodoxe*, 52–56. Evdokimov emphasizes, "For Maximus, Cyril of Alexandria could not in any way teach that the Son is cause of the Spirit" (ibid., 56 [my translation]). Here Lewis Ayres's cautionary remarks are helpful: for Gregory, "It is, however, the divine power that is 'through' the Son, not the Spirit. The Spirit's dependence on the Son serves to distinguish Spirit and Son, but it is allowed to do little more. Gregory allows that this *taxis* describes Trinitarian causality and in at least two places *en passant* comments seem to ascribe the Son a mediating role between Father and Spirit. But in a manner that reveals the strongly apophatic context within which he thinks that any comments about the Spirit's procession should be taken, Gregory sees the unity of nature between the three persons to be our primary faith commitment" (Ayres, "Innovation and *Ressourcement* in Pro-Nicene Pneumatology," 201). Ayres grants that Gregory describes the Spirit "as *always* 'receiving' from the Son and as *always* being 'sent'" (ibid., 202). See also André de Halleux, "'Manifesté par le fils': Aux origins d'une formule pneumatologique" and "Cyrille, Théodoret et le 'Filioque,'" in *Patrologie et oecuménisme*, 338–66 and 367–95.

130. Siecienski, *Filioque*, 84.

For Siecienski, then, it would be a mistake to attempt to read Aquinas's position as parallel to (even if in different language from) Maximus's position. This is because, in his view, the Latin scholastics, and Aquinas preeminently among them, transferred "the Father's hypostatic properties to the Son" by positing that the Father communicated his spirative power to the Son.[131] Siecienski holds that Aquinas's insistence upon "one principle" should be jettisoned on the grounds that it cannot really be squared with the Father's monarchy, given Aquinas's emphasis on the unity of the spiration (despite the two persons spirating). He argues that Aquinas's approach logically leads to the claim that "the Spirit derived his ἐκπόρευσις from the Son" as well as from the Father, since an emphasis on "one principle" and one spiration hardly lends itself to distinguishing ἐκπόρευσις from προϊέναι.[132] For Siecienski, in short, Aquinas's language cannot avoid making the Son "responsible for the Spirit's ἐκπόρευσις" and undermining the Father's proper status as the "sole cause" of the Spirit.[133] Siecienski concludes that the most the Latin West can take from Maximus is that "the *filioque* was an orthodox (albeit clumsy) way of articulating an important theological truth—the προϊέναι of the Spirit through the Son in the trinitarian order [τάξις]."[134] But the West must not suppose that Maximus and Aquinas can coincide.

By contrast, as Siecienski recognizes, the Pontifical Council approvingly cites both Maximus and Aquinas. The Pontifical Council also accepts the formulation of "one principle" as found in paragraph 248 of the *Catechism of the Catholic Church*: "The eternal order of the divine persons in their consubstantial communion implies that the Father, as the 'principle without principle' (DS 1331), is the first origin of the Spirit, but also that as Father of the only Son, he is, with the Son, the single principle from which the Spirit

---

131. Ibid., 86. Evdokimov comments that "Augustine emphasizes that it is *principally* from the Father, as the premier and absolute principle, that the Holy Spirit proceeds. But since the Father and the Son are *one*, and all that the Father has, the Son also has, they constitute a single principle of the procession of the Holy Spirit. The principle of the Monarchy is not thereby suppressed; there are not two principles, two sources of the Holy Spirit. The monarchy, one can say, is shared between the Father and the Son united in the same nature in order to form only a single Principle of procession. . . . Likewise, according to Saint Thomas, the Father and the Son together produce a spiration; therefore there is only One Spirator" (Evdokimov, *L'Esprit-Saint dans la tradition orthodoxe*, 56–57 [my translation]). Aquinas, however, states in a more nuanced fashion, "If we consider the spirative power, the Holy Spirit proceeds from the Father and the Son as they are one in the spirative power, which in a certain way signifies the nature with the property. . . . But if we consider the *supposita* of the spiration, then we may say that the Holy Spirit proceeds from the Father and the Son, as distinct" (I, q. 36, a. 4, ad 1). See Emery, "Procession of the Holy Spirit According to St. Thomas Aquinas," 219–25.

132. Siecienski, *Filioque*, 84.

133. Ibid., 86.

134. Ibid.

proceeds (Second Council of Lyons, DS 850)."[135] According to the Pontifical Council, nonetheless, Maximus's care in distinguishing ἐκπόρευσις and
προϊέναι should instruct the West today. The *filioque* must not be transposed
into the Greek version of the Niceno-Constantinopolitan Creed. But, *pace*
Siecienski, the Pontifical Council holds that the *filioque* and the doctrine of
the Father and Son as "one principle," as understood in the West, are not in-
exorably opposed to what Maximus had in view in differentiating ἐκπόρευσις
and προϊέναι.

In my view, despite his own sharp criticisms of Aquinas and the *filioque*,
Lossky helps us to see why an inexorable opposition between East (Maximus)
and West (Aquinas) need not obtain. Lossky's criticisms of Bulgakov demonstrate that causality and the order of origin must be retained in interpreting what has been revealed about the Son and Holy Spirit. If this is so, then
arguably the appeal to opposed relations of origin in the communication
of the divine essence, including with respect to the sharing of the spirative
power and to the Spirit's procession, also has a place. The Father's unique
monarchy, his full power to beget his perfect likeness in all but paternity, and
the distinctiveness of the Son and Spirit are at stake for the West as for the
East. Although Aquinas does not understand the significance that the term
"ἐκπόρευσις" has for the East, his view certainly does not require us to deny
that there are two persons spirating: the spirative power does not act by itself
in the one spiration, and the Father and Son are not explicitly amalgamated.
Nor does Aquinas suppose that the Father's monarchy is absent in the Spirit's
procession. On the contrary, Aquinas holds that "the Holy Spirit proceeds
from the Father immediately, as from Him, and mediately, as from the Son,"
and that "if we consider the *supposita* of the spiration, then we may say
that the Holy Spirit proceeds from the Father and the Son, as distinct [*ut
sunt plures*]."

---

135. *Catechism of the Catholic Church*, §248. David Coffey, a proponent of the *filioque*,
points out that "as a theological question it is distinct from the issue of its retention in the
Western version of the Nicene Creed. . . . Unilaterally inserted, it could be unilaterally removed
in a gesture of ecumenical good will as the recent North American agreed statement suggests.
However, before this is done the Western churches, acting together and ecumenically so as not
to cause further offense (this time in the West), should carefully weigh the pastoral implications
of dropping from the Creed an article that has been confessed in good faith for a millennium"
(Coffey, *"Did You Receive the Holy Spirit When You Believed?,"* 44). Both in its openness and in
its caution, this position seems right to me. The *filioque* remains important because, as Coffey
says, "the key to an understanding of the Spirit, the most mysterious and elusive of the three
divine persons, is the relationship he bears to the other two persons" (ibid.). With respect to
what it means for the Spirit to be the mutual love of the Father and Son, see Congar, *I Believe
in the Holy Spirit*, 1:90, indebted to the studies of H.-F. Dondaine; and Emery, *Trinitarian
Theology of Saint Thomas Aquinas*, 233–44.

Far from being rationalistic, Aquinas's approach is rooted in his reading of Scripture and of the councils of the church. Reflecting upon the implications of the Son receiving all that the Father is (Matt. 11:27; John 16:15), Aquinas affirms that filiation cannot differ from paternity except with respect to the specific relation of paternity, which constitutes the Father's distinct person-hood. Aquinas's position avoids instrumentalizing the Son or subordinating either the Son or the Holy Spirit. In defending the *filioque*, Aquinas seeks to preserve the revealed distinctiveness of the Holy Spirit in the one God, as well as the Spirit's intimacy with the Father's Word. Even when arguing philosophically, on the basis of relations of origin, he is seeking to illuminate the scriptural testimony that the incarnate Son "is the Word, not any sort of word, but one who breathes forth Love," the greatest Gift.[136] Admittedly, Aquinas's approach does not resolve the difference between East and West about whether later councils convened by the pope have the authority to interpret earlier councils, nor can Aquinas be expected to resolve the debates over the proper interpretation of the relevant scriptural texts (indeed, historical-critical scholars often argue that both East and West are wrong).[137] But the concerns behind the East's defense of the Father as solely "responsible for the Spirit's ἐκπόρευσις" are not antithetical to Aquinas's position, once it is recognized that "ἐκπόρευσις" functions not least as a way of insisting upon the Spirit's procession immediately from the Father, which is a different point (in Aquinas's terms) from the unity of spiration.

Thus I hope to have shown that Aquinas—perhaps I should say *even* Aquinas, given the criticisms his position has incurred and given his own criticisms and occasional serious misunderstandings of the position of his Greek con-temporaries—does not bring to a rationalistic end what David Bentley Hart, speaking of the trinitarian theologies of the Greek and Latin fathers, has called the "deep and astonishingly rich unity between our traditions, a unity too easily forgotten or obscured when we devote ourselves to interpreting the

---

136. I, q. 43, a. 5, ad 2. For the implications of this in Christian spirituality, see Michael Downey, *Altogether Gift: A Trinitarian Spirituality* (Maryknoll, NY: Orbis, 2000), 36–37. See also the ecumenically hopeful conclusions (at least with regard to Augustine) of David Bent-ley Hart, "The Hidden and the Manifest: Metaphysics after Nicaea," in Demacopoulos and Papanikolaou, *Orthodox Readings of Augustine*, 191–226. For Hart, it is correct to hold (as both Augustine and Gregory of Nyssa do) that "the image of God in creation—and in rational natures in particular—must be an actual communication of the light of God's own inward life, his own eternal Image of himself within the trinitarian mystery" (ibid., 222).

137. On the biblical evidence set forth by Aquinas, see also the excellent treatment by Emery, "The Procession of the Holy Spirit *a Filio* according to St. Thomas Aquinas," 225–35. For favorable discussion of the *filioque* from the vantage point of contemporary biblical scholar-ship, see Mauro Meruzzi, "Lo Spirito Santo nel Vangelo di Giovanni. E alcune note sul verbo ἐκπορεύομαι in Gv 15, 26," in *Il Filioque*, 167–98.

past in the light of our later separation."[138] Like the Greek fathers, Aquinas advocates caution in approaching the mystery of the Spirit's distinctiveness. His intention of preserving and defending the Spirit's revealed distinctiveness along relational lines in the Trinitarian *ordo*, while taking care not to negate the Father's monarchy or to isolate the Spirit from either the Father or the Son, accords with the goals of Maximus and the earlier Greek fathers.

Without claiming to know the intimate details of the inner life of the Trinity, then, it seems possible to conclude with Aquinas (and Augustine) that the Word, as the Word of the Father, "breathes forth Love." Put more boldly, the Spirit manifests the fecundity of the love of the Father and Son: the fruit of their exchange is inexhaustible communion. In the chapters that follow, I trace this personal fruit, the Holy Spirit, in his invisible and visible missions to Jesus Christ and the church, and so in his eschatological gift of communion in love.

138. Hart, "The Hidden and the Manifest," 226.

THE HOLY SPIRIT AND JESUS CHRIST

Bruce Marshall has remarked with regard to the Trinity, "The language of 'immanent' and 'economic' has become so pervasive in Catholic trinitarian theology that to question it might seem tantamount to questioning faith in the Trinity itself."[1] As Marshall points out, however, the use of these two terms was not standard prior to modern times. He traces the terms back to Franz Anton Staudenmaier in the nineteenth century. The Greek fathers contrasted the *oikonomia* and *theologia*, but did not refer to an "economic," let alone a "theological," Trinity. Marshall grants that we require a "conceptual means for apprehending the distinctions among the divine persons, and their unity as God, other than the means we use to apprehend the totality of their activity in creation and redemption."[2] But he proposes that for this task, the traditional distinction between the processions and missions of the divine persons remains the best approach. The processions enable us to distinguish the persons without eviscerating the divine unity, while the missions add "a specific relationship to the creature" without conflating the economy of salvation with the intratrinitarian life.[3] Since the missions are the processions with

---

1. Bruce D. Marshall, "The Unity of the Triune God: Reviving an Ancient Question," *The Thomist* 74 (2010): 1–32, at 8.
2. Ibid., 19.
3. Ibid. Thus, challenging Karl Rahner's axiom "the immanent Trinity is the economic Trinity and vice versa" (not least as taken up by such theologians as Wolfhart Pannenberg and Jürgen Moltmann), John Zizioulas observes that "if these views are considered from the

a temporal term, the missions display what generally appears under the rubric "economic Trinity." The theology of the missions allows for a conceptually clearer link with (and distinction from) the eternal processions than can be obtained from the economic/immanent contrast.[4]

Ralph Del Colle has urged that we should "understand both 'who Christ is' and 'what Christ has done' from the perspective of the third article of

---

angle of Trinitarian freedom, the conclusion would be that whatever happens in the economy is logically determined by what God is in his essence and vice versa" (Zizioulas, "Trinitarian Freedom: Is God Free in Trinitarian Life?," in *Rethinking Trinitarian Theology*, ed. Giulio Maspero and Robert J. Woźniak [London: T&T Clark, 2012], 193–207, at 204). Zizioulas accepts, of course, that the "immanent" and "economic" Trinity are not two different Trinities, but he emphasizes that the way God "reaches beyond himself is dictated by the special conditions of those he wishes to reach (creation and humanity), as condescensions for their sake, and not by any inner logical or ontological necessity. . . . The economy manifests God's freedom precisely by showing that God is free to become what he is not rather than what he is in his own being. By projecting what God has done for our sake in the economy into what he is eternally in his Trinitarian being we implicitly undermine his freedom to become what he eternally is not" (ibid., 205–6). For a similar response to Rahner's axiom, see David Bentley Hart, *The Beauty of the Infinite: The Aesthetics of Christian Truth* (Grand Rapids: Eerdmans, 2003), 155–59. See also the helpful examination of the Cappadocians, Augustine, and Maximus on *theologia/oikonomia* and *missio* in Philipp Gabriel Renczes, "Scope of Rahner's Fundamental Axiom in the Patristic Perspective: A Dialogue of Systematic and Historical Theology," in Maspero and Woźniak, *Rethinking Trinitarian Theology*, 254–88. For Maximus, Renczes remarks, "the human being cannot claim to be able to know the Economic and the Immanent Trinity in the dynamic relation of one to the other (not to mention the relation between the divine work and the divine being), but only as it offers itself to man as gift" (ibid., 285). For the opposite emphasis on the missions as opening up the "history of the Trinity," see Jürgen Moltmann, *The Church in the Power of the Spirit: A Contribution to Messianic Ecclesiology*, trans. Margaret Kohl (Minneapolis: Fortress, 1993), 56–65. Moltmann goes so far as to say, "The unity of the triune God is the goal of the uniting of man and creation with the Father and the Son in the Spirit," and "The history of the Son and of the Spirit therefore brings about, even for God himself within the Trinity, an experience, something 'new'" (ibid., 62). For Moltmann, "The history of God's suffering in the passion of the Son and the sighings of the Spirit serves the history of God's joy in the Spirit and his completed felicity in the end" (ibid., 64). For a particularly cogent response to Moltmann, see William J. Hill, OP, *The Three-Personed God: The Trinity as a Mystery of Salvation* (Washington, DC: Catholic University of America Press, 1982), 166–75.

4. As Marshall observes, "If there is going to be a divine mission, the coming forth of a divine person which has a *creature* as its term (or more precisely, which terminates in a change wrought in the creature by a new relation to that person), it has to include the eternal procession by which that divine person is already constituted and in which he already has his unique personal identity. In fact, if a divine person is to have a mission at all, the temporal coming forth of sent from sender in which the mission consists must be the very same coming forth as the eternal procession by which that person originates from the Father (and, as the case may be, from the Son)" (Marshall, "Unity of the Triune God," 22). See also Gilles Emery, OP, "*Theologia* and *Dispensatio*: The Centrality of the Divine Missions in St. Thomas's Trinitarian Theology," *The Thomist* 74 (2010): 515–61; Matthew Levering, "Christ, the Trinity, and Predestination: McCormack and Aquinas," in *Trinity and Election in Contemporary Theology*, ed. Michael T. Dempsey (Grand Rapids: Eerdmans, 2011), 244–73.

the creed: 'I believe in the Holy Spirit, the Lord and Giver of Life.'"[5] So long as we equally appreciate the mission of the Son and do not fall into a Spirit-monism or a competition between Son and Spirit, this position seems right to me, since the incarnate Son was conceived in Mary's womb "of the Holy Spirit" (Matt. 1:20), and he was filled with the Holy Spirit.[6] As Miroslav Volf and Maurice Lee put it, "The identity and mission of *Christ* were fundamentally shaped by the *Spirit*."[7] On this basis, therefore, the present chapter focuses on the Holy Spirit's missions to Jesus Christ for the salvation of the world. I begin by exploring the relationship of Jesus to the Spirit according to the biblical scholar James D. G. Dunn. Unlike myself, Dunn does not affirm the distinctive, divine status of the Spirit and of the Son.[8]

5. Ralph Del Colle, *Christ and the Spirit: Spirit-Christology in Trinitarian Perspective* (Oxford: Oxford University Press, 1994), 3. Del Colle firmly distances himself from what he calls "the most comprehensive form of Spirit-christology—namely, that which posits Spirit as the divine element in the person of Christ. The Spirit then may be either a substitution for or identical with the divine Logos" (ibid., 4). Occasionally Del Colle describes his own Spirit-Christology in ways from which I demur, as when he states, "What believers receive as the grace of God through the presence and power of the Holy Spirit is constitutive of the person of Christ and consistent with the self-communication of God, itself an expression of the intra-trinitarian relations" (ibid., 126). Here it is better to insist that the person of Christ is the divine Son who comes forth from the Father.

6. Thus Yves Congar, OP, forcefully remarks, "If I were to draw but one conclusion from the whole of my work on the Holy Spirit, I would express it in these words: no Christology without pneumatology and no pneumatology without Christology" (Congar, *The Word and the Spirit*, trans. David Smith [London: Geoffrey Chapman, 1986], 1 [cf. 27, 71–72]).

7. Miroslav Volf and Maurice Lee, "The Spirit and the Church," in *Advents of the Spirit: An Introduction to the Current Study of Pneumatology*, ed. Bradford E. Hinze and D. Lyle Dabney (Milwaukee: Marquette University Press, 2001), 382–409, at 384. They identify "a *triplicity* of relations that is of fundamental significance for ecclesiology: the relation between the Spirit and the church, the relation between Christ and the church, and a complex relation between the Spirit and Christ in which Christ appears both as bearer and giver of the Spirit" (ibid.).

8. See particularly Dunn's *Christology in the Making: A New Testament Inquiry into the Origins of the Doctrine of the Incarnation*, 2nd ed. (London: SCM, 1989), although Dunn's foreword to the second edition (xi–xxxix) defends some sense of "trinitarian orthodoxy" as well as the view that "Jesus Christ is he whom the Word of God *became* in the incarnation" (xxxi–xxxii). In the same foreword, Dunn continues to deny that pre-Johannine New Testament texts affirm the preexistence of a divine Son of God. Dunn is especially concerned to avoid the "bitheism or tritheism of which Judaism and Islam accuse Christianity" (xxxi). For a persuasive response to Dunn on the topic of the preexistence of the Son according to the Synoptic Gospels, see Simon J. Gathercole, *The Pre-Existent Son: Recovering the Christologies of Matthew, Mark, and Luke* (Grand Rapids: Eerdmans, 2006). See also Dunn, *Christianity in the Making*, vol. 1, *Jesus Remembered* (Grand Rapids: Eerdmans, 2003), 708–24, where he presents Jesus's view of his Sonship as quite compatible with a merely human status; and Dunn's *Did the First Christians Worship Jesus? The New Testament Evidence* (Louisville: Westminster John Knox, 2010), where he argues that the New Testament texts that are often taken as evidence for early Christian belief in the divinity of Jesus are instead likely to have been simply testimonies to the fact that "the depth and profundity of God has been so fully revealed in and through Christ"

But Dunn nonetheless provides valuable assistance in appreciating the biblical testimony to Jesus's powerful experience of the Spirit. More than any other contemporary biblical scholar, Dunn has made a point of emphasizing and creatively exploring the Spirit's role in the life of Jesus. In Dunn's focus (especially in his early work) upon Jesus's experience, I find helpful insight into the way that the Gospels' portraits of Jesus convey a man indwelt and impelled by the Spirit of God.[9]

In this exegetical light, I retrieve Thomas Aquinas's theology of the Holy Spirit's visible and invisible missions to Jesus.[10] My central argument is that Aquinas's theological portrait of Jesus's humanity as *uniquely* Spirit-filled accords with, even as it can be enriched by, the fundamental thrust of Dunn's research. Aquinas goes beyond Dunn not only by identifying the Son and Spirit as distinct divine persons but also in his reflections about how the Spirit's missions to Jesus undergird his sinlessness, knowledge, and works of charity and power, including his exorcisms and miracles. As John Zizioulas puts it from his own theological perspective, "Christ is not Christ unless He is an existence in the Spirit, which means an *eschatological existence*."[11] I hope to make clear that this eschatological existence, in its supreme self-giving love for the salvation of the people of God, is stamped uniquely by the Love and Gift of the Spirit.[12] The Spirit's missions empower the incarnate Son for his public ministry and paschal mystery, whose outcome

---

or to the "powerful significance" of "Jesus's Lordship" (ibid., 136). For Dunn, Jesus can be said to embody "God's 'identity'" in the sense of "embodying the creative and redemptive purpose and energy of God" (ibid., 143), but Dunn essentially limits the descriptor "God" to the Father and urges that Jesus (the Son) is the one in and through whom Christians should worship God rather than being himself worthy of worship.

9. As Declan Marmion and Rik Van Nieuwenhove observe in summative fashion, "The Synoptic Gospels see Jesus as one anointed by the Spirit—the Messiah—and portray his understanding of the Spirit in traditional prophetic terms as the dynamic power of God working in and through him. . . . In Luke's Gospel each aspect of Jesus's life and ministry is animated by the Spirit. Even Jesus's conception, when the Spirit comes upon Mary (Luke 1:35), indicates that there never was a time in his history when Jesus was not imbued with the Spirit" (Marmion and Van Nieuwenhove, *An Introduction to the Trinity* [Cambridge: Cambridge University Press, 2011], 43–44). They add that Jesus "had not only a unique sense of his relationship to his God as Abba, he also knew himself as a unique bearer of the Spirit. . . . In *giving* the Spirit he goes beyond the prophets and acts from the side of God. Through his ministry the bestowal of the Spirit takes on a definitive quality heralding a new people and a new creation" (ibid., 45).

10. For a work of Catholic spirituality that emphasizes the Spirit's missions to Jesus, see Columba Marmion, OSB, *Christ, the Life of the Soul*, trans. Alan Bancroft (Bethesda, MD: Zaccheus, 2005), 138–44.

11. John Zizioulas, "Apostolic Continuity and Orthodox Theology: Towards a Synthesis of Two Perspectives," *St. Vladimir's Theological Quarterly* 19 (1975): 75–108, at 85.

12. As Yves Congar puts it, "It is primarily in Christ that the 'two hands' of the Father, the Word and the Breath, are united" (Congar, *Word and the Spirit*, 62).

is the visible pouring out of the Spirit upon the apostles at Pentecost. The Spirit's missions to Jesus, therefore, always have in view the Spirit's missions to the church.[13]

James D. G. Dunn on Jesus and the Holy Spirit

Dunn's Jesus and the Spirit *(1975)*

In his *Jesus and the Spirit*, Dunn acknowledges his debt to Albert Schweitzer and Johannes Weiss and especially to their emphasis on the eschatological proclamation of Jesus.[14] The Jesus reconstructed by Schweitzer and Weiss proclaimed the imminent arrival of the kingdom of God. Dunn reasons that Jesus's "message was rooted in his own *sense* that something new and final

13. In chap. 6 of *The Word and the Spirit*, Congar criticizes Aquinas's theology of Christ and salvation for giving insufficient attention to "the action of the Holy Spirit" and for lacking "a full recognition of the historical character of the economy of salvation" (ibid., 86–87). It seems to me that Congar's criticisms, while valid for certain less central elements of Aquinas's exposition of Christ, are most definitely not valid for Aquinas's exposition viewed as a whole. In addition to the present chapter, see Matthew Levering, *Christ's Fulfillment of Torah and Temple: Salvation according to Thomas Aquinas* (Notre Dame, IN: University of Notre Dame Press, 2002).

14. See Johannes Weiss, *Jesus' Proclamation of the Kingdom of God*, ed. and trans. Richard H. Hiers and D. Larrimore Holland (Philadelphia: Fortress, 1971); Albert Schweitzer, *The Quest of the Historical Jesus: A Critical Study of Its Progress from Reimarus to Wrede*, trans. W. Montgomery (Minneapolis: Fortress, 2001). More proximately, see C. K. Barrett, *The Holy Spirit and the Gospel Tradition*, 2nd ed. (London: SPCK, 1966). Barrett approaches the problem of Jesus's and the church's relation to the Holy Spirit by stating, "It cannot be too frequently or too strongly emphasized that the thought of Jesus was cast in an eschatological mould, and that it cannot be understood if it is considered apart from that mould" (ibid., 4). From a perspective that strikes me as an exaggeration, Barrett holds that Jesus's "silence with regard to the Spirit" can be understood in terms of his eschatological self-understanding: "He could not in the time of his ministry speak of his own plenary inspiration, nor unmistakably reveal it, because that would have meant the betrayal of the Messianic secret. He did not bestow the Spirit upon his followers, because that gift was a mark of the fully realized Kingdom of God, and did not lie within the province of the germinal Kingdom which corresponded to his veiled Messiahship. He did not prophesy the existence of a Spirit-filled community, because he did not foresee an interval between the period of humiliation and that of complete and final glorification" (ibid., 160). For Barrett, by contrast to Dunn (and to my own view), the connection between Jesus and the Spirit was made not by Jesus but by the postresurrection community that, contrary to its original expectations of the immediate arrival of the kingdom, experienced the gift of the Spirit while awaiting Jesus's return. See also Brian Gaybba, *The Spirit of Love: Theology of the Holy Spirit* (London: Geoffrey Chapman, 1987), 20–21. Gaybba addresses the problem of Jesus's relative silence about the Holy Spirit, and he agrees with Dunn's insistence upon Jesus's awareness of God's power or Spirit within him. For background, see Wendell Willis, "The Discovery of the Eschatological Kingdom: Johannes Weiss and Albert Schweitzer," in *The Kingdom of God in 20th-Century Interpretation*, ed. Wendell Willis (Peabody, MA: Hendrickson, 1987), 1–14.

was happening in him and through him."[15] If Jesus had such a sense, however, why did he have it, and why did he give credence to it? Dunn argues that the answer, so far as can be gleaned from the New Testament, consists in Jesus's awareness of the active, eschatological presence of the Spirit in himself. As Dunn says, "We have a number of sayings of Jesus which throw considerable light on his self-consciousness at this point, above all on *his consciousness of eschatological power, of God's Spirit upon him and working through him.*"[16] Dunn identifies three sets of passages in particular: passages related to Jesus's exorcisms, to the prophecy found in Isaiah 61, and to Jesus's baptism at the Jordan.

Historical-critical scholars have no problem accepting that Jesus was well known as a successful exorcist. This being so, a question follows: How did Jesus himself account for his success as an exorcist? In Matthew 12:28 and Luke 11:20, the evangelists preserve a saying of Jesus that seeks to explain his success as an exorcist, and that Dunn takes to be part of "Q," the hypothetical common source behind these Synoptic Gospels. Matthew 12:28 presents Jesus's saying as follows: "But if it is by the Spirit of God that I cast out demons, then the kingdom of God has come upon you." Luke 11:20 presents the same saying, but has "the finger of God" rather than "the Spirit of God." Dunn argues for the priority of Matthew's version, despite the fact that many scholars consider Luke's to be prior on the grounds that the Spirit is prominent in Luke's Gospel, and he would not have altered the saying to "finger" had "Spirit" been present in the source material. In response to such scholars, Dunn points out that Matthew here retains "kingdom of God" rather than changing it to "kingdom of heaven," an indication that Matthew is not in this verse changing his source material. Furthermore, Matthew characteristically presents Jesus as the new Moses, the new lawgiver, and Matthew therefore would have been likely to keep "finger of God" in order to preserve the link to Exodus 8:19. In Dunn's view Luke's strong exodus typology might have easily led him to change "Spirit" to "finger." In addition, Dunn thinks that Luke held that the Spirit was not subordinate to Jesus prior to his resurrection and ascension.

Dunn goes on to observe that, in either case, Jesus was referring to the power of God, a hallmark of the eschatological age. Thus Jesus certainly "believed that he cast out demons by the power of God."[17] It follows that

---

15. James D. G. Dunn, *Jesus and the Spirit: A Study of the Religious and Charismatic Experience of Jesus and the First Christians as Reflected in the New Testament* (London: SCM, 1975), 43.
16. Ibid.
17. Ibid., 47.

Jesus's consciousness included "an *awareness* of an *otherly* power working through him, together with the *conviction* that this power was *God's* power."[18] In Jesus's exorcistic action, God was at work through Jesus. Surely this sense of divine power acting through him—of divine Spirit—gave Jesus a strong sense of authority.

As Dunn points out, this sense of divine power must be combined with the eschatological expectations that Jesus, in his own way, shared with other Jews of his time. In various ways, many Jews were expecting the inbreaking of God's kingdom, and Jesus was no exception. In this context, the overcoming of demons would naturally be taken as a sign of the eschatological age. Dunn argues, "So far as Jesus was concerned, the exercise of this power was *evidence that the longed-for kingdom of God had already come upon his hearers*; his exorcisms demonstrated that the last days were already present."[19] Although there were other Jewish exorcists contemporary with Jesus, moreover, Jesus did not associate his exorcisms with theirs but instead emphasized that the power (or Spirit) of God was working through *him*. In this regard, Dunn highlights Jesus's saying about the binding of the strong man, in Matthew 12:29; Mark 3:27; Luke 11:21. All three versions are similar; I quote Mark's: "But no one can enter a strong man's house and plunder his goods, unless he first binds the strong man; then indeed he may plunder his house." According to Dunn, Jesus saw the power (Spirit) of God working through him to bind Satan and indeed to be "that binding of the powers of evil which was looked for at the end of the age. The final battle was already joined and Satan was already being routed (cf. Luke 10.18)."[20] The point is that Jesus saw his own actions as being the precise ones through which the power (Spirit) of God was working. He experienced, then, in his own person the power of "the eschatological Spirit" enabling him to perform the deeds that were inaugurating the eschatological age.[21] As Dunn states, "*The eschatological kingdom was present for Jesus only because the eschatological Spirit was present in and through him.*"[22]

---

18. Ibid.
19. Ibid.
20. Ibid., 48.
21. Ibid.
22. Ibid. By contrast, Barrett comments,

   Jesus himself thought of his power to perform mighty works, and of his own status and divine mission, as an anticipation of the future; here and there his future glory as Messiah, and the power of the Kingdom, shone through the veil of their present humiliation and obscurity. The Church, however, as was natural, looked upon this same power and status as the fruit of the Spirit of God resting upon the Messiah. Hence, inevitably, there arose a tendency to change the centre of gravity of Jesus's eschatological teaching, accommodating it to the standpoint of the post-resurrection community, and at the same time introducing into his words, either by the creation of new sayings or by the modification

Dunn draws a similar lesson from Jesus's teaching, attested in Matthew 12:31; Mark 3:29; Luke 12:10, that rejection of the Holy Spirit is an unforgivable sin, whereas rejection of the "Son of Man," according to Matthew and Luke, will be forgiven. Historical-critical scholars debate which version (Mark or Q) has priority, and Dunn leaves this debate unresolved. But he argues against the view that the saying reflects tensions in the early community rather than Jesus's own words, and instead he locates the saying in the context of Jesus's exorcisms. As he puts it, "His power to cast out demons was the Spirit of God. Therefore criticism of his exorcisms was a speaking against God's Spirit."[23] To speak against God's Spirit is here to deny God's power to accomplish the eschatological victory through Jesus. For Dunn, Jesus's confidence that the Spirit had returned to Israel, and that the Spirit was working through him, was rooted in his experience of successfully performing exorcisms. Indeed, Jesus was so confident about his possession of the Spirit that he considered anyone speaking against him to be speaking against the Spirit. Dunn remarks, "Here we see coming to clear expression Jesus's sense of the awfulness, the numinous quality, the eschatological finality of the power which possessed him."[24]

Turning to Isaiah 61, Dunn repeats his emphasis on Jesus's sense of his own new, definitive spiritual power—God's power, the Spirit—in relation to his sense of authority and proclamation of the kingdom. Dunn does not consider Luke 4:18–21, with its open messianic claim, to be authentic.[25] But in Luke 6:20–26 (paralleled in Matt. 5:3–6), he finds another allusion to Isaiah 61, and he deems this to be authentic. The list of those who are "blessed" is an eschatological list, a depiction of the eschatological age. Its inclusion of the "poor" and those who weep indicates the influence of Isaiah

---

of already existing logia, teaching about the Spirit. The effect of this was to depict the Lord himself as a "spiritual" man. But this process was checked by the conviction, at once historical and theological, that "the Spirit was not yet; because Jesus was not yet glorified" (John 7.39); which is the last word that may be said about the Holy Spirit in the Synoptic Gospels. (Barrett, *Holy Spirit and the Gospel Tradition*, 162)

23. Dunn, *Jesus and the Spirit*, 52.

24. Ibid., 53.

25. For the problematizing of the criteria of authenticity, see, for example, Anthony Le Donne's insistence—discomfiting historical-critical scholars and theologians alike—that with respect to the Gospels we cannot really sift what is historically "authentic" from what is not. For discussion, see the essays in Chris Keith and Anthony Le Donne, eds., *Jesus, Criteria, and the Demise of Authenticity* (London: T&T Clark, 2012). See also Le Donne, *Historical Jesus: What Can We Know and How Can We Know It?* (Grand Rapids: Eerdmans, 2011); Le Donne, *The Historiographical Jesus: Memory, Typology, and the Son of David* (Waco: Baylor University Press, 2009). Even if Le Donne somewhat overstates his case, it should not surprise that biblical "authenticity," even solely with regard to historicity, cannot be measured by historical-critical tools alone.

61. By proclaiming this list of beatitudes, Dunn says, Jesus is laying claim to be the one who has "been anointed by the Spirit of God, commissioned to proclaim the good news of the end-time kingdom," and to inaugurate this kingdom.[26] Another, more explicit allusion to Isaiah 61 comes in Luke 7:18–23 (paralleled in Matt. 11:2–6), where Jesus tells the disciples of John the Baptist, "Go and tell John what you have seen and heard: the blind receive their sight, the lame walk, lepers are cleansed, and the deaf hear, the dead are raised up, the poor have good news preached to them. And blessed is he who takes no offense at me" (vv. 22–23). After reviewing scholarly doubts about the authenticity of this saying, Dunn argues that the key point is that the eschatological answer fits the eschatological question posed by John the Baptist. Jesus is indeed claiming to act with the power or Spirit of God. Dunn's conclusion is that Jesus considered the eschatological kingdom to be present not only in his exorcisms, but also in his teaching or preaching. As Dunn puts it, "The power which he experienced in himself, the power which became evident in his healings (in his exorcisms in particular) and especially in his proclamation of the good news to the poor, was in Jesus's view the eschatological Spirit operating in and through him."[27] Recall that Dunn is seeking to explain why Jesus seems to have felt so sure that God was bringing about the eschatological age in and through Jesus himself. Dunn's answer, again, is that Jesus bears witness to a unique experience of the Spirit, to "an overwhelming conviction that *he* himself *is* the one anointed by the end-time Spirit."[28]

Reflecting upon the connection between Sonship and Spirit in the Gospel of Mark's presentation of Jesus's baptism at the Jordan (Mark 1:9–11), Dunn argues that since "it is certain that Jesus believed himself to be empowered by the Spirit and thought of himself as God's son [though not, for Dunn, God's divine Son]," his baptism at the Jordan might well have been the moment where "these convictions crystallized" in Jesus's mind.[29] Dunn adds that John the Baptist and Jesus differed on the timing of the kingdom, which for Jesus has in some sense already been inaugurated. On this basis Dunn reasons, "The break between John and Jesus must therefore have been occasioned by Jesus's awareness of the Spirit: the eschatological Spirit

---

26. Dunn, *Jesus and the Spirit*, 55.

27. Ibid., 61. For discussion, see Bruce W. Longenecker, "Rome's Victory and God's Honour: The Jerusalem Temple and the Spirit of God in Lukan Theodicy," in *The Holy Spirit and Christian Origins: Essays in Honor of James D. G. Dunn*, ed. Graham N. Stanton, Bruce W. Longenecker, and Stephen C. Barton (Grand Rapids: Eerdmans, 2004), 90–102, at 100–102.

28. Dunn, *Jesus and the Spirit*, 62.

29. Ibid., 63.

was already upon him—therefore John's message and ministry was already superseded."[30] Jesus's baptism could have been the moment, then, when Jesus became aware of the Spirit and thus also of his Sonship. Furthermore, when Jesus is asked later in the Gospel of Mark about his authority for doing such deeds, Jesus counters by asking his questioners to answer whether John's baptism was from God or not. Jesus's respect for John's baptism may come from his own experience of the Spirit at his baptism. Dunn nonetheless considers that "it remains quite probable that Jesus never spoke directly of what happened at the Jordan, but made some allusions which have provided the basis of the earliest account."[31] These allusions would have indicated the event's importance for Jesus's experience of the Spirit and for his conviction of his Sonship.

With respect to Jesus's baptism, Dunn finds that Jesus likely "experienced an insurge of spiritual power and became aware that he was being anointed with the eschatological Spirit of God. . . . It is quite likely that Jesus was convinced that at his baptism he had heard God's voice addressing him as son and setting him apart for a special task."[32] But, although Dunn thinks that the baptism has this significance, he does not thereby rule out the possibility that Jesus may have been conscious of the Spirit's presence and of his own Sonship well before his baptism. The rather scant historical evidence does not allow for anything like certitude about when Jesus became aware of the power of the eschatological Spirit working through him. Dunn adds that we should consider Jesus's "consciousness of sonship and consciousness of Spirit as two sides of the one coin."[33] In this regard, he points to the Spirit's leading Jesus into the wilderness to undergo temptations that have to do with Jesus's Sonship; to the evil spirits who recognize Jesus (the exorcist) as the Son of God; and to Jesus's sense of his own authority stemming not only from the Spirit but also from the Father. Summing up the results of his inquiry, Dunn observes that the texts that testify to Jesus's spiritual experience—admittedly few though these texts are—make clear that "*Jesus thought of himself as God's son and as anointed by the eschatological Spirit, because in prayer he experienced God as Father and in ministry he experienced a power to heal which he could only understand as the power of the end-time*

---

30. Ibid., 64. Dunn also observes that, by contrast to the imagery of judgment used by John the Baptist to foretell the Spirit-filled Messiah, Jesus emphasizes grace and mercy. In Dunn's view, "The power which he [Jesus] experienced working through his ministry was a power to heal not to destroy" (ibid., 61). One can see connections here with Aquinas's theology of the Spirit as "Love" and "Gift."
31. Ibid., 65.
32. Ibid.
33. Ibid., 66.

and an inspiration to proclaim a message which he could only understand as the gospel of the end-time."[34]

Dunn's "The Spirit of Jesus" (1988)

In "The Spirit of Jesus," Dunn begins with the observation that Jesus must have been an impressive and unusual figure, or else a movement would hardly have coalesced around him. During his lifetime, Jesus's impact came about due to his exorcisms and teachings, which included appropriating to himself an unusual degree of authority regarding the coming of God's kingdom. Dunn's question is how Jews of Jesus's day would have interpreted such a figure. He identifies five possible answers. First, they might have seen Jesus as a prophet, or perhaps the final prophet, "one anointed with the Spirit to bring about the revelation for the new age (Isa. 61:1–4), an age in which the prophetic Spirit would be dispersed much more widely (Joel 2:28–29)."[35] Second, they might have considered him to be Enoch or Elijah returning from heaven, or even perhaps a figure such as Moses, Ezra, or Melchizedek. Elijah, certainly, was expected by Jews of Jesus's day to return from heaven, and the other figures were prominent in eschatological texts of the day. Third, they might have thought him to be an angel, such as Gabriel, who appeared to Mary. Fourth, they might have identified him with Sophia or the Logos, since personified Wisdom (Sophia) appears in Proverbs and Sirach, and since Philo presents the divine Logos in personal terms. Fifth, they might have supposed that Jesus had been the beneficiary of a visionary journey into heaven such as that experienced by Daniel. In Jesus's day, Dunn points out, "Such journeys were attributed to several great names from Israel's past—including Enoch, Adam, Abraham, and Levi . . . with particular interest in Moses' ascent of Sinai as a type of ascent to heaven."[36] Jesus's contemporaries seem to have been interested in *merkabah* or chariot mysticism revolving around Ezekiel 1, and "Paul himself speaks of a visionary journey to heaven in 2 Corinthians 12:2–4 which he enjoyed."[37]

---

34. Ibid., 67.

35. James D. G. Dunn, "The Spirit of Jesus," in *The Christ and the Spirit: Collected Essays of James D. G. Dunn*, vol. 2, *Pneumatology* (Grand Rapids: Eerdmans, 1998), 329–42, at 330.

36. Ibid., 333.

37. Ibid., 334. See also Dunn's response to reductionary emphasis on Jewish apocalyptic and *merkebah* mysticism, in Dunn, *Christology in the Making*, xxiii–xxvi. For a reduction of Paul's Christology to *merkabah* mysticism, see, for example, two representative works published after Dunn's "Spirit of Jesus": Alan F. Segal, *Paul the Convert: The Apostolate and Apostasy of Saul the Pharisee* (New Haven: Yale University Press, 1990); John Ashton, *The Religion of Paul the Apostle* (New Haven: Yale University Press, 2000). See also Christopher Rowland's

Dunn argues that most of these categories, although possible, can be shown to be highly unlikely. Had Jesus been an angel, for example, he would have been expected to stay only a short while. Had Jesus been a man who received a heavenly journey, he would have been expected to maintain "a great reserve in speaking of what had been seen and heard."[38] The New Testament writings distinguish clearly between Jesus and angels, and these writings never depict Jesus's knowledge as deriving from a visionary journey that was given to the man Jesus; indeed, John 3:12–13 explicitly rules out this possibility. Jesus seems to have presented himself as the Danielic "son of man," but "there is no indication that anyone thought he was identifying himself with a heavenly being who had come from heaven to earth."[39] Jesus himself ruled out the view that his power is that of Elijah; instead he associated John the Baptist with this role, without supposing John to be literally Elijah. The transfiguration narratives describe Jesus appearing with both Moses and Elijah, and so he is not to be identified with either. In Dunn's view, "There is little likelihood that any of Jesus's contemporaries thought that Wisdom would appear in human form."[40]

Dunn argues, therefore, that the category worth focusing upon is that of "*the* final prophet, or alternatively, that of the Messiah anointed with the Spirit."[41] In the Gospels of Mark and Luke, Jesus refers to himself as a prophet, and Mark clearly presents him as a prophet like Moses. Jesus claims that his power to expel demons comes from the Spirit of God. In all the Gospels, and in Acts as well, the earliest Christians proclaim Jesus to have been anointed with the Spirit. Dunn finds "a massive consistency about the picture which emerges. Jesus, the anointed one, inspired by the Spirit, was the end-time prophet who (with John the Baptist) broke the long drought of the Spirit and introduced the new age of the Spirit in himself and his mission."[42]

This portrait of Jesus as the final prophet, anointed by the Spirit to introduce the eschatological age, should not, in Dunn's view, be supposed to compete with Jesus as the incarnation of Wisdom or the Logos. The Gospel of John, of course, explicitly describes Jesus as the incarnation of the preexistent Logos, and the identification of Jesus with Wisdom appears in Matthew and Paul. But as Dunn emphasizes, even in the Gospel of John, where Jesus is the incarnation of the preexistent Logos, Jesus still needs the Spirit. Thus

---

groundbreaking work, *The Open Heaven: A Study of Apocalyptic in Judaism and Early Christianity* (London: SPCK, 1982).

38. Dunn, "Spirit of Jesus," 334.
39. Ibid., 336.
40. Ibid., 333.
41. Ibid., 334.
42. Ibid., 335.

John the Baptist says, "I saw the Spirit descend as a dove from heaven, and it remained on him. I myself did not know him; but he who sent me to baptize with water said to me, 'He on whom you see the Spirit descend and remain, this is he who baptizes with the Holy Spirit'" (John 1:32–33).[43] Dunn notes that the evangelist John "must have retained this emphasis, not only because it was firmly rooted in the tradition, but also because it said something of continuing importance for his understanding of Jesus and the Spirit."[44]

Dunn also considers that in Second Temple Judaism "Wisdom, Logos, and Spirit were all in very large measure synonymous," although I am not sure that the texts that he cites—Wisdom 9:1–2 and 9:17—in fact serve to show this.[45] But the main point that he has in view here is indisputable: in the New Testament, a careful distinction is made between Jesus and the Spirit. For Dunn, the distinction between Jesus and the Spirit serves to underscore the fact that those who encountered Jesus, rather than turning to explanations such as the return of Elijah, the coming of an angel, or a heavenly journey, explained Jesus's extraordinary authority and power by identifying Jesus as a Spirit-filled prophet, indeed as "a man inspired by the Spirit in full and final measure."[46] This sense of Jesus as a prophet, or rather as the final prophet, is not replaced even by the view that Jesus is incarnate Wisdom or incarnate Logos. The Spirit's role in empowering Jesus remains in full force.

Dunn then asks whether Jesus's relation to the Spirit changes after his resurrection and ascension. He first notes that the fact that Jesus's disciples used "resurrection" to describe what happened to him is significant. They could have employed heavenly journey imagery, or imagery such as is found in Second Temple narratives about the ascensions of Enoch, Moses, or Elijah. Instead, they presented Jesus as resurrected in such a way as to be the inauguration of the general resurrection of the dead. According to Dunn, the ascended Jesus's intercessory role is one that is given elsewhere in Second Temple literature to protagonists such as the archangels, Melchizedek, and Abel. But the ascended Jesus has a role that the others do not seem to have: he is "Lord and dispenser of the Spirit" (cf. Acts 2:33; John 15:26).[47] Having inaugurated the eschatological age, the risen and ascended Jesus now acts through the Spirit, so that it is by the Spirit that believers are united with

43. Regarding the symbolism of the dove, see especially George T. Montague, SM, *The Holy Spirit: Growth of a Biblical Tradition; A Commentary on the Principal Texts of the Old and New Testaments* (New York: Paulist Press, 1976), 240–41.

44. Dunn, "Spirit of Jesus," 336.

45. Ibid., 337.

46. Ibid., 338.

47. Ibid., 339.

Jesus. Citing various texts, including 1 Corinthians 6:17, Acts 16:7, Romans 8:9, Galatians 4:6, Philippians 1:19, and 1 Peter 1:11, Dunn urges us to "think of what was being claimed: that the Spirit of God, the Holy Spirit, was to be identified as the Spirit of Jesus. The cosmic power of God, the mysterious and miracle-working action of God in his world, could now be known simply as the Spirit which inspired Jesus and which came from Jesus."[48]

During his earthly life, in other words, Jesus is propelled by the Spirit; as risen and ascended to the right hand of God the Father, Jesus now sends the Spirit and exercises lordship over the Spirit. What Dunn identifies here is described by Hans Urs von Balthasar, from a different theological perspective, as "Trinitarian inversion."[49] In his earthly life, Balthasar says, the Son "entrusts himself to the activity of the Spirit in accord with the Father's will," whereas "the exalted Lord is given manifest power, even in his humanity, to breathe forth the Spirit."[50] Dunn argues that the first Christians blended the *exalted* Jesus and the Spirit in the same way that they did Jesus and Wisdom/Logos (by which Dunn does not intend to imply the divinity of the exalted Jesus). As a central text in this regard, Dunn cites 1 Corinthians 15:45, "the last Adam became a life-giving spirit," or, in Dunn's own translation, "became life-giving Spirit."[51] Although even with regard to the exalted Jesus Dunn accepts that there is still "a continuing distinction between Jesus and the Spirit," Dunn allows that we are dealing here with a strong identification of the exalted Jesus and the Spirit: we no longer experience Jesus as distinct from the Spirit, but rather we experience "Jesus through the Spirit, or even Jesus as the Spirit."[52]

This way of putting it—which is also found in Dunn's *Jesus and the Spirit*[53]—seems to me to be a stretch, both because of an overreliance on

48. Ibid.

49. Hans Urs von Balthasar, *Theo-Drama: Theological Dramatic Theory*, vol. 3, *The Dramatis Personae: Persons in Christ*, trans. Graham Harrison (San Francisco: Ignatius, 1992), 183.

50. Ibid., 186, 189. Balthasar asks, "Does this 'inversion' not disrupt the order of hypostases in God assumed in Catholic theology?" (ibid., 190). He answers in a highly complex fashion, arguing (unpersuasively in my view) that "it is only when the Son has risen and returned home to the Father that, together with the Father, he can openly represent a single principle of spiration" (ibid., 191). But I agree with Balthasar's basic point nonetheless, which is that "the Son, on the basis of his eternal origin, *really* receives power to breathe forth the Spirit. Similarly, in his incarnation, he already has *within him* a docility vis-à-vis the Spirit; the Spirit is *in* him in fullness (John 3:34), so that the Son can surrender himself to the guiding Spirit *above* him without any sense of heteronomy. What we have termed 'inversion' is ultimately only the projection of the immanent Trinity onto the 'economic' plane, whereby the Son's 'correspondence' to the Father is articulated as 'obedience'" (ibid.).

51. See Dunn, "Spirit of Jesus," 339.

52. Ibid., 340.

53. See especially Dunn, *Jesus and the Spirit*, 318–26. Dunn observes, "The point for us is that *Paul equates the risen Jesus with the Spirit who makes alive*. . . . He deliberately says that

1 Corinthians 15:45 and because there is a large difference between experiencing the exalted "Jesus through the Spirit" and experiencing Jesus "as the Spirit."[54] Yet Dunn is certainly right that the exalted Jesus, in his humanity, is "Lord of the Spirit" and sends the Spirit upon believers.[55] Likewise—and this is the crucial point that Dunn makes—"Because Jesus was the man of the Spirit, we can now recognize the Spirit as the Spirit of Jesus."[56] Since Jesus was a "prophet" and "a man like us," we should attend to his experience of the Spirit. Dunn comments in this regard, "We can thrill to his experience of spiritual anointing and empowering, his success in healing by the power of the Spirit. . . . The character of a Spirit-filled, Spirit-shaped ministry still retains

---

Jesus by his resurrection became that Spirit which believers experience as the source and power of their new life and new relationship with God. As from his resurrection Jesus may be known by men only as life-giving Spirit" (ibid., 322). Dunn goes on to say that "*when Paul wants to find the distinctive mark of Spirit-given experience, he finds it not in the charismatic Spirit as such, nor in the eschatological Spirit as such, but in the Jesus Spirit, the Spirit whose characteristics are those of Christ. . . .* The only charismata, the only charismatic Spirit Paul wants to know about is the Spirit of Christ, that is Christ the life-giving Spirit" (ibid., 324–25). For criticism of Dunn in this regard, see Grant Macaskill, *Union with Christ in the New Testament* (Oxford: Oxford University Press, 2013), 28–30, 158–59, 198–201, 218, and elsewhere. As Macaskill notes, "Those attempts to understand the divinity of Jesus to be constituted by the Spirit and therefore of the same species as that of the Christian have simply failed to do justice to those ways by which Luke's account distinguishes the two" (ibid., 200). While recognizing that the Spirit-Christologies of David Coffey and Ralph Del Colle (whose approach is essentially that of Coffey [see Del Colle's chaps. 4 and 5]) are much more nuanced than this, Macaskill nonetheless considers their arguments to be undermined by their dependence on Dunn's perspective. See David Coffey, *Grace: The Gift of the Holy Spirit* (Manly: Catholic Institute of Sydney, 1979); Coffey, *"Did You Receive the Holy Spirit When You Believed?" Some Basic Questions for Pneumatology* (Milwaukee: Marquette University Press, 2005), 75–82; Del Colle, *Christ and the Spirit*, 141–47, 157–79. While accepting the exegetical accuracy of Dunn's statements that "the divinity of the incarnate Christ is a function of the Holy Spirit" and "the risen humanity of Jesus is a function of the Spirit," Del Colle critiques certain common understandings of these statements, and the point he wishes to make is that "Jesus' filial relation to God and his pneumatically inspired and empowered mission are directly related without implying identity" (Del Colle, *Christ and the Spirit*, 168–69). Michel René Barnes points out that "Spirit Christology may be found in the writings of Tertullian, Hippolytus, Novatian, Cyprian, Lactantius, the Council of Western Serdica (343), Phoebadius, and Hilary" (Barnes, "Latin Trinitarian Theology," in *The Cambridge Companion to the Trinity*, ed. Peter C. Phan [Cambridge: Cambridge University Press, 2011], 76). On the fate of early Christian Spirit-Christology, see also Barnes, "The Beginning and End of Early Christian Pneumatology," *Augustinian Studies* 39 (2008): 169–86, at 180–84.

54. Dunn comments, "Too often we invest too much weight in the incarnation, at the cost of a proper appreciation of the resurrection. It is as though at the first Christmas Christ became incarnate Spirit, as well as incarnate Wisdom and Logos, without further development in the relationship. But when we see how at Easter the man of the Spirit became Lord of the Spirit, we can give a fuller weight to Easter, without denying the significance of Christmas" (Dunn, "Spirit of Jesus," 342).

55. Ibid., 340.

56. Ibid., 341.

clear lines and features, particularly in the first three Gospels."[57] Whenever Jesus's powerful awareness of the Spirit's work in and through him began, it is Jesus's own uniquely powerful experience of the Spirit that grounds our recognition of the Holy Spirit as the Spirit of Jesus, the Spirit who now unites us to the exalted Jesus. Because the earthly Jesus (and, in a lesser way, the exalted Jesus) is distinct from the Spirit, there can be no complete identification of Jesus and the Spirit, and thus, as Dunn recognizes, the distinctiveness of Father, Son, and Spirit can be upheld.[58]

Dunn's Jesus Remembered (2003)

Most recently, in *Jesus Remembered*, Dunn takes a somewhat different approach. Here he argues regarding Jesus's baptism that "the Liberal attempts to read here an experience of Jesus, Jesus's own experience of being commissioned by God, are undermined by the character of the account itself."[59] In Dunn's view, the character of the accounts of Jesus's baptism by John suggests that this tradition does not stem from Jesus himself. Those who originally formulated this tradition, Dunn says, did so from a perspective of faith, and it is therefore necessary to ask why they formulated the tradition as they did. In answer, Dunn observes that they seem to have done so because Jesus too saw his mission as rooted in the work of the Holy Spirit and the blessing of the Father: "Jesus himself probably claimed to have been anointed with the Spirit (Isa. 61.1), and thought of his relationship to God as son to father."[60]

Is there a way of reconstructing when Jesus might have experienced this anointing of the Spirit? Did his first or decisive experience of the Spirit occur at his baptism? Certainly "it was the baptism of Jesus which was early seen to mark both the beginning of Jesus's mission and the parting of the ways between Jesus and John."[61] Therefore, as Dunn says, those who wrote down these traditions were naturally inclined to make Jesus's baptism the starting point of his unique experience of the Spirit. But when the tradents composed his birth narratives, they focused even in these narratives on "his birth from the Spirit and sonship of God."[62] Dunn concludes that although we can say

57. Ibid.
58. I should note that Dunn is not thereby affirming the coequal divinity of the Father, Son, and Holy Spirit.
59. Dunn, *Christianity in the Making*, vol. 1, *Jesus Remembered*, 374–75.
60. Ibid., 376. For Dunn, this does not imply, by any means, that Jesus saw himself as the coequal divine Son of the Father.
61. Ibid.
62. Ibid.

that the followers of Jesus always experienced him as "Spirit-inspired and God's intimate," we cannot say when Jesus's own experience of these realities began.[63] Certainly, both in the birth narratives and in the narratives of Jesus's baptism, there is no "thought of Jesus *becoming* Messiah or son of God at that point. In both cases the thought is of Jesus as Spirit-endowed and son of God from the beginning—whether the beginning of his mission, or the beginning of his life."[64] But the latter option does not receive positive support from Dunn, since he thinks that we simply cannot know the answer. We can surely surmise that Jesus had a strong experience of the Spirit during his ministry, but "whether we can speak of Jesus himself experiencing the Spirit and sonship prior to his mission is quite obscure (despite Luke 2.49)."[65] Dunn adds that Luke 2:49, which attests to Jesus's awareness of his sonship at the age of twelve, is hagiography that provides no historical ground for supposing that Jesus's unique experience of the Spirit began earlier than his baptism.[66]

Toward the end of his book, Dunn remarks that the question of Jesus's self-understanding was a largely unpopular one in the twentieth century, due to the prominence of this question among "the nineteenth-century Liberals, as characterized by Schleiermacher's conception of Jesus's 'God-consciousness' and by the preoccupation with Jesus's 'messianic consciousness.'"[67] As he points out, "The reaction . . . has been to deny the possibility of gaining access to the self-consciousness of a historical person."[68] In *Jesus Remembered*, by contrast to his earlier work, Dunn accepts this methodological limitation, at least insofar as he seeks the "remembered Jesus" rather than claiming to be able to locate Jesus per se. But he argues nonetheless, quite rightly in my view, that the issue of Jesus's self-understanding cannot be suppressed. Evidence regarding the impact made by Jesus (i.e., the remembered Jesus) inevitably

63. Ibid.

64. Ibid., 376–77.

65. Ibid., 377.

66. For the significance of the Holy Spirit in Luke's Christology, see Louis Bouyer, *The Eternal Son: A Theology of the Word of God and Christology*, trans. Simone Inkel and John F. Laughlin (Huntington, IN: Our Sunday Visitor, 1978), 256–61.

67. Dunn, *Jesus Remembered*, 616. Dunn later observes, "In all this we are touching on what Bultmann described as 'the immediacy of [Jesus'] eschatological consciousness' coming to expression in such material, somewhat surprisingly given Bultmann's overall reaction to Liberal attempts to penetrate into Jesus's self-consciousness. Today, when eschatology is being reinterpreted in more social and political terms, Bultmann's description has been largely left behind. But if self-awareness can legitimately be detected behind certain assertions (and ways of acting), then Bultmann's observation remains valid. We are unlikely to appreciate Jesus's kingdom teaching and his mission as a whole unless we are willing to recognize that Jesus claimed (was remembered as claiming) a distinctive, and distinctively eschatological, empowering for his mission, as evidenced particularly in his healings and exorcisms" (ibid., 696).

68. Ibid., 616.

leads to questions about what Jesus's intentions were and how Jesus understood his own power and authority, not least in his acts of exorcism.

Dunn keeps his conclusions in this regard generally modest. He does again point out, however, that "Jesus seems to have regarded his successful exorcisms as the defeat (or evidence of the defeat) of Satan. . . . He laid claim to a plenitude of power" beyond that of other exorcists.[69] Furthermore, even if now only with respect to the remembered Jesus, Dunn finds that "it was the fact that Jesus achieved his success by the *Spirit/finger of God* which demonstrated or proved that the *kingdom of God* had come upon them."[70] This leads him to repeat the view expressed in *Jesus and the Spirit* that Jesus must have understood himself as possessed of "a special anointing by the Spirit (Isa. 61.1)," especially in light of his frequent teaching on the basis of his personal authority.[71] Echoing his earlier insights, Dunn finds that there is a "tantalising possibility that Jesus deliberately claimed a degree of distinctiveness for his mission, for all its thoroughly Jewish character, which left both hearers and disciples struggling for words to express the significance of what they were seeing and hearing."[72] When he turns to the possible "titles" in terms of which Jesus might have understood his mission (e.g., "Messiah" and Danielic "son of man"), he argues that Jesus focused on proclaiming the kingdom of God and gave little attention to his own significance or identity. Yet he does think that we can rightly speak of Jesus's "conviction of being God's eschatological agent at the climax of God's purposes for Israel, his sense of intimate sonship before God and of the dependence of his disciples on him, and his probably strong hope for final acknowledgment as the man who was playing the decisive role in bringing the kingdom to fulfilment and consummation."[73]

In making this statement, however, Dunn no longer appeals to Jesus's experience of the Spirit; his approach is much less experiential than it was in *Jesus and the Spirit*. As he observes with regard to his hypothesis that Jesus saw his death as a covenant sacrifice, "Much of this is speculative. How could it not be when we are trying to do the impossible—to 'get inside' the head of a historical figure?"[74] With respect to Jesus's self-understanding, Dunn makes a similar point: "We cannot even be sure that Jesus asked a question like 'Who am I?' let alone that he thought it important to articulate a particular

69. Ibid., 694.
70. Ibid.
71. Ibid. (cf. 702).
72. Ibid., 704.
73. Ibid., 762.
74. Ibid., 818.

answer."[75] Regarding whether Jesus taught that he was God's Son, and in particular what meaning we should attribute to Matthew 11:27 // Luke 10:22, Dunn likewise remarks that "such a discussion is unavoidably caught in the inadequacies of the historical method. For its natural recourse is to search out precedents and parallels to help explain particular and distinctive data. And the tendency or temptation is to conform the data to the precedents, to explain by explaining away the less obviously explicable elements."[76] Biblical scholarship contextualizes texts, but does not thereby necessarily draw us closer to the realities contained therein.

Although I understand the reasons that have led Dunn away from the quest to understand Jesus's own experience, I find his emphasis on Jesus's experience of the Spirit—which we observed even in *Jesus Remembered*, albeit in a muted form—to be of particular value. It seems to me that Dunn's effort to speak in some way about Jesus's awareness of the eschatological Spirit is commendable and indeed necessary. Reflection on Jesus the eschatological prophet inevitably has to choose: either Jesus's exalted self-understanding was delusional, or Jesus received some real and unique "mission" of the Spirit (allowing for the Gospels' somewhat diverse understandings of the Spirit). Even though historical research cannot resolve the problem, since no historian can enter into Jesus's consciousness, Dunn rightly directs our attention to Jesus's sense of the Spirit working powerfully in and through him to inaugurate the kingdom of God, as evidenced by his exorcisms, miracles, and especially his resurrection.[77] A central task for Christian theology of the Holy Spirit, then, is to reflect upon Jesus and the Spirit.[78] In this reflection, as Raniero Cantalamessa

75. Ibid., 707.

76. Ibid., 717. See also Dunn's reflections on history, historiography, and faith (ibid., 17–136).

77. Graham Tomlin draws particular attention to Jesus's miracles, accomplished by "the Spirit coming upon him and working through him," as evidence of the inbreaking of the kingdom of God (Tomlin, *The Prodigal Spirit: The Trinity, the Church and the Future of the World* [London: Alpha International, 2011], 47–53, at 53). Yet Tomlin sharply separates the church from the kingdom, rather than allowing that the church, while not yet the full kingdom, is in certain ways the inaugurated kingdom: "The church can thus be understood as the community of people filled with the Holy Spirit, and dedicated to the agenda of the kingdom of God as manifest in the ministry of Jesus. . . . The church is not the kingdom—any experience of the frailty and imperfection of the average church acts as an all too vivid reminder of that—but it always has the kingdom as its goal and purpose" (ibid., 58–59). Even so, he holds that the "new reality" brought about by Pentecost "can be both experienced and identified" in the church (ibid., 59).

78. Gordon D. Fee is nonetheless right to point out that "Paul thinks of the Spirit *primarily* in terms of the Spirit's relationship to God (the Father, although he never uses this imagery of this relationship). Not only does he more often speak of the 'Spirit of God' than of the 'Spirit of Christ,' but God is invariably the subject of the verb when Paul speaks of human reception of the Spirit" (Fee, *God's Empowering Presence: The Holy Spirit in the Letters of Paul* [Peabody, MA: Hendrickson, 1994], 835). A similar point is made by Marianne Meye

says, "A somewhat new picture of Jesus is disclosed to the eye of faith . . . , an image radiating spiritual energy and courage: the Jesus anointed with the Holy Spirit and power, who courageously takes on the powers of darkness; the Jesus of the early moments of his mission; the Jesus who acts to usher in the kingdom of God."[79]

Aquinas on the Missions of the Holy Spirit to Jesus Christ

Dunn's work has special value in emphasizing exegetically that we cannot (and do not) have a biblical Christology without a thoroughgoing pneumatology. Not surprisingly, Thomas Aquinas's theology of Jesus Christ is likewise strongly attuned to the Spirit's missions to Jesus—what Boris Bobrinskoy terms the Spirit's "plenary presence in Christ," which "reveals and actualizes the mystery of salvation."[80] Aquinas takes a theological approach to the scriptural testimony to the relationship of Jesus and the Spirit. He focuses on the relationship of the Word and Spirit in the incarnation, and he argues for the plenitude of the Spirit's invisible mission to the incarnate Word already at the instant of his conception. He emphasizes the elevation of Jesus's intellect and will by the Spirit, so that Jesus intimately knows the Father and undertakes his vocation with supreme obedience, love, and holiness. He interprets the visible missions of the Spirit to Jesus at Jesus's baptism and transfiguration as expressive of Jesus's unique power to communicate grace and truth and to make his people holy.

It may seem that this approach cannot do justice to the eschatological emphases that we noted in Dunn. When Aquinas investigates the missions

---

Thompson with regard to the Gospel of John; see Thompson, *The God of the Gospel of John* (Grand Rapids: Eerdmans, 2001), 183–88. Indeed, she argues that outside the Farewell Discourse, "the Spirit is primarily the means or mode by which God acts in the world," rather than a distinct figure (ibid., 184), but she notes that this should be understood in the same way that we discern the Word's sameness to God and distinction from God: "The Word can be construed, on the one hand, as the spoken expression of God's thought, and, on the other hand, as virtually distinct from God. . . . So also the Spirit of God can be spoken of, on the one hand, as the very life-giving breath of God, and, on the other hand, as a distinct agent of God" (ibid., 185).

79. Raniero Cantalamessa, OFMCap, *The Holy Spirit in the Life of Jesus: The Mystery of Christ's Baptism*, trans. Alan Neame (Collegeville, MN: Liturgical Press, 1994), 36. Cantalamessa elsewhere remarks, "No one comes to Pentecost other than by way of Easter" (Cantalamessa, *Sober Intoxication of the Spirit: Filled with the Fullness of God*, trans. Marsha Daigle-Williamson [Cincinnati: Servant, 2005], 12).

80. Boris Bobrinskoy, *The Mystery of the Trinity: Trinitarian Experience and Vision in the Biblical and Patristic Tradition*, trans. Anthony P. Gythiel (Crestwood, NY: St. Vladimir's Seminary Press, 1999), 94.

of the Holy Spirit to Jesus Christ, does he find (with Dunn) a miracle-worker and teacher who is experientially aware of the unique power and plenitude of the Spirit working in and through him? Put another way, does Aquinas's understanding of the Spirit's invisible and visible missions to Jesus befit the unique character of Jesus's vocation?

Aquinas on the Divine Missions: Clarifications

As a first step, some clarifications are in order with respect to what Aquinas means by divine "missions." It might seem that the Son and Spirit undertake a "mission" in the same way that humans go on mission. If this were so, then a divine mission would require some kind of change, motion, or movement on the part of the Son and Spirit. One might imagine the Son and Spirit bursting forth from the "immanent Trinity" and occupying new terrain in the world.

In order to correct this potential misunderstanding, Aquinas begins with God's mysteriously simple, infinite actuality as the transcendent source of all finite being. God's transcendence implies a perfect immanence: God is perfectly and fully present everywhere, while being spatially contained nowhere. For this reason, the Son and Holy Spirit need not move to new places. As Aquinas observes in the *Summa theologiae*, movement "has no place in the mission of a divine person; for the divine person sent neither begins to exist where he did not previously exist, nor ceases to exist where he was. Hence such a mission takes place without a separation."[81] Instead, the change described by a divine "mission" consists in a creature gaining a new real relation to the Son or Holy Spirit, a relation of intimacy that elevates the creature into a participation in the trinitarian communion.

A second possible misunderstanding has to do with the Father's not being sent. Does this mean that rational creatures receive a relationship with the Son and Spirit but not with the Father, or at least not directly with the Father? In answer, Aquinas explains that the Father is not sent because, in the order of processions, the Father is always the origin. But this does not mean that we do not attain to a relationship with the Father. On the contrary, when the Son and Spirit are sent ("mission"), they are not separated from the Father. Aquinas states that "although the effect of grace is also from the Father, who dwells in us by grace, just as the Son and the Holy Spirit, still he is not described as being sent, for he is not from another."[82]

81. I, q. 43, a. 1, ad 2.
82. I, q. 43, a. 4, ad 2. In the Gospel of John, Jesus says, "If a man loves me, he will keep my word, and my Father will love him, and we will come to him and make our home with him" (John 14:23).

A third possible misunderstanding consists in the view that the intratrinitarian *processions* of the Son and Spirit constitute one "coming forth," to which the *missions* of the Son and Spirit add a second "coming forth." On this view, the Father begets the Son and (with the Son) spirates the Spirit, and then has to undertake another round of action by now sending the Son and Spirit into the world. But as Aquinas emphasizes, the Son's being begotten and the Son's mission belong to the same coming forth from the Father. The only difference is that the begetting has an eternal term, and the sending has a temporal term. Aquinas notes that a divine mission "includes the eternal procession, with the addition of a temporal effect. For the relation of a divine person to his principle must be eternal. Hence the procession may be called a twin procession, eternal and temporal, not that there is a double relation to the principle, but a double term, temporal and eternal."[83] The point is that the procession and mission are not two coming forths, but *one* with "a double term."

83. I, q. 43, a. 2, ad 3. For an engagement with my reading of Aquinas on this point (and with Gilles Emery's interpretation as well, which my reading dovetails), see Bruce L. McCormack, "Processions and Missions: A Point of Convergence between Thomas Aquinas and Karl Barth," in *Thomas Aquinas and Karl Barth: An Unofficial Catholic-Protestant Dialogue*, ed. Bruce L. McCormack and Thomas Joseph White, OP (Grand Rapids: Eerdmans, 2013), 99–126, drawing upon Matthew Levering, "Christ, the Trinity, and Predestination: McCormack and Aquinas," in *Trinity and Election in Contemporary Theology*, ed. Michael T. Dempsey (Grand Rapids: Eerdmans, 2011), 244–73. McCormack suggests that my position is at odds with that of Bruce Marshall, who distinguishes in his "The Dereliction of Christ and the Impassibility of God" (in *Divine Impassibility and the Mystery of Human Suffering*, ed. James F. Keating and Thomas Joseph White, OP [Grand Rapids: Eerdmans, 2009], 246–98) between the intradivine processions as "necessary" and the temporal divine missions as "contingent." In McCormack's view, Marshall's distinction inevitably divides the processions from the missions (turning the missions into new processions, as it were), but I do not think that such a division in fact follows from this distinction—a distinction with which I fully agree. McCormack states that "God . . . is contingently necessary and necessarily contingent. He is contingently necessary in that the one act in which he gives to himself the kind of freedom he enjoys (a freedom 'for us') is an act that makes necessary (essential) to him all that it contains. He is necessarily contingent in that he has and exercises no 'freedom' prior to this act which makes necessary, so that all his freedom in relation to us is an expression of who and what he 'necessarily' is" (McCormack, "Processions and Missions," 121n58). But the processions are not, on my view, "the one act in which he gives to himself the kind of freedom he enjoys." This is a misinterpretation of the divine actuality, which is not constituted by the processions. Additionally, if this "one [free] act . . . is an act that makes necessary (essential) to him all that it contains," the divine act seems retroactively to delete the conditions of its own possibility, which raises the question of whether we are dealing with the same God. For McCormack, certainly, "the Father does not *preexist* the decision in which he both constitutes himself as triune and turns toward the human race in the Son and the Spirit" (ibid., 121). But the Father does not "[constitute] himself as triune" by a "decision" of free will; for discussion of this point, see, for example, I, q. 41, a. 2. McCormack also criticizes John Webster for insisting upon a certain asymmetry between "immanent" and "economic" teachings about God, but, in my view, Webster is correct.

Fourth, it may seem that while the Son has a visible mission—the incarnation—the Holy Spirit does not. In Aquinas's view, the Spirit in fact possesses a visible mission, but in a more diverse way than does the Son. The Spirit's visible mission "was directed to Christ, to the apostles, and to some of the early saints on whom the church was in a way founded."[84] Thus visible missions of the Spirit take place when the Spirit appears in the form of a dove at Christ's baptism and in the form of a cloud at Christ's transfiguration. A visible mission of the Spirit also occurs, in the form of breath, when the risen Jesus "breathed on them [the apostles], and said to them, 'Receive the Holy Spirit'" (John 20:22), and at Pentecost a visible mission of the Spirit occurs in the form of tongues of fire.[85] Yet, the main mission of the Spirit is invisible. This mission occurs whenever, by sanctifying grace, "the rational creature is perfected so that it can freely use not only the created gift itself, but enjoy also the divine person himself."[86] It follows that the great gift that the Holy Spirit gives is not solely grace, but rather is the Holy Spirit himself. Aquinas remarks, "Sanctifying grace disposes the soul to possess the divine person,"

84. I, q. 43, a. 7, ad 6. Gilles Emery, OP, comments that for Aquinas, "The visible missions of the Son and Spirit thus involve a dual disclosure: they manifest the procession of the person, and they manifest the donation of this person in grace, in the 'invisible mission.' And so the 'visible mission' contains three threads: (1) the divine person's eternal procession; (2) the divine person's new presence; and (3) the disclosure of the eternal origin and new presence through a visible sign. The 'invisible mystery' of the processions and of grace is manifested to witnesses by these visible signs" (Emery, *The Trinitarian Theology of Saint Thomas Aquinas*, trans. Francesca Aran Murphy [Oxford: Oxford University Press, 2011], 406–7).

85. See I, q. 43, a. 7, ad 6. For discussion of Aquinas on John 20:22, see Denis-Dominique le Pivain, FSSP, *L'action du saint-Esprit dans le Commentaire de l'Évangile de saint Jean par saint Thomas d'Aquin* (Paris: Téqui, 2006), 96–100, 155–56. For Augustine, as Michel René Barnes says, "Christ breathing upon the apostles and saying, 'Receive the Holy Spirit' means that the Holy Spirit proceeds from him—and in a literal way. At the Johannine Pentecost the Holy Spirit comes from—even *out of*—the Son; this is the 'insufflation' Augustine speaks of. John 20:22 provides a description of the Spirit not simply as the 'Spirit *of*' the Son or Lord, but of the Spirit proceeding from him" (Barnes, "Augustine's Last Pneumatology," *Augustinian Studies* 39 [2008]: 223–34, at 224–25). I should also note the position of David Coffey, summarized with approbation by Ralph Del Colle: "Coffey distinguished between the bestowal of the Spirit on Jesus and the bestowal upon human beings. In the latter case, the bestowal is sacramental—i.e., mediated by a categorial historical agent—while in the former case it is strictly a transcendental action of God without any mediation. When he further examines the sending of the Holy Spirit by Christ and the Spirit's bestowal by the Father—the terms respectively preferred by Coffey for each person's role—he distinguishes the transcendental and categorial aspects of the outpouring of the Holy Spirit upon believers. The Father is the agent of the transcendental anointing and the Son of the categorial anointing" (Del Colle, *Christ and the Spirit*, 125). It seems to me to be a mistake to assign Christ (the incarnate Son) a strictly "categorial" agency while assigning the Father a "transcendental" agency.

86. I, q. 43, a. 3, ad 1. See Kenneth M. Loyer, *God's Love through the Spirit: The Holy Spirit in Thomas Aquinas and John Wesley* (Washington, DC: Catholic University of America Press, 2014), 154–58.

so that "the Holy Spirit is possessed by man, and dwells within him, in the very gift itself of sanctifying grace."[87] When this happens, we are healed from sin and filled with charity.

Fifth, it may seem that whereas the Holy Spirit has both a visible and an invisible mission, the Son has only a visible mission. On the contrary, Aquinas considers that the Son has an invisible mission, which is manifested in the illumination of our minds. Given that "the Son is . . . not any sort of Word, but one who breathes forth Love," Aquinas holds that "the Son is sent not in accordance with every and any kind of intellectual perfection, but according to the intellectual illumination, which breaks forth into the affection of love."[88] When the Son is sent in this way, we know him experientially and have a real relation to him. Drawing upon Augustine, Aquinas comments that the invisible mission of the Son "implies a certain experimental knowledge; and this is properly called wisdom [*sapientia*], as it were a sweet knowledge [*sapida scientia*]."[89] The invisible mission of the Son involves, on the part of those who receive this mission, coming to know the Son. Moreover, there is never an invisible mission of the Son without a corresponding invisible mission of the Spirit.

Sixth, it might appear that everyone in a state of grace is constantly receiving an enduring, stable invisible mission of the Son and Spirit. Aquinas clarifies, however, that what he means by an invisible mission takes place only when the Son and Spirit do something *new* in a rational creature. The invisible mission of the Spirit is not the same thing as an ongoing state of grace. Rather, the invisible mission of the Spirit *establishes* the intimate relationship with the Spirit that grounds the ongoing state of grace. The invisible "mission" of the Spirit initiates either "the indwelling of grace" or "a certain renewal by grace."[90] Aquinas's position here fits with Graham Tomlin's observation, from a different theological perspective, that "the Spirit creates something new in human nature."[91] It is the element of newness—for example, a new zeal or

87. I, q. 43, a. 3 and ad 2.
88. I, q. 43, a. 5, ad 2.
89. I, q. 43, a. 5, ad 2.
90. I, q. 43, a. 6. For background, focused not on the missions per se but on Augustine's transformative pneumatology and the reception of this pneumatology in the later fathers, see Thomas L. Humphries Jr., *Ascetic Pneumatology from John Cassian to Gregory the Great* (Oxford: Oxford University Press, 2013). As Humphries observes, for Augustine, "The Holy Spirit reforms the [fallen] human will, giving it not only true freedom, but also enabling it to love with God's love. Because the Spirit is the love of God, when Christians are filled with the Spirit (for example at baptism), they receive the ability to love with divine love. New possibilities are opened for the human will because it is no longer bound by an existence subject to sin, but can truly love with God's love, which is given through the Holy Spirit" (ibid., 80).
91. Tomlin, *Prodigal Spirit*, 31.

spiritual fervor—that signals the reception of a further invisible mission. The Spirit's invisible mission involves a new coming of the Spirit into the soul, a new relation of the soul to the Holy Spirit.

Jesus and the Missions of the Holy Spirit

When Aquinas applies all this to Jesus Christ, we encounter something that resonates with the uniqueness of Jesus's eschatological vocation but nonetheless seems to undermine a richly pneumatological Christology: Jesus Christ received only one invisible mission of the Holy Spirit. In fact, according to Aquinas, Jesus received the Spirit's invisible mission far less often than does the lowliest saint. Even the blessed in heaven regularly receive the Spirit's invisible mission, not only "at the very beginning of their beatitude" but also, Aquinas supposes, "by the further revelation of mysteries; which goes on till the day of judgment."[92] It may seem, then, that Jesus is sadly deprived of the fresh activity of the Spirit.

By affirming that Jesus received the invisible mission of the Spirit only at the instant of his conception, Aquinas aims to account for the unique plenitude and power of the Spirit's invisible mission to Jesus, shaping Jesus's entire life from the outset by relating him in all ways to the Spirit. The unique plenitude of the Spirit's invisible mission to Jesus enables Jesus, during his lifetime, to be fully and utterly a man of the Spirit so as to fulfill his eschatological task. The coming of the Spirit to Jesus's human nature attunes him supremely to Love and Gift, and does so precisely in the unfolding of his historical existence. If we recall that "the Son is the Word, not any sort of word, but one who breathes forth Love,"[93] we can see how fitting it is that the invisible mission of the Spirit uniquely enrich the incarnate Son at the very outset of his life. Impelled by the Spirit, Jesus manifests self-giving love in literally everything that he does in the flesh. The fact that the Spirit makes only one invisible mission to Christ, therefore, does not mean that the Spirit makes contact only once with the incarnate Son; on the contrary, it means that at every instant of his life, the incarnate Son is utterly related to the Spirit who moves him to accomplish his vocation.

The plenitude of the Spirit's invisible mission to Jesus fits well with what the Gospels teach about Jesus's conception in Mary's womb. As evidence of the Spirit's intimate involvement in the incarnation of the Son, Luke 1:35 reports the words of the angel Gabriel to Mary: "The Holy Spirit will come upon you, and the power of the Most High will overshadow you; therefore the

92. I, q. 43, a. 6, ad 3.
93. I, q. 43, a. 5, ad 2.

child to be born will be called holy, the Son of God." Matthew 1:18 succinctly says of the Virgin Mary, "she was found to be of child by the Holy Spirit."[94] Aquinas gives three reasons for the fittingness of this attribution of the creation of Christ's humanity to the Holy Spirit. The first reason has to do with the Spirit's personal property as "Love" in the trinitarian communion. According to this reason, Luke and Matthew highlight the Spirit's role in the incarnation because "that the Son of God took to himself flesh from the Virgin's womb was due to the exceeding love of God."[95] The second reason consists in the fact that the incarnation was God's sheer gift, not merited in any way by the human nature of Jesus. The third reason is that the incarnate Son is to be "called holy, the Son of God." Citing Galatians 4:6 and Romans 1:4, Aquinas observes that it is the Holy Spirit who makes humans holy (as the eschatological people of God must be). He affirms that "just as other men are sanctified spiritually by the Holy Spirit, so as to be the adopted sons of God, so was Christ conceived in sanctity by the Holy Spirit, so as to be the natural Son of God."[96]

Yet Aquinas denies that the Holy Spirit *alone* created the humanity of Jesus. The conception of Jesus's humanity does not involve a proper *mission* of the Holy Spirit, since it is a work of the whole Trinity, whereas the sanctification of Jesus's humanity involves such a mission.[97] Aquinas also considers that the preeminent reason for Jesus's reception of a perfect invisible mission of the Spirit was "the union of his soul with the Word of God. For the nearer any recipient is to an inflowing cause, the more does it partake of its influence."[98] If Jesus in his human nature received an automatic invisible mission of the Spirit due to "the union of his soul with the Word," then this would seem to undervalue the Spirit's role. Given Aquinas's emphasis on the Trinity and the Word, the question is whether he has truly appreciated the role of the Spirit that Dunn identified, namely Jesus's "*awareness* of an *otherly* power working through him, together with the *conviction* that this power was *God's* power"—what N. T. Wright calls Jesus's experience of "being guided, driven along, by YHWH's spirit."[99]

94. See III, q. 32, a. 1, *sed contra* for the citation of Luke 1:35.
95. III, q. 32, a. 1.
96. III, q. 32, a. 1.
97. Aquinas also states, "The mission refers to the Person assuming, who is sent by the Father; but the conception refers to the body assumed, which is formed by the operation of the Holy Spirit" (III, q. 32, a. 1, ad 2).
98. III, q. 7, a. 1. See Jean-Pierre Torrell, OP, "La grâce du Christ," in Thomas Aquinas, *Somme théologique: Le Verbe incarné*, vol. 2, *3a, Questions 7–15*, trans. Jean-Pierre Torrell (Paris: Cerf, 2002), 395–415.
99. Dunn, *Jesus and the Spirit*, 47; N. T. Wright, *Jesus and the Victory of God* (Minneapolis: Fortress, 1996), 648.

Discussing the role of the Spirit in the incarnation. Aquinas note that the "grace of union"—the incarnation of the Son—"precedes the habitual grace of Christ, not in order of time, but by nature and in thought."[100] It follows that the visible mission of the Son *logically* "precedes" the invisible mission of the Spirit in Jesus, not only because of the order of procession/mission in the Trinity, but also because "grace is caused in man by the presence of the Godhead, as light in the air by the presence of the sun," and "the presence of God in Christ is by the union of human nature with the divine person. Hence the habitual grace of Christ is understood to follow this union, as light follows the sun."[101] But there is no temporal separation between the two missions: as soon as Christ exists, he is filled at that same instant with the Spirit for the sake of his eschatological vocation. Indeed, as Khaled Anatolios observes in his study of Nicene theology, it is the Son who sends the Spirit whom he receives as man: "The perfect and reciprocally referencing co-activity of Son and Spirit is manifest in the incarnation, wherein the Son both divinely gives the Spirit and humanly receives it, thus enabling human reception of the Spirit."[102]

The above account of the Spirit's uniquely full invisible mission to the incarnate Son at the instant of his conception rules out the adoptionist Christology with which Dunn has sometimes been associated. The Spirit's work does not in itself bring about Christ's Sonship, even though Christ's Sonship includes from the outset the Spirit's work. It is not *because* the Spirit descends upon Jesus at his baptism that the voice of the Father from heaven is moved to proclaim, "This is my beloved Son" (Matt. 3:17). On the contrary, at his conception Jesus already is the Christ and Emmanuel ("God with us") who "will save his people from their sins" (Matt. 1:21, 23), and at his birth he receives the magi's worship (Matt. 2:11). It is neither imaginable nor biblical that the Word could have been active in the incarnation only after the Spirit's activity, or that the Word incarnate could have lacked the Spirit's full gift of "glory as of the only Son from the Father" (John 1:14), a gift whose purpose is to enable us "to become children of God" (John 1:12).

100. III, q. 7, a. 13. On the "grace of union," see Jean-Miguel Garrigues, "The 'Natural Grace' of Christ in St. Thomas," in *Surnaturel: A Controversy at the Heart of Twentieth-Century Thomistic Thought*, ed. Serge-Thomas Bonino, OP, trans. Robert Williams (Ave Maria, FL: Sapientia Press of Ave Maria University, 2009), 103–115; Thomas Joseph White, OP, "The Crucified Lord: Thomistic Reflections on the Communication of Idioms and the Theology of the Cross," in McCormack and White, *Thomas Aquinas and Karl Barth*, 157–92, at 173–74. For this topic in Aquinas's *Commentary on the Sentences*, see Inos Biffi, *I Misteri di Cristo in Tommaso d'Aquino*, vol. 1, *La Costruzione della Teologia* (Milan: Jaca, 1994), 89–92.

101. III, q. 7, a. 13.

102. Khaled Anatolios, *Retrieving Nicaea: The Development and Meaning of Trinitarian Doctrine* (Grand Rapids: Baker Academic, 2011), 287.

Certainly Dunn does not presume an incarnation or even a distinct "person" of the Spirit; all this is theological and creedal language. But what Dunn wishes to uphold, especially in his early work, is the Spirit's activity in and through Jesus, as manifested by the eschatological power and authority of Jesus's words and deeds. Dunn emphasizes that Jesus must have experienced a strong interior presence of the Spirit guiding and empowering him. Theologically, Aquinas wishes to uphold the very same thing, although he does so not simply in light of the biblical testimony to Jesus's words and deeds but also in light of the biblical testimony to Jesus's divine Sonship. The point is that Jesus's Sonship cannot be understood without appreciating and underscoring the unique plenitude of the Spirit in Jesus. The missions of Son and Spirit are connected in such a way that the Son's humanity receives uniquely and superabundantly the mission of the Spirit, precisely because, as Anatolios remarks, "the Spirit is the one in whom the relation between the Father and the Son is extended outward."[103] We can indeed say—and here we are following Dunn's essential insight, rooted in the Synoptic Gospels—that the Spirit uniquely shapes and leads Jesus so that "we might no longer be enslaved to sin" but rather might be "alive to God in Christ Jesus" (Rom. 6:6, 11).

To return to the issue with which we began, however, does it suffice to say that Jesus receives the invisible mission of the Holy Spirit only once, at the instant of his conception? As we have seen, given the unfathomably great character of the incarnation, Aquinas considers the incarnation of the Son to bring with it a superabundant sanctification of the humanity of the Son by the Holy Spirit. This fullness of the Spirit's invisible mission does not go away but rather informs Jesus's humanity in radical holiness throughout his growth, maturation, and public ministry. The point that unites Aquinas and Dunn here consists in the radical and unique character of the Spirit's presence in Jesus, which nourishes and sustains Jesus's eschatological words and deeds as befits his supreme vocation.

Aquinas's conclusions about the unique plenitude of the Spirit's invisible mission to Jesus have to do centrally with Jesus's knowledge and will, since it is by his self-sacrificial love that he saves those whom he knows, as Jesus indicates in John 10:14–15: "I know my own and my own know me, as the Father knows me and I know the Father; and I lay down my life for the sheep." With regard to Jesus's will, the key element is Jesus's holiness and thus the purity of his love. Aquinas quotes Jesus's words in John 8:46, "Which of you

---

103. Ibid. For this same point, see also Michael Allen and Scott R. Swain, *Reformed Catholicity: The Promise of Retrieval for Theology and Biblical Interpretation* (Grand Rapids: Baker Academic, 2015), 28.

convicts me of sin?"[104] He also quotes 1 Peter 2:22, "He [Jesus] committed no sin; no guile was found on his lips," and 2 Corinthians 5:21, where Paul says that Jesus "knew no sin."[105] His sinlessness is not merely for his own sake but rather bears specifically upon the salvation of the people of God: "For our sake he made him to be sin who knew no sin, so that in him we might become the righteousness of God" (2 Cor. 5:21).[106] Aquinas could also have quoted Hebrews 4:15, which describes Jesus as "one who in every respect has been tempted as we are, yet without sinning."

In order for Jesus's sacrificial death on the cross to accomplish our redemption, Aquinas argues, Jesus could not have been in need of redemption. Aquinas finds useful here not only the New Testament texts about Jesus's sinlessness, but also Sirach 34:19's remark that "the Most High is not pleased with the offerings of the ungodly."[107] If Jesus had been one of the ungodly, then Jesus's self-offering on the cross could not have been the eschatological expiation, marked by supreme Love and Gift, of the sins of all those who "have sinned and fall short of the glory of God" and who "are justified by his grace as a gift, through the redemption which is in Christ Jesus, whom God put forward as an expiation by his blood, to be received by faith" (Rom. 3:23–25).[108] Empowered by the Spirit, Jesus must have been free to give himself perfectly in love. As Jesus says in the Gospel of John, "every one who commits sin is a slave to sin. The slave does not continue in the house for ever; the son continues for ever. So if the Son makes you free, you will be free indeed" (John 8:34–36).

The sinlessness envisioned here is no mere absence of evildoing. Rather, it is a positive attunement of Jesus's human will and passions to the divine will in every respect, for the sake of the eschatological reconciliation of the world to God. Jesus's sinlessness, in this positive sense, involves a "pre-eminent"

104. III, q. 15, a. 1, *sed contra*.

105. III, q. 15, a. 1.

106. Frank J. Matera observes, "The sense is that God placed Christ in the sinful human condition so that humanity might experience the righteous condition that comes with God's righteousness" (*II Corinthians: A Commentary* [Louisville: Westminster John Knox, 2003], 128).

107. III, q. 15, a. 1.

108. For the view—mistaken on more than one level—that the Holy Spirit suffered on the cross, see D. Lyle Dabney, "*Pneumatologia Crucis*: Reclaiming *Theologia Crucis* for a Theology of the Spirit Today," *Scottish Journal of Theology* 53 (2000): 511–24. For Aquinas on the suffering of the incarnate Son, see the following essays published in Keating and White, *Divine Impassibility and the Mystery of Human Suffering*: Gilles Emery, OP, "The Immutability of the God of Love and the Problem of Language concerning the 'Suffering of God,'" 27–76; Thomas G. Weinandy, OFMCap, "God and Human Suffering: His Act of Creation and His Acts in History," 99–116; Paul Gondreau, "St. Thomas Aquinas, the Communication of Idioms, and the Suffering of Christ in the Garden of Gethsemane," 214–45; Marshall, "Dereliction of Christ and the Impassibility of God," 246–98.

reception of the gifts of the Holy Spirit (as befits the humanity of the Word) whereby the powers of the soul gain "a natural aptitude to be moved by the Holy Spirit," who is Love and Gift.[109] As Dunn also recognizes, it is not sufficient to think of the Spirit as an exterior force, as though when the Spirit "drove" Jesus "into the wilderness" (Mark 1:12; cf. Luke 4:1, cited by Aquinas) the Spirit did so like a big wind. On the contrary, the Spirit works interiorly in Jesus, and Jesus is supremely receptive to these promptings of the Spirit—a receptiveness that requires the unique fullness of the invisible mission of the Spirit to Jesus, by which Jesus receives the spiritual gifts that enable him to be obedient to the Holy Spirit. Jesus's powers of exorcism and miracle working, strongly emphasized by Dunn as evidence of Jesus's unique experience of the Spirit, also flow from the fullness of the invisible mission of the Spirit to him. Aquinas terms the powers of exorcism and miracle-working "gratuitous graces" and notes that they "are ordained for the manifestation of faith and spiritual doctrine" to the world.[110]

The Spirit's mission to Jesus is always ordered to those whom Jesus came to redeem, and thus to the kingdom of God. The two texts that Aquinas highlights in this respect are 1 Timothy 2:5, "For there is one God, and there is one mediator between God and men, the man Christ Jesus, who gave himself as a ransom for all," and John 1:16, "And from his fulness have we all received, grace upon grace." Since Jesus is the one mediator, Aquinas observes, "it behooved him to have grace which would overflow upon others."[111] He further cites Ephesians 4:7: "grace was given to each of us according to the measure of Christ's gift."[112] The point that Aquinas has in view is not far from Dunn's insistence that Jesus's experience of the Spirit be accounted for in biblical scholarship, since our own experience of the Spirit is inseparable from the uniquely powerful mission of the Spirit to Jesus. The connection between the grace of the Holy Spirit in Christ and in believers is underscored by Aquinas through a citation of Ephesians 3:8: "To me [Paul], though I am the very least of all the saints, this grace was given, to preach to the Gentiles the unsearchable riches of Christ."[113]

---

109. III, q. 7, a. 5. For discussion, see Servais Pinckaers, OP, *The Sources of Christian Ethics*, trans. Mary Thomas Noble, OP (Washington, DC: Catholic University of America Press, 1995), 151–55 (drawing upon Augustine); Pinckaers, "Morality and the Movement of the Holy Spirit: Aquinas's Doctrine of *Instinctus*," in *The Pinckaers Reader: Renewing Thomistic Moral Theology*, ed. John Berkman and Craig Steven Titus, trans. Mary Thomas Noble, OP, et al. (Washington, DC: Catholic University of America Press, 2005), 385–95.

110. III, q. 7, a. 7.

111. III, q. 7, a. 1.

112. III, q. 7, a. 10.

113. III, q. 7, a. 10.

What about the challenge posed by the Gospel of Luke's statement that "Jesus increased in wisdom and in stature, and in favor with [καὶ χάριτι παρὰ] God and man" (Luke 2:52)? Aquinas's Latin Bible translates χάρις here as "*gratia.*" In Aquinas's view, as we have seen, an increase in grace normally involves a new mission of the Holy Spirit, which Jesus did not need since Jesus received the fullness of grace at his conception. Aquinas points out that in this passage from Luke the increase in "grace" or "favor with God and man" is linked explicitly with Jesus's increasing age, as Jesus grows from a twelve-year-old boy to a mature man in his early thirties. As a mature man, Jesus performed deeds that fully manifested the unique relationship with the Spirit that he enjoyed, and so Aquinas reasons that Luke's statement indicates that "Christ increased in wisdom and grace even as in age, since in the course of time he did more perfect works."[114] Due to the Spirit's invisible mission to him, Jesus exhibited during his public ministry such virtues as charity, humility, obedience, courage, and justice, and Jesus did so in a manner obviously much increased from what he showed as a youth.[115] Had he lacked the plenitude of the Spirit's mission from the outset, he could not have displayed this increased grace or favor nearly as powerfully as he did.

Granted that the invisible mission of the Spirit wondrously elevated Jesus's human will so as to establish him in radical holiness , what about his human intellect? According to Scripture, Jesus revealed what the prophets and wise persons of every time and place desired to know, namely the divine Father (and thus also the Son). For Aquinas, Jesus's intimate knowledge of the Father requires that Jesus must have possessed glorified intelligence, so that he could commune with the Father in a suprarational mode—but without this communion preventing his intelligence from also operating in the normal graced human ways.[116] Aquinas speaks of "the dignity of this [Jesus's] soul,

114. III, q. 7, a. 12, ad 3.
115. See III, q. 7, a. 2; III, q. 46, a. 3.
116. For a comprehensive and persuasive defense of the truth of Aquinas's position, see Simon Francis Gaine, OP, *Did the Saviour See the Father? Christ, Salvation and the Vision of God* (London: Bloomsbury, 2015). See also Thomas Joseph White, OP, "Dyotheletism and the Instrumental Human Consciousness of Jesus," *Pro Ecclesia* 17 (2008): 396–422; White, "The Voluntary Action of the Earthly Christ and the Necessity of the Beatific Vision," *The Thomist* 69 (2005): 497–534; Joseph Wawrykow, "Grace," in *The Theology of Thomas Aquinas*, ed. Rik Van Nieuwenhove and Joseph Wawrykow (Notre Dame, IN: University of Notre Dame Press, 2005), 192–221, at 216–18. An influential and still useful earlier defense of Aquinas's position appears in Jacques Maritain, *On the Grace and Humanity of Jesus*, trans. Joseph W. Evans (New York: Herder and Herder, 1969), though Gaine's criticisms of certain aspects of Maritain's approach are on target. For a critique of Aquinas's position, see Thomas G. Weinandy, OFMCap, "Jesus's Filial Vision of the Father" and "Thomas Joseph White's Beatific Vision of the Incarnate Son: A Response,"

whose operations were to attain so closely to God by knowledge and by love."[117] Clearly Jesus's human intellect, in itself, could not and did not possess divine intelligence. In order for Jesus to humanly know his Father intimately and to communicate this knowledge propositionally, then, his human intellect was uniquely raised and elevated by the Word and Spirit. In this regard, Aquinas relies heavily on the Gospel of John, which admittedly counts little as a historical source in Dunn's work.[118]

Of course, there are sayings in the Synoptic Gospels and Paul that also point to Jesus's uniquely rich knowledge for the sake of our salvation. For example, Jesus proclaims that "no one knows the Father except the Son and any one to whom the Son chooses to reveal him" (Matt. 11:27 [cf. Luke 10:22]). Similarly, there are Jesus's extraordinary statements that "he who loses his life for my sake will find it," and that "he who receives me receives him who sent me" (Matt. 10:39–40). How could Jesus know such things unless his knowledge of the Father were inexpressibly intimate? For his part, Paul insists that "the Son of God . . . loved me and gave himself for me" (Gal. 2:20).[119] Indeed, given the soul's unity, the powerful working of the Holy Spirit can hardly be expected to have an extraordinary influence upon Jesus's will without also, in conjunction with the Word, enlightening his human intellect so that he might accomplish his eschatological mission.

In Aquinas's view, Jesus possessed the fullness of infused and acquired knowledge. Aquinas is motivated here both by the theological tradition and by texts such as John 2:25, "he knew all men and needed no one to bear witness of man; for he himself knew what was in man."[120] Although Aquinas grants that Jesus advanced in acquired knowledge, in accord with Luke 2:52 (as interpreted by Ambrose), Aquinas thinks that Jesus from his conception "had perfect infused knowledge of all things."[121] This seems to me to be a

---

in *Jesus: Essays in Christology* (Ave Maria, FL: Sapientia Press of Ave Maria University, 2014), 279–92 and 293–301.

117. III, q. 7, a. 1.

118. Although see Dunn, "Let John Be John: A Gospel for Its Time," in *The Gospel and the Gospels*, ed. Peter Stuhlmacher (Grand Rapids: Eerdmans, 1991), 293–322. For how to interpret the Gospel of John in relation to the other Gospels, see Peter Stuhlmacher, "Spiritual Remembering: John 14:26," in Stanton, Longenecker, and Barton, *Holy Spirit and Christian Origins*, 55–68; Heinrich Schlier, *Besinnung auf das Neue Testament*, 2nd ed. (Freiburg: Herder, 1967), 264–71; Udo Schnelle, *Das Evangelium nach Johannes* (Leipzig: Evangelische Verlagsanstalt, 1998), 21.

119. See III, q. 47, a. 2, ad 1.

120. See III, q. 10, a. 2.

121. III, q. 12, a. 2. R. Michael Allen states that for Aquinas, "the perfection of humanity occurred in Mary's womb, quite apart from Jesus's own activity (though, of course, the paschal activity of Christ accomplishes the sacrificial ministry of Christ). Thomas upholds a punctiliar view of the perfection of human nature in Christ, whereas the texts of Luke's Gospel and the

mistake, despite the testimony of John 2:25. We need not hold that Jesus possessed perfect infused knowledge, though his infused or prophetic knowledge surely was extensive. Aquinas is nonetheless correct to highlight the unique fullness of the Spirit's invisible mission to Jesus at the instant of his conception, shaping Jesus's entire life in accord with the Spirit's mode of Love and Gift.[122]

In this regard, recall Dunn's remark that "Jesus's own experience of anointing and ministry empowered by the same Spirit/power of God may in itself have convinced him that God's longed-for (final) manifestation of his royal rule was already in evidence and that its full manifestation could therefore not be long delayed."[123] If this conviction was not delusional—and Jesus's resurrection indicates that it was not—the Spirit's mission to Jesus must have been truly unique in its plenitude and power. In his later work, Dunn accepts that not only in the narratives of Jesus's baptism but also in the narratives of Jesus's birth "the thought is of Jesus as Spirit-endowed and son of God from the beginning— whether the beginning of his mission, or the beginning of his life."[124] Aquinas would certainly agree, while insisting that Jesus's mission of mercy begins at

---

Epistle to the Hebrews point toward a dynamic and gradual maturation of humanity in the person of the Word" (Allen, *The Christ's Faith: A Dogmatic Account* [London: T&T Clark, 2009], 61). Although I agree with Allen that Aquinas errs in holding that Jesus possessed perfect acquired and infused knowledge, I consider that the fact that the Holy Spirit's mission to Jesus at his conception was uniquely full does not rule out the "dynamic and gradual maturation" of Jesus's humanity, since the mission of the Holy Spirit opens up the humanity of the Word through the virtues and gifts of the Spirit, rather than freezing it in an ahistorical state. Allen argues that Jesus's possession of the beatific vision, if true, would mean that Jesus was ignorant of nothing, which seems to be contradicted by certain biblical texts. But Jesus's beatific vision pertains to his intimate knowledge of the Father and of his own Sonship; beatific vision does not account for Jesus's conceptual knowledge, which must be accounted for in terms of acquired and infused/prophetic knowledge. In affirming Jesus's beatific knowledge, I disagree with Allen's view that mere faith could suffice for Jesus's uniquely intimate knowledge of his Father. In his more recent "'From the Time He Took on the Form of a Servant': The Christ's Pilgrimage of Faith," *International Journal of Systematic Theology* 16 (2014): 4–24, Allen argues that Christ's faith should be understood, like ours, as a pilgrimage guided (in Christ's case perfectly) by the Holy Spirit: "The lifelong fidelity of the Son manifests the covenantal fellowship enjoyed by the incarnate one with his heavenly Father by the Spirit. . . . The Son and Father relate in a willed and covenantal manner: the Father expresses his will, and the Son submits to that determination; the Father outlines the expectations of the covenant, and the Son fulfills those conditions" (ibid., 22–23) through his faithful love, his constantly trusting "faith in the Father's promise" (ibid., 23). What is missing here is the scope of Jesus's intimate and revelatory knowledge of his Father, which goes far beyond mere fidelity. Indeed, the fidelity that Allen describes would be described by Aquinas primarily in terms of charity or obedience rather than in terms of knowledge. See also Gaine, *Did the Saviour See the Father?*, chap. 5.

122. The difference (in my view quite slight) between my position and Aquinas's is that I argue for a "unique fullness" that needed no increase from a new invisible mission of the Spirit, whereas Aquinas argues for a fullness that is perfect in all possible ways.

123. Dunn, *Jesus Remembered*, 479.

124. Ibid., 377.

his conception, and while holding to a doctrine of the eternal existence of the Son of God (and thus of the incarnation) that Dunn does not share.

Why did Jesus twice receive a *visible* mission of the Holy Spirit? As Aquinas understands the New Testament testimony, Jesus received the visible mission of the Spirit at his baptism and at his transfiguration. Prior to this, there had been no visible mission of the Spirit in human history, even to the patriarchs and people of Israel. Why had there not been? In light of the economy of salvation, in which Jesus comes to "show us the Father" (John 14:9), Aquinas offers the answer that "the visible mission of the Son was to be accomplished before that of the Holy Spirit; since the Holy Spirit manifests the Son, as the Son manifests the Father."[125] The visible missions of the Spirit manifest Jesus to be the Father's beloved Son.

Aquinas seeks reasons of fittingness for the Spirit's taking the visible forms of a dove and of a cloud. The first visible mission of the Spirit to Jesus occurs at his baptism, when the Spirit descends upon Jesus "like a dove" (Matt. 3:16). Why should the Spirit come to Jesus in a visible form at Jesus's baptism? In Aquinas's view, the visible mission of the Spirit at Jesus's baptism helps to show that Jesus possesses "the authority of the giver of grace by spiritual regeneration."[126] With respect to the Spirit's appearing specifically in the form of a dove, Aquinas emphasizes Jesus's purpose to make us into children of God. A dove fits with this purpose, because a dove, as a "fruitful [*fecundum*] animal," begets many baby doves in its image, thereby constituting a large flock. The Spirit's visible mission in the form of a dove thereby directs our attention not only to the fact of Jesus's authority as the giver of sacramental grace, but also to the fact that we must be born again by being "regenerated to the likeness of the only Begotten" so as to belong to the kingdom that Jesus.[127]

In the second visible mission, at Jesus's transfiguration, the Spirit takes the form of "a bright cloud" (Matt. 17:5). The transfiguration occurs directly after Peter has confessed that Jesus is "the Christ, the Son of the living God" (Matt. 16:16) and after Jesus has begun "to show his disciples that he must go to Jerusalem and suffer many things from the elders and chief priests and scribes, and be killed, and on the third day be raised" (Matt. 16:21). Aquinas reasons that the "bright cloud" serves symbolically to exhibit the "exuberance of doctrine" (*exuberantiam doctrinae*), the refulgence of the truth of Christ.[128]

---

125. I, q. 43, a. 7, ad 6. As Gilles Emery notes, "The Holy Spirit is not the Giver but the *Gift himself*, spread in human hearts. And so the visible indicators of the Holy Spirit do not display him as the Giver but as sanctifying Gift" (Emery, *Trinitarian Theology of Saint Thomas Aquinas*, 410).

126. I, q. 43, a. 7, ad 6.

127. I, q. 43, a. 7, ad 6.

128. I, q. 43, a. 7, ad 6.

On this view, the Spirit's visible mission in the form of a bright cloud highlights the divine authority of Jesus's teaching, which God the Father confirms when he speaks from the bright cloud, "This is my beloved Son, with whom I am well pleased; listen to him" (Matt. 17:5). Jesus's ability to give his church true sacraments and true teaching, an ability that is made manifest by the visible missions of the Spirit to Jesus, thus reflects the kingdom-building purpose of the Spirit's invisible mission to Jesus.[129]

Yet, does Aquinas err by positing a category "visible mission" that places mere *manifestations* of the Holy Spirit alongside the *incarnation* of the Son? After all, the Spirit only very briefly and temporarily appears as a dove or a cloud. He certainly does not become hypostatically united with the nature of a dove, let alone a cloud. The dove only signifies the Holy Spirit, or the grace of the Holy Spirit, descending upon Jesus. It may seem that such signification should not be included in the same category ("visible mission") that describes the incarnation of the Son.[130]

In response to this concern, Aquinas says more about the symbolism that we find in the Spirit's visible missions to Jesus. For example, the traits of doves direct us toward the gifts of the Holy Spirit, such as "the gift of fortitude, wherewith the saints build their nest, i.e., take refuge and hope, in the death wounds of Christ, who is the Rock of strength."[131] The dove is gentle, like all who share in the reconciliation won by Jesus. The dove is "loving and gregarious," like those who are united in the mystical body of Christ.[132] In these ways, the visible mission of the Spirit in the form of a dove helps to display the incarnate Son's mission of bringing about the adoption of sons

129. Aquinas underscores that the primary reason for supposing that Jesus possesses "habitual grace" is "on account of the union of his soul with the Word of God. For the nearer any recipient is to an inflowing cause, the more does it partake of its influence. . . . And hence it was most fitting that his soul should receive the influx of divine grace" (III, q. 7, a. 1). Aquinas goes on to explain in ad 2 of this article: "To Christ, inasmuch as he is the natural Son of God, is due an eternal inheritance, which is the uncreated beatitude through the uncreated act of knowledge and love of God, i.e., the same whereby the Father knows and loves himself. Now the soul was not capable of this act, on account of the difference of natures. Hence it behooved it to attain to God by a created act of fruition which could not be without grace. Likewise, inasmuch as he was the Word of God, he had the power of doing all things well by the divine operation. And because it is necessary to admit a human operation, distinction from the divine operation, . . . it was necessary for him to have habitual grace, whereby this operation might be perfect in him."

130. Indebted to Augustine, Aquinas holds that such things as the burning bush that Moses saw (Exod. 3:2–3), and the rock from which water miraculously flowed (Exod. 17:6), were not visible missions of the Holy Spirit, on the grounds that the bush and the rock preexisted their use as signs rather than being created directly and immediately for the purpose of manifesting the Spirit. See I, q. 43, a. 7, ad 2.

131. III, q. 39, a. 6, ad 4.

132. III, q. 39, a. 6, ad 4.

and daughters of God. Aquinas also points out that the Spirit's visible missions fit with Jesus's mission of freeing humans from sin and elevating us to participate in the divine life.[133] Thus the Spirit's visible mission in the form of a dove primarily signifies liberation from sin, as befits its connection with Jesus's baptism. For its part, the Spirit's visible mission in the form of a bright cloud primarily signifies elevation to the divine life, as befits its connection with Jesus's transfiguration. Aquinas explains that "just as in baptism he [the whole Trinity] confers innocence, signified by the simplicity of the dove, so in the resurrection will he give his elect the clarity of glory and refreshment from all sorts of evil, which are signified by the bright cloud."[134]

In short, the category "visible mission" fits both the Son and Spirit, because the Spirit's visible mission serves to show forth the Son's visible mission, and both are for the sake of the church as the (inaugurated but not yet consummated) kingdom of God. The visible missions of the Spirit manifest Jesus's redemptive and prophetic tasks in the inauguration of the kingdom of God, and therefore it is hardly the case that the invisible mission of the Spirit to Jesus at his conception is the only mission that matters. At Jesus's baptism and transfiguration, the Spirit shows us who Jesus is and what we should hope for from him; and in this way, by these visible anointings, the Spirit shows us that Jesus is truly the anointed one from his very conception in Mary's womb.[135]

Conclusion

James Dunn and Thomas Aquinas make a rather unlikely pair. Dunn is a Protestant Christian and a New Testament historian who has little use for the church's dogma or hierarchy. Dunn's historical-critical research follows

133. See III, q. 1, a. 2, where Aquinas speaks first of the incarnate Son's furthering us in good, and then of the incarnate Son's withdrawing us from evil.

134. III, q. 45, a. 4, ad 2.

135. I disagree, therefore, with Cantalamessa's suggestion that the visible missions of the Spirit to Jesus become obscured and relativized by the insistence (itself fully biblical) upon the plenitude of the invisible mission of the Spirit at Jesus's conception. Without properly appreciating the significance of the visible missions, Cantalamessa argues, "The concept of Jesus' anointing as the work of the Holy Spirit does not disappear from theology, but is transferred from the baptism in the Jordan to the moment of the incarnation, eventually becoming identified, purely and simply, with the incarnation itself. . . . Among the Latins, with the advent of Scholasticism the mystery and the very concept of Christ's anointing by action of the Holy Spirit on the day of his baptism disappears completely from theology, never figuring as a separate topic in any of the various *Summae*, starting with that of St. Thomas" (Cantalamessa, *The Holy Spirit in the Life of Jesus*, 9). Cantalamessa's view is a caricature that arises from lack of attention to the theology of the visible missions of the Spirit to Jesus, in light of the biblical portrait of Jesus as "holy, the Son of God" (Luke 1:35) from his conception.

a method quite different from that of Aquinas's biblical commentaries, let alone his *Summa theologiae*. Guided by the creedal confessions of the church, Aquinas assumes that the New Testament's references to the Spirit refer to a distinct divine person, whereas Dunn considers that New Testament authors often have simply the divine power in view. Indeed, Aquinas's reflections on Jesus and the Spirit are in certain ways about as far from Dunn's historical-critical reconstruction as one can get.

In this chapter, however, I have proposed that Aquinas's theology of the Holy Spirit's missions to Jesus can fruitfully be paired with Dunn's exegetical emphasis on interpreting Jesus in light of the testimony to Jesus's experience of the Spirit. This can be done, at least, once one allows for Aquinas's and Dunn's contrasting understandings of the ontological status of the Son and Spirit. As Dunn recognizes, Jesus's powerful experience of the Spirit is all too often neglected in historical-critical reconstruction. Denuded of the Spirit, Jesus can easily seem delusional or fanatical, and the New Testament's testimony to him can appear unconscionably exaggerated.[136] By contrast, when we recall the testimony to Jesus's extraordinary experience of being propelled by the Spirit, his words and deeds become more intelligible, as does the New Testament's testimony. Historical work, of course, generally has little place for the personal agency of the Holy Spirit, and historians are loath to make historically unverifiable claims about Jesus's interior experience. This is why Dunn's approach offers much to theology: he is willing to take the Spirit seriously as a profound factor in the words and deeds of Jesus, and even, at least in his early work, to foreground the Spirit. Jesus the eschatological prophet is understandable on Christian terms only so long as the Holy Spirit is centrally in the picture.

In turn, Aquinas's theology of the missions of the Spirit has much to offer contemporary biblical exegesis. Of course, it is possible to study Aquinas's theology of the divine processions and missions without inquiring into how this might relate to the study of Jesus and the Spirit that arises from historical inquiry into the New Testament texts. Aquinas's theology, however, would then be at risk of losing its biblical sap. When placed in conversation with Dunn's historical-critical reconstructions, Aquinas's approach offers a way of accounting for the unique plenitude of Jesus's experience of the Spirit. Aquinas finds this experience to be at the very root of Jesus's vocation. The plenitude of the Spirit's invisible mission to Jesus at

---

136. For a recent popular book along these lines, depicting a revolutionary Jesus whose goal was to overthrow Roman rule, see Reza Aslan, *Zealot: The Life and Times of Jesus of Nazareth* (New York: Random House, 2013).

his conception, unfolding over the course of Jesus's life in his virtues and "gratuitous graces," helps to make sense of the New Testament witness to Jesus's sinlessness, his untutored wisdom, and the powers of exorcism and miracle-working that so impress Dunn. The gifts of the Holy Spirit shed light on Jesus's openness to the prompting of the Spirit, his wonderful understanding of his fellow humans, his intimate knowledge of his Father, and his intense life of prayer. Above all, the missions of personal Love and Gift to Jesus help to account for Jesus's supreme charity, culminating in his radical gift of self on the cross.

The distinction between the invisible and visible missions of the Spirit to Jesus is also valuable, not least for its explanation that the visible missions of the Spirit serve to demonstrate Jesus's unique authority (as the incarnate Son) to give grace and to teach all people. The visible missions are understandable, furthermore, in light of the unique plenitude of the invisible mission of the Spirit to Jesus Christ. Thus for Aquinas as for Dunn, appreciating Jesus's eschatological words and deeds—the wonderful power of the one who "humbled himself and became obedient unto death" (Phil. 2:8)—requires thoroughly appreciating the Spirit's work in and through him, even though Aquinas and Dunn understand Philippians 2 (and Jesus's Sonship) in contrasting ways.[137]

Dunn is not alone among biblical scholars in recognizing the role of the Spirit in Jesus's life. As I noted above, N. T. Wright comments that Jesus "saw his whole work as being guided, driven along, by YHWH's spirit (what prophet would not?)," and Wright equally appreciates "the possibility"—indeed for Wright the likelihood—"of Jesus's having a particular intimacy with the one he called 'father'" as part of Jesus's unique vocation.[138] In his *Jesus and the Victory of God*, however, Wright's remarks about the Spirit's work are quite spare and sparse. Wright should make much more than he does of the fact that Jesus's vocation—namely "to do and be, for Israel and the world, that which according to scripture only YHWH himself could do and be"[139]—would have required the uniquely powerful interior presence of the Spirit in order to enable someone sane to embrace it.

Aquinas's approach to Jesus and the Spirit has been fruitfully developed by Hans Urs von Balthasar. Balthasar states, "It is unquestionable that the Spirit

137. For Dunn's perspective on Philippians 2, see, for example, *Christology in the Making*, 114–21. For discussion of Aquinas's perspective on Philippians 2, see Matthew Levering, *Paul in the* Summa Theologiae (Washington, DC: Catholic University of America Press, 2014), chap. 9.

138. Wright, *Jesus and the Victory of God*, 648, 650.

139. Ibid., 653.

rested *over* him [Jesus] and that he knew that the Spirit dwelt *in* him: this is manifest in the sovereign authority of his deeds and words."[140] Balthasar grants that "we have no way of inspecting Jesus's consciousness of this inseparable bond with the Spirit"—no way, that is, other than through the authority of his actions and teaching, to which Dunn likewise appeals.[141] To the note of Jesus's "sovereign authority," Balthasar adds the further Johannine note of Jesus's obedience to the Father. He observes, "Jesus is aware that he has received a mission from the Father and is its complete embodiment in the world. . . . He knows that he has identified himself in complete inner freedom with a task that has been *given* him and must be carried out at all costs; in other words, it calls for total obedience."[142] Such obedience, to the point of *completely* embodying a mission, could not be accomplished without the power of the Spirit. Balthasar adds regarding Jesus's awareness of mission, "We cannot conceive that this awareness ever had a beginning."[143] This seems right, especially in light of birth narratives and the numerous texts in the New Testament that testify to the preexistence of the Son.

What Aquinas provides is a unified and profound arrangement of trinitarian processions and missions, the virtues and gifts of the Spirit, habitual grace and the gratuitous graces, and Jesus's sinless humanity and supreme charity on the cross. In Aquinas, Jesus's intimate knowledge of the Father, his miracle working, and his prophetic wisdom are bound together with his supreme charity through the invisible mission of the Holy Spirit, who is Love and Gift in person. The visible missions of the Spirit to Jesus at his baptism and transfiguration point toward the interior reality of Jesus, who is the divine Son and therefore uniquely possesses the fullness of the Spirit for the sake of our salvation. Aquinas's approach remains notably close to Scripture, which presents Jesus as led and anointed by the Spirit, as working signs and wonders, as teaching authoritatively and knowing his Father in a way far beyond mere conceptual knowledge, as the sinless exemplar of charity and the one mediator of salvation, and as the preexistent Son who, after his resurrection and exaltation, sends the Spirit upon his disciples. As Gilles Emery puts it, Aquinas's approach "regards Christ and the Holy Spirit in their unity and in their relations."[144]

140. Hans Urs von Balthasar, *Theo-Logic: Theological Logical Theory*, vol. 3, *The Spirit of Truth*, trans. Graham Harrison (San Francisco: Ignatius, 2005), 173.

141. Ibid.

142. Balthasar, *Theo-Drama: Theological Dramatic Theory*, vol. 3, *The Dramatis Personae*, 183.

143. Ibid.

144. Gilles Emery, OP, *The Trinity: An Introduction to Catholic Doctrine on the Triune God*, trans. Matthew Levering (Washington, DC: Catholic University of America Press, 2011), 193. Emery is speaking specifically of Aquinas's doctrine of the missions.

To look upon Christ and the Spirit in this way, of course, requires attending to the Spirit's upbuilding of the "body of Christ" (1 Cor. 12:27), the church, which occurs preeminently in the "the higher gifts" and in the "still more excellent way" (1 Cor. 12:31) that is love. The next chapter, therefore, addresses the Holy Spirit's visible and invisible missions to the church, in relation to the meaning of Jesus's eschatological actions and prophecies.

THE HOLY SPIRIT AND THE CHURCH

How should we understand the Holy Spirit's activity in constituting, building, and sustaining the church?[1] It might be helpful to begin with John the Baptist, who prophesies about Christ Jesus that "he will baptize you with the Holy Spirit and with fire. His winnowing fork is in his hand, and he will clear his threshing floor and gather his wheat into the granary, but the chaff he will burn with unquenchable fire" (Matt. 3:12). These words directly precede Jesus's baptism by John and Jesus's anointing by "the Spirit of God" (Matt. 3:16), as well as Jesus's being led by the Spirit to endure temptation in the wilderness. Prior to this, the evangelist Matthew has already reported that an angel told Joseph in a dream, "Do not fear to take Mary your wife, for that which is conceived in her is of the Holy Spirit" (Matt. 1:20).

According to the Gospel of Matthew, then, Jesus is "of the Holy Spirit," and he comes to bring about the eschatological baptism "with the Holy Spirit

---

1. Brian Gaybba (joined, in this regard, by many other commentators) sets the context for this chapter by observing, "When one turns to the New Testament, it is immediately obvious that one is faced with people who are convinced that the longed-for day of the outpouring of the Spirit on all had arrived. . . . The way the Spirit is referred to makes it clear that the early Christians regarded the Spirit as permanently present in the community. In both Acts and Paul's letters, the community is Spirit-filled and its individuals enjoy the permanent presence of the Spirit. In its ordinary peaceful life, the Church is 'filled with the consolation of the Holy Spirit' (Acts 9:31). The Church is a house in which God dwells in the Spirit (Eph. 2:22), and Christians are temples of the Spirit (1 Cor. 6:19)" (Gaybba, *The Spirit of Love: Theology of the Holy Spirit* [London: Geoffrey Chapman, 1987], 13).

and with fire." Arguably, his "winnowing fork" is his cross. As he instructs his disciples, "whoever would be great among you must be your servant, and whoever would be first among you must be your slave; even as the Son of man came not to be served but to serve, and to give his life as a ransom for many" (Matt. 20:26–28). Charity, as manifested supremely by Jesus's cross, separates those who love God from those who love the world. At Caesarea Philippi, Peter stands among the latter, despite his confession of Jesus as the "the Christ, the Son of the living God" (Matt. 16:16). When Jesus describes his coming passion and resurrection, "Peter took him and began to rebuke him, saying, 'God forbid, Lord! This shall never happen to you'" (Matt. 16:22). Jesus responds by warning Peter that "you are not on the side of God, but of men" (Matt. 16:23).

Jesus's eschatological baptizing "with the Holy Spirit and with fire" can also be seen in his actions toward and prophecies about the temple.[2] In the Gospel of Mark, a day after his triumphant entrance into Jerusalem in preparation for his last Passover, Jesus "entered the temple and began to drive out those who sold and those who bought in the temple, and he overturned the tables of the money-changers and the seats of those who sold pigeons" (Mark 11:15). This symbolic action recalls Zechariah's prophesy regarding the day of the Lord, on which day the Lord will return to Zion to reign forever: "I will pour out on the house of David and the inhabitants of Jerusalem a spirit of compassion and supplication, so that, when they look on him whom they have pierced, they shall mourn for him. . . . And there shall no longer be a trader in the house of the LORD of hosts on that day" (Zech. 14:21). Shortly after cleansing the temple, Jesus prophesies the destruction of the temple: "Do you see these great buildings? There will not be left here one stone upon another, that will not be thrown down" (Mark 13:2). After his arrest, false witnesses accuse Jesus without knowing the real truth of their statement: "We heard him say, 'I will destroy this temple that is made with hands, and in three days I will build another, not made with hands'" (Mark 14:58).

Jesus's eschatological baptizing "with the Holy Spirit and with fire" should therefore be understood not only in relation to his cross, but also in relation to

2. For various exegetical perspectives on Jesus (and his body the church) as the eschatological temple, see Grant Macaskill, *Union with Christ in the New Testament* (Oxford: Oxford University Press, 2013), 147–91; Nicholas Perrin, *Jesus the Temple* (Grand Rapids: Baker Academic, 2010); Timothy C. Gray, *The Temple in the Gospel of Mark: A Study in Its Narrative Role* (Grand Rapids: Baker Academic, 2010); Paul M. Hoskins, *Jesus as the Fulfillment of the Temple in the Gospel of John* (Milton Keynes: Paternoster, 2006); G. K. Beale, *The Temple and the Church's Mission: A Biblical Theology of the Dwelling Place of God* (Downers Grove, IL: InterVarsity, 2004); Mary L. Coloe, *God Dwells with Us: Temple Symbolism in the Fourth Gospel* (Collegeville, MN: Liturgical Press, 2001).

the community of believers united by the Spirit in Jesus's body—the temple "not made with hands."[3] Even so, it may seem that some of Jesus's eschatological prophecies leave little or no room for the church—whether one conceives the church as present wherever the true gospel is preached and the true sacraments practiced, or whether one conceives the church (as I do) to be the Catholic Church, ecumenically related to other Christian communions in various degrees.[4] In one prophetic text, for example, Jesus tells his disciples that "you will not have gone through all the towns of Israel, before the Son of man comes" (Matt. 10:23). Similarly, he assures his disciples that "there are some standing here who will not taste death before they see the Son of man coming in his kingdom" (Matt. 16:28), and he promises that "this generation will not pass away till all these things take place" (Matt. 24:34). These passages are especially puzzling because at the same time he suggests that the "close of the age" (Matt. 24:3) is not yet imminent, since there must first be wars, famines, and earthquakes in different parts of the world, and "this gospel of the kingdom will be preached throughout the whole world, as a testimony to all nations; and then the end will come" (Matt. 24:14 [cf. Matt. 10:18]). Jesus also observes that "of that day and hour no one knows, not even the angels of heaven, nor the Son, but the Father only," and that "the Son of man is coming at an hour you do not expect" (Matt. 24:36, 44).

What are we to make of this? The kingdom is here, since it "has come upon you"; and yet the kingdom is something that we will enter in the future. The eschatological end and the return of Jesus will come before all the disciples have died, and yet it will take much longer than this, since the gospel must first be preached throughout the whole world. Jesus knows when he is going to return, and yet he says that only the Father knows. Can these various claims be squared with one another or with Jesus's preparations for his church, the inaugurated kingdom and eschatological temple?

In my view, the key to squaring these claims is to recognize that even now, the church participates in Jesus's "hour" (John 2:4), his eschatological fulfillment of all things by his paschal mystery. During this time, which is already the "last hour" (1 John 2:18) and yet which also prepares for the "last time"

---

3. Along these lines, Grant Macaskill notes that Peter's speech in Acts 4 "reflects the basic conviction that the eschatological temple has come into existence and that the Messiah is part of its structure" (Macaskill, *Union with Christ in the New Testament*, 165). See also the succinct summary of the Holy Spirit's work in Jesus and the church in Michael Kyne, SJ, "The Holy Spirit and Prayer," in *The Spirit in Action: Papers Read at the Second Catholic Dogma Course Roehampton 1967*, ed. Robert Butterworth, SJ (Langley, UK: St. Paul Publications, 1968), 143–49, at 144–45.

4. For the latter view of the church, see the Second Vatican Council's *Lumen Gentium* and *Unitatis Redintegratio*, along with Pope John Paul II's encyclical *Ut Unum Sint*.

(1 Pet. 1:5) of the final judgment and new creation, Jesus's Spirit-filled church lives by sharing in his holy self-offering to the Father. The church does so by eucharistic worship, almsgiving, and proclaiming the good news to the whole world.[5] In these ways, the Spirit-filled church participates in the work of its Spirit-filled Lord. The world remains the same—there are wars, famines, and earthquakes—but yet it is also completely changed, since the inaugurated kingdom of God (and the risen Christ himself) is now present in the world through the outpouring of the Holy Spirit upon the messianic community.[6]

Can Jesus's eschatological discourses be appropriately read in this way, with an emphasis on the Spirit's mission to the church as the inaugurated kingdom of God? With Jürgen Moltmann, can we affirm that "as the historical community of Christ . . . the church is the eschatological creation of the Spirit"?[7] In order to frame this question more sharply, I begin by examining three portraits of Jesus as an eschatological prophet of the kingdom of God, offered by the biblical scholars N. T. Wright, James D. G. Dunn, and Dale Allison, respectively. I set forth Allison's position in particular detail, since Allison, like Albert Schweitzer, holds that Jesus wrongly predicted the imminent end of the world. After noting Hans Urs von Balthasar's helpful response to this problematic, I argue that however one comes down regarding the question of whether Jesus anticipated a literal, imminent end to the world, it is surely the case that unless the Holy Spirit has been poured out, then Jesus was

---

5. For further discussion, see Matthew Levering, *Jesus and the Demise of Death: Resurrection, the Afterlife, and the Fate of Christians* (Waco: Baylor University Press, 2012), chap. 4.

6. As Raniero Cantalamessa says, in a manner that should not be taken to exclude the work of the incarnate Son, "The experience of the Spirit in the Church is nothing other than what we call the tradition of the church" (Cantalamessa, *The Mystery of Pentecost*, trans. Glen S. Davis [Collegeville, MN: Liturgical Press, 2001], 3). This requires, however, that we understand the "experience of the Spirit" in a more differentiated manner than one finds in Karl Rahner, SJ's insistence that "transcendental experience that allows God to be present is always . . . experience of the Holy Spirit" (Rahner, *The Spirit in the Church*, trans. John Griffiths et al. [New York: Seabury, 1979], 16).

7. Jürgen Moltmann, *The Church in the Power of the Spirit: A Contribution to Messianic Ecclesiology*, trans. Margaret Kohl (Minneapolis: Fortress, 1993), 33. Despite their rhetorical power, some of Moltmann's formulations in the same section are exaggerated or off-kilter—for example, his claims that "through the Spirit the believer is determined by the divine future," and that "the church is the concrete form in which men experience the history of Christ" (ibid., 34–35). In both cases, distinctions would need to be made that Moltmann does not make. I agree, however, with Moltmann's insistence that "the true perception that the messianic history of Christ from his incarnation to his exaltation is the work of the eschatological Spirit must not pass by Christ's death on the cross" (ibid., 37). See also the emphasis on relationality and on the Spirit as "the life principle of the church" in Bernd Jochen Hilberath, "Identity through Self-Transcendence: The Holy Spirit and the Fellowship of Free Persons," in *Advents of the Spirit: An Introduction to the Current Study of Pneumatology*, ed. Bradford E. Hinze and D. Lyle Dabney (Milwaukee: Marquette University Press, 2001), 265–94.

wrong. Certainly, Jesus could not have poured out the Spirit unless Jesus also rose from the dead. Yet it is the Spirit's outpouring that is the fundamental mark of the inaugurated kingdom that Jesus repeatedly prophesied. Jesus's eschatological prophecies make sense only if the Spirit has been poured out so that the world is both ended and not ended.

Theologically, then, much depends on our construal of the Holy Spirit and the church. Yet what is involved in adequately describing the church as Spirit-filled? The second section of this chapter proposes that Thomas Aquinas's theology of the Spirit's missions to the church is particularly suitable for conveying the intensity and intimacy of the church's reception of the eschatological Spirit.[8] Along these lines, Yves Congar states, "Both in its life and in its origin, the Church is the fruit of two 'divine missions,' in the exact and very profound sense in which Thomas Aquinas uses this phrase."[9] Indeed, I will suggest that Aquinas places the focus precisely where it must be if the eschatological people (and thus reign) of God truly has been inaugurated by Jesus of Nazareth. Put another way, we can be sure that the church today is *not* the eschatological community that Jesus understood himself to be inaugurating, unless the church today is formed by the Holy Spirit in extraordinary ways. By helping to articulate the numerous ways in which the Holy Spirit even now constitutes, strengthens, and works through the church, Aquinas offers us a

8. In his study of Aquinas's ecclesiology, George Sabra states quite surprisingly, "Pneumatology is not very developed in Thomas and is not very explicit either" (Sabra, *Thomas Aquinas' Vision of the Church* [Mainz: Matthias Grünewald Verlag, 1987], 105). Earlier, however, Sabra had warned against inferring "that Thomas attributed little importance to the Spirit in ecclesiology and the economy of salvation as a whole" (ibid., 94). For the scope of Aquinas's pneumatology, see also Gilles Emery, OP, "The Holy Spirit in Aquinas's Commentary on Romans," in *Reading Romans with St. Thomas Aquinas*, ed. Matthew Levering and Michael Dauphinais (Washington, DC: Catholic University of America Press, 2012), 127–62; Bruce D. Marshall, "What Does the Spirit Have to Do?," in *Reading John with St. Thomas Aquinas: Theological Exegesis and Speculative Theology*, ed. Michael Dauphinais and Matthew Levering (Washington, DC: Catholic University of America Press, 2005), 62–77.

9. Yves Congar, OP, *I Believe in the Holy Spirit*, trans. David Smith (New York: Crossroad, 1997), 2:7; see his full discussion on 7–8. For the correlation of the work of the Son and Spirit, see also Martin Sabathé, *La Trinité rédemptrice dans la* Commentaire de l'Évangile de saint Jean *par Thomas d'Aquin* (Paris: Vrin, 2011), 182–85. Note also the comment of Avery Dulles, SJ: "Any solid ecclesiology must be rooted in the two divine processions, those of the Son and the Holy Spirit, which are continued in their respective missions" (Dulles, "The Trinity and Christian Unity," in *God the Holy Trinity: Reflections on Christian Faith and Practice*, ed. Timothy George [Grand Rapids: Baker Academic, 2006], 69–82, at 82). The Spirit's missions to the church are related to, but not a mere continuation of, the Spirit's missions to Jesus Christ; in this regard I differ somewhat from Heribert Mühlen's view that the church is the continuation not of the incarnation but of Christ's anointing by the Spirit. See Mühlen, *Una Mystica Persona: Die Kirche als das Mysterium der heilsgeschichtlichen Identität des heiligen Geistes, eine Person in vielen Personen* (Munich: Schöningh, 1968).

plausible vision of the eschatological community that Jesus thought himself to be inaugurating—the community of those who receive the Spirit and come to recognize Jesus as the risen Lord, the Son who calls us into communion with the Father.[10]

To those who consider medieval theology to be out of touch both with the eschatological fervor of the first Christians and with their enthusiasm for the Spirit's presence, Aquinas may seem to be an unlikely exemplar of the proper valuation of the outpouring of the eschatological Spirit upon the church.[11] Graham Tomlin, for example, argues that "functions attributed to the Spirit (transformation, healing etc.) came to be attributed instead to divine *grace*, especially within the sacramental theology of the Middle Ages. As a result, within medieval theology, pneumatology was largely lost within the theology of grace, and does not play a prominent role in the theological discussion of that time."[12] Similarly, surely with Aquinas in view, Kilian

10. For studies of Aquinas's theology of the church, see Jean-Pierre Torrell, OP, *Saint Thomas Aquinas*, vol. 2, *Spiritual Master*, trans. Robert Royal (Washington, DC: Catholic University of America Press, 2003), chap. 8; Yves Congar, OP's collection of essays *Thomas d'Aquin: Sa vision de théologie et de l'Église* (London: Variorum Reprints, 1984); Martin Grabmann, *Die Lehre des heiligen Thomas von Aquin von der Kirche als Gotteswerk* (Regensburg: G. J. Manz, 1903); John Mahoney, SJ, "'The Church of the Holy Spirit' in Aquinas," *Heythrop Journal* 15 (1974): 18–36; Sabra, *Thomas Aquinas' Vision of the Church*; Avery Dulles, SJ, "The Church according to Thomas Aquinas," in *A Church to Believe In* (New York: Crossroad, 1982), 149–92. Congar argues that because the *Summa theologiae* lacks a treatise on the church, it lacks an integrative consideration of the church's various elements "as forming a collective reality of mediation of the grace of the Holy Spirit and of Christ," that is to say, a "consideration of the Church as Communion, and a Communion of local and particular churches"—although Aquinas does appreciate the diversity of local churches. See Congar, "Vision de l'Église chez S. Thomas d'Aquin," *Revue des sciences philosophiques et théologiques* 44 (1960): 523–41, at 536 (my translation). I take up these issues in relation to Aquinas in Matthew Levering, *Christ and the Catholic Priesthood: Ecclesial Hierarchy and the Pattern of the Trinity* (Chicago: Hillenbrand, 2010).

11. Those who have such a view of medieval theology should consult E. Benz, "Joachim-Studien, III. Thomas von Aquin und Joachim de Fiore. Die katholische Antwort auf die spiritualistische Kirchen- und Geschichtsanschauung," *Zeitschrift für Kirchengeschichte* 53 (1934): 52–116. See also Henri de Lubac, SJ, *La postérité spirituelle de Joachim de Flore*, vol. 1, *De Joachim à Schelling* (Paris: Éditions Lethielleux, 1979); Raoul Manselli, *La "Lectura super apocalipsim" di Pietro di Giovanni Olivi: Ricerche sull' escatologismo medioevale* (Rome: Istituto Storico Italiano per il Medioevo, 1955). John Mahoney notes, regarding Aquinas's critique of the Joachimites, "To say, as they did, that the Gospel of Christ is not the Gospel of the kingdom was, he considered, the utmost foolishness (*stultissimum*). And to claim that the Holy Spirit is yet to come in all his fullness is a vanity (*vanitas*) today, Aquinas judged, as great as were the vanities (*istae vanitates*) of the Montanists and the Manichees who in their day had held the same view" (Mahoney, "'The Church of the Holy Spirit' in Aquinas," 30) (cf. *Summa theologiae* I-II, q. 106, a. 4).

12. Graham Tomlin, *The Prodigal Spirit: The Trinity, the Church and the Future of the World* (London: Alpha International, 2011), 15. For further examples of contemporary biblical scholars and theologians, including Larry Hurtado and John Howard Yoder, who mistakenly

McDonnell states that "Augustine tends, as do his heirs both ancient and modern, to refer to grace in contexts where theologians of the East speak of the Spirit."[13]

It is true that like St. Paul, Aquinas freely appeals to "grace," but not to the detriment of the role of the Holy Spirit. Appreciating the full scope of Aquinas's pneumatology should therefore illumine the continuity of the church's self-understanding as the eschatological kingdom inaugurated by Jesus. It should also help us to value properly the Spirit's work as Love and Gift. For as Paul makes clear, it is the "Spirit of Jesus Christ" (Phil. 1:19) who, having filled Jesus with his Love and Gift, now fills Jesus's Body, the church—the inaugurated kingdom of God—with "the grace of the Lord Jesus Christ" (Phil. 4:23).[14]

---

criticize patristic/medieval ecclesiology for lacking eschatological fervor, see Levering, *Jesus and the Demise of Death*, chap. 4. Citing Gary Badcock's *Light of Truth and Fire of Love: A Theology of the Holy Spirit* (Grand Rapids: Eerdmans, 1997), 67–75, Tomlin argues that the root of the problem was Augustine's theology of the Spirit: "Augustine seems to subsume the Spirit into the relationship between the Father and the Son, which leads to the question of whether the Spirit is anything different from the divine substance itself, or even whether the Spirit is less than personal—a bond and not a person. . . . [Augustine's] approach can be read as endorsing a view of the Trinity that leaves the Spirit as passive, impersonal and subordinate" (Tomlin, *Prodigal Spirit*, 15). From the medieval period, Tomlin takes Aquinas's *Summa theologiae* as the exemplar of the bad fruits of Augustine's approach. Tomlin states critically, "Aquinas's *Summa Theologica* treats the Holy Spirit under the general section entitled 'Father, Son and Holy Ghost' (Ia.33–43). In the *Tertia Pars*, there is a section on 'The Incarnate Word' and 'Our Lady,' but none on the Holy Spirit. The theme of the Spirit is revisited in the section on virtues and the moral life later on in the *Summa*, yet it seems to be primarily located in the ethical rather than more strictly theological section of the work" (ibid., n4). A more complete misreading of Aquinas on the Holy Spirit could hardly be found. For a response to concerns such as Tomlin's, see, for example, Bruce D. Marshall, "*Ex Occidente Lux*? Aquinas and Eastern Orthodox Theology," in *Aquinas in Dialogue: Thomas for the Twenty-First Century*, ed. Jim Fodor and Frederick Christian Bauerschmidt (Oxford: Blackwell, 2004), 19–46.

13. Kilian McDonnell, OSB, *The Other Hand of God: The Holy Spirit as the Universal Touch and Goal* (Collegeville, MN: Liturgical Press, 2003), 223. According to McDonnell, "Augustine scarcely spoke of the Holy Spirit except where he could not avoid it, such as when he found the Spirit in a citation he had invoked in order to support a thesis on which he had already decided" (ibid.).

14. Aquinas would agree with Gordon D. Fee's insistence that "to be a trinitarian of the Pauline kind means to be a person of the Spirit; for it is through the Spirit's indwelling that we know God and Christ relationally, and through the same Spirit's indwelling that we are being transformed into God's own likeness 'from glory to glory' (2 Cor. 3:18)" (Fee, "Paul and the Trinity: The Experience of Christ and the Spirit for Paul's Understanding of God," in *The Trinity: An Interdisciplinary Symposium on the Trinity*, ed. Stephen T. Davis, Daniel Kendall, SJ, and Gerald O'Collins, SJ [Oxford: Oxford University Press, 1999], 49–72, at 72). Aquinas would also agree with Fee's warning that "our trinitarianism is terribly defective if we spend our labours on the ontological questions in such a way as to lose the essential narrative about God and salvation that raised those questions in the first place" (ibid.).

Jesus the Eschatological Prophet of the Kingdom of God: Exegetical Views

N. T. Wright: Jesus, the Kingdom of God, and the Temple

What are the fundamental elements of Jesus's eschatological preaching according to N. T. Wright, whose reading of the scriptural witness to Jesus is deeply indebted to Schweitzer? Wright considers Jesus to have taught the imminence, indeed the immanent presence, of the kingdom of God. At the same time, as Wright shows, Jesus also warned about the upcoming eschatological tribulation and called upon people to repent. From this perspective, Jesus's "announcement of the kingdom was a warning of imminent catastrophe, a summons to an immediate change of heart and direction of life, and invitation to a new way of being Israel. Jesus announced that the reign of Israel's god, so long awaited, was now beginning."[15] According to Wright, the people of Israel in Jesus's day were anticipating and awaiting a renewed covenant, a restored creation through the defeat of evil, the end of Israel's exile, and the return of YHWH to Zion/temple as King—and these are precisely the elements foretold in Jesus's parables and foreshadowed by his mighty works, his exorcisms and miracles.

Wright argues, therefore, that Jesus was deliberately inaugurating the kingdom of God. It is important, however, to distinguish the kingdom (and Jewish "apocalyptic" in general) from "the end of the space-time universe."[16] Wright considers that Schweitzer, in presuming that Jesus preached the literal end of the world, adopted "a bizarre literalistic reading of what the first century knew to be thoroughly metaphorical."[17] In fact, the kingdom of God entails not the end of the world but the renewal of this world through the restoration of Israel.[18] Wright notes that even in the welcome that Jesus gave to sinners, he was already establishing this kingdom, by allowing them to bypass the sacrificial and legal system so as to receive forgiveness directly from him, through whom "the eschatological work of the spirit of YHWH" was taking place.[19] Wright also pays attention to Jesus's parables, such as Mark 4:30–32, the parable of the mustard seed. For Wright, the mustard seed's growth into "the greatest of all shrubs" (Mark 4:32) has to do with Jesus's ministry in Israel, which may not look like the coming restoration of Israel but "is in fact its strange beginning."[20] By his cross and resurrection, then, Jesus renews the

---

15. N. T. Wright, *Jesus and the Victory of God* (Minneapolis: Fortress, 1996), 172.
16. Ibid., 81.
17. Ibid.
18. See, for example, ibid., 209, 214.
19. Ibid., 273.
20. Ibid., 241. By comparison, Joseph Ratzinger interprets this parable (and other similar ones) as being about the gradual spread of the kingdom of God—"Jesus' presence and action," his eschatological reign of cruciform love—during the period between its inauguration and

covenant, conquers evil, brings an end to Israel's exile, and establishes himself as the exalted King not only of Israel but of the whole world. The kingdom of God is thereby fully inaugurated, even if not yet consummated.

When Wright reads explicitly apocalyptic texts such as Mark 13, where Jesus speaks about an imminent end-time tribulation that will be followed by "the Son of man coming in clouds with great power and glory" (Mark 13:26), Wright finds in them a prophecy of the final destruction of the temple of Jerusalem that occurred in AD 70. Regarding the apocalyptic imagery of Mark 13 ("the sun will be darkened, and the moon will not give its light, and the stars will be falling from heaven, and the powers in the heavens will be shaken" [Mark 13:24–25]), Wright holds that such imagery is not meant literally, as Schweitzer thought. On the contrary, "no Jews whose opinions are known to us thought that their god was about to bring the space-time world, including land and Temple, to a sudden end."[21] Why, then, did Jesus (and/or Mark) use such bold cosmic imagery? Wright suggests that the reason was to prepare the people of Israel for the occurrence of "startling and 'cosmically' significant events, such as the fall of great empires, *within* the space-time world."[22] With respect to such passages as Matthew 10:23, "you will not have gone through all the towns of Israel, before the Son of man comes," Wright adds that Jesus, speaking prophetically, has in view his own decisive vindication. Wright sums up the position he is advocating: "Already present in Jesus's ministry, and climactically inaugurated in his death and resurrection, the divine kingdom will be manifest within a generation, when Jesus and his followers are vindicated in and through the destruction of Jerusalem."[23]

---

consummation (Ratzinger, *Jesus of Nazareth: From the Baptism in the Jordan to the Transfiguration*, trans. Adrian Walker [New York: Doubleday, 2007], 60). For Ratzinger, Jesus's kingdom proclamation is Jesus's announcement that "this is the hour when God is showing himself in history as its Lord, as the living God, in a way that goes beyond anything seen before. . . . In Jesus, God is now the one who acts and who rules as Lord—rules in a divine way, without worldly power, rules through the love that reaches 'to the end' (John 13:1), to the Cross" (ibid., 56, 61). The kingdom of God consists in God's reigning in love through Jesus and thereby establishing "a new family" based upon following Jesus and enjoying communion with him (and his Father) through the grace of the Holy Spirit (ibid., 61).

21. Wright, *Jesus and the Victory of God*, 513.

22. Ibid.

23. Ibid., 365. Similarly, regarding Luke 9:27 (cf. Mark 9:1; Matt. 16:28), "there are some standing here who will not taste death before they see the kingdom of God," Wright comments,

> This constitutes a further clear promise of future victory and vindication. Like the eager followers of the many other prophets and messianic figures who flit through the pages of first-century Jewish history, Jesus' hearers would have understood their leader to be promising them the final victory for which the nation as a whole was longing. The great new exodus would occur: the real "return from exile," the return of YHWH to Zion, the rebuilding of the Temple, the defeat of the forces of evil—all of this would

In Paul (for instance, 1 Cor. 15:20–28), Wright finds the already/not yet, or immanent/imminent, dimension of the kingdom that the risen Jesus has established. He explains that for Paul, writing to the first Christian communities, the kingdom is now "already a reality in which the Messiah's people partake. They have already been created as 'a kingdom, and priests' [Rev. 1:6], precisely through the work of the Messiah."[24] But the kingdom is also a future reality: the full resurrection of the dead, the final judgment, and the consummation of all things in the new creation has not yet happened.[25] Christian communities today, then, are still in this situation. As the people of the Messiah, Christian communities today share in the immanent reality of the kingdom and await the fullness of this kingdom in the final eschatological consummation of all things. This kingdom will be a renewed cosmos, not an ethereal Platonic heaven.

James D. G. Dunn: Jesus, the Kingdom of God, and the Spirit

The same passages are read somewhat differently by James Dunn, although his position is broadly similar to that of Wright. Taking up the problem of what exactly Jesus meant in his difficult and sometimes seemingly contradictory eschatological preaching, Dunn observes, "The phrase 'kingdom of God' [or: 'kingdom of heaven'] occurs regularly in the Evangelists' recollection of Jesus's words—thirteen times in Mark, another nine times in the material shared by Matthew and Luke (q/Q), a further twenty-eight times in tradition

---

be contained within the promise. And it would happen within their lifetimes. Political and revolutionary leaders down the ages have said much the same, albeit without the specific first-century Jewish theological overtones. To read this saying as though it were a prediction of Jesus' "return," or of the "parousia" in some Schweitzerian end-of-the-world sense, is simply to fail to think historically. (ibid., 470)

24. Ibid., 217.

25. Wright emphasizes, "The point of the present kingdom is that it is the first-fruits of the future kingdom; and the future kingdom involves the abolition, not of space, time, or the cosmos itself, but rather of that which threatens space, time, and creation, namely, sin and death" (ibid., 218). Wright also emphasizes that the kingdom expectations of the Jewish people have been redefined by Jesus, so that the community of the risen Lord "self-consciously sees itself as the time when the covenant purpose of the creator, which always envisaged the redemption of the whole world, moves beyond the narrow confines of a single race (for which national symbols were of course appropriate), and calls into being a trans-national and trans-cultural community. Further, it sees itself as the time when the creator, the covenant god himself, has returned to dwell with his people, but not in a Temple made with hands" (ibid., 219). In this way, Wright addresses the obvious point that the "early Christian kingdom-language has little or nothing to do with the vindication of ethnic Israel, the overthrow of Roman rule in Palestine, the building of a new Temple on Mount Zion, the establishment of Torah-observance, or the nations flocking to Mount Zion to be judged and/or to be educated in the knowledge of YHWH" (ibid.). He has in view Albert Schweitzer's argument that Jesus's kingdom expectations failed.

distinctive of Matthew, and a further twelve times in tradition attested only by Luke."[26] By contrast, in the earliest New Testament author, Paul, the image of the kingdom of God rarely appears, although in a few cases Paul speaks of inheriting the kingdom. On this basis, Dunn concludes that the emphasis on the kingdom of God can be reliably traced to Jesus himself, rather than solely to the evangelists.

Dunn then inquires into what the "kingdom of God" might mean. From the intertestamental literature, he explores Qumran, the *Sybilline Oracles*, the *Psalms of Solomon*, and the *Testament of Moses*. In general, these texts foresee a divine (and sometimes messianic) kingship in Jerusalem that will bring peace to the whole creation. Dunn lists fourteen elements that are found as characteristics of Jewish eschatological hope at this period, although of course not each of the fourteen elements occurs in every text: ingathering of the twelve tribes (return from exile), abundant prosperity, a messiah, a renewed covenant, a new temple, YHWH's return to Zion, the gentiles coming to Jerusalem to worship and give alms to YHWH, Israel inheriting not only the promised land but the whole earth, a period of tribulation, cosmic disturbances, the defeat of evil and of Satan, the final judgment, the resurrection, and the punishment of the wicked in Sheol. If these elements tended to belong to Jewish eschatological hope during the time of Jesus, what elements were central, what elements did Jesus have in view, and did Jesus understand any of his eschatological language to be "metaphorical" and/or to include the traditional flexibility of Israelite prophetic discourse?

In seeking to answer these questions, Dunn observes at the outset that Jesus certainly spoke "of the kingdom as *yet to come* but also *already present*."[27] Dunn also rejects any "grand narratives," such as Wright's organizing of all the intertestamental material around the return from exile and YHWH's return to Zion. He emphasizes the theme of eschatological reversal of status, noting that already Jesus thought that the poor were receiving blessing. With regard to the coming kingdom, he points out that discipleship itself is understood in terms of eschatological suffering or tribulation, and he notes that Jesus's preaching contains the "expectation of impending judgment," a judgment that will often involve reversal and that will include reward for those who have followed Jesus.[28] Like Wright, Dunn underscores the metaphorical and polyvalent character of the images that Jesus employed for the coming kingdom of God. After all, Jesus was attempting to evoke a highly complex

---

26. James D. G. Dunn, *Christianity in the Making*, vol. 1, *Jesus Remembered* (Grand Rapids: Eerdmans, 2003), 384.

27. Ibid., 405.

28. Ibid., 420.

reality, not attempting to pin down the nature of the "kingdom of God" in a scientific or empirical fashion.

With regard to texts that suggest the kingdom has in some sense already come in or through Jesus, Dunn pays special attention to Jesus's understanding of his success as an exorcist. For Jesus, Dunn concludes, Satan's rule had been broken and the eschatological "harvest" was ready for reaping, but the fullness of God's triumphant kingdom remained in the future.[29] Dunn finds too that it is likely that Jesus intended "to gather around himself the core of a reconstituted Israel," represented by the twelve disciples/apostles and constituting a new temple or house of God, with special attention to the poor and perhaps also with inclusion of the gentiles.[30] Dunn argues that the connecting link between Jesus's eschatology and that of the earliest Christians can be found in the role of the Spirit. Jesus believed himself to be acting powerfully by the Spirit, and the earliest Christians believed that their shared experience of the Spirit was "the 'first instalment' of the kingdom whose full inheritance was yet outstanding."[31] For Dunn, therefore, once misunderstandings rooted in the metaphorical complexity of Jesus's language have been cleared away, it is the work of the Spirit that requires central attention.

Dale C. Allison Jr.: The Mistaken Prophet of the Kingdom

Yet was any of this expectation of either an immanent or an imminent kingdom real? Can it be correlated with any actual reality, notwithstanding the views of Jesus and his enthusiastic first followers? Dale Allison opens his discussion of Jesus's eschatological preaching by saying, "I wish I could believe that Jesus, as one theologian from the nineteenth century put it, 'thrust aside apocalyptic questions, or gave them an ideal turn, and floated them away on the current of spiritual religion.' But I do not."[32] Allison voices this wish because he thinks that Jesus promoted an apocalyptic eschatology that did not, in fact, come to pass. Second Temple proponents of this eschatology, including Jesus, believed that God would very soon, after a final tribulation, overcome evil and restore Israel by means of the resurrection of the dead, the final judgment, and the establishment of the kingdom of God. In Allison's view, therefore, Jesus mistakenly imagined a "profound discontinuity

29. See ibid., 466.
30. Ibid., 513; cf. 539.
31. Ibid., 479.
32. Dale C. Allison Jr., *Constructing Jesus: Memory, Imagination, and History* (Grand Rapids: Baker Academic, 2010), 31. He is citing James Martineau, *The Seat of Authority in Religion*, 4th ed. (London: Longmans, Green, 1898), 322.

between the present and the future" and supposed that the end—the final consummation of all things—was literally about to happen.[33] Among the texts that Allison cites to make this case are Mark 4:25; 8:27–30, 35; 9:1, 43–45, 49; 10:17, 23–25, 29–31; 13:3–23, 30, 33–37; 14:58; Matthew 5:12, 22; 6:10, 19–21; 10:15, 23, 28, 32–36; 11:2–4, 22, 24; 12:36; 13:36–43, 47–50; 18:6–9; 22:13, 34–35; 23:15, 33; 24:37–44; 25:30–46; Luke 4:16–19; 7:18–23; 10:14; 11:45–51; 12:5, 33–34; 17:1–2, 26–30, 34–35; 18:8. Though Allison recognizes that according to some of these texts "something dramatic and unprecedented has begun to unfold," he focuses upon the texts that indicate the imminent "coming judgment."[34] At the same time, he points out similarities between Jesus's eschatological preaching and what we find in other Second Temple texts, such as 11QMelchizedek (from Qumran), *1 Enoch, 4 Ezra*, the *Apocalypse of Abraham*, and the *Sibylline Oracles*.

Allison denies that the evidence allows room for thinking, as Wright does, that Jesus envisioned an imminent (very soon) destruction of Jerusalem's temple, to be followed by a much later final judgment and consummation of all things. Instead, Allison argues that Jesus, like the previous Israelite prophets—and like his mentor John the Baptist—was solely interested in the near future.[35] As Allison observes, this fits with the earliest writing in the New Testament, 1 Thessalonians, which is concerned with the *delay* of the eschaton (1 Thess. 4–5). Thus Allison suggests that the first Christians remained in Jerusalem, rather than returning to Galilee or going elsewhere, because they thought of themselves as living in the last days and "believed that Jesus would return quickly" to bring an end to the world.[36] Believing that Jesus had been raised, the first Christians supposed that the general resurrection would happen very soon.[37]

Turning to Mark 13, where Jesus gives full voice to his eschatological vision, Allison compares this chapter to the description of Jesus's passion in Mark 14–16. He finds that what Jesus describes as happening to the temple

---

33. Allison, *Constructing Jesus*, 32.
34. Ibid., 37, 39.
35. See ibid., 45.
36. Ibid., 50.
37. See ibid., 58. Allison adds, "Easter faith may have been born after the crucifixion, but it was conceived before. Schweitzer saw the truth: the 'resurrection appearances' are 'intelligible' only if they were 'based upon the expectation of the resurrection, and this again as based on references of Jesus to the resurrection.' Without antecedent expectation of the imminent resurrection of the dead in general, there would have been no proclamation of the resurrection of Jesus in particular" (ibid., 59). This seems an overly strong claim. He is citing Albert Schweitzer, *The Quest of the Historical Jesus: A Critical Study of Its Progress from Reimarus to Wrede*, trans. W. Montgomery (Minneapolis: Fortress, 2001), 343.

and to the disciples is paralleled by what happens to Jesus. On this basis, he concludes that these chapters imply that "the last days of Jesus belong to or proleptically instantiate the latter days," that is to say, the apocalyptic end.[38] In Matthew 27:51–53 and John 16:21–22 (and John 12:31), furthermore, we encounter clearly eschatological motifs associated directly with Jesus's passion. Indeed, Jesus's passion seems to be presented implicitly as the eschatological tribulation. This event, according to the Gospel of John, will result in the pouring forth of the Holy Spirit (a mark of the eschatological age) upon the world, who will execute the "judgment" that conquers Satan. As Jesus states in the Gospel of John, "If I do not go away, the Counselor will not come to you; but if I go, I will send him to you. And when he comes, he will convince the world of sin and righteousness and of judgment: of sin, because they do not believe in me; of righteousness, because I go to the Father, and you will see me no more; of judgment, because the ruler of this world is judged" (John 16:7–11). Paul too presents the crucifixion as the supreme eschatological event, inaugurating the new creation under the reign of the messianic king. On this view, Jesus is the "first fruits" (1 Cor. 15:20), whose resurrection begins the eschatological harvest and points to the general resurrection of the dead.

Since the world seemingly went on as it was, why did the first Christians speak in this way? Allison reasons that the most logical explanation is that this is simply the way of all apocalyptic movements, which if necessary invent or reinterpret past events so as to make them correspond as much as possible to their prior expectations. He cites the examples of the Seventh-day Adventists (1844) and the Jehovah's Witnesses (1874 and 1914). Historically speaking, Allison finds it likely that Jesus's adherents, given the stories that were circulating about an empty tomb and appearances of Jesus, would naturally "have sought to correlate their apocalyptic expectations with what had actually transpired. They would have interpreted his death as eschatological tribulation and his vindication as resurrection from the dead."[39] In Luke-Acts and the Gospel of John, Allison identifies a further predictable step: the denial that Jesus himself expected an imminent end, in the literal sense of the new creation. Luke 19:11, for example, states that the disciples "supposed that the kingdom of God was to appear immediately" (cf. Acts 1:6); Luke then portrays Jesus as correcting them by means of a parable.[40] In John 21:20–23,

38. Allison, *Constructing Jesus*, 60–61.
39. Ibid., 65.
40. On the meaning of the "kingdom of God," especially the question of whether Jesus imagined it to be a territorial place, see ibid., 164–204. Allison concludes that in the Synoptics, the kingdom of God is "a realm as well as a reign; it is a place and a time yet to come in which God will reign supreme" (ibid., 201). For background to the contemporary discussion, see

similarly, Allison locates an attempt to correct Mark 13:30, where Jesus says that "this generation will not pass away before all these things take place."[41]

Allison grants that his reconstruction is not the only possibility. It could indeed be that Jesus knew and taught that the ordinary course of history would continue for some significant time. But Allison suggests that it is simpler to hold otherwise, and to conclude that Luke and John were correcting a rather serious problem. Certainly, "Luke affirms that, during Jesus's ministry, the disciples expected the end to come soon," and it is simpler to suppose that they thought this because their teacher, Jesus, mistakenly did too—as we find in Mark 13 and elsewhere.[42]

Allison goes on to discuss Jesus's selection of twelve disciples, a number that he identifies as indicating a deliberate eschatological choice on Jesus's part. In this respect, he discusses in detail the widely popular eschatological hopes common among first-century Jews, including the restoration of the twelve tribes, rule over the gentiles, a new temple, a renewed Jerusalem, and the purification of God's people. Indeed, he suggests that "Origen probably was right: around the time of Jesus, many had used the Scriptures to calculate the time of the redemption."[43] He observes that Jews of Jesus's day were influenced by the fact that "portions of the Hebrew Bible, which by the first century included all the additions to the prophetic books as well as Daniel, foretell the defeat of Israel's enemies, the influx of the Diaspora, the transformation of the land of promise into a paradise, and the realization of God's perfect will throughout the world."[44] All this makes it even more likely, Allison suggests, that Jesus himself shared in these apocalyptic expectations. Citing a variety of Synoptic texts, Allison argues that Jesus in fact

---

Norman Perrin, *The Kingdom of God in the Teaching of Jesus* (London: SCM, 1963); Norman Perrin, *Jesus and the Language of the Kingdom: Symbol and Metaphor in New Testament Interpretation* (Philadelphia: Fortress, 1976).

41. Raymond E. Brown comments that
   the Johannine portrait of the ministry of Jesus in terms of partially realized eschatology means that for John many of the features which the Synoptic Gospels relate to the second coming have already been made realities on earth in and through Jesus, for example, eternal life and the gift of divine sonship (i. 12; xvii. 3). In particular, Jesus' coming into the world as man represents the basic element of world judgement (iii. 19) that an earlier and simpler theology associated almost exclusively with the second coming. As part of this realized judgement the presence of the Paraclete puts the world on trial and proves the world wrong about Jesus. And so, unexpectedly, in the Paraclete Jesus has fulfilled his promise that all these things would take place before this generation passed away. (Brown, "The Paraclete in the Fourth Gospel," *New Testament Studies* 13 [1966–67]: 113–32, at 132)

42. Allison, *Constructing Jesus*, 67.

43. Ibid., 77n204.

44. Ibid., 78.

saw himself as fulfilling Scripture's eschatological prophecies, so that "the early Christian habit of drawing upon eschatological prophecies in Scripture owed something to Jesus's own outlook."[45] If Jesus did this, he certainly was not the first person to read himself into Scripture's prophecies, nor was he the last.[46] Allison shows that "Pacific cargo cults, Jewish messianic groups, Amerindian prophetic movements, and Christian sects looking for the immediate end of the present world display a host of features that reappear in the early traditions about Jesus."[47]

Allison admits that Jesus in the Gospels says things that do not seem rooted in an apocalyptic worldview (i.e., one that anticipates an imminent end), but he points out that few people have a perfectly consistent worldview. He contends that logical consistency is not what we should expect from Jesus. Here Allison's argument depends upon minimizing the acuity of Jesus's teachings. He states, "His mind . . . was poetic, and his mental universe, filled as it was with invisible spirits and informed by the cosmology of the Hebrew Scriptures, was mythological. He composed parables. He issued warnings. He appealed to religious sentiment. He busied himself neither with defining his terms nor with constructing syllogisms for the intellect."[48] Jesus's inconsistency or unpredictability, including saying and doing striking and paradoxical things that shocked his audience, would have served only to enhance his charisma. This explains, Allison thinks, how Jesus was able to announce "that the kingdom of God has come (Matt. 12:28 // Luke 11:20 [Q]; Luke 17:20–21)" while also

45. Ibid., 82.
46. See ibid., 82n227.
47. Ibid., 85. Here he is summarizing conclusions from an earlier book: Allison, *Jesus of Nazareth: Millenarian Prophet* (Philadelphia: Fortress, 1998), 78–94. He notes,
> Elisabeth Schüssler Fiorenza has objected that my use of a millenarian model in *Jesus of Nazareth* "stands social-scientific method on its head" by seeking to "prove" my "reconstruction of a thoroughly eschatological Jesus by parallelizing and 'proof-texting' it with reference to the cross-cultural model of millennialism" (*Jesus and the Politics of Interpretation* [New York: Continuum, 2000], 106–14). This is not, however, what I took myself to be doing there (or what I take myself to be doing here). I came to a particular understanding of Jesus on the basis of general historical reflections and exegesis of the texts. Only after this . . . did I observe that my findings could be correlated with a cross-cultural model formulated by anthropologists and sociologists. Similarly, in this chapter, as likewise in my own biography of Jesus, the millenarian model comes not at the beginning but at the end. It is the capstone, not the foundation. It is not intended to "prove" anything. It simply shows that my apocalyptic Jesus is all the more credible because he resembles other apocalyptic figures who are even better documented. (Allison, *Constructing Jesus*, 86n239)

48. Allison, *Constructing Jesus*, 92. Along these lines, Allison observes that Jesus's "tradition was not Greco-Roman philosophy, but popular Galilean Judaism. He was not a scholastic logician, but heir to a religion that at all periods displayed 'incongruous and inconsistent elements'" (ibid.).

"teaching others to pray for its coming (Matt. 6:10 // Luke 11:2 [Q])."[49] Allison gives other examples of first-century Jewish persons and movements (as well as later persons and movements) that combine imminent eschatological expectations with sapiential/halakic teaching. There is no reason to presuppose "a disjunction between imminent eschatology and serious attention to everyday lives and conventions."[50] Jesus could have spoken the parable of the good Samaritan and believed, at the same time, that the broken world was about to end (in a literal sense) and to be replaced by the kingdom of God.[51]

In this light, Allison analyzes such texts as Luke 17:20–21: "Being asked by the Pharisees when the kingdom of God was coming, he answered them, 'The kingdom of God is not coming with signs to be observed; nor will they say, "Lo, here it is!" or "There!" for behold, the kingdom of God is in the midst of you'"; and Luke 11:20: "But if it is by the finger of God that I cast out demons, then the kingdom of God has come upon you." He notes that even if these texts are authentic or traceable to Jesus, it is important to keep in mind that Jesus could have said these things without abandoning an imminent eschatology: "to affirm that the kingdom has arrived is not to say that it is already all that it will be."[52] Again, it would be a mistake to expect Jesus to be consistent in his eschatology.[53] Paul himself uses the phrase "the kingdom of God" in a variety of ways, some having to do with the present, others with the future. Jesus would likely have done the same, especially in light of scriptural texts (notably Daniel) that depict God's kingdom as both present and still to come. God's kingdom could also be in the process of coming, as in Isaiah 40–66, *Jubilees*, and the Apocalypse of Weeks in *1 Enoch*. Jesus could have conceived of himself as the one who, by the power of God's Spirit, was bringing an end to the dominion of Satan. In so doing, Jesus would have been playing the part of the messenger of Isaiah 52:7 and 61:1–3. He would also have been conceiving of the kingdom (present and very soon to come) in the same way as later Jewish eschatological figures and leaders such as Severus, Abraham Abulafia, Isaac Abravanel, Menachem Schneerson, and R. Abraham Kook.

49. Ibid., 93.
50. Ibid., 96.
51. Allison argues that none of Jesus's parables exclude an apocalyptic worldview, although "most of the parables do not compel an apocalyptic reading" (ibid., 117).
52. Ibid., 100–101.
53. In this regard Allison critiques both Marcus Borg and Albert Schweitzer for trying to make all the texts mean the same thing: "To label Jesus an apocalyptic or millenarian prophet is not to say that everything he said or did should or can be explained in these terms, nor does it require that he cannot be characterized in still other, and even seemingly contradictory, ways" (ibid., 135).

The key point for Allison, which he repeats at the conclusion of his discussion, is that Jesus was a false eschatological prophet. Allison states, "Like the historical Zoroaster, the historical Jesus foretold a resurrection of the dead, a universal divine judgment, and a new, idyllic world with evil undone, all coming soon."[54] Obviously, none of this happened.[55]

Jesus's "Hour" and the Holy Spirit

Hans Urs von Balthasar offers yet another way of reading Jesus's eschatological sayings. Like Wright and Dunn, he aims to defuse the claim that Jesus was a failed eschatological prophet. He focuses especially upon Jesus's awareness of his eschatological mission. On this basis, he argues that "it does not matter so much whether and how far Jesus may have spoken of a continuing world-time after his exaltation."[56] According to Balthasar, parsing Jesus's sayings about whether the world will or will not continue much longer is to miss the point, which is that Jesus saw his destiny as completing all things once and for all. From this perspective, Jesus's resurrection and second coming belong to one and the same event, rather than being fundamentally divisible. Whether or not Jesus spoke of an interim time between the resurrection and second coming, such an interim time is misunderstood if Jesus's own sense of *definitive completion* is not placed at the forefront. Jesus's focus was entirely upon his eschatological "hour," which had already begun during his lifetime and which completely governs whatever further historical time there will be. Given that "the core of apocalyptic" is

54. Ibid., 157.
55. Allison, in his commentary on Matthew's Gospel (coauthored with W. D. Davies), argues that in Matthew 28:18–20, "the command to go and make disciples" and "the assurance of Christ's presence" are "redactional," invented by Matthew (W. D. Davies and Dale C. Allison Jr., *A Critical and Exegetical Commentary on the Gospel according to Saint Matthew*, vol. 3, *Commentary on Matthew XIX–XXVIII* [London: T&T Clark, 1997], 678). Yet, even so, Allison and Davies say of Matthew 28:16–20, "The grand denouement, so consonant with the spirit of the whole Gospel because so full of resonances with earlier passages, is, despite its terseness, almost a compendium of Matthean theology" (ibid., 687). At least the evangelist Matthew, then, thought that Jesus's imminent eschatology in Matthew 10:23 could be squared with Jesus's preparation for his church. The same is true for Matthew 16:18, regarding which Davies and Allison remark that "the universal church is in view" and that "the numerous parallels between Jesus and Moses entail that the church had its origins in a new exodus" (Davies and Allison, *A Critical and Exegetical Commentary on the Gospel according to Saint Matthew*, vol. 2, *Commentary on Matthew VIII–XVIII* [London: T&T Clark, 1991], 629). They conclude that "these words harmonize with the other promises in which Jesus foresees at least some of his disciples surviving to the end, despite eschatological tribulation" (ibid., 634).
56. Hans Urs von Balthasar, *Theo-Drama: Theological Dramatic Theory*, vol. 3, *The Dramatis Personae: Persons in Christ*, trans. Graham Harrison (San Francisco: Ignatius, 1992), 99.

"the imminent expectation of God's final judgment of the old world, and therefore the change of aeon to a new world," Balthasar considers that this apocalyptic judgment is so concentrated in Jesus that "his final 'hour' contains the entirety of world-time, whether or not the latter continues to run, chronologically, 'after' his death."[57]

If Balthasar is right about Jesus's "hour," the charge of false prophecy that stands at the core of Allison's approach loses its force. Yet, what is so determinative about Jesus's "hour"? Why should we suppose that his "hour" governs and indeed "contains the entirety of world-time"? Balthasar's answer to this question is rich and complex, and deserves a lengthy consideration that I cannot give here. He recognizes, however, that Jesus's concentration upon his hour does not exclude the Holy Spirit. For Jesus's "hour" (or mission) to be determinative as the completion of all worldly time, it must be something into which the Spirit calls the whole world. The question, then, is not only what constitutes Jesus's "hour" and what his "hour" accomplishes, but also whether the eschatological Spirit has truly been poured out upon the messianic community by the exalted Jesus at the right hand of the Father.[58] Only in light of this question, as Dunn particularly shows, can we make sense of Jesus's words and imagery about the immanent and imminent kingdom,

---

57. Ibid., 110–11; for Balthasar's whole discussion see 59–122. The exegetes and theologians with whom Balthasar engages on this topic include A. Schweitzer, J. Weiss, R. Bultmann, G. W. Kümmel, J. Héring, R. Schnackenburg, E. Linnemann, E. Käsemann, E. Stauffer, J. A. T. Robinson, E. Grässer, A. Vögtle, A. Strobel, B. Rigaux, R. Pesch, M. Hengel, O. Cullmann, A. Feuillet, C. J. Cadoux, E. Fuchs, H. Conzelmann, W. Thüsing, C. H. Dodd, H. Kessler, G. Lohfink, and E. Schweizer. For briefer discussions of this topic, see also Balthasar, *Theo-Drama: Theological Dramatic Theory*, vol. 2, *The Dramatis Personae: Man in God*, trans. Graham Harrison (San Francisco: Ignatius, 1990), 64–66; Balthasar, *The Glory of the Lord: A Theological Aesthetics*, vol. 7, *Theology: The New Covenant*, trans. Brian McNeil, CRV, ed. John Riches (San Francisco: Ignatius, 1989), 115–26.

58. Rudolf Schnackenburg strongly distinguishes the early Christian community from the Qumran community, and he also argues against the view (found, as we have seen, in Allison) that "the early Church was dominated by an imminent expectation in the sense of one with a fixed date" (Schnackenburg, *The Church in the New Testament*, trans. W. J. O'Hara [New York: Seabury, 1965], 122). Rather, he considers that the early church's eschatological eagerness, rooted in Christ's resurrection and the experience of the outpouring of the Spirit, "excluded any apocalyptic calculation of the end and disregarded the question of the date of the Parousia" and thus underwent no crisis when Jesus's second coming did not yet happen (ibid.). Nonetheless, Schnackenburg emphasizes that "the fundamentally eschatological attitude of the primitive Church is to be noted; it is conscious of being God's eschatological redeemed community, and of being this because the promised Messias has appeared in Jesus of Nazareth, because he has been raised up by God to his right hand and has sent the Holy Spirit to his Church. . . . The early Church's conviction of the eschatological outpouring of the Holy Spirit above it and in it is so apparent from various points of view, that this bond with God's Spirit must be regarded as another essential feature of the Church and one which is very closely connected with its eschatological character" (ibid., 118–19, 123).

about the temple, about the seed that "grows up and becomes the greatest of all shrubs" (Mark 4:32), and about the exalted Jesus's presence and absence.

It follows that an inaugurated kingdom, filled with the Spirit and putting "forth large branches, so that the birds of the air can make nests in its shade" (Mark 4:32), is what we should expect to find during the period in which human history answers to Jesus' accomplishment of his "hour."[59] Many New Testament texts, of course, suggest that Jesus had in view just such a Spirit-filled community, the "reign of God" that is already even now "the coming and final presence of God *with* God's people, the reconstitution of the people as unforsakably *God's*."[60]

The testimony of Paul—who Allison deems "no objective witness"[61]—merits attention here. In what may be the earliest New Testament writing, 1 Thessalonians, Paul appeals to the powerful presence of the Spirit in the community of believers: "Our gospel came to you not only in word, but also in power and in the Holy Spirit and with full conviction" (1 Thess. 1:5). Paul encourages the Thessalonians to live in holiness, and he notes that "whoever disregards this, disregards not man but God, who gives his Holy Spirit to you" (1 Thess. 4:8).[62]

The Holy Spirit is a constant presence in Paul's mature letters as well. In Romans, Paul confesses that "God's love has been poured into our hearts

59. Recall how Jesus is mocked on the cross: "He saved others; he cannot save himself. Let the Christ, the King of Israel, come down now from the cross, that we may see and believe" (Mark 15:31–32). Here Jesus appears as "the King of Israel" who "saved others" but who, on the cross, is being exposed as a fraud with respect to his kingdom proclamation. But his disciples, a few days later, do indeed "see and believe" the risen Jesus, who thereby stands revealed as the true King of Israel, the one who has in fact inaugurated the kingdom of God. Attempting to forestall interpretation in this direction, Allison repeatedly links the memories of Jesus's followers not with the work of God in Israel, but with the memories of UFO enthusiasts, the Seventh-day Adventists, the Jehovah's Witnesses, the Lubavitcher community, and numerous other disappointed eschatological/apocalyptic/messianic movements over the centuries. Allison does not deny on historical grounds that Jesus could have been resurrected, although he develops an extended historical case for the view that Jesus's followers saw hallucinatory visions.

60. Miroslav Volf and Maurice Lee, "The Spirit and the Church," in Hinze and Dabney, *Advents of the Spirit*, 382–409, at 386, drawing upon Wright, *Jesus and the Victory of God*, 615. My approach in chaps. 4 and 5 is broadly similar to Volf and Lee's approach, although my focus is on the Spirit rather than on ecclesiology per se, and although they are content to rely upon biblical scholarship rather than to draw upon Aquinas. They emphasize that Jesus subverted the normal modes of politics in establishing the kingdom of God "as now present in his person through the offer of grace" (Volf and Lee, "Spirit and the Church," 388), given his instantiation of a fellowship based not on power and subjugation but on forgiveness and love.

61. Allison, *Constructing Jesus*, 158.

62. For discussion, see James W. Thompson, *The Church according to Paul: Rediscovering the Community Conformed to Christ* (Grand Rapids: Baker Academic, 2014), 25–26. Regarding the Thessalonian church, Thompson notes that "the Holy Spirit played a decisive role in the founding of the church" and that Paul presents the church as "the community that lives by the power of the Spirit" (ibid., 25).

through the Holy Spirit who has been given to us" (Rom. 5:5); Paul exhorts the Roman Christians to recognize that "you are not in the flesh, you are in the Spirit, if the Spirit of God really dwells in you" (Rom. 8:9);[63] Paul explains that "all who are led by the Spirit of God are sons of God" (Rom. 8:14); and Paul remarks that "the Spirit intercedes for the saints according to the will of God" (Rom. 8:27). In 1 Corinthians, Paul states that "the Spirit searches everything, even the depths of God" (1 Cor. 2:10); Paul asserts that he is "taught by the Spirit" and that he communicates "spiritual truths to those who possess the Spirit" (1 Cor. 2:13); Paul affirms that "you were washed, you were sanctified, you were justified in the name of the Lord Jesus Christ and in the Spirit of our God" (1 Cor. 5:11); Paul comments that "no one can say 'Jesus is Lord' except by the Holy Spirit" (1 Cor. 12:3); Paul proclaims that "by one Spirit we were all baptized into one body—Jews or Greeks, slaves or free—and all were made to drink of one Spirit" (1 Cor. 12:13); and Paul cautions, "since you are eager for manifestations of the Spirit, strive to excel in building up the church" (1 Cor. 14:12). In 2 Corinthians, Paul rejoices that God "has put his seal upon us and given us his Spirit in our hearts as a guarantee" (2 Cor. 1:22); and Paul describes the current epoch as "the dispensation of the Spirit" (2 Cor. 3:8). Paul asks the Galatian Christians rhetorically, "Does he who supplies the Spirit to you and works miracles among you do so by works of the law, or by hearing with faith?" (Gal. 3:5).[64]

Many more examples from Paul could be cited, but it should already be evident that when the book of Acts describes the Spirit's outpouring at Pentecost, this conveys the earliest Christians' sense of their situation. As Acts depicts the event, the disciples were gathered together for prayer when suddenly "they were all filled with the Holy Spirit and began to speak in other tongues, as the Spirit gave them utterance" (Acts 2:2–4). According to Acts, Peter connects this outpouring of the Spirit with the prophecy of Joel regarding the

---

63. In Romans 8:9, the first use of "Spirit" could be lowercase, although I have allowed the RSV's capitalization to stand. For the argument that in the contrast flesh/Spirit, "Spirit" should always be capitalized, see Cantalamessa, *Mystery of Pentecost*, 56–58.

64. For discussion of the Holy Spirit in Paul and specifically in Galatians, see, for example, Gordon D. Fee, *God's Empowering Presence: The Holy Spirit in the Letters of Paul* (Peabody, MA: Hendrickson, 1994); D. J. Lull, *The Spirit in Galatia: Paul's Interpretation of Pneuma as Divine Power* (Chico, CA: Scholars Press, 1980); Rodrigo J. Morales, *The Spirit and the Restoration of Israel: New Exodus and New Creation Motifs in Galatians* (Tübingen: Mohr Siebeck, 2010); Friedrich Wilhelm Horn, *Das Angeld des Geistes: Studien zur paulinischen Pneumatologie* (Göttingen: Vandenhoeck & Ruprecht, 1992); Alexander J. M. Wedderburn, "Pauline Pneumatology and Pauline Theology," in *The Holy Spirit and Christian Origins: Essays in Honor of James D. G. Dunn*, ed. Graham N. Stanton, Bruce W. Longenecker, and Stephen C. Barton (Grand Rapids: Eerdmans, 2004), 144–56; Anthony C. Thiselton, *The Holy Spirit—In Biblical Teaching, through the Centuries, and Today* (Grand Rapids: Eerdmans, 2013), 70–94.

last days—here, presumably, the days between the redemptive eschatological tribulation (Jesus' cross) and the final eschatological consummation, already presaged in Jesus' resurrection.[65] In Joel 2:28, quoted by Peter, God promises to "pour out my Spirit upon all flesh, and your sons and your daughters shall prophesy, and your young men shall see visions, and your old men shall dream dreams" (Acts 2:17).[66] Peter proclaims that Jesus, at the right hand of the Father, now is pouring out the Spirit upon those who believe in him, so as to prepare them for the final judgment.[67] Peter therefore exhorts his audience,

65. See Brant Pitre, *Jesus, the Tribulation, and the End of the Exile: Restoration Eschatology and the Origin of the Atonement* (Grand Rapids: Baker Academic, 2005); Pitre, *Jesus and the Last Supper* (Grand Rapids: Eerdmans, 2015). The latter book gives a strong historical-critical rationale for supposing that Jesus prepared for a time—marked by the inaugurated eschatological community's celebration of the Eucharist—between Jesus's inauguration of the kingdom and its consummation. See *Jesus and the Last Supper*, 515–16, for a succinct summary of Pitre's case. See also David W. Pao, *Acts and the Isaianic New Exodus* (Grand Rapids: Baker Academic, 2002), chap. 4, where he remarks, "The portrayal of the early Christian community in Acts as an eschatological community of the Spirit needs no elaborate demonstration. The connection between the outpouring of the Spirit in Acts 2 and the arrival of the eschatological age is signaled by the insertion of the phrase 'in the last days' . . . from Isa. 2:1 at the beginning of the quotation from Joel (Acts 2:17)" (131). Commenting on Acts 3:19's reference to "times of refreshing," Pao shows that this refers to the outpouring of the Spirit and the restoration of Israel (see ibid., 133). See also George T. Montague, SM, *The Holy Spirit: Growth of a Biblical Tradition; A Commentary on the Principal Texts of the Old and New Testaments* (New York: Paulist Press, 1976), 271–301; Alan J. Thompson, *The Acts of the Risen Lord Jesus: Luke's Account of God's Unfolding Plan* (Downers Grove, IL: InterVarsity, 2011), chap. 3.

66. For background, see Erika Moore, "Joel's Promise of the Spirit," in *Presence, Power and Promise: The Role of the Spirit of God in the Old Testament*, ed. David G. Firth and Paul D. Wegner (Downers Grove, IL: IVP Academic, 2011), 245–56. For debate about whether the "Spirit of prophecy" is also a soteriological agent in Luke-Acts, see Max Turner, "The Spirit and Salvation in Luke-Acts," in Stanton, Longenecker, and Barton, *Holy Spirit and Christian Origins*, 103–16. Turner's opponents hold that the Spirit in Luke-Acts is solely involved in prophetic and missiological empowering. For this view, see W. W. Menzies and R. P. Menzies, *Spirit and Power: Foundations of Penetcostal Experience; A Call to Evangelical Dialogue* (Grand Rapids: Zondervan, 2000). For an earlier statement of Max Turner's view, see his *Power from on High: The Spirit in Israel's Restoration and Witness in Luke-Acts* (Sheffield: Sheffield Academic Press, 1996). My focus on the Spirit as Love and Gift includes, of course, the gifts of knowledge and wisdom that guide Jesus and that also guide believers and the whole church in the process of handing on the gospel and developing doctrine. For further emphasis (indebted especially to Menzies and to Roger Stronstad) on the Holy Spirit's inspiration of prophetic speech throughout the history of Israel and the church, see Gary Tyra, *The Holy Spirit in Mission: Prophetic Speech and Action in Christian Witness* (Downers Grove, IL: IVP Academic, 2011).

67. As Ju Hur points out with respect to this aspect of Peter's speech, "The exalted Jesus, sitting at the right hand of God in heaven and thus sharing the power and authority to send the Spirit of God, is characterized as 'Lord of the Spirit' (cf. 16.7; 8.39) in terms analogous to Yahweh's relationship to the Spirit in the Jewish Bible. In this respect, *the pentecostal Spirit is now understood to be dispensed or caused by the risen Jesus*; this may explain why Jesus's disciples empowered/inspired by the Spirit are to be characterized as *testifying about Jesus*. That is, the Spirit is to be presented as causing them to bear witness to the risen Jesus through their mighty

"Repent, and be baptized every one of you in the name of Jesus Christ for the forgiveness of your sins; and you shall receive the gift of the Holy Spirit" (Acts 2:38).

This gift of the eschatological Spirit, connected with faith in Jesus, is omnipresent in the first half of Acts.[68] Going forth to pray in the temple, Peter and John perform a miraculous healing in the name of Jesus Christ, just as Jesus performed healings and exorcisms by the power of the Spirit. Arrested and brought before the Jewish leaders, Peter, "filled with the Holy Spirit" (Acts 4:8), proclaims the power of "the name of Jesus Christ of Nazareth" (Acts 4:10).[69] Those Christians who lie to the community, and who do not live as true Christians, are identified as having lied "to the Holy Spirit" and having "tempted the Spirit of the Lord" (Act 5:3, 9). The apostles describe themselves as united with the Holy Spirit in their witness: "we are witnesses to these things, and so is the Holy Spirit whom God has given to those who obey him" (Acts 5:32).

During his martyrdom, the deacon Stephen has a vision of the ascended Jesus: "But he, full of the Holy Spirit, gazed into heaven and saw the glory of God, and Jesus standing at the right hand of God" (Acts 7:55). Peter and John travel from Jerusalem to Samaria, where they pray for and lay hands on people who had believed in the gospel, and the result is that these people "received the Holy Spirit" (Acts 8:17). After Saul's vision of Jesus on the road to Damascus, Ananias brings Saul into the Christian community: "Brother Saul, the Lord Jesus who appeared to you on the road by which you came, has sent me that you may regain your sight and be filled with the Holy Spirit" (Acts 9:17). Despite persecutions and dissensions, therefore, Luke is able to conclude, "So the church throughout all Judea and Galilee and Samaria had peace and was built

---

words and deeds" (Hur, *A Dynamic Reading of the Holy Spirit in Luke-Acts* [London: T&T Clark, 2004], 233–34). Similarly, Martin Hengel argues that Luke-Acts, as a "double work," nonetheless "covers the one history of Jesus Christ. . . . The division of the work into two parts necessarily followed from the distinction between the activity of the earthly Jesus and his work as exalted Lord, who acts through the spirit in the preaching of his messengers" (Hengel, *Acts and the History of Earliest Christianity*, trans. John Bowden [Philadelphia: Fortress, 1979], 59).

68. Alan Thompson observes, "Luke is emphasizing in a variety of ways that the pouring out of the Holy Spirit is to be understood as the fulfilment of God's promise for the last days. The fulfilment of this promise of the Spirit is therefore part of the evidence that the kingdom of God has been inaugurated. The reason for this pouring out of the promised Holy Spirit, however, is because the Lord Jesus has risen from the dead and ascended to reign at the right hand of the Father" (Thompson, *Acts of the Risen Lord Jesus*, 129).

69. For a study of Acts's depiction of the relationship of Jewish believers (Peter and, more broadly, the church in Jerusalem) to other Jews and to non-Jewish believers, see Richard P. Thompson, *Keeping the Church in Its Place: The Church as Narrative Character in Acts* (New York: T&T Clark, 2006); Coleman A. Baker, *Identity, Memory, and Narrative in Early Christianity: Peter, Paul, and Recategorization in the Book of Acts* (Eugene, OR: Pickwick, 2011).

up; and walking in the fear of the Lord and in the comfort of the Holy Spirit it was multiplied" (Acts 9:31).[70] In the remainder of Acts, the Holy Spirit is shown to be guiding and governing both the church and history (cf. Acts 13:52; 15:28; 16:6–7; 19:21; 20:23; 20:28; 21:11; 28:24). In all this, the Holy Spirit is seen to be powerfully at work precisely in the ways that Paul describes in his letters.

How, then, might we summarize the significance that historical research about Jesus's eschatological sayings should have for theologians, whose starting point is faith? Appreciating Jesus's eschatological words and deeds should lead us to attend ever more fully to the Spirit's work in the church. The Spirit does not replace the risen Jesus in the inaugurated eschatological kingdom, but rather mediates his presence, so that "the church can, like a bride, both stand over against Christ and be most intimately united with him."[71] Recognizing, in Boris Bobrinskoy's words, that "the gift of the Spirit is constituent of the new life of Jesus' apostles," theologians must articulate the thoroughgoing character of the Spirit's work in the inaugurated kingdom.[72] How should this

---

70. Raniero Cantalamessa emphasizes that in Luke/Acts, "the Holy Spirit is first of all the Spirit of prophecy. It is the power that guarantees the progress of the Word from Jerusalem all the way to the ends of the earth" (Cantalamessa, *Mystery of Pentecost*, 21). The Holy Spirit ensures that *God's* Word is proclaimed across time and space. As Cantalamessa goes on to say, however, "Love is the 'warm breath,' the spiritual fire, that transports the word, and we know that love is given 'through the Holy Spirit' (Rom. 5:5). Also and especially in this sense—that is, to the extent that it is love—the Holy Spirit is the power of the word, the secret of proclaiming it" (ibid., 31). Cantalamessa's perspective would enhance Luke Timothy Johnson's emphasis on Luke's "characterization of the first-generation church in terms of a prophetic manner of life—being led by the spirit, sharing possessions, engaging in an itinerant mission, exercising servant leadership, bearing powerful witness before religious and state authorities" (Johnson, *Prophetic Jesus, Prophetic Church: The Challenge of Luke-Acts to Contemporary Christians* [Grand Rapids: Eerdmans, 2011], 4). For Johnson, Luke-Acts should not be seen as instantiating a hierarchical church; instead, Luke-Acts is open to all sorts of ecclesiologies, so long as they embody a "prophetic manner of life" along the lines that Johnson envisions. He states that "Acts assumes the simple sort of local leadership for assemblies that were found also in Hellenistic synagogues: boards of elders with supervisors, who managed the financial and forensic affairs of the community. . . . We find no sign of hierarchy, of sacramental system, or of a theological rationalization for ecclesial structure" (ibid., 70). This seems true if one (mistakenly) excludes the role and ministry of the disciples/apostles, not least in Luke 22 and Acts 15. When Johnson addresses hierarchy in the contemporary church, his view is far too negative (see ibid., 128–29) and appears to be shaped by his own bones of contention rather than by the text of Luke-Acts. See also the strong emphasis on the Spirit as the "Spirit of prophecy," with appreciation of the prophetic Spirit's soteriological role in empowering the holiness and life of the community, in Max Turner, *The Holy Spirit and Spiritual Gifts: In the New Testament Church and Today*, rev. ed. (Peabody, MA: Hendrickson, 2009).

71. Volf and Lee, "Spirit and the Church," 391. On the relationship of the kingdom and the church, see Avery Dulles, SJ, "The Church and the Kingdom: A Study of Their Relationship in Scripture, Tradition, and Evangelization," *Letter & Spirit* 3 (2007): 23–38.

72. Boris Bobrinskoy, *The Mystery of the Trinity: Trinitarian Experience and Vision in the Biblical and Patristic Tradition*, trans. Anthony P. Gythiel (Crestwood, NY: St. Vladimir's Seminary Press, 1999), 102.

be done? In what ways should the church's life, and the life of the members of the church, be expected to display the work of Christ's Spirit?

Thomas Aquinas can assist us in answering this question. Indeed, now that historical-critical scholars over the past century have highlighted Jesus's status as an eschatological prophet of the (immanent and imminent) kingdom of God, Aquinas's manner of discussing the church becomes even more propitious. Aquinas treats the church not in a distinct treatise, but fully in relation to Christ and his Spirit, and with a focus on the infused virtues and gifts and on the sacramental actions of the crucified Lord at the right hand of the Father. The coming fullness of God's kingdom—perfect beatitude and charity—is always present to Aquinas as he reflects upon the church on earth.

In what follows, therefore, I examine Aquinas's theology of the church as the inaugurated eschatological community of believers being configured by the Holy Spirit to the crucified and risen Christ, who is the risen and exalted king.[73] Kenneth Loyer has recently urged that the study of Aquinas be enriched by "renewed attention to sanctification and other aspects of Aquinas's rich spiritual theology that is generally underemphasized by his interpreters."[74] Although interpreters over the centuries have in fact made much of Aquinas's "spiritual theology," it is certainly the case that his detailed

73. Robert W. Jenson observes, "The common factor in Western problems with the Spirit, one may suggest, is a tendency of the Spirit simply to disappear from theology's description of God's triune action, often just when he might be expected to have the leading role" (Jenson, *Systematic Theology*, vol. 1, *The Triune God* [Oxford: Oxford University Press, 1997], 153). This is the very opposite of what happens in Aquinas's theology.

74. Kenneth M. Loyer, *God's Love through the Spirit: The Holy Spirit in Thomas Aquinas and John Wesley* (Washington, DC: Catholic University of America Press, 2014), 243. For an excellent recent study of sanctification, noted by Loyer, see Edgardo A. Colón-Emeric, *Wesley, Aquinas, and Christian Perfection: An Ecumenical Dialogue* (Waco: Baylor University Press, 2009). See also the important contributions of Charles Raith II, *Aquinas and Calvin on Romans: God's Justification and Our Participation* (Oxford: Oxford University Press, 2014); A. N. Williams, *The Ground of Union: Deification in Aquinas and Palamas* (Oxford: Oxford University Press, 1999); as well as the classic treatise of Réginald Garrigou-Lagrange, OP, *Christian Perfection and Contemplation, according to St. Thomas Aquinas and St. John of the Cross*, trans. Sr. M. Timothea Doyle (St. Louis: Herder, 1937). Loyer values Aquinas especially for "pinpointing the trinitarian context in which penumatology is rightly located. This context not only illuminates the trinitarian basis of the doctrine of the Holy Spirit but also gives sanctification, the Spirit's appropriated work, its proper ground and goal in the triune God. . . . God loves us with the same love with which God loves himself, and that love is the person of the Holy Spirit. Furthermore, as Aquinas articulates in his account of the missions of the divine persons, through the gift of sanctifying grace God dwells in us as in God's own temple. We are thus consecrated to God, and made holy in and by the Holy Trinity. Loving us by his Spirit and actually dwelling in us through sanctifying grace, God has made possible for us a participation in his triune life through the Spirit" (Loyer, *God's Love through the Spirit*, 273–74). It is noteworthy too that Loyer brings together Wesley and Aquinas on merit; see ibid., 244–51.

conception of the Spirit-filled church, marked by radical participation in divine Love and Gift, needs retrieval today. Exegetical focus upon Jesus's eschatological claims about the immanent and imminent kingdom of God have made it even more necessary to highlight the Spirit's outpouring upon the apostolic community—an outpouring that certainly did not put an end to sin but did work ongoing transformation, as Paul's experiences with his churches attest.

Thomas Aquinas on the Kingdom, the Church, and the Holy Spirit

Aquinas and the Kingdom

When Aquinas speaks about the kingdom in his *Commentary on the Gospel of St. Matthew*, he remarks that in the Gospels, the "kingdom" is identified with four different things. The first meaning has to do with the indwelling of Christ in us through the grace of the Holy Spirit: "the kingdom of God is in the midst of you" (Luke 17:21). Since this indwelling causes our deification, it is an eschatologically oriented reality: "By the indwelling of grace, the way to the heavenly kingdom is begun in us."[75]

The second meaning of the "kingdom" in the Gospels appears, Aquinas thinks, in Matthew 21:43, where Jesus is teaching in the temple. Jesus warns his audience that "the kingdom of God will be taken away from you and given to a nation producing the fruits of it." Aquinas interprets this to mean that the Scripture (the law and the prophets) will be taken away, in the sense of no longer being interpreted authoritatively by the people of Israel. The law, Aquinas observes, "leads to a kingdom."[76] Since Scripture leads us into the kingdom of God, Scripture is in a certain way synonymous with this kingdom, when it is canonized and rightly interpreted in the church of Jesus Christ. This second sense of "kingdom" emphasizes that the inaugurated eschatological kingdom involves not simply the interior indwelling of the Trinity, but exterior teaching as well, preeminently Scripture. The eschatological people of God proceeds toward the consummation of all things by means of interior and exterior instruction: God leads us authoritatively through Scripture into Scripture's covenantal kingdom of holiness.

75. Thomas Aquinas, *Commentary on the Gospel of St. Matthew*, trans. Paul M. Kimball (Camillus, NY: Dolorosa, 2012), 88. As Miroslav Volf and Maurice Lee put it, "In coming to persons, the Spirit of God breaks through the self-enclosed worlds they inhabit; the Spirit renews, recreates, them, and sets each on a road toward becoming a site of the eschatological reign of God" (Volf and Lee, "Spirit and the Church," 394).

76. Aquinas, *Commentary on the Gospel of St. Matthew*, 88.

The third meaning of "kingdom," according to Aquinas, is the church on earth. As an example of this meaning, he points to Matthew 13:47, where Jesus says that "the kingdom of heaven is like a net which was thrown into the sea and gathered fish of every kind; when it was full, men drew it ashore and sat down and sorted the good into vessels but threw away the bad." This "kingdom" originally contains both good and bad, as does the church on earth. Lastly, the fourth meaning of "kingdom" is the heavenly court or heavenly banquet, as in Matthew 8:11, where Jesus says that "many will come from east and west and sit at table with Abraham, Isaac, and Jacob in the kingdom of heaven."[77]

It should be clear, then, that Aquinas recognizes not only the centrality of "kingdom" in Jesus's preaching, but also what Allison identifies as Jesus's inconsistent eschatology (immanent and imminent). Jesus's eschatology is immanent in that the Trinity dwells in us and insofar as the church is the kingdom even now, whereas Jesus's eschatology is imminent insofar as Scripture (the law and Gospel) helps us to press forward toward the consummation of the kingdom that will be the "heavenly banquet."

This fourfold exposition of "kingdom" appears in Aquinas's commentary on Matthew 3:2, which records John the Baptist's exhortation "Repent, for the kingdom of heaven is at hand." This is the first reference to the kingdom in Matthew's Gospel. It also is a sign of the basic continuity between Jesus and the eschatological prophet John, a continuity accepted by Aquinas. Aquinas recognizes that Jesus's kingdom preaching allows for a wider range of meaning for the word "kingdom," because of the addition of an immanent dimension to the sense of eschatological imminence.

In his *Commentary on the Sentences*, Aquinas offers additional insight into his theology of the kingdom of God. He notes that the kingdom of God can be spoken of in two ways. The first way is "of the congregation of those who walk by faith, and thus the Church militant is called the kingdom of God."[78]

---

77. Pitre notes that "for Jesus, as in Second Temple Jewish apocalyptic literature, the kingdom of God was not only an eschatological reality to be tasted at the 'end of the world,' but a heavenly reality that already existed in the invisible transcendent realm" (Pitre, *Jesus and the Last Supper*, 516).

78. For the full passage, see Aquinas, *Scriptum super libros Sententiarium*, lib. 4, d. 49, q. 1, a. 2, qc. 5 co.: "Unde et regnum Dei, quasi antonomastice, dupliciter dicitur: quandoque congregatio eorum qui per fidem ambulant; et sic Ecclesia militans regnum Dei dicitur: quandoque autem illorum collegium qui jam in fine stabiliti sunt; et sic ipsa Ecclesia triumphans regnum Dei dicitur; et hoc modo esse in regno Dei idem est quod esse in beatitudine. Nec differt, secundum hoc, regnum Dei a beatitudine, nisi sicut differt bonum commune totius multitudinis a bono singulari uniuscujusque." The translations in the main text are my own. I thank Gilles Emery for pointing out this text to me.

In this way, the church on earth is the kingdom of God even now, insofar as the church even now is governed by Jesus Christ and bound together in faith and charity by his Holy Spirit. Secondly, the kingdom of God sometimes denotes "the assembly of those who are already established in the end, and in this way the kingdom of God is said to be the church triumphant, so that to be in the kingdom of God is the same as to be in beatitude."[79] This second sense is crucial to Aquinas's understanding of the kingdom: Aquinas identifies the kingdom with beatitude, either the imperfect beatitude that we possess by faith informed by charity or the perfect beatitude of heaven.[80]

In the *Summa theologiae*, Aquinas does not devote specific questions either to the "kingdom" or to the church. Instead, his focus is on the rule of the exalted Christ at the right hand of the Father and on the sending of the Spirit, whom he identifies as Love and Gift in person. This focus fits with Aquinas's eschatological perspective, especially in light of the centrality of beatitude (and charity) in the *Summa*.[81] He affirms that "the Gospel of Christ is . . . the Gospel of the kingdom."[82] He also argues that "a third epoch began with the Resurrection," namely the epoch of "the New Law, which is the Law of love" (and of the Spirit) and in which the saving power of the gospel is communicated in creedal faith and the sacraments.[83] For Aquinas, furthermore, Jesus's

79. Ibid.

80. For an essentially similar perspective, see Scot McKnight, *Kingdom Conspiracy: Returning to the Radical Mission of the Local Church* (Grand Rapids: Brazos, 2014), 92–95 (in his chapter titled "No Kingdom outside the Church").

81. For the central importance of beatitude (and the beatitudes of the Sermon on the Mount) in the *Summa*, see especially Servais Pinckaers, OP, *The Sources of Christian Ethics*, trans. Mary Thomas Noble, OP (Washington, DC: Catholic University of America Press, 1995).

82. I-II, q. 106, a. 4, ad 4. Here he is responding to Joachim of Fiore's millennialism and to similar movements from the early church (such as Montanism). For Aquinas's theology in relation to the challenge posed by Joachim, see Sabra, *Thomas Aquinas' Vision of the Church*, 80–84; Jürgen Moltmann, "Christliche Hoffnung: Messianisch oder transzendent? Ein theologisches Gespräch mit Joachim von Fiore und Thomas von Aquin," *Münchener Theologische Zeitschrift* 33 (1982): 241–60.

83. III, q. 53, a. 2; I-II, q. 107, a. 1, ad 2. (Aquinas adds here that "there were some in the state of the Old Testament who, having charity and the grace of the Holy Spirit, looked chiefly to spiritual and eternal promises: and in this respect they belonged to the New Law.") For discussion of Aquinas's view of Christ and the church as "the entrance . . . of the eschatological into the historical," see Congar, "Vision de l'Église chez S. Thomas d'Aquin," 529 (my translation); cf. 535. Congar notes that for Aquinas, "the eschatological value par excellence" (ibid., 532) is found in the missions of the Holy Spirit, since Aquinas "attributes to the Holy Spirit the whole movement of the return to God" (ibid.). For further background, see Congar, "Le sens de l' 'économie' salutaire dans la 'théologie' de S. Thomas d'Aquin (*Somme Théologique*)," in *Festgabe Joseph Lortz*, vol. 2, *Glaube et Geschichte*, ed. E. Iserloh and P. Mann (Baden-Baden: Verlag Bruno Grimm, 1957), 73–122, at 83–91; Jean-Pierre Torrell, OP, "Saint Thomas et l'histoire: État de la question et pistes de recherches," in *Nouvelles recherches thomasiennes* (Paris: J. Vrin, 2008), 131–75, at 139.

resurrection inaugurates the final consummation, the "eternity of glory."[84] Jesus rose victorious, so that the scars of his crucifixion now stand as "trophies of his power"—a royal power that is not domination but perfect love.[85] When this kingdom is consummated, all will be based on charity; those who possess "greater charity . . . shall also attain greater glory from the divine vision."[86] Aquinas prefers here to speak of the risen Jesus's "glory" rather than kingship, but he goes on to refer to "the glory of his majesty," thereby showing that the kingdom imagery remains central.[87]

Jesus ascends in his glorified flesh to the right hand of the Father, infinitely beyond any merely human kingship. Discussing whether Jesus ascended above the angels, Aquinas quotes Ephesians 1:21 (to which I add v. 20), which affirms that God "raised him [Jesus] from the dead and made him sit at his right hand in the heavenly places, far above all rule and authority and power and dominion, and above every name that is named, not only in this age but also in that which is to come."[88] Jesus, says Aquinas, is our heavenly high priest (see Heb. 7:25) who has been "established in his heavenly seat as God and Lord" so that "he might send down gifts upon men," through the Gift of the Holy Spirit who "is love drawing us up to heavenly things [cf. John 16:7]."[89] Jesus's high-priestly work prepares "the way for our ascent into heaven" (see John 14:2).[90] This depiction of Jesus's heavenly priesthood makes clear that the consummation of the the kingdom of God, like its inauguration, depends upon Jesus.[91]

84. III, q. 53, a. 2.

85. III, q. 54, a. 4, ad 1.

86. III, q. 55, a. 1, ad 3.

87. III, q. 55, a. 3; III, q. 55, a. 6, ad 4.

88. III, q. 57, a. 5, *sed contra*.

89. III, q. 57, a. 6; III, q. 57, a. 1, ad 3. As Grant Macaskill puts it, "The Spirit given at Pentecost is poured out by Jesus in his exalted state, ruling at the right hand of God over an established kingdom that he now governs as enthroned Messiah" (Macaskill, *Union with Christ in the New Testament*, 200).

90. III, q. 57, a. 6.

91. The Eucharist is particularly significant here, as Pitre (in accord with Aquinas) points out. Pitre states that

> if the Last Supper was indeed an eschatological Passover meal, in which Jesus identified himself as the eschatological Passover lamb, whose blood would be poured out and whose body would be eaten by the eschatological priests of a new cult, then the implication is that he intended to establish not only a new people, but a new cultus. This new act of "remembrance," however, would no longer look back to the exodus of the twelve tribes from Egypt, but forward to the eschatological ingathering of Israel and the nations into the heavenly and eschatological reality of God's kingdom, into which Jesus himself would enter in advance, in adntication of the day when he would drink the fruit of the vine new with his disciples in the kingdom of God. (Pitre, *Jesus and the Last Supper*, 517)

In question 58 of the *tertia pars*, a question devoted to Jesus's sitting at the right hand of the Father, Aquinas makes explicit recourse to kingdom language about Jesus. To sit at the right hand of the Father, Aquinas says, means to rule or reign with the Father, "just as [in human courts] he who sits at the king's right hand helps him in ruling and judging."[92] Jesus shares in the Father's kingship. Aquinas explains that "to sit on the right hand of the Father is nothing else than to share in the glory of the Godhead with the Father, and to possess beatitude and judiciary power, and that unchangeably and royally."[93] As Son, Jesus by nature shares in the Father's power; as man, hypostatically united to the divine nature in the Son, Jesus is elevated to this position.[94] There is no literal throne in heaven, but Aquinas explains that nonetheless "throne" is an appropriate image: "By the *throne* is meant the judiciary power which Christ has from the Father: and in this sense he is said *to sit in the Father's throne*."[95] To his apostles, and indeed to all the saints, Jesus gives their own distinctive share in his throne or judiciary power, which is none other than the reign of self-sacrificial love. In this regard, Aquinas quotes Matthew 19:28, where Jesus tells the apostles that "in the new world, when the Son of man shall sit on his glorious throne, you who have followed me will also sit on twelve thrones, judging the twelve tribes of Israel."[96] Aquinas does

---

As Pitre adds,

> the cleavage of opinion over whether Jesus "founded the church" is inextricably bound up with the debate over the origin of the eucharist. If this study is correct, and Jesus the Jewish prophet saw himself as establishing the new sacrifice of a new cult—or, to put it another way, the new Passover of a new Temple—then the answer must be yes. For it is as impossible to isolate the church from the eucharist as it is to isolate Israel from the Passover. This is the community Jesus envisioned when he commanded the disciples to do what he did in remembrance of him. (ibid.)

Pitre rightly remarks that his research

> provides a powerful challenge to those who would follow Schweitzer in holding that Jesus expected the cataclysmic "end of the world" to happen immediately after his death. That is of course why the words of institution were dismissed by Schweitzer's followers and continue to be ignored (or dismissed as insignificant) to this very day by those who argue for such a Jesus. By contrast, as I have tried to demonstrate, it is precisely Jesus' embrace of apocalyptic eschatology that enables us to explain how it is that he both expected the kingdom to be inaugurated by his passion and death and commanded his disciples to celebrate a ritual enactment of his redemptive death in his absence. (ibid., 516)

See also the conclusions of Nicholas Perrin, *Jesus the Temple*, 183–90.

92. III, q. 58, a. 1.

93. III, q. 58, a. 2.

94. Aquinas explains, "Christ's humanity according to the conditions of his nature has not the glory or honor of the Godhead, which it has nevertheless by reason of the Person with whom it is united" (III, q. 58, a. 3, ad 1).

95. III, q. 48, a. 4, ad 3.

96. III, q. 48, a. 4, ad 3.

not think that Jesus envisioned the eschatological consummation literally as twelve thrones in Jerusalem, although he recognizes that some of the people of Israel may have thought in this direction. Rather, our incorporation into Jesus and our sharing in his intimacy with the Father by charity (and beatitude) require a more spiritual, though still fully embodied, understanding of the kingdom of God.

Aquinas adds that even though Jesus was "established king by God," he did not wish "to exercise judiciary power over temporal concerns, since he came to raise men to divine things."[97] The eschatological kingdom therefore is still to be consummated. Here Aquinas quotes Matthew 28:18, "All authority in heaven and on earth has been given to me," to which Aquinas adds the point that "as to the exercise of this power, all things are not yet subject to him: this will come to pass in the future, when he shall fulfil his will regarding all things, by saving some and punishing others."[98] Thus Jesus will fully consummate the kingdom only at the final judgment. Aquinas notes that although we are judged when we die (see Heb. 9:27), we cannot be fully judged until everything that our lives have influenced has taken place—in other words, until time has come to an end. Only then can "a perfect and public judgment" be made.[99]

The Eschatological Age, the Mission of the Holy Spirit, and the Apostles

But why is there a delay or interim period between Jesus's pasch and the final consummation? Aquinas, following Luke 18:8, says that "the charity of many will grow cold at the end of the world."[100] Why then the delay? Aquinas obviously does not think that Jesus miscalculated. On the contrary, he thinks that Jesus's pasch did indeed inaugurate the kingdom, because the church is built up by the Spirit that Jesus pours out.[101] The final consummation has not yet arrived, however, because the preaching of the gospel has not yet

97. III, q. 59, a. 4, ad 1.
98. III, q. 59, a. 4, ad 2.
99. III, q. 59, a. 5.
100. III, q. 1, a. 5.
101. Jesus's pasch, however, does not bring about the eschatological age of the Spirit in the sense that the people of Israel (and/or the gentile nations) previously simply lacked the Holy Spirit. Aquinas is quite clear that people before the time of Christ received the Spirit's invisible mission. Speaking of the saints of the Old Testament, he comments that even if they had no explicit faith in Christ, "they did, nevertheless, have implicit faith through believing in divine providence, since they believed that God would deliver mankind in whatever way was pleasing to him" (II-II, q. 2, a. 7, ad 3). Aquinas strongly affirms both the importance of the church's public proclamation of the gospel and the fact that at all times there have been people who have observed, by the invisible missions of the Son and Spirit, "the law of grace": "at all times there have been some persons belonging to the New Testament" (I-II, q. 106, a. 4, ad 2).

produced "its full effect" in all those whom God wishes to unite to himself.[102] Yet, even now believers are living in a communion of love with the Trinity, as his temples (John 14:23; 1 Cor. 3:16; 6:19). Since this communion is what the "kingdom" is, "no state of the present life can be more perfect than the state of the New Law."[103]

Aquinas emphasizes that Jesus made no promise about the length of the period prior to the final consummation. Although Jesus promised his disciples that "when the Spirit of truth comes, he will guide you into all the truth" (John 16:13), Aquinas points out that the Spirit did not teach the apostles "about all future events," since, as the risen Jesus told the apostles, "It is not for you to know the times or seasons which the Father has fixed by his own authority" (Acts 1:7).[104]

How does the risen Jesus sustain his eschatological church during this period? In Aquinas's view, the apostles received two visible missions of the Holy Spirit that continue to ground the ongoing ministry of the church by uniting the church in a participatory way to the source of the church's life, namely Jesus's own eschatological work of mercy on the cross. The first visible mission of the Spirit, Aquinas says, occurred when the risen Jesus "breathed on them [the disciples], and said to them, 'Receive the Holy Spirit. If you forgive the sins of any, they are forgiven; if you retain the sins of any, they are retained'" (John 20:22–23). Certainly most biblical scholars would not think that this passage in John stands up to historical scrutiny, nor would biblical scholars today suppose that in Jesus's breath we have a "visible mission" of the Holy Spirit. But the point is that Jesus's eschatological mission is participated in by the apostles through the Spirit whom he bestows on them, so as to prepare a people (Jews and gentiles) in the Messiah/new Temple for

---

102. I-II, q. 106, a. 4, ad 4. For a cognate perspective, see Christopher J. H. Wright, *The Mission of God: Unlocking the Bible's Grand Narrative* (Downers Grove, IL: InterVarsity Press, 2006).

103. I-II, q. 106, a. 4. Aquinas had earlier remarked that "the New Law . . . consists chiefly in the grace of the Holy Spirit: which it behooved not to be given abundantly until sin, which is an obstacle to grace, had been cast out of man through the accomplishment of his redemption by Christ" (I-II, q. 106, a. 3). See Luc-Thomas Somme, OP, "La rôle du Saint-Esprit dans la vie chrétienne, selon saint Thomas d'Aquin," *Sedes Sapientiae* 26 (1988): 11–29; Yves Congar, OP, "Le Saint-Esprit dans la théologie thomiste de l'agir moral," reprinted (with original pagination, 9–19) as chap. 11 of Congar, *Thomas d'Aquin: Sa vision de théologie et de l'Église* (London: Variorum, 1984); Ulrich Kühn, *Via caritatis: Theologie des Gesetzes bei Thomas von Aquinas* (Göttingen: Vandenhoeck & Ruprecht, 1965), 192–97.

104. I-II, q. 106, a. 4, ad 2. For historical-critical analysis of the "spirit of truth," in light of the Qumran literature, see John R. Levison, *Filled with the Spirit* (Grand Rapids: Eerdmans, 2009), 383–90. Levison notes that for the Gospel of John, "the irenic function of guiding the community into truth, of interpreting the past afresh, is directed internally only to the community. The spirit of truth, the paraclete, will have an altogether different impact on the world by bringing it to trial because it cannot receive, see, or know the spirit of truth" (ibid., 384).

the final eschatological consummation. As Jesus says to his apostles, "As the Father has sent me, even so I send you" (John 20:21). Insofar as Jesus has won the victory over sin and death, the kingdom has arrived (see John 19:30), but it has not been fully consummated, because God wills to build up the body of Christ missiologically by the addition of further members over the course of history.

The character of the church as the inaugurated kingdom—one of the four meanings of "kingdom" that Aquinas identifies in his *Commentary on Matthew*—is made clear not least by the fact that when Jesus breathes out the Spirit upon the disciples, the disciples receive a share (always under Jesus's authority) in his power to forgive sin. In this way, they mediate the merciful power of the crucified and risen Lord to his people. Raymond Brown speaks here of "the power to isolate, repel, and negate evil and sin, a power given to Jesus in his mission by the Father and given in turn by Jesus through the Spirit to those whom he commissions."[105] Francis Moloney observes more broadly, "The gift of the Spirit-Paraclete will render the absent Jesus present within the worshiping community. . . . The mission of the disciples renders present the holiness of the absent Jesus."[106] Their unique role in the church, like every mission in the church, does not come without cost; thus the risen Jesus tells Peter, after prophesying Peter's death on a cross, "Follow me" (John 21:19 [cf. Mark 8:34–35 for the point that all Jesus's followers must live a life of self-sacrifice]).[107] Enabled by Jesus's anointing to mediate to the whole community the power of cross, the sacramental ministry of the apostles nourishes and builds up the church, just as Jesus instructs Peter three times, "Feed my lambs," "Tend my sheep," "Feed my sheep" (John 21:15–17).

Aquinas specifies that the visible mission of the Spirit to the apostles in the breath of Jesus has the purpose of manifesting "the power of their ministry in the dispensation of the sacraments."[108] As for the sacraments themselves, they "derive their power specially from Christ's passion, the virtue of which

---

105. Raymond E. Brown, SS, *The Gospel according to John XIII–XXI* (Garden City, NY: Doubleday, 1970), 1044.

106. Francis J. Moloney, SDB, *The Gospel of John* (Collegeville, MN: Liturgical Press, 1998), 533.

107. Nonetheless, the sacramental participation of the apostles in Jesus's priestly mission does not depend upon their personal holiness, since their participation is not for their own sake but rather is for the building up of the whole community into Christ.

108. I, q. 43, a. 7, ad 6. Grant Macaskill remarks, "The presence and activity of the Spirit . . . ensure that the sacraments are understood as a true participation in Christ, by which his narrative becomes truly realized in believers" (Macaskill, *Union with Christ in the New Testament*, 217). See also Michael Bossy, SJ, "The Holy Spirit and the Sacraments," in Butterworth, *Spirit in Action*, 71–78.

is in a manner united to us by our receiving the sacraments. It was in sign of this that from the side of Christ hanging on the cross there flowed water and blood, the former of which belongs to Baptism, the latter to the Eucharist, which are the principal sacraments."[109] Not simply individually but as the people of God, we are drawn by the sacraments into Jesus's eschatological movement from tribulation to glory. As Aquinas says, following the lead of Pseudo-Dionysius, "heavenly glory . . . is the universal end [goal] of all the sacraments."[110]

The second and final visible mission of the Holy Spirit to the apostles, if we follow Aquinas's understanding of the New Testament texts, occurred at Pentecost. Admittedly, many biblical scholars today posit that the Johannine breath of Jesus and the Lukan Pentecost—assuming that something truly happened—describe the same event. Along these lines, Andrew Lincoln remarks that "the giving of the Spirit to the disciples here in John has been called the 'Johannine Pentecost.' Whereas Luke spreads out the events chronologically and distinguishes between the episodes of resurrection, ascension, and giving of the Spirit, John brings them all together on one day."[111] Lincoln also points to connections with Genesis 2:7, "The Lord God . . . breathed into his nostrils the breath of life"; Wisdom of Solomon 15:11, "breathed into him a living spirit"; and Ezekiel 37:5, "I will cause breath to enter you, and you shall live."[112]

We need not decide whether there were in fact two "visible missions" of the Spirit or just one.[113] Either way, the connections with Genesis, Wisdom

---

109. III, q. 62, a. 5.

110. III, q. 66, a. 1, ad 1. Again, Pitre's *Jesus and the Last Supper* is highly important here.

111. Andrew T. Lincoln, *The Gospel according to Saint John* (London: Continuum, 2005), 500.

112. Ibid., 501. Marianne Meye Thompson points out, "Virtually all interpretations of these two accounts [John 20 and Acts 2] assume that the New Testament speaks of one definitive gift of the Holy Spirit to the church" (Thompson, "The Breath of Life: John 20:22–23 Once More," in Stanton, Longenecker, and Barton, *Holy Spirit and Christian Origins*, 69–78, at 70). This is not the case for Aquinas. Following the interpretation of John 20 proposed by Rudolf Schnackenburg and James Dunn, Thompson argues for "the possibility that the description of the 'breathing' of the Spirit in John 20 deliberately evokes the creation of humankind in Genesis: just as God breathed the breath of life into humankind, so now Jesus 'breathes' the divine breath of life into the disciples, representative of God's renewed people, the 'children of God' who are born by 'water and Spirit' (1:12–13; 3:3, 5). Although John does not use the word 'baptize' in ch. 20, it is likely that this scene narrates the fulfillment of the promise that Jesus will baptize with the Holy Spirit (1:33), since Jesus has been glorified (7:37–39) and the Spirit has been sent; thus new birth by the Spirit (3:3, 5) is now possible" (ibid., 71). Thompson goes on to suggest that John 20:22–23 signifies the fulfillment of Ezekiel 36–37, Isaiah 32:15–17, and Isaiah 44:3–6, passages in which "the outpouring of the Spirit effects eschatological re-creation and renewal" (ibid., 73). In her *The God of the Gospel of John* (Grand Rapids: Eerdmans, 2001), 172, Thompson links John 20:22 with Isaiah 57:16, where God tells Israel, "For I will not contend for ever, nor will I always be angry; for from me proceeds the spirit, and I have made the breath of life."

113. For further discussion, see Cantalamessa, *Mystery of Pentecost*, 34–36.

of Solomon, and Ezekiel show that Aquinas is correct to underscore the significance of the risen Jesus's breath. The book of Acts presents a different image, that of a "sound . . . like the rush of a mighty wind" (Acts 2:2). This "mighty wind" (or sound of wind) comes "from heaven" (Acts 2:2); it has evident affinities, then, with the risen Jesus's breath. All of a sudden, those in the house are enveloped by visible evidence of the wind's presence: "tongues as of fire, distributed and resting on each one of them" (Acts 2:3). In Acts's portrait of this first Pentecost, the visible mission of the Spirit as "tongues as of fire" results not in the reception of a "sacramental" power to mediate to the community the forgiveness won by Jesus's pasch—as in Jesus's promise, "If you forgive the sins of any, they are forgiven" (John 20:23)—but in the reception of power to teach and evangelize even among those who speak foreign languages. The Spirit's second visible mission, his extraordinary gifting, equips the apostles for their unique teaching mission. The inaugurated kingdom is marked by sacraments and teaching (preeminently inspired Scripture, interpreted by the church) that enable all people truly to hear, share in, and be configured by the gospel of Jesus Christ.

Luke Timothy Johnson observes that the connection made in Acts 2 is not between creation and new creation (as in John 20), but rather with the giving of the law at Sinai. Regarding Acts 2:2–4, Johnson points out that "nowhere is the same cluster of symbols found all together except in the LXX description of Sinai (Exod 19:16), with its repeated emphasis on the *sound*, and the 'descending of God upon it in fire [Exod 19:18].'"[114] This fits with Aquinas's emphasis that the "New Law" is "chiefly the grace itself of the Holy Spirit, which is given to those who believe in Christ."[115] The Spirit descends upon the messianic community to bestow the New Law. Aquinas's authority for this claim is Romans, where Paul speaks of the law or "principle of faith" (Rom. 3:27) and praises "the law of the Spirit of life in Christ Jesus" (Rom. 8:2). Closely connected with the grace of the Holy Spirit is the teaching of the gospel, since, as Aquinas says, the grace of the Spirit "is given to those who believe in Christ." Aquinas explains that "the faithful needed to be instructed" about all things pertaining to the life of grace, and this instruction came "both by word and writing, both as to what they should believe and as to what they should do."[116] This is precisely what the apostles were equipped to do by the Spirit's visible mission in fiery

---

114. Luke Timothy Johnson, *The Acts of the Apostles* (Collegeville, MN: Liturgical Press, 1992), 46. See also Montague, *Holy Spirit*, 280–82; note esp. 282: "The first Christian Pentecost was the eschatological Sinai event where the promised covenant of the Spirit was given."

115. I-II, q. 106, a. 1.

116. I-II, q. 106, a. 1.

tongues at Pentecost. As Johnson makes clear, the apostles ("the Twelve," with Matthias replacing Judas) "began to speak in other tongues" under the inspiration of the Spirit (Acts 2:4) and did so as the eschatological people of God, restored by Jesus but not yet fully consummated. Johnson comments, "Just as the Twelve represent the nucleus of the people that is being restored, so does this audience represent all the lands to which the Jews had been dispersed."[117]

Note that the two ways that are signified by the two visible missions of the Spirit—the apostolic sacramental ministry and teaching—go together. Thus Acts 2:42 describes the earliest Christians as devoting "themselves to the apostles' teaching and fellowship, to the breaking of bread and the prayers." The "breaking of bread" here is the Eucharist, although what that meant for the earliest church is, of course, debated.[118] But what is not in doubt is the

---

117. Johnson, *Acts of the Apostles*, 47. Johnson concludes that for Luke (the author of Acts), "Jesus is the prophet who sums up all the promises and hopes of the people before him; in his apostolic successors, that promise and hope (now sealed by the Spirit) will be carried to all the nations of the earth" (ibid.).

118. The connection between the "breaking of bread" and the Eucharist (or ritual remembrance of the Last Supper) is denied by James D. G. Dunn; see Dunn, *Christianity in the Making*, vol. 2, *Beginning from Jerusalem*, 199. His view is eccentric, however. For a variety of perspectives on the "breaking of bread" and the earliest Eucharist, see Pitre, *Jesus and the Last Supper*; Macaskill, *Union with Christ in the New Testament*, 201–16; N. T. Wright, *Jesus and the Victory of God*, 554–63; David Lincicum, "Sacraments in the Pauline Epistles," in *The Oxford Handbook of Sacramental Theology*, ed. Hans Boersma and Matthew Levering (Oxford: Oxford University Press, 2015), 97–108; Xavier Léon-Dufour, SJ, *Sharing the Eucharistic Bread: The Witness of the New Testament*, trans. Matthew J. O'Connell (New York: Paulist Press, 1987); John Koenig, *The Feast of the World's Redemption: Eucharistic Origins and Christian Mission* (Harrisburg, PA: Trinity Press International, 2000); Ben Witherington III, *Making a Meal of It: Rethinking the Theology of the Lord's Supper* (Waco: Baylor University Press, 2007). Koenig argues that for Jesus, "the visionary meal hosted by God for Moses and Israel's elders offered a preview of the kingdom banquet. His own last supper, then, would have functioned as a necessary link between the events of Exodus 24 and that final banquet. But Jesus also believed that if this ultimate flowering of God's covenant was to reveal itself before the whole world, thereby bringing human history to its fulfillment, his blood would have to flow" (Koenig, *Feast of the World's Redemption*, 39). The profound incorporation into Jesus signaled by the New Testament texts is rejected by Koenig: "That Paul and the synoptic Gospels, still in a Jewish orbit, would be able to show Jesus connecting bread and wine with his body and blood in such a direct manner must mean that the verb 'is' (absent in Aramaic but present in the Greek) meant something other than simplistic identification. Jewish sensibilities, including those of Jewish believers, would not have allowed for a medieval doctrine of transubstantiation" (ibid., 38). Absent such incorporation, which I find to be fundamental, the most that Koenig can say (with respect to the relationship of the Last Supper and Jesus's kingdom proclamation) is that Jesus's words and actions at the Last Supper indicate that Jesus had gained "a sharpened vision of God's cosmic feast in the perfected kingdom" and that Jesus supposed that his self-offering would "open the doors of the banquet hall to Israel and the nations" (ibid., 42).

fact that the apostles' teaching and sacramental ministry were at the center of the earliest church.[119]

Aquinas underscores that union with Jesus comes about through both faith and the sacraments. He states, for example, that "Christ's Passion works its effect in them to whom it is applied, through faith and charity and the sacraments of faith."[120] Likewise, he notes that the sacraments do not work their redemptive and deifying effect without faith: "the power of the sacrament which is ordained unto the remission of sins is derived principally from faith in Christ's Passion."[121] In this regard he cites Romans 3:25, where Paul depicts Jesus as having been "put forward as an expiation by his blood, to be received by faith." The role of faith (which requires teaching: "faith comes from what is heard, and what is heard comes by the preaching of Christ" [Rom. 10:17]) and the role of the sacraments are complementary; both are involved in our union with Jesus Christ.

The Holy Spirit's Invisible Missions, Sanctifying Grace, and the Theological Virtues

The two visible missions of the Spirit, then, describe the Spirit's work of manifesting the incarnate Son and configuring humans to his self-giving love: by enabling the apostles' true teaching of the gospel, and by establishing the sacramental ministry of the church. The next step, then, is to trace the Holy Spirit's presence in the theology of faith and the other virtues, and in the theology of the sacraments. Since Aquinas has no separate theology of the church, he moves directly from Christ's passion, resurrection, and ascension to the sacraments, which draw us toward the state of glory, the eschatological consummation.[122] Citing Galatians 3:27, where Paul speaks of putting on Christ through baptism, Aquinas comments that "through the sacraments of the New Law man is incorporated with Christ."[123] Likewise, Christ is the source of our grace and virtues, "since all have received grace on account of his grace."[124]

119. See Richard Bauckham, *Jesus and the Eyewitnesses: The Gospels as Eyewitness Testimony* (Grand Rapids: Eerdmans, 2006).

120. III, q. 49, a. 3, ad 1.

121. III, q. 62, a. 5, ad 2.

122. See III, q. 61, a. 4.

123. III, q. 62, a. 1. See Macaskill, *Union with Christ in the New Testament*, 192–218. As Macaskill observes, "It is clear in the use of baptism imagery in Paul . . . that the participatory dimension is not confined to the presence of the Spirit, but also involves the symbolism of the believer as being incorporated into, or included in, the death of Christ" (ibid., 195).

124. III, q. 8, a. 1.

Throughout history, there have been countless invisible missions of the Spirit to believers—whether those believers have known Christ implicitly (even simply by believing in God's existence and providence) or explicitly. As noted in the previous chapter, the invisible mission of the Spirit to humans takes place when "the divine person is in the rational creature in a new mode."[125] This occurs through the gift of what Aquinas calls "sanctifying grace," which "disposes the soul to possess the divine person."[126] To receive sanctifying grace is none other than to come to possess the indwelling Holy Spirit, and indeed the Father and Son as well.[127] According to Aquinas, "grace" is a "participation of the divine goodness"; it qualifies the soul supernaturally (i.e., above the capacities of created nature) so that the soul "may be moved by Him [God] sweetly and promptly to acquire eternal good."[128] Aquinas compares grace to a "light" and remarks that the infused virtues, including faith, "are derived from and are ordained to this light."[129] Grace qualifies the essence of the soul, whereas the (infused) virtues are perfections of the soul's powers. Aquinas explains that "man in his intellective power participates in the divine knowledge through the virtue of faith, and in his power of will participates in the divine love through the virtue of charity."[130]

Since the Holy Spirit proceeds as Love and "love has the nature of a first gift, through which all free gifts are given," Aquinas observes that "the gift itself of grace is from the Holy Spirit."[131] When we enter into the state of sanctifying grace, or when we reach a new level of fervor or undertake a new act of grace (such as prophesying), this involves the invisible mission of the

125. I, q. 43, a. 3.

126. I, q. 43, a. 4, ad 2. See Reinhard Hütter, "'Thomas the Augustinian'—Recovering a Surpassing Synthesis of Grace and Free Will," in *Dust Bound for Heaven: Explorations in the Theology of Thomas Aquinas* (Grand Rapids: Eerdmans, 2012), 249–82; Joseph Wawrykow, "Grace," in *The Theology of Thomas Aquinas*, ed. Rik Van Nieuwenhove and Joseph Wawrykow (Notre Dame, IN: University of Notre Dame Press, 2005), 192–221; Wawrykow, *God's Grace and Human Action: "Merit" in the Theology of Thomas Aquinas* (Notre Dame, IN: University of Notre Dame Press, 1995), 164–77.

127. For background, see Francis L. B. Cunningham, OP, *The Indwelling of the Trinity: A Historico-Doctrinal Study of the Theory of St. Thomas Aquinas* (Dubuque, IA: Priory, 1955); Javier Prades, *"Deus specialiter est in sanctis per gratium": El misterio de la inhabitación de la Trinidad en los escritos de santo Tomás* (Rome: Gregorian University Press, 1993); Luc-Thomas Somme, *Fils adoptifs de Dieu par Jésus Christ: La filiation divine par adoption dans la théologie de saint Thomas d'Aquin* (Paris: Vrin, 1997).

128. I-II, q. 110, a. 2.

129. I-II, q. 110, a. 3.

130. I-II, q. 110, a. 4. See Michael S. Sherwin, OP, *By Knowledge and by Love: Charity and Knowledge in the Moral Theology of St. Thomas Aquinas* (Washington, DC: Catholic University of America Press, 2005).

131. I, q. 38, a. 2; I-II, q. 112, a. 1; I, q. 43, a. 3, ad 2. Note also I, q. 43, a. 5, ad 1: "All the gifts, considered as such, are attributed to the Holy Spirit, forasmuch as He is by His nature the first Gift, since He is Love."

Spirit.[132] Our day-to-day spiritual lives do not, of course, always require a new invisible mission of the Spirit.

The charity that unites the members of the church eschatologically with the Lord Jesus, Aquinas says, "is a participation of the infinite charity which is the Holy Spirit" and "is the friendship of man for God."[133] As Aquinas observes, "the Holy Spirit directs man's will by the gift of charity, so as to move it directly to some supernatural good."[134] The eschatological people of God are configured by charity not into a triumphalistic body but into a cruciform body (cf. John 15:12–14).[135] Aquinas states that "our love for God is proved to be all the stronger through carrying a man's affections to things which are furthest from him, namely, to the love of his enemies."[136] Surely this is impossible unless, as Paul says, "the law of the Spirit of life in Christ Jesus has set me free from the law of sin and death" (Rom. 8:2), so that we "who have the first fruits of the Spirit groan inwardly as we wait for adoption as sons, the redemption of our bodies" (Rom. 8:23).

Aquinas emphasizes that "charity is given, not according to our natural capacity, but according as the Spirit wills to distribute his gifts."[137] This means

132. The blessed in heaven enjoy an invisible mission "at the very beginning of their beatitude" and also "by the further revelation of mysteries; which goes on till the day of judgment" (I, q. 43, a. 6, ad 3).

133. II-II, q. 24, a. 7; II-II, q. 23, a. 1. See especially Guy Mansini, OSB, "Aristotle and Aquinas's Theology of Charity in the *Summa Theologiae*," in *Aristotle in Aquinas's Theology*, ed. Gilles Emery, OP, and Matthew Levering (Oxford: Oxford University Press, 2015), 121–38; Sherwin, *By Knowledge and by Love*, chap. 5; Loyer, *God's Love through the Spirit*, 147–51. See also the connection with Jesus's cross (and the justice restored by Jesus's work of satisfaction) emphasized by Daniel Schwartz, *Aquinas on Friendship* (Cambridge: Cambridge University Press, 2007), 142–61. For Aquinas's response to Peter Lombard's view that our charity *is* the Holy Spirit, with attention also to Aquinas's response to Richard Fishacre's position on this topic, see Geertjan Zuijdwegt, "'*Utrum caritas sit aliquid creatum in anima*': Aquinas on the Lombard's Identification of Charity with the Holy Spirit," *Recherches de théologie et philosophie médiévales* 79 (2012): 39–74. See also Philipp W. Rosemann, "*Fraterna dilectio est Deus*: Peter Lombard's Thesis on Charity as the Holy Spirit," in *Amor amicitiae: On the Love That Is Friendship: Essays in Medieval Thought and Beyond in Honor of the Rev. Professor James McEvoy*, ed. Thomas A. F. Kelly and Philipp W. Rosemann (Leuven: Peeters, 2004), 409–36.

134. II-II, q. 8, a. 4. See Romanus Cessario, OP's anti-Pelagian reflections in his *Introduction to Moral Theology* (Washington, DC: Catholic University of America Press, 2001), 224–27.

135. See Michael J. Gorman, *Becoming the Gospel: Paul, Participation, and Mission* (Grand Rapids: Eerdmans, 2015).

136. II-II, q. 27, a. 7. See Gerald W. Schlabach, *For the Joy Set before Us: Augustine and Self-Denying Love* (Notre Dame, IN: University of Notre Dame Press, 2001), 40–42. See also Miroslav Volf, *Free of Charge: Giving and Forgiving in a Culture Stripped of Grace* (Grand Rapids: Zondervan, 2005).

137. II-II, q. 24, a. 3, *sed contra*. On this topic, and indeed on almost all matters pertaining to Aquinas's theology of charity, see Francis de Sales's extraordinary *Treatise on the Love of God*, trans. Henry Benedict Mackey, OSB (Rockford, IL: Tan, 1997).

that the eschatological people of God depend entirely for their characteristic trait—their conformity to Jesus Christ in charity—upon the free action of the Holy Spirit.[138] Aquinas often simply speaks of "grace," but he is careful here to credit the "grace of the Holy Spirit," since it is the Holy Spirit "who infuses charity" and since "the quantity of charity depends . . . only on the will of the Holy Spirit" who, as Paul says (cited by Aquinas), "apportions to each one individually as he wills" (1 Cor. 12:11).[139]

The result of the Holy Spirit moving our wills so that they freely move in charitable friendship with God is joy. Aquinas observes that "joy is caused in us by the Holy Spirit," and in confirmation he quotes Romans 14:17: "For the kingdom of God does not mean food and drink but righteousness and peace and joy in the Holy Spirit."[140] It is this righteousness, peace, and joy that mark the kingdom of God even in its unconsummated and imperfect manifestation on earth, during which time sin continues to afflict the members of the church. Aquinas even goes so far as to claim that such "joy has no admixture of sorrow."[141] This is indeed an eschatological church, filled with the joy of the risen Lord. In charity, Aquinas states, "we rejoice in the divine good considered in itself," and this gives us a true joy, uncontaminated with human sorrows.[142] Nonetheless, Aquinas recognizes that the eschatological church on pilgrimage does indeed have sorrow, since we lament all those things in our lives and in the lives of others that hinder "the participation of the divine good."[143]

Indeed, the sorrow that inevitably marks our earthly lives reminds us that this life is not our goal. The kingdom of God is not fully present, even though it is not absent either. Paul yearns for the fullness of the eschatological kingdom: "Here indeed we groan, and long to put on our heavenly dwelling, so that by putting it on we may not be found naked. For while we are still in this tent, we sigh with anxiety; not that we would be unclothed, but that we would be further clothed, so that what is mortal may be swallowed up by life" (2 Cor. 5:2–4). Paul adds that it is the Holy Spirit in us who guarantees

---

138. Note that Aquinas sees no tension between the Holy Spirit's freedom and the sacramental, magisterial, and dogmatic structures of the church (or, for that matter, the canonized words of Scripture). For the opposite view, see Simeon Zahl, "The Spirit and the Cross: Engaging a Key Critique of Charismatic Pneumatology," in *The Holy Spirit in the World Today*, ed. Jane Williams (London: Alpha International, 2011), 111–29.

139. II-II, q. 24, a. 3.

140. II-II, q. 28, a. 1. On joy, see my *The Betrayal of Charity: The Sins That Sabotage Divine Love* (Waco: Baylor University Press, 2011), chap. 3.

141. II-II, q. 28, a. 2, *sed contra*.

142. II-II, q. 28, a. 2.

143. II-II, q. 28, a. 2.

that the fullness of the kingdom of God will be ours. He states, "He who has prepared us for this very thing is God, who has given us the Spirit as a guarantee" (2 Cor. 5:5). Yet Paul also frequently proclaims his own joy and exhorts his churches to "rejoice in the Lord" (Phil. 3:1); in fact, he strongly emphasizes this joy: "Rejoice in the Lord always; again I will say, Rejoice" (Phil. 4:4). Aquinas comments regarding the combination of joy and sorrow that we experience as we await the eschatological consummation, "Although in this unhappy abode we participate, after a fashion, in the divine good, by knowledge and love, yet the unhappiness of this life is an obstacle to a perfect participation in the divine good: hence this very sorrow, whereby a man grieves for the delay of glory, is connected with the hindrance to a participation of the divine good."[144] The joy that we have from charity is not itself mixed with sorrow, but nonetheless, insofar as we and those whom we love do not yet fully share in the divine good, we have sorrow.

In the Gospel of John, Jesus himself speaks of joy in connection with the eschatological kingdom. In his Farewell Discourse, Jesus explains to his disciples, "These things I have spoken to you, that my joy may be in you, and that your joy may be full" (John 15:11). Citing this passage, Aquinas argues that the fullness of joy (happiness) is not possible in this world, since "as long as we are in this world, the movement of desire does not cease in us, because it still remains possible for us to approach nearer to God by grace."[145] The fullness of joy pertains to the fully realized eschatological kingdom. We are destined to enter into God's own joy, an inexpressibly glorious gift. In the fully realized eschatological kingdom, all our desires will be fulfilled, "so that the joy of the blessed is full to perfection—indeed over-full, since they will obtain more than they were capable of desiring."[146] Our full entrance into the kingdom is presaged, Aquinas thinks, by Jesus's parable of the talents, in which the master tells one of the servants, "Well done, good and faithful servant; you have been faithful over a little, I will set you over much; enter into the joy of your master" (Matt. 25:21).[147]

Just as for Aquinas "joy is caused in us by the Holy Spirit," so also is faith. Citing 1 Corinthians 12:7 with regard to the knowledge of divine mysteries possessed by the patriarchs and prophets of Israel, Aquinas notes that "the manifestation of the Spirit is given to such men for the common good . . . so that the knowledge of faith was imparted to the Fathers who were instructors in the faith, so far as was necessary at the time for the instruction of

144. II-II, q. 28, a. 2, ad 3.
145. II-II, q. 28, a. 3.
146. II-II, q. 28, a. 3.
147. See II-II, q. 28, a. 3.

the people, either openly or in figures."[148] The Holy Spirit infused faith's knowledge in the patriarchs and prophets, but only insofar as was suitable for the time. Aquinas explains that it would be a mistake to think that the prophets spoke solely by the Spirit, rather than by the whole Trinity, since all the Trinity's actions *ad extra* are the actions of the whole Trinity (otherwise the persons would not be distinct solely with regard to their eternal relations). But it is right to appropriate the inspiration of the prophets to the Holy Spirit. Similarly, Aquinas adds, "The sanctification of a creature by grace, and its consummation by glory, is also effected by the gift of charity, which is appropriated to the Holy Spirit."[149]

Is the doctrine of "trinitarian appropriation," however, simply a mask, a way of covering over Scripture's insistence that the Holy Spirit uniquely acts in the world? The basis for appropriation is a creaturely similitude: since the Holy Spirit proceeds as Love, the divine infusion of created charity is specially appropriated to the Holy Spirit, to whom charity particularly configures us.[150]

148. II-II, q. 1, a. 7, ad 3.
149. II-II, q. 1, a. 8, ad 5. For discussion, see Sabathé, *La Trinité rédemptrice dans la* Commentaire de l'Évangile de saint Jean *par Thomas d'Aquin*, 549–57. For approaches that, while different, are united by a desire to accentuate the Spirit's distinctive activity toward creatures, see Dionysius Petavius, SJ, *Dogmata Theologica*, vol. 3, book 8 (Paris: Vivès, 1865), 481–87; Matthias Joseph Scheeben, *Gesammelte Aufsätze* (Freiburg: Herder, 1967), 169–299, responding to four critical essays by T. Granderath, SJ; Maurice de la Taille, SJ, "Actuation créée par Acte incréé," *Recherches de science religieuse* 18 (1928): 253–68; Karl Rahner, SJ, "Some Implications of the Scholastic Concept of Uncreated Grace," in *God, Christ, Mary and Grace*, trans. Cornelius Ernst, OP (Baltimore: Helicon, 1961), 319–46. For a helpful exposition of Scheeben's position (and Granderath's), see Somme, *Fils adoptifs de Dieu par Jésus Christ*, 246–65. See also the discussion of this issue in David Coffey, *"Did You Receive the Holy Spirit When You Believed?" Some Basic Questions for Pneumatology* (Milwaukee: Marquette University Press, 2005), 10–42. Coffey points out that while both de la Taille and Rahner "moved in the direction of Petavius, neither recovered his full position. Neither was prepared to say that just as the divine Word exercised a unique function in relation to the humanity of Christ, so the Holy Spirit exercised a unique function in the matter of grace" (ibid., 20). In Coffey's view (though not in mine), Petavius was right: "The sense in which the Holy Spirit can be said to communicate himself to the exclusion of the Father and the Son is that which I assert with Petavius, namely, that the Holy Spirit alone exercises quasi-formal causality in grace, and hence unites himself with the human spirit in a unique way that allows him to mediate the presence and action of the Father and the Son" (ibid., 102).
150. See I, q. 39, aa. 7–8. On trinitarian appropriation, see especially Gilles Emery, OP, *The Trinitarian Theology of Saint Thomas Aquinas*, trans. Francesca Aran Murphy (Oxford: Oxford University Press, 2011), 312–37; Bruce D. Marshall, "Action and Person: Do Palamas and Aquinas Agree about the Spirit?," *St. Vladimir's Theological Quarterly* 39 (1995): 379–409, at 399–401. Marshall warns against construing "'appropriation' as a linguistic and epistemological convenience whereby we distinguish the divine persons by assigning roles and attributes differently to each, but must recognize that our ascription has no relation to the 'real'—that is, entirely undifferentiated—way in which the persons of the Trinity possess their shared attributes and actions" (Marshall, "Action and Person," 400). Instead, Marshall notes that "appropriations are natural

The Holy Spirit's personal property is uniquely implicated in this divine action of infusing charity, to the extent that this action particularly assimilates us to (and makes manifest) the Holy Spirit's personal property, even though the same action also comes from the Father and the Son.[151] Since the Holy Spirit proceeds as Gift, grace likewise is specially appropriated to the Holy Spirit. When we receive grace and charity, furthermore, we gain a new, real relation to the Holy Spirit. Grace enables us to experience or enjoy the Holy Spirit himself. As Gilles Emery puts it in his exposition of Aquinas's trinitarian theology: "The personality of the Holy Spirit is Love, and this is why he spreads love: from within the heart of the Trinity, he joins human beings to the property personal to him."[152]

---

and ontological—they are 'drawn,' as it were, by God—and just for this reason manifest and yield knowledge of the *propria*, the eternal and person-constituting characteristics, of the Father, the Son, and the Holy Spirit" (ibid.). See also Anselm Kyongsuk Min, "God as the Mystery of Sharing and Shared Love: Thomas Aquinas on the Trinity," in *The Cambridge Companion to the Trinity*, ed. Peter C. Phan (Cambridge: Cambridge University Press, 2011), 87–106, at 100–104.

151. Gilles Emery explains that the persons are constituted not only by pure relation (to one another), but also by the common nature in which they subsist; so, even if the divine action is shared, it still belongs to the persons. He emphasizes too that in the inseparable action of the persons *ad extra*, in which they act "in virtue of their common divine nature," "each person acts within the distinct mode of his relationship to other persons within this common action" (Emery, *Trinitarian Theology of Saint Thomas Aquinas*, 349). At the same time, he warns against imagining that the bestowal of grace, for example, can be attributed to the Holy Spirit "as if the Holy Spirit himself brought about this grace independently of the other divine persons," for example through a "quasi-formal causality," in which the Holy Spirit takes on a "quasi-formal" role in the human person so as to be "the immanent principle" of the human person's acts of charity (ibid., 348). I agree with Emery's position that "quasi-formal causality" cannot apply to the Holy Spirit in his temporal mission, both on the grounds that God (as transcendent) cannot function like a form of a creature, and on the grounds that the persons act as one *ad extra* (rather than the Holy Spirit acting "alone"). See also the critique of Rahner's notion of quasi-formal causality, as rooted in an idealist/Hegelian framework, in William J. Hill, OP, *The Three-Personed God: The Trinity as a Mystery of Salvation* (Washington, DC: Catholic University of America Press, 1982), 287–96. Hill argues, rightly in my view, that a better approach is to hold that "all *causal* activity upon finite persons is exercised by the Three through the commonality of their nature. Then, at the interior of this causal scheme, the persons communicate themselves in the sense of offering themselves to be known and loved in their personal distinctness. This is accomplished by an extension of their inner relating to one another to include finite persons and is the import of Aquinas's teaching that 'the Holy Spirit is the love whereby the Father loves the Son, and also the love whereby he loves the creature' [I *Sent.*, d. 14, q. 1, a. 1]" (Hill, *The Three-Personed God*, 295). David Coffey responded to Hill in his "A Proper Mission of the Holy Spirit," *Theological Studies* 47 (1986): 227–50; see the summary of this debate in Ralph Del Colle, *Christ and the Spirit: Spirit-Christology in Trinitarian Perspective* (Oxford: Oxford University Press, 1994), 128–33. For the activity of the Trinity in the incarnation, see Thomas G. Weinandy, OFMCap, *Does God Change?* (Still River, MA: St. Bede's Publications, 1985). See also, for an appreciative extension of Coffey's view, Steven M. Studebaker, *From Pentecost to the Triune God: A Pentecostal Trinitarian Theology* (Grand Rapids: Eerdmans, 2012), 162–66.

152. Emery, *Trinitarian Theology of Saint Thomas Aquinas*, 262. Similarly, Emery earlier observes (as cited above in chap. 2) that the Holy Spirit is "the divine person 'closest to us,'

Regarding faith, Aquinas emphasizes that the truth of the creedal content of faith is assured by the Holy Spirit, who governs the church. Quoting John 16:13, "When the Spirit of truth comes, he will guide you into all the truth," Aquinas states with respect to the creed that "the universal Church cannot err, since she is governed by the Holy Spirit, who is the Spirit of truth: for such was our Lord's promise to his disciples."[153] Among these creedal doctrines, of course, are found truths about the mysteries of Jesus Christ and the Trinity. Aquinas points out that our faith in Jesus Christ requires faith in the Holy Spirit: "The mystery of Christ includes . . . that he renewed the world through the grace of the Holy Spirit, and again, that he was conceived by the Holy Spirit."[154] The Spirit who works to bring forth Jesus Christ and to bring forth the church is the same Spirit who guides the doctrines of the church about the realities of faith (including the realities of Jesus Christ and

---

so to speak, the one who is most intimate with us, because he is given to us. It is through him that we receive the Father and the Son, and it is through him that we receive all gifts" (ibid., 258). Emery goes on to explain that for Aquinas, the action of the Son and Spirit accomplish the same effects in us (since they are inseparable actions) but do so according to the distinct personal mode of each person. For the doctrine of trinitarian appropriation, see esp. ibid., 364–404. Emery explains that the missions produce a "grasp of the Son and Holy Spirit within their sending," a fruition that consists in "an authentic 'enjoyment' of the persons" or an experiencing of the persons (ibid., 394). Ontologically, grace is the effect of the action of the whole Trinity, but "the gifts of grace refer us to the three divine persons as distinct from each other, and grasped in their proper peculiarity, one as Father, the other as Son, and the third as the Holy Spirit issuing from Father and Son. Within this second frame, it is not a matter of appropriation, but of a relation to three divine persons, each grasped in the distinct personality proper to him" (ibid., 404). See also Emery, "The Personal Mode of Trinitarian Action in St. Thomas Aquinas," in *Trinity, Church, and the Human Person: Thomistic Essays*, trans. Mary Thomas Noble, OP, et al. (Naples, FL: Sapientia Press of Ave Maria University, 2007), 115–53; Torrell, *Saint Thomas Aquinas*, vol. 2, *Spiritual Master*, 94–98; F. Elisondo Aragón, "Conocer por experiencia: Un studio de sus modos y valoración en la *Summa theologica* de Tomás de Aquino," *Revista Espagnola de Teologia* 52 (1992): 5–50; 189–229; Jeremy D. Wilkins, "Trinitarian Missions and the Order of Grace According to Thomas Aquinas," in *Philosophy and Theology in the Long Middle Ages: A Tribute to Stephen F. Brown*, ed. Kent Emery Jr., Russell L. Friedman, and Andreas Speer (Leiden: Brill, 2011), 689–708, at 692–95.

153. II-II, q. 1, a. 9. See Romanus Cessario, OP, *Christian Faith and the Theological Life* (Washington, DC: Catholic University of America Press, 1996), 63–76; Reinhard Hütter, "'A Forgotten Truth?'—Theological Faith, Source and Guarantee of Theology's Inner Unity," in Hütter, *Dust Bound for Heaven*, 313–46; Stephen F. Brown, "The Theological Virtue of Faith: An Invitation to an Ecclesial Life of Truth (IIa IIae, qq. 1–16)," in *The Ethics of Aquinas*, ed. Stephen J. Pope (Washington, DC: Georgetown University Press, 2002), 221–31. For the extent of the Spirit's guidance of the church, in light of the Second Vatican Council's *Dei Verbum* and with antihierarchical Christian movements such as Pentecostalism in view, see also Yves Congar, OP, *The Word and the Spirit*, trans. David Smith (London: Geoffrey Chapman, 1986), chaps. 4–5. Congar emphasizes that "the Spirit is totally relative to Jesus. . . . His activity is relative to the truth that Jesus was and is" (ibid., 44).

154. II-II, q. 2, a. 8.

of the church). The eschatological church is thoroughly pneumatological, then, as can be seen in the content of the church's faith.

The Gifts of the Holy Spirit

The gifts of the Holy Spirit are another significant element of Aquinas's construal of the eschatological church.[155] Aquinas comments that these "gifts" have to do with a principle of extrinsic motion in us, and specifically with our disposition "to follow well the promptings of God."[156] What is at stake, according to Aquinas, is what it means to be "led by the Spirit of God" and thus to be adopted "sons of God" (Rom. 8:14). To be led by the Spirit requires not only rationality elevated by faith and love, but also "the prompting or motion of the Holy Spirit," or "special promptings from God."[157] The gifts of the Holy Spirit are not these promptings, but instead dispose us or "make us amenable" to the Spirit's promptings, the promptings of personal Love and Gift.[158]

Following the theological tradition, Aquinas considers that the seven gifts of the Holy Spirit are enumerated in Isaiah 11:2–3. Two in particular attach to the virtue of faith, namely understanding and knowledge. How do these gifts contribute to the portrait of the eschatological church of the Holy Spirit? The purpose of the natural light of understanding, Aquinas says, consists in penetrating "into the heart of things."[159] The gift of understanding follows upon faith, which enlightens the mind supernaturally. What the gift of understanding does is to enable us not merely to assent to the propositions of faith as true, but also to perceive the relationship of particular truths of faith to the end or goal of deification. Our mind becomes taken up by the end (beatitude or happiness) that God has willed for us, and we come to understand other things in relation to this end. In this way our understanding becomes "easily moved by the Holy Spirit," as our mind is configured more profoundly to God's eternal law for our flourishing.[160] Through the gift of understanding, then, our mind's assent to supernatural truth under the prompting of the

---

155. See Congar, "Vision de l'Église chez S. Thomas d'Aquin," 535. On the gifts of the Holy Spirit, see especially Cessario, *Introduction to Moral Theology*, 205–12; Cessario, *Christian Faith and the Theological Life*, 159–80; Torrell, *Saint Thomas Aquinas*, vol. 2, *Spiritual Master*, 206–15. See also Bernard Lonergan, SJ, *Grace and Freedom*, ed. F. E. Crowe, SJ, and R. M. Doran, SJ (Toronto: University of Toronto Press, 2000), 44–49.

156. I-II, q. 68, a. 1, ad 3.

157. I-II, q. 68, a. 2; cf. ad 2.

158. I-II, q. 68, a. 2, ad 3.

159. II-II, q. 8, a. 1. See Cessario, *Christian Faith and the Theological Life*, 171–76.

160. II-II, q. 8, a. 5; cf. II-II, q. 8, a. 3.

Spirit becomes easy, and this also aids our will's movement to right action, which depends upon knowing the end.

For its part, the gift of knowledge has to do with a "sure and right judgment" about the creaturely matters pertaining to faith.[161] We need knowledge of what creatures are and how to order them to the supernatural end we know in faith. Experience teaches how difficult this is, since we are always falling into sin by cleaving to creatures in some way. The Spirit's gift of knowledge, then, corresponds to and strengthens the supernatural virtue of faith by enabling us rightly to esteem creatures and to live in accordance with what we know in faith.

The eschatological church, in other words, is not a "mere" waiting for Christ's return and for the consummation of the kingdom. Rather, the community of believers must hold tightly to the goal revealed in Christ, lest its focus turn away from the Lord. Thus the Holy Spirit's powerful presence is of absolute necessity. This is the place to note, as well, that in his discussion of faith Aquinas attends to Jesus's rather obscure statement that "whoever says a word against the Son of man will be forgiven; but whoever speaks against the Holy Spirit will not be forgiven, either in this age or in the age to come" (Matt. 12:32). While granting that the sin against the Holy Spirit could be a literal blasphemy against the Spirit (John Chrysostom's view) or final impenitence (Augustine's view), Aquinas concurs with Peter Lombard's list of six kinds of sin against the Holy Spirit or against the effects of the Holy Spirit in us: "despair, presumption, inpenitence, obstinacy, resisting the known truth, envying our brother's spiritual good."[162] The point for our purposes is that we can act against the Holy Spirit, and we do so by actions that negate faith, hope, and charity. Such separation from Christ's eschatological community, however, does not in this life "close the way of forgiveness and healing to an all-powerful and merciful God."[163]

---

161. II-II, q. 9, a. 1; cf. II-II, q. 9, a. 2. See Cessario, *Christian Faith and the Theological Life*, 176–80.

162. II-II, q. 14, a. 2, obj. 1.

163. II-II, q. 14, a. 3. On Christ's mercy, see Guy Mansini, OSB, "Mercy 'Twice Blest,'" in *John Paul II and St. Thomas Aquinas*, ed. Michael Dauphinais and Matthew Levering (Naples, FL: Sapientia Press of Ave Maria University, 2006), 75–100. A misleading path is taken by Walter Kasper, *Mercy: The Essence of the Gospel and the Key to Christian Life*, trans. William Madges (New York: Paulist Press, 2014). He argues that "within the parameters of the metaphysical attributes of God, there is scarcely room for a concept of mercy" (ibid., 11), but in fact Aquinas easily locates mercy within the divine love. For Kasper, "Mercy must be understood as God's own justice and as his holiness" (ibid., 13), but the concept of mercy—namely, filling up what is lacking—differs from the concept of justice; they are not synonyms when applied to God. Kasper rightly insists that "a church without charity and without mercy would no longer be the church of Jesus Christ" (ibid., 158). His simplifications, however, exaggerate the demise

Other gifts of the Holy Spirit include filial fear, which renders us more "amenable" to the Spirit's motion and prompts us to revere and cleave to God; wisdom, which provides knowledge of divine realities; counsel, by which the Holy Spirit's counsel takes the place of our research; filial piety, which enables us to recognize ourselves as God's children; and fortitude, in which the Holy Spirit strengthens us to complete the work that we have been given. With regard to the gift of wisdom, Aquinas cites two texts from 1 Corinthians 2 that suggest to him that knowledge of divine realities comes only through the Holy Spirit: "the Spirit searches everything, even the depths of God" (1 Cor. 2:10) and "the spiritual man judges all things" (1 Cor. 2:15). Aquinas associates the gift of counsel with the virtue of prudence. The Holy Spirit counsels the members of the eschatological people of God, "just as, in human affairs, those who are unable to take counsel for themselves, seek counsel from those who are wiser."[164] Piety toward God is a "gift" insofar as it is specifically "that piety, whereby, at the Holy Spirit's instigation, we pay worship and duty to God as our Father."[165] Lastly, the gift of fortitude allows the Holy Spirit to move us with a unique confidence, an assurance that we will in fact attain our goal of eternal life. Through the gift of fortitude, the Holy Spirit renders the eschatological people of God confident that God will reward us, rather than being fearful that the promised consummation will elude us.

Aquinas says each believer is fueled by infused moral virtues, as well. Naturally acquired moral virtues do not suffice for the Christian, because our prudence and justice, for example, must be "proportionate" to the theological virtues such as faith and love. The Holy Spirit's action upon us is radical and thorough.[166]

If anything, Aquinas's encomium to the Holy Spirit's thoroughgoing presence in the ecclesial body of Christ risks being unbelievable to anyone who has ever met a Christian. Of course, Aquinas is aware of how deep sin goes in the human person, and it is in this context that his insistence upon the scope of the Spirit's presence must be understood. His theology of the Spirit's activity in the church is an exposition of Paul's dictum that "where sin increased, grace abounded all the more, so that, as sin reigned in death, grace also might reign through righteousness to eternal life through Jesus Christ our Lord" (Rom.

---

of mercy in Catholic theology and produce a truncated vision of the church's mediation of Christ's mercy, as can be seen in his claim that "[w]e stand, therefore, before the task of pulling mercy out of the Cinderella existence into which it has fallen in traditional theology" (ibid., 13).

164. II-II, q. 52, a. 1 and ad 1.

165. II-II, q. 121, a. 1.

166. On the infused moral virtues, see Romanus Cessario, OP, *The Moral Virtues and Theological Ethics* (Notre Dame, IN: University of Notre Dame Press, 1991), 102–25.

5:20–21). The purpose of the time between the inauguration and consummation of the kingdom is to build up disciples of Jesus by the Holy Spirit, that
is to say, to configure people from all nations to Jesus's self-giving love. This
is the explanation of the outpouring of the Spirit that Aquinas places at the
heart of his theology of Christian life.

The Sacraments and the Holy Spirit

For Aquinas, as we have seen, "grace is attributed to the Holy Spirit, inasmuch as it is through love that God gives us something gratis, which is
the very nature of grace: while the Holy Spirit is love."[167] This is the direction from which to read Aquinas's theology of the sacraments, which—as
is evident from the New Testament's multiple references to baptism and the
Eucharist—are central, in the plan of Jesus, to the inaugurated but not yet
consummated kingdom of God. Aquinas reasons that the sacraments of the
New Law must "cause grace" because "through the sacraments of the New
Law man is incorporated with Christ," which can happen only by grace.[168]

Aquinas's treatment of baptism brings out the active role of the Holy
Spirit, not least through the biblical texts that he cites. For example, he
quotes John the Baptist's promise that the coming Messiah "will baptize
you with the Holy Spirit and with fire" (Matt. 3:11); John the Baptist's
statement that "he who sent me to baptize with water said to me, 'He on
whom you see the Spirit descend and remain, this is he who baptizes with
the Holy Spirit'" (John 1:33); and Jesus's instruction to Nicodemus that

---

167. III, q. 63, a. 3, ad 1.

168. III, q. 62, a. 1. See John P. Yocum, "Sacraments in Aquinas," in *Aquinas on Doctrine: A
Critical Introduction*, ed. Thomas G. Weinandy, OFMCap, Daniel A. Keating, and John P. Yocum
(London: T&T Clark, 2004), 159–81; Liam Walsh, OP, "Sacraments," in Van Nieuwenhove
and Wawrykow, *The Theology of Thomas Aquinas*, 326–64, at 344–47; Bernhard Blankenhorn,
OP, "The Place of Romans 6 in Aquinas's Doctrine of Sacramental Causality: A Balance of
History and Metaphysics," in *Ressourcement Thomism: Sacred Doctrine, the Sacraments,
and the Moral Life*, ed. Reinhard Hütter and Matthew Levering (Washington, DC: Catholic
University of America Press, 2010), 136–49; John F. Gallagher, *Significando Causant: A Study
of Sacramental Causality* (Fribourg: Fribourg University Press, 1965). For an emphasis on the
connection between pneumatology (and spirituality) and the sacraments, see Ola Tjørhom, *Visible Church—Visible Unity: Ecumenical Ecclesiology and "The Great Tradition of the Church"*
(Collegeville, MN: Liturgical Press, 2004), 101–9. Michael Bossy, SJ, sums up the central point:
"Christ became present on earth when the power of the Holy Spirit came upon Our Lady. The
Spirit led him through his life and death to the Father. His presence on earth continues by the
power of the Holy Spirit acting in the sacraments of the Church and guiding the people of God
on their pilgrimage to the Father" (Bossy, "The Holy Spirit and the Sacraments," 78). See also,
for what follows, Liam Walsh, OP, *Sacraments of Initiation: A Theology of Life, Word, and
Rite*, 2nd ed. (Chicago: Hillenbrand, 2011).

"unless one is born of water and the Spirit, he cannot enter the kingdom of God" (John 3:5).[169] In the book of Acts too we see that at the invocation of the name of Christ at baptism, "the Holy Spirit was given" to the baptized.[170] With regard to the rite of baptism, Aquinas appeals to the Holy Spirit's governance of the church's practice of the sacraments: "The Church is ruled by the Holy Spirit, who does nothing inordinate."[171] Infant baptism, rooted in the faith of the church, provides an instance of this working of the Spirit in the church. Aquinas states that "the faith of one, indeed of the whole Church, profits the child through the operation of the Holy Spirit, who unites the Church together, and communicates the goods of one member to another."[172]

Aquinas also discusses baptism of the Spirit, namely the "baptism" that can occur outside the sacramental rite. This occurs whenever "a man receives the effect of baptism by the power of the Holy Spirit, not only without baptism of water, but also without baptism of blood: forasmuch as his heart is moved by the Holy Spirit to believe in and love God and to repent of his sins."[173] The Holy Spirit's centrality is obvious here. Regarding those who experience baptism of the Spirit and then are later able to receive the actual sacrament of baptism, Aquinas observes that they thereby "receive a yet greater fulness of grace and virtues."[174]

Aquinas remarks that the sacrament of baptism "derives its efficacy, both from Christ's Passion and from the Holy Spirit."[175] Indeed, he points out that Christ's passion itself "derives its efficacy from the Holy Spirit," and as evidence he cites Hebrews 9:14: "how much more shall the blood of Christ, who through the eternal Spirit offered himself without blemish to God, purify your conscience from dead works to serve the living God."[176]

169. See III, q. 66, aa. 3, 5, 9. See Michael Dauphinais, "Christ and the Metaphysics of Baptism in the *Summa Theologiae* and the *Commentary on John*," in *Rediscovering Aquinas and the Sacraments: Studies in Sacramental Theology*, ed. Matthew Levering and Michael Dauphinais (Chicago: Hillenbrand, 2009), 14–27.

170. III, q. 66, a. 6, ad 1. See Cessario, *The Moral Virtues and Theological Ethics*, 118–19.

171. III, q. 66, a. 10, *sed contra*. This means not that the church makes no mistakes of any kind (which is far from the case), but rather that the Holy Spirit ensures that the church does not err in its definitive teachings about the Christian faith, including about baptism. Thus it should not be taken to imply that *whatever* the church does is thereby authorized by the Holy Spirit.

172. III, q. 68, a. 9, ad 2. See Gilles Emery, OP, "Le baptême des petits enfants," *Nova et Vetera* 87 (2012): 7–23; Walsh, *Sacraments of Initiation*, 132–44.

173. III, q. 66, a. 11.

174. III, q. 69, a. 4, ad 2.

175. III, q. 66, a. 11, ad 1.

176. III, q. 66, a. 12, obj. 3.

For our purposes, what is notable is the active and central place of the Holy Spirit in Aquinas's theology of Christ and the eschatological church. The Holy Spirit fills Christ Jesus and gives his pasch salvific efficacy due to the supreme love with which Jesus dies, and the Holy Spirit works to unite us sacramentally to Jesus's saving pasch and thereby to join us to Jesus's self-offering in love. With respect to baptism, "the power of the Holy Spirit acts in the baptism of water through a certain hidden power; in the baptism of repentance by moving the heart; but in the baptism of blood [martyrdom] by the highest degree of fervor of dilection and love."[177] The Holy Spirit causes in Jesus, and in us, the love that makes us willing to give our lives for others.

The sacrament of confirmation too displays the power of the Holy Spirit in the eschatological people of God, who are being configured to Christ during this interim period before the consummation of the kingdom. Citing Jesus's words in John 15:7, "if I do not go away, the Counselor will not come to you; but if I go, I will send him to you," Aquinas argues that Jesus instituted the sacrament of confirmation by promising its content: namely, "the fulness of the Holy Spirit."[178] Conformity to Christ, Aquinas points out, requires a "fulness" with regard to the Spirit's presence in one's life.[179] After all, the Spirit was profoundly active in Jesus, as Aquinas underscores by quoting John 1:14; Luke 3:22; and Luke 4:1, the last of which describes Jesus as "full of the Holy Spirit." The purpose of the sacrament of confirmation is to make us full of the grace of the Holy Spirit and thus ever more configured to Christ.

Aquinas explains that the sacrament of confirmation is given when we have reached an age of social maturity, so that in our interactions with

---

177. III, q. 66, a. 12.

178. III, q. 72, a. 1, ad 1. Liam Walsh comments, "It is well to note that when Aquinas comes to study individual sacraments, he never sets out to 'prove' from the Scriptures or the Tradition that Christ instituted each of the seven sacraments. Rather, he tries to find a place in the Word of God where the significance of what the Church of his day was doing is seen to have been determined by God" (Walsh, "Sacraments," 337). See the comprehensive study of this topic according to Aquinas (in light of other medieval theologians) in Bertrand-Marie Perrin, *L'Institution des sacrements* (Paris: Parole et Silence, 2008). For discussion of the sacrament of confirmation, see, for example, Robert C. Miner, "Aquinas on the Sacrament of Confirmation," in Levering and Dauphinais, *Rediscovering Aquinas and the Sacraments*, 28–38; Walsh, *Sacraments of Initiation*, 145–214. See also Benedikt Tomás Mohelník, OP, *'Gratia augmenti': Contribution au débat contemporain sur la confirmation* (Fribourg: Academic Press Fribourg, 2005). Walsh notes the influence of Rabanus Maurus upon Aquinas's view of confirmation, and he remarks that for Aquinas, the fullness of the Holy Spirit "is the reality that was given at Pentecost: there it was given visibly but not in a sacramental rite" (Walsh, *Sacraments of Initiation*, 187).

179. For discussion, see Marshall, *"Ex Occidente Lux?,"* 22–23.

others we might have the "spiritual strength" that comes from "the fulness of the Holy Spirit."[180] The sacrament employs holy oil because "the
grace of the Holy Spirit is signified by oil," which was used for anointing in
Israel.[181] The centrality of the Holy Spirit's agency in Christian life could
hardly be clearer. Aquinas goes on to say that the actual sacrament was not
administered during apostolic times, since the reality was given directly. As
he comments, "Christ, by the power which he exercises in the sacraments,
bestowed on the apostles the reality of this sacrament, i.e., the fulness of
the Holy Spirit, without the sacrament itself."[182] The sacrament was not
needed, because Christ filled them with the Spirit through the tongues of
fire. The apostles too found that they did not need this sacrament, because
"when the apostles imposed their hands, and when they preached, the fulness of the Holy Spirit came down under visible signs on the faithful."[183] As
an example, Aquinas cites Acts 11:15, where Peter reports, "As I began to
speak, the Holy Spirit fell on them just as on us at the beginning."[184] Later
generations, however, found a need for the material sacrament.

The key point is the fullness of the Holy Spirit in the eschatological church—
and this despite (or indeed because of, given our great need for the Spirit)
the ongoing troubles with sin that Paul already finds in his churches. With
reference to the matter of the sacrament (in this case, oil and balm), Aquinas
contrasts baptism and confirmation: "Baptism is bestowed that spiritual life
may be received simply. . . . But this sacrament is given that we may receive
the fulness of the Holy Spirit, whose operations are manifold."[185] Even the
fact that olive oil is used in this sacrament strikes Aquinas as a sign of the
Spirit-filled character of the church. He suggests that "the olive-tree itself,
through being an evergreen, signifies the refreshing and merciful operation

180. III, q. 72, a. 2. Here Susan K. Wood's cautionary remark is apropos: "Sacraments are
not just seven anthropological markers of lifetime passages such as birth, puberty, sickness,
and marriage, but relate to the two fundamental sacraments, baptism and Eucharist, in their
functions of reconciliation and building up the church as a messianic saving community. Sacraments give access to participation in this plan of salvation, anamnesis (memorial) and epiclesis
being essential to each of them. Anamnesis recalls the saving event of Jesus's death and resurrection so that it is actually present today, and epiclesis makes it effective through the power
of the Spirit" (Wood, "The Trinity in the Liturgy, Sacraments, and Mysticism," in Phan, *The
Cambridge Companion to the Trinity*, 381–96, at 384). Wood provides insightful reflection on
the references to the Holy Spirit in the rites of each of the sacraments.

181. III, q. 72, a. 2. On the sign-character of the sacraments, see Benoît-Dominique de
La Soujeole, OP, "The Importance of the Definition of Sacraments as Signs," in Hütter and
Levering, *Ressourcement Thomism*, 127–35; Walsh, "Sacraments," 333–40.

182. III, q. 72, a. 2, ad 1.

183. III, q. 72, a. 2, ad 1.

184. See III, q. 72, a. 2, ad 1.

185. III, q. 72, a. 2, ad 2.

of the Holy Spirit."[186] Only a Spirit-filled church would have the courage to confess faith in Jesus Christ even at the cost of martyrdom. Aquinas cites the example of the apostles, who prior to Pentecost had stayed largely in an upper room, but who after Pentecost emerged to proclaim the gospel boldly due to their possession of "the fulness of the Holy Spirit."[187] He concludes that "the Holy Spirit is given to the baptized for strength: just as he was given to the apostles on the day of Pentecost."[188] This strengthening grace of the Holy Spirit, given after baptism, *is* confirmation.

Indeed, the sacrament of confirmation provides a new mission of the Spirit to the recipient of this sacrament, which, like baptism, bestows sanctifying grace.[189] Aquinas specifies that "sanctifying grace is given not only for the remission of sin, but also for growth and stability in righteousness."[190] Regarding confirmation, he also insists that all members of the church are called to receive the Holy Spirit, Love and Gift, in this sacrament. He draws encouragement for his view from Acts 2:2, where the Spirit "filled the house," and Acts 2:4, "they were all filled with the Holy Spirit." The Spirit's strengthening activity through this sacrament, in other words, must fill the whole "house," and all the members, of the eschatological people of God. Only in this way can the church suitably engage in the "spiritual combat"—the charitable sufferings and sacrifices—by which we follow the path of Jesus Christ.[191]

The Eucharist is by no means less Spirit-filled than baptism or confirmation; thus Aquinas calls the Eucharist "spiritual food" that brings about "spiritual refreshment."[192] Denis-Dominique le Pivain remarks that Aquinas, "who is known as the poet of the Eucharist, develops his discourse on this sacrament from a perspective not only Christological, which goes without saying, but also ecclesiological and pneumatological."[193] From the fact that the Eucharist is the body and blood of Christ, and is the church's participation in Christ's pasch, Aquinas draws the Spirit-related conclusion that "just as by coming into the world, he [Christ] visibly bestowed the life of grace upon the world,

---

186. III, q. 72, a. 2, ad 3.
187. III, q. 72, a. 5.
188. III, q. 72, a. 7.
189. See III, q. 72, a. 7; I, q. 43, a. 6, ad 4.
190. III, q. 72, a. 7, ad 1.
191. See III, q. 72, a. 9.
192. III, q. 73, a. 1 and ad 1. As Susan Wood says, then, "Christ is not just an external exemplar of Christian living. In the sacraments Christians are joined to Christ in the power of the Spirit and actually participate in his paschal mystery of dying and rising. Christ's trinitarian pattern of life becomes theirs" (Wood, "Trinity in the Liturgy, Sacraments, and Mysticism," 382).
193. Denis-Dominique le Pivain, FSSP, *L'action du saint-Esprit dans le Commentaire de l'Évangile de saint Jean par saint Thomas d'Aquin* (Paris: Téqui, 2006), 161.

according to John i. 17, *Grace and truth came by Jesus Christ*, so also, by coming sacramentally into man, [Christ] causes the life of grace, according to John vi. 58: *He that eateth me, the same also shall live by me.*"[194] Thus in the Eucharist Christ gives us the "life of grace," which is the grace of the Holy Spirit—the same Spirit that filled Christ in his earthly life and that fills the glorified Christ now. It is for this reason, Aquinas suggests, that Jesus can say, "the bread which I shall give for the life of the world is my flesh" (John 6:51).[195]

The presence of the grace of the Holy Spirit in the sacrament of the Eucharist is also shown by the giving of this sacrament under the form of bread and wine. In this regard, Aquinas explains that "this sacrament does for the spiritual life all that material food does for the bodily life, namely, by sustaining, giving increase, restoring, and giving delight."[196] We are "spiritually gladdened, and as it were inebriated with the sweetness of the divine goodness."[197] The Eucharist thereby kindles the act of charity in us, and we become true selfless lovers.[198] In this way, just as Jesus promises in John 6, the Eucharist "bestows on us the power of coming unto glory."[199]

When he turns to the sacrament of penance, Aquinas connects it strongly with the Holy Spirit. He writes that "in this sacrament man regains the Holy Spirit whom he had lost."[200] Along the same lines, he says that "whosoever have done penance, have been illuminated, and have received the gift of the Holy Spirit."[201] Through the sacrament of penance, we are healed of mortal

194. III, q. 79, a. 1. Macaskill comments on the eucharistic imagery (which he connects strongly with faith) in the Gospel of John: "The Eucharist points to a personal appropriation of all that is held out in the Son, which brings real life to the believer. It is very much the imagery of making Jesus one's own" (Macaskill, *Union with Christ in the New Testament*, 216).

195. See III, q. 79, a. 1, *sed contra*.

196. III, q. 79, a. 1.

197. III, q. 79, a. 1, ad 2.

198. See III, q. 79, a. 4. On the Holy Spirit and the Eucharist in Aquinas, with special attention to charity, see Loyer, *God's Love through the Spirit*, 162–65.

199. III, q. 79, a. 2. Attention could be paid here also to the eucharistic liturgy as our entrance into the world to come; see, for example, Alexander Schmemann, *For the Life of the World: Sacraments and Orthodoxy* (Crestwood, NY: St. Vladimir's Seminary Press, 2002), esp. 26–46; Reinhard Hütter, *Suffering Divine Things: Theology as Church Practice*, trans. Doug Stott (Grand Rapids: Eerdmans, 2000), 119–20. For the eucharistic liturgy as our sharing in Christ's sacrificial self-offering to the Father, and thus as our sharing in the cruciform love that marks the risen Christ's reign at the right hand of the Father, see Matthew Levering, *Sacrifice and Community: Jewish Offering and Christian Eucharist* (Oxford: Blackwell, 2005), chap. 5. See also the overview offered by Mauro Gagliardi, *Introduzione al mistero eucaristico: Dottrina, liturgia, devozione* (Rome: Edizioni San Clemente, 2007).

200. III, q. 84, a. 4.

201. III, q. 84, a. 10. Romanus Cessario states, "Like the gifts of the Holy Spirit, which constitute the special and privileged endowments of the Christian believer, the three-personed God remains the principal and unique source of spiritual benefit and growth for the members of

sin by a new infusion of habitual or sanctifying grace—a new mission of the Spirit—and we are healed of venial sin by a new "movement of grace or charity."[202] Aquinas observes that "there can be no infusion of grace without an actual movement of the free-will towards God and against sin."[203]

The *Summa theologiae* breaks off in the middle of Aquinas's discussion of the sacrament of penance.[204] But I have already said enough to show that Aquinas's theology of the church, both with respect to the Spirit's interior effects in us and with respect to the sacraments of the church, bears witness to a messianic community that owes its (liturgical) life to the exalted Jesus, who, as Peter tells the crowd at Pentecost, "received from the Father the promise of the Holy Spirit" and "has poured out this which you see and hear" (Acts 2:33). Aquinas's church is indeed the eschatological church of the "last days" when God, through Christ, "will pour out my Spirit upon all flesh" (Acts 2:17 [cf. Joel 2:28]).

Conclusion

Dale Allison presses the point that certain claims of Jesus identify him as a false eschatological prophet, such as Matthew 10:23: "You will not have gone through all the towns of Israel, before the Son of man comes." As we have seen, this passage is difficult to square with other eschatological texts such as Matthew 24:36, "But of that day and hour no one knows, not even the angels of heaven, nor the Son, but the Father only."[205] Moreover, the same Gospel envisions the formation of the church, guided by the exalted Christ, who works through "the Spirit of God" (Matt. 12:28). Jesus praises Peter for his confession of Jesus as the Messiah: "Blessed are you, Simon Bar-jona! For flesh and blood has not revealed this to you, but my Father who is in heaven. And I tell you, you are Peter, and on this rock I will build my church, and the powers of death shall not prevail against it" (Matt. 16:17–18).

Christ's Body. So the sacraments point to God. And in the sacrament of penance, especially, we discover how the Trinity effects a sacrament of salvation for those who remain united with the incarnate Son" (Cessario, "Christian Satisfaction and Sacramental Reconciliation," in Levering and Dauphinas, *Rediscovering Aquinas and the Sacraments*, 65–75, at 74).

202. III, q. 87, a. 2.

203. III, q. 87, a. 2.

204. Thus I do not here include a discussion of the Holy Spirit and the sacrament of marriage, a topic that is well treated by John Mahoney, SJ, "Holy Spirit and Married Life," in Butterworth, *Spirit in Action*, 102–14.

205. For Aquinas's discussion of this text, a favorite one for Arian thinkers, see III, q. 10, a. 2, ad 1. For other perspectives, see Balthasar's emphasis on Jesus's concentration upon his "hour," and Thomas Joseph White, OP's "Dyotheletism and the Instrumental Human Consciousness of Jesus," *Pro Ecclesia* 17 (2008): 396–422.

Mark 13 exemplifies the difficulty of squaring such passages. In Mark 13:5–7, Jesus suggests that there is going to be some time before the end: "Take heed that no one leads you astray. Many will come in my name, saying, 'I am he!' and they will lead many astray. And when you hear of wars and rumors of wars, do not be alarmed; this must take place, but the end is not yet." Jesus tells his disciples that before the end comes, "the gospel must first be preached to all the nations" (Mark 13:10). In the same chapter of Mark, however, Jesus seems to indicate that the end will come quite soon, and that it will have to do with temple sacrilege: "But when you see the desolating sacrilege set up where it ought not to be (let the reader understand), then let those in Judea flee to the mountains. . . . For in those days there will be such tribulation as has not been from the beginning of the creation which God created until now, and never will be" (Mark 13:14, 19). Jesus concludes that this tribulation will be followed by cosmic dissolution and by the arrival of "the Son of man coming in clouds with great power and glory" (Mark 13:26), and furthermore that "this generation will not pass away before all these things take place" (Mark 13:30).

For Allison, rather than appealing to immanent and imminent dimensions of the kingdom's arrival (allowing for the consummation of the kingdom to be far off, yet fully present in Jesus's "hour"), Jesus must be seen to be simply contradictory and misguided in the way that end-time prophets such as R. Abraham Kook have been. This viewpoint, however, requires assuming that the living God's work in Israel was not in fact reaching a crescendo in Jesus's life, as well as assuming that Jesus's eschatological preaching did not receive divine confirmation through his resurrection, ascension, and Pentecostal outpouring of the Spirit.[206] This viewpoint also requires depreciating the sapiential power of Jesus's teachings and his institution of the Eucharist as what Brant Pitre calls "the mechanism of the eschatological restoration of Israel."[207] The reductionary tenor of Allison's approach is indicated by his statement that Jesus's "mind . . . was poetic, and his mental universe, filled as it was with invisible spirits and informed by the cosmology of the Hebrew Scriptures, was

---

206. On the historical plausibility of Jesus's resurrection, see N. T. Wright, *The Resurrection of the Son of God* (Minneapolis: Fortress, 2003); James D. G. Dunn, *Christianity in the Making*, vol. 1, *Jesus Remembered* (Grand Rapids: Eerdmans, 2003); Dale C. Allison Jr., *Resurrecting Jesus: The Earliest Christian Tradition and Its Interpreters* (New York: T&T Clark, 2005). See also, for discussion of the positions of these scholars (although I mistakenly attribute to Allison a certitude about the hallucinatory origins of the disciples' experiences of the risen Jesus, whereas in fact he thinks that historical research cannot arrive at certitude in this matter), Levering, *Jesus and the Demise of Death*, chap. 2. See also Luke Timothy Johnson, *Prophetic Jesus, Prophetic Church*, 182–83.

207. Pitre, *Jesus and the Last Supper*, 516.

mythological."[208] It is not clear that a belief in angels and demons, let alone belief in the God of Israel (the center of Jesus's "mental universe"), should be classified as "mythological" as a matter of historical assessment. Allison sets Jesus's teachings rather summarily to the side, as seen in his remark that Jesus "composed parables. He issued warnings. He appealed to religious sentiment."[209] This reduces Jesus's profound teachings merely to what we might expect to come forth from any religious fanatic of his time (or of later times).

As we saw, N. T. Wright seeks to defend the truth of Jesus's eschatological teaching in Matthew 10:23 and its fit with Jesus's other eschatological statements. He argues that Jesus is likely referring to his vindication through the Romans' destruction of the Jerusalem temple in AD 70. According to Wright, Jesus is not speaking literally, but rather is prophesying his full and final vindication. For Dunn, Jesus's discourse about the imminent and immanent kingdom of God is to be read with the leeway that one should give to prophetic imagery. Dunn gives particular attention to Jesus's sense of acting with the power of the eschatological Spirit. Hans Urs von Balthasar suggests that Jesus is focused upon his eschatological "hour"; historical time continues, but does so now only in reference to Jesus's definitive fulfillment of all things. Somewhat like Wright, Thomas Aquinas thinks that Matthew 10:23 has to do with the Son of man's coming at his resurrection, after which he will send the disciples beyond the boundaries of the "towns of Israel," in accord with the risen Jesus's command to the eleven disciples to "go therefore and make disciples of all nations" (Matt. 28:19).[210]

In light of these competing exegetical paths, I observed that how one interprets Jesus's eschatological sayings is inextricably tied to one's estimation of the events after Jesus's death. In this regard, Dunn's attention to the Spirit seems especially helpful. The dialectic between immanent and (in some sense) imminent eschatology is found both in Jesus's sayings and in the worldview of the early church, since the early church considered the outpouring of the Spirit to be the firstfruits of the eschatological consummation. Dunn underscores the significance of Jesus's and the early Christians' understanding of the church as the new temple filled with the Spirit. If the Spirit was truly poured out upon the early Christians, then the vision of Jesus the eschatological prophet has indeed come to pass.

This interior outpouring of the Spirit connects believers with Christ the exalted King, and it takes sacramental form in baptism and the Eucharist as ways of uniting and configuring the restored people of God to their King.

208. Allison, *Constructing Jesus*, 92.
209. Ibid.
210. Aquinas, *Commentary on the Gospel of St. Matthew*, 381.

Filled with the Spirit, believers are bound together as one church, in faith, charity, and obedience to the Spirit's promptings. By approaching the church from this perspective, emphasizing the visible and invisible missions of the Holy Spirit and our ordering to the state of glory by means of the infused virtues and the sacraments, Aquinas offers an eschatological perspective on the church that complements contemporary New Testament exegesis. His discussion of the missions of the Holy Spirit highlights the transformative power and interior intimacy of the Spirit's upbuilding of the church.

We saw this first and foremost in Aquinas's theology of the kingdom of God, inclusive of the indwelling of grace, inspired Scripture, the church on earth, and the heavenly banquet or consummated kingdom. At the right hand of the Father, Jesus now reigns as judge and king; the marks of his royal dignity over his kingdom are his wounds. The gospel, for Aquinas, is "the gospel of the kingdom."[211] Aquinas's theology of history too displays a sense for the eschatological power of Jesus's pasch, since Jesus's resurrection inaugurates the epoch of grace. Jesus's return is delayed—if "delayed" is the right word, since the Spirit did not teach the church about the timing of the parousia—in order that the gospel can have its full effect over time and space due to the Spirit publicly manifesting the incarnate Son. The Spirit comes upon the apostles in two visible missions, as breath (John 20:22–23) and as tongues of fire (Acts 2); the former signals the apostles' participation in Jesus's power through their ability to bestow the sacraments, and the latter signals the apostles' sharing in Jesus's power to teach. The invisible missions of the Spirit sanctify believers, not least by infusing virtues such as charity and faith as well as the gifts of the Holy Spirit, by which believers live in accord with the Spirit's movements.[212] The sacraments too mediate the invisible Spirit in distinctive ways, as I showed by exploring Aquinas's theology of baptism, confirmation, the Eucharist, and penance.

The extraordinary presence of the Spirit in believers' lives, the manifold interlacing ways in which the Spirit shapes us, becomes crystal clear in Aquinas's presentation. In this manner, the work of biblical scholars and theologians attentive to Albert Schweitzer's eschatological Jesus invites a rereading of classical Christian theology of the Holy Spirit in the church. This rereading involves nothing less than a renewed awareness of the Love and Gift to which believers, filled with the eschatological Spirit of Jesus, joyfully bear witness by means of lives of repentance and self-giving love: "For the kingdom of God does not consist in talk but in power" (1 Cor. 4:20).

211. I-II, q. 106, a. 4, ad 4.
212. Indeed, William Hill argues that there is a certain "priority of the Spirit over the Son in the missions *ad extra*. The ground for this is simply the primacy of divine love in all negotiations with creatures" (Hill, *Three-Personed God*, 296).

The Holy Spirit
and the Unity of the Church

In the first of his six sermons on the Holy Spirit, John of Avila, whose life spanned the years of the Reformation divisions, begins by encouraging us to imitate the apostles' longing for the Holy Spirit. He notes that "we would do well to imitate them [the apostles], since we are one with them, one church and one in union with Jesus Christ."[1] As evidence for the truth of this unity, John appeals to Song of Songs, which he reads as a dialogue between Christ and the church. Christ says of the church, "My dove, my perfect one, is only one" (Song 6:9). The embodied bride of Christ, his "dove," possesses unity so as to be "one in union with Jesus Christ."[2]

1. John of Avila, *The Holy Ghost*, trans. Ena Dargan (Chicago: Scepter, 1959), 11.
2. Ephraim Radner, in his "The Holy Spirit and Unity: Getting Out of the Way of Christ," *International Journal of Systematic Theology* 16 (2014): 207–20, articulates many of the same concerns about what he calls "modern pneumatological expansionism" that I put forward in this chapter. Citing *The Work of the Spirit: Pneumatology and Pentecostalism*, ed. Michael Welker (Grand Rapids: Eerdmans, 2006), Radner notes that "we see numerous attempts to apply *sui generis* pneumatological elements to Christian life: diversity, openness and so on. The 'Spirit is' power, *is* futurity, *is* life. One of the major attempts to discuss the pneumatological character of Christian unity, the 2002 Bose Conference on the Spirit and Ecumenism, itself slipped into this current, as it seamlessly moved from an initial discussion of the cross of Christ to an enumeration of pneumatic 'gifts' necessary for unity that lifted up elements of 'diversity' and 'manifoldness' and 'openness' as undefined categories untethered to any scriptural descriptives" (Radner, "Holy Spirit and Unity," 218). Radner's solution to this problem, a solution with which

Can we today follow John of Avila's emphasis on unity when reflecting on the Holy Spirit's upbuilding of the church? In his *God the Spirit*, Michael Welker grants that "the Spirit of God places people in the community of conscious solidarity."[3] He holds that in the church, despite "seeming insignificance and de facto corruption, the Spirit of God joins together people called to communion with Christ. . . . Here a powerful communion is being formed."[4] At the same time he emphasizes that "the Spirit of valid life is by no means at work and detectable only in visible churches," since the Spirit is "more or less clearly and unambiguously recognizable in many religious and secular environments."[5] Welker does not propose that the Spirit's work aims to form one visible church, whether by uniting the many visible churches or by leading members of the diverse churches to recognize and submit to an existing one true church.[6] He depicts the Spirit as entering into conflictual

---

I concur, is to insist upon giving christological form—and thus embodied particularity—to church unity. Yet when Radner spells out the details of his solution, I find them problematic, even though I am grateful for Radner's powerful witness to the degree of conflict and brokenness within the church's life.

3. Michael Welker, *God the Spirit*, trans. John F. Hoffmeyer (Minneapolis: Fortress, 1994), 282. Along similar lines, Amos Yong notes that "the incarnational union of divine and human in Christ by the Spirit leads to the pentecostal creation of the body of Christ composed of many human members by that same Spirit" (Yong, *Spirit-Word-Community: Theological Hermeneutics in Trinitarian Perspective* [Burlington, VT: Ashgate, 2002], 32). While affirming the unity of this "body," Yong focuses on the overcoming of "differences of race and ethnicity, gender, and social class" (ibid., 33). He emphasizes that the earliest church was marked by the surmounting of "gender barriers" and "social divides" (ibid.), so that "the gospel levels out the differences that are marginalizing" (ibid., 34). Yong goes on to say much more about the Spirit—including that the Spirit is the one who communicates God's wisdom and that "the Spirit is the power of life in creation" (ibid., 43)—but it is noteworthy that his account of the unity of the church offers specifics about race, gender, and class rather than about the actual embodied, institutional unity that characterizes human social groups. Again, of course, Yong certainly affirms—as one would expect from a theologian of his caliber—that the Holy Spirit is "the Spirit of fellowship or communion," and that "the Spirit created *homo sapiens* for community, and true community is to be experienced in the new body of Christ, the *ekklēsia*. This is also the fellowship of the Spirit whereby human beings live in the mutual sociality of having all things in common, breaking and sharing bread, praying, and worshipping together" (ibid., 46).

4. Welker, *God the Spirit*, 309.

5. Ibid., 308.

6. For Ephraim Radner, in his *A Brutal Unity: The Spiritual Politics of the Christian Church* (Waco: Baylor University Press, 2012), "division is bound to Christ's very coming and presence" (ibid., 428), so that the church's "unity" is found only as "the solidarity of God with the godless" (ibid., 445), in God's self-emptying solidarity with the godlessness, rebellions, and blasphemy that intrinsically and inevitably characterize the church itself. He argues that only a church that recognizes that its unity is fundamentally a kenotic solidarity with sinners (Christ's kenotic stance, though from the side of the sinful church), and thus a unity of "love that bears the enemy himself or herself" (ibid., 460), can be an honest church. Such a church will be united by Christ's self-emptying solidarity with sinners, not by doctrine, truth, or structure: "The procedures of the church will never guarantee or provide either unity *or* truth. They will, however,

situations and turning them into situations of reconciliation and blessing, but he does not speak of visible unity in one church. He is particularly concerned with how the Holy Spirit is operative in situations in which conflict between people of different traditions is replaced by a pluralistic harmony between such groups—a harmony that does not mean that the groups become fully united by any means, but that does result in a salutary end to generations of conflict.

In his *Pneumatology*, Veli-Matti Kärkkäinen praises Welker for recognizing that "the one Spirit of God opens himself into a myriad of experiences: the Eastern churches' vision of deification in the Spirit; the Pentecostal/Charismatic yearning for power in the Spirit; the Roman Catholic insistence on the infallibility of the church through the Spirit; the green pneumatologies' hope for the preservation of the earth by spiritual resources"—and many other similar testimonies "to the endless bounty and richness of the Spirit's agenda in God's creation."[7] The one thing that the Spirit does not seem able to do, on

---

offer the necessary framework of life together in which truth and unity emerge as the course of God's own self-giving, often as modes of witness distinct from them and suffered because of them" (ibid., 445). But I think that the New Testament's view of church unity conveys a far more "positive" sense of the unity in charity and truth that is enabled for the apostolic (sacramental, hierarchical, and institutional) church by the crucified, risen, and ascended Lord and his Spirit. Radner assumes that such unity does not historically exist (as has become especially evident since the Reformation, in his view), and he suggests that those who claim otherwise are wearing disastrously prideful and exclusionary blinders. Thus "unity in truth" about the realities of faith must be kenotically abandoned, on the grounds that these realities will uphold themselves: "If, as the character of authoritative consensus would demand, we are in fact called to hold on to and uphold our Eucharists, ministerial orders, sound doctrine, and whatever else marks the 'essentials' of our gospel and ecclesial integrity, we cannot allow these to determine our unity in truth. These demand nothing of our acts to maintain their integrity. Rather, we hold on to these things insofar as we accept their repudiation as painful, insofar as conscience is suffered in the body's *paradosis*" (ibid., 446). In my view—though I would need to make my case in much more detail—his position turns Christian faith into an ethical stance and set of pragmatic practices, rooted in imitation of Christ. For the issues involved, see, for example, Reinhard Hütter, "'A Forgotten Truth?'—Theological Faith, Source and Guarantee of Theology's Inner Unity," in *Dust Bound for Heaven: Explorations in the Theology of Thomas Aquinas* (Grand Rapids: Eerdmans, 2012), 313–46. For Radner's view of apostolicity and church order, see *Brutal Unity*, 169–219, 399–403.

7. Veli-Matti Kärkkäinen, *Pneumatology: The Holy Spirit in Ecumenical, International, and Contextual Perspective* (Grand Rapids: Baker Academic, 2002), 177. From the perspective of trinitarian ontology, Gisbert Greshake makes a claim that perhaps has a similar resonance: "Unity of relationality, of love, and not unity of the substance or a collectivity: that is the new Christian unity concept, which gains ground in the light of the Revelation of the triune God" (Greshake, "Trinity as 'Communio,'" in *Rethinking Trinitarian Theology: Disputed Questions and Contemporary Issues in Trinitarian Theology*, ed. Giulio Maspero and Robert J. Woźniak [London: T&T Clark, 2012], 331–45, at 338). Although Greshake clearly intends to invest "substance" and "collectivity" with negative connotations, the danger is that an amorphous "relationality" here can replace (surely not in accord with Greshake's intention) actual collective unity between persons who, substantially speaking, are quite distinct. For Greshake, a

this view, is to unify the church in a visible communion. Kärkkäinen remains concerned with church unity, understood, however, in a manner that does not require actual visible unity in one church. He states, "We receive the Spirit through the church, which represents continuity with others who came before us. As the bond of love, the Spirit unites us with the rest of the church, and as the eschatological gift, with the purposes of God's coming new creation."[8]

Welker's and Kärkkäinen's depictions of the Spirit's work make clear that the Spirit's main work will not be to unify people into one visible church, people who would otherwise have worshiped separately had not the Spirit touched their hearts. Put another way, by contrast to John of Avila, they do not seem to expect that the Spirit's coming impels human beings, filled with the gift of love and a spirit of repentance, to come together in visible sacramental and institutional unity as the eschatological community of Jesus Christ, which on earth is always in need of the Spirit's powerful work of reform and renewal for enriching and expanding the bond of unity, but which nonetheless is truly one in the Spirit.[9]

"collectivity" exists in a situation "in which all differences are churned together" (ibid., 341). In his trinitarian theology and theology of creation, he emphasizes, "Being-in-relation reveals itself then as the most profound nature of reality" (ibid.). I would add that the distinction between "being" and "relation" must be retained for either of the concepts to be intelligible, not only with respect to the divine undividedness, absolute simplicity, and transcendental unity, but also with respect to the distinction of persons who are nonetheless utterly the same in their divinity. Yet Greshake is certainly right to say, "The one divine nature exists only in the dynamic living exchange between Father, Son and Spirit" (ibid.).

8. Kärkkäinen, *Pneumatology*, 176.

9. Ola Tjørhom rightly observes with regard to contemporary ecumenism that "instead of visible structured unity, the main emphasis seems to be put increasingly on a static 'diversity' which is based on a typically 'postmodern' worshiping of limitless plurality and which allows the churches to maintain their denominational or even parochial identities and so to 'remain as they are'" (Tjørhom, *Visible Church—Visible Unity: Ecumenical Ecclesiology and "The Great Tradition of the Church"* [Collegeville, MN: Liturgical Press, 2004], 74 [cf. 80]). Against such emphasis, Tjørhom argues, "Since diversity has its limits in the Church's life and one such limit is our obligation to unity, it must be clearly stated that unity is theologically, ecclesiologically, and ecumenically prior to diversity" (ibid., 89). For Tjørhom, the Holy Spirit certainly "creates and sustains diversity" in the church, but nonetheless the Spirit is "the source and guardian of visible unity," not least by "holding and knitting our diversities together within the framework of communion" (ibid., 90). Tjørhom adds that "church unity is not an isolated end in itself, but must always be understood as unity in and for the world" (ibid., 93). See also the reflections on the Spirit and the church's unity in Brian Gaybba, *The Spirit of Love: Theology of the Holy Spirit* (London: Geoffrey Chapman, 1987), 27–28. The contrary perspective is articulated by John McIntyre: "It has always seemed to me inappropriate that uniformity should be implicitly assumed, when not overtly promulgated, as the ideal of ecumenical relations, especially when a fair case could be made for the retention of the existing denominations along the lines of the Pauline image [see 1 Cor. 12] but minus, of course, the thinly-veiled mutual disparagement" (McIntyre, *The Shape of Pneumatology: Studies in the Doctrine of the Holy Spirit* [Edinburgh: T&T Clark, 1997], 4).

Obviously, the issues here are complex. But it does seem to me that much is lost if, when thinking of the Spirit's work, we suppose that this work need not centrally include an efficacious interior impulsion to visible and institutional unity in one church.[10] The Spirit's powerful and unceasing gift of love should produce concrete ecclesial unity. Put another way, we can hardly expect the Spirit to leave multiplicity as he finds it. Rather, if the Spirit is truly Love and Gift, then the Spirit cannot fail to unite humans into the one body of Jesus Christ.[11] This will be so even if for various reasons many people who share in the Spirit are not visibly united in the one church during their earthly lives, and it will also be so even at historical moments when the church is most in need of a renewal of holiness and a deepening of unity. As Anselm Kyongsuk Min evocatively remarks, "The personhood of the Spirit lies precisely in the power and activity of relating, reconciling, and in general creating communion and solidarity in the life of both the immanent and economic Trinity."[12]

No Christian theologian, to my knowledge, goes so far as to deny the Holy Spirit's unitive mission in the church. Likewise, although some Christian theologians in the past have mistakenly limited salvation to the visible confines of the church,[13] it is important to affirm that the Spirit is at work

10. As Grant Macaskill points out, "The imagery of the church as eschatological temple is consistently linked to the unity of the church. At the heart of this is the distinctive eschatological identity of the church as a new reality containing both Jew and Gentile. The union of these with one another is founded upon their union with the Messiah and their shared experience of the Spirit" (Macaskill, *Union with Christ in the New Testament* [Oxford: Oxford University Press, 2013], 170). Emmanuel Durand, OP, extends this point to encompass perichoretic unity: "Ecclesial communion therefore proves to be entirely relative to Trinitarian perichoresis which, as both its model and final cause, is mediated by the closely related missions of Christ and the Holy Spirit" (Durand, "Perichoresis: A Key Concept for Balancing Trinitarian Theology," in Maspero and Woźniak, *Rethinking Trinitarian Theology*, 177–92, at 192). Durand references Heribert Mühlen, *Una mystica persona: Eine Person in vielen Personen* (Paderborn: Schöningh, 1964).

11. This unity does not, of course, exclude real multiplicity. As Avery Dulles, SJ, points out, "The unity of the Church, far from being monolithic, includes a great variety of ecclesial types, oriental and occidental, having their own liturgical and spiritual traditions. . . . The Church, as Christ's body, must possess different organs and members (1 Cor. 12:12–31). The Holy Spirit apportions different gifts to different groups so that the universal church may be built up in vigor and unity" (Dulles, "The Trinity and Christian Unity," in *God the Holy Trinity: Reflections on Christian Faith and Practice*, ed. Timothy George [Grand Rapids: Baker Academic, 2006], 69–82, at 81).

12. Anselm Kyongsuk Min, "Solidarity of Others in the Power of the Holy Spirit: Pneumatology in a Divided World," in *Advents of the Spirit: An Introduction to the Current Study of Pneumatology*, ed. Bradford E. Hinze and D. Lyle Dabney (Milwaukee: Marquette University Press, 2001), 416–43, at 418. The Spirit's work of unity always consists in deepening the charity of believers, and therefore this work can at times be "subversive" and surprising, but never in a deconstructive way.

13. This mistaken position is quite different from affirming that all salvation requires unity with Christ, and thus with his church, at least through some kind of implicit faith. For discussion,

among diverse peoples bringing them to salvation even though they do not adhere to the visible church of Christ. Certainly the Holy Spirit is connected not only with unity but also—and at the same time—with multiplicity.[14] But if we do not place the emphasis on the unity that the Holy Spirit brings, then we seriously underestimate the biblical testimony to the unitive power of the Spirit's work.[15] Lukas Vischer rightly observes that we cannot "expect from

see Avery Dulles, in his *Church and Society: The Laurence J. McGinley Lectures, 1988–2007* (New York: Fordham University Press, 2008), "Christ among the Religions" and "Who Can Be Saved?," 360–72 and 522–34. In the latter essay Dulles suggests that the phrase "implicit faith" is inadequate: "Wisely, in my opinion, the popes and councils have avoided talk about implicit faith, a term that is vague and ambiguous. They do speak of persons who are sincerely seeking for the truth and of others who have found it in Christ. They make it clear that sufficient grace is offered to all and that God will not turn away those who do everything within their power to find God and live according to his law. We may count on him to lead such persons to the faith needed for salvation" (Dulles, "Who Can Be Saved?," 530). Granting the vagueness of "implicit faith," I think that the approach taken by Thomas Aquinas in *Summa theologiae* II-II, q. 2, a. 7, ad 3 and elsewhere remains useful, so long as it is clearly extended to the epoch after Christ's coming. See also Stephen Bullivant, *The Salvation of Atheists and Catholic Dogmatic Theology* (Oxford: Oxford University Press, 2012), including his critique (unpersuasive in my view) of "implicit faith" on 184; Ralph Martin, *Will Many Be Saved? What Vatican II Actually Teaches and Its Implications for the New Evangelization* (Grand Rapids: Eerdmans, 2012), esp. 36–53 for its examination of Aquinas's viewpoint and its later development; Francis Sullivan, SJ, *Salvation outside of the Church? Tracing the History of the Catholic Response* (Eugene, OR: Wipf & Stock, 2002); Roch Kereszty, OCist, *Christianity among Other Religions: Apologetics in a Contemporary Context* (New York: Alba House, 2006).

14. See the 2007 Ravenna Statement of the Joint International Commission for the Theological Dialogue between the Roman Catholic Church and the Orthodox Church: http://www .vatican.va/roman_curia/pontifical_councils/chrstuni/ch_orthodox_docs/rc_pc_chrstuni_doc _20071013_documento-ravenna_en.html.

15. See also Tjørhom, *Visible Church—Visible Unity*, 64–65, 74–93. On page 74 Tjørhom quotes an important passage from the Roman Catholic/Lutheran Joint Commission, *Facing Unity: Models, Forms and Phases of Catholic-Lutheran Church Fellowship* (Geneva: Lutheran World Federation, 1985), §3: "Unity needs a visible outward form which is able to encompass the element of inner differentiation and spiritual diversity as well as the element of historical change and development." See also Harding Meyer, *That All May Be One: Perceptions and Models of Ecumenicity*, trans. William G. Rusch (Grand Rapids: Eerdmans, 1999); Yves Congar, OP, *Diversity and Communion*, trans. John Bowden (Mystic, CT: Twenty-Third Publications, 1985), esp. chap. 16 on "'Reconciled Diversity.' How Would Möhler Have Reacted?," In *Diversity and Communion*, 150, Congar quotes an insightful passage from Yves de Montcheuil, SJ, "La liberté et la diversité dans l'Unité," in *L'Église est une: Hommage à Moehler*, ed. Pierre Chaillet (Paris: Bloud & Gay, 1939), 234–54, at 252, where de Montcheuil notes that the Catholic Church "has always rejected these attempts at ecumenism which at root are only an attempt to realize a federation of schisms, each of which agrees to recognize the legitimacy of the others." Congar and de Montcheuil are indebted to Johann Adam Möhler's *Unity of the Church or the Principle of Catholicism: Presented in the Spirit of the Church Fathers of the First Three Centuries*, trans. Peter C. Erb (Washington, DC: Catholic University of America Press, 1995). In Chaillet, *L'Église est une*, see also the essays by A.-D. Sertillanges, OP, Karl Adam, Joseph-Rupert Geiselmann, Pierre Chaillet, SJ, Stephan Lösch, and Yves Congar.

the New Testament a consistent doctrine of the unity of the church," in the sense of a fully developed doctrine of church order, but we can expect from the New Testament a consistent insistence that the church is in fact one.[16] Vischer strongly affirms the New Testament's insistence upon the church's concrete unity: "There can be only one church of Jesus Christ. All the images used in the New Testament confirm it: the church is one body, one people, one temple, one bride. Separation is contrary to the nature of the church."[17]

In making the case for the primacy of the Holy Spirit's unifying mission, I first examine Kendall Soulen's *The Divine Name(s) and the Holy Trinity*, whose main thesis consists in an urgent call for the church to recognize the ongoing value of the divine name "YHWH."[18] My discussion of Soulen's book

16. Lukas Vischer, "Difficulties in Looking to the New Testament for Guidance," in Lukas Vischer, Ulrich Luz, and Christian Link, *Unity of the Church in the New Testament and Today*, trans. James E. Crouch (Grand Rapids: Eerdmans, 2010), 7–27, at 12.

17. Ibid., 26. Vischer's aim is to restore the unity of the separated churches, and he favors doing this through the model of a "conciliar fellowship," which he thinks "best reflects the witness of the New Testament" (ibid., 27). In the same volume, Christian Link restates the thesis of Walter Bauer (without here citing him): "The widely held idea that an originally existing unity was destroyed in the course of the centuries due to the guilt of Christians is much too simple, and we need to abandon it. The New Testament shows us a different picture. Even stronger than the unifying forces, there are sundering centrifugal forces that determine the earliest stage of Christianity" (Link, "The Unity Movement: Christian Fellowship in the Oecumene," in Vischer, Luz, and Link, *Unity of the Church in the New Testament and Today*, 163–248, at 193). But can or should we suppose that the "sundering centrifugal forces" are stronger and more determinative than the "unifying forces," above all the Holy Spirit? For a historical argument against Link's position, in the form that it takes in Bauer (and in Bart Ehrman), see Andreas J. Köstenberger and Michael J. Kruger, *The Heresy of Orthodoxy: How Contemporary Culture's Fascination with Diversity Has Reshaped Our Understanding of Early Christianity* (Wheaton: Crossway, 2010). See also Walter Bauer, *Orthodoxy and Heresy in Earliest Christianity*, ed. Robert A. Kraft and Gerhard Krobel, 2nd ed. (Mifflintown, PA: Sigler, 1996).

18. See R. Kendall Soulen, *The Divine Name(s) and the Holy Trinity*, vol. 1, *Distinguishing the Voices* (Louisville: Westminster John Knox, 2011). For a somewhat similar argument—though much less nuanced and with a different name in view—see Kornel Zathureczky, *The Messianic Disruption of Trinitarian Theology* (Lanham, MD: Lexington, 2009). Zathureczky focuses not on the name "YHWH" but on the name "Jesus Messiah." He argues that Christians should now speak of "Jesus Messiah" rather than "Jesus Christ," in order to recall the messianic character of Christianity and thereby avoid the totalitarian and universalizing temptation of this-worldly Christendoms. In my view, Jesus instituted a new way of naming God/YHWH, specifically by including us, in the Holy Spirit, in his filial naming of God as Father. Christopher Seitz states insightfully, "YHWH, the Holy One of Israel, is the Father, and the Son, and the Holy Spirit not because such was required for a proper estimate of Jesus Christ as God or the Spirit as God, but because this was held to be what the literal sense of the Old Testament required when its deliverances were properly grasped, in the light of Christ, as conveyed by the Holy Spirit" (Seitz, "The Trinity in the Old Testament," in *The Oxford Handbook of the Trinity*, ed. Gilles Emery, OP, and Matthew Levering [Oxford: Oxford University Press, 2011], 28–39, at 38). Even so, I agree with Soulen that Christians should honor and remember God's name "YHWH." The name "YHWH" reminds Christians that God's oneness, as confessed by Israel

focuses on the connections that Soulen makes between the Holy Spirit and multiplicity. In light of Soulen's emphasis on multiplicity, I turn to Thomas Aquinas for an exposition of the Holy Spirit's relationship to unity. Aquinas offers insight into the Spirit's characteristic work of building up the church as a visible communion of self-giving charity, a visible unity that is never an autonomous possession of the church but instead must always be received anew from the Spirit.[19]

Kendall Soulen and the Holy Spirit

The Holy Spirit, the "Pneumatological" Pattern of Divine Naming, and Multiplicity

Arguing that the New Testament and the Niceno-Constantinopolitan Creed develop three patterns of naming the Trinity, Kendall Soulen terms these three patterns "theological," "christological," and "pneumatological." Although my main interest here is in what Soulen associates with the "pneumatological" pattern, it will help if I describe all three. The "theological" pattern is oriented, via the Shema, toward the mysterious and undefinable Tetragrammaton: "One God, the Father, from whom are all things and for whom we exist" (1 Cor. 8:6). Soulen states that the "theological" pattern expresses "the essentially anonymous God who receives every divine predicate even as he transcends them all."[20] The "christological" pattern revolves around Jesus

---

in the Shema (Deut. 6:4) and by the prophets (cf. Isa. 43:10), does not mean a less personal, less loving, less communicative God.

19. See, among other studies, Denis-Dominique le Pivain, FSSP, *L'action du saint-Esprit dans le Commentaire de l'Évangile de saint Jean par saint Thomas d'Aquin* (Paris: Téqui, 2006), 158–61; E. Vauthier, "Le Saint-Esprit principe d'unité de l'Église d'après Saint Thomas d'Aquin: Corps mystique et inhabitation du Saint-Esprit," *Mélanges de science religieuse* 5 (1948): 175–96; 6 (1949): 57–80; George Sabra, *Thomas Aquinas' Vision of the Church* (Mainz: Matthias Grünewald Verlag, 1987), 100–104. Sabra considers Aquinas to be "the last great representative of a predominantly theological conception of Church unity," since "with Boniface VIII this theological conception of unity begins to yield place to one where juridical and sociological ideas dominate" (Sabra, *Thomas Aquinas' Vision of the Church*, 104). It is important, of course, not to place a theological conception of church unity in opposition to juridical and sociological elements that also characterize church unity. Le Pivain notes that for Aquinas, "The unity of the Church consists in this: it is 'unity of charity and unity of faith,' 'unity of faith and of sacraments.' This unity produces two fruits, both flowing from the action of the Holy Spirit. On the one hand, he gives peace, a complete peace, exterior and interior, peace with one's neighbor and with God, peace in oneself. . . . On the other hand, it is accompanied by the joy that 'is obtained by unity of mind'" (Le Pivain, *L'action du saint-Esprit*, 161). Le Pivain points out that the unifying work of the Spirit is attributed to him because he is Love in person.

20. Soulen, *Divine Name(s) and the Holy Trinity*, 54.

Christ and the way in which he names his Father. The name "Father, Son, and Holy Spirit" comes from the words of Jesus and has its intelligibility in light of his Sonship. Jesus promises that the Father "will give you another Counselor, to be with you forever" (John 14:16); this Counselor is the Holy Spirit. Indeed, it is not only the Father but also the Son who sends the Spirit: "If I do not go away, the Counselor will not come to you; but if I go, I will send him to you" (John 16:7). In short, both the mysterious Tetragrammaton and the "philosophical" attributes of God (being, good, one, etc., attributes whose meaning is analogous and therefore utterly ineffable) belong to the "theological" pattern, while the "christological" pattern names the Trinity as Father, Son, and Holy Spirit.

The "pneumatological" pattern, then, describes the way in which Christians have used multiple images to name the Trinity. The sheer variety of triads, rooted in the imagination of Christian authors as they sought to make the Trinity intelligible, forms the "pneumatological" pattern. Soulen observes that like some Hellenistic philosophers, Christians believe that God is transcendent and unnamable. It follows that even though names of creaturely perfections can be aptly applied to God when stripped of their creaturely limitations, humans nonetheless cannot conceive of the infinite reality that these names describe. Like the worshipers of pagan gods, however, Christians allow for many names for God. Christians do not follow the pagans in attempting to worship the one God under many aspects or names, such as Zeus, Apollo, and Athena. But once freed from myth, metaphorical names serve an important purpose. Thus the Old Testament names God "Mighty Warrior, Rock, King, God, my Shepherd, a Stronghold, Powerful, Upright, Pure, and so on."[21]

Metaphorical names proliferate in Christian naming of the Trinity. To give just one example among many, Basil the Great describes the Trinity as Glory, Image, and Light.[22] Regarding such names, Soulen comments, "Here, then, we encounter the Bible's own native version of divine polyonymy, in the plethora of divine names that stand in apposition to the divine name. These names elucidate the divine name without competing with it or taking its place."[23] Soulen thinks that without a proper appreciation of the other two modes of naming the Trinity, this "pneumatological" mode moves in a pagan direction. But in the context of the "theological" and "christological" modes, the proliferation of "pneumatological" metaphorical names can be understood and appreciated.

21. Ibid., 56.
22. See Basil the Great, *On the Holy Spirit*, trans. Stephen Hildebrand (Yonkers, NY: St. Vladimir's Seminary Press, 2011), 26.64, p. 103.
23. Soulen, *Divine Name(s) and the Holy Trinity*, 56.

Soulen grounds the connection between the Holy Spirit and multiplicity in the event of Pentecost. When the Holy Spirit came upon the apostles, they "began to speak in other tongues, as the Spirit gave them utterance" (Acts 2:4). Assembled in Jerusalem for the Jewish feast of Pentecost, the people wondered how this group of Galileans could speak so fluently to "each of us in his own native language," so that "we hear them telling in our own tongues the mighty works of God" (Acts 2:6, 11). The pattern by which we imaginatively form triadic names for the Trinity is, as Soulen says, "characterized by the extraordinary variety of its linguistic expressions drawn from the breadth of human experience across time and space."[24] This "extraordinary variety" seems to fit with how the Holy Spirit moved the apostles to proclaim in many different languages the saving works of God.

In the Niceno-Constantinopolitan Creed, Soulen observes, this variety is instanced in the phrase "God of God, light of light, true God of true God." This phrase specifically sought to counter Arian theology, and Soulen connects this with the way in which the "pneumatological" pattern of naming the Trinity exhibits a "high degree of context-sensitivity."[25] Thus the Holy Spirit's eliciting of a multiplicity of tongues for the purpose of evangelization suggests to Soulen a particular pattern of trinitarian naming, one that values imagination, context, and multiplicity. He adds that the name "Holy Spirit" can be read in any one of the three modes: in the theological mode, it points to the Tetragrammaton because of the ineffability of "holiness" and its association with YHWH; in the christological mode, it flows from Jesus's usage and is related to Father and Son; and in the pneumatological mode, it uses terms that are generic and that are thereby open to a multiplicity of interpretation.

In addition to the passage from Acts, Soulen justifies his connection between the Holy Spirit and multiplicity on the grounds of Luke 19:37–40. That passage describes Jesus's triumphant entrance into Jerusalem on Palm Sunday. First, "the whole multitude of the disciples began to rejoice and praise God with a loud voice for all the mighty works that they had seen" (Luke 19:37). They proclaim Jesus as the "King" who enters Jerusalem "in the name of the Lord" (Luke 19:38). Second, Jesus responds to the Pharisees who ask Jesus to moderate the praise that his disciples are giving him: "I tell you, if these were silent, the very stones would cry out" (Luke 19:40). The "multitude" of disciples, the many "mighty works" to which they testify, and the notion of the stones crying out all indicate, in Soulen's view, the role

24. Ibid., 20.
25. Ibid., 42.

and character of the Holy Spirit. As he observes, "The Holy Spirit magnifies 'all the deeds of power' (Luke 19:37) that proceed from God, speaking through a multiplicity of cries and shouts and voices. It is free to speak not only through humans, but also through rocks, even as it is permanently tied to neither. It speaks by enabling others to speak, freeing them to bless the one whom God has blessed, and to receive his blessings in turn."[26]

Here Soulen shows how his use of the adjective "pneumatological" fits with his doctrine of the Holy Spirit. Just as the "pneumatological" pattern of divine naming encourages multiple names, drawn from human imagination, that fit particular contexts, so also the Holy Spirit speaks in a multitude of ways. The Son speaks in Jesus Christ, but the Spirit can speak through many different humans, as well as through rocks (if the Spirit so wishes). The Spirit's speaking belongs to the Spirit in a manner that differs from how Jesus's speaking is that of the Son. The Son speaks by his own words; the Spirit speaks by enabling and liberating others' words, so that others are able to worship the Son who is blessed by the Father. Whereas when we think of the Son we think of one voice, when we think of the Spirit we must think of the work by which many voices come to praise the Son (and through the Son, the Father) in diverse ways. The Holy Spirit is associated with freedom because he is not tied down to one voice, but instead frees many voices to praise God. Soulen states, "The Spirit speaks *indirectly*, through the inspired voices of those blessed by God."[27]

The multiplicity that Soulen has in view is by no means a chaotic multiplicity. On the contrary, it is a multiplicity that is *united* by divine blessing. In his theology of the Holy Spirit, Soulen argues that the Holy Spirit's "voice resonates with the mystery of *divine blessing* that surrounds and glorifies the divine life."[28] The Holy Spirit's voice makes itself heard in many voices because divine blessing manifests itself in a multitude of humans (and other creatures). The characteristic mark of the Holy Spirit's work consists in a multitude of people experiencing and proclaiming the gift of divine blessing. The presence of the Holy Spirit can be known when many people testify to blessings received from God. The Holy Spirit's "voice" is never separated from those of the Father and the Son, since the blessing that we receive is a trinitarian one. Yet the voice of the Holy Spirit has a special connection with the multiplicity of languages, perspectives, and persons in whom God's blessing is instantiated.

26. Ibid., 169–70.
27. Ibid., 168; for Old Testament context, see 158.
28. Ibid., 176.

Since this connection with multiplicity characterizes the Holy Spirit, the pattern of trinitarian naming that merits the title "pneumatological" also must be connected with multiplicity. Soulen describes the "pneumatological" pattern as having "a special affinity with open-ended enlistment of ordinary forms of speech," that is, with metaphor.[29] It is the breadth made possible by metaphor that, for Soulen, best depicts the way in which the Holy Spirit's gift of blessing manifests itself in a multitude of different persons at so many different places and times. Because of the breadth of this mediation of divine blessing, the multiplicity associated with the Spirit is "open-ended" and linked with the "ordinary." The Holy Spirit pushes into the realm of daily life by sharing divine blessing, and we hear the Holy Spirit's distinctive "voice" when we hear human voices praising God in accessible and context-specific images.

Again, the many voices of the Galilean followers of Jesus at the feast of Pentecost exemplify what Soulen has in view. Their many voices, Soulen observes, reflect the "distinctive tenor" of the Holy Spirit's voice.[30] The Holy Spirit comes not upon one or two, but upon many, "enabling everyone to speak ordinary languages in an extraordinary way."[31] The Holy Spirit does two things: it transforms many persons, and it makes the "ordinary" extraordinary. The transformation of Jesus's first followers leads to the transformation of many others: "The miracle of Pentecost is as much about the capacity of the nations to *hear* the message of the Galileans, as it is about the backwater countryfolk themselves."[32] When they hear the message, they proclaim "the mighty works of God" (Acts 2:11), a Greek phrase that Soulen argues refers as much to the glory of God as to his works. The Holy Spirit leads the crowd to rejoice with the apostles in God and his mighty works; Soulen imagines "the plenitude of divine names and praises that filled the air."[33] Multiplicity and plenitude are the marks of the Holy Spirit and of pneumatological naming of God.

Peter, in his speech at Pentecost, proposes that his audience can know the Spirit because Christ has poured out the Spirit, or specifically because Christ "has poured out this which you see and hear" (Acts 2:33). Soulen reasons, then, that the Spirit is in a certain sense equivalent with "this which you see and hear": "The phrase names the Spirit in terms of what the assembly has experienced for itself: the hurly-burly in the streets, the strange eloquence of peasants, and the wonder of hearing of God's splendors recounted in one's

29. Ibid.
30. Ibid., 185.
31. Ibid.
32. Ibid., 186.
33. Ibid.

own native tongue."[34] Naming the Spirit comes through the multiplicity of the Spirit's effects and through the Spirit's transformation of the ordinary into something extraordinary. Soulen concludes that "it is characteristic of the Holy Spirit to rest on the ordinary wherever it may be, bless it, and transform it into praise" of God and his works.[35]

Late in his book, Soulen devotes a full chapter to exploring the pneumatological pattern of trinitarian speech, "characterized by a limitless ability to unfurl the blessings of the triune life in ever new forms of speech, which multiply and coexist while always leaving room for more."[36] The emphasis again is on limitless multiplicity. Jesus's signs of power and parables, not least when read figuratively, provide examples of this fruitful multiplicity. So does the use of metaphors in describing God the Trinity. Soulen defines the pneumatological pattern of divine naming "as a kind of nonidentical *repetition* of God's name and its ineffable cloud of connotation" and as a way of praising "God's superabundant glory and blessing, conveyed by a limitless variety of terms drawn from many spheres of life."[37] The pneumatological pattern's presence in the Old Testament is found in such names as "El-Roi," "Elohim," "El," "El-Olam," "El-Shaddai," and "Lady Wisdom." The pneumatological pattern's presence in the New Testament is reflected the Gospel of John's "I am" sayings, where Jesus names himself as Bread of Life, Light of the World, True Vine, and so forth. With Origen, Soulen argues that in this sense, God has countless names. Jesus also is named Son, Son of God, Word, Lord, Christ, and Image, among other names.

This multiplicity of names is reflected in the creativity of the saints and liturgies of the church (as well as in the creativity of numerous contemporary theologians), with their gift for devising triads of names applied to the Trinity. Praising this multiplicity and elevation of the ordinary, Soulen observes that "a great advantage of this pattern of naming is precisely the extraordinary breadth with which it intersects human language and experience in the world."[38] Like the Holy Spirit, the pneumatological pattern transforms the ordinary in its countless individual instantiations. The Holy Spirit and the pneumatological pattern have no fear of multiplicity, creativity, and adaptability, but instead embrace and employ—as at Pentecost—"the general forms of speech

34. Ibid., 188.
35. Ibid., 189. Soulen aptly describes this a bit further on: "The Spirit, who gathers up the wounded words of ordinary life and transforms them into hymns to the everlasting Trinity" (ibid., 193).
36. Ibid., 233.
37. Ibid., 240.
38. Ibid., 251.

and possibilities of speech present in the discourse of all peoples, tribes, and nations."[39] The multiplicity associated with the Holy Spirit can be seen in how the Holy Spirit appears in the world; this occurs "in an endless variety of ways, now as a dove descending, now as the sound of wind roaring, now as tongues of fire dancing, now as the gift of speech in ecstasy."[40] But this multiplicity, it should be noted, does not undermine the Holy Spirit's "constancy," since the Holy Spirit always comes forth from the Father and bestows new life.[41]

The Holy Spirit and Unity

Is Soulen right to associate the Spirit so strongly with multiplicity, while not equally emphasizing the Spirit's association with unity in truth and charity? Soulen does not deny, of course, that pneumatological multiplicity coheres; nor does he think that the forgetting of the Tetragrammaton utterly destroyed the church's ability to praise the Triune God. A gentle moderation is the hallmark of Soulen's rhetoric. Even so, I think that more attention to the Spirit's promotion of unity in truth, to the Spirit as the bond of love, would be beneficial. The Spirit unites humans to the incarnate Son. The Spirit enables the church to "remember" all that Jesus said (see John 14:26) and to receive the harmonious "peace" that Christ brings (John 14:27).[42] The Spirit is "the Spirit

39. Ibid., 252.

40. Ibid., 254.

41. Ibid. As a contemporary example of the "pneumatological" mode of trinitarian naming, Soulen cites Elizabeth Johnson, CSJ's *She Who Is: The Mystery of God in Feminist Theological Discourse* (New York: Crossroad, 1992). For Soulen, Johnson "is a champion of the unsubstitutable importance of the pneumatological pattern of naming the three persons by using an open-ended variety of context-specific ternaries that always leaves room for more" (ibid., 105–6). Soulen notes, however, that Johnson's treatment of the Tetragrammaton does not give sufficient place to the "theological" mode of naming, with the result that her book is open to the accusation that she turns all divine names into culturally constructed metaphors. Indeed, Soulen finds, "For Johnson, the differences between the three patterns are only passing distinctions, for all ultimately express the pneumatological pattern, which celebrates the nameless God of many names" (ibid., 118). Whether Johnson's book contributes to a strong pneumatology is doubtful to me; for one thing, she envisions the church's history as one in which the Holy Spirit's presence has been quite weak.

42. In quoting John 14:26, it is worth recalling the perspective that historical-critical scholarship brings to bear on this text, as, for example, in the work of David E. Aune:

> Christians believed, as did the Judaism from which they emerged, that because they were the people of God they had received special wisdom and insight from God (1 Cor. 1:18–31; Eph. 1:9; *Barn.* 5:3; Ignatius *Eph.* 14:1; Polycarp *Phil.* 12:1). This special insight was often attributed to the revelatory influence of the Spirit of God, believed to be present as the eschatological gift of God in the midst of the believing community (1 Cor. 2:6–16; 1 John 2:20, 27). Various phases of early Christianity understood this gift of divine insight in very particular ways. The Johannine community, for example, was convinced the Spirit enabled them to understand the true meaning of the words of

of truth" (John 15:26; 16:13), and even though truth divides, it also and more importantly unites. It is the Spirit who, sent by the Father, unites the church.

In the Gospel of John, Jesus emphasizes unity in a manner that surely has the Spirit's work in view, now that Jesus is giving his disciples the Spirit. In his Farewell Discourse, he states, "The glory which you [the Father] have given me I have given to them, that they may be one even as we are one, I in them and you in me, that they may become perfectly one, so that the world may know that you have sent me and have loved them even as you have loved me" (John 17:22–23).[43] Whatever else it might mean, Jesus's statement certainly does not envision a multitude of Christian churches that are not even in communion with one another. Rather, Jesus has given his disciples "glory" from the Father so that "they may become perfectly one" for the sake of the conversion of the world. This emphasis on ecclesial unity, a unity in truth and love, is further underscored by the "peace" (John 20:21) that the risen Jesus gives to his disciples when he breathes the Spirit on them and sends them forth into the world. The peace given by Christ is connected with the church's ability, in the Spirit, to mediate the forgiveness won by Christ, an ability that offers hope for renewed unity to a world fragmented by sin: "Receive the Holy Spirit. If you forgive the sins of any, they are forgiven; if you retain the sins of any, they are retained" (John 20:22–23).

When the Holy Spirit comes upon the people at Pentecost, we again find unity emphasized in a manner that needs at least as much attention as does multiplicity.[44] The Spirit comes upon the disciples when "they were all together in one place" (Acts 2:1). The result of the Spirit being poured upon the disciples is that "the multitude came together," even if this means simply that a crowd gathered (Acts 2:6). Peter delivers his speech not merely to a differentiated multitude, but to "all the house of Israel" (Acts 2:36). Furthermore, Peter urges them to be baptized so as to receive forgiveness in Christ Jesus and to

---

Jesus (John 14:26; 16:12–15; cf. 2:22; 12:16). Here "charismatic exegesis" focuses on the oral transmission of the Jesus traditions, presumably to legitimate the particular understanding of that tradition cherished by the Johannine church. (Aune, "Charismatic Exegesis in Early Judaism and Early Christianity," in *Apocalypticism, Prophecy, and Magic in Early Christianity: Collected Essays* [Grand Rapids: Baker Academic, 2008], 280–99, at 294–95)

The key underlying question here is whether the Holy Spirit is real, a question that historical-critical scholarship brackets.

43. For discussion, see Durand, "Perichoresis," 190–91.

44. See Raniero Cantalamessa, *The Mystery of Pentecost*, trans. Glen S. Davis (Collegeville, MN: Liturgical Press, 2001), chap. 1: "'And They Began to Speak in Different Tongues': The Lukan Pentecost and the Spirit of Unity." Cantalamessa states that for Luke (and for Paul in 1 Cor. 12:13), "the Spirit that came upon the apostles at Pentecost and that since then continues to guide the path of the Church in history is fundamentally a Spirit of unity" (ibid., 5).

"receive the gift of the Holy Spirit" (Acts 2:38). Peter proclaims this word of unity "to you and to your children and to all who are far off, every one whom the Lord our God calls to him" (Acts 2:39). When the people receive baptism, they enter fully into the unity of the church, a sacramental unity in truth and love: "And they devoted themselves to the apostles' teaching and fellowship, to the breaking of bread and the prayers. . . . And all who believed were together and had all things in common" (Acts 2:42, 44).

This emphasis on unity continues throughout Acts; consider Paul's farewell speech to the Ephesian elders, in which he urges, "Take heed to yourselves and to all the flock, in which the Holy Spirit has made you guardians, to feed the church of the Lord which he obtained with his own blood" (Acts 20:28).[45] The same emphasis appears also in the letters of Paul. Paul gives praise to "the Spirit of holiness" (Rom. 1:4), and holiness is unitive. Paul affirms that "we have peace with God through our Lord Jesus Christ" because "God's love has been poured into our hearts through the Holy Spirit who has been given to us" (Rom. 5:1, 5). The Spirit of God unites us as God's children: "All who are led by the Spirit of God are sons of God" (Rom. 8:14). The Spirit unites us in the truth that Jesus is Lord: "No one can say 'Jesus is Lord' except by the Holy Spirit" (1 Cor. 12:3). Even in giving diverse gifts, the Spirit works for the "common good" (1 Cor. 12:7) and draws together those who "are inspired by one and the same Spirit" (1 Cor. 12:11). Paul highlights the connection between the Holy Spirit, baptism, and the unity of the church: "For by one Spirit we were all baptized into one body—Jews or Greeks, slaves or free—and all were made to drink of one Spirit" (1 Cor. 12:13).[46] The key is that the Holy Spirit builds up the church (see 1 Cor. 14:12). For this reason, "the fruit of the Spirit is love, joy, peace, patience, kindness, goodness, faithfulness, gentleness, self-control" (Gal. 5:22–23).[47] These fruits are unitive.

---

45. See also Stanley E. Porter's chapter on "Paul and the Holy Spirit in Acts," in *The Paul of Acts: Essays in Literary Criticism, Rhetoric, and Theology* (Tübingen: Mohr-Siebeck, 1999), 67–97, esp. 86–89.

46. On 1 Corinthians 12 (and its context), note Macaskill, *Union with Christ in the New Testament*, 158: "Paul's concern in these verses is to emphasize the singularity of the Spirit and the consequent unity of the body. These, of course, are the same concerns that we observed in Ephesians and that we have seen also to govern Paul's association of the temple and Spirit in 1 Cor 3:16–17. Similarly, we have seen the connection between the body and the temple in 1 Cor 6:15–19. . . . Christ is the one whose identity governs and integrates the body: the church is baptized 'into' (εἰς) his body, thus being located 'in him' and, as such, identified as the body *of Christ*. The Spirit is portrayed, as in Ephesians, as being in the role of the one who actualizes."

47. See John M. G. Barclay, "Grace and the Transformation of Agency in Christ," in *Redefining First-Century Jewish and Christian Identities: Essays in Honor of Ed Parish Sanders*, ed. Fabian E. Udoh et al. (Notre Dame, IN: University of Notre Dame Press, 2008), 372–89, at 383.

An emphasis on unity does not undermine an appreciation for multiplicity, and so my point is not to negate the positive things that Soulen says. The two go hand in hand, since ecclesial unity involves multiple individuals who share their diverse gifts. Yet interpreting the event of Pentecost (for example) in light of its insistence on unity as the "gift of the Holy Spirit" (Acts 2:38) makes a difference for how we understand pneumatological multiplicity. Soulen, as we saw, thinks of the pattern of trinitarian speech associated with the Holy Spirit as "characterized by a limitless ability to unfurl the blessings of the triune life in ever new forms of speech, which multiply and coexist while always leaving room for more."[48] I agree that there should exist (and that there does exist) a profusion of metaphorical and analogical triads by which the church names the Trinity. But this emphasis on limitless multiplicity should be combined with an equal emphasis on the concrete unity in truth and love brought about by the Holy Spirit.[49] It seems to me that any pattern meriting the name "pneumatological" needs to be as much or more about this unity, across time and space, as it is about multiplicity.

In making this case, Thomas Aquinas's theology of the Holy Spirit and unity (divine and ecclesial) has much to offer. George Sabra observes that it is "a forceful and clear position of Thomas' that the constitutive action of

48. Soulen, *Divine Name(s) and the Holy Trinity*, 233.

49. As Raniero Cantalamessa puts it, "The Church is universal not only when it aims to reach 'the ends of the earth' but also when it tends towards its center which is the head of the body, the risen Christ. In this sense, universality and unity coincide and the Spirit of unity is also the Spirit of universality of the Church" (Cantalamessa, *Mystery of Pentecost*, 6). Discussing the "pneumatic ecclesiology" of Jacques Benigne Bossuet, whom he terms "a firm Roman Catholic chauvinist," Ephraim Radner suggests that Bossuet in effect substitutes the papacy for the Holy Spirit and turns the church's words, in toto, into the speech of the Holy Spirit; see Radner, "Holy Spirit and Unity," 211–12. Radner comments, "Under this scheme, 'unity' becomes synonymous with the Roman church itself, organized under and led by the pope. . . . Of course, this begs the question as to whether institutional and confessional cohesion *do* constitute 'unity' in Christ" (ibid., 212). Certainly, "institutional and confessional cohesion" is not the sole constituent of "'unity' in Christ," but I do not see why such cohesion would not be a significant constituent of unity in Christ. In my view, the New Testament makes clear that it is so, and the church fathers also considered it to be so. Further, why should there not be a Petrine ministry that, within the apostolic church, serves unity—though this does not entail that "unity" is strictly "synonymous with the Roman church itself, rather than with the Spirit's work in Christ's Body"? It seems unfair to deem Bossuet a "Roman Catholic chauvinist," despite his flaws, just as it would be unfair to call Radner, with his deeply Anglican ecclesiology, an "Anglican chauvinist." These points are important not least because Radner deems Newman to be "Bossuet's direct ecclesiological heir" (ibid., 212n25). See Jacques Benigne Bossuet, *Exposition de la doctrine de l'Eglise Catholique sur les matiéres de controverse* (Paris: Guillaume Desprez, 1747); Bossuet, *Histoire des variations des églises protestantes*, 2 vols. (Paris: Sebastien Mabre-Cramoisy, 1688).

unifying the church is fundamentally the work of the Spirit."[50] In the following section, therefore, I employ Aquinas to investigate the unifying work of the Spirit, just as in the next chapter I take up his approach to the Spirit's sanctifying work (always in conjunction with the work of the incarnate Son). The most evident aspect of the Holy Spirit, of course, is that the Holy Spirit is neither the Son nor the Father. Aquinas wisely cautions against applying the term "diversity" (*diversitas*) to the divine persons, since the term is too easily taken to mean formal diversity (and thus diversity of essence).[51] The fact that the Spirit is neither the Father nor Son, however, certainly bears witness to an extraordinary multiplicity or plurality in God, without implying that God is divisible or quantitative.[52]

Despite the plurality entailed by the distinct personhood of the Spirit, Aquinas argues that the Holy Spirit is on the side of unity, both with respect to God and to the church. In this regard, Aquinas's pneumatology accords with the approach that we find in much contemporary Catholic ecclesiology. Thus Vatican II's Decree on Ecumenism, *Unitatis redintegratio*, connects the

50. Sabra, *Thomas Aquinas' Vision of the Church*, 104. See also Yves Congar, OP, *I Believe in the Holy Spirit*, trans. David Smith (New York: Crossroad, 1997), 3:123.

51. Note Thomas Aquinas, *De potentia* q. 9, a. 8, esp. ad 2:
> Although some doctors of the Church use the term difference [*differentiae*] in reference to God, it should not be employed as a general rule, or enlarged upon: because difference denotes a distinction of form, and this is impossible in God since God's form is his nature according to Augustine. But we must explain the term *difference* as standing for a *distinction* of the slightest kind: since some things are described as distinct in respect of a mere relation or even only logically. Again if we meet with the term diversity in connection to God, we must explain it in the same way: for instance, if we find it stated that the Person is diverse from that of the Son, we must take *diverse* to denote *distinct*. Yet in speaking of God we must be more wary of using the word *diverse* than the word *different*, because diversity refers more to an essential division: inasmuch as any multiplication whatsoever of forms causes a difference, whereas diversity arises only from substantial forms. (Aquinas, *On the Power of God* [*De Potentia*], trans. the English Dominican Fathers [Eugene, OR: Wipf & Stock, 2004], 3:148–49)

52. Discussing whether numerical terms are predicated "positively" of God the Trinity, Aquinas notes that just as unity can be either numerical or transcendental,
> there is a kind of division which altogether transcends the genus of quantity, and this is division according to formal opposition which has nothing to do with quantity. . . . Whereas the unity that is convertible with being, adds nothing to being except the negation of division, not that it signifies indivision only, but substance with indivision: for *one* is the same as individual being. In like manner the plurality that corresponds to this unity adds nothing to the *many things* except distinction, which consists in each one not being the other: and this they have not from anything added to them but from their proper forms. . . . Accordingly then, while *one* adds to *being* one negation inasmuch as a thing is undivided in itself; *plurality* adds two negations, inasmuch as a certain thing is undivided in itself, and distinct from another. (*De potentia* q. 9, a. 7 [Aquinas, *On the Power of God*, 3:141–42])

Holy Spirit with the unity of the church and the unity of the Trinity: "This is the sacred mystery of the unity of the Church, in Christ and through Christ, with the Holy Spirit energizing its various functions. The highest exemplar and source of this mystery is the unity, in the Trinity of persons, of one God, the Father and the Son in the Holy Spirit."[53] By examining how Aquinas connects the Holy Spirit with unity, we can gain deeper insight into this trinitarian ecclesiology of Love and Gift.

Aquinas on the Holy Spirit and the Church: Unity and Multiplicity

The Holy Spirit in the Triune God

Aquinas remarks that since the Holy Spirit differs from the Father and Son only by relative opposition according to the order of origin, the Spirit does not divide the unity of God. Certainly, each divine person possesses the divine essence in a distinct way according to his personal mode. For example, "The Son has the same omnipotence as the Father, but with another relation; the Father possessing power as *giving* signified when we say that he is able to beget; while the Son possesses the power of *receiving*, signified by saying that he can be begotten."[54] When Aquinas states that the divine persons are best construed as subsisting relations according to the order of origin, it is important to keep in view that relation in God is not an "accident," let alone something "adjacent" to the divine essence.[55] From this it follows that "in God essence is not really distinct from person; and yet . . . the persons are really distinguished from each other."[56] Put another way, the divine persons

---

53. *Unitatis Redintegratio*, §2, in *Vatican Council II*, vol. 1, *The Conciliar and Post Conciliar Documents*, new revised edition, ed. Austin Flannery, OP (Northport, NY: Costello, 1996), 452–70, at 455. Avery Dulles comments in this regard, "The fellowship of Christians cannot exactly replicate that of the divine persons. As human beings, we are distinct substances, and our relationships are, unlike those in the Godhead, accidents. We can acquire or lose these relationships without ceasing to be ourselves. Only in a metaphorical sense can we become, in the terminology of Acts 4:32, one in heart and soul. We are, and shall eternally remain, distinct substances with our own minds and wills" (Dulles, "Trinity and Christian Unity," 75). Dulles therefore considers "the unity of the divine persons as an ideal for us to approach from afar, the asymptotic goal of our hopes and endeavors" (ibid.).

54. I, q. 42, a. 6, ad 3.

55. I, q. 42, a. 6, ad 3.; cf. I, q. 29, a. 4.

56. I, q. 39, a. 1. For the common critique that this position makes Aquinas an essentialist, note Paul S. Fiddes, *Participating in God: A Pastoral Doctrine of the Trinity* (Louisville: Westminster John Knox, 2000), 35: "Aquinas explains the self-existence or subsistence of the relationships by the fact that they are identical with the one essence of God. They subsist because they are *the same* as the one divine substance which itself has self-existence. This gives ample warrant to the suspicion of Eastern theologians that talk of 'subsistent relations' is simply in aid of

are constituted by relative opposition in the order of origin, but these distinct relations (persons) subsist in the divine essence and indeed simply are the divine essence. The Holy Spirit's personal distinction from the Father and Son, therefore, does not mean that the Spirit lacks absolute identity, with respect to essence, with the Father and Son. The distinction of persons does not divide the unity of essence.[57]

In a second way too the Holy Spirit is on the side of unity in God. Namely, as we saw in our first two chapters, the procession of the Son as Word is complemented by the procession of the Spirit as Love. All three persons love, since God is love; in this sense "love" belongs to the divine essence. But the Father and the Son spirate Love, and the Spirit proceeds personally as Love. If the Spirit is "Love proceeding," then the Spirit is also "the bond of the Father and Son, inasmuch as he is Love."[58]

But why would the Father and the Son need a "bond" to unite them? It is not as though the Father would be separated from the Word without this Love. The Spirit does not bridge a chasm that has opened up or would otherwise open up between the Father and the Son.[59] Rather, the relation of Father to Son (and

---

the typical Western stress on the unity of God's essence; the 'relations' seem to be swallowed up into the one essence with the loss of any real threeness and 'otherness' of persons within God." On this point, see Gilles Emery, OP, "Essentialism or Personalism in the Treatise on God in St. Thomas Aquinas?," in *Trinity in Aquinas*, trans. Teresa Bede et al., 2nd ed. (Naples, FL: Sapientia Press of Ave Maria University, 2006), 165–208.

57. For discussion, see Gilles Emery, OP, *The Trinitarian Theology of Saint Thomas Aquinas*, trans. Francesca Aran Murphy (Oxford: Oxford University Press, 2007), 128–45; Declan Marmion and Rik Van Nieuwenhove, *An Introduction to the Trinity* (Cambridge: Cambridge University Press, 2011), 119–22; Denys Turner, *Thomas Aquinas: A Portrait* (New Haven: Yale University Press, 2013), 117–31; James E. Dolezal, "Trinity, Simplicity and the Status of God's Personal Relations," *International Journal of Systematic Theology* 16 (2014): 79–98. As Dolezal puts it, "The real identity between the divine essence and persons and between the persons and their distinguishing relations, which seems to be required by the doctrine of simplicity, does not necessarily do violence to the reality of the relations and distinctions among the divine persons. It only requires that we not regard these persons as distinct substances, or the relations as accidents, in God" (Dolezal, "Trinity, Simplicity and the Status of God's Personal Relations," 98).

58. I, q. 37, a. 1, ad 3.

59. For an example of this view, see Jürgen Moltmann, *The Trinity and the Kingdom* (San Francisco: Harper & Row, 1981). Hans Urs von Balthasar similarly speaks of "dereliction as a mode of eternal communion between Father and Son in the Spirit" (Balthasar, *Theo-Drama: Theological Dramatic Theory*, vol. 5, *The Last Act*, trans. Graham Harrison [San Francisco: Ignatius, 1998], 268). Balthasar approvingly quotes Adrienne von Speyr's statement that "since the Spirit is not separated like the Son from the Father, he can establish union in the separation of the Son without abolishing the separation" (*Last Act*, 262, from von Speyr's *John: Discourses of Controversy; Meditations on John 6–12*, trans. Brian McNeil [San Francisco: Ignatius, 1993], 381–82). For Balthasar's critique of Moltmann for conceiving of the cross as "the locus of the Trinity's authentic actualization," so that "God is entangled in the world process and becomes a tragic, mythological God," see Balthasar, *Theo-Drama: Theological Dramatic Theory*, vol. 4,

Son to Father) "is expressed in the Holy Spirit, as Love."[60] Aquinas explains that "the Father loves himself and the Son with one Love, and conversely."[61] Fully speaking himself in the Word, the Father loves what he speaks (and thus all that he himself is) as good; in this respect Aquinas comments that "the Holy Spirit proceeds as the love of the primal goodness whereby the Father loves himself and every creature."[62] The Word loves the Father as good with this same Love, since the Father and his Word differ only with respect to the relation paternity-filiation. As Aquinas remarks, therefore, "since the Father loves himself and the Son with one Love, and conversely, there is expressed in the Holy Spirit, as Love, the relation of the Father to the Son, and conversely, as that of the lover to the beloved."[63] The Father and the Son mutually love each other in the Holy Spirit, and so they are together the principle of the Spirit, although the Father is so as the primal source of the Son and thus also of the Spirit. For our purposes here, the point is that the Spirit can be called both the "mutual Love" of the Father and Son and the "bond" between the Father and Son, not in the sense of linking what would otherwise be separated, but in the sense of "proceeding from both."[64]

The Action, trans. Graham Harrison (San Francisco: Ignatius, 1994), 321–22. In the same place, Balthasar affirms that the Father's begetting of the Son, as "an action of absolute love," "implies such an incomprehensible and unique 'separation' of God from himself that it *includes* and grounds every other separation—be it never so dark and bitter"—a "distinction between Father and Son that is maintained and bridged by the Holy Spirit" (*Last Act*, 325, 327).

60. I, q. 37, a. 1, ad 3. Emmanuel Durand comments on this text, "The paternal-filial relation, which implies the love that characterizes its origin, is manifested in the Holy Spirit himself. . . . The generation of the Son is characterized by the relationship of perfect natural likeness that exists between the Father and the Son. In this respect, the Son is called the Image of the Father in a proper manner. However, the property of likeness in the Father-Son relation is not fully characterized if it is not understood as a basis for a communion of love. It is only in the Son that the Father recognizes the perfect (filial) image of his (paternal) goodness. This is accompanied by a love that is the measure of this unique likeness" (Durand, "Perichoresis," 188–89).

61. I, q. 37, a. 1, ad 3.
62. I, q. 37, a. 2, ad 3.
63. I, q. 37, a. 1, ad 3.
64. I, q. 37, a. 1, ad 3. Kenneth M. Loyer observes, "The Spirit is properly mutual love because the very love that the Spirit *in se* is, love in person who proceeds from the Father and the Son as the love of God's own goodness, constitutes the Spirit's relation to the Father and the Son, a relation rooted in love" (Loyer, *God's Love through the Spirit: The Holy Spirit in Thomas Aquinas and John Wesley* [Washington, DC: Catholic University of America Press, 2014], 140). See also the criticism posed against Aquinas's position by Catherine Osborne, "The *nexus amoris* in Augustine's Trinity," *Studia Patristica* 22 (1987): 309–14, at 310. In Osborne's view, Aquinas leaves it unclear whether the Holy Spirit really is a "bond" between the Father and Son, since (as Loyer puts it) "a bond is not something that proceeds but something that unites; it is a medium between what it joins together" (Loyer, *God's Love through the Spirit*, 115). Loyer observes that for Aquinas, "In the sense of origin the Spirit is love in person but not love as medium or bond, whereas in the sense of relation the Spirit, as mutual love, is the

Aquinas clarifies that the Spirit is not the cause or source of the Father and Son's love for each other. Yet he also wants to affirm that the Father and Son love each other by or through the Spirit. This cannot mean merely that the Spirit is a sign of their love or that the love that pertains to the divine essence is appropriated to the Spirit.[65] Instead, Aquinas argues that the preposition "by" here functions in the same way as when we say, "fire warms by heating."[66] Strictly speaking, fire warms by the heat that is the "form" of the fire, whereas heating is "an action proceeding from the fire."[67] Along similar lines, the Father and Son love each other by the Spirit, not in the sense that the Spirit is the source of their love or the "form" of divine love, but in the sense that the Spirit proceeds as Love from the Father and the Son. Aquinas concludes in this regard, "As therefore we say that a tree flowers by its flower, so do we say that the Father, by the Word or the Son, speaks himself and his creatures; and that the Father and the Son love each other and us, by the Holy Spirit, or by Love proceeding."[68] The Holy Spirit is unitive precisely because he proceeds, as Love, from the Father and the Son, as the fruit or imprint of their communion. As Gilles Emery puts it, the Holy Spirit is "the imprint of love which blossoms from the unity of Father and Son. In this sense, to love is to breathe Love; and the bloom of Love is the Holy Spirit. . . . The *communion* of Father and Son and the *procession* of the Holy Spirit are so wholly

---

medium uniting Father and Son in their perfect and eternal communion of love" (ibid., 116). *Pace* Osborne, Loyer argues that Aquinas successfully holds in balance the two perspectives, procession/origin and relation. For further discussion, see John Baptist Ku, OP, *God the Father in the Theology of St. Thomas Aquinas* (New York: Peter Lang, 2013), 260–68.

65. On the Spirit as a "sign" of love between the Father and Son according to Aquinas, see Ku, *God the Father in the Theology of St. Thomas Aquinas*, 274–78. In this section Ku draws especially on Aquinas's *Commentary on the Gospel of John*.

66. I, q. 37, a. 2. For discussion of Aquinas's argument here (and of the positions of the theologians against whom Aquinas is arguing, including Simon of Tournai and William of Auxerre), see Emery, *Trinitarian Theology of Saint Thomas Aquinas*, 238–42. See also the helpful discussion in Ku, *God the Father in the Theology of St. Thomas Aquinas*, 268–74; as well as Walter H. Principe, "St. Bonaventure's Theology of the Holy Spirit with Reference to the Expression 'Pater et Filius diligent se Spiritu Sancto,'" in *S. Bonaventura 1274–1974*, vol. 4, *Theologica*, ed. J. G. Bougerol (Grottaferrata, Italy: Colegio S. Bonaventura, 1974), 243–69; Principe, "Odo Rogaldus: A Precursor of St. Bonaventure on the Holy Spirit as *Effectus Formalis* in the Mutual Love of the Father and Son," *Medieval Studies* 39 (1977): 498–505.

67. I, q. 37, a. 2.

68. I, q. 37, a. 2. See also Loyer, *God's Love through the Spirit*, 123. Aquinas adds in answer to an objection, "Hence we cannot say that the Father spirates by the Holy Spirit, or begets by the Son. But we can say that the Father speaks by the Word, as by the Person proceeding, and speaks by the speaking, as by a notional act; forasmuch as *to speak* imports a determinate person proceeding; since *to speak* means to produce word. Likewise to love, taken in a notional sense, means to produce love; and so it can be said that the Father loves the Son by the Holy Spirit, as by the person proceeding, and by Love itself as a notional act" (I, q. 37, a. 2, ad 2).

caught up with one another that the communion is inconceivable without the procession of the Holy Spirit."[69]

It will be helpful to see how this view of the Holy Spirit as the "bloom of Love," blossoming from the communion of the Father and Son, differs from how the Spirit is often conceived in contemporary trinitarian theology. Antonio López, indebted to Claude Bruaire and Hans Urs von Balthasar, states this contemporary conception well: "The Father confirms the Son's reception and reciprocation of the gift with the further gift of the Holy Spirit, who, by hypostasizing God's unity, makes God's absolute act be because through him shines forth the fullness of its unity."[70] Here the Holy Spirit, as the last of the three persons, "hypostatizes" or brings about the fullness of "God's absolute act" in its unity, a unity that is constituted by the persons' gifting as sealed by the gift of the Spirit. Aquinas, by contrast, does not hold that the persons (let alone the Spirit) make the being and unity of God to be by their notional acts, which Emmanuel Perrier has helpfully analyzed in terms of "fecundity in God."[71] On the contrary, each person is fully God, fully Act, and the notional acts distinguish the persons only from one another—crucial as this is—rather

69. Emery, *Trinitarian Theology of Saint Thomas Aquinas*, 243; see also Loyer, *God's Love through the Spirit*, 138; Ku, *God the Father in the Theology of St. Thomas Aquinas*, 273. Ku goes on to emphasize that Aquinas's "understanding of the Holy Spirit as mutual love shows that Thomas does not regard the Holy Spirit as somehow posterior to the Father-Son relationship. Thomas very clearly affirms the simultaneous inter-relatedness of all three persons in his explanation that the very relationship of the Father to the Son 'is implied in the Holy Spirit.' To grasp the relationship between the Father and the Son, an understanding of the Holy Spirit's procession as Love is obligatory" (*God the Father in the Theology of St. Thomas Aquinas*, 263).

70. Antonio López, *Gift and the Unity of Being* (Eugene, OR: Cascade, 2014), 246. López continues, "If the tripersonal movement of gift expresses God's unity, and without unity there is no being, it is the person of the Holy Spirit who fully accounts for God's *esse*" (ibid.). The problem with this approach is that it accounts for God's unity and being in terms of "the tripersonal movement of gift." At first glance, something similar may seem to be found in Pope John Paul II's observations, in his encyclical *Dominum et vivificantem*, "that in the Holy Spirit the intimate life of the Triune God becomes totally gift, an exchange of mutual love between the divine Persons and that through the Holy Spirit God exists in the mode of gift" (Pope John Paul II, *Dominum et vivificantem*, in *The Encyclicals of John Paul II*, ed. J. Michael Miller, CSB [Huntington, IN: Our Sunday Visitor, 2001], 244–302, at §10, p. 250). But these observations may rightly mean that in the Holy Spirit, who is Gift, the divine nature subsists in the mode of Gift. I fully agree with the central conclusion that Pope John Paul II draws: "It is the Holy Spirit who is *the personal expression* of this self-giving, of this being-love. He is Person-Love. He is Person-Gift. Here we have an inexhaustible treasure of the reality and an inexpressible deepening of the concept of *person* in God, which only divine revelation makes known to us" (ibid.). Likewise, expositing Aquinas's theology, Emery states, "The Father also gives himself, and the Son is no less given, but the Holy Spirit holds this as his personal property: to be Gift formally belongs to his distinct character. This is why the Father and the Son are given to us *in the Holy Spirit*" (Emery, *Trinitarian Theology of Saint Thomas Aquinas*, 257).

71. See Emmanuel Perrier, OP, *La fécondité en Dieu* (Paris: Parole et Silence, 2009), esp. chap. 3.

than establishing the divine being and unity, which the Father communicates to the Son and Spirit in the sharing of the divine nature.

This is important, because if the being and unity of the Triune God came about through the persons' notional acts, then the Father would not be able to communicate the divine nature to the Son; the Father himself would be less than fully divine, as would the Son and Spirit, since all that they are comes from the Father. As Bruce Marshall, drawing upon John of Damascus, has repeatedly pointed out, the Father can give to the Son and Holy Spirit only what the Father himself possesses.[72] For his part, López also recognizes that "what the Spirit can give is not something that either the paternal or the filial donation lacks. Just as the Son says all that the Father gives by being other from him, so the Holy Spirit says *anew* the divine *esse* that both the Father and the Son are."[73] Yet this clarification, though significant, cannot be squared with López's earlier claim that the Spirit, "by hypostatizing God's unity, makes God's absolute act be." The truth of the Trinity hinges upon the fact that the Father's divine being and unity is eternally shared or communicated, rather than constituted, in the "tripersonal movement of gift."[74] When Aquinas

72. See, for example, Bruce D. Marshall: "The Filioque as Theology and Doctrine: In Reply to Bernd Oberdorfer," *Kerygma und Dogma* 50 (2004): 271–88, at 280–81; Marshall, "The Absolute and the Trinity," *Pro Ecclesia* 23 (2014): 147–64. For the point at issue, note also John of Damascus, *An Exact Exposition of the Orthodox Faith* 1.8, in John of Damascus, *Writings*, trans. Frederic H. Chase Jr. (Washington, DC: Catholic University of America Press, 1958), 184: "For the Father is uncaused and unbegotten, because He is not from anything, but has His being from Himself and does not have from any other anything whatsoever that He has. . . . Because of the Father, the Son and the Spirit have everything that they have, that is to say, because of the fact that the Father has them, excepting the being unbegotten, the begetting, and the procession." Thus the mutual love of the Father and Son does not mean that the Father receives from the Son something that the Father lacked. Aquinas clarifies, "The Holy Spirit proceeds both from the Father to the Son and from the Son to the Father, not as recipients but as objects of love. For the Holy Spirit is said to proceed from the Father to the Son inasmuch as he is the love whereby the Father loves the Son; and in the same way it may be said that the Holy Spirit proceeds from the Son to the Father inasmuch as he is the love whereby the Son loves the Father" (*De potentia*, q. 10, a. 4, ad 10 [Aquinas, *On the Power of God*, 3:206]). For discussion, see Ku, *God the Father in the Theology of St. Thomas Aquinas*, 266–67.

73. López, *Gift and the Unity of Being*, 246.

74. Ibid. In accord with the dialectical character of his approach, López goes on to emphasize, "That God is himself a tripersonal gift does not mean that he is the cause of himself. He does not bring himself out from nothingness. Instead, God *is*, because he is nothing but eternal beginning, an unpreceded beginning that expresses itself *anew* in a Word in which he is, which exists only in the one who utters it, a reciprocal *indwelling* where the Holy Spirit fruitfully seals the unity of the two who remain eternally other from each other. The third hypostasis, remembering the gratuitous donation, binds and opposes one to the other by letting the one be in the other" (ibid., 247–48). At the same time, López affirms that the persons' gifting constitutes the divine unity: "The gift that constitutes the unity of the absolute spirit is utterly free precisely because it gives *and* because it receives and reciprocates the gift of itself

states that the relation of Father to Son (and Son to Father) "is expressed in the Holy Spirit, as Love," therefore, he has in view not the sealing of the divine unity-in-love, but rather the breathing forth of the Holy Spirit as the Love of the Father and Son, the consubstantial trinitarian communion in which the Spirit is integrally related to the Father and the Son as their mutual Love.[75] The Spirit is on the side of unity in the trinitarian communion, but this does not imply that the gift of the Spirit perfects the unity of the divine being that the persons are. Instead, in Emery's words, "The communion (the union or unity) of the Father and Son is twofold: the unity of nature of the three persons and the unity of the Spirit."[76]

The Holy Spirit and the Church's Unity

Commenting on John 14:26, where Jesus promises his disciples that the Father will send the Paraclete, or Holy Spirit, in Jesus's name, Aquinas explains the name "Paraclete" in terms of consolation and love. Again we hear the note of unity in connection with the Spirit: it is the Spirit-Paraclete who comforts us in the midst of trials, and the Spirit does so "because he is love, and causes us to love God and give him great honor."[77] The Spirit, as Love, unites us with God by causing us to love God, who is the source of our being. The Spirit also unites us to God by giving us hope of forgiveness, so that we do not despair because of the sins we have committed.[78] Reflecting on the name

completely, that is, according to the 'ever-greaterness' unique to God's *Trinitas*. . . . Because of the relationship between gratuity and fecundity, the unity of the triune gift is to let oneself be in another as other, a triune letting-be that reveals itself as an ever-new and eternally delightful indwelling" (ibid., 251).

75. I, q. 37, a. 1, ad 3. See especially Gilles Emery, OP, "Qu'est-ce que la 'communion trini-taire'?," *Nova et Vetera* (Swiss ed.) 89 (2014): 258–83. Emery draws attention in this regard to the convergence of Aquinas's thought with that of the *Catechism of the Catholic Church*, 2nd ed. (Vatican City: Libreria Editrice Vaticana, 1997).

76. Emery, "Qu'est-ce que la 'communion trinitaire'?," 274 (cf. 267–77, drawing upon a wide array of Aquinas's writings). Earlier Emery notes that in Aquinas's *Commentary on the Sentences*, "on the one hand, the Father and Son are united *formally* by essential love; on the other hand, the Father and Son are united '*quasi* formally' by the Love who is the Holy Spirit. The expression '*quasi* formally' signifies that the Holy Spirit is not the principle who gives their unity to the Father and to the Son (it is not the Holy Spirit who formally brings about the unity of the Father and Son), but the Holy Spirit *proceeds* from the Father and Son as their mutual Bond of love: the Holy Spirit is 'Love proceeding,' coming forth from all eternity from the communion of the Father and Son" (ibid., 264).

77. Thomas Aquinas, *Commentary on the Gospel of John: Chapters 13–21*, trans. Fabian Larcher, OP, and James A. Weisheipl, OP, ed. Daniel Keating and Matthew Levering (Washington, DC: Catholic University of America Press, 2010), no. 1955, p. 85.

78. On the Spirit's relation to hope, see also Gaybba, *Spirit of Love*, 30. Radner argues that in the New Testament and the monastic tradition (and even often in Augustine), "pneumatological

"Holy Spirit," Aquinas adds that "he is the Spirit because he moves hearts to obey God," and "he is Holy because he consecrates us to God."[79] The Holy Spirit moves us to unity with God through charity and gift of self, and thus to a unity in holiness and life.[80]

---

reflection ends by tethering unity to the exercise of certain practices, broadly construed, but particularly given. . . . Charismatic pneumatological unity within this tradition of concrete communal life is practice-oriented. And to this degree, it is also bound necessarily to the christological particulars of both the Scriptures and Christ's own existence" (Radner, "Holy Spirit and Unity," 210–11). Insofar as Radner insists upon the inseparability of the Holy Spirit from Jesus Christ, I agree with him (I take it that this is what he means by his claim that "allowing the Spirit theologically to define Christian unity ends by subverting that unity" [ibid., 211]). But the primacy that Radner gives to practices, inevitably over against doctrine, strikes me as untenable and imbalanced, not least on christological grounds.

79. Aquinas, *Commentary on the Gospel of John: Chapters 13–21*, no. 1955, p. 86. Sabra identifies two ways in which Aquinas conceives of the Spirit's work of unifying the church: through the infused theological virtues, and through the indwelling of the Spirit. As Sabra observes, "How to reconcile these two notions of unity has given rise to a debate in Thomas studies. This has taken the form of a question about the nature of the soul of the church: is it created or uncreated grace (Holy Spirit) which is the soul of the church, hence the principle of unity?" (Sabra, *Thomas Aquinas' Vision of the Church*, 101). If we put to the side the question of the "soul" of the church—as Sabra urges us to do—we can see that the infused virtues (the grace of the Holy Spirit) and the indwelling of the Holy Spirit are two sides of the same coin. Thus Sabra notes that for Aquinas "the Holy Spirit dwells in a rational creature through sanctifying, i.e., created, grace. Moreover, the possession of sanctifying grace disposes (*disponit*) the soul to receive the Divine Person, thus the two belong together. To say that the Holy Spirit is the principle of unity through indwelling does not at all exclude the first kind of unity based on the action of the grace of the Spirit through the theological virtues" (ibid., 102). For the view that the Holy Spirit (uncreated grace) is the soul of the church, see Cantalamessa, *Mystery of Pentecost*, 7; see also Pope Leo XIII, *Divinum illud munus* (1897), §6 (available at www.vatican.va); as well as Veli-Matti Kärkkäinen's mistaken assumption that this analogy "makes the church and its structures absolute, divine in their origin, while the only task of the Spirit is to 'animate' the already existing ecclesiastical apparatus" (Kärkkäinen, *Pneumatology*, 73–74). For clarifications regarding the limits of this analogy, see Congar, *I Believe in the Holy Spirit*, 1:154; on the patristic provenance and value of the analogy, note Congar, *I Believe in the Holy Spirit*, 2:18: "the most important affirmation is that which claims that the Holy Spirit himself plays, in the Church, the part played by the soul. Perhaps a better way of expressing this idea is that identically and personally the same Spirit, *idem numero*, is both in the Head, Christ, and in his Body, the Church or its members, that is, us as believers." For his part, Jean-Pierre Torrell comments, "The Holy Spirit cannot directly fulfill the role of a soul [vis-à-vis the church], but he indirectly fulfills it through his gifts," since justification/sanctification and the divine indwelling are "attributed preferentially to the Holy Spirit" (Torrell, *Saint Thomas Aquinas*, vol. 2, *Spiritual Master*, trans. Robert Royal [Washington, DC: Catholic University of America Press, 2003], 193). On this topic Torrell appreciatively cites Charles Journet, *L'Église du Verbe incarné: Essai de théologie spéculative* (Paris: Desclée de Brouwer, 1951), 2:510–80.

80. Emery points out, "In his meditation on mutual Love, St. Augustine had seen the bond of Father and Son as that in which unity and sanctity are given to be shared within the Church. Thomas pursues this close association between theology and the economy: it is through the Love which proceeds from them that the Father and the Son love one another and *love us*" (Emery, *Trinitarian Theology of Saint Thomas Aquinas*, 242).

In the same place, Aquinas further identifies the unifying role of the Holy Spirit, in discussing the reason why Jesus states that the Father will send the Spirit "in my name" (John 14:26). Observing that Jesus comes in the Father's name, and the Spirit in Jesus's name, Aquinas reasons that the basis for this is the consubstantiality of the three persons. More than this, however, the Son's and the Spirit's missions are aimed at the unity of humans with the Triune God. Aquinas observes that "just as the Son, coming in the name of the Father, subjects his faithful to the Father—'and has made them a kingdom and priests to our God' (Rev. 5:10)—so the Holy Spirit conforms us to the Son because he adopts us as children of God: 'You have received the spirit of adoption, by which we cry out 'Abba!' Father' (Rom. 8:15)."[81] The Spirit's work is to unite us to the Father by conforming us to the incarnate Son, who is the free and active head of the church. Thus Yves Congar comments that the exalted "Lord Jesus and the Holy Spirit have *together* been the authors of the Body, in other words, of the Church in its unity, but Christ is the author as the Head of that Body, homogeneous with its members, in a way that is absolutely his own and strictly personal."[82] In all of this, love is at the center. Aquinas remarks that peace is appropriated to the Spirit because the Spirit "is love, which is the cause of peace."[83] Unity in multiplicity is, arguably, the mark of the Spirit.

In what way, however, does the Holy Spirit enable humans truly to imitate or participate in the unity of God? After all, the unity of God is not like any

81. Aquinas, *Commentary on the Gospel of John*, no. 1957, p. 87. Compare this to Dulles's view, drawing upon *Lumen Gentium*, that "the church's visible aspect, with its personal hierarchical structures, shows forth the first mission, that of the Son (LG 8). And in its interiority the church shows forth the second mission by being the dwelling place of the Holy Spirit, who bestows his charisms and establishes the sense of interpersonal fellowship or communion. Under both aspects, the church is a sign and instrument of unity—unity among human beings of all races and nations, and between them and the Triune God" (Dulles, "Trinity and Christian Unity," 82). Dulles cautions against trading a christocentric ecclesiology for a Spirit-centered ecclesiology, since both Christ and the Holy Spirit are central, and the church is indeed the body of Christ (see ibid., 73). Although in this book I am emphasizing the Spirit, I certainly agree with Dulles and have emphasized the Son in an earlier ecclesiological study: Matthew Levering, *Christ and the Catholic Priesthood: Ecclesial Hierarchy and the Pattern of the Trinity* (Chicago: Hillenbrand, 2010).

82. Congar, *I Believe in the Holy Spirit*, 2:20. Jeremy Wilkins points out in this regard, "The Word incarnate is the author of sanctification because he gives the Spirit. The divine Word is not just any kind of word, but *verbum spirans amorem*. Similarly, the Word incarnate is properly head of the Church because he operates both mediately through the order of the Church, and immediately through the inner gift of the Spirit" (Wilkins, "Trinitarian Missions and the Order of Grace according to Thomas Aquinas," in *Philosophy and Theology in the Long Middle Ages: A Tribute to Stephen F. Brown*, ed. Kent Emery Jr., Russell L. Friedman, and Andreas Speer [Leiden: Brill, 2011], 689–708, at 693).

83. Aquinas, *Commentary on the Gospel of John*, no. 1961, p. 88.

creaturely unity. In the *Summa*, Aquinas notes that, strictly speaking, "*one* does not add any reality to *being*; but is only a negation of division: for *one* means undivided *being*."[84] Creaturely being is finite, and therefore creaturely unities are finite. To be "one," for a creature, means to be one among many. In this sense, oneness in creatures can be said to "add" something to the concept of creaturely being, namely the accident of quantity. But God's unity is not a finite oneness; God's unity simply expresses the undividedness of his being, his infinite actuality. Likewise, God's Trinity expresses not quantitative divisibility, but rather the distinction of one person from another. The Triune God utterly transcends all numbered sets of quantities. God and the entire cosmos are not two (or more) things, and the divine persons, while distinct from each other, are the indivisible God. Since God the Trinity is infinite actuality, there is nothing that can make him into a quantitative multitude.

Aquinas observes that in the cosmos, diverse things are ordered to one another in a complex manner, and this would not be possible unless there were one orderer. This point provides the connection between the divine unity and the Holy Spirit's unitive work in humans. The Holy Spirit orders us into a unity like that of the cosmos, a unity that *shows* that our triune orderer is one. The body of Christ is just such a unity. Commenting on Ephesians 4:3–4, where Paul urges the community "to maintain the unity of the Spirit in the bond of peace" since "there is one body and one Spirit," Aquinas notes that unity need not always be good, since people can be united, for a time, in evildoing. It is unity in doing good, then, that is "the unity of the Spirit," and such unity is preserved through "the bond of peace." Aquinas explains the unity achieved by the work of the Spirit: "charity is a union of souls. Now the fusion of material objects cannot last unless it is held by some bond. Similarly, the union of souls through love will not endure unless it is bound. Peace proves to be a true bond."[85] Peace is an effect of charity, which is infused in us by the grace of the Holy Spirit, and peace also requires justice.[86]

An important element here is the notion that humans must be bound together in self-giving love in order to flourish, not only naturally but supernaturally (as the body of Christ). In the *Summa*, Aquinas quotes both Augustine and Dionysius to the effect that everything desires peace. Like Augustine, Aquinas defines peace as the "tranquillity of order," a condition in which all

84. I, q. 11, a. 1.

85. Thomas Aquinas, *Commentary on the Letter of Saint Paul to the Ephesians*, trans. Matthew L. Lamb, no. 194, in Aquinas, *Commentary on the Letters of Saint Paul to the Galatians and Ephesians*, ed. J. Mortensen and E. Alarcón (Lander, WY: Aquinas Institute for the Study of Sacred Doctrine, 2012), 268.

86. See II-II, q. 29, a. 3.

our desires are fulfilled and set at rest.[87] He points out that "even those who seek war and dissension, desire nothing but peace, which they deem themselves not to have."[88] Charity establishes humans in peace, because charity orders our wills so that we truly love God and neighbor, and do not cleave selfishly to anything contrary to their good or ours. As Aquinas observes, the twofold union required by peace comes about through charity because charity refers all our desires toward God and because charity ensures that "we wish to fulfil our neighbor's will as though it were ours."[89] Commenting on Ephesians 4:4, Aquinas observes that the church is "one body" in the sense of an ordered unity of many members, and is "one Spirit" in the sense of possessing "a spiritual consensus through the unity of your faith and charity."[90]

Similarly, commenting on 1 Corinthians 12:12, Aquinas notes that Aristotle, in book 5 of the *Metaphysics*, distinguishes three ways of being "one": transcendental unity, which utterly excludes multitude; unity by reason of continuity, which "excludes actual multitude but not potential" (such as the unity of a line); and the unity of a whole, which comprises multitude.[91] It is this third way, the unity of a whole, that constitutes the unity of any body, including Christ's "body," the church. We are made a unity in Christ "by the power of the Holy Spirit."[92] Aquinas explains that the Holy Spirit does this through the sacrament of baptism, as well as through the interior action of grace (beyond that given by baptism) and through the eucharistic blood of Christ that "is consecrated by the Spirit."[93] The resulting "mystical body"—the church—"represents a likeness to a natural body," because the various human members serve the mystical body in a manner comparable to how the various powers of the soul serve a natural body.[94]

After commenting on verses 14–26, where Paul elaborates the connection between the members of a natural body and the members of the church, Aquinas arrives at Paul's conclusion in 1 Corinthians 12:27, which in Aquinas's version reads, "Now you are the body of Christ, and members of

87. See II-II, q. 29, aa. 1–2.

88. II-II, q. 29, a. 2, ad 2.

89. II-II, q. 29, a. 3. On a natural level, humans are inclined to live in society rather than alone, and dissension harms human flourishing; see, for example, I-II, q. 94, a. 2; II-II, q. 37, a. 1; II-II, q. 40, a. 1.

90. Aquinas, *Commentary on the Letter of Saint Paul to the Ephesians*, no. 195, p. 268.

91. Thomas Aquinas, *Commentary on the First Letter of Saint Paul to the Corinthians*, trans. Fabian Larcher, no. 732, in Aquinas, *Commentary on the Letters of Saint Paul to the Corinthians*, ed. J. Mortensen and E. Alarcón (Lander, WY: Aquinas Institute for the Study of Sacred Doctrine, 2012), p. 276.

92. Ibid., no. 734, p. 277.

93. Ibid.

94. Ibid., no. 737, p. 278.

a member [*et estis membra de membro*]." For our purposes, this phrase "members of a member" is particularly significant. Aquinas notes that in his human nature, Jesus Christ is one member among the many members of the church, even if Jesus is the head. In his divine nature, however, Jesus "does not have the nature of a member or of a part, since he is the common good of the entire universe."[95] Since Jesus is one person, the Son or Word, as a divine person he shares in the unity of God. On the basis of these principles (which Aquinas sets forth in order to interpret "members of a member"), we can go further and conclude that we participate in the unity of God by being united to the divine person Jesus Christ, in his communion with the Father in the Love of the Holy Spirit. Along these lines, Aquinas states in the *Summa* that Christ's humanity bestows on us "the full participation of the divinity, which is the bliss of man and end of human life," and he quotes Augustine's remark that "God was made man, that man might be made God."[96] Here, we can appreciate Antonio López's insistence that "the concrete singular cannot be himself if he does not gratuitously receive and reciprocate the gift of being."[97] The unity of the body of Christ—our unity—comes about when, in Christ, we "receive and reciprocate" God's gifts through the power of personal Gift-Love. Unity is found in a communion in Christ and the Spirit that imitates and participates in the trinitarian communion.[98]

Law, Love, and Unity

When he treats "peace" in the *Summa*, Aquinas takes Psalm 119:165 as his *sed contra* in support of the view that peace is an effect of charity: "Great peace have those who love your law."[99] The combination here of love, law, and peace is significant. Earlier in the *Summa*, Aquinas treats the various kinds of law, including the Mosaic law. He argues that "the proper effect of

---

95. Ibid., no. 753, p. 283.

96. III, q. 1, a. 2. See also Aquinas's reflections on Christ's headship, for example his statement that "the interior influx of grace is from no one save Christ, whose manhood, through its union with the Godhead, has the power of justifying" (III, q. 8, a. 6). Aquinas makes clear that we cannot compare our graced participation in God with Christ's grace of hypostatic union, except in the sense that both are God's gratuitous gift; see III, q. 7, a. 13, ad 3.

97. López, *Gift and the Unity of Being*, 260.

98. López puts this situation eloquently: "On the one hand, the offering of the transfiguring and divine love in and through Jesus Christ, who sends the Holy Spirit along with the Father, is the unforeseeable, unmerited, and surprising denial of man's claim to be everything for himself. It is a radically uncalled-for gift. On the other hand, the offering of this unexpected gift is the fruit of the Father's eternally faithful giving" (ibid., 260–61).

99. II-II, q. 29, a. 3, *sed contra*.

law is to lead its subjects to their proper virtue."[100] Recall that human unity comes from having fully virtuous desires, so that our loves are rightly ordered and we are one with God and neighbor. God, Aquinas observes, moves us to good in two ways: God "instructs us by means of his law, and assists us by his grace."[101] The Mosaic law and the "law" of the new covenant in Christ have the same end or goal, since Christ fulfills the Mosaic law and reconfigures it around himself.[102] Aquinas contrasts the end of human law with the end of divinely revealed law: "The end of human law is the temporal tranquility of the state, which end law effects by directing external actions, as regards those evils which might disturb the peaceful condition of the state. On the other hand, the end of the divine law is to bring man to that end which is everlasting happiness."[103] This "everlasting happiness" is our perfect unity with God and neighbor.

Aquinas remarks in this vein that "the end of grace is the union of the rational creature with God," and "the principle of habitual grace, which is given with charity, is the Holy Spirit, who is said to be sent inasmuch as he dwells in the mind by charity."[104] We find our perfect or everlasting happiness when we are filled with perfect charity in eternal life, so that we are sharing in the life of God—a sharing that does not take away our multiplicity or diversity, but that unites us with the Triune God and with our fellow humans. As Aquinas puts it, therefore, "the Holy Spirit is likened to the heart, since he invisibly quickens and unifies the Church."[105] The Love and Gift that is Holy Spirit makes us "fit to partake of everlasting happiness," because our healing from sin and elevation to the divine life "cannot be done save by the grace of the Holy Spirit, whereby *charity*, which fulfills the law, . . . *is spread abroad in our hearts* (Rom. v. 5): since *the grace of God is life everlasting* (Rom. vi. 23)."[106]

It is in this light that Aquinas views the unity that God sought to accomplish in his chosen people, Israel, through electing them and giving them a law to govern their moral, cultic, and judicial lives. Aquinas observes, "The more a man is united to God, the better his state becomes: wherefore the more the Jewish people were bound to the worship of God, the greater their excellence over other peoples."[107] Not surprisingly, Aquinas envisions Israel as a priestly people among the nations, comparable to the role of the priests among the

100. I-II, q. 92, a. 1.
101. I-II, q. 90, prologue.
102. See I-II, q. 107, aa. 1–2.
103. I-II, q. 98, a. 1.
104. III, q. 7, a. 12; III, q. 7, a. 13.
105. III, q. 8, a. 1, ad 3.
106. I-II, q. 98, a. 1.
107. I-II, q. 98, a. 5, ad 2.

laity in the church. Israel is closer to God because God has united Israel to himself in a unique way, but Israel is not closer because of its own merits; and Israel's closeness to God is for the service of all the nations.[108]

The Mosaic law accomplishes two things that especially show Israel's priestly mission of service to all nations. First, the Mosaic law bears witness to Christ, who reconciles and unites all peoples—an eschatological unity of which the church is the firstfruits but whose fullness will be seen only at the end of time. Second, the Mosaic law withdraws "men from idolatrous worship" and establishes "them in the worship of one God," not least through the commandment "Hear, O Israel: The LORD our God is one LORD; and you shall love the LORD your God with all your heart, and with all your soul, and with all your might" (Deut. 6:4–5).[109] In these two ways, the Mosaic law reveals the intended unity in holiness of the human race; we are created in order to be united in the worship of the true God through Christ and his Spirit. Indeed, the very giving of a law exhibits God's unifying purpose, God's will to overcome our sinful division, discord, and strife. Since a law contains general precepts governing a whole people, rather than consisting in a few rules to set in order the life of a few individuals, God waited to give the Mosaic law until Abraham's descendants had multiplied and had been led out of slavery by God's power.

Through the Mosaic law, God forms his chosen people in holiness, even though God does not allow his people to suppose that this law suffices to make them holy. Instead, God wills "to give such a law as men by their own forces could not fulfill, so that, while presuming on their own powers, they might find themselves to be sinners, and being humbled might have recourse to the help of grace."[110] Certainly Aquinas thinks that the holy men and women of Israel sought and received God's grace. He holds that many Israelites, and gentiles as well, were sustained in charity by the grace of the Holy Spirit through implicit, and in some cases explicit, faith in the coming redeemer.[111]

---

108. See I-II, q. 98, aa. 4–5.

109. I-II, q. 98, a. 2; I-II, q. 100, a. 10.

110. I-II, q. 98, a. 2, ad 3.

111. See II-II, q. 2, a. 7. Aquinas is not clear regarding whether there can be implicit faith after Christ's coming among people whom the church's preaching has not reached. For discussion, see Sabra, *Thomas Aquinas' Vision of the Church*, 166–68. Aquinas's perspective can and should be developed so as to make clear that implicit faith, or something like it, is still possible. As Brian Gaybba remarks,

> The fact that the apostolic community linked Spirit and Church did not mean that it never saw the Spirit as active outside the Christian fold. But it did mean for them that any action of the Spirit outside their community had as its purpose the leading of people to Christ and his Church. A good example of this is the story about Cornelius in Acts 10. We read there how the Spirit descended on Cornelius and his household even before

Thus he concludes that "the ancient Fathers belong to the same Church as we."[112] The key point is that the body of Christ is simply the unity of all people (and angels) who possess charity. Aquinas thinks that since the end or goal of the law is charity, we can say that "the whole Law is comprised in this one commandment, *You shall love your neighbor as yourself*, as expressing the end of all commandments: because love of one's neighbor includes love of God, when we love our neighbor for God's sake."[113] The formation of a united people is the purpose of the Mosaic law and, on a worldwide scale, is the purpose of the eschatological grace of the Holy Spirit that Israel's Messiah pours forth.

In his *Summa theologiae* and *Summa contra gentiles*, Aquinas devotes no questions or articles explicitly to the topic of the church. Instead, he focuses on the person and work of the divine Son in his incarnation, and on the sacraments. Throughout these discussions, as we saw in chapters 4 and 5, the Holy Spirit is central. As Jean-Pierre Torrell states of the Spirit, "Bond of love between the Father and the Son, it belongs to Him in a special way to realize in the Body of believers their coming together in charity."[114] In the *Summa contra gentiles*, Aquinas observes that "since we are made lovers of God by the Holy Spirit, and every beloved is in the lover as such, by the Holy Spirit necessarily the Father and the Son dwell in us also."[115] In this trinitarian ecclesiology, the church's unity as a communion in charity comes about through the Spirit, who is the Love of the Father and Son.

In the *Summa contra gentiles*, Aquinas also gives various reasons for the unity of the church specifically as led by the bishop of Rome, "who is head of the entire Church."[116] Most important, in my view, is Aquinas's connection of the church on earth with the heavenly church united in glorious worship as the beginnings of the new creation. Aquinas states, "The militant Church . . . derives from the triumphant Church by exemplarity; hence, John in the Apocalypse (21:2) saw 'Jerusalem coming down out of heaven'; and Moses was told to make everything 'according to the pattern that was shewn

---

they were baptized. What is more, they were Gentiles—and this fact astonished the Jewish believers. However, the whole point of the Spirit's intervention was, we are told, to lead Cornelius and his household to Christ and the Christian community—and to show the Jewish believers that Christ and his community were for everybody, Jews as well as Gentiles. (Gaybba, *Spirit of Love*, 26)

112. III, q. 8, a. 3, ad 3.

113. I-II, q. 99, a. 1, ad 2.

114. Torrell, *Spiritual Master*, 193.

115. Thomas Aquinas, *Summa contra gentiles* 4.21, trans. Charles J. O'Neil (Notre Dame, IN: University of Notre Dame Press, 1975).

116. Aquinas, *Summa contra gentiles* 4.76.

thee in the mount' (Exod. 25:40; 26:30). But in the triumphant Church one presides, the one who presides over the entire universe—namely, God."[117] Aquinas's argument here goes from the Triune God to the incarnate Son Jesus Christ, who is head of the church, and from Christ to his apostolic ministers, with Peter at their head.[118] The divine unity requires the unity of the multiple people whom God calls to worship him in charity, a unity that will ultimately comprise the multiplicity of the entire universe as God's new creation.[119] As Paul says of this glorious unity, "the creation itself will be set free from its bondage to decay and obtain the glorious liberty of the children of God. We know that the whole creation has been groaning in travail together until now; and not only the creation, but we ourselves who have the first fruits of the Spirit groan inwardly as we wait for adoption as sons" (Rom. 8:22–23).[120]

117. Aquinas, *Summa contra gentiles* 4.76. See also Thomas Aquinas, "Sermon 5: Ecce Rex Tuus," in Aquinas, *The Academic Sermons*, trans. Mark-Robin Hoogland, CP (Washington, DC: Catholic University of America Press, 2010), 62–78.

118. For an exposition and defense of Aquinas's theology of the papacy, see Levering, *Christ and the Catholic Priesthood*, chap. 4.

119. Michael Northcott fears that a proper "sense of the work of the Spirit—as moving from the sacraments and the life of holiness to the restoration of creation and of human and creaturely relations—was increasingly attenuated in the West, especially in the second millennium, when a strong contrast between Eastern and Western pneumatology opened up" (Northcott, "Holy Spirit," in *Systematic Theology and Climate Change: Ecumenical Perspectives*, ed. Michael S. Northcott and Peter M. Scott [London: Routledge, 2014], 51–68, at 58) (cf. 60 for his concern about "the loss of the symbolism of the *artos* or 'whole loaf' in Western [Eucharistic] practice"). Without granting the historical reality of this "strong contrast," I very much agree that charity involves rightly ordered relations with nonrational creation, since all creation is being renewed together. See also Sigurd Bergman, "Invoking the Spirit amid Dangerous Environmental Change," in *God, Creation and Climate Change: Spiritual and Ethical Perspectives*, ed. Karen L. Bloomquist (Minneapolis: Lutheran University Press, 2009), 159–74. Bergmann proposes that we should "reimagine the church as an agglomeration of local places and a global space for creative experiments in the arts of survival in environmentally changing contexts" (ibid., 174). In response to such proposals, my concern is that this would reduce the church to merely another human institution, among the numerous other institutions devoted to experimenting "in the arts of survival in environmentally changing contexts." The church's mission is much more radical than this, even though environmental flourishing is an important part of the church's social teaching. The danger of reducing the radicality of divine revelation is apparent in Bergmann's view (which she mistakenly attributes to Gregory of Nyssa and Gregory of Nazianzus) that "we should be silent about God's essence, which we cannot know, but speak positively about God's actions in creation, which we can experience bodily" (ibid., 167). See also, for a position similar to Bergmann's, Ernst Conradie, *The Church and Climate Change* (Pietermaritzburg: Cluster, 2008).

120. For Aquinas on the new creation, see Matthew Levering, *Jesus and the Demise of Death: Resurrection, the Afterlife, and the Fate of Christians* (Waco: Baylor University Press, 2012). Antonio López rightly underscores the Spirit's work of unity vis-à-vis the whole of creation (López, *Gift and the Unity of Being*, 285–86).

Conclusion

Contrasting the disunity of Babel with the unity of Pentecost, Raniero Canta-lamessa observes: "Everyone wants unity. After the word 'happiness,' there is probably no other word that answers to such a compelling need of the human heart as the word 'unity.'"[121] Is the church, however, really an instrument of unity, or should human unity instead be sought outside any particular religious body? In this regard, the comparative theologian Diana Eck has portrayed the world as a household, encompassing a tremendous diversity of persons and traditions.[122] For Eck, the image of a household is preferable to that of a body, because a body is unavoidably hierarchical (head and feet). As she puts it, "A household may also have its hierarchies, but they are not the built-in hierarchies of the body. They will be open to challenge and negotiation. There is no household without its arguments, but its foundation is undergirding love and its language the two-way language of dialogue."[123] The unity she envisions is nonhierarchical, or at least is dialogically and fluidly hierarchical.

In Eck's view, this world-unity is urgently needed; the only alternative to unity is terrible conflict, misunderstanding, and war (including religious war). But she argues that the world-unity cannot be based either upon one

121. Cantalamessa, *Mystery of Pentecost*, 9. Drawing upon Aquinas, Cantalamessa notes that this desire for unity arises from the finitude and poverty of our being; we therefore seek a greater fullness of being. He comments further, "Everybody wants unity, everybody desires it from the bottom of their hearts; however, it is so difficult to attain that even in the most suc-cessful marriages the moments of true and total oneness—not only of the flesh but also of the spirit—are rare enough and are, in fact, only moments. Why is this so? In general, it is because although we wish that there be unity, we wish it to be centered around our own point of view. . . . By contrast, in the unity of Pentecost or the unity according to the Spirit, one puts God at, or better accepts God as, the center" (ibid., 10–11). He then quotes Aquinas to underscore this point about the proper way to seek unity: "St. Thomas Aquinas calls the love of God 'aggrega-tive' and the love of self 'disgregative.' He writes, 'The love of God is aggregative inasmuch as it brings human desire back from multiplicity to a single thing; self-love, on the other hand, disperses (*disgregat*) human desire in the multiplicity of things. In fact, a human being loves himself by desiring for themselves temporal goods that are many and diverse.' Thus, the love of God not only brings about unity among different people but also within one single person, an internal not just an external unity" (ibid., 11, citing *Summa theologiae* II-II, q. 73, a. 1, ad 3).

122. See Diana L. Eck, *Encountering God: A Spiritual Journey from Bozeman to Banaras* (Boston: Beacon, 2003). For the same sense of a diverse extended family, although without the image of the household, see Francis X. Clooney, SJ, *Comparative Theology: Deep Learning across Religious Borders* (Oxford: Wiley-Blackwell, 2010), 106. By comparison to Eck, Clooney devotes more effort to emphasizing his Christian location. Eck draws her image from Gandhi's experiment in communal living and from Martin Luther King Jr.'s speech "The World House." See Martin Luther King Jr., *Where Do We Go from Here: Chaos or Community?* (Boston: Beacon, 1967). For ecumenical reflections on the church as the family of God the Father, adopted sons and daughters in the Son by the Holy Spirit, see Dulles, "Trinity and Christian Unity," 69–71.

123. Eck, *Encountering God*, 228.

particular religious tradition or upon the sum of the world's religious traditions, each of which claims a fundamental exclusivity even while also being
open in certain ways to religious others. Instead, "The underlying foundation
of the world household will finally have to be pluralism."[124] Eck explains that
our shared human identity is the foundation for true unity. Although we can
still identify with our particular religious traditions, these traditions must
not deny or impede recognition of our fundamental unity as human beings.

Eck is well aware, of course, that "many religious traditions have their
own distinctive visions of the imagined community of diverse peoples," and
she notes that for Christians "the dominant image of the community coming
into being is the Kingdom of God."[125] Her own vision of world unity draws
in significant ways from this Christian image. She observes, for instance, that
the kingdom of God "would not secure its identity by dominion or exclusion, but was imagined to be an open house for all the peoples of the earth,
coming from the East and West, North and South, to eat at table together."[126]
The kingdom of God is expected to come into being on this very earth, albeit
through a new creation, and this kingdom of divine blessing "is much wider
than the church. It is the Kingdom of God, not of the Christian church."[127]

124. Ibid.
125. Ibid.
126. Ibid., 230.
127. Ibid. This strong disjunction between the "kingdom of God" and "the Christian church"
neglects the way in which the church on earth is related to the eschatological church. The two
are not separate entities, even though the former is not fully the latter. Vatican II's Dogmatic
Constitution on the Church, *Lumen Gentium*, addresses this issue by stating,

> To carry out the will of the Father Christ inaugurated the kingdom of heaven on earth
> and revealed to us his mystery; by his obedience he brought about our redemption.
> The Church—that is, the kingdom of Christ already present in mystery—grows visibly
> through the power of God in the world. . . . The mystery of the holy Church is already
> brought to light in the way it was founded. For the Lord Jesus inaugurated his Church
> by preaching the Good News, that is, the coming of the kingdom of God, promised over
> the ages in the scriptures: "The time is fulfilled, and the kingdom of God is at hand"
> (Mark 1:15; Matt. 4:17). This kingdom shone out before men in the word, in the works
> and in the presence of Christ. The word of the Lord is compared to a seed which is sown
> in a field (Mark 4:14); those who hear it with faith and are numbered among the little
> flock of Christ (Luke 12:32) have truly received the kingdom. Then, by its own power
> the seed sprouts and grows until the harvest (cf. Mark 4:26–29). The miracles of Jesus
> also demonstrate that the kingdom has already come on earth: "If I cast out devils by
> the finger of God, then the kingdom of God has come upon you" (Luke 11:20; cf. Matt.
> 12:28). But principally the kingdom is revealed in the person of Christ himself, Son of
> God and Son of Man, who came "to serve and to give his life as a ransom for many"
> (Mark 10:45). When Jesus, having died on the cross for men, rose again from the dead,
> he was seen to be constituted as Lord, the Christ, and as Priest for ever (cf. Acts 2:36;
> Heb. 5:6; 7:17–21), and he poured out on his disciples the Spirit promised by the Father
> (cf. Acts 2:23). Henceforward the Church, endowed with the gifts of her founder and

Is Eck's vision of a world-unity inspired by recognition of our common humanity and of shared divine blessing more fitting than an emphasis on seeking unity in and through the church? It should be noted, first, that Eck's critical vision of the limitations of "the Christian church" seems to adopt an integralist view of the institutional church, one that the church itself has rejected as unchristian. As described by David L. Schindler, "integralism is a program for effecting a (religious) unity, or wholeness, arbitrarily and through relations of power. Such an integration will by definition exclude those who do not share the same arbitrary relation to God: integralism is the progenitor of sectarianism."[128] Schindler observes that this kind of unity is the very opposite of the church's path of following Christ in self-giving charity.

Furthermore, it seems that Eck misapprehends, at a deeper level, the significance of the church's quest for unity. Eck's vision of a world-unity based on the recognition of our common humanity neglects the human need for forgiveness, for mercy, which requires the historical action of the living God to overcome our brokenness and the harm that we have done to others. We need the God of mercy, in Jesus Christ and the Holy Spirit, to heal our alienated condition and establish for us a relationship of love and justice by a transformative gift of love. As Antonio López puts it, only "the light of the unforeseeable, ever-renewing embrace of God allows human beings to welcome each other."[129] Related to this, it is also unclear how the god/God invoked by Eck wills to be related to us in our suffering and death. If death is the end—that is to say, if our death results in the everlasting annihilation of our conscious existence—then earthly things constitute our only chance for

faithfully observing his precept of charity, humility and self-denial, receives the mission of proclaiming and establishing among all peoples the kingdom of Christ and of God, and she is, on earth, the seed and the beginning of that kingdom. While she slowly grows to maturity, the Church longs for the completed kingdom and, with all her strength, hopes and desires to be united in glory with her king. (Vatican II, *Lumen Gentium*, §§3, 5, in *Vatican Council II*, vol. 1, *The Conciliar and Postconciliar Documents*, ed. Austin Flannery, OP, rev. ed. [Northport, NY: Costello, 1998], 351–53)

128. David L. Schindler, "The Religious Sense and American Culture," in *A Generative Thought: An Introduction to the Works of Luigi Giussani*, ed. Elisa Buzzi (Montreal: McGill-Queen's University Press, 2003), 84–102, at 93. See also Peter J. Bernardi, SJ, *Maurice Blondel, Social Catholicism, and Action Française: The Clash over the Church's Role in Society during the Modernist Era* (Washington, DC: Catholic University of America Press, 2008). Pope Pius XI condemned *Action Française*, with its integralist perspective, in 1926.

129. López, *Gift and the Unity of Being*, 294. López rightly adds that "to welcome Christ's mercy means to change. God's love is powerful enough to change the human being. Through his Holy Spirit, God opens him up from within to the life God wants to share with him (Ezek. 36:26). . . . When the Holy Spirit gives the sinner the eyes of love to look at his own ingratitude in the light of the crucified-risen Christ, the person is brought to see that the evil he generated or permitted is not greater than God's virginal love" (ibid., 295).

happiness, in which case real unity is surely an illusion; we must compete for earthly goods in the short span of time that we have. All is different, however, if death opens up an everlasting personal communion with the living God and with one another. One of the constitutive elements of our shared humanity is the desire to seek, find, and be related to the living God, who alone has the power to unite us. Eck's proposal founders, then, not least because it offers an insufficient account of our shared humanity.

Nonetheless, Eck's goal of bringing humans together is laudable and should help us to see why Soulen's emphasis on relating the Holy Spirit to fruitful multiplicity is of value. Recall that Soulen characterizes the "pneumatological" pattern of divine naming as a way of praising "God's superabundant glory and blessing, conveyed by a limitless variety of terms drawn from many spheres of life."[130] Aquinas also recognizes that the Holy Spirit engages individual people, across societies and cultures, from within their "limitless variety."[131] In Aquinas's theology of the Holy Spirit, however, we find a greater focus on unity (both in the Triune God, and in the Spirit's mission) than we find in Soulen and many other theologians today. Soulen seeks a Christian way of naming the positive dimension of the enormous religious and cultural pluralism that one encounters in the world, and the Holy Spirit provides him with a way of naming this pluralism and claiming it for Christ. But what can go missing from such an account, if only by being put on the back burner, is the Spirit's role as bond of unity and the Spirit's work of healing and unifying humans in charity. Without the charity given by the Spirit, no true or enduring unity (or peace) is possible. Nor can the Spirit's work in the world be conceived without a real, visible unity—so that it can truly be said, with Miroslav Volf and Maurice Lee, that "the Spirit fashions the church into a site of reconciled and mutually enriching diversity," "a catholic community with a multiplicity of charismatic ministries."[132]

Aquinas values multiplicity as part of the beauty and goodness of God's creation and new creation. Oliva Blanchette comments that Aquinas's "theo-

130. Soulen, *Divine Name(s) and the Holy Trinity*, 240.

131. Thus Aquinas allows for the salvation of gentiles who, without explicitly believing in Christ, had "implicit faith through believing in divine providence, since they believed that God would deliver mankind in whatever way was pleasing to him, and according to the revelation of the Spirit to those who knew the truth" (II-II, q. 2, a. 7, ad 3). For further discussion, see Anselm K. Min, *Paths to the Triune God: An Encounter between Aquinas and Recent Theologies* (Notre Dame, IN: University of Notre Dame Press, 2005), chap. 2.

132. Miroslav Volf and Maurice Lee, "Spirit and the Church," in Hinze and Dabney, *Advents of the Spirit*, 382–409, at 394–95. As Cantalamessa puts it, "The unity of the Spirit must continually recreate and renew because the 'disaggregative' forces of egoism and the action of the one whom the Scripture defines as 'the devil,' *diabolos*, he who divides, continually lay in wait to ensnare it" (Cantalamessa, *Mystery of Pentecost*, 17).

logical principle of unity" does not lead Aquinas "into any kind of monism or reductionism. Quite the contrary, he is led to emphasize the greatest pluralism and diversity possible."[133] Indeed, radical distinction (in the Trinity) and diversity (among creatures, not least in the church) are evident divine and human realities. With respect to both the trinitarian God and to creatures, it is far more difficult to show real unity. Denys Turner therefore underscores that "all possible hint of multiplicity is driven out" from Aquinas's theology of God, so that when Aquinas treats the divine Trinity, he makes sure that "none of the ways that could conflict with or imply qualification of the absoluteness of God's uniqueness and simplicity is defended."[134] Similarly, when treating human beings, Aquinas makes clear that real unity in Christ is truly possible, and he does this by appeal to the Holy Spirit and especially to the infusion of charity or self-giving love with its effects of mercy and joy. As Volf and Lee remark, "Since the very being of the church is grounded in God's self-giving and constituted by that self-giving's being made present to those who believe by the Spirit, the life of the church must be modeled on God's self-giving, by which God has reconciled humans to himself."[135]

Nonetheless, it might seem as though the Holy Spirit takes second place when Aquinas appeals so strongly to the hierarchical image of the "body of Christ" and to the leadership of the bishops led by the bishop of Rome as a sign and means of the church's unity.[136] In this regard, Volf and Lee insist that "no principle and unalterable hierarchical relations obtain between the members" of the church, and they warn against "a hierarchical line of super- and subordination."[137] As I argue in *Christ and the Catholic Priesthood*, however, the church's mutuality and hierarchy are not opposed, even when it is the hierarchy's task to settle a dispute, because hierarchy instructs us in the receptivity that is the great sign of self-giving love, a willingness to hear the humble Word of God who comes to us through the mediation of our fellow sinners, rather than to insist in pride upon the self-sufficiency or superiority of our own words and judgment.[138] Thus in order to heal our pride and to unite us in his inaugurated kingdom, Jesus separated out the Twelve from among his many followers and gave them the commission to be hierarchical servants of all, and to Peter he said, "Feed my sheep" (John 21:17). A sharp division between the "Spirit" of

---

133. See Oliva Blanchette, *The Perfection of the Universe according to Aquinas: A Teleological Cosmology* (University Park: Pennsylvania State University Press, 1992), 118.

134. D. Turner, *Thomas Aquinas*, 118–19.

135. Volf and Lee, "Spirit and the Church," 401.

136. On this point, see Dulles, "Trinity and Christian Unity."

137. Volf and Lee, "Spirit and the Church," 397.

138. See Levering, *Christ and the Catholic Priesthood*, a book that is deeply indebted both to Hans Urs von Balthasar and Aquinas.

mutual love and hierarchical "institution" works only when one assumes that the Holy Spirit distances himself from the apostolic church.[139]

Does this mean that the Holy Spirit ensures that all is pure love and smooth sailing in the church? On the contrary, human sin often opposes the Holy Spirit, bringing evildoing and strife into the church itself. The unity of the church is obviously, indeed painfully, not as full as it should be. With a deeply repentant spirit, Christians must be continually involved in and committed to ecumenism. Nonetheless, the Spirit does not fail in establishing ecclesial unity, so that, as *Lumen Gentium* puts it, Christ's church truly "subsists in the Catholic Church."[140] Such unity in love, which stands as a witness against triumphalist pride of all kinds, is not the suppression of diversity but rather the

---

139. See Matthew Levering, *Engaging the Doctrine of Revelation: The Mediation of the Gospel through Church and Scripture* (Grand Rapids: Baker Academic, forthcoming), chap. 3.

140. *Lumen Gentium*, §8, in Flannery, *Vatican Council II*, 357. For discussion, see Avery Dulles, SJ, "Nature, Mission, and Structure of the Church," in *Vatican II: Renewal within Tradition*, ed. Matthew L. Lamb and Matthew Levering (Oxford: Oxford University Press, 2008), 25–36, at 28; Joseph Ratzinger, "The Ecclesiology of the Constitution *Lumen Gentium*," in *Pilgrim Fellowship of Faith: The Church as Communion*, ed. Stephan Otto Horn and Vinzenz Pfnür, trans. Henry Taylor (San Francisco: Ignatius, 2005), 123–52, at 147–49. Ratzinger states,

> With the *subsistit* formula, Vatican II intended—in line with the Catholic tradition—to say something the exact opposite of "ecclesiological relativism": there is a Church of Jesus Christ. He himself willed her existence, and ever since Pentecost the Holy Spirit is constantly creating her, despite all human failures, and preserves her in her substantial identity. The institution is not an unavoidable—although theologically irrelevant or even damaging—external phenomenon; it is, in its essential core, a part of the concrete character of the Incarnation. The Lord is keeping his word: "The gates of hell shall not prevail against it." . . . *Subsistere* is a special variant of *esse*. It is 'being' in the form of an independent agent. That is exactly what is concerned here. The Council is trying to tell us that the Church of Jesus Christ may be encountered in this world as a concrete agent in the Catholic Church. (Ratzinger, "Ecclesiology of the Constitution *Lumen Gentium*," 147)

Note also Thomas P. Rausch, SJ, *Towards a Truly Catholic Church: An Ecclesiology for the Third Millennium* (Collegeville, MN: Liturgical Press, 2003), 221: "Unity if it is to be real must be visible." As Rausch goes on to say, "The Church is not a Platonic idea. It is a real, historical community, the people of God, showing God's historical relationship with humankind. As the Body of Christ, the Church makes visible in human history the presence of the risen Jesus among his own for the sake of the world" (ibid.). Rausch's viewpoint is otherwise rather far from Ratzinger's, especially in Rausch's sympathy with the proposal of Heinrich Fries and Karl Rahner, SJ, that true communion (and a fully "catholic" Church, rooted in ecumenical desire for unity as well as in a loose synodal governing structure) need involve only a very limited set of doctrinal agreements. In response to Fries and Rahner, see Joseph Ratzinger, *Church, Ecumenism and Politics: New Essays in Ecclesiology*, trans. Robert Nowell (New York: Crossroad, 1988), 122–34. On *koinōnia*/communion, see also the Anglican theologian Nicholas Sagovsky, *Ecumenism, Christian Origins and the Practice of Communion* (Cambridge: Cambridge University Press, 2000), written before issues related to homosexuality tested once again whether the archbishop of Canterbury is able truly to play a sufficiently unifying role in matters of faith and morals. On the church's unity, in light of ecumenism, see also the Congregation for the Doctrine of the Faith's *Mysterium ecclesiae* (June 24, 1973), at www.vatican.va.

opposite. As Ola Tjørhom says, "The Spirit does not only generate diversity but also holds and binds our diversities together within the one body of the Church," so that "true and sustainable diversity is always taken up into the service of unity in that it is directed toward building community."[141]

Is this simultaneous affirmation of both unity and diversity, however, too idealistic in its insistence upon the unity of Christ's church in history, a unity that is concretized in the eucharistic liturgy (in which we share in Jesus's sacrificial self-offering to the Father in the Spirit) under the guidance of the bishops as successors of the apostles?[142] It will be clear that discussion of the Holy Spirit and the church's unity leads inevitably to investigation of another "mark" of the church, holiness. The church of Jesus Christ receives the ever-surprising gift of unity, sealed by the bond of love, through the Gift and Love of the Spirit.[143] Given the divisiveness of sin, however, an *intrinsically* unholy church could hardly be a real unity, no matter what theologians might claim about the Spirit's work. In the next chapter, therefore, I turn to the question of the church's holiness—or lack thereof.

141. Tjørhom, *Visible Church—Visible Unity*, 89. See also James W. Thompson, *The Church according to Paul: Rediscovering the Community Conformed to Christ* (Grand Rapids: Baker Academic, 2014), 149.

142. For discussion of many of the themes that arise here, see my *Christ and the Catholic Priesthood*, especially my dialogue with theologians such as Nicholas Afanasiev, John D. Zizioulas, and Nicholas M. Healy. On the Eucharist, see my *Sacrifice and Community: Jewish Offering and Christian Eucharist* (Oxford: Blackwell, 2005).

143. By contrast, as Reinhard Hütter observes with evident contemporary application, "in both the 'Kantian church' of moral motivation and the 'Schleiermacherian church' of religious communication, the moral and/or religious subject antecedes the church. The fixed point is the subject to whom the 'church' stands in a function relationship of service—be it of a moral or religious kind" (Hütter, "The Church: The Knowledge of the Triune God: Practices, Doctrine, Theology," in *Knowing the Triune God: The Work of the Spirit in the Practices of the Church*, ed. James J. Buckley and David S. Yeago [Grand Rapids: Eerdmans, 2001], 23–47, at 25). Attention to the risen Christ's eschatological sending of the Holy Spirit averts individualism of this kind. This essay contains, in brief form, Hütter's strong critique of Barth's theology of the Holy Spirit (ibid., 30–31). Against Barth's actualism, Hütter insists that "as the work of the Spirit, the church participates in the Spirit's sanctifying mission" (ibid., 39). For Hütter, at Pentecost, "A new public was created; the *ekklesia* of the eschatological polis (Heb. 13:14) was gathered. After initial struggles, it became increasingly clear that it was not the life according to the *mizvot* anymore that constituted and informed this public most fundamentally. Rather, the *ekklesia* was constituted and informed, christologically and pneumatologically, by the *kerygma* and by peculiar practices (especially the breaking of the bread and baptism)" (ibid., 41). Hütter ends this insightful essay on a quite beautiful note that expresses my own sense of the relationship of the Holy Spirit and the church: "The Spirit and the Spirit's works are precisely the guarantee that the knowledge of God, which we suffer by being engaged by them [i.e., by the Spirit's works], is a knowledge neither at our disposal nor of our making, but the beginning of a final 'clothing,' a last 'suffering' that will include that knowledge of God of which the apostle Paul says: 'Then I will know fully, even as I have been fully known' (1 Cor. 13:12)" (ibid., 47).

THE HOLY SPIRIT
AND THE HOLINESS OF THE CHURCH

Does the Holy Spirit make the church "holy"? In the prophets, we frequently find both condemnations of the moral failings of the people of Israel (and of the nations), and God's eschatological promise to make his people holy.[1] In Zechariah's prophecy, for example, God promises that on the day of the Lord, when God will fulfill his covenantal promises to Israel, "there shall be a fountain opened for the house of David and the inhabitants of Jerusalem to cleanse them from sin and uncleanness" (Zech. 13:1). Through Isaiah, God promises that the eschatological fulfillment will accomplish the marriage between God and Israel, so that "as the bridegroom rejoices over the bride, so shall your God rejoice over you" (Isa. 62:5). God promises to the "daughter of Zion," to Israel, that "your salvation comes; behold, his reward is with him," and this reward means that Israel "shall be called The holy people, The redeemed of the LORD" (Isa. 62:11–12). The first Christians understood the

---

1. For discussion of the theme of the "holy people" of God, see Jo Bailey Wells, *God's Holy People: A Theme in Biblical Theology* (Sheffield: Sheffield Academic Press, 2000); Pancratius C. Beentjes, "'Holy People': The Biblical Evidence," in *A Holy People: Jewish and Christian Perspectives on Religious Communal Identity*, ed. Marcel Poorthuis and Joshua Schwartz (Leiden: Brill, 2006), 3–15. See also, for a more popular introduction to this theme in biblical theology, Michael Dauphinais and Matthew Levering, *Holy People, Holy Land: A Theological Introduction to the Bible* (Grand Rapids: Brazos, 2005).

church to be this eschatological people, the restored "Israel of God" (Gal. 6:16) constituted around the Messiah, in whom "the dividing wall of hostility" between Jews and gentiles (Eph. 2:14) has come to an end: "You are fellow citizens with the saints and members of the household of God, built upon the foundation of the apostles and prophets, Christ Jesus himself being the cornerstone, in whom the whole structure is joined together and grows into a holy temple in the Lord; in whom you also are built into it for a dwelling place of God in the Spirit" (Eph. 2:19–22).[2]

In the Apostles' Creed and the Niceno-Constantinopolitan Creed, the early Christians confessed the church to be "one, holy, catholic, and apostolic." Yet what did they mean by attributing this "holiness" to the church? Were Christians ever particularly holy? The book of Acts joyfully describes the

---

2. Does this mean that the Jewish people, the descendents of Abraham, Isaac, and Jacob, are no longer "a people holy to the Lord" (Deut. 7:6), having been replaced by the eschatological church of Christ? This concern is raised in Erik Borgman, "The Ambivalent Role of the 'People of God' in Twentieth Century Catholic Theology: The Examples of Yves Congar and Edward Schillebeeckx" and especially Simon Schoon, "'Holy People': Some Protestant Views," both in Poorthuis and Schwartz, *Holy People*, 263–77 and 279–306. Schoon concludes that "the Church may be called *also*—as one of many different names and metaphors—'People of God,' when the Church is ready to acknowledge that it is not the first and not the only one to be chosen as God's People. It is not *the* People of God, but *a* People of God. . . . The Church as *ekklesia* represents the eschatological people of God as they are gathered in worship and as they witness to the hope for the coming kingdom of God. It is 'holy' when it reflects the holiness of God in the name of Jesus Christ" (Schoon, "'Holy People,'" 303). I do not make this distinction between "the people of God" and "a people of God," but that does not mean that I consign the Jewish people to the dustbin of salvation history or deny that they are now "a people holy to the Lord." In his *Aquinas on Israel and the Church: The Question of Supersessionism in the Theology of Thomas Aquinas* (Eugene, OR: Pickwick, 2014), Matthew A. Tapie argues that in my writings on Israel and the church, "the main concern of the Jewish thinkers regarding the paramount question of supersessionism is bypassed—whether God intends carnal Israel to exist or be replaced by the Church" (47). He suggests that my view is a "replacement" theology, and he points out, "By Levering's own account, Aquinas's teaching in Ia-IIae q. 103.4 has exactly the problematic consequences that Isaac, Soulen, and Wyschogrod foresee. It is not clear how the covenant *with* the Jews can be 'ongoing' if Jewish identity is abrogated. From Wyschogrod's view, the claim that the ceremonial law is dead implies that God no longer wills the Jewish people to live as Jews but rather, to live as some other people. Therefore, Levering's interpretation of Aquinas's teaching amounts to economic supersessionism since it assumes Christ's fulfillment of the ceremonial law renders it obsolete" (ibid., 35, 37). Certainly I believe that Jesus is the Messiah of Israel and of all people, that he calls all people to union with him in the church, and that he has fulfilled the Mosaic law and reconfigured it around himself. But the ongoing Jewish people, who do not accept Jesus as the Messiah, is not thereby rejected, cursed, or in mortal sin. In God's plan, it is right and spiritually salutary for the ongoing Jewish people, as God's elect people, to observe the Mosaic law, even if the invitation to faith in Jesus as Israel's Messiah should not be excluded or assumed to be of no value. My position is indebted to Aquinas's nuanced theology of history and implicit faith, as well as to contemporary teaching of the Catholic Church. See especially Gavin D'Costa, *Vatican II: Catholic Doctrines on Jews and Muslims* (Oxford: Oxford University Press, 2014).

sending of the Holy Spirit upon the apostles, who were "gathered all together in one place" when a sound "like the rush of a mighty wind . . . filled all the house where they were sitting" and "tongues as of fire" rested upon them (Acts 2:1–3). Recall that the Holy Spirit enables the apostles to proclaim the gospel to Jews who were visiting Jerusalem from other countries. Although these Jews were divided by language and nationality, they "came together" when they heard the sound of the Spirit's outpouring, and "each one heard them [the apostles] speaking in his own language" (Acts 2:6).[3] The work of the Holy Spirit here appears as one of unifying or restoring Israel, through the ingathering of the Jewish people (and, in due time, of gentiles as well). As we learn from Peter's Pentecost speech as set forth in Acts, this unifying work belongs to the fulfillment of God's promise, through the prophet Joel, to "pour out my Spirit upon all flesh" in the last days, prior to the final consummation of the kingdom brought about by the "day of the Lord" (Acts 2:17, 20 [cf. Joel 2:28–32]).

When those who hear Peter's speech ask to receive this Holy Spirit, Peter replies that they should repent of sin and be baptized so as to receive the Holy Spirit, who unites them to Christ and to one another. The book of Acts reports that "all who believed were together and had all things in common" (Acts 2:44). According to Acts, the first Christians manifest their faith in the risen Jesus "with glad and generous hearts, praising God and having favor with all the people" (Acts 2:46–47). The Holy Spirit produced an extraordinary unity of love: "Those who believed were of one heart and soul" and shared everything with one another, as "with great power the apostles gave their testimony to the resurrection of the Lord Jesus, and great grace was upon them all" (Acts 4:32–33).

Even Acts admits, however, that tension and sin soon powerfully beset the inaugurated eschatological community. Ananias and Sapphira claim to have given all the money that they received from selling a tract of land, but in fact they have given only a part. When confronted with their lie, they fall down dead. They have lied "to the Holy Spirit" (Acts 5:3), and the results are fatal. In the narrative of Acts, this example of wickedness is soon followed by strife. The first recorded strife among believers occurs when "the Hellenists murmured against the Hebrews because their widows were neglected in the daily distribution" (Acts 6:1).

Despite this sinfulness and strife, Acts continues to insist upon the holiness of the nascent church. After the episode with Ananias and Sapphira, Peter and the apostles are arrested and questioned by the high priest and the Sanhedrin.

3. For discussion, see Darrell L. Bock, *Acts* (Grand Rapids: Baker Academic, 2007), 102–4.

In response to the questioning, they insist that the Holy Spirit is with those who believe in the risen Lord (see Acts 5:30–32). Likewise, the deacon Stephen speaks with "wisdom and the Spirit" and is "full of faith and of the Holy Spirit" (Acts 6:5, 10).[4] After Stephen's martyrdom, the Holy Spirit continues to fuel the growth of the church through the preaching of Peter and John, soon followed by Saul/Paul. Shortly after Act's depiction of the conversion of Paul, we find the following summary: "So the church throughout all Judea and Galilee and Samaria had peace and was built up; and walking in the fear of the Lord and in the comfort of the Holy Spirit it was multiplied" (Acts 9:31). The church enjoys "peace" precisely because the church is holy, "walking in the fear of the Lord and in the comfort of the Holy Spirit." Just prior to this summary, however, Acts reports that Paul's preaching in Jerusalem so roused the ire of the Hellenists that they "were seeking to kill him," with the result that Paul had to be sent back to Tarsus by his fellow Christians (Acts 9:29–30). What kind of peace and holiness is this?

In his letters, Paul bears witness to the same tension between holiness and strife in the eschatological church of Christ. He tells the Corinthians that "there must be factions among you in order that those who are genuine among you may be recognized" (1 Cor. 11:19). In the Gospel of Matthew too Jesus teaches that "it is necessary that temptations come, but woe to the man by whom the temptation comes!" (Matt. 18:7), and he suggests that even in the church it will be necessary to forgive our brethren not "seven times, but seventy times seven" (Matt. 18:22). At the same time, Jesus promises that "the powers of death shall not prevail against" the church (Matt. 16:18). In the book of Revelation, the seer John receives the command to write down his vision and to "send it to the seven churches" (Rev. 1:11). Many of these churches are plagued by wickedness and strife, including the church in Thyatira that harbors a false prophetess and the church at Laodicea that is "neither cold nor hot" (Rev. 3:15). Yet in the very midst of the seven churches, depicted in the vision as "seven lampstands" (Rev. 1:20), John sees the exalted Christ, fully victorious. God permits his church to be peopled by sinners such as ourselves, and yet the church truly mediates Christ's truth and is filled with Christ's Spirit.

4. For the difficulty of ascertaining whether the "Spirit" here refers to Stephen's virtuous human spirit or the indwelling divine Holy Spirit, see John R. Levison, *Filled with the Spirit* (Grand Rapids: Eerdmans, 2009), 242–45. Levison comments, "On the one hand, this description of Stephen does fit beautifully within a tradition represented by Micah, Elihu, Job, Ben Sira, and Daniel in the tale of Susannah, in which the spirit, the powerful spirit-breath within, inspires cogent speech and stirs compelling debate. On the other hand, the transformation of a speaker by a fresh filling with the spirit is familiar territory in Acts; the holy spirit has just transformed an unlearned Peter into an impressive speaker (Acts 4:8–13)" (ibid., 244).

Can a church composed of sinners and rived by strife be, at the same time, holy and at peace? At first glance, it hardly seems right to talk about Christian holiness (or unity) when there is so much evidence to the contrary. Indeed, some scholars consider that Christian talk of the church as one and holy has been simply a delusion, of the kind that Stephen Greenblatt (following Lucretius) identifies in another context as "the fantasy of attaining something that exceeds what the finite mortal world allows."[5] Is the church's holiness merely a dangerous fantasy?[6]

Answering in the affirmative, the Anglican theologian Ephraim Radner argues that in fact the church is in what Catholics would describe as "mortal" sin. In Radner's view, "the Holy Spirit has taken leave of the divided Church" due to the church's mortal sin of division.[7] Nonetheless, he considers that "we must yet stay loyal to the Church's empty precincts," because it is in our utter sin and impoverishment that the Lord Jesus wills to meet us.[8] Along

5. Stephen Greenblatt, *The Swerve: How the World Became Modern* (New York: W. W. Norton, 2011), 196.

6. This question has become a hot topic today, not least due to horrific revelations of the sexual abuse of children by priests, and also due to the decisions of bishops who simply moved the abusive priests from one parish to another. For an effort to respond to these revelations by changing the episcopal governance of the church, on the grounds that the involvement of the laity in church governance would mitigate such failures (which seems to me to be historically implausible, not least since the sins of the Catholic laity are also scandalous), see Stephen J. Pope, ed., *Common Calling: The Laity and Governance of the Catholic Church* (Washington, DC: Georgetown University Press, 2004). See also Stephen J. Pope, "Accountablity and Sexual Abuse in the United States: Lessons for the Universal Church," *Irish Theological Quarterly* 69 (2004): 73–88; Christopher Ruddy, "Ecclesiological Issues behind the Sexual Abuse Crisis," *Origins* 37 (5 July 2007): 119–26.

7. Ephraim Radner, *The End of the Church: A Pneumatology of Christian Division in the West* (Grand Rapids: Eerdmans, 1998), 10. As he says at the outset of his book, "Within the divided Church, the hearing of Scripture, pneumatic existence, the guidance of the ministry, the taste of communion, even the savor of penitence itself—all this is reduced to the insensible shell of ecclesial mortality, whose presentation on the stage of history, borne listlessly by time as in the image of our Savior's deposition from the Cross, itself provides, by grace, a vehicle of inspired penance" (ibid., 1). See Bruce D. Marshall's important, and appreciative, review essay on Radner's book, "The Divided Church and Its Theology," *Modern Theology* 16 (2000): 377–96; Marshall's perspective here sheds light on the path by which a few years later Marshall became a Catholic. See also Radner's *A Brutal Unity: The Spiritual Politics of the Christian Church* (Waco: Baylor University Press, 2012), which I discuss above. Although I disagree with both of Radner's books, not least because I hold that the church retains real (though obviously not full) unity, I value them for their extraordinary erudition and clear-sighted attention to the often deplorable concrete history of Christianity and to the painfulness and scope of Christian division. See also his wonderfully balanced "Anglicanism on Its Knees," *First Things* 243 (May 2014): 45–50, where he remarks that the current situation in worldwide Anglicanism means that his "own particular understanding of the Christian's vocation to a painful 'standing beside' erring brethren and enemies will be tested, as it already has been to some smaller extent"—although he does not suggest that his ecclesiastical or theological position will change (ibid., 49).

8. Radner, *End of the Church*, 10.

broadly similar lines, the Catholic theologian Nicholas M. Healy finds that despite the idealistic proclamations of theologians, the actual church has frequently been in a state of sinful alienation from God, since "the power of sin is manifested not only in the actions of individuals but in the Christian communal body, when the latter fosters practices, valuations and beliefs in its membership that are incompatible with the gospel."[9] Other recent Catholic theologians, such as Karl Rahner and Francis Sullivan, hold that the church sins, even though Rahner and Sullivan consider that the church can also be said to be "holy" in an eschatological sense, insofar as God promises to guide and govern the church unto salvation.[10]

9. Nicholas M. Healy, *Church, World and the Christian Life: Practical-Prophetic Ecclesiology* (Cambridge: Cambridge University Press, 2000), 7. The period around 1300 is an example for Healy of a time when the church as a whole was in grave sin. Another such time occurred around the time of the Holocaust, which involved, Healy says, "the corporate failure of the church to witness to its Lord" (ibid., 8). The key for Healy is that the church must "acknowledge that it is part of the fallen world" (ibid., 9). I can certainly agree with Healy when he says, "As Christians, then, we have not only to fight against the power of sin in the fallen world, we must fight against it in the midst of our ecclesial body and within ourselves" (ibid.). But in an undifferentiated way, he concludes that "sin and error . . . are part of the church's theological and concrete identity prior to the eschaton" (ibid., 11). He suggests that the traditional Catholic doctrine of the church's holiness is fundamentally a form of works-righteousness: "Claiming an essential perfection suggests too easily, to those within the church as well as to those looking on from outside, that the church thinks there is something deep down within itself—something about who we are—that is worth at least a little bit of glorying" (ibid., 11). See also Healy's "Practices and the New Ecclesiology: Misplaced Concreteness?," *International Journal of Systematic Theology* 5 (2003): 287–308.

10. See two essays by Karl Rahner, SJ: "The Church of Sinners" and "The Sinful Church in the Decrees of Vatican II," in *Theological Investigations*, vol. 6, *Concerning Vatican Council II*, trans. K. H. Kruger and B. Kruger (London: Darton, Longman & Todd, 1969), 253–69 and 270–94; and Francis A. Sullivan, SJ, "Do the Sins of Its Members Affect the Holiness of the Church?," in *In God's Hands: Essays on the Church and Ecumenism in Honour of Michael A. Fahey, SJ*, ed. Jaroslav Z. Skira and Michael S. Attridge (Leuven: Leuven University Press, 2006), 247–68. Against idealized or hypostatized views of the church, Rahner argues that the actual, historical church can and does sin, and he attributes this view to the Second Vatican Council, most significantly in the council's teaching that the church always needs purification (which would not be possible if the church was not in some way the subject of sin). Yet Rahner also holds that the church is "indefectibly holy." As Sullivan summarizes Rahner's position, "Rahner insists that this true holiness, precisely as indefectible, is given to the church as a whole, not to the individual members as such. Rahner sees this indefectible holiness as the effect of the predestination by God of efficacious grace for the church as a whole, which brings it about that her holiness, and not her sinfulness, is her decisive and determining factor" (Sullivan, "Do the Sins of Its Members Affect the Holiness of the Church?," 258). For Rahner, the "holiness" of the church means that God efficaciously guides and governs it, despite its many sins, unto salvation. Sullivan makes much of the fact that *Lumen Gentium* and Pope John Paul II suggest that the church's holiness, at least as it is manifested to the world, is negatively impacted or sullied by the sins (including "social sins") of the members. To my mind, the position of Rahner and Sullivan involves an extrinsicist view of the church's relationship to the incarnate

For the Mennonite theologian Jeremy Bergen, a quick survey of what the church has used its power to accomplish over the course of history makes it impossible to deny that the church is fundamentally a sinful church. Bergen has his eye not simply on history as a broad category in which the church exists but on "the particular history in which the church acted as an agent in the torture of other Christians in sixteenth-century Europe, in the teaching of contempt for the Jews or in providing theological justifications for the enslavement of Africans."[11] When Bergen says "the church acted," he means

---

Son and the Holy Spirit. This is shown not least in Sullivan's argument for privileging "people of God" over against "mother" as an image of the church, and in his statement (true as far as it goes, but not going far enough) that the church "is a people led by human leaders, who are fallible in every decision they make except when they solemnly define a doctrine of faith or morals" (ibid., 267). See also Bishop Stephen Laszlo, "Sin in the Holy Church of God," in *Council Speeches of Vatican II*, ed. Hans Küng, Yves Congar, and Daniel O'Hanlon (Glen Rock, NJ: Paulist Press, 1964); and Joseph A. Komonchak, "Preparing for the New Millennium," *Logos* 1 (1997): 34–55.

11. Jeremy M. Bergen, *Ecclesial Repentance: The Churches Confront Their Sinful Pasts* (London: T&T Clark, 2011), 215. See also such works as Bradford E. Hinze, "Ecclesial Repentance and the Demands of Dialogue," *Theological Studies* 61 (2000): 207–38; Ruud G. W. Huysmans, "The Inquisition for Which the Pope Did Not Ask Forgiveness," *The Jurist* 66 (2006): 469–82; John T. Noonan Jr., *A Church That Can and Cannot Change: The Development of Catholic Moral Teaching* (Notre Dame, IN: University of Notre Dame Press, 2005). I respond to Noonan's line of reasoning in chap. 6 of my *Engaging the Doctrine of Revelation: The Mediation of the Gospel in Church and Scripture* (Grand Rapids: Baker Academic, 2014). Taking a position similar to Noonan's, Hinze argues that

> ecclesial repentance requires in certain cases doctrinal change. . . . If the Catholic Church as a collectivity, and not simply as a group of individuals, has sinned and needs to repent, then the Church as corporate entity and institution must be open to conversion and change in its modes of discourse and action. The role of dialogue in the process of conversion, repentance, and reconciliation and correlatively in the process of tradition has a special place, for dialogue serves not only as the impetus and means for the transmission and reception of tradition, but also for changing and applying tradition in new and unprecedented ways. If this is true, then doctrinal change is not always linear and based on manifest continuities. Any doctrinal change, it is now widely acknowledged, reflects a discontinuity-in-continuity. There are occasions, presumably rare, when the discontinuity that is called for is more pronounced, where the interpretation of the Scriptures and the practices called for are innovative and different. Yet even here calls for discontinuous changes in the Catholic tradition are motivated by a desire to affirm a more basic continuity with the gospel and are advanced as a faithful response to the Triune God of Christian faith. This call to ongoing conversion and purification lies at the heart of the gospel. (Hinze, "Ecclesial Repentence and the Demands of Dialogue," 237–38)

The question is what is included in, and meant by, "the gospel" and thus "a more basic continuity with the gospel." It is unclear how Hinze can be so sure that "the gospel" includes his doctrine of the church, and it is equally unclear how we can now know that definitive Catholic Church teaching, taught precisely as an interpretation and proclamation of the gospel, is false and must be rejected on the basis of "the gospel." Hinze's idea that the holiness of the church would be negated if "the Catholic Church as a collectivity . . . has sinned" indicates that he misunderstands the traditional doctrine of the holiness of the church.

that ordained leaders, acting on behalf of the church, acted in sinful ways or in ways that implicated the church as a whole in social sins, such as slavery.

For Bergen, like Radner, there is a way of resolving the tension. The answer involves Jesus Christ's radical solidarity with sinners: "The holiness of the Church may be understood in a specifically christological way. In the midst of the church's own sin, the Holy Spirit acts to conform the penitent Church evermore to Christ's body—that body on the cross which is God's endurance of sin and victory over it."[12] The more sinful the church is, the more the church is united to the sorrowful Christ who bears it, endures it, and overcomes it.

In my view, there is a better way forward. As I will show, Cyprian, Augustine, and Thomas Aquinas invite us to distinguish between, on the one hand, a church that is holy in its definitive teachings and sacraments, and, on the other hand, the members of the church, who are still sinners despite being in the process of sanctification. In this way, which requires further explication, we can maintain both sides of the tension that we found in Acts and elsewhere in the New Testament between real holiness and real strife. Before retrieving this approach to the holiness of the eschatological church of Christ, however, I will attend to the important alternative view advocated by Reformed theology, represented here by the contemporary theologians Kevin Vanhoozer and Todd Billings and by the Reformer John Calvin.[13] Their emphasis on the ongoing sinfulness of the church's members and on the church's utter dependence upon God for any holiness it possesses is deeply salutary. As T. F. Torrance aptly describes this participatory dependence, "The holiness of the church is its relation to God, its participation in the fellowship of the divine being and life and truth. . . . *Holy* church refers to a unique relation to God, in which as one and holy (the *Una Sancta*) the church is drawn into the holiness of God himself, into the fellowship of the holy Trinity, partaking of that fellowship through the Holy Spirit."[14]

12. Bergen, *Ecclesial Repentance*, 286.

13. For further Reformation background, see David S. Yeago, "*Ecclesia Sancta, Ecclesia Peccatrix*: The Holiness of the Church in Martin Luther's Theology," *Pro Ecclesia* 9 (2000): 331–54.

14. Thomas F. Torrance, *Atonement: The Person and Work of Christ*, ed. Robert T. Walker (Downers Grove, IL: IVP Academic, 2009), 385 (see 341 for the provenance of this text). Along these lines, Torrance helpfully adds, "*Holy* church refers to the ontological grounding of the being of the church in the self-impartation and self-revelation of God to it, thus sharing with it his own holy life and informing and purifying its mind with his divine truth. . . . Holy church means that the church is church through God alone, having its own unique ground and its own unique end in God. Hence however much the church in history and on earth may be conditioned by involvement in this or that society, nation or race, the church stands out against all that as distinct, in holy relation to holy God through the Holy Spirit" (ibid., 385–86). As Torrance says, Jesus Christ alone "has divine nature, but through union with him in his human nature, hallowed and sanctified by the truth of God, the church is marvellously made a partaker of

Reformed Theology and the Church's Holiness

Kevin Vanhoozer and Todd Billings

Drawing upon Martin Luther's definition of the Christian, Kevin Vanhoozer describes the church as "*simil justus et peccator.*"[15] In saying this, Vanhoozer aims to appreciate the Spirit's work in the church, without supposing that "every church doctrine mediate[s] the presence of God."[16] It is crucial for Vanhoozer that the church not displace the centrality of God in the drama of salvation, which he thinks tends to happen all too often. He has in view especially the Catholic Church's claim to be able to interpret Scripture infallibly and even, guided by the Spirit, to teach dogmas that are not explicitly present in Scripture.[17] Yet this concern about an inflated church does not lead Vanhoozer to minimize the work of the Holy Spirit in building Christ's church. He states that "the Spirit is 'the hand of God' who leads believers to the truth, enables believers to walk the way, and bestows on believers the gift of life."[18] The Spirit inspires the writing of Scripture and enables persons to hear, accept, and obey God's Word. Thus, for Vanhoozer, "The Spirit's special role is to make Christ's communicative action—in particular, the commissioned canonical testimony of the apostles—efficacious, transforming communication into a species of communion."[19] The Spirit leads the church toward holiness, but the church is not yet the holy bride that eschatologically it will be. Vanhoozer explains, "The Spirit ministers the word in order to build up all things—especially the church—into Christ."[20]

---

divine nature. Hence the holiness of the church is the holiness of Christ in which it shares by grace, being anointed with his anointing, sanctified with his sanctification, and so sharing in his holy relation to the Father through the Holy Spirit. This holiness is actualised in the church through the communion of the Holy Spirit. He only is the Spirit of holiness, he only the Spirit of truth; and therefore it is only through his presence and power in the church that it partakes of the holiness of Jesus Christ" (ibid., 386).

15. Kevin J. Vanhoozer, *The Drama of Doctrine: A Canonical-Linguistic Approach to Christian Theology* (Louisville: Westminster John Knox, 2005), 188.

16. Ibid.

17. On the church's "infallibility," see especially Yves Congar, OP, *I Believe in the Holy Spirit*, trans. David Smith (New York: Crossroad, 1997), 2:46. See also Matthew Levering, *Mary's Bodily Assumption* (Notre Dame, IN: University of Notre Dame Press, 2014).

18. Vanhoozer, *Drama of Doctrine*, 198.

19. Ibid., 199.

20. Ibid., 201. Vanhoozer later comments, "As the theater of the gospel, the church must be formed by word and Spirit to be the place, and the people, where not only vital but life-giving speech and action are on public display" (ibid., 406–7). He goes on to say that "the life of Jesus celebrated in the liturgy is in turn formed in those who worship in spirit and in truth. In this way the liturgy, like theology, is conducive to spirituality: to recognizing the truth of 'what is' in Jesus Christ. Specifically, liturgical worship enables a participatory knowledge of this truth through its ritual performance of the gospel" (ibid., 409). He concludes this section with another

Is the church, then, fundamentally still *awaiting* reconciliation? No. Vanhoozer remarks in this regard, "The church does not have to work for reconciliation. Reconciliation has already been accomplished; its reality is in Christ."[21] But the church, composed of Christ's followers, must be further configured to this reality of reconciliation and holiness that Christ has made present once and for all. In this sense the church's task is to "suffer" the effects of its preaching and teaching of the (biblical) gospel: the church is to repent and be increasingly configured to Christ. This occurs through the Holy Spirit and thus also through the Spirit-inspired Scripture: "The Spirit is the one through whom we become 'thickly related' to Christ by believing Scripture's assertions, obeying its commands, and trusting its promises."[22] The goal is union with Christ—something that is happening now, but that is still imperfect due to sin.

In two recent books, *Union with Christ* and *The Word of God for the People of God*, Todd Billings offers a similar Reformed account of the church's sanctification or "holiness." He emphasizes the value of the church while retaining an awareness of its sinfulness and its ongoing need for transformation. The starting points for Billings's theology are God's righteousness in Christ and God's free justification of the sinner. On this view, God first "legally" adopts us by imputing Christ's righteousness to us even though we are sinners. This is "forensic" justification, by which God simply claims us as his children in Christ. Only then can a process of sanctification begin. Billings describes sanctification as "a transformative process by the Spirit."[23] This process is not fueled by our striving, since we cannot save ourselves or make ourselves holy. Instead, it is fueled by utter dependence upon Christ and a complete embrace of his righteousness. Although justification and sanctification must be kept distinct in order to avoid works-righteousness, they are separated formally rather than temporally. When God makes us his children "legally" through adoption in Christ, God helps "us enter into our new identity as God's children by the Spirit's power."[24]

---

stirring commendation of the role of the church: "The church is a celebratory theater that, through its liturgy and its life, inserts its members into the drama of redemption. This drama is *really present* in the life of the church, and the liturgy helps us to see, taste, imagine, and *live* it. *What the church finally celebrates in the liturgy is historical and eschatological reality: the reality of the already/not yet presence of Jesus Christ in our midst*" (ibid., 410).

21. Ibid., 201.

22. Ibid., 202.

23. J. Todd Billings, *Union with Christ: Reframing Theology and Ministry for the Church* (Grand Rapids: Baker Academic, 2011), 27.

24. Ibid., 29. See also 107–9, where Billings describes "the double grace of justification and sanctification, gifts that are inseparable yet distinct, received by the Spirit in union with Christ" (107) and emphasizes that "this new life does not make our own *works* the ground or content of the gospel. Our works, even our works of justice in the way of Jesus Christ, are not, in themselves,

But the sanctification that we experience now is limited; we are still sinners. Billings argues that being children of God is "a reality that belongs to the future and is experienced now as a foretaste of God's future," because even though God has made us his children, "the full reality of adoption is not yet."[25] Billings further emphasizes that apart from our union with Christ, we can do nothing. We have no autonomous righteousness, no autonomous claim upon God in any way whatsoever. In this sense, Billings finds the discourse of "total depravity" and the "bondage of the will" to be helpful. It is only in Christ, through the Holy Spirit, that we receive the gift of sanctification. Billings affirms that "communion with the Spirit is what makes our faith and action our own. . . . God *does* use our will, our mind, our ministry, and our efforts to preach the gospel and to live faithful Christian lives."[26] But the credit is not half God's and half ours. On the contrary, we could do absolutely nothing without God, and if we do bear fruit, then the credit belongs to Christ and the Holy Spirit. We do not need to be anxious about our holiness because we know that it is a work of God in us through the righteousness of Jesus Christ, not a work whose source is our own will. Christian action has no "space that is autonomous from the Spirit's work."[27] God reveals in Scripture both that "only by the Spirit's effectual work can one move toward communion with God" and that we can trust that "the Spirit's work is effectual."[28]

So long as holiness is not seen as an autonomous possession, then, Billings gladly affirms that the Holy Spirit can and does truly sanctify believers, even if our limited degree of sanctification is only a foretaste of the perfection that we will receive in eternal life. As believers, we receive "the Spirit-empowered activation of our lives for love of God and neighbor."[29] If all congregations were simply unholy, it would make no sense to challenge congregations to be holy, as Billings does.[30] But the church is also always in need of reform. God's word in Scripture challenges the church (and individual believers) to be more deeply configured to Christ. Billings states, "God's word empowers the reshaping of the church because, on this side of the *eschaton*, the church

---

the good news" (107). Along the same lines, Billings goes on to say, "Moreover, obedience to the law is not done as an anxious work for our salvation or as a bold, heroic human action; obedience to the law takes place in the context of Spirit-empowered freedom and gratitude to God, who has been revealed as a gracious Father through the adoption that believers receive in Christ" (ibid., 112).

25. Ibid., 31.
26. Ibid., 46.
27. Ibid., 48.
28. Ibid., 49.
29. Ibid., 108.
30. See ibid., 95.

is always in need of further transformation through Scripture."[31] On the one hand, then, "The kingdom is amongst us"; on the other hand, "until the consummation of God's kingdom, his disciples will continue to struggle with sin."[32]

It would be a mistake, in Billings's view, either to imagine that the church has not been guided by the Spirit in its scriptural interpretation or to suppose that the church has always been right. He explains that "the Spirit is always speaking a word to call the church to further transformation through Scripture, yet the church's tradition also reflects the Spirit's work in a people whom God has united to Jesus Christ."[33] If the latter were not true, then the church could hardly be said to be the "mystical body of Christ," as in fact the church is.[34] Certainly, the church is not perfect. The church is "a people who find true life by participating more and more in Jesus Christ through the Spirit."[35] Billings carefully keeps Scripture and the Spirit above the church, so that neither ends up being merely "the possession of the church."[36] Yet he also emphasizes that the early and medieval church should not be simply rejected by Protestants. He calls upon his fellow Protestants to be active in "discerning the Spirit's work in and through the church throughout its history and across cultures."[37]

Billings argues that when the first Protestants identified themselves as "catholic," they were self-consciously recognizing the Spirit's work over the centuries and identifying themselves "with the early ecumenical councils and creeds of the church, assuming that the Spirit was active in leading the church 'into all truth' through these decisions."[38] Thus the Nicene Creed, while obviously predating the Reformation and its ecclesiological reforms, should be recognized as containing "a deposit of the Spirit's work, a standard by which the universal church could discern a faithful interpretation of Scripture from

---

31. J. Todd Billings, *The Word of God for the People of God: An Entryway to the Theological Interpretation of Scripture* (Grand Rapids: Eerdmans, 2010), 68.

32. Ibid., 205. Billings sees the church as "called to be a sign of the [eschatological] kingdom" (ibid., 222).

33. Ibid., 198.

34. Ibid., 161.

35. Ibid. See also, from a Pentecostal perspective aiming to develop a fully "pneumatological doctrine of justification by faith" (179), Frank D. Macchia, "Justified in the Spirit: Implications on the Border of Theology and Science," in *The Spirit in Creation and New Creation: Science and Theology in Western and Orthodox Realms*, ed. Michael Welker (Grand Rapids: Eerdmans, 2012), 179–91; as well as Macchia's fuller treatment of the Holy Spirit and justification in his *Justified in the Spirit: Creation, Redemption, and the Triune God* (Grand Rapids: Eerdmans, 2010).

36. Billings, *Word of God for the People of God*, 133.

37. Ibid.

38. Ibid.

an aberrant one."[39] To deny this work of the Spirit among pre-Reformation Christian communities, Billings suggests, would be to fail "to believe God's promise through Scripture to send the Spirit to the church to lead her into all truth, to bind together the church as Christ's body, to give her gifts and bear fruit through the Spirit's power."[40] According to Scripture, the Spirit's work is always communal, not simply individual. At the same time, it is also true that the patristic and especially the medieval church erred profoundly. Billings observes that "the Spirit speaks freely through Scripture . . . and is not strictly constrained by the church's past interpretation."[41] The church must not "arrogate to itself the role of being the final standard for scriptural interpretation."[42] That would be to confuse the church with the Spirit, so that the Spirit could no longer correct the sinful church.

John Calvin

We can anticipate that Vanhoozer's and Billings's positions on the church's sanctification or holiness will be close to John Calvin's, but Calvin's position nonetheless has its own distinctive emphases worth identifying here. As background, let me first set forth Calvin's defense of the divinity of the Holy Spirit. In book 1 of his *Institutes of the Christian Religion*, Calvin inquires into the basis upon which we proclaim the Holy Spirit to be God.[43] He does not think that we need to begin with the New Testament. The Spirit's divinity was already fairly clear in Genesis 1:2, where we find "not only that the beauty

39. Ibid., 133–34. Thus the early church provides us with a Spirit-given "tradition." See also the essays in Timothy George, ed., *Evangelicals and the Nicene Faith: Reclaiming the Apostolic Witness* (Grand Rapids: Baker Academic, 2011). On the relationship of the universal church and the local church, see James W. Thompson, *The Church according to Paul: Rediscovering the Community Conformed to Christ* (Grand Rapids: Baker Academic, 2014), 175–82, 202–6.

40. Billings, *Word of God for the People of God*, 134.

41. Ibid., 135.

42. Ibid. On this point, see the final chapter of Matthew Levering, *Participatory Biblical Exegesis: A Theology of Biblical Interpretation* (Notre Dame, IN: University of Notre Dame Press, 2008).

43. For background, see Scott R. Swain, "The Trinity in the Reformers," in *The Oxford Handbook of the Trinity*, ed. Gilles Emery, OP, and Matthew Levering (Oxford: Oxford University Press, 2011), 227–39; A. Baars, "The Trinity," in *The Calvin Handbook*, ed. H. J. Selderhuis (Grand Rapids: Eerdmans, 2009), 245–57; John McIntyre, *The Shape of Pneumatology: Studies in the Doctrine of the Holy Spirit* (Edinburgh: T&T Clark, 1997), 109–33; Thomas F. Torrance, "Calvin's Doctrine of the Trinity," *Calvin Theological Journal* 25 (1990): 165–93. The Catholic theologian Brian Gaybba argues that "with Calvin there is a rediscovery—in the West at any rate—of a biblical idea virtually forgotten since patristic times. It is the idea of the Spirit as God in action" (Gaybba, *The Spirit of Love: Theology of the Holy Spirit* [London: Geoffrey Chapman, 1987], 100). Although this claim does not hold up historically, it nonetheless testifies to a central aspect of Calvin's theology of the Holy Spirit.

which the world displays is maintained by the invigorating power of the Spirit, but that even before this beauty existed the Spirit was at work cherishing the confused mass" so as to create it and sustain it in being.[44] Already in Genesis, then, Moses has signaled to us that the Spirit is the Creator God. The Spirit's divine sharing in the work of redemption is also expressed in the Old Testament. Calvin cites Isaiah 48:16, which in his version associates the Lord God and the Spirit in the work of sending the prophet.[45] The Spirit is the one who "searches everything, even the depths of God" and who "comprehends the thoughts of God" (1 Cor. 2:10–11). The Spirit reveals to Paul the "secret and hidden wisdom of God" (1 Cor. 2:7), though it is only God who can make humans "dumb, or deaf, or seeing, or blind" (Exod. 4:11). The Spirit is the author and source of "the varieties of gifts" (1 Cor. 12:4) for the upbuilding of the church, all of which "are inspired by one and the same Spirit, who apportions to each one individually as he wills" (1 Cor. 12:11). The Spirit could not possibly have such power and authority unless he were God.

Calvin notes that Scripture explicitly associates the name of God with the Spirit. We are "God's temple" because the "Spirit of God" dwells in us (1 Cor. 3:16); if so, then the Spirit is God dwelling in us and making us God's temple. Similarly, in Acts, Peter rebukes Ananias for lying "to the Holy Spirit" (Acts 5:3), and Peter describes this as lying not "to men but to God" (Acts 5:4). One and the same lie is thus described as being "to the Holy Spirit" and "to God." The Holy Spirit must therefore be God. Also in Acts, Paul quotes Isaiah 6:9–10, a discourse that Isaiah attributes to the Lord but that Paul attributes to the Holy Spirit (Acts 28:25–27). The Lord God and the Holy Spirit must therefore be the same God. The same conjunction is made in Isaiah 63:10, which connects the Lord's anger with the fact that the people "grieved his holy Spirit."[46] Further, if all kinds of sin will be forgiven except "blasphemy against the Spirit" (Matt. 12:31), then the Spirit surely cannot be a mere creature.

44. John Calvin, *Institutes of the Christian Religion*, trans. Henry Beveridge (Grand Rapids: Eerdmans, 1989), 1:122.

45. In the RSV, by contrast, Isaiah 48:16 reads "And now the Lord GOD has sent me and his Spirit."

46. Richard E. Averbeck notes that Isaiah 63:10 is one of three instances (including Ps. 51:11 and Isaiah 63:11) in which the Spirit is described in the Old Testament as the "Spirit of holiness" (*rûaḥ qōdeš*). Averbeck points out that the Septuagint "translates this combination of words with the same expression the New Testament uses for what we render as 'Holy Spirit' (i.e., the noun *pneuma*, 'Spirit,' followed by the adjective *hagion*, 'Holy')." See Averbeck, "Breath, Wind, Spirit and the Holy Spirit in the Old Testament," in *Presence, Power and Promise: The Role of the Spirit of God in the Old Testament*, ed. David G. Firth and Paul D. Wegner (Downers Grove, IL: IVP Academic, 2011), 25–37, at 25–26.

Calvin further remarks that believers experience the Spirit's presence in both creation and redemption. No creature could be present to the created order as the Spirit is; the Spirit's "transfusing vigour into all things, breathing into them being, life, and motion, is plainly divine."[47] We see the movement, energy, and order of created things, a manifestation that reveals the Spirit's presence. We also experience internally the Spirit's transformative presence. This internal and external testimony fits with what Scripture teaches us about the Spirit's divinity.

There are other biblical testimonies to the divinity of the Holy Spirit, including the baptismal formula in Matthew 28:19. The distinction between Father, Son, and Holy Spirit—while remaining an ineffable mystery—appears clearly throughout the Gospel of John. To illuminate these biblical testimonies, the church fathers appropriate "energy and efficacy of action" to the Spirit, and Augustine (followed by the church in the West) conceives of the Spirit in terms of the analogy of mind, knowledge, and will. Calvin approves of these analogies, even though they are obviously of less value than Scripture. He affirms the *filioque* on the grounds that Scripture depicts the Spirit as being both of the Father and of the Son, as for instance in Romans 8:9, where Paul calls the Spirit the "Spirit of God" and the "Spirit of Christ." He accepts Augustine's view that the distinction of persons signifies distinct relations in the order of origin rather than distinct substances, and he devotes a lengthy section to refuting the antitrinitarian theology of Servetus.

On the basis of this defense of the Holy Spirit as fully divine and as relationally distinct from the Father and Son, Calvin in the first chapter of book 3 of the *Institutes* develops his theology of the work of the Holy Spirit. Christ is our Head, and we are members of Christ; and it is due to "the secret efficacy of the Spirit . . . that we enjoy Christ and all his blessings."[48] When the Holy Spirit unites us to Christ, we receive the salvation won by Christ. Citing 1 Corinthians 6:11, Calvin argues that our justification and sanctification come in Christ and by the Spirit. He describes the Spirit as "the bond by which Christ effectually bonds us to himself."[49] In book 1, he laid weight upon our internal experience of the Spirit enlightening and sanctifying us through his gifts; now he emphasizes the Spirit's role in uniting us to Christ. Although he does not here draw out this unitive role through a discussion of the Father and Son's mutual Love, he certainly thinks of the Spirit's work in the economy of salvation primarily in terms of uniting or bonding.

47. Calvin, *Institutes of the Christian Religion*, 1:122.
48. Calvin, *Institutes of the Christian Religion*, 1:463.
49. Calvin, *Institutes of the Christian Religion*, 1:463.

Calvin notes that the prophets promised that in "the kingdom of Christ . . . the Spirit would be poured out in richer abundance."[50] Now that Christ has inaugurated his kingdom, the "Spirit of sanctification" has been given to us to be "the seed and root of heavenly life in us."[51] In this regard, Calvin again cites Romans 8:9, in addition to various other passages from the Pauline Epistles, the Gospel of John, and the prophets. The "energy of the Holy Spirit" is "the special life that Christ breathes into his people."[52] The emphasis here is not simply on sanctification but on *communal* sanctification. Christ's "people," his "kingdom," is filled with the Holy Spirit. God does this freely, and our righteousness is God's free work. Calvin states that it is the Spirit's "secret irrigation that makes us bud forth and produce the fruits of righteousness."[53] When we receive the Spirit, we "are restored to the full vigour of life."[54] The Spirit purifies us from sin and inflames us with desire for God. Calvin describes our sanctification—and thus the church's sanctification—in powerful terms: we receive "all heavenly riches"; God "exerts his power" and rules us "by his motion and agency"; Christ accomplishes a "sacred marriage" with us so that "we become bone of his bone, and flesh of his flesh"; and Christ "keeps us under him" so that the church is truly his body (obedient to the commands of the Head).[55] This is a strong account of the church's sanctification and righteousness in Christ and the Spirit! We receive all this, Calvin notes, by faith, which is the Holy Spirit's gift in us. Through the Holy Spirit, Christ enlightens us and regenerates us: we become "new creatures," "cleansed from all pollution," "holy temples to the Lord."[56]

It would seem then that, for Calvin, the Holy Spirit makes the church holy. In the first chapter of book 4 of the *Institutes*, Calvin clarifies this point. On the one hand, when the church lacks truth and holiness, it is definitely no church. Truth and holiness come to the church from Christ's and the Spirit's work in "the ministry of the word and sacraments."[57] Wherever the word and sacrament are properly found, the church exists; wherever they are lacking, we must speak of "the death of the Church."[58] In Calvin's view, this death

50. Calvin, *Institutes of the Christian Religion*, 1:463.
51. Calvin, *Institutes of the Christian Religion*, 1:463.
52. Calvin, *Institutes of the Christian Religion*, 1:464.
53. Calvin, *Institutes of the Christian Religion*, 1:465.
54. Calvin, *Institutes of the Christian Religion*, 1:465.
55. Calvin, *Institutes of the Christian Religion*, 1:465. See Mark Garcia, *Life in Christ: Union with Christ and Twofold Grace in Calvin's Theology* (Carlisle, UK: Paternoster, 2008).
56. Calvin, *Institutes of the Christian Religion*, 1:466.
57. Calvin, *Institutes of the Christian Religion*, 2:304.
58. Calvin, *Institutes of the Christian Religion*, 2:305. In his *Brutal Unity*, Ephraim Radner takes this further and argues on theological and especially historical grounds that all the

has happened in the church that remains under the jurisdiction of Rome: "If the true Church is 'the pillar and ground of the truth' (1 Tim. iii.15), it is certain that there is no Church where lying and falsehood have usurped the ascendancy. Since this is the state of matters under the Papacy, we can understand how much of the Church there survives."[59] Calvin goes on to specify that under the papacy the ministry of the word has been replaced by "a perverted government, compounded of lies" and that the ministry of the sacraments (especially the Eucharist) has been replaced by "the foulest sacrilege" and "intolerable superstitions."[60] The true church, therefore, is indeed holy; without sufficient holiness, the church will die.

However, Calvin makes clear that he is not suggesting that the church requires a perfect holiness in order to exist. The work of the Holy Spirit does not establish a perfect church prior to the eschaton. So long as the ministry of the word and sacraments "exists entire and unimpaired," the church exists despite other defects.[61] Even when the ministry of the word and sacraments is itself infected by minor defects, the church still exists. Arguing against the radical Reformers, Calvin strongly warns that "we arrogate too much to ourselves, if we presume forthwith to withdraw from the communion of the Church, because the lives of all accord not with our judgment, or even with the Christian profession."[62] After all, the holy prophets did not withdraw from the church (the Israel of God) despite the great corruption and idolatry that they found. Christ himself, along with the apostles, did not withdraw from the religion of the Jerusalem temple, despite "the desperate impiety of

churches—Protestant, Catholic, and Orthodox—are unholy (and thus, in Calvin's terms, dead), but also that God does not abandon his covenant. Radner states, "To be 'one Church' is to be joined to the unity of the Son to the Father, who, in the Spirit, gives himself away (Heb. 9:14), not in some general flourish of self-denial, but to and for the sake of his enemies, the 'godless,' for their life (Rom. 4:5; 5:6; 5:10; 1 Cor. 15:22; Eph. 2:12). Not that the church in fact does this. She does not, and hence she is not one, and finally therefore she is not who she is meant to be. But though she is faithless, yet 'he remains faithful' (1 Tim. 2:13). The woefulness of Christian witness in this world is measured by the distance between these two realities; so too is measured the mercy of God" (Radner, *Brutal Unity*, 1–2).

59. Calvin, *Institutes of the Christian Religion*, 2:305. For contemporary application of this principle (in light of battles over sexual teaching within the Presbyterian Church [U.S.A.]), see James C. Goodloe IV, "The Church: One and Holy," *Theology Today* 66 (2009): 203–16, at 208–10. When treating the unity and catholicity of the church, Calvin observes, "For although the sad devastation which everywhere meets our view may proclaim that no Church remains, let us know that the death of Christ produces fruit, and that God wondrously preserves his Church, while placing it as it were in concealment. Thus it was said to Elijah, 'Yet I have left me seven thousand in Israel' (1 Kings xix.18)" (Calvin, *Institutes of the Christian Religion*, 2:282).

60. Calvin, *Institutes of the Christian Religion*, 2:305.

61. Calvin, *Institutes of the Christian Religion*, 2:304.

62. Calvin, *Institutes of the Christian Religion*, 2:296.

the Pharisees" and "the dissolute licentiousness of manners which everywhere prevailed."[63] Those who reject the church because of even a "minutest blemish," therefore, are wrongly expecting the church on earth to be the eschatological Jerusalem.[64] So long as "the word of God is preached and the sacraments are administered," we have no right to leave the church even if a large number of our fellows—or of our pastors—are unworthy.[65] Calvin states that the "sacred rites are not less pure and salutary to a man who is holy and upright, from being at the same time handled by the impure."[66]

Like Augustine, Calvin argues that "the Scriptures speak of the Church in two ways."[67] The first way consists in the church as God sees it, "the Church as it really is before God."[68] This church contains all the elect, and more particularly all "who by the gift of adoption are sons of God, and by the sanctification of the Spirit true members of Christ."[69] The second way consists in the church as we see it. This church contains many who profess to be members of Christ but who in fact are not, and these persons cause scandal by their false witness. The one church is both visible and invisible.[70] The true church is the invisible church (which God alone sees), but this church is in fact the same church as the visible church, even if some of the members differ.[71] God has willed that for the duration of human history, the elect and the reprobate are to be mingled in the one visible church. With respect to this visible church (which is the one church), Calvin states that this church is our "Mother," and he observes that being able to recognize the visible church is crucial because "there is no other means of entering into life unless she conceive us in the

63. Calvin, *Institutes of the Christian Religion*, 2:296.
64. Calvin, *Institutes of the Christian Religion*, 2:297.
65. Calvin, *Institutes of the Christian Religion*, 2:297.
66. Calvin, *Institutes of the Christian Religion*, 2:297.
67. Calvin, *Institutes of the Christian Religion*, 2:288.
68. Calvin, *Institutes of the Christian Religion*, 2:288.
69. Calvin, *Institutes of the Christian Religion*, 2:288.
70. On the unity of the church according to Calvin, see Lukas Vischer, *Pia Conspiratio: Calvin on the Unity of Christ's Church* (Geneva: John Knox International Reformed Center, 2000).
71. For discussion of Calvin on the church's visibility, see, for example, Emidio Campi, "Calvin's Understanding of the Church," *Reformed World* 57 (2007): 290–305. This view differs significantly from that of John Owen, at least as Ephraim Radner presents Owen's position: "True Christian unity, for Owen, is not given in a congregation, not even in a more faithful congregation. Rather, faithful congregations are to be joined and supported because they are aimed at the proper form of unity's invisible—spiritual—status. Christian unity [for Owen] describes the condition in which we are in 'union' with Christ as one body 'spiritually,' in the Spirit, which is analogous to a soul; and this lies *behind* all churches, and all institutional means and practices" (Radner, "The Holy Spirit and Unity: Getting Out of the Way of Christ," *International Journal of Systematic Theology* 16 [2014]: 207–20, at 217). See John Owen, *Pneumatologia, or, A Discourse concerning the Holy Spirit* (London: Nathaniel Ponder, 1674).

womb and give us birth, unless she nourish us at her breasts, and, in short, keep us under her charge and government" until we die and enter into eternal life.[72] Citing numerous biblical texts from both Testaments, Calvin is quite clear that "beyond the pale of the church no forgiveness of sins, no salvation, can be hoped for."[73]

As we have seen, Calvin considers that the true visible church of his own time is not the church under papal jurisdiction, which was the church in which he was raised. That false church is dead and deadly, due to the work of Satan.[74]

72. Calvin, *Institutes of the Christian Religion*, 2:283. For the sacramental and soterio-logical implications of this passage, see Julie Canlis, *Calvin's Ladder: A Spiritual Theology of Ascent and Ascension* (Grand Rapids: Eerdmans, 2010), 238. On Calvin's description of the church as our "mother," see Neil Pronk, "Calvin's Doctrine of the Church," in *Calvin for Today*, ed. Joel R. Beeke (Grand Rapids: Reformation Heritage, 2009), 139–54, at 147–48. On the church's jurisdictional power, see Marta García-Alonso, "Calvin and the Ecclesiastical Power of Jurisdiction," *Reformation & Renaissance Review* 10 (2008): 137–55. In García-Alonso's view, Luther's undoing of the medieval Catholic Church's "doctrine of universal papal power" (vis-à-vis the state) was generally beneficial, but nonetheless risked leaving the church under the dominance of the state (ibid., 138). In this context, "It was Calvin chiefly who managed to balance the critique of papal *plenitudo potestatis* with the demand for some degree of jurisdiction for a church which, in this way, reclaimed its institutional dimension. . . . Calvin progressively [beginning with the third edition of the *Institutes*] abandons the Lutheran doctrine of the Church in favour of an institutional Church that reasserts part of its old pow-ers" (ibid.). At stake was both the church's doctrinal authority and the church's discipline or punishment of sin, ultimately by excommunication (and by the execution of heretics). Calvin helped to establish the Genevan Consistory, composed of representatives of the Reformed Church and the Genevan state, to ensure attendance at Reformed worship services (as well as stamping out certain Catholic practices and beliefs) and to excommunicate citizens for such sins as adultery, drunkenness, blasphemy, gambling, dancing, usury, and heresy. See also John Witte Jr., "Moderate Religious Liberty in the Theology of John Calvin," *Calvin Theological Journal* 31 (1996): 359–403.

73. Calvin, *Institutes of the Christian Religion*, 2:283.

74. Regarding Satan's attacks upon the true ministry of the word and sacraments, Calvin comments, "To his wiles it was owing that for several ages the pure preaching of the word disap-peared" (Calvin, *Institutes of the Christian Religion*, 2:290). Faced with the radical Reformers' rejection of his own church, Calvin expresses alarm and calls for a careful test:

How perilous, then, nay, how fatal the temptation, when we even entertain a thought of separating ourselves from that assembly in which are beheld the signs and badges which the Lord has deemed sufficient to characterise his Church! We see how great caution should be employed in both respects. That we may not be imposed upon by the name of Church, every congregation which claims the name must be brought to that test as to a Lydian stone. If it holds the order instituted by the Lord in word and sacraments there will be no deception; we may safely pay it the honour due to a church: on the other hand, if it exhibit itself without word and sacraments, we must in this case be no less careful to avoid the imposture than we were to shun pride and presumption in the other. When we say that the pure ministry of the word and pure celebration of the sacraments is a fit pledge and earnest, so that we may safely recognise a church in every society in which both exist, our meaning is, that we are never to discard it so long as these remain, though it may otherwise teem with numerous faults. Nay, even in the administration

Rather, the visible church of his own time is, for Calvin, the reformed church in which the true ministry of the word and the sacraments can be observed. Even this true, visible church contains many who are not truly members of Christ and whose sins cause scandal. But this true church can be known and recognized in the world: it is "the whole body of mankind scattered throughout the world, who profess to worship one God and Christ, who by baptism are initiated into the faith; by partaking of the Lord's Supper profess unity in true doctrine and charity, agree in holding the word of the Lord, and observe the ministry which Christ has appointed for the preaching of it."[75]

Regarding the visible church, then, God wills for us to charitably acknowledge as our fellow Christians not only those who appear most worthy to our eyes but also all "who by confession of faith, regularity of conduct, and participation in the sacraments, unite with us in acknowledging the same God and Christ."[76] The universal visible church on earth is present in all the local congregations that truly "have the ministry of the word, and honour the administration of the sacraments."[77] As Calvin famously puts it, "Wherever we see the word of God sincerely preached and heard, wherever we see the sacraments administered according to the institution of Christ, there we cannot have any doubt that the church of God has some existence, since his promise cannot fail, 'Where two or three are gathered together in my name, there am I in the midst of them' (Matth. xviii.20)."[78] No one can be justified

---

of word and sacraments defects may creep in which ought not to alienate us from its communion. (Calvin, *Institutes of the Christian Religion*, 2:290–91)

75. Calvin, *Institutes of the Christian Religion*, 2:288.

76. Calvin, *Institutes of the Christian Religion*, 2:288–89.

77. Calvin, *Institutes of the Christian Religion*, 2:289. See Kilian McDonnell, *John Calvin, the Church, and the Eucharist* (Princeton, NJ: Princeton University Press, 1967); B. A. Gerrish, *Grace and Gratitude: The Eucharistic Theology of John Calvin* (Minneapolis: Fortress, 1993).

78. Calvin, *Institutes of the Christian Religion*, 2:289. Calvin goes on to explain further, For such is the value which the Lord sets on the communion of his Church, that all who contumaciously alienate themselves from any Christian society, in which the ministry of his word and sacraments is maintained, he regards as deserters of religion. So highly does he recommend her authority, that when it is violated he considers that his own authority is impaired. For there is no small weight in the designation given to her, "the house of God," "the pillar and ground of the truth" (1 Tim. iii.15). By these words Paul intimates, that to prevent the truth from perishing in the world, the Church is its faithful guardian, because God has been pleased to preserve the pure preaching of his word by her instrumentality, and to exhibit himself to us as a parent while he feeds us with spiritual nourishment, and provides whatever is conducive to our salvation. Moreover, no mean praise is conferred on the Church when she is said to have been chosen and set apart by Christ as his spouse, "not having spot or wrinkle, or any such thing" (Eph. v.27), as "his body, the fulness of him that filleth all in all" (Eph. i.23). Whence it follows, that revolt from the Church is denial of God and Christ. Wherefore there is the more necessity to beware of a dissent so iniquitous; for seeing by it we aim as far as in us lies at the

in withdrawing from the church in its local instantiation, so long as the marks of the church—the truthful ministry of word and sacraments—are present.

Calvin points out that the way in which Paul handled his churches should instruct us. So long as they retained the true ministry of the word and sacraments, Paul did not separate from them. As Calvin observes, "Among the Corinthians it was not a few that erred, but almost the whole body had become tainted" by a variety of grave sins; yet Paul still "acknowledges and heralds them as a Church of Christ, and a society of saints."[79]

What then of the holiness of the church? Calvin's opponents emphasize that since the true church is holy, "there is no church where there is not complete purity and integrity of conduct."[80] Calvin reminds them, however, that the holiness of the church is perfect only in God's eyes, since God knows the final church of the elect. The visible church on earth contains persons in various degrees of sanctification, and it also contains insincere persons who profess Christian faith without truly believing. Calvin cites Jesus's various parables that make clear that "the Church will labour under the defect of being burdened with a multitude of wicked until the day of judgment."[81] Those who deny this burden—for example, Donatists and Anabaptists—have failed to attend sufficiently to Jesus. In this regard, Calvin notes that "there always have been persons who, imbued with a false persuasion of absolute holiness, as if they had already become a kind of aerial spirits, spurn the society of all in whom they see that something human still remains."[82] In fact, as Calvin says, "the holiest sometimes make the most grievous fall," whereas open sinners often repent and seek amendment.[83]

Going deeper into the particular sense in which the church is "holy," Calvin notes that we certainly cannot deny the truth of Paul's statement in Ephesians 5:25–27 that "Christ loved the church and gave himself up for her, that he might sanctify her, having cleansed her by the washing of water with the word, that he might present the church to himself in splendor, without spot or wrinkle or any such thing, that she might be holy and without blemish."[84]

---

destruction of God's truth, we deserve to be crushed by the full thunder of his anger. No crime can be imagined more atrocious than that of sacrilegiously and perfidiously violating the sacred marriage which the only begotten Son of God has condescended to contract with us. (Calvin, *Institutes of the Christian Religion*, 2:290)

See also Goodloe, "The Church," 205.

79. Calvin, *Institutes of the Christian Religion*, 2:293.
80. Calvin, *Institutes of the Christian Religion*, 2:292.
81. Calvin, *Institutes of the Christian Religion*, 2:292.
82. Calvin, *Institutes of the Christian Religion*, 2:292.
83. Calvin, *Institutes of the Christian Religion*, 2:295.
84. Calvin, *Institutes of the Christian Religion*, 2:295.

That said, the key point is that Christ is even today sanctifying the church by the Holy Spirit. The church on earth still has both "spot" and "wrinkle"; the church on earth is not perfect.

In what sense, then, can the church be said to be holy? Have prophecies such as Joel 3:17 ("Jerusalem shall be holy") and Isaiah 35:8 ("it shall be called the Holy Way") not in fact been fulfilled by Christ? Calvin argues that they have been fulfilled but not yet perfectly fulfilled. Their perfect fulfillment awaits the eschaton. The church "daily advances, but as yet has not reached the goal."[85] The church is "holy" because the hearts of its true members cry out for perfect holiness. Calvin here has recourse to the legal imagery that he uses also for justification. The church is holy not only because the Holy Spirit is in the process of sanctifying believers but also because God imputes holiness to the church. In this case, however, the free imputation is based upon the church's striving toward holiness under the sanctifying power of the Holy Spirit. As Calvin explains regarding the members of the church, "With their whole heart they aspire after holiness and perfect purity: and hence, that purity which they have not yet fully attained is, by the kindness of God, attributed to them."[86] Calvin admits that the instances of Christians truly seeking holiness have, over the centuries, been "too rare."[87] But it is in these instances that the holy church is found. The holy church is present where, under the impulse of the Holy Spirit, believers eagerly seek perfect holiness, since God imputes the attribute "holy" to the church on this basis. In every time and place, furthermore, there have been (and will be) such believers: "At no period since the world began has the Lord been without his Church, nor ever shall be till the final consummation of all things."[88]

How does Calvin know that in every age God raises up his true church, which strives for holiness and to which God imputes the attribute of holiness? In Pauline language, Calvin emphasizes that, despite our terrible fallenness, God "always sanctifies some vessels to honour, that no age may be left without experience of his mercy."[89] We know this because of God's covenantal promises. Calvin cites in particular God's covenants with Israel and with David (as recorded in Pss. 132:13–14; 89:3–4; Jer. 31:35–36), but Calvin's point extends to the beginning of the world, since otherwise there would have been a time when there was no holy church in the world. Despite the fall, God's free covenantal love has always been mercifully present.

85. Calvin, *Institutes of the Christian Religion*, 2:295.
86. Calvin, *Institutes of the Christian Religion*, 2:295.
87. Calvin, *Institutes of the Christian Religion*, 2:295.
88. Calvin, *Institutes of the Christian Religion*, 2:296.
89. Calvin, *Institutes of the Christian Religion*, 2:296.

In sum, Calvin, Vanhoozer, and Billings strongly affirm that the Holy Spirit is sanctifying the church. They rightly emphasize that no *autonomous* holiness is possible for the church. Since the members of the church are still sinners, and since the church can and does err (although the church also gets many things right, guided by the Spirit), the church can at best be called "holy" only due to God's imputation. In this sense, as Calvin makes clear, the "holy" church is present wherever believers are striving for sanctification through true preaching and true sacraments.

Cyprian, Augustine, and Thomas Aquinas on the Holiness of the Church

Cyprian of Carthage

Thus far our attention has been focused upon Reformed theology. How does the Reformed perspective compare with the teaching of the church fathers about the holiness of the church? Although the fathers tend to have little to say about the church per se,[90] an exception is the third-century African bishop Cyprian, who wrote a treatise *On the Unity of the Church* in response to the schism of Novatian. In this treatise, Cyprian bemoans the fact that even after "the advent of Christ, after light has come to the nations, and saving rays have shone for the preservation of men, that the deaf might receive the hearing of spiritual grace, the blind might open their eyes to God, the weak might grow strong again with eternal health, the lame might run to the church," nonetheless there are people, namely heretics and schismatics, who wish to divide the church.[91] Such people thereby separate themselves and their followers from the one true church, and offer "perfidy under the pretext of faith, antichrist under the name of Christ."[92]

Cyprian's rejection of the notion that more than one church can exist has biblical grounds. He cites Matthew 16:18 ("you are Peter, and on this rock I will build my church, and the powers of death shall not prevail against it") and John 21:17 ("Feed my sheep") as evidence of Jesus's concern for the unity of his church, a unity that Jesus instituted by singling out Peter from among the Twelve. Cyprian comments, "Assuredly the rest of the apostles were also

90. For an example of this spareness, see John of Damascus, *An Exact Exposition of the Orthodox Faith*, in John of Damascus, *Writings*, trans. Frederic H. Chase Jr. (Washington, DC: Catholic University of America, 1958), 165–406. Augustine, of course, writes extensively about the church, though he does not compose an ecclesiological treatise in any strict sense.

91. Cyprian, *Treatise I: On the Unity of the Church*, trans. Ernest Wallis, in *Fathers of the Third Century: Hippolytus, Cyprian, Caius, Novatian, Appendix*, ed. A. Cleveland Coxe (Peabody, MA: Hendrickson, 1994 [1886]), 421–29, at 422.

92. Cyprian, *On the Unity of the Church*, 422.

the same as was Peter, endowed with a like partnership both of honour and power; but the beginning proceeds from unity."[93] He connects this unity with holiness. In this regard he quotes Song of Songs 6:9: "My dove, my perfect one, is only one, the darling of her mother, flawless to her that bore her." He interprets the beloved, the "dove," to be the church; Christ is speaking to his church. His church is "one." With respect to the church's unity and holiness, Cyprian also cites Ephesians 4:4–5: "There is one body and one Spirit, just as you were called to the one hope that belongs to your call, one Lord, one faith, one baptism, one God and Father of us all." Cyprian compares the church spread all over the world to the sun and its rays; the rays cannot separate from the sun. Similarly, he alludes to Jesus's and Paul's analogy of a tree (or vine) and its branches; the branch that is cut off from the unity of the tree/vine will die (see Rom. 11:16–24; John 15:1–8). As Paul says about Israel and the gentiles, "If the root is holy, so are the branches" (Rom. 11:16). Cyprian also makes use of the image of many rivers with one source (cf. Ezek. 47; Zech. 14:8; John 7:37–39; Rev. 22:1–2), as well as the image of one mother with many children: "She is one mother, plentiful in the results of fruitfulness: from her womb we are born, by her milk we are nourished, by her spirit [the Holy Spirit] we are animated."[94]

Turning specifically to the holiness of the church, Cyprian states, "The spouse of Christ cannot be adulterous; she is uncorrupted and pure."[95] Here he is using imagery from Ephesians 5, where Christ's bride is the church and Christ cleanses "her by the washing of water with the word," that is to say, by baptism. His imagery also evokes the numerous Old Testament texts where Israel is depicted as God's adulterous but beloved wife. Israel's "adultery" consists in worshiping other gods and breaking God's law, despite God's covenantal love for his elect people. For example, God tells the prophet Ezekiel that the people of Israel "have committed adultery, and blood is upon their hands; with their idols they have committed adultery; and they have even offered up to them for food the sons whom they had borne to me" (Ezek. 23:37). God tells the prophet Hosea that "my people inquire of a thing of wood, and their staff gives them oracles. For a spirit of harlotry has led them astray, and they have left their God to play the harlot. They sacrifice on the tops of the mountains, and make offerings upon the hills" (Hos. 4:12–13). Cyprian is arguing that the church, our spiritual mother, is not in the same situation as Israel was. The church is not adulterous. Through Christ, the church truly

93. Cyprian, *On the Unity of the Church*, 422.
94. Cyprian, *On the Unity of the Church*, 423.
95. Cyprian, *On the Unity of the Church*, 423.

worships the living God. The church's pure worship, in Christ, constitutes her holiness and our pathway to eternal life: "She knows one home; she guards with chaste modesty the sanctity of one couch. She keeps us for God. She appoints the sons whom she has born for the kingdom."[96] The reason why the church's unity and holiness cannot be broken is found for Cyprian in God's sustaining power, rather than in anything that belongs to the church apart from God. Cyprian asks rhetorically, "Does any one believe that this unity which thus comes from the divine strength and coheres in celestial sacraments, can be divided in the Church?"[97]

Along the same lines, Cyprian compares the "sacrament of unity" to the fact that Christ's tunic remained whole rather than being cut apart.[98] Recall that, according to the Gospel of John, Christ's "tunic was without seam, woven from top to bottom; so they said to one another, 'Let us not tear it, but cast lots for it to see whose it shall be'" (John 19:23–24). After quoting this text, Cyprian observes that by contrast to this undivided unity, Abijah the prophet divided his garments in order to symbolize the division of the people of Israel. During the reign of Solomon, after Solomon's "wives turned away his heart after other gods" (1 Kings 11:4), Abijah put on a new garment and went out to meet Jeroboam, who served under Solomon as the head of "all the forced labor of the house of Joseph" (1 Kings 11:28). In a symbolic action, Abijah ripped the garment into twelve pieces and gave ten to Jeroboam, signifying the ten northern tribes that would break away from the two southern tribes after the death of Solomon. Cyprian notes that Jesus's seamless, untorn tunic indicates Jesus's will for his church: the church's unity cannot be broken as Israel's was. Jesus's tunic "bore with it a unity that came down from the top, that is, that came from heaven and the Father, which was not to be at all rent by the receiver and the possessor, but without separation we obtain a whole and substantial entireness."[99]

Does schism, then, surprise God or foil God's plan for his church's unity? Cyprian holds that the answer is no; God permits schism, because by allowing us free will, he allows us to go astray. We can leave the unity of the church, but we cannot negate it. Paul himself, a firm defender of the church's unity, acknowledges that there will be divisions. In a text quoted by Cyprian, Paul

96. Cyprian, *On the Unity of the Church*, 423.
97. Cyprian, *On the Unity of the Church*, 423.
98. Cyprian, *On the Unity of the Church*, 423. Regarding Cyprian on the church as the *sacramentum unitatis*, Ola Tjørhom notes, "This signifies that the Church is the place where unity in Christ is lived and also that it emerges as a sign of unity for the world" (Tjørhom, *Visible Church—Visible Unity: Ecumenical Ecclesiology and "The Great Tradition of the Church"* [Collegeville, MN: Liturgical Press, 2004], 48).
99. Cyprian, *On the Unity of the Church*, 423.

tells the Corinthians that "when you assemble as a church, I hear that there are divisions among you; and I partly believe it, for there must be factions among you in order that those who are genuine among you may be recognized" (1 Cor. 11:18–19). These factions cannot break the church's real unity, but they are nonetheless terribly sad and obviously to be avoided if at all possible. Cyprian quotes Paul's exhortation to the Corinthians: "I appeal to you, brethren, by the name of our Lord Jesus Christ, that all of you agree and that there be no dissensions among you, but that you be united in the same mind and the same judgment" (1 Cor. 1:10). Paul would not appeal for unity were not unity truly possible. Paul urges the Corinthians to avoid dissensions or schisms, but he does not suppose that the presence of such things would destroy the church's unity.

Cyprian also links the church's unity to holiness by considering the Eucharist. In Exodus 12:46, God commands Moses and Aaron about the Passover lamb, "In one house shall it be eaten; you shall not carry forth any of the flesh outside the house; and you shall not break a bone of it." This Passover lamb prefigures Jesus Christ, whose bones were not broken on the cross (John 19:32–33). Thus the eucharistic memorial of the true Passover lamb cannot be taken outside the "house," that is, the church. Cyprian states, "The flesh of Christ, and the holy of the Lord, cannot be sent abroad, nor is there any other home to believers but the one Church."[100] The church is holy because the church contains the holy Eucharist, the "flesh of Christ." Cyprian also argues that the church enjoys "unanimity" and "concord," so that no one should suppose "that the good can depart from the Church."[101] Those who are "genuine" (1 Cor. 11:19) can be known by whether they preserve unity: "Thus the faithful are approved, thus the perfidious are detected."[102] The evil depart from the church by worshiping outside the church; by acting "in opposition to Christ's priests" and separating "from the company of His clergy and people," they become "an enemy of the altar, a rebel against Christ's sacrifice."[103]

In Cyprian's treatise, then, two themes appear regarding the holiness of the church. First, this holiness is rooted in the sacraments, especially the Eucharist (although Cyprian uses "sacrament" also in the sense of a holy sign of a divine reality). The church's holiness is a divine gift that pertains to holy worship: the church is holy because, in Christ, the church's worship is holy. This worship is Christ's gift to us, since it is a share in the true Passover lamb. Because of the unity of this divinely given worship, it is not possible for the church to be divided in the way that Israel was divided from Judah.

---

100. Cyprian, *On the Unity of the Church*, 424.
101. Cyprian, *On the Unity of the Church*, 424.
102. Cyprian, *On the Unity of the Church*, 424.
103. Cyprian, *On the Unity of the Church*, 427.

Second, there is real goodness in those who remain in the "concord" of the church, since they are bound together by the Holy Spirit's gift of charity. Citing 1 John 4:16, Cyprian observes that "he who has not charity has not God."[104] Nonetheless, Cyprian is aware that in the visible church there will be those who pretend to be Christian but in fact are not. All who remain in the church are not thereby holy. Cyprian holds both that the church "is joined into a substantial unity of body by the cement of concord" and that we must seek "to be peacemakers, gentle in heart, simple in speech, agreeing in affection, faithfully linked to one another in the bonds of unanimity."[105]

Without admitting that the unity of the church has been broken, Cyprian recognizes that there has been a certain declension from the perfection of the apostolic church. He quotes the passages from Acts that portray the apostolic church as being "of one heart and soul" (Acts 4:32). For Cyprian, the church of Acts was better than the third-century church because it was more loving, as manifested in its perfect sharing of possessions. Unlike the apostolic church, the third-century church is weak in charitable almsgiving. Cyprian observes with sadness that "we do not even give the tenths from our patrimony; and while our Lord bids us sell, we rather buy and increase our store. Thus has the vigour of faith dwindled away among us; thus has the strength of believers grown weak."[106] While defending the unity and holiness of the church, therefore, Cyprian grants that its third-century members are not holy in the sense of perfect holiness, by any means. If the unity and holiness of the church depended for Cyprian upon the holiness of its members, then he could not have dared to write that in the third-century church (and not only among Novatian and his followers), "There is no faith in the fear of God, in the law of righteousness, in love, in labour; none considers the fear of futurity, and none takes to heart the day of the Lord, and the wrath of God, and the punishments to come upon unbelievers, and the eternal torments decreed for the faithless."[107]

Augustine of Hippo

Augustine's theology of the church's unity and holiness is in many ways like Cyprian's.[108] In his *De symbolo ad catechumenos* (a brief commentary

---

104. Cyprian, *On the Unity of the Church*, 426.
105. Cyprian, *On the Unity of the Church*, 429.
106. Cyprian, *On the Unity of the Church*, 429.
107. Cyprian, *On the Unity of the Church*, 429.
108. See also Ephraim Radner's discussion of Cyprian's and Augustine's ecclesiology in his chapter "The Sins of the Church" in *Brutal Unity*. He notes that for Cyprian, "in a sense it is incorrect to use the phrase 'church division' to describe ecclesial contention, since in fact the Church cannot be divided: what appears to be division is in fact the disclosure of the God/Satan

on the creed), Augustine discusses the church's holiness by pointing to the fact that the church successfully opposes all heresies and cannot be conquered by any of them. The church's doctrine remains pure, undefiled by falsehood. Referencing Matthew 16:18 ("the gates of Hell shall not prevail against it"), John 15:2 ("Every branch of mine that bears no fruit, he takes away"), and 1 John 1:19 ("They went out from us, but they were not of us; for if they had been of us, they would have continued with us"), Augustine observes, "As for heresies, they went all out of it [the church], like unprofitable branches pruned from the vine: but itself abides in its root, in its Vine, in its charity."[109]

---

distinction, of the inside/outside chasm, of truth/falsehood, chosen/rejected, or religion/heresy in their integral oppositions" (Radner, *Brutal Unity*, 128). The question then becomes who is inside and who outside; those outside have failed to obey legitimate authority. Radner observes that since both sides brand the other as outsiders, one must ask which commands are the right ones to obey. For Radner, "This is precisely the problem with vying interpretations of obedience: as always, prior appeals to authoritative definition of what is included in obedience steer the debate among contending parties, usually therefore toward just those areas of polity and decision making that eventually seem all too human in their ordering and outcome" (ibid.). Radner goes on to say, "It is not clear that Augustine could image a divided 'Church as such,' even if he might consider one that was visibly variegated in its moral character" (ibid., 129). This is correct, but for Radner, it means that violence is inbuilt into Augustine's (and Cyprian's) understanding of the church: "The tension between the imperfections of ecclesial temporality and the firm identification of the *ecclesia* itself meant that unity could be construed coercively, in the sense of the providential factors that might drive a people to remain 'together' and, by contrast, the condemnatory factors that might pull them apart" (ibid.). Radner contrasts the "providential coercive" model (Catholic) with the "elective" model (Protestant), and he raises concerns about both, since "neither tradition was able to envisage a 'Church as such' that was in fact 'divided' among itself and that was thus 'as such' mired in actions colored by sin and violence as given in division in particular" (ibid., 130). Radner urges that we recognize that in fact the "body of Christ" (1 Cor. 12:27)—"For God's temple is holy, and that temple you are" (1 Cor. 3:17)—is "as such" sinful and wicked. We must recognize "the sins of the Church's own self as informing the receipt of God's love. . . . Hence, the Church's unity is established in and because of her sins, not in themselves but as they stand in relation to God as creator and redeemer in Christ Jesus. The oneness of God is just *this* oneness with the sinful Church" (ibid., 460). In this way, Radner intensifies the Reformed position, emphasizing how our sinfulness requires and belongs to our utter dependence on Christ. His book demonstrates that ecclesiology can be and has been used as a violent tool to assert our (whoever the "we" is) superiority over other Christians. But the abuse of ecclesiology—like the abuse of monotheism that scholars such as Jan Assmann have identified—should not rule out construals of God's gifting that are more persuaded than is Radner about the Spirit-given holiness and unity (in charity and truth) of the church, despite the terrible divisions among Christians that have never been absent. We should fully admit the shared character of blame for ongoing Christian division even while also attempting to be faithful to the unity, holiness, catholicity, and apostolicity that, in faith, believers (certainly Catholic and Orthodox believers) consider the church to receive continuously from Jesus Christ. For Assmann's work, marked by strong condemnation of religions influenced by ancient Israel, see most recently Jan Assmann, *The Price of Monotheism*, trans. Robert Savage (Stanford, CA: Stanford University Press, 2010).

109. Augustine, *On the Creed: A Sermon to the Catechumens (De Symbolo ad catechumenos)*, trans. C. L. Cornish, in *Augustin: On the Holy Trinity, Doctrinal Treatises, Moral Treatises*, ed. Philip Schaff (Peabody, MA: Hendrickson, 1994 [1887]), 369–75, at 374.

The church is holy in its doctrine because it abides in Christ and his love; the branches receive the Spirit of the vine. As branches of the vine, the church is holy because the vine is holy.[110]

Like Cyprian, Augustine makes clear that, despite the forgiveness of sins accomplished by baptism, the members of the church are not perfectly holy. After the fall, venial sin plagues those who are being sanctified. Exhorting his audience to "guard your Baptism even unto the end," Augustine explains, "I do not tell you that you will live here without sin; but they are venial, without which life is not."[111] In Augustine's view, we cannot live without committing some lesser or venial sins, which are purified by prayer. The holiness of the church comes about not because of our perfect holiness, but because of the true doctrine that the church, united to Christ, preserves against all heresy.

In his *City of God*, Augustine affirms that after the fall the human mind no longer was able to cleave to (or even endure) the divine light, and so "the mind had to be trained and purified by faith."[112] The remedy that God provided was Jesus Christ. As Augustine puts it, "in order to give man's mind greater confidence in its journey towards the truth along the way of faith, God the Son of God, who is himself the Truth, took manhood without abandoning his godhead, and thus established and founded this faith, so that man might have a path to man's God through the man who was God."[113] Those who follow this path of humble faith and love compose the "City of God" on pilgrimage in the world. The delight of those on this path "is to worship God rather than to be worshipped instead of God."[114] Those who reject this path and cling to pride constitute the "City of Man." But Augustine emphasizes that the "City of God," although it is the church, is not strictly coterminous with the church in membership. On the contrary, the two cities, which have existed since Cain and Abel, are "intermixed with one another in this present world."[115]

---

110. As Graham Tomlin remarks, "The Augustinian view was that the holiness of the church derives not from its members but from Christ. The church is holy because it is the bride of Christ, however holy or unholy its members happen to be at any particular time" (Tomlin, *The Prodigal Spirit: The Trinity, the Church and the Future of the World* [London: Alpha International, 2011], 165). Tomlin agrees with this view: "The church is first and foremost holy because it belongs to Christ. Its holiness does not derive from itself, but from its relation to God in Christ. . . . God's gift of holiness enables holiness to grow as an embedded quality within Christian people" (ibid., 166).

111. Augustine, *On the Creed*, 374.

112. Augustine, *City of God*, trans. Henry Bettenson (New York: Penguin, 1984), 11.2, p. 430.

113. Augustine, *City of God* 11.2, pp. 430–31.

114. Augustine, *City of God* 11.1, p. 429.

115. Augustine, *City of God* 10.32, p. 426. Regarding Jews and gentiles prior to Christ's coming, Augustine holds that God gave his chosen people the advantage of true worship and

In Christ, therefore, the members of the church suffer persecution, and not only from those outside the visible church. Like Calvin, Augustine acknowledges that "there are always some, inside indeed there are many, who by their unprincipled behaviour torment the feelings of those who live devout lives."[116] Professed Christians who behave wickedly bring shame upon the church and make evangelization more difficult. Dissensions, heresies, and schisms obscure the true gospel and cause grief in the hearts of the faithful. Imitating Christ's patience with Judas, however, Christians on the path of sanctification must put up with the wicked in their midst. Indeed, Augustine suggests that God permits the church to endure such turmoil precisely so as to share in Christ's humiliation on the path to glorification. It is for this reason that "many reprobates are mingled in the Church with the good, and both sorts are collected as it were in the dragnet of the gospel."[117]

When people leave the church due to heresy or schism, this action does not destroy the church's unity, since the church's unity does not depend on having all people remain within the church. In *City of God*, Augustine makes clear that he agrees with Cyprian that the church's unity is constituted by God, and that its center is true worship. "The Heavenly City on pilgrimage in this world," Augustine says, "does not create false gods. She herself is the creation of the true God, and she herself is to be his true sacrifice."[118] True worship is the offering of ourselves in love to God, and this worship is accomplished in Christ and thus in the eucharistic liturgy. God creates the church, by the Holy Spirit, precisely as this participation in Christ's sacrificial love.[119] Commenting on the Holy Spirit's work according to Romans and 1 John, Augustine observes, "If a person loves his brother, the Spirit of God is abiding in him."[120] The Holy Spirit causes our charity. Augustine goes on to show that the Holy Spirit sanctifies us through the church's holy sacraments, and that Christ came to gather the church in love.

---

prophecies of Christ and the church, but that even gentiles could and did come to an implicit, saving faith in Christ by God's grace.

116. Augustine, *City of God* 18.51 p. 834.

117. Augustine, *City of God* 18.49 p. 832.

118. Augustine, *City of God* 18.54 p. 842.

119. See Augustine, *City of God* 19.23, p. 889; 21.15, p. 993. As Yves Congar remarks, "The fact that Christian worship must be spiritual does not mean that it cannot be sensible, corporeal" (Congar, *I Believe in the Holy Spirit*, 2:54). The fact that the sacraments are "outward" does not make them powerless in the order of grace. For the latter argument, which misunderstands Augustine as merely a Neoplatonist, see Phillip Cary, *Outward Signs: The Powerlessness of External Things in Augustine's Thought* (Oxford: Oxford University Press, 2008), as well as the profound response to Cary by John C. Cavadini, "The Darkest Enigma: Reconsidering the Self in Augustine's Thought," *Augustinian Studies* 38 (2007): 119–32.

120. Augustine, *Homilies on the First Epistle of John*, trans. Boniface Ramsey, ed. Daniel E. Doyle, OSA, and Thomas Martin, OSA (Hyde Park, NY: New City Press, 2008), homily 6, p. 97.

On this basis, Augustine concludes that holiness (love) is inseparable from the unity that is the church: "Let us hold onto the unity of the Church, let us hold onto Christ, let us hold onto charity. Let us not be torn away from the members of his bride, let us not be torn away from the faith, so that we may glory in his presence, and we shall remain secure in him, now through faith and then through sight, the pledge of which we have as the gift of the Holy Spirit."[121] By causing love in Christ's members, the indwelling Holy Spirit ensures that sanctity or holiness already belongs to the church, even if not perfectly. The Holy Spirit ensures the church's holiness by sustaining it in holy doctrine (the truth of faith) and in holy sacramental worship, which consists preeminently in the eucharistic offering of the whole Christ (head and members) to God in faith and love. By knowing and loving God in true worship, we already "glory in his presence" as his holy church, even though we are not yet fully sanctified and even though the visible church contains some members who are members in name only.

Thomas Aquinas

It is clear that Cyprian's and Augustine's positions differ from the Reformed theologians, but not by denying the imperfection of the members of the church. Like the Reformed theologians whom we surveyed, Cyprian and Augustine underscore the church's continual dependence upon God's gifts. Unlike the Reformed theologians, however, they suggest that this condition of dependence coexists with the absolute holiness and truth of the church's doctrine and sacraments. Can Thomas Aquinas add anything to this discussion?

Let me first draw attention to the *secunda-secundae pars* of his *Summa theologiae*, where he treats the virtue of faith. In his discussion of the articles of faith contained in the creed, Aquinas makes clear that the creed does not

---

121. Augustine, *Homilies on the First Epistle of John,* homily 9, p. 144; cf. homily 10, p. 153. In light of the unity of Christ with his bride/body (expressed by Augustine through the notion of *totus Christus*), John Milbank argues regarding the holiness of the church, "The relationship of the Spirit and the Bride [the church] has, then, a double aspect: first, the one atonement by Christ makes possible a human atoning process; second, because Christ yet *depends* upon this process (that is to say, cannot be sinless himself without the sinless *reception* of himself by Mary/*ecclesia*) and because only the sinless God can make the true, suffering response to Christ (Christ, as God, *cannot* depend on anything created) the Spirit has her own form of *kenosis* in the Church" (Milbank, "The Second Difference," in *The Word Made Strange: Theology, Language, Culture* [Oxford: Blackwell, 1997], 171–93, at 186). I think that Milbank is not putting it quite right when he says that Christ "cannot be sinless himself without the sinless *reception* of himself by Mary/*ecclesia*," but Milbank is nonetheless on the right track in describing what Christ and the Holy Spirit have in fact accomplished. Milbank notes that "the infinite response of the Spirit to the Son is now *eschatologically identical* with the setting of all human beings on the path of deification, itself a work of inter-human participation and exchange" (ibid., 185).

replace Scripture as the "rule of faith," but rather the creed truthfully and succinctly explicates Scripture so that the gospel "might the more easily be proposed to all, lest anyone might stray from the truth through ignorance of the faith."[122] In the same place, Aquinas turns to the creed's confession that "we believe in one, holy, catholic, and apostolic Church." Drawing upon Augustine, he points out that "the Catholic Church is merely a created being," and so we should not believe "in" it, since we should only believe "in" God.[123] It seems, therefore, that the creed is deeply misleading, even idolatrous, insofar as it seems to elevate the church to a divine status as an object of faith.

In response to this objection to the creed (among others), Aquinas responds first that the creed "is published by the authority of the universal Church," and this church "cannot err, since she is governed by the Holy Spirit, who is the Spirit of truth: for such was our Lord's promise to his disciples (Jo. xvi. 13): 'When he, the Spirit of truth, is come, he will teach you all truth.'"[124] With regard to the specific question of the creed's confession that "we believe in one, holy, catholic, and apostolic Church," then, he emphasizes that in fact this confession has the Holy Spirit as its primary object. It is the Spirit who makes the church holy; the church as a human institution has no power to make itself holy. Thus, "If we say: '"In" the holy Catholic Church,' this must be taken as verified in so far as our faith is directed to the Holy Spirit, who sanctifies the Church; so that the sense is: 'I believe in the Holy Spirit sanctifying the Church.'"[125] When we speak of the church's holiness, we are praising the Holy Spirit, rather than praising the merely human powers of the church. For Aquinas, then, to confess the church's holiness is simply to confess the Holy Spirit's work in the inaugurated kingdom of God.[126]

During Lent of 1273, the year before his death, Aquinas authored a short sermon-commentary on the Apostles' Creed.[127] When he turns to the creed's

---

122. II-II, q. 1, a. 9, obj. 1 and *respondeo*.

123. II-II, q. 1, a. 9, obj. 5.

124. II-II, q. 1, a. 9, *sed contra*.

125. II-II, q. 1, a. 9, ad 5.

126. Note John Mahoney, SJ's point that for Aquinas "the whole function of the Church as a worshipping community in all its activities is quite simply to dispose men to the reception of the grace of the Holy Spirit and to give expression to that grace in the lives of its members" (Mahoney, "'The Church of the Holy Spirit' in Aquinas," *Heythrop Journal* 15 [1974]: 18–36, at 27).

127. Herwi Rikhof has rightly observed that this sermon-commentary "contains a wealth of theological insights and can therefore serve well as a frame and a starting point for examining Thomas' views on the Church" (Rikhof, "Thomas on the Church: Reflections on a Sermon," in *Aquinas on Doctrine: A Critical Introduction*, ed. Thomas G. Weinandy, OFMCap, Daniel A. Keating, and John P. Yocum [London: T&T Clark, 2004], 199–223, at 199). For reflections on Aquinas's preaching, with occasional reference to his sermon-commentary on the Apostles' Creed, see Jean-Pierre Torrell, OP, "La pratique pastorale d'un théologien du XIIIe siècle:

affirmation of the "holy catholic church," Aquinas discusses the characteristics of the church, including unity and holiness. At the outset of his discussion, he compares the church to a body-soul organism: the church's "body"
is its many members, while the church's soul, which gives life and operation
to the body, is the Holy Spirit.[128] The church is guided and governed by the
Holy Spirit. Aquinas also describes the church as "the congregation of the
faithful."[129] He conceives of this assembly as an assembly for learning God's
ways. In this regard he quotes Sirach 51:23: "Draw near to me, you who are
untaught, and lodge in my school."

Like Cyprian (and John of Avila), Aquinas grounds his discussion of the
church's unity in Song of Songs 6:9: "My dove, my perfect one, is only one."
Aquinas is aware that Christians have divided many times, but he denies that
this has negated the church's unity. The division that characterizes heretical
sects shows that they are not the one church.[130] Although ecumenically we

Thomas d'Aquin prédicateur," in *Recherches thomasiennes: Études revues et augmentées* (Paris:
J. Vrin, 2000), 282–314.

128. On this point, see Yves Congar, OP, "Vision de l'Église chez S. Thomas d'Aquin," *Revue
des sciences philosophiques et théologiques* 44 (1960): 523–41, at 532–33; George Sabra, *Thomas
Aquinas' Vision of the Church* (Mainz: Matthias Grünewald Verlag, 1987), 103–4. Sabra remarks
with respect to later Thomistic discussion, "The jump to a discussion of the Holy Spirit as
causa formalis of the church and the enthusiastic affirmation about the church being a kind of
incarnation of the Spirit are indeed very foreign to Thomas' thought on this matter. The point
of this particular analogy is very simple: just as a soul animates and unifies a body, so the Holy
Spirit vivifies and unites the church. The Spirit is the life and principle of unity in the mystical
body. One should not make more out of this harmless and straightforward analogy, for, after
all, to the heart are also ascribed the same functions of unification and animation when Thomas
calls the Spirit the heart of the church" (Sabra, *Thomas Aquinas' Vision of the Church*, 104).

129. Thomas Aquinas, *The Sermon-Conferences of St. Thomas Aquinas on the Apostles'
Creed*, trans. and ed. Nicholas Ayo, CSC (Notre Dame, IN: University of Notre Dame Press,
1988), 125. Aidan Nichols comments that "Thomas's key term for the Church is *congregatio
fidelium*, 'the congregation of the faithful,' but owing to his high view of faith this option has
exalted consequences. For Thomas faith, so we noted, is the beginning of glory. It is a disposition or capacity that has no rationale other than God himself considered as uncreated Truth,
the God who plants in us, precisely by faith, the seeds of his own self-knowledge, seeds which
will come to flower in the face-to-face vision of him in heaven. Thomas's view of the Church as
congregatio fidelium leads him to treat her as homogeneous with the universal or cosmic assembly
of the elect, those who will see God—including even the elect angels" (Nichols, *Discovering
Aquinas: An Introduction to His Life, Work and Influence* [London: Darton, Longman & Todd,
2002], 121). See also Sabra, *Thomas Aquinas' Vision of the Church*, 50–58; Congar, "Vision de
l'Église chez S. Thomas d'Aquin," 525–26. Sabra argues that alongside *congregatio fidelium*,
Aquinas also privileges the designation *corpus mysticum* (Sabra, *Thomas Aquinas' Vision of
the Church*, 69–71).

130. A greater emphasis on the failures of each "side" in Christian division is appropriate.
As Pope John Paul II observes in his encyclical *Ut Unum Sint*, today "there is an increased sense
of the need for repentance: an awareness of certain exclusions which seriously harm fraternal
charity, of certain refusals to forgive, of a certain pride, of an unevangelical insistence on

would need to say more than Aquinas does here, nonetheless we can agree with his fundamental point that the unity of the church comes from three sources, all of which flow from the Holy Spirit: unity of faith ("all Christians who belong to the body of the church have the same belief"); unity of hope ("the hope of obtaining eternal life"); and unity of love (of God and neighbor). As befits a unity produced by the Holy Spirit, the church's unity is primarily a spiritual unity, albeit a spiritual unity that has a visible institutional effect, since the church's many members are drawn together by these supernatural virtues for the purpose of learning from Christ.

With respect to the creed's description of the church as "holy," Aquinas first remarks that the church is a holy congregation. Aquinas is aware, of course, that the visible church includes wicked persons. But Scripture makes clear that the church possesses a real sanctity through the indwelling of the Holy Spirit in believers. In this regard Aquinas quotes 1 Corinthians 3:17: "For God's temple is holy, and that temple you are."[131] Although we are imperfect,

---

condemning the 'other side,' of a disdain born of an unhealthy presumption" (*Ut Unum Sint*, §15, in *The Encyclicals of John Paul II*, ed. J. Michael Miller, CSB [Huntington, IN: Our Sunday Visitor, 2001], 782–831, at 789). The Second Vatican Council's Decree on Ecumenism, *Unitatis Redintegratio*, affirms the "perfect unity" of "holy Church" as an ongoing gift of Christ and the Holy Spirit to the apostolic community led by Peter (§2), while at the same time stating, "In this one and only Church of God from its very beginnings there arose certain rifts, which the Apostle strongly censures as damnable. But in subsequent centuries much more serious dissensions appeared and large communities became separated from full communion with the Catholic Church—for which, often enough, men of both sides were to blame. However, one cannot charge with the sin of the separation those who at present are born into these communities and in them are brought up in the faith of Christ, and the Catholic Church accepts them with respect and affection as brothers" (§3). See *Unitatis Redintegratio*, in *Vatican Council II*, vol. 1, *The Conciliar and Post Conciliar Documents*, new rev. ed., ed. Austin Flannery, OP (Northport, NY: Costello Publishing Company, 1996), 452–70, at 454–55. In addition, Avery Dulles, SJ, rightly draws attention to the baptismal unity of Christians as the body of the Christ: "In several of his letters Paul makes it clear that all the baptized are incorporated into Christ and thus are made members of his body. . . . If baptism is the rite of incorporation, we must conclude that all baptized believers are one in the body of Christ, which is the church. Vatican II's Decree on Ecumenism acknowledges this: 'All those justified by faith through baptism are incorporated into Christ. They therefore have a right to be honored by the title of Christian, and are properly regarded as brothers and sisters in the Lord by the children of the Catholic Church' (Unitatis redintegratio 3; cf. 22). Because we think of the church comprehensively as the body of Christ, our ecclesiology ought to be broadly ecumenical" (Dulles, "The Trinity and Christian Unity," in *God the Holy Trinity: Reflections on Christian Faith and Practice*, ed. Timothy George [Grand Rapids: Baker Academic, 2006], 69–82, at 71). As Dulles well recognizes, the significance of unity of faith should not thereby be minimized. See Dulles, "Nature, Mission, and Structure of the Church," in *Vatican II: Renewal within Tradition*, ed. Matthew L. Lamb and Matthew Levering (Oxford: Oxford University Press, 2008), 25–36, at 28–29 (on *Lumen Gentium*).

131. This section of Aquinas's commentary on the Apostles' Creed is discussed briefly but appreciatively by Yves Congar in *I Believe in the Holy Spirit*, 2:53. Congar points out that although "nothing is said about a holy Church in the New Testament," nonetheless such texts

insofar as the Holy Spirit dwells in us, we truly possess holiness (even if not perfectly); otherwise we could not be described as God's holy temple. Since this is the case, the church of believers must be holy. Paul does not mean simply that some individuals are God's holy temple. Rather, the Holy Spirit indwells individuals precisely as members of Christ, united to him by faith and love: "Now you are the body of Christ and individually members of it" (1 Cor. 12:27). This "body of Christ" is the church.

Aquinas points out that if the church were not holy, then it could not be contrasted with wicked assemblies. The church would merely be yet another congregation of sinners. Aquinas quotes the psalmist's statement, "I hate the company of evildoers, and I will not sit with the wicked" (Ps. 26:5). As Aquinas knew, the psalmist goes on to describe his love for the temple worship: "I wash my hands in innocence, and go about your altar, O LORD, singing aloud a song of thanksgiving, and telling all your wondrous deeds. O LORD, I love the habitation of your house, and the place where your glory dwells" (Ps. 26:6–8). The temple is characterized by the presence of God's glory and by true worship of God, unlike the "company of evildoers" that lacks God's presence and is antithetical to God's goodness. Christ's church too is characterized by the indwelling Holy Spirit and by true worship in Christ, and so it differs profoundly from the "company [or assembly] of evildoers." This is so even though the members of Christ are still venial sinners, and even though there are false Christians who are outwardly, but not inwardly, members of the church.

In addition to defending the holiness of the church by these arguments, Aquinas holds that the church is holy because the church is the place of our sanctification. If the church were not holy, then we would not need the church for sanctification. But in fact, by God's will, our sanctification is inseparable from the church. In the church, Aquinas observes, believers are sanctified by washing in the blood of Christ, by the anointing of the Holy Spirit, by the indwelling Trinity, and by the invoking of God's name for our salvation. The washing and anointing suggest the sacraments of baptism and confirmation; the indwelling Trinity and invoking of God's name suggest the basis, pattern, and truth of Christian worship.

Aquinas first remarks that just as a church building is consecrated by being cleansed, so also the members of the church are "washed in the blood of Christ."[132] The reference here is to the sacrament of baptism, which unites

---

as Ephesians 5:26–27, 1 Corinthians 3:16, 1 Peter 2:5 (and 2:9), and Ephesians 2:21 show that the church is holy (ibid., 2:52, 54–56).

132. Aquinas, *The Sermon-Conferences of St. Thomas Aquinas on the Apostles' Creed*, 127. James Monti notes, "The magnificent gothic cathedrals and churches built for the liturgical rites of medieval Europe were themselves the subject of what became by far the longest and most

us to Christ's passion and takes away original sin. It may seem a stretch to connect what happens to believers with what happens to the church building, as if the latter had anything to do with the church's holiness. But for Aquinas, the church building itself, as the house of God, has iconographic significance.[133] The church building suggests, by its structure and orientation, both the church's communal participation in Christ's pasch and the church's eschatological expectation of Christ's return in glory. The symbolism present in the consecration of a church building indicates the basis for the real sanctity of the church, namely Christ's sanctifying us through his blood.

Regarding our being washed in the blood of Christ, Aquinas cites Ephesians 5:25–27 (which Calvin also quoted), and Hebrews 13:12: "Jesus also suffered outside the gate in order to sanctify the people through his own blood." Ephesians 5:25–27 explicitly depicts the church as sanctified by Christ. While Hebrews 13:12 does not explicitly describe the church, it does refer to Jesus's suffering to "sanctify the people."[134] Hebrews 13:14–15 goes on to say that "here we have no lasting city, but we seek the city which is to come. Through him then let us continually offer up a sacrifice of praise to God." Lest this "sacrifice of praise" seem to be merely the duty of each individual rather than of the whole church, recall that Hebrews 13:17 adds, "Obey your leaders and submit to them; for they are keeping watch over your souls, as men who will have to give account."[135] Jesus died in order "to sanctify the people"; the church is that people, and its members are called to "offer up a sacrifice of praise to God."

The second way in which the members of the church are sanctified, according to Aquinas, is by "a spiritual anointing."[136] Here Aquinas points out

---

complex of the Church's ceremonies—the rite of consecrating a new church. . . . The medieval liturgical commentators speak of this multistaged solemn blessing of a newly constructed House of God as an analogy for the three-staged infusion of the theological virtues into the Christian soul, a comparison traceable to Saint Augustine" (Monti, *A Sense of the Sacred: Roman Catholic Worship in the Middle Ages* [San Francisco: Ignatius, 2012], 15–16).

133. See Thomas Aquinas, *Summa theologiae*, trans. by the Fathers of the English Dominican Province (Westminster, MD: Christian Classics, 1981) III, q. 83, a. 3. Aquinas explains in ad 2: "The house in which this sacrament [the Eucharist] is celebrated denotes the Church, and is termed a church; and so it is fittingly consecrated, both to represent the holiness which the Church acquired from the Passion, as well as to denote the holiness required of them who have to receive this sacrament."

134. For the significance of Hebrews in Aquinas's theology of salvation, see the succinct remarks of Romanus Cessario, OP, "Aquinas on Christian Salvation," in Weinandy, Keating, and Yocum, *Aquinas on Doctrine*, 117–37, at 125–26.

135. For discussion of Aquinas's commentary on Hebrews 13:17, see Antoine Guggenheim, *Jésus Christ, grand prêtre de l'ancienne et de la nouvelle alliance: Étude théologique et herméneutique du commentaire de saint Thomas d'Aquin sur l'Épître aux Hébreux* (Paris: Parole et Silence, 2004), 581–82.

136. Aquinas, *The Sermon-Conferences of St. Thomas Aquinas on the Apostles' Creed*, 127.

that when a church building is being consecrated, it is anointed with holy oil. Similarly, the sacramental anointing of the members of the church consecrates the church as holy. By this anointing, the members of the church become like Christ, who was anointed by the Holy Spirit. To be "Christ" means to be "anointed." Aquinas remarks that if we did not receive this anointing that makes us holy, we "would not be Christians," since we would not be like the anointed one, Christ.[137] In support of the role of the anointing in making us holy, Aquinas cites 1 Corinthians 6:11: "you were washed, you were sanctified, you were justified in the name of the Lord Jesus Christ and in the Spirit of our God"; and 2 Corinthians 1:21: "It is God who establishes us with you in Christ, and has commissioned [Vulgate "*unxit* (anointed)"] us."[138] For Aquinas, 1 Corinthians 6:11 suggests that the baptismal washing is followed by sanctification through anointing. Similarly, 2 Corinthians 1:21 appears to give a central role to anointing.

The contexts of these two verses are also worth noting, although Aquinas does not comment on them here. In 1 Corinthians 6, Paul is urging the Corinthians not to take their legal cases "before the unrighteous instead of the saints" (1 Cor. 6:1), and indeed entirely to avoid legal cases against one another. The church consists of the "saints," but they are still prone to acting in the ways of the world. In 2 Corinthians 1, Paul is speaking of his apostolic commission to teach and govern; he says of himself that God "has put his seal upon us and given us his Spirit in our hearts as a guarantee" (2 Cor. 1:22). Both passages refer to the anointing or sanctifying work of the Holy Spirit and show that it pertains not solely to individuals but also to the church as an interconnected and hierarchical body. In addition, in both passages Paul discusses the Holy Spirit's sanctifying or anointing work in the context of his criticisms of the Corinthians' notable lack of holiness. The holiness of the church does not depend upon the perfect sanctity of the members of the church, and indeed some of them are members in name only (see 1 Cor. 5:2).

The third way that the church is made holy is through the indwelling Trinity. Aquinas has already argued, as we have seen, that the congregation of the faithful is washed in Christ's blood and anointed by his Spirit so as to be the temple of God. Connecting this with the indwelling Trinity, he now

---

137. Aquinas, *The Sermon-Conferences of St. Thomas Aquinas on the Apostles' Creed*, 127. For background to Aquinas's reading of 1 and 2 Corinthians, see Daniel A. Keating, "Aquinas on 1 and 2 Corinthians: The Sacraments and Their Ministers," in *Aquinas on Scripture: An Introduction to His Biblical Commentaries*, ed. Thomas G. Weinandy, OFMCap, Daniel A. Keating, and John P. Yocum (London: T&T Clark, 2005), 127–48.

138. See Rikhof, "Thomas on the Church," 204.

observes that "wherever God dwells, that place is holy."[139] Again he gives two biblical citations, this time both from the Old Testament: Genesis 28:17, in which Jacob, having dreamt of a ladder reaching from earth to heaven and having received YHWH's covenantal blessing, proclaims that this place is "none other than the house of God" and "the gate of heaven"; and Psalm 93:5, where the psalmist says, "Your decrees are very sure; holiness befits your house, O Lord, for evermore." Jacob's awed proclamation comes as he is leaving Canaan, the promised land where God will dwell with his people. Psalm 93 describes the glorious sovereignty of the Creator God and concludes by suggesting that a people with such a powerful and wise sovereign will be holy. God dwells in his people as a sanctifying power, not as a passive inhabitant. Furthermore, the indwelling of the Trinity is not simply an individual experience but rather is the fulfillment of God's covenantal promises to his people.

The fourth and final aspect noted by Aquinas is that the church sanctifies its members by invoking the name of God. Why does the invocation of God add anything? Aquinas cites a prophecy that Jeremiah received during a period of terrible drought in Judah. The prophecy begins with the mourning of Judah, with a lament that pleads with God to act. God is committed to punishing his rebellious people, but Jeremiah intercedes for the people and begs God, "We acknowledge our wickedness, O Lord, and the iniquity of our fathers, for we have sinned against thee. Do not spurn us, for thy name's sake; do not dishonor thy glorious throne; remember and do not break thy covenant with us" (Jer. 14:20–21). The verse that Aquinas quotes comes earlier, at the end of the prophecy's first lament: "Yet thou, O Lord, art in the midst of us, and we are called by thy name; leave us not" (Jer. 14:9). The point is that the people of Israel are "called by thy name"; God has placed his "name" upon this people by associating them intimately with himself and by making himself present to them in truth. Even though they are sinners, God has united himself to them in the sense of making them the bearers of his holy "name." Christians too have been baptized and anointed in God's name, now revealed as Father, Son, and Holy Spirit. God has placed his "name" on us and has made us (both individually and as the church) his temple. In Christ, we bear the saving name of God. On this basis Aquinas warns against sin: "We should be careful, lest after such a sanctification we soil through sin our

139. Aquinas, *The Sermon-Conferences of St. Thomas Aquinas on the Apostles' Creed*, 127. Rikhof comments that "the shortness of the statement and treatment, 'the Church is named holy through the indwelling of the Trinity,' should not mislead us. This is the centre of Thomas' vision. The mystery of the Church is the presence of Father-Son-Spirit among us and in us" (Rikhof, "Thomas on the Church," 205).

soul, which is the temple of God."[140] The consequences of rebelling against the holy God are spiritually fatal. Aquinas quotes Paul's admonition, "Do you not know that you are God's temple and that God's Spirit dwells in you? If any one destroys God's temple, God will destroy him" (1 Cor. 3:16–17).[141]

Aquinas thus defends the holiness of the church by attending to the church's sources: "the blood of Christ" and "the grace of the Holy Spirit." Baptism and confirmation (and other sacraments) enable the members of the church to receive the saving power of Christ's passion and to be filled with the grace of the Holy Spirit. God the Trinity dwells in the church, and where he dwells is holy. God has placed his "name" upon the church, which therefore is his holy temple.[142]

We can understand something more of Aquinas's position from his commentary on Ephesians 5:25–27.[143] Aquinas makes clear that the church that lacks "spot or wrinkle" (Eph. 5:27) is primarily the eschatological church, the perfect church as it will be at the consummation of all things. When Christ presents to himself the church "in splendor" (Eph. 5:27), this refers, Aquinas says, to the church composed of members whose bodies and souls have been glorified. He cites Philippians 3:21 (to which I add v. 20): "Our commonwealth is in heaven, and from it we await a Savior, the Lord Jesus Christ, who will change our lowly body to be like his glorious body." The blessed in heaven will be perfect, and will have no "spot"; in this regard Aquinas applies two psalms that describe the blameless person who walks with God (Ps. 101:6 and Ps. 119:1). Neither will the blessed in heaven have any "wrinkle," that is, any suffering.

140. Aquinas, *The Sermon-Conferences of St. Thomas Aquinas on the Apostles' Creed*, 129.

141. For discussion of 1 Corinthians 3:16–17, see Grant Macaskill, *Union with Christ in the New Testament* (Oxford: Oxford University Press, 2013), 154–55. Macaskill comments that Paul's "deployment of the temple image is not an isolated move, but is part of a consistent argument that the church is Spirit-filled and led, and cannot be governed by human standards of wisdom, status, and power" (ibid., 155).

142. Although Aquinas does not cite it here, one thinks of 2 Samuel 7:13–14, where God says of David's son, "He shall build a house for my name, and I will establish the throne of his kingdom for ever. I will be his father, and he shall be my son"; and 1 Kings 8:27–30, "But will God indeed dwell on the earth? Behold, heaven and the highest heaven cannot contain thee; how much less this house which I have built! Yet have regard to the prayer of thy servant and to his supplication, O LORD my God, hearkening to the cry and to the prayer which thy servant prays before thee this day; that thy eyes may be open night and day toward this house, the place of which thou hast said, 'My name shall be there,' that thou mayest hearken to the prayer which thy servant offers toward this place. And hearken thou to the supplication of thy servant and of thy people Israel, when they pray toward this place; yea, hear thou in heaven thy dwelling place; and when thou hearest, forgive."

143. For an erudite historical contextualization of Aquinas's *Commentary on Ephesians*, see Mark Edwards, "Aquinas on Ephesians and Colossians," in Weinandy, Keating, and Yocum, *Aquinas on Scripture*, 149–65.

Yet Aquinas also thinks that the passage can refer to the church of grace, the church on earth that is not yet perfect. From this perspective, the church has no "spot" in the sense that the true members of the church on earth are not in a state of mortal sin. The church on earth is already "in splendor" because of the dignity of following God by the grace of the Holy Spirit. The church also already lacks any "wrinkle," if by "wrinkle" one means "duplicity of purpose," which would be a mortal sin and thus would be far from "those who are rightly united with Christ and the Church."[144] The church even now is "holy" by its "aspiration [*intentionem*]."[145] Aquinas suggests that the church is also without blemish, insofar as the members of the church manifest a real sanctity and "every kind of purity."[146] Through the grace of the Holy Spirit, even now Christ presents the church "to himself in an immaculate state."[147]

Aquinas connects this holiness with the sacrament of baptism, in accord with the logic of Ephesians 5:25–27. Regarding the cleansing that Christ brings "by the washing of water" (Eph. 5:26), Aquinas explains that Paul is here speaking of baptism, which has its "power from the passion of Christ."[148] In this respect Aquinas cites two prophetic texts about the day of the Lord: Ezekiel 36:25: "I will sprinkle clean water upon you, and you shall be clean from all your uncleannesses"; and Zechariah 13:1: "On that day there shall be a fountain opened for the house of David and the inhabitants of Jerusalem to cleanse them from sin and uncleanness." Baptism constitutes the "fountain" or sprinkling "of clean water" that, by enabling us to share in Christ's passion, causes our cleansing from sin. Aquinas quotes Paul in this regard: "Do you not know that all of us who have been baptized into Christ Jesus were baptized into his death? We were buried therefore with him by baptism into death" (Rom. 6:3–4).[149] The role of baptism in this work of salvation is made even clearer by the risen Christ's commanding his disciples to baptize all nations "in the name of the Father and of the Son and of the Holy Spirit" (Matt. 28:19).[150]

---

144. Thomas Aquinas, *Commentary on Saint Paul's Epistle to the Ephesians*, trans. Matthew L. Lamb (Albany, NY: Magi, 1966), 5.8, p. 220.

145. Aquinas, *Commentary on Saint Paul's Epistle to the Ephesians* 5.8, p. 220.

146. Aquinas, *Commentary on Saint Paul's Epistle to the Ephesians* 5.8, p. 220.

147. Aquinas, *Commentary on Saint Paul's Epistle to the Ephesians* 5.8, p. 219.

148. Aquinas, *Commentary on Saint Paul's Epistle to the Ephesians* 5.8, p. 219.

149. For the significance of Romans 6:3–4 in Aquinas's theology of baptism, see Bernhard Blankenhorn, OP, "The Place of Romans 6 in Aquinas's Doctrine of Sacramental Causality: A Balance of History and Metaphysics," in *Ressourcement Thomism: Sacred Doctrine, the Sacraments, and the Moral Life*, ed. Reinhard Hütter and Matthew Levering (Washington, DC: Catholic University of America Press, 2010), 136–49; and Matthew Levering, *Paul in the Summa Theologiae* (Washington, DC: Catholic University of America Press, 2014), chap. 3.

150. See also the patristic reflections on Matthew 28:19 in Joseph T. Lienhard, SJ, "The Baptismal Command (Matthew 28:19–20) and the Doctrine of the Trinity," in *The Holy*

In this way, Christ's passion makes the people of God fit for marriage with God, since "it would be highly improper for the immaculate bridegroom to wed a soiled bride."[151] Aquinas emphasizes that Christ came for the purpose of bringing about "the Church's purity."[152] On the one hand, Aquinas agrees with Calvin that the church can be called holy, in its "appearance through faith," through its "aspiration" or "intention," its sincere striving in the process of sanctification.[153] Like Calvin, Aquinas recognizes the ongoing sinfulness of the church's members, even though he distinguishes these sins as venial. On the other hand, Aquinas insists that the church already, by the grace of the Holy Spirit, is "immaculate." Such holiness depends upon the missions of the Son and Spirit, which constitute the church as the temple of God.[154] As with Aquinas's view that humans merit condignly when the primary agent of the action is the Holy Spirit dwelling within them, I interpret Aquinas to mean that the church is immaculately holy not insofar as its works flow from mere humans (who are imperfect), but insofar as its works (such as baptism) flow from Christ and the Holy Spirit.

Aquinas fully recognizes that the sins of the church's members, including the seeming members who are interiorly separated from the church by mortal sin, sadly mar the face of the church and make it difficult to perceive the church's holiness. Almost any of the *Summa theologiae*'s questions on the vices would suffice to show that Aquinas is not overly idealistic about human nature after baptism. I will focus here very briefly on his treatment

---

Trinity in the Life of the Church, ed. Khaled Anatolios (Grand Rapids: Baker Academic, 2014), 3–14.

151. Aquinas, *Commentary on Saint Paul's Epistle to the Ephesians*, 219.

152. Aquinas, *Commentary on Saint Paul's Epistle to the Ephesians*, 219. Note also Joseph Ratzinger's observation about the relationship of the church and the kingdom: "the gathering and cleansing of men for the Kingdom of God is part of this Kingdom" (Ratzinger, *Called to Communion: Understanding the Church Today*, trans. Adrian Walker [San Francisco: Ignatius, 1996], 21–22).

153. Aquinas, *Commentary on Saint Paul's Epistle to the Ephesians*, 220.

154. See also Levering, *Engaging the Doctrine of Revelation*, chap. 1. T. F. Torrance eloquently makes a similar point:

> Because the holiness of the church is its participation through the Spirit in the self-sanctification of Christ that has already been completed, the church is holy in a once and for all sense. Just as justification is not something that is to be repeated for it has taken place once and for all, so the sanctification of the church is already complete in Christ and is the enduring reality into which it is unrepeatably initiated in baptism and in which it is continually participant in holy communion. In Christ the holiness of the church is unshakeable and incorruptible. In him it is sinless and perfect, without spot or wrinkle, for it is clothed with his righteousness and sanctified with his holiness in truth. The church cannot fail in regard to its holiness because that holiness comes from the head of the church and is not a holiness which comes or accrues from its members. (Torrance, *Atonement*, 387)

of the sin of simony and on his account of the virtue of fraternal correction. With regard to simony, he displays a large acquaintance with the contours of this sin that especially plagued the wealthy medieval church. He notes that "the Pope can be guilty of the vice of simony, like any other man," and he warns that the pope would commit simony by accepting "money from the income of any church in exchange for a spiritual thing" or "by accepting from a layman moneys not belonging to the goods of the Church."[155] He knows that "it happens sometimes that someone maliciously hinders a person from obtaining a bishopric or some like dignity," and he knows that there are priests who are "unwilling to baptize without being paid."[156] He knows that there are instances in which a cleric buys "off the opposition of [his] rivals, before acquiring the right to a bishopric or any dignity or prebend."[157] He specifies, as one who is aware of the opposite practice, that "those who in certain churches are appointed to instruct the clerics of that church and other poor persons, and are in receipt of an ecclesiastical benefice for so doing, are not allowed to receive anything in return."[158] He observes even that "sometimes a person obtains admission to a monastery by simony."[159] If this sort of thing was going on even among those devoted to priestly service and to religious life, then one can hardly have a particularly hopeful view of what must have been going on throughout the church. In the *secunda-secundae*, Aquinas's discussion of the many other vices that plague laypeople, religious, and clergy shows that he knows well what problems afflict baptized Christians.

Aquinas also speaks of fraternal correction as a most important virtue for Christians, which would hardly be the case if the church were holy in an undifferentiated or empirically verifiable sense. He expects that people will have to correct their prelates, although he encourages them "to do so in a becoming manner, not with impudence and harshness, but with gentleness

155. II-II, q. 100, a. 1, ad 7. John Mahoney comments that Aquinas was well aware of the possible misuse of authority, which is nevertheless intended to be a ministry of the Spirit. And he was at one with tradition and his own age in seeing simoniacal abuses and the sale of "the gifts of the Holy Spirit" as the most striking instance of such misuse, implying as it did that the Spirit was a servant or slave to be bought and sold. There are other abuses of authority, of course, but Aquinas's central objection to all of them is that they usurp the role of the Holy Spirit in his own Church, and this is perhaps best expressed in his exegesis of Jesus's warning on authority in Matt. 20:25–8, a passage in which Aquinas carefully points out the chiastic structure and the central phrase "It shall not be so among you." (Mahoney, "'Church of the Holy Spirit' in Aquinas," 23)
156. II-II, q. 100, a. 2, obj. 5 and ad 1.
157. II-II, q. 100, a. 2, obj. 5 and ad 5.
158. II-II, q. 100, a. 3, ad 3.
159. II-II, q. 100, a. 6, obj. 5.

and respect."[160] The pope may need to be corrected publicly, as Paul corrected Peter (see Gal. 2). Aquinas urges us first to correct our brethren's sins privately, unless the sins are "public sins" that "should be denounced in public."[161] Even if we are sinners, we can still rightly correct our sinful brethren, so long as we do so humbly. In this discussion, Aquinas clearly supposes that the need for fraternal correction will arise rather frequently. In the *tertia pars*, likewise, Aquinas treats at length the situation of wicked persons who present themselves to receive various sacraments, as well as the problem of wicked priests administering the sacraments.

His view of the church, in other words, is not rose-colored. Instead, he recognizes fully the extent of sin among baptized persons, and thus among the human agents of the church. His affirmation of the holiness of the church does not depend upon denying the venial sins of the church's members or the mortal sins of those who profess Christianity but cut themselves off (invisibly) from the church by their sins. In this regard, Aquinas stands fully within the perspective of Cyprian and Augustine, even while he also shares Calvin's emphasis that the church is holy insofar as it is striving for holiness. Aquinas repeatedly highlights the sacrament of holy baptism and the church's status as God's temple, and he describes the church as even now "immaculate" in a way that underscores the power of the missions of the Spirit. As Michael Allen and Scott Swain rightly remark, "The Spirit . . . is the principle of theology, the infinite ocean and transcendent fountain of divine truth. The church is not that ocean; the church is not that fountain."[162]

Conclusion

As we observed, Kevin Vanhoozer, drawing upon Luther, names the church "*simil justus et peccator.*"[163] The Spirit is at work justifying and sanctifying the people of God, but we are not yet holy, we are not yet what we should be. We are being sanctified, but we are still sinners. According to Vanhoozer, the same point holds for the church itself: it is striving toward God under the

---

160. II-II, q. 33, a. 4.
161. II-II, q. 33, a. 7.
162. Michael Allen and Scott R. Swain, *Reformed Catholicity: The Promise of Retrieval for Theology and Biblical Interpretation* (Grand Rapids: Baker Academic, 2015), 33. For Allen and Swain, it is Scripture, inspired by the Spirit, that participates truly in the ocean/fountain. The church has a role but does not participate in the ocean/fountain in any manner that parallels Scripture's participation, because the church often has fallen away (even in definitively proclaimed doctrine) from the truth of Scripture.
163. Vanhoozer, *Drama of Doctrine*, 188.

guidance of the Holy Spirit, but it is imperfect and fallen, so that we should not imagine, for example, that "every church doctrine mediate[s] the presence of God."[164] Billings too considers that although the church is being sanctified by the Spirit, nonetheless the church remains sinful and in need of reformation: "God's word empowers the reshaping of the church because, on this side of the *eschaton*, the church is always in need of further transformation through Scripture."[165] The fact is that believers are sinners, and "until the consummation of God's kingdom, his disciples will continue to struggle with sin."[166]

For Calvin, since the true members of the church are in fact imperfect, despite their striving for holiness, it follows that the holiness of the church depends on God's imputation. In this sense, Calvin considers that there has always been a holy church. At all times and places, even when the visible church has been at its most wicked (mired in an idolatrous worship and false teaching, in the pre-Reformation period), God has always ensured the existence of a remnant of believers who strive for holiness, and thus the true proclamation of the Word and the true celebration of the sacraments (baptism and the Eucharist) have never completely ceased. God imputes the attribute "holiness" to this remnant church. For Calvin "all sin is mortal, because it is rebellion against the will of God, and necessarily provokes his anger; and because it is a violation of the Law, against every violation of which, without exception, the judgment of God has been pronounced."[167]

How do the positions of Cyprian, Augustine, and Aquinas on the holiness of the church accord with and differ from these Reformed perspectives?

---

164. Ibid.

165. Billings, *Word of God for the People of God*, 68.

166. Ibid., 205.

167. Calvin, *Institutes of the Christian Religion*, 1:362. In accord with Calvin's emphasis on the sanctification and imputed holiness of the church, R. Michael Allen holds that the church is "a creaturely, reconciled, and gradually renewed people," but he prefers to speak of "the ungodly church" rather than the holy church (Allen, *Justification and the Gospel: Understanding the Contexts and Controversies* [Grand Rapids: Baker Academic, 2013], 160–61). See also Kilian McDonnell, OSB's emphasis that "it was the goal of Calvin's theological endeavor to restore divinity to God," in the sense of restoring a full appreciation of God's absolute sovereignty: "The church which sets itself up as an absolute, not only above judgment but equal with the judge, rendering judgment, canonizing and anathematizing, as by a power which she possesses inwardly, as a self-contained atomized source, has nothing to do with the church of Christ. Indeed, the church, though she is the body of Christ, cannot make laws which bind in conscience; this is a divine prerogative which the church cannot usurp. She can and must witness to and proclaim God's laws, but she herself has no power to bind consciences. . . . The body of Christ has ears only for the Words of Christ, and she gives recognition to no other voice and to no other command" (McDonnell, *John Calvin, the Church, and the Eucharist*, 168, 171–72). McDonnell goes on to remark that "Calvin rejected the spiritualist ideal of a sinless church and also denied the right to leave a church simply because of its moral inadequacies" (ibid., 175).

Cyprian grounds his reflections upon the image of the church as the mother of all the faithful (an image also cherished by Calvin): "She is one mother, plentiful in the results of fruitfulness: from her womb we are born, by her milk we are nourished, by her spirit we are animated."[168] The church, whose head is Christ, nourishes and animates believers with her own "milk" and "spirit." The grace of the Holy Spirit builds up the church in the holiness that believers receive in Christ. But for Cyprian, by contrast to Calvin, "The spouse of Christ cannot be adulterous; she is uncorrupted and pure."[169] The church has no "adulterous" worship, not least because of its possession of the true and holy Eucharist, the "flesh of Christ." The holiness of the church is not merely imputed, but rather is already perfectly (liturgically) real.

For his part, in his *On the Creed*, Augustine gives special emphasis to the link between the church's holiness (as affirmed by the Apostles' Creed) and the church's true doctrine. After quoting 1 Corinthians 3:17, where Paul describes Christians as God's holy temple, Augustine states, "This same is the holy Church, the one Church, the true Church, the catholic Church, fighting against all heresies: fight, it can: be fought down, it cannot."[170] The holiness of the church is found in its true doctrine. Like Cyprian, Augustine also connects the church's holiness with its sacramental worship. Thus, in his *City of God*, he emphasizes that the church "does not create false gods. She herself is the creation of the true God, and she herself is to be his true sacrifice."[171]

Aquinas draws a repeated link to the sacrament of baptism, by which the church is cleansed through the power of Christ's passion. The members of the church receive the indwelling of the Trinity (the divine missions), so that the church can truly be the holy temple of God upon which God places his name. As Aquinas emphasizes, the members of the church are holy only in an imperfect sense, insofar as they are without mortal sin and strive toward full union with God. Yet even on earth, the church is rightly said to be "immaculate," since the church is God's temple, and insofar as it is God who works in and through his temple to sanctify believers in the truth of his name (as God does in baptism, for example), the church is holy.

Thus while Cyprian, Augustine, and Aquinas can agree with Reformed theologians about the sinfulness of the church's members on earth in the process of sanctification, they disagree with Reformed theologians about whether the church is (in the words of *Lumen Gentium*) "unfailingly holy" (*indefectibiliter*

---

168. Cyprian, *On the Unity of the Church*, 423.
169. Cyprian, *On the Unity of the Church*, 423.
170. Augustine, *On the Creed* 374.
171. Augustine, *City of God* 54, p. 842.

sancta).[172] This unfailing holiness is a mark of the Holy Spirit's outpouring in the body of the incarnate Son; it is a testimony to the real "peace" enjoyed by the messianic people of the Lord Jesus Christ as described in Acts. If the church's holiness is not fully affirmed, then the tension between real peace and real strife that we found in Acts is lost, and the power of the Spirit's eschatological outpouring upon Christ's church is dissipated. The church can faithfully mediate Christ's truth and nourish his body sacramentally only because the church is truly a holy temple, marked by the ongoing eschatological outpouring of the Spirit. Yet Cyprian, Augustine, and Aquinas can agree with the Reformed theologian T. F. Torrance's statement that "so long as it [the church] lives in this world that passes away and partakes of its sinful patterns and forms, it is involved in error and wrong," so long as in these "sinful patterns and forms" and "error and wrong" Torrance did not include the church's sacramental constitution and definitive doctrine.[173]

172. *Lumen Gentium*, §39, in Flannery, *Vatican Council II*, 396. Earlier, *Lumen Gentium* states, "Christ, 'holy, innocent and undefiled' (Heb. 7:26) knew nothing of sin (2 Cor. 5:21), but came only to expiate the sins of the people (cf. Heb. 2:17). The Church, however, clasping sinners to her bosom, at once holy and always in need of purification, follows constantly the path of penance and renewal" (*Lumen Gentium*, §8, in ibid., 358). See also *Lumen Gentium*, §40, in ibid., 397; §48, in ibid., 408.

173. Torrance, *Atonement*, 388. Torrance makes his position hard to pin down. He states, "Regarded merely in itself the church on earth can err, can fail, can become heretical, can be weak and sickly. Yet the church cannot be regarded merely in itself, for its true life is in Christ who has bound it to himself in a holy and everlasting covenant, in which he sanctifies it with his holiness, establishes it in his truth, maintains it as his very own body and will present it at last to himself in all the perfection and purity of the divine life which he imparts to it" (ibid., 389). The question is whether the church has in fact erred, failed, and become heretical. All parties can agree that "regarded merely in itself" the church can do these things, but Torrance rightly says that "the church cannot be regarded merely in itself." Torrance insists that the "church cannot dissociate itself from the sinners that make up its membership or reckon itself untarnished by their sin and error and so separate itself from them" (ibid., 371), but this point can be taken in diverse ways. Certainly the church is tarnished by its members' "sin and error," but the question is whether this "sin and error" cuts right to the church's sacramental constitution and definitive doctrine. Torrance rightly places the eucharistic liturgy (along with baptism) at the center of his account of the church as Christ's body: "Although the church is sanctified and consecrated in Christ and his self-consecration on its behalf, its constituent members remain sinners constantly in need of his pardon and healing and sanctifying, and therefore until he comes again they must be ever renewed in their membership of his body through participation in his body and blood, individually and corporately. Thus it is in holy communion that the church ever becomes what Christ in his grace has made it, when he loved it and gave himself over for it and adopted it as his own body" (ibid., 371). Torrance's account of the body of Christ begins by separating Christ quite strongly from his members, but ends by emphasizing union and communion. Torrance states,

> When we speak of the church as the body of Christ meaning the whole Christ, head and members, we must speak of it as sinless and perfectly holy, for then we speak of the church in its concentration in Christ himself. But when we speak of the church as the

Is it possible to specify any further how the church is holy, other than by broadly affirming that it is holy as ontologically and efficaciously participating in the missions of the Son and Holy Spirit? In this regard, contemporary Catholic theologians offer different answers. Like the fathers and Aquinas, Avery Dulles focuses upon the point that the church is united to Christ as her head by the Holy Spirit, and so the church's "doctrines, sacraments, and ministries are objectively holy (or 'sacred') because they are supernatural gifts coming from God and conveying the grace of God."[174] As for the holiness of the members of the church on earth, this is real but imperfect.

Jean-Hervé Nicolas and Aidan Nichols add the argument that the outpouring of the Spirit at Pentecost sanctified the apostles in such a way that "the unfailing mediatorial action of the church—holy Church—in initiating people into holiness begins with the apostles and on their foundation."[175] For their part, Hans Urs von Balthasar and Joseph Ratzinger propose that the immaculate personality of the church as the true bride of Christ began with Mary at the cross, "when through Mary's faith, hope, and love, now reconfigured by the Sacrifice of the cross, holy Church as the Mother of sinners—but not herself sinful—came to be."[176] Mary, of course, was also present in the upper room at Pentecost.

From a somewhat different angle, Roch Kereszty considers that the "church of the perfect, the immaculate dove, can in the full sense be only the heavenly

---

body of Christ meaning the body of sinners with which he identified himself in life and death, so that through the crucifixion of the body of sin he might raise it a glorious body clothed with his own holiness and purity, then we speak of the church as constantly in need of forgiveness and constantly directed away from itself to find in Christ alone its justification and its sanctification. Yet it is this very body, constituted out of sinful men and women, that Christ appropriates as his very own and brings into such union and communion with himself that, in spite of sin, he dwells within it and heals and hallows it and makes it the instrument of his saving love among all nations. (ibid.)
See also Levering, *Engaging the Doctrine of Revelation*, chaps. 1–6.

174. Avery Dulles, SJ, "Church," in *The Blackwell Companion to Catholicism*, ed. James J. Buckley, Frederick Christian Bauerschmidt, and Trent Pomplun (Oxford: Blackwell, 2007), 326–39, at 332. For the same position see Yves Congar, OP, *True and False Reform in the Church*, trans. Paul Philibert, OP (Collegeville, MN: Liturgical Press, 2011).

175. Aidan Nichols, OP, *Figuring Out the Church: Her Marks, and Her Masters* (San Francisco: Ignatius, 2013), 54–55. Nichols cites Nicolas, *Synthèse dogmatique*, 698.

176. Nichols, *Figuring Out the Church*, 55–56. Nichols cites Hans Urs von Balthasar and Joseph Ratzinger, *Mary: The Church at the Source* (San Francisco: Ignatius, 2005). Note also Hans Urs von Balthasar's observation: "The Church, purified through the 'washing of water' in baptism, becomes the *immaculata* (Eph. 5:26); but this means that she becomes what she always already was in Mary" ("Mary and the Holy Spirit," in *Explorations in Theology*, vol. 5, *Man Is Created*, trans. Adrian Walker [San Francisco: Ignatius, 2014], 176–83, at 182). For the same position, eloquently expressed, see Antonio López, *Gift and the Unity of Being* (Eugene, OR: Cascade, 2014), 281–82.

church: the immaculate Virgin Mary in the most perfect way and around her all the saints sharing in her holiness."[177] The church on earth is not perfect or immaculate in the fullest way possible, not least because the church on earth contains sinners. Yet for Kereszty, the church here on earth is sustained in holy sacraments, holy teaching, and holy offices, "because they are the ways in which the one Bride of Christ operates, the Bride Mother with whom and through whom Christ sanctifies through the Holy Spirit all those who are open to his grace."[178] The church as the "Bride Mother" is holy and nourishes believers in holy sacraments and holy teaching.

Benoît-Dominique de La Soujeole proposes that the solution consists in the Holy Spirit's indwelling of all the members of Christ's church. This indwelling gives the church a corporate personality. De La Soujeole states in this regard, "The Church subsists in her members in such wise as the Holy Spirit dwells in them, the Holy Spirit who unites them in a way just as the soul unites the members of a body. The infallible and indefectible character of the faith of the Church relates to this mystical unity."[179] Since the indwelling Spirit is the

177. Roch Kereszty, OCist, "'*Sacrosancta Ecclesia*': The Holy Church of Sinners," *Communio* 40 (2013): 663–79, at 670. *Lumen Gentium* observes, "The one mediator, Christ, established and ever sustains here on earth his holy Church, the community of faith, hope and charity, as a visible organization through which he communicates truth and grace to all men. But, the society structured with hierarchical organs and the mystical body of Christ, the visible society and the spiritual community, the earthly Church and the Church endowed with heavenly riches, are not to be thought of as two realities. On the contrary, they form one complex reality which comes together from a human and a divine element" (*Lumen Gentium*, §8, in Flannery, *Vatican Council II*, 357). See also Jacques Servais, SJ, "The Confession of the *Casta Meretrix*," *Communio* 40 (2013): 642–62. On this topic, see also the overview of the positions of Charles Journet, Yves Congar, and Karl Rahner provided by Francis A. Sullivan in his "Do the Sins of Its Members Affect the Holiness of the Church?," Sullivan cites Yves Congar, OP, *Sainte Église: Études et approches ecclésiologiques* (Paris: Cerf, 1963); Congar, *L'Église Une, Sainte, Catholique et Apostolique* (Paris: Cerf, 1970); Charles Journet, *Théologie de l'Église* (Paris: Desclée de Brouwer, 1958); and Karl Rahner's "The Church of Sinners" and "The Sinful Church in the Decrees of Vatican II." Sullivan agrees with Congar's strong criticisms of Journet's argument that the church is holy (and sinless) insofar as the Holy Spirit, and created charity, is acting in the members of the church, so that when the members sin, they are in that respect not acting qua church. But Sullivan is also dubious about Congar's distinction between "the Church herself" and the members of the church, although Sullivan appreciates that Congar is willing to attribute "historical faults" (but not sins) to the church. Sullivan advocates Rahner's position that the church sins. For a similar survey of Journet, Congar, and Rahner, in light of Vatican II and Pope John Paul II's statements and actions regarding ecclesial repentance during the Jubilee Year of 2000 (also treated in Sullivan's essay), see Bergen, *Ecclesial Repentance*, 209–24.

178. Kereszty, "*Sacrosancta Ecclesia*," 674.

179. Benoît-Dominique de La Soujeole, OP, "The Economy of Salvation: Entitative Sacramentality and Operative Sacramentality," *The Thomist* 75 (2011): 537–54, at 549. See also John Saward, "*L'Église a ravi son coeur*: Charles Journet and the Theologians of *Ressourcement* on the Personality of the Church," in *Ressourcement: A Movement for Renewal in Twentieth-Century*

divine principle of the church's actions of sacramental worship and of definitive proclamation of the gospel (just as the indwelling Spirit is the divine principle of a graced person's good actions), the church is holy.

Each of these approaches to the holiness of the church has strengths and weaknesses, and for our purposes we need not decide between them. With Reformed theologians, we must grant that the church on earth is always in great need of repentance and renewal, as history shows.[180] Yet the church is also truly holy. This sacramental and doctrinal holiness is never an autonomous possession (as if the church were thereby placed over the gospel), but rather is always a testimony to the ongoing outpouring of the eschatological Spirit of Christ in his body, an outpouring that ensures that the church faithfully mediates to each generation the power and truth of Christ's pasch. Thanks to the eschatological activity of the incarnate Son and Spirit in the church, "The Church subsists in the Holy Spirit . . . in all the most decisive acts of her existence here below: fidelity in the faith and the authentic sacraments."[181] The church's members on earth are sinners, but the Spirit never ceases to unite the church in "the permanence of the *sancta* [holy things]."[182] As Khaled Anatolios eloquently states, "Jesus gives us the Spirit and the Spirit gives us Jesus as Lord and we are thus enfolded into the circle of mutual trinitarian glorification."[183]

Catholic Theology, ed. Gabriel Flynn and Paul D. Murray (Oxford: Oxford University Press, 2012), 125–37.

180. See Pope John Paul II, *The Purification of Memory*, www.vatican.va. For discussion of this aspect of John Paul II's pontificate, see, for example, Michael R. Marrus, "Papal Apologies of Pope John Paul II," in *The Age of Apology: Facing Up to the Past*, ed. Mark Gibney et al. (Philadelphia: University of Pennsylvania Press, 2008), 259–70. See also the International Theological Commission's document "Memory and Reconciliation: The Church and Faults of the Past," *Origins* 29, no. 39 (March 16, 2000): 625–44. The International Theological Commission attributes the church's holiness to the missions of Son and the Holy Spirit and holds that the church's holiness guarantees the effective proclamation of the gospel and sanctification of believers. For discussion of this document in light of *Lumen Gentium*, see Herwi Rikhof, "The Holiness of the Church," in Poorthuis and Schwartz, *Holy People*, 321–35, at 329–34. For Rikhof, "From the conclusion [made by the document] that sin *in* the church has effects on the entire church, one could infer that therefore the church is to be called sinful. That inference is not drawn, but it is not clear why not" (ibid., 334). In my view, the answer consists in what it means to call the church "holy"; it is a confession of the Triune God's work in and through the church. See also the critical reflections of Bernard P. Prusak, "Theological Considerations—Hermeneutical, Ecclesiological, Eschatological regarding *Memory and Reconciliation: The Church and the Faults of the Past*," *Horizons* 32 (2005): 136–51.

181. Benoît-Dominique de La Soujeole, OP, *Introduction to the Mystery of the Church*, trans. Michael J. Miller (Washington, DC: Catholic University of America Press, 2014), 561.

182. Ibid., 626.

183. Khaled Anatolios, *Retrieving Nicaea: The Development and Meaning of Trinitarian Doctrine* (Grand Rapids: Baker Academic, 2011), 288.

Indeed, it is this ongoing divine gifting that makes the visible and institutional church to be "a holy nation, God's own people," ruled by the Lord Jesus Christ at the right hand of the Father, and built up in the Holy Spirit by the "kiss of love" that is the greatest gift (1 Pet. 2:9; 5:14).[184] Preeminently in the liturgy of the Eucharist, where the scriptural word is proclaimed and the incarnate Word is sacramentally made present, we participate through the Spirit in Christ's self-offering for the life of the world, and the church becomes what it is.

184. For 1 Peter on the church as the eschatological temple, though not yet fully consummated, see Macaskill, *Union with Christ in the New Testament*, 159–62. See also Joel B. Green, "Faithful Witness in the Diaspora: The Holy Spirit and the Exiled People of God according to 1 Peter," in *The Holy Spirit and Christian Origins: Essays in Honor of James D. G. Dunn*, ed. Graham N. Stanton, Bruce W. Longenecker, and Stephen C. Barton (Grand Rapids: Eerdmans, 2004), 282–95. Ola Tjørhom states eloquently, "The holiness of the Church depends primarily on the fact that it belongs to God the Father, in the sense that he has called it into being through Christ and that it is the space of his continued action for the redemption of humankind in the Holy Spirit. Since everything that belongs to God is holy, it follows that the Church's holiness does not derive from our efforts or our longing for perfection, but from God's ultimate perfection and grace" (Tjørhom, *Visible Church—Visible Unity*, 65). For Tjørhom, this means that "holiness can be and has been maintained within the Church even when it has failed its God-given purpose" (ibid.). I would agree, so long as such failure is not understood to distort the holiness and truth of the church's sacraments and definitive teachings. Tjørhom makes this same point when he adds, "A church that gives in to heresy immediately ceases to be a 'pillar and bulwark of the truth' (1 Tim 3:15)" (ibid., 67).

Conclusion

To name the Holy Spirit "Love" and "Gift" is admittedly rather bold. These names are not explicit in Scripture, by contrast to the Son's name "Word." They can be obtained by means of scriptural exegesis, but only from scriptural exegesis attuned to the likelihood that God intends to instruct us richly about his Spirit. In Scripture, the Holy Spirit is repeatedly associated with gift, as well as with love, the greatest gift. But the Spirit is also repeatedly associated with truth, although in enlightening us with truth, the Spirit specifically unites us to the Son. Even if the case can be made for naming the Spirit Love and Gift in the economy of salvation, the claim that the Spirit is *properly* Love and Gift—in the same way that the Son is Word—is more difficult. We have seen that the Son also is given by the Father; how then is the Spirit alone properly Gift? How can we say that the Spirit proceeds properly as Love, given that the Son is surely beloved by the Father? Indeed, how can we dare to say anything about the inexhaustible mystery of the Father, Son, and Holy Spirit, who are one God and yet distinct?

I have argued that naming the Spirit Love and Gift is, nonetheless, biblically and theologically justified. Discussing Augustine and Aquinas, Gregory Collins remarks that "their *filioquism* emerges as much more soteriologically orientated than rationalistically speculative: they wanted to justify how the Holy Spirit of salvation history is also the Spirit of the eternal Logos in the bosom of the Trinity."[1] The name Word illumines the distinctive personhood of the Son and the immanent character of the Son's coming forth from the

---

1. Gregory Collins, OSB, "Three Modern 'Fathers' on the *Filioque*: Good, Bad, or Indifferent?," in *The Holy Spirit in the Fathers of the Church*, ed. D. Vincent Twomey, SVD, and Janet E. Rutherford (Dublin: Four Courts, 2010), 164–84, at 171.

Father. Likewise, the fact that Scripture repeatedly connects the Spirit with gift, love, and communion is a strong indication of the Spirit's distinctive trinitarian properties. When we learn that "God's love [or the love of God] has been poured into our hearts through the Holy Spirit who has been given to us" (Rom. 5:5), we encounter and experience the Spirit as Love and Gift in his work of uniting us to Christ and one another in the body of Christ. There is no reason to suppose that this way of encountering and experiencing the Spirit tells us nothing about who the Spirit eternally is in relation to the Father and Son. The names "Love" and "Gift" are apt for differentiating the Spirit's procession from the Father from that of the Word, in a manner that fully manifests the Spirit's intimacy with the Son. The Holy Spirit is "Love proceeding" as the inexhaustible communion of the Father and Son, and as the one who (never without the Son) engenders charitable communion in history, preeminently in the eschatological community's participatory offering of the holy Eucharist, head and members. The Spirit proceeds immediately from the Father and mediately from the Son, even though the Father and Son are not differentiated from each other by this spiration.

Although the names Love and Gift can seem dull to those who have become accustomed to them, in fact they offer a precious and dramatic glimpse into the mystery of the Trinity. When theologians go still further by envisioning the Spirit as a uniquely surpassing love who crowns the interaction of the Father and Son, or by adding to the Spirit active causal roles in the order of origin, they have not understood the specific boldness and limitations of the analogy and of the biblical testimony that grounds it. Ironically, though such theologians are seeking to be bolder in their trinitarian theology, their approaches lead to a trinitarian theology that is much less bold in terms of its ability to identify distinctive personal properties of the Holy Spirit without dividing the Godhead. As Yves Congar points out, Bernard of Clairvaux's marvelous image of the Spirit as the mutual kiss of the Father and Son succeeds only insofar as it remains within "the order of images" rather than the order of analogy (as Bernard fully recognizes), since otherwise our trinitarian speech would collapse under the weight of anthropomorphism.[2] In contemporary trinitarian theology, anthropomorphism has become a serious threat, with the result that the cautious gains of earlier trinitarian theology—in terms of identifying distinctive threeness without losing transcendental oneness—are being jeopardized, often without theologians even being aware of the impact of their new formulations upon the framework that supports naming the Spirit Love and Gift.

2. Yves Congar, OP, *The Word and the Spirit*, trans. David Smith (London: Geoffrey Chapman, 1986), 108–9.

While striving to be bolder about what there is little scriptural basis to be bold about, many contemporary theologians are becoming less bold about what there is significant biblical justification to be truly bold about, namely the Spirit's work (never separated from the Son's) in making the church one and holy, as befits the church's mediation of the gospel. The economic power of the Spirit as personal Love and Gift is being shortchanged.

For example, in their recent textbook *The Holy Spirit*, LeRon Shults and Andrea Hollingsworth identify three areas in which, they predict, Christian pneumatology will develop in the coming decades. The first has to do with the relationship of matter and spirit. Specifically, since the Holy Spirit creates matter and is graciously present to (and in) matter, the Holy Spirit will be increasingly linked with ecology and with bodily as well as spiritual liberation. The second has to do with relational personhood or the fact that persons are never mere autonomous individuals. Personhood is constituted through communal relationships. The Holy Spirit establishes communities in which we are liberated for love. The third has to do with new concepts of "force" or "power" that focus on free causation of unpredictable future events. The Holy Spirit comes into the world to accomplish a liberative and eschatological work for the world.

It will be evident that what is largely missing from this picture is the concrete unity and holiness of the universal church. Shults and Hollingsworth conclude, "The disturbing and comforting presence of the Spirit of the trinitarian God is good news indeed, for our embodied desire for an open future of peaceful communion is constituted, upheld, and fulfilled by this all-embracing advent of the infinitely life-giving eschatological force that renews all things by calling them into a transformative participation in the life of Eternity."[3] If the Spirit is so wondrously powerful and transformative, however, why is the Spirit unable today to accomplish the most significant work that the New Testament attributes to it, namely building up the church in visible unity and holiness? If the Holy Spirit cannot unite believers spiritually and institutionally across time and space, building upon the apostolic foundation established by Jesus Christ, then why should anyone take Christians at their word when they proclaim the mighty eschatological deeds that the Spirit is accomplishing?[4]

3. F. LeRon Shults and Andrea Hollingsworth, *The Holy Spirit* (Grand Rapids: Eerdmans, 2008), 95.

4. In *Who Is the Holy Spirit? A Walk with the Apostles* (Brewster, MA: Paraclete, 2011), the Pentecostal theologian Amos Yong argues that in the book of Acts we see emerging "a fully mutual (rather than hierarchical) community" (53), in which there is "no need for a priesthood (the Twelve were not of the tribe of Levi)" (83) and in which the breaking of the bread (or Eucharist) is an "open table" (183). But to make these claims already involves a portrait of Christian unity that is, at best, not embodied in an institutional form over space and time. Even if one assumes

Where, in other words, is this "open future of peaceful communion," if there is not even a publicly identifiable church that possesses unity and holiness thanks to the grace of the Holy Spirit? If Christians cannot be united in one visible community, then why should anyone imagine that the "all-embracing advent of the infinitely life-giving eschatological force" is anything but mere rhetoric pouring forth from theologians who are professionally committed to writing such stuff?[5]

Gary Badcock observes with regard to the Holy Spirit's place in Christian theology, "The plea for a revitalized theology of the Spirit who 'blows where he wills' is a recurring theme in theology. It has been prominent in theology in recent times, but the recognition that the Spirit is, on the one hand, a relatively neglected theme in Christian theology, and yet, on the other, the essential basis of Christian faith and life is much older."[6] I consider that the

---

that a fully hierarchical church emerged only in the second century, it is clear that the church that canonized Scripture and promulgated the early creeds was hierarchical. Yong praises the "Spirit who empowered Jesus and the early Christians to confront the principalities and powers of their day" and speaks of the church's "ongoing faithfulness" thanks to "the power of the Spirit" (ibid., 190), but it would seem that the embodied, institutional church of the first millennium (and the second) would in fact be testimony, on Yong's view of what Christianity entails, to the Spirit's inability to unite Christians in fidelity. There is also the question, even supposing an appeal to canonical Scripture, of how Yong knows that the Spirit-guided church was not intended to be hierarchical and how Yong knows what the Eucharist was intended to be (since his views go against the decisions of the early church). At the same time, let me stress my admiration for Yong's fundamental project, which he describes as follows: "If we can see how the Holy Spirit empowered Jesus and his followers to announce in their words and enact in their deeds the arrival of the coming kingdom of God, this might help us to discern and participate in the work of the Holy Spirit in the world today" (ibid., xii–xiii). For a succinct account of the rise of Pentecostalism out of Wesleyanism, see Brian Gaybba, *The Spirit of Love: Theology of the Holy Spirit* (London: Geoffrey Chapman, 1987), 106–10.

5. In a similar vein, Ola Tjørhom warns against presenting "a picture of the Spirit as vague and elusive, a pneumatology that resembles the spiritualities of the religious marketplace" (Tjørhom, *Visible Church—Visible Unity: Ecumenical Ecclesiology and "The Great Tradition of the Church"* [Collegeville, MN: Liturgical Press, 2004], 99). As Tjørhom says, "The work of the Holy Spirit in mediating Christ does not occur in thin air. This work is done through outward, empirically recognizable means—word and sacrament—and in a particular place, the Church" (ibid.). He adds that as "the Spirit of creation, the Holy Spirit also points toward the ultimate liberation and restoration of God's creation" (ibid.).

6. Gary D. Badcock, *Light of Truth and Fire of Love: A Theology of the Holy Spirit* (Grand Rapids: Eerdmans, 1997), 1. In 1956 George S. Hendry stated, "It has become almost a convention that those who undertake to write about the Holy Spirit should begin by deploring the neglect of this doctrine in the thought and life of the Church today" (Hendry, *The Holy Spirit in Christian Theology*, rev. ed. [Philadelphia: Westminster, 1956], 11). More strongly, Henry P. Van Dusen claims, "With a few inconsequential exceptions, there has been hardly a period in the Church's history, hardly a school of Christian theology, hardly an individual theologian who has given to the Holy Spirit the attention which its importance as an aspect of the Godhead, according to the historic creeds 'co-eternal' and 'co-equal' with the Father and the Son, merited" (Van Dusen, foreword to *The Holy Spirit and Modern Thought: An Inquiry into*

contemporary widespread sense of theological "neglect" of the Spirit—a neglect that is far more perceived than real, as becomes apparent to anyone who tries to write on the topic—may come from our shame at our own lack of holiness and our embarrassment about the church's seemingly obvious lack of unity and holiness. Paul instructs us that "the fruit of the Spirit is love, joy, peace, patience, kindness, goodness, faithfulness, gentleness, self-control" (Gal. 5:22–23), but who among us truly has all these, or has them when it matters most and is most difficult? Christians are divided against each other: Catholics cannot agree with Orthodox, and neither can agree with Reformed, and so on. Personal enmities and hardened disagreements of all kinds are found even among those who, to an outsider, would seem most likely to be in concord with one another.

Indeed, the church is and has always been obscured by the sins of its members. Does this refute the gospel story of (in David Hart's words) "a divine source of all being that is also infinite self-outpouring love, of a physical universe restored and glorified in an eternal Kingdom of love and knowledge, and of a God who dwells among us so that we might dwell in him"?[7] Certainly, in this life it remains all too easy to grieve the Spirit, all too easy to place ourselves among "those who live according to the flesh" and "set their minds on the things of the flesh" (Rom. 8:5), and who are thereby in slavery to sin and death. But the Spirit constantly comes to us as Gift and Love, revitalizing anew

---

the Historical, Theological, and Psychological Aspects of the Christian Doctrine of the Holy Spirit, by Lindsay Dewar [New York: Harper, 1960], vii–xi, at viii). See also G. J. Sirks, "The Cinderella of Theology: The Doctrine of the Holy Spirit," Harvard Theological Review 50 (1957): 77–89; Robert W. Jenson, "You Wonder Where the Spirit Went," Pro Ecclesia 2 (1993): 296–303; Eugene F. Rogers Jr., After the Spirit: A Constructive Pneumatology from Resources outside the Modern West (Grand Rapids: Eerdmans, 2005). By contrast, even while raising various pneumatological concerns (particularly with regard to ecclesiology), Yves Congar points out, "The Holy Spirit has been very much alive in Catholicism since the Counter-Reformation and the restoration after the French revolution" (Congar, I Believe in the Holy Spirit, trans. David Smith [New York: Crossroad, 1997], 1:154). Likewise, Lyle Dabney observes (in 2001) that "in the last three decades we have witnessed a dramatic increase in the number of serious works on Pneumatology. Gone are the days when Hendrikus Berkhof could begin his Warfield Lectures at Princeton in 1964 with the complaint that even in the Anglo-Saxon literature one could discover little of substance on the topic" (Dabney, "Why Should the Last Be First? The Priority of Pneumatology in Recent Theological Discussion," in Advents of the Spirit: An Introduction to the Current Study of Pneumatology, ed. Bradford E. Hinze and D. Lyle Dabney [Milwaukee: Marquette University Press, 2001], 240–61, at 240). Dabney argues, mistakenly in my view, that pneumatology must now be given a place of primacy over the theology of the other two persons. See also Bruce D. Marshall, "What Does the Spirit Have to Do?," in Reading John with St. Thomas Aquinas: Theological Exegesis and Speculative Theology, ed. Michael Dauphinais and Matthew Levering (Washington, DC: Catholic University of America Press, 2005), 65–77.

7. David Bentley Hart, Atheist Delusions: The Christian Revolution and Its Fashionable Enemies (New Haven: Yale University Press, 2009), 212.

the power of the gospel. When we respond in repentance and love by giving ourselves to others, we find ourselves "aglow with the Spirit" (Rom. 12:11), and we learn experientially that "the kingdom of God does not mean food and drink but righteousness and peace and joy in the Holy Spirit" (Rom. 14:17).

This "peace and joy" is an ecclesial reality, not merely an individual one. As John Webster observes, "The Father wills that *ex nihilo* there should come into being a creaturely counterpart to the fellowship of love which is the inner life of the Holy Trinity."[8] God the Father has accomplished this in a historical and personal way, beginning with the election and formation of his people Israel. By his sending of Israel's Messiah, the incarnate Son, and by the Son's sending of the Spirit, the visible fellowship of the church has come to be.

What can be rightly expected of this church, which *Lumen Gentium* calls "the kingdom of Christ already present in mystery" and "the seed and the beginning of that kingdom"?[9] In his encyclical *Ut Unum Sint*, Pope John Paul II states that although the church is ceaselessly "called to be renewed in the spirit of the Gospel," the church even now is filled with "the gift of holiness" and rejoices in the possession of a real "unity, which the Lord has bestowed on his Church" and that "belongs to the very essence of this community."[10] Yet John Paul II recognizes that "full and visible unity" is not yet present, and he deplores "the often grave crises which have shaken her [the church], the infidelity of some of her ministers, and the faults into which her members daily fall."[11] If "full and visible unity" is not present, however, then is unity itself truly present?

Ephraim Radner answers that unity is in a certain way present, but not holiness. The unity comes from God's decision to be one with his sinful people in the very midst of their sinfulness. Radner states that "the Church's unity is established in and because of her sins, not in themselves but as they stand in relation to God as creator and redeemer in Christ Jesus."[12] In Jesus Christ,

8. John Webster, "On Evangelical Ecclesiology," in *Confessing God: Essays in Christian Dogmatics II* (London: T&T Clark, 2005), 153–93, at 153. Webster fears, however, that "a potent doctrine of the church's relation to God as both participatory and mediatorial" will obscure "God's utter difference from creatures even in his acts towards and in them" (ibid., 163). The solution for Webster is to locate the church concretely under the cross and to emphasize the work of the Holy Spirit as pure grace, rather than as "some kind of coordination of divine and creaturely elements" (ibid., 181).

9. *Lumen Gentium* §§3 and 5, in *Vatican Council II*, vol. 1, *The Conciliar and Post Conciliar Documents*, new revised edition, ed. Austin Flannery, OP (Northport, NY: Costello, 1996), 350–426, at 351 and 353.

10. Pope John Paul II, *Ut Unum Sint*, in *The Encyclicals of John Paul II*, ed. J. Michael Miller, CSB (Huntington, IN: Our Sunday Visitor, 2001), 782–831, at §3, p. 783; §9, p. 786.

11. Ibid., §11, p. 787; and §99, p. 829.

12. Ephraim Radner, *A Brutal Unity: The Spiritual Politics of the Christian Church* (Waco: Baylor University Press, 2012), 460.

God has chosen to be one with sinful humanity, and the church's oneness is precisely the oneness of a sinful church with which God has chosen to be united as the redeemer and reconciler of sin. Radner speaks of "the giving over of and standing beside of God's self within a 'community of enemies,' such that its communal reality is established by the One whose life is love that bears the enemy himself or herself."[13]

For his part, Webster warns against an "ecclesiology that makes the work of the Church an actualization of or sharing in the divine presence and action, rather than a testimony to that presence and action."[14] From a Reformed perspective, Webster does not deny that the church should be called holy, but this holiness must be understood as utterly dependent upon God and thus as *extrinsic* to the church, rather than as something that belongs in a way to the church. He states, "The Church is holy; but it is holy, not by virtue of some ontological participation in the divine holiness, but by virtue of its calling by God, its reception of the divine benefits, and its obedience of faith."[15] The church is holy because God elects the church. The sinful church hears the call of the gospel and accepts the gospel's precepts and judgment of sin. On this view, the holiness of the church is "alien" and is made known by the church's penitence, the church's response to the fact that "the promise and command of the gospel have already broken into its life and disturbed it, shaking it to the core."[16] The church is holy insofar as it recognizes that it has nothing, including holiness, that it can call its own, and thus insofar as it begs for mercy and praises God.[17]

Webster's condemnation of ecclesiastical sinfulness corresponds all too accurately to the sinfulness that we find in the members of the church, priests and laity (including ourselves). But in my view, as I have made clear, more must be said about the ways that the Spirit as Love and Gift efficaciously enables the church to participate and mediate the sanctifying power and life-giving truth of Christ. The eschatological people upon whom the exalted Christ pours out his Spirit do more than testify in repentance and praise to the promise and command of the gospel. We see the church doing more when the council of Jerusalem states that "it has seemed good to the Holy Spirit and to us to lay upon you no greater

13. Ibid.
14. John Webster, *Holiness* (Grand Rapids: Eerdmans, 2003), 55.
15. Ibid., 57. He goes on to say that "visible holiness is *confessed* of the Church; and that confession is not a recognition of a property which the Church has *in se*, but an acknowledgement of that which it is by virtue of the sovereign work of the triune God" (ibid., 71).
16. Ibid., 73.
17. See ibid., 75. Webster is aware of the criticism that can be posed to this view of the Spirit's work; indeed, he describes this criticism nicely in surveying responses to Barth's ecclesiology. See Webster, "On Evangelical Ecclesiology," 178.

burden than these necessary things" (Acts 15:28).[18] Jesus gathered the Twelve
to be the eschatological Israel, the inaugurated kingdom that eucharistically
celebrates Jesus's pasch until he comes. This church receives "the keys of the
kingdom of heaven," and against this church "the powers of death shall not
prevail" (Matt. 16:18–19). The intimacy of the risen Jesus with his church is
profound: "I am with you always, to the close of the age" (Matt. 28:20). Possessed of all authority, Jesus sent his disciples forth to baptize all nations and
to teach "them to observe all that I have commanded you" (Matt. 28:20). The
church is able to do this faithfully because Jesus acts in and through the church
as its Head, and because the Spirit of Jesus is active in guiding the church.

Indeed, Jesus tells the disciples that "it is to your advantage that I go away,
for if I do not go away the Counselor [Paraclete] will not come to you; but if I
go, I will send him to you" (John 16:7). As Boris Bobrinskoy comments, "The
consolation of the disciples by the promise of the Comforter seals the teaching
of Jesus."[19] But Jesus's going away would hardly have been to their advantage
unless the Spirit's work, as Love and Gift, is efficacious. By the power of the
Spirit, then, the church mediates the truth and sanctification brought by Jesus
Christ, the very "peace" that Jesus alone gives: "Jesus said to them again,
'Peace be with you. As the Father has sent me, even so I send you.' And when
he had said this, he breathed on them, and said to them, 'Receive the Holy
Spirit. If you forgive the sins of any, they are forgiven; if you retain the sins of
any, they are retained'" (John 20:21–23). Jesus is "the Lord's Christ," the one
who brings about "the consolation of Israel" (Luke 2:25–26). It is no wonder
that when the Christ comes to Israel, he inaugurates the messianic kingdom
by his words and deeds, and pours out the Spirit as promised by God through
the prophets. As Peter says in his speech at Pentecost, "Being therefore exalted
at the right hand of God, and having received from the Father the promise of
the Holy Spirit, he has poured out this which you see and hear" (Acts 2:33).[20]

18. On the historicity of Acts 15, see Richard Bauckham, "James and the Jerusalem Church,"
in The Book of Acts in Its Palestinian Setting, ed. Richard Bauckham (Grand Rapids: Eerdmans, 1995), 415–80, esp. 455–56. For helpful insights into the relationship between authority,
experience, Scripture, and study in Acts 15, see John R. Levison, Inspired: The Holy Spirit and
the Mind of Faith (Grand Rapids: Eerdmans, 2013), 112–16. With charismatic (Pentecostal)
churches in view, he observes, "According to the story of the Jerusalem Council, then, the holy
spirit inspires communities by means of, rather than apart from, the rigors of the mind, the
sustained and scrupulous examination of an important issue that expresses—and determines—
the character of the church" (ibid., 115).

19. Boris Bobrinskoy, The Mystery of the Trinity: Trinitarian Experience and Vision in
the Biblical and Patristic Tradition, trans. Anthony P. Gythiel (Crestwood, NY: St. Vladimir's
Seminary Press, 1999), 83.

20. See John Breck, "'The Two Hands of God': Christ and the Spirit in Orthodox Theology,"
St. Vladimir's Theological Quarterly 40 (1996): 231–46, at 236.

When the apostolic community proclaims the gospel, then, it does so with the Holy Spirit acting in and through it. This certainly does not mean that everything that the church does is of the Holy Spirit, but it does mean that the church can rely upon the Holy Spirit's efficacious guidance in the faithful mediation of divine revelation.[21] Of course, as Guy Mansini observes, "The human mediation of the truth of Christ by erring, forgetful, and sinful men makes this mediation seem frail."[22] Nonetheless, Jesus instructs his disciples that "the gospel must first be preached to all nations. And when they bring you to trial and deliver you up, do not be anxious beforehand what you are to say; but say whatever is given you in that hour, for it is not you who speak, but the Holy Spirit" (Mark 13:10–11). By ensuring the church's faithful preaching of the gospel to all nations—and thereby guiding the development of doctrine, as Mansini emphasizes—the Holy Spirit makes the church to be "the household of God, which is the church of the living God, the pillar and bulwark of the truth" (1 Tim. 3:15).[23] Indeed, 1 Timothy 4:1–3 tells us that the Holy Spirit

21. Alasdair I. C. Heron warns that in the medieval West, the Catholic Church displaced the Holy Spirit, a disaster that was "encouraged by the imposing authority of ecclesiastical tradition, by the intensifying claims of the papacy, and above all by the enormous development of the doctrine of grace as an objective, supernatural power mediated through the sacraments. . . . Divine grace dispensed through the ministrations of the church tends now in effect to replace the Spirit, which is located and spoken of primarily in the context of the eternal Trinity" (Heron, *The Holy Spirit* [Philadelphia: Westminster, 1983], 97). This presumes that in elevating the church's role in the mediation of the grace of the Holy Spirit, we effectively denigrate the Holy Spirit. But the Holy Spirit's work is precisely to build up the church as a communion of love. One assumes that Heron is cautioning against a mentality that seeks to encounter not the Spirit, but rather solely the church—a mentality that rejoices in the church's greatness rather than in the greatness of the living God. Wherever such an attitude exists, it must be entirely rejected, but so should the notion that the Spirit and church exist in an oppositional, zero-sum relationship, as though the flourishing of the institutional church (the embodied, concrete church) were not a preeminent work of the Holy Spirit. See also the discussion of the Eucharist, the pope, and the Virgin Mary as "substitutes for the Holy Spirit" in some Catholic piety in recent centuries in Congar, *I Believe in the Holy Spirit*, 1:160–66. Rather than merely setting up oppositional frameworks, Congar affirms that to praise Mary is, when rightly understood, also to praise the Holy Spirit for his work in Mary. See also Hans Urs von Balthasar, "Mary and the Holy Spirit," in *Explorations in Theology*, vol. 5, *Man Is Created*, trans. Adrian Walker (San Francisco: Ignatius, 2014), 176–83.

22. Guy Mansini, OSB, "Ecclesial Mediation of Grace and Truth," *The Thomist* 75 (2011): 555–83, at 583.

23. For discussion of this text in light of 2 Timothy 2:19–21 and Numbers 16:5, and for emphasis that 1 Timothy 3:15 is affirming "the stability of a church that cannot be destroyed by the false teachers," see James W. Thompson, *The Church according to Paul: Rediscovering the Community Conformed to Christ* (Grand Rapids: Baker Academic, 2014), 215–20, at 217. By contrast, Luke Timothy Johnson argues that the "the pillar and bulwark of the truth" refers not to "the church of the living God" but to "how one ought to behave in the household of God" (1 Tim. 3:15); see Johnson, *The First and Second Letters to Timothy: A New Translation with Introduction and Commentary* (New York: Doubleday, 2001), 231–32. Johnson grants that

prepares the church to expect deviations from the gospel, which the Spirit will correct through the church's faithful teaching, however contentious the debates may be by which the church arrives at and sustains this teaching. We read, "Now the Spirit expressly says that in later times some will depart from the faith by giving heed to deceitful spirits and doctrines of demons, through the pretensions of liars whose consciences are seared, who forbid marriage and enjoin abstinence from foods which God created to be received with thanksgiving by those who believe and know the truth."[24]

The intensity of the Holy Spirit's ongoing outpouring in the church, for the sake of the world, is signaled also by Paul's statement to the Corinthians that "since you are eager for manifestations of the Spirit, strive to excel in building up the church" (1 Cor. 14:12). There is no doubt that the Spirit allows for dangerous and even scandalous "factions" and "divisions" in the church (1 Cor. 11:18–19). Even so, Paul envisions one visible, institutional, and Spirit-filled church with multiple offices and gifts, united by the "still more excellent way" (1 Cor. 12:31) of love. Paul portrays the variety of vocations that one finds in the one church, "Now you are the body of Christ and individually members of it. And God has appointed in the church first apostles, second prophets, third teachers, then workers of miracles, then healers, helpers, administrators, speakers in various kinds of tongues" (1 Cor. 12:27–28). This unity in diversity manifests the Spirit's activity. Paul states in the same context, "To each is given the manifestation of the Spirit for the common good" (1 Cor. 12:7). Our unity in the church, thanks to the Spirit, is built up in the eucharistic liturgy, which is a real communion or participation in Christ (see 1 Cor 10:16–17).[25]

Luke Timothy Johnson remarks, therefore, that the earliest Christians "considered themselves caught up by, defined by, a power not in their control but rather controlling them, a power that derived from the crucified and raised

---

his reading is uncommon, and for the standard reading he directs us to A. T. Hanson, "The Foundation of Truth: 1 Timothy 3:15," in Hanson, *Studies in the Pastoral Epistles* (London: SPCK, 1968), 5–20; and P. H. Towner, *The Goal of Our Instruction: The Structure of Theology and Ethics in the Pastoral Epistles* (Sheffield: JSOT Press, 1989), 131–35.

24. Johnson cautions, "Especially in the polemical rhetoric within first-century Judaism, the charge and countercharge of demonism was common. It is a form of rhetorical hardball that is both dangerous and distressing to contemporary tastes. It was, however, the common coinage of antiquity" (Johnson, *First and Second Letters to Timothy*, 239). For amplification of this point—although in my view with too little attention to the spiritually dangerous aspects of worshiping finite, creaturely gods—see Luke Timothy Johnson, *Among the Gentiles: Greco-Roman Religion and Christianity* (New Haven: Yale University Press, 2009), esp. 1–9.

25. See Mansini, "Ecclesial Mediation of Grace and Truth," 575–77; Pope John Paul II, *Ecclesia de eucharistia*, Vatican translation (Boston: Pauline Books and Media, 2003), chap. 2; Pope Benedict XVI, *Deus caritas est* (Vatican City: Libreria Editrice Vaticana, 2006), §§13–14.

Messiah Jesus."[26] What kind of "power" is this? In seeking to answer this question, my first chapter argued that the Holy Spirit should, on biblical grounds, be known and named as Love and Gift both in the economy of salvation and in his eternal distinctiveness within the Trinity. Augustine was our exegetical guide into these names, although the fundamental insight is already found in Hilary of Poitiers's remark that "the words, *God is Spirit* [John 4:24], do not alter the fact that the Holy Spirit has a name of his own, and that He is the Gift to us."[27] In two further chapters, Thomas Aquinas helped us to see how these names express, with proper caution as well as suitable boldness, the ineffable mystery of the Spirit's eternal procession. I then turned to the missions of the Holy Spirit, Love and Gift, to Jesus Christ and to the church. Chapter 4 took up James Dunn's emphasis that Jesus was an eschatological prophet who considered himself to be interiorly impelled by the Spirit, and in this light I argued that Aquinas's theology of the Holy Spirit's mission to Jesus provides a helpful way of describing the unique presence and plenitude of the Spirit in Jesus Christ. It is in and through the Holy Spirit that Christ is able to give himself supremely in perfect love. Chapter 5 examined the approaches of contemporary biblical scholars to Jesus's eschatological prophecies. Jesus thought that the kingdom of God was both immanent and imminent, and he could have been correct only if he did indeed pour out the eschatological Spirit upon the apostolic community. In this regard, Aquinas helps us to appreciate theologically how the Spirit touches and guides every aspect of Christian life, making the individual and communal lives of repentant believers into a sharing in Christ's Gift of Love.

Boris Bobrinskoy comments that "the Spirit, in a permanent Pentecost, ensures the presence of Christ in the Church."[28] The greatest signs of the Holy Spirit's activity, outside the life of Jesus, are therefore not charismatic activities such as speaking in tongues or even performing miracles—though the Holy Spirit does cause such good things to happen—but rather are the unity and holiness of the church as the body of Christ. Chapter 6 argued that the church of the Holy Spirit must be one, since when human beings love one another, they form visible bonds of unity. In recent literature on the Holy Spirit we often find the Holy Spirit depicted as blessing multiplicity, diversity, and pluralism. While true to an extent, this approach

26. Luke Timothy Johnson, *Religious Experience in Earliest Christianity: A Missing Dimension in New Testament Studies* (Minneapolis: Fortress, 1998), 184.

27. Hilary of Poitiers, *De Trinitate*, trans. E. W. Watson, E. N. Bennett, and S. C. Gayford, in *St. Hilary of Poitiers: Select Works*, ed. W. Sanday, *Nicene and Post-Nicene Fathers*, vol. 9 (Peabody, MA: Hendrickson, 1995), 40–233, at 60 (2:31).

28. Bobrinskoy, *Mystery of the Trinity*, 72.

underestimates the unity accomplished by the Gift of Love. In chapter 7, I noted that Reformed theologians rightly underscore that the church's members on earth are not fully holy, but rather are in need of repentance and sanctification. Yet, as I argued, the church is truly holy because the missions of the Son and Holy Spirit enable the church to mediate the holy teaching and sanctifying power of Christ, and thereby to show itself to be as God's true temple.

In focusing upon Love and Gift, I do not mean to deny that there are other ways of describing what the Spirit brings about in the people of God. In fact, a number of these ways are connected specifically with truth; for example, the Spirit inspires the prophets and inspires the Scriptures. The Spirit leads the community into all truth and enables us to bear witness to the truth in times of testing. Even charismatic gifts, such as speaking in tongues, ultimately have to do with the conveyance of divine truth.[29] Is it right, then, to privilege the names "Love" and "Gift" as I have done?

In John 14:15–17, in Jesus's Farewell Discourse, Jesus tells his disciples, "If you love me, you will keep my commandments. And I will pray the Father, and he will give you another Counselor, to be with you for ever, even the Spirit of truth, whom the world cannot receive, because it neither sees him nor knows him; you know him, for he dwells with you, and will be in you." The relationship between love and the "Spirit of truth" is instructive here. The "Spirit of truth" is in us when we love Jesus and obey his commandment of love. This Spirit of truth, Jesus goes on to say, will "bring to your remembrance all that I have said to you" and "will take what is mine and declare it to you" (John 14:26; 16:14). The Spirit bears witness to the Son and to the Son's mission of proclaiming and enacting the truth about God. When the Spirit is given to us, we are able to love and thereby to bear true witness to Jesus Christ.[30] In this regard, Gilles Emery comments that the Holy Spirit gifts us with knowledge of the truth, and thus enlightens us, because he "is the principle of all participation in the Son-Truth, in the order of natural knowledge and that of grace."[31] Emery explains, however, that the Holy Spirit does this by way of love. He states, "By the impulse of love that he communicates, the Holy Spirit leads us to seek the truth and adhere to it; he disposes men to receive

29. See Gaybba, *Spirit of Love*, 17–18.

30. See Francis Watson, "The Gospel of John and New Testament Theology," in *The Nature of New Testament Theology: Essays in Honour of Robert Morgan*, ed. Christopher Rowland and Christopher Tuckett (Oxford: Blackwell, 2006), 248–62.

31. Gilles Emery, OP, "Trinity and Truth: The Son as Truth and the Spirit of Truth in St. Thomas Aquinas," in *Trinity, Church, and the Human Person: Thomistic Essays*, trans. Mary Thomas Noble, OP, et al. (Naples, FL: Sapientia Press of Ave Maria University, 2007), 73–114, at 114.

the truth and inscribes it upon their hearts."[32] This way of putting it shows well the connection of personal Love (the Holy Spirit) and truth.

About the Spirit's characteristic work, the Reformed theologian T. F. Torrance emphasizes the community-building dimension, "The personalising incorporative activity of the Spirit creates, not only reciprocity between Christ and ourselves, but a community of reciprocity among ourselves, which through the Spirit is rooted in and reflects the trinitarian relations in God himself."[33] Put succinctly, in a manner that may serve as the conclusion to this book, the Spirit, who is Love and Gift, binds together the eschatological church in the self-giving love of Christ, who is Truth in person.

In his magisterial three-volume collection of studies on the Holy Spirit, *I Believe in the Holy Spirit*, Yves Congar comments with regard to Thomas Aquinas, "A whole book could be written on his pneumatology. Such a book would contain at least four chapters: (1) the great principles of the theology of faith in the Trinity; (2) the procession of the Holy Spirit *a Patre et Filio tanquam ab uno principio*; (3) the theme of the Holy Spirit as the mutual love of the Father and the Son . . . ; (4) the part played by the Holy Spirit in the life of the Christian and the Church."[34] I have sought to develop these themes, or at least to offer an introduction to them, in the present book, in gratitude to "the Spirit who moved Christ and the apostles to utter their words and who still moves the Church, the structured People of God, to keep and meditate on them."[35] But this investigation would be worth nothing if we could not also experience the Holy Spirit as Love and Gift and thereby gain a real apprehension, in Congar's words, "of what concerns Christ, of what his acts and words mean for us."[36]

Our Creator, "the LORD, who made heaven and earth" (Ps. 115:15), desires to give us this experience—the experience of gratuitous mercy, of loving and being loved, of the full freedom and joy of the gift of self, of abundant life and indeed of "a spring of water welling up to eternal life" (John 4:14). In this life, surely a valley of tears as well as an extraordinary journey of friendship and discovery, we often call out to God, asking him to have mercy upon us

32. Ibid.
33. Thomas F. Torrance, *The Trinitarian Faith: The Evangelical Theology of the Ancient Catholic Church* (Edinburgh: T&T Clark, 1988), 250.
34. Congar, *I Believe in the Holy Spirit*, 3:116.
35. Congar, *Word and the Spirit*, 29.
36. Ibid. For discussion of Aquinas on Christ and the Spirit in relation to the church, see ibid., 61–62.

and to make himself fully known to us. Can we really say that "we rejoice in our sufferings, knowing that suffering produces endurance, and endurance produces character, and character produces hope" (Rom. 5:3–4)? If we seek to rely on our own endurance and character, we will hardly "rejoice in our sufferings." But in our sufferings, when we turn (sometimes in desperation) to Christ, we find that "hope does not disappoint us, because God's love has been poured into our hearts through the Holy Spirit who has been given to us" (Rom. 5:5). "For he who sows to his own flesh will from the flesh reap corruption; but he who sows to the Spirit will from the Spirit reap eternal life" (Gal. 6:8).

BIBLIOGRAPHY

Alexakis, A. "The *Epistula ad Marinum Cypri Presbyterum* of Maximus the Confessor (*CPG* 7697.10) Revisited: A Few Remarks on Its Meaning and Its History." *Byzantinische Zeitschrift* 94 (2001): 545–54.

Allen, R. Michael. *The Christ's Faith: A Dogmatic Account*. London: T&T Clark, 2009.

———. "'From the Time He Took on the Form of a Servant': The Christ's Pilgrimage of Faith." *International Journal of Systematic Theology* 16 (2014): 4–24.

———. *Justification and the Gospel: Understanding the Contexts and Controversies*. Grand Rapids: Baker Academic, 2013.

Allen, R. Michael, and Scott R. Swain. *Reformed Catholicity: The Promise of Retrieval for Theology and Biblical Interpretation*. Grand Rapids: Baker Academic, 2015.

Allison, Dale C., Jr. *Constructing Jesus: Memory, Imagination, and History*. Grand Rapids: Baker Academic, 2010.

———. *Jesus and the Politics of Interpretation*. New York: Continuum, 2000.

———. *Jesus of Nazareth: Millenarian Prophet*. Philadelphia: Fortress, 1998.

———. *Resurrecting Jesus: The Earliest Christian Tradition and Its Interpreters*. New York: T&T Clark, 2005.

Anatolios, Khaled. "The Canonization of Scripture in the Context of Trinitarian Doctrine." In Emery and Levering, *The Oxford Handbook of the Trinity*, 15–26.

———, ed. *The Holy Trinity in the Life of the Church*. Grand Rapids: Baker Academic, 2014.

———. "Personhood, Communion, and the Trinity in Some Patristic Texts." In Anatolios, *The Holy Trinity in the Life of the Church*, 147–64.

———. *Retrieving Nicaea: The Development and Meaning of Trinitarian Doctrine*. Grand Rapids: Baker Academic, 2011.

Andreopoulos, Andreas. "The Holy Spirit in the Ecclesiology of Photios of Constantinople." In Twomey and Rutherford, *The Holy Spirit in the Fathers of the Church*, 164–84.

Anselm of Canterbury. *Monologion*. Translated by Simon Harrison. In Anselm of Canterbury, *The Major Works*, edited by Brian Davies, OP, and G. R. Evans, 3–81. Oxford: Oxford University Press, 1998.

Aragón, F. Elisondo. "Conocer por experiencia: Un studio de sus modos y valoración en la *Summa theologica* de Tomás de Aquino." *Revista Espagnola de Teologia* 52 (1992): 5–50.

Ashton, John. *The Religion of Paul the Apostle*. New Haven: Yale University Press, 2000.

———. "The Spirit and the Church." In Butterworth, *The Spirit in Action*, 11–30.

Aslan, Reza. *Zealot: The Life and Times of Jesus of Nazareth*. New York: Random House, 2013.

Assmann, Jan. *The Price of Monotheism*. Translated by Robert Savage. Stanford, CA: Stanford University Press, 2010.

Augustine. *City of God*. Translated by Henry Bettenson. New York: Penguin, 1984.

———. *Homilies on the First Epistle of John*. Translated by Boniface Ramsey. Hyde Park, NY: New City Press, 2008.

———. *On the Creed: A Sermon to the Catechumens (De Symbolo ad catechumenos)*. Translated by C. L. Cornish. In *Augustin: On the Holy Trinity, Doctrinal Treatises, Moral Treatises*, edited by Philip Schaff, 369–75. Peabody, MA: Hendrickson, 1994 (1887).

———. *The Trinity*. Translated by Edmund Hill, OP. Hyde Park, NY: New City Press, 1991.

Aune, David E. "Charismatic Exegesis in Early Judaism and Early Christianity." In *Apocalypticism, Prophecy, and Magic in Early Christianity: Collected Essays*, 280–99. Grand Rapids: Baker Academic, 2008.

Averbeck, Richard E. "Breath, Wind, Spirit and the Holy Spirit in the Old Testament." In Firth and Wegner, *Presence, Power and Promise*, 25–37.

Ayres, Lewis. *Augustine and the Trinity*. Cambridge: Cambridge University Press, 2010.

———. "Augustine on the Trinity." In Emery and Levering, *The Oxford Handbook of the Trinity*, 123–36.

———. "Innovation and *Ressourcement* in Pro-Nicene Pneumatology." *Augustinian Studies* 39 (2008): 187–206.

———. "Into the Cloud of Witnesses: Catholic Trinitarian Theology Beyond and Before Its Modern 'Revivals.'" In Maspero and Woźniak, *Rethinking Trinitarian Theology*, 4–25.

———. *Nicaea and Its Legacy: An Approach to Fourth-Century Trinitarian Theology*. Oxford: Oxford University Press, 2004.

———. "*Sempiterne Spiritus Donum*: Augustine's Pneumatology and the Metaphysics of Spirit." In Demacopoulos and Papanikolaou, *Orthodox Readings of Augustine*, 127–52.

———. "*Spiritus Amborum*: Augustine and Pro-Nicene Theology." *Augustinian Studies* 39 (2008): 207–21.

———. "'There's Fire in That Rain': On Reading the Letter and Reading Allegorically." In *Heaven on Earth? Theological Interpretation in Ecumenical Dialogue*, edited by Hans Boersma and Matthew Levering, 33–51. Oxford: Wiley-Blackwell, 2013.

Ayres, Lewis, and Michel René Barnes. "Introduction and Acknowledgments." *Augustinian Studies* 39 (2008): 165–67.

Baars, A. "The Trinity." In *The Calvin Handbook*, edited by H. J. Selderhuis, 245–57. Grand Rapids: Eerdmans, 2009.

Badcock, Gary. *Light of Truth and Fire of Love: A Theology of the Holy Spirit*. Grand Rapids: Eerdmans, 1997.

Bailleux, Émile. "L'Esprit du Père et du Fils selon saint Augustin." *Revue Thomiste* 77 (1977): 5–29.

Baker, Coleman A. *Identity, Memory, and Narrative in Early Christianity: Peter, Paul, and Recategorization in the Book of Acts*. Eugene, OR: Pickwick, 2011.

Balthasar, Hans Urs von. *The Glory of the Lord: A Theological Aesthetics*. Vol. 7, *Theology: The New Covenant*. Edited by John Riches. Translated by Brian McNeil, CRV. San Francisco: Ignatius, 1989.

———. "The Holy Spirit as Love." In *Explorations in Theology*. Vol. 3, *Creator Spirit*, translated by Brian McNeil, CRV, 117–34. San Francisco: Ignatius, 1993.

———. "Mary and the Holy Spirit." In *Explorations in Theology*. Vol. 5, *Man Is Created*, translated by Adrian Walker, 176–83. San Francisco: Ignatius, 2014.

————. *Theo-Drama: Theological Dramatic Theory*. Vol. 2, *The Dramatis Personae: Man in God*. Translated by Graham Harrison. San Francisco: Ignatius, 1990.

————. *Theo-Drama: Theological Dramatic Theory*. Vol. 3, *The Dramatis Personae: Persons in Christ*. Translated by Graham Harrison. San Francisco: Ignatius, 1992.

————. *Theo-Drama: Theological Dramatic Theory*. Vol. 4, *The Action*. Translated by Graham Harrison. San Francisco: Ignatius, 1994.

————. *Theo-Drama: Theological Dramatic Theory*. Vol. 5, *The Last Act*. Translated by Graham Harrison. San Francisco: Ignatius, 1998.

————. *Theo-Logic: Theological Logical Theory*. Vol. 2, *Truth of God*. Translated by Adrian J. Walker. San Francisco: Ignatius, 2004.

————. *Theo-Logic: Theological Logical Theory*. Vol. 3, *The Spirit of Truth*. Translated by Graham Harrison. San Francisco: Ignatius, 2005.

Balthasar, Hans Urs von, and Joseph Ratzinger. *Mary: The Church at the Source*. San Francisco: Ignatius, 2005.

Barclay, John M. G. "Grace and the Transformation of Agency in Christ." In *Redefining First-Century Jewish and Christian Identities: Essays in Honor of Ed Parish Sanders*, edited by Fabian E. Udoh et al., 372–89. Notre Dame, IN: University of Notre Dame Press, 2008.

Barnes, Michel René. "Augustine's Last Pneumatology." *Augustinian Studies* 39 (2008): 223–34.

————. "The Beginning and End of Early Christian Pneumatology." *Augustinian Studies* 39 (2008): 169–86.

————. "Divine Unity and the Divided Self: Gregory of Nyssa's Trinitarian Theology in Its Psychological Context." *Modern Theology* 18 (2002): 475–96.

————. "Irenaeus's Trinitarian Theology." *Nova et Vetera* 7 (2009): 67–106.

————. "Latin Trinitarian Theology." In Phan, *The Cambridge Companion to the Trinity*, 70–83.

Barrett, C. K. *The Holy Spirit and the Gospel Tradition*. 2nd ed. London: SPCK, 1966.

Barth, Karl. *Church Dogmatics*. Vol. I, *The Doctrine of the Word of God*, Part 1. Translated by G. W. Bromiley. Edited by G. W. Bromiley and T. F. Torrance. 2nd ed. Edinburgh: T&T Clark, 1975.

Basil the Great. *On the Holy Spirit*. Translated by Stephen Hildebrand. Yonkers, NY: St. Vladimir's Seminary Press, 2011.

Bauckham, Richard. "James and the Jerusalem Church." In *The Book of Acts in Its Palestinian Setting*, edited by Richard Bauckham, 415–80. Grand Rapids: Eerdmans, 1995.

———. *Jesus and the Eyewitnesses: The Gospels as Eyewitness Testimony.* Grand Rapids: Eerdmans, 2006.

———. *Jesus and the God of Israel:* God Crucified *and Other Studies on the New Testament's Christology of Divine Identity.* Grand Rapids: Eerdmans, 2008.

Bauer, Walter. *Orthodoxy and Heresy in Earliest Christianity.* Edited by Robert A. Kraft and Gerhard Krobel. 2nd ed. Mifflintown, PA: Sigler, 1996.

Beale, G. K. *The Temple and the Church's Mission: A Biblical Theology of the Dwelling Place of God.* Downers Grove, IL: InterVarsity, 2004.

Beeley, Christopher A. "Divine Causality and the Monarchy of God the Father in Gregory of Nazianzus." *Harvard Theological Review* 100 (2007): 199–214.

———. *Gregory of Nazianzus on the Trinity and the Knowledge of God: In Your Light We Shall See Light.* Oxford: Oxford University Press, 2008.

Beentjies, Pancratius C. "'Holy People': The Biblical Evidence." In Poorthuis and Schwartz, *A Holy People*, 3–15.

Begg, Christopher T. "The Peoples and the Worship of Yahweh in the Book of Isaiah." In *Worship and the Hebrew Bible*, edited by M. P. Graham, R. R. Marrs, and S. L. McKenzie, 35–55. Sheffield: Sheffield Academic Press, 1999.

Benedict XVI, Pope. *Deus Caritas Est.* Vatican City: Libreria Editrice Vaticana, 2006.

Benz, E. "Joachim-Studien, III. Thomas von Aquin und Joachim de Fiore. Die katholische Antwort auf die spiritualistische Kirchen- und Geschichtsanschauung." *Zeitschrift für Kirchengeschichte* 53 (1934): 52–116.

Bergen, Jeremy M. *Ecclesial Repentance: The Churches Confront Their Sinful Pasts.* London: T&T Clark, 2011.

Bergmann, Sigurd. "Invoking the Spirit amid Dangerous Environmental Change." In *God, Creation and Climate Change: Spiritual and Ethical Perspectives*, edited by Karen L. Bloomquist, 159–74. Minneapolis: Lutheran University Press, 2009.

Bernardi, Peter J., SJ. *Maurice Blondel, Social Catholicism, and Action Française: The Clash over the Church's Role in Society during the Modernist Era.* Washington, DC: Catholic University of America Press, 2008.

Biffi, Inos. *I Misteri di Cristo in Tommaso d'Aquino.* Vol. 1, *La Costruzione della Teologia.* Milan: Jaca Book, 1994.

Bilaniuk, Petro B. T. *Theology and Economy of the Holy Spirit: An Eastern Approach*. Bangalore: Dharmaram, 1980.

Billings, J. Todd. *Union with Christ: Reframing Theology and Ministry for the Church*. Grand Rapids: Baker Academic, 2011.

———. *The Word of God for the People of God: An Entryway to the Theological Interpretation of Scripture*. Grand Rapids: Eerdmans, 2010.

Blanchette, Oliva. *The Perfection of the Universe according to Aquinas: A Teleological Cosmology*. University Park: Pennsylvania State University Press, 1992.

Blankenhorn, Bernhard, OP. "The Place of Romans 6 in Aquinas's Doctrine of Sacramental Causality: A Balance of History and Metaphysics." In Hütter and Levering, *Ressourcement Thomism*, 136–49.

Blenkinsopp, Joseph. *Ezekiel*. Louisville: John Knox, 1990.

———. *A History of Prophecy in Israel: From the Settlement in the Land to the Hellenistic Period*. Philadelphia: Westminster, 1983.

———. "Second Isaiah—Prophet of Universalism." *Journal for the Study of the Old Testament* 41 (1988): 83–103.

Bobrinskoy, Boris. "The *Filioque* Yesterday and Today." In Vischer, *Spirit of God, Spirit of Christ*, 133–48.

———. *The Mystery of the Trinity: Trinitarian Experience and Vision in the Biblical and Patristic Tradition*. Translated by Anthony P. Gythiel. Crestwood, NY: St. Vladimir's Seminary Press, 1999.

Bock, Darrell L. *Acts*. Grand Rapids: Baker Academic, 2007.

Boff, Leonardo. *Trinity and Society*. Translated by Paul Burns. Maryknoll, NY: Orbis, 1988.

Bok, Nico den. *Communicating the Most High: A Systematic Study of Person and Trinity in the Theology of Richard of St. Victor († 1173)*. Paris: Brepols, 1996.

Bonner, Gerald. "St. Augustine's Doctrine of the Holy Spirit." *Sobornost* 4 (1960): 51–66.

Borgman, Erik. "The Ambivalent Role of the 'People of God' in Twentieth Century Catholic Theology: The Examples of Yves Congar and Edward Schillebeeckx." In Poorthuis and Schwartz, *A Holy People*, 263–77.

Bossuet, Jacques Benigne. *Exposition de la doctrine de l'Eglise Catholique sur les matiéres de controverse*. Paris: Guillaume Desprez, 1747.

———. *Histoire des variations des églises protestantes*. 2 vols. Paris: Sebastien Mabre-Cramoisy, 1688.

Bossy, Michael, SJ. "The Holy Spirit and the Sacraments." In Butterworth, *The Spirit in Action*, 71–78.

Boulnois, M.-O. *Le paradoxe trinitaire chez Cyrille d'Alexandrie*. Paris: Études Augustiniennes, 1994.

Bourassa, François, SJ. "'Dans la communion de l'Esprit Saint': Étude théologique," Parts I–III. *Science et Esprit* 34 (1982): 31–56, 135–49, 239–68.

———. "Le Saint-Esprit unite d'amour du Père et du Fils." *Sciences ecclésiastiques* 14 (1962): 375–416.

Bouyer, Louis. *The Eternal Son: A Theology of the Word of God and Christology*. Translated by Simone Inkel and John F. Laughlin. Huntington, IN: Our Sunday Visitor, 1978.

———. *Le Consolateur: Esprit-Saint et vie de grace*. Paris: Cerf, 1980.

Brachet, J.-Y., and Emmanuel Durand. "La réception de la 'Clarification' de 1995 sur le '*Filioque*.'" *Irénikon* 78 (2005): 47–109.

Breck, John. "'The Two Hands of God': Christ and the Spirit in Orthodox Theology." *St. Vladimir's Theological Quarterly* 40 (1996): 231–46.

Briggman, Anthony. *Irenaeus of Lyons and the Theology of the Holy Spirit*. Oxford: Oxford University Press, 2012.

Brown, Raymond E., SS. *The Gospel according to John XIII–XXI*. Garden City, NY: Doubleday, 1970.

———. "The Paraclete in the Fourth Gospel." *New Testament Studies* 13 (1966–1967): 113–32.

Brown, Stephen F. "The Theological Virtue of Faith: An Invitation to an Ecclesial Life of Truth (IIa IIae, qq. 1–16)." In *The Ethics of Aquinas*, edited by Stephen J. Pope, 221–31. Washington, DC: Georgetown University Press, 2002.

Bruaire, Claude. *L'être et l'esprit*. Paris: Presses Universitaires de France, 1983.

Brueggemann, Walter. *Isaiah 40–66*. Louisville: Westminster John Knox, 1998.

Bulgakov, Sergius. *The Bride of the Lamb*. Translated by Boris Jakim. Grand Rapids: Eerdmans, 2002.

———. *The Comforter*. Translated by Boris Jakim. Grand Rapids: Eerdmans, 2004.

Bullivant, Stephen. *The Salvation of Atheists and Catholic Dogmatic Theology*. Oxford: Oxford University Press, 2012.

Butterworth, Robert, SJ, ed. *The Spirit in Action: Papers Read at the Second Catholic Dogma Course Roehampton 1967*. Langley, UK: St. Paul Publications, 1968.

Byrne, Brendan, SJ. *Romans*. Collegeville, MN: Liturgical Press, 1996.

Calvin, John. *Institutes of the Christian Religion*. Translated by Henry Beveridge. Grand Rapids: Eerdmans, 1989.

Campi, Emidio. "Calvin's Understanding of the Church." *Reformed World* 57 (2007): 290–305.

Canlis, Julie. *Calvin's Ladder: A Spiritual Theology of Ascent and Ascension*. Grand Rapids: Eerdmans, 2010.

Cantalamessa, Raniero, OFMCap. *The Holy Spirit in the Life of Jesus: The Mystery of Christ's Baptism*. Translated by Alan Neame. Collegeville, MN: Liturgical Press, 1994.

———. *The Mystery of Pentecost*. Translated by Glen S. Davis. Collegeville, MN: Liturgical Press, 2001.

———. *Sober Intoxication of the Spirit: Filled with the Fullness of God*. Translated by Marsha Daigle-Williamson. Cincinnati: Servant, 2005.

Cardman, Francine. "The Holy Spirit and the Apostolic Faith, A Roman Catholic Response." In *Spirit of Truth: Ecumenical Perspectives on the Holy Spirit*, edited by Theodore Stylianopoulos and S. Mark Heim, 59–80. Brookline, MA: Holy Cross Orthodox Press, 1986.

Cary, Phillip. *Outward Signs: The Powerlessness of External Things in Augustine's Thought*. Oxford: Oxford University Press, 2008.

Catechism of the Catholic Church. 2nd ed. Vatican City: Libreria Editrice Vaticana, 1997.

Cattoi, Thomas. "The Relevance of Gregory of Nyssa's *Ad Ablabium* for Catholic-Orthodox Ecumenical Dialogue on the Trinity and the Church." In Anatolios, *The Holy Trinity in the Life of the Church*, 183–98.

Cavadini, John C. "The Darkest Enigma: Reconsidering the Self in Augustine's Thought." *Augustinian Studies* 38 (2007): 119–32.

Cessario, Romanus, OP. "Aquinas on Christian Salvation." In Weinandy, Keating, and Yocum, *Aquinas on Doctrine*, 117–37.

———. *Christian Faith and the Theological Life*. Washington, DC: Catholic University of America Press, 1996.

———. "Christian Satisfaction and Sacramental Reconciliation." In Levering and Dauphinais, *Rediscovering Aquinas and the Sacraments*, 65–75.

———. *Introduction to Moral Theology*. Washington, DC: Catholic University of America Press, 2001.

———. *The Moral Virtues and Theological Ethics*. Notre Dame, IN: University of Notre Dame Press, 1991.

Chaillet, Pierre, ed. *L'Église est une: Hommage à Moehler*. Paris: Bloud & Gay, 1939.

Clément, Olivier. *L'essor du christianisme oriental*. Paris: Presses Universitaires de France, 1964.

―――. *Orient-Occident: Deux passeurs, Vladimir Lossky et Paul Evdokimov*. Geneva: Labor et Fides, 1989.

Clooney, Francis X., SJ. *Comparative Theology: Deep Learning across Religious Borders*. Oxford: Wiley-Blackwell, 2010.

Coakley, Sarah. *God, Sexuality, and the Self: An Essay "On the Trinity."* Cambridge: Cambridge University Press, 2013.

―――. "'Persons' in the 'Social' Doctrine of the Trinity: A Critique of Current Analytic Discussion." In Davis, Kendall, and O'Collins, *The Trinity*, 123–44.

Coffey, David. *Deus Trinitas: The Doctrine of the Triune God*. Oxford: Oxford University Press, 1999.

―――. *"Did You Receive the Holy Spirit When You Believed?" Some Basic Questions for Pneumatology*. Milwaukee: Marquette University Press, 2005.

―――. *Grace: The Gift of the Holy Spirit*. Manly: Catholic Institute of Sydney, 1979.

―――. "A Proper Mission of the Holy Spirit." *Theological Studies* 47 (1986): 227–50.

―――. "The Roman 'Clarification' of the Doctrine of the Filioque." *International Journal of Systematic Theology* 5 (2003): 3–21.

―――. "Spirit Christology and the Trinity." In Hinze and Dabney, *Advents of the Spirit*, 315–38.

Collins, Gregory, OSB. "Three Modern 'Fathers' on the *Filioque*: Good, Bad, or Indifferent?" In Twomey and Rutherford, *The Holy Spirit in the Fathers of the Church*, 164–84.

Coloe, Mary L. *God Dwells with Us: Temple Symbolism in the Fourth Gospel*. Collegeville, MN: Liturgical Press, 2001.

Colón-Emeric, Edgardo A. *Wesley, Aquinas, and Christian Perfection: An Ecumenical Dialogue*. Waco: Baylor University Press, 2009.

Congar, Yves, OP. *Diversity and Communion*. Translated by John Bowden. Mystic, CT: Twenty-Third Publications, 1985.

―――. *I Believe in the Holy Spirit*. Translated by David Smith. 3 vols. New York: Crossroad, 1997.

―――. *L'Église Une, Sainte, Catholique et Apostolique*. Paris: Cerf, 1970.

———. "Le Saint-Esprit dans la théologie thomiste de l'agir moral," reprinted (with original pagination, 9–19) as chapter 11 of Yves Congar, OP, *Thomas d'Aquin: Sa vision de théologie et de l'Église*. London: Variorum Reprints, 1984.

———. "Le sens de l' 'économie' salutaire dans la 'théologie' de S. Thomas d'Aquin (*Somme Théologique*)." In *Festgabe Joseph Lortz*. Vol. 2, *Glaube et Geschichte*, edited by E. Iserloh and P. Mann, 73–122. Baden-Baden: Verlag Bruno Grimm, 1957.

———. *Sainte Église: Études et approches ecclésiologiques*. Paris: Cerf, 1963.

———. *Thomas d'Aquin: Sa vision de théologie et de l'Église*. London: Variorum Reprints, 1984.

———. *True and False Reform in the Church*. Translated by Paul Philibert, OP. Collegeville, MN: Liturgical Press, 2011.

———. "Vision de l'Église chez S. Thomas d'Aquin." *Revue des sciences philosophiques et théologiques* 44 (1960): 523–41.

———. *The Word and the Spirit*. Translated by David Smith. London: Geoffrey Chapman, 1986.

Congregation for the Doctrine of the Faith. *Mysterium Ecclesiae* (June 24, 1973). www.Vatican.va.

Conradie, Ernst. *The Church and Climate Change*. Pietermaritzburg: Cluster, 2008.

Cook, Stephen L. *Prophecy and Apocalypticism: The Post-Exilic Social Setting*. Minneapolis: Fortress, 1995.

Cross, Richard. "Latin Trinitarianism: Some Conceptual and Historical Considerations." In McCall and Rea, *Philosophical and Theological Essays on the Trinity*, 201–13.

———. "Medieval Trinitarianism and Modern Theology." In Maspero and Woźniak, *Rethinking Trinitarian Theology*, 26–43.

———. *The Metaphysics of the Incarnation: Thomas Aquinas to Duns Scotus*. Oxford: Oxford University Press, 2002.

Cunningham, Francis L. B., OP. *The Indwelling of the Trinity: A Historico-Doctrinal Study of the Theory of St. Thomas Aquinas*. Dubuque, IA: Priory, 1955.

Cyprian of Carthage. *Treatise I: On the Unity of the Church*. Translated by Ernest Wallis. In *Fathers of the Third Century: Hippolytus, Cyprian, Caius, Novatian, Appendix*, edited by A. Cleveland Coxe, 421–29. Peabody, MA: Hendrickson, 1994 (1886).

Dabney, D. Lyle. "*Pneumatologia Crucis*: Reclaiming *Theologia Crucis* for a Theology of the Spirit Today." *Scottish Journal of Theology* 53 (2000): 511–24.

———. "Why Should the Last Be First? The Priority of Pneumatology in Recent Theological Discussion." In Hinze and Dabney, *Advents of the Spirit*, 240–61.

Daley, Brian E., SJ. "Conclusion: A God in Whom We Live: Ministering the Trinitarian God." In Anatolios, *The Holy Trinity in the Life of the Church*, 217–31.

———. "The Fullness of the Saving God: Cyril of Alexandria on the Holy Spirit." In *The Theology of St. Cyril of Alexandria*, edited by Thomas G. Weinandy, OFMCap, and Daniel A. Keating, 113–48. London: T&T Clark, 2003.

———. "Revisiting the 'Filioque': Part One, Roots and Branches of an Old Debate." *Pro Ecclesia* 10 (2001): 31–62.

———. "Revisiting the 'Filioque': Part Two, Contemporary Catholic Approaches." *Pro Ecclesia* 10 (2001): 195–212.

Dauphinais, Michael. "Christ and the Metaphysics of Baptism in the *Summa Theologiae* and the *Commentary on John*." In Levering and Dauphinais, *Rediscovering Aquinas and the Sacraments*, 14–27.

Dauphinais, Michael, Barry David, and Matthew Levering, eds. *Aquinas the Augustinian*. Washington, DC: Catholic University of America Press, 2007.

Dauphinais, Michael, and Matthew Levering. *Holy People, Holy Land: A Theological Introduction to the Bible*. Grand Rapids: Brazos, 2005.

Davies, G. I. "The Destiny of the Nations in the Book of Isaiah." In *Le Livre d'Isaïe*, edited by J. Vermeylen, 93–120. Leuven: Leuven University Press, 1989.

Davies, W. D., and Dale C. Allison Jr. *A Critical and Exegetical Commentary on the Gospel according to Saint Matthew*. Vol. 2, *Commentary on Matthew VIII–XVIII*. London: T&T Clark, 1991.

———. *A Critical and Exegetical Commentary on the Gospel according to Saint Matthew*. Vol. 3, *Commentary on Matthew XIX–XXVIII*. London: T&T Clark, 1997.

Davis, Stephen T., Daniel Kendall, SJ, and Gerald O'Collins, SJ, eds. *The Trinity: An Interdisciplinary Symposium on the Trinity*. Oxford: Oxford University Press, 1999.

D'Costa, Gavin. "Christ, the Trinity, and Religious Plurality." In *Christian Uniqueness Reconsidered: The Myth of a Pluralistic Theology of Religions*, edited by Gavin D'Costa, 16–29. Maryknoll, NY: Orbis, 1990.

―――. *Christianity and World Religions: Disputed Questions in the Theology of Religions*. Oxford: Blackwell, 2009.

―――. *The Meeting of Religions and the Trinity*. Maryknoll, NY: Orbis, 2000.

―――. "The Trinity in Interreligious Dialogues." In Emery and Levering, *The Oxford Handbook of the Trinity*, 573–84.

―――. *Vatican II: Catholic Doctrines on Jews and Muslims*. Oxford: Oxford University Press, 2014.

Decrees of the Ecumenical Councils. Vol. 1, *Nicaea I to Lateran V*, edited by Norman P. Tanner, SJ. Washington, DC: Georgetown University Press, 1990.

Decrees of the Ecumenical Councils. Vol. 2, *Trent to Vatican II*, edited by Norman P. Tanner, SJ. Washington, DC: Georgetown University Press, 1990.

Dei Verbum. In *Decrees of the Ecumenical Councils*, vol. 2, *Trent to Vatican II*, edited by Norman P. Tanner, SJ, 971-81. Washington, DC: Georgetown University Press, 1990.

Del Colle, Ralph. *Christ and the Spirit: Spirit-Christology in Trinitarian Perspective*. Oxford: Oxford University Press, 1994.

―――. "Oneness and Trinity: A Preliminary Proposal for Dialogue with Oneness Pentecostalism." *Journal of Pentecostal Theology* 10 (1997): 85–110.

―――. "'Person' and 'Being' in John Zizioulas' Trinitarian Theology: Conversations with Thomas Torrance and Thomas Aquinas." *Scottish Journal of Theology* 54 (2001): 70–86.

―――. "Reflections on the *Filioque*." *Journal of Ecumenical Studies* 34 (1997): 202–17.

dell'Osso, Carlo. "*Filioque* in Massimo il Confessore." In *Il Filioque. A mille anni dal suo inserimento nel Credo a Roma (1014-2014)*, edited by Mauro Gagliardi, 147-64. Vatican City: Libreria Editrice Vaticana, 2015.

Demacopoulos, George, and Aristotle Papanikolaou, eds. *Orthodox Readings of Augustine*. Crestwood, NY: St. Vladimir's Seminary Press, 2008.

Destivelle, Hyacinthe, OP. *The Moscow Council (1917–1918): The Creation of the Conciliar Institutions of the Russian Orthodox Church*. Edited by Michael Plekon and Vitaly Permiakov. Translated by Jerry Ryan. Notre Dame, IN: University of Notre Dame Press, 2014.

Díaz, Miguel H. "The Life-Giving Reality of God from Black, Latin American, and US Hispanic Theological Perspectives." In Phan, *The Cambridge Companion to the Trinity*, 259–72.

Dolezal, James E. "Trinity, Simplicity and the Status of God's Personal Relations." *International Journal of Systematic Theology* 16 (2014): 79–98.

Downey, Michael. *Altogether Gift: A Trinitarian Spirituality*. Maryknoll, NY: Orbis, 2000.

Dulles, Avery, SJ. "Church." In *The Blackwell Companion to Catholicism*, edited by James J. Buckley, Frederick Christian Bauerschmidt, and Trent Pomplun, 326–39. Oxford: Blackwell, 2007.

———. "The Church according to Thomas Aquinas." In *A Church to Believe In*, 149–92. New York: Crossroad, 1982.

———. *Church and Society: The Laurence J. McGinley Lectures, 1988–2007*. New York: Fordham University Press, 2008.

———. "The Church and the Kingdom: A Study of Their Relationship in Scripture, Tradition, and Evangelization." *Letter & Spirit* 3 (2007): 23–38.

———. "Nature, Mission, and Structure of the Church." In *Vatican II: Renewal within Tradition*, edited by Matthew L. Lamb and Matthew Levering, 25–36. Oxford: Oxford University Press, 2008.

———. "The Trinity and Christian Unity." In George, *God the Holy Trinity*, 69–82.

Dunn, James D. G. *Christianity in the Making*. Vol. 1, *Jesus Remembered*. Grand Rapids: Eerdmans, 2003.

———. *Christianity in the Making*. Vol. 2, *Beginning from Jerusalem*. Grand Rapids: Eerdmans, 2009.

———. *Christology in the Making: A New Testament Inquiry into the Origins of the Doctrine of the Incarnation*. 2nd ed. London: SCM, 1989.

———. *Did the First Christians Worship Jesus? The New Testament Evidence*. Louisville: Westminster John Knox, 2010.

———. *Jesus and the Spirit: A Study of the Religious and Charismatic Experience of Jesus and the First Christians as Reflected in the New Testament*. London: SCM, 1975.

———. "Let John Be John: A Gospel for Its Time." In *The Gospel and the Gospels*, edited by Peter Stuhlmacher, 293–322. Grand Rapids: Eerdmans, 1991.

———. "The Spirit of Jesus." In *The Christ and the Spirit: Collected Essays of James D. G. Dunn*. Vol. 2, *Pneumatology*, 329–42. Grand Rapids: Eerdmans, 1998.

Durand, Emmanuel, OP. *La périchorèse des personnes divines: Immanence mutuelle, réciprocité et communion*. Paris: Cerf, 2005.

———. "Perichoresis: A Key Concept for Balancing Trinitarian Theology." In Maspero and Woźniak, *Rethinking Trinitarian Theology*, 177–92.

Durrwell, François-Xavier, CSsR. *The Holy Spirit of God: An Essay in Biblical Theology*. Translated by Benedict Davies, OSU. London: Geoffrey Chapman, 1986.

———. *Jésus, Fils de Dieu dans l'Esprit Saint*. Paris: Desclée, 1997.

Eck, Diana L. *Encountering God: A Spiritual Journey from Bozeman to Banaras*. Boston: Beacon, 2003.

Edwards, Mark. "Aquinas on Ephesians and Colossians." In Weinandy, Keating, and Yocum, *Aquinas on Scripture*, 149–65.

Elowsky, Joel C., ed. *We Believe in the Holy Spirit*. Downers Grove, IL: IVP Academic, 2009.

Emery, Gilles, OP. "The Dignity of Being a Substance: Person, Subsistence, and Nature." *Nova et Vetera* 9 (2011): 991–1001.

———. "Essentialism or Personalism in the Treatise on God in St. Thomas Aquinas?" In Emery, *Trinity in Aquinas*, 168–208.

———. "The Holy Spirit in Aquinas's Commentary on Romans." In *Reading Romans with St. Thomas Aquinas*, edited by Matthew Levering and Michael Dauphinais, 127–62. Washington, DC: Catholic University of America Press, 2012.

———. "The Immutability of the God of Love and the Problem of Language Concerning the 'Suffering of God.'" In Keating and White, *Divine Impassibility and the Mystery of Human Suffering*, 27–76.

———. *La Trinité créatrice: Trinité et Création dans les commentaires aux Sentences de Thomas d'Aquin et de ses précurseurs Albert le Grand et Bonaventure*. Paris: Vrin, 1995.

———. "Le baptême des petits enfants." *Nova et Vetera* 87 (2012): 7–23.

———. "The Personal Mode of Trinitarian Action in St. Thomas Aquinas." In Emery, *Trinity, Church, and the Human Person*, 115–53.

———. "The Procession of the Holy Spirit *a Filio* according to St. Thomas Aquinas." In Emery, *Trinity in Aquinas*, 209–69.

———. "Qu'est-ce que la 'communion trinitaire'?" *Nova et Vetera* (Swiss edition) 89 (2014): 258–83.

———. Review of *Jésus, Fils de Dieu dans l'Esprit Saint*, by François-Xavier Durrwell. *Revue Thomiste* 98 (1998): 471–73.

———. Review of *The Father's Spirit of Sonship*, by Thomas G. Weinandy. *Revue Thomiste* 96 (1996): 152–54.

———. Review of *The Theological Epistemology of Augustine's* De Trinitate, by Luigi Gioia. *Revue Thomiste* 109 (2009): 321–23.

―――. "*Theologia* and *Dispensatio*: The Centrality of the Divine Missions in St. Thomas's Trinitarian Theology." *The Thomist* 74 (2010): 515–61.

―――. "Trinitarian Theology as Spiritual Exercise in Augustine and Aquinas." In Dauphinais, David, and Levering, *Aquinas the Augustinian*, 1–40.

―――. *The Trinitarian Theology of Saint Thomas Aquinas*. Translated by Francesca Aran Murphy. Oxford: Oxford University Press, 2011.

―――. *The Trinity: An Introduction to Catholic Doctrine on the Triune God*. Translated by Matthew Levering. Washington, DC: Catholic University of America, 2011.

―――. "Trinity and Truth: The Son as Truth and the Spirit of Truth in St. Thomas Aquinas." In Emery, *Trinity, Church, and the Human Person*, 73–114.

―――. *Trinity, Church, and the Human Person: Thomistic Essays*. Translated by Mary Thomas Noble, OP, et al. Naples, FL: Sapientia Press of Ave Maria University, 2007.

―――. *Trinity in Aquinas*. Translated by Teresa Bede et al. 2nd ed. Naples, FL: Sapientia Press of Ave Maria University, 2006.

Emery, Gilles, OP, and Matthew Levering, eds. *Aristotle in Aquinas's Theology*. Oxford: Oxford University Press, 2015.

―――. *The Oxford Handbook of the Trinity*. Oxford: Oxford University Press, 2011.

Evans, Craig A. "Jesus and the Continuing Exile of Israel." In *Jesus and the Restoration of Israel: A Critical Assessment of N. T. Wright's Jesus and the Victory of God*, edited by Carey C. Newman, 77–100. Downers Grove, IL: InterVarsity, 1999.

Evdokimov, Paul. *L'Esprit-Saint dans la tradition orthodoxe*. Paris: Cerf, 1969.

Fahey, Michael, SJ. "Son and Spirit: Divergent Theologies between Constantinople and the West." In Küng and Moltmann, *Conflicts about the Holy Spirit*, 15–22.

Farrell, Joseph P. "A Theological Introduction to the Mystagogy of Saint Photios." In Saint Photios, *The Mystagogy of the Holy Spirit*, translated by Joseph P. Farrell, 17–56.

Fee, Gordon D. *God's Empowering Presence: The Holy Spirit in the Letters of Paul*. Peabody, MA: Hendrickson, 1994.

―――. "Paul and the Trinity: The Experience of Christ and the Spirit for Paul's Understanding of God." In Davis, Kendall, and O'Collins, *The Trinity*, 49–72.

Felmy, Karl Christian. "The Development of the Trinity Doctrine in Byzantium (Ninth to Fifteenth Centuries)." In Emery and Levering, *The Oxford Handbook of the Trinity*, 210–22.

Ferguson, Sinclair B. *The Holy Spirit*. Downers Grove, IL: InterVarsity, 1996.

Fiddes, Paul S. *Participating in God: A Pastoral Doctrine of the Trinity*. Louisville: Westminster John Knox, 2000.

Firth, David G., and Paul D. Wegner, eds. *Presence, Power and Promise: The Role of the Spirit of God in the Old Testament*. Downers Grove, IL: IVP Academic, 2011.

Fitzmyer, Joseph, SJ. *The Acts of the Apostles: A New Translation with Introduction and Commentary*. New York: Doubleday, 1998.

———. *Romans: A New Translation with Introduction and Commentary*. New York: Doubleday, 1993.

Flannery, Austin, OP, ed. *Vatican Council II*. Vol. 1, *The Conciliar and Post Conciliar Documents*. New rev. ed. Northport, NY: Costello Publishing Company, 1996.

Flogaus, Reinhard. "Inspiration—Exploitation—Distortion: The Use of St. Augustine in the Hesychast Controversy." In Demacopoulos and Papanikolaou, *Orthodox Readings of Augustine*, 63–80.

Ford, David F. "In the Spirit: Learning Wisdom, Giving Signs." In J. Williams, *The Holy Spirit in the World Today*, 42–63.

Fox, Patricia A. "Feminist Theologies and the Trinity." In Phan, *The Cambridge Companion to the Trinity*, 274–90.

Francis de Sales. *Treatise on the Love of God*. Translated by Henry Benedict Mackey, OSB. Rockford, IL: Tan, 1997.

Fredriksen, Paula. *Sin: The Early History of an Idea*. Princeton, NJ: Princeton University Press, 2012.

Friche, Pauline. "L'Esprit Saint comme Don: Étude dans le *De Trinitate* d'Augustin et la *Somme de théologie* de Thomas d'Aquin." Master's thesis, University of Fribourg, 2014.

Friedman, Russell L. "Medieval Trinitarian Theology from the Late Thirteenth to the Fifteenth Centuries." In Emery and Levering, *The Oxford Handbook of the Trinity*, 197–208.

———. *Medieval Trinitarian Thought from Aquinas to Ockham*. Cambridge: Cambridge University Press, 2010.

Gagliardi, Mauro. *Introduzione al Mistero Eucaristico: Dottrina, Liturgia, Devozione*. Rome: Edizioni San Clemente, 2007.

Gaine, Simon Francis, OP. *Did the Saviour See the Father? Christ, Salvation and the Vision of God*. London: Bloomsbury, 2015.

Gallagher, Clarence, SJ. "Authority and the Spirit." In Butterworth, *The Spirit in Action*, 79–91.

Gallagher, John F. *Significando Causant: A Study of Sacramental Causality*. Fribourg: Fribourg University Press, 1965.

Galot, Jean, SJ. "L'origine éternelle de l'Esprit Saint." *Gregorianum* 78 (1997): 501–22.

Garcia, Mark. *Life in Christ: Union with Christ and Twofold Grace in Calvin's Theology*. Carlisle, UK: Paternoster, 2008.

García-Alonso, Marta. "Calvin and the Ecclesiastical Power of Jurisdiction." *Reformation & Renaissance Review* 10 (2008): 137–55.

Garrigou-Lagrange, Réginald, OP. *Christian Perfection and Contemplation, according to St. Thomas Aquinas and St. John of the Cross*. Translated by Sr. M. Timothea Doyle. St. Louis: Herder, 1937.

Garrigues, Jean-Miguel. "À la suite de la clarification romaine: Le *Filioque* affranchi du 'filioquisme.'" *Irénikon* 69 (1996): 189–212.

———. "La Clarification sur la procession du Saint-Esprit." *Irénikon* 68 (1995): 501–6.

———. *Le Saint-Esprit sceau de la Trinité: Le* Filioque *et l'originalité trinitaire de l'Esprit dans sa personne et dans sa mission*. Paris: Cerf, 2011.

———. *L'Esprit qui dit 'Père!' et le problème du filioque*. Paris: Téqui, 1981.

———. "The 'Natural Grace' of Christ in St. Thomas." In *Surnaturel: A Controversy at the Heart of Twentieth-Century Thomistic Thought*, edited by Serge-Thomas Bonino, OP, translated by Robert Williams, 103–15. Ave Maria, FL: Sapientia Press of Ave Maria University, 2009.

———. "A Roman Catholic View of the Position Now Reached in the Question of the *Filioque*." In Vischer, *Spirit of God, Spirit of Christ*, 149–63.

Gathercole, Simon J. *The Pre-Existent Son: Recovering the Christologies of Matthew, Mark, and Luke*. Grand Rapids: Eerdmans, 2006.

Gavrilyuk, Paul L. *The Suffering of the Impassible God: The Dialectics of Patristic Thought*. Oxford: Oxford University Press, 2004.

Gaybba, Brian. *The Spirit of Love: Theology of the Holy Spirit*. London: Geoffrey Chapman, 1987.

George, Timothy, ed. *Evangelicals and the Nicene Faith: Reclaiming the Apostolic Witness*. Grand Rapids: Baker Academic, 2011.

————, ed. *God the Holy Trinity: Reflections on Christian Faith and Practice*. Grand Rapids: Baker Academic, 2006.

Gerber, Chad Tyler. *The Spirit of Augustine's Early Theology: Contextualizing Augustine's Pneumatology*. Burlington, VT: Ashgate, 2012.

Gerrish, B. A. *Grace and Gratitude: The Eucharistic Theology of John Calvin*. Minneapolis: Fortress, 1993.

Gioia, Luigi, OSB. *The Theological Epistemology of Augustine's* De Trinitate. Oxford: Oxford University Press, 2008.

Gondreau, Paul. "St. Thomas Aquinas, the Communication of Idioms, and the Suffering of Christ in the Garden of Gethsemane." In Keating and White, *Divine Impassibility and the Mystery of Human Suffering*, 214–45.

Goodloe, James C., IV. "The Church: One and Holy." *Theology Today* 66 (2009): 203–16.

Gorman, Michael J. *Becoming the Gospel: Paul, Participation, and Mission*. Grand Rapids: Eerdmans, 2015.

————. *Cruciformity: Paul's Narrative Spirituality of the Cross*. Grand Rapids: Eerdmans, 2001.

Grabmann, Martin. *Die Lehre des heiligen Thomas von Aquin von der Kirche als Gotteswerk*. Regensburg: G. J. Manz, 1903.

Gray, Timothy C. *The Temple in the Gospel of Mark: A Study in Its Narrative Role*. Grand Rapids: Baker Academic, 2010.

Green, Joel B. "Faithful Witness in the Diaspora: The Holy Spirit and the Exiled People of God according to 1 Peter." In Stanton, Longenecker, and Barton, *The Holy Spirit and Christian Origins*, 282–95.

Greenblatt, Stephen. *The Swerve: How the World Became Modern*. New York: W. W. Norton, 2011.

Gregory of Nazianzus. *On God and Christ: The Five Theological Orations and Two Letters to Cledonius*. Translated by Lionel Wickham. Crestwood, NY: St. Vladimir's Seminary Press, 2002.

Greshake, Gisbert. "Trinity as 'Communio.'" In Maspero and Woźniak, *Rethinking Trinitarian Theology*, 331–45.

Guggenheim, Antoine. *Jésus Christ, grand prêtre de l'ancienne et de la nouvelle alliance: Étude théologique et herméneutique du commentaire de saint Thomas d'Aquin sur l'Épître aux Hébreux*. Paris: Parole et Silence, 2004.

Gunton, Colin. "'The Spirit Moved over the Face of the Waters': The Holy Spirit and the Created Order." In *Spirit of Truth and Power: Studies in*

Christian Doctrine and Experience, edited by D. F. Wright, 56–72. Edinburgh: Rutherford House, 2007.

Guretzki, David. *Karl Barth on the Filioque*. Burlington, VT: Ashgate, 2009.

Habets, Myk. *The Anointed Son: A Trinitarian Spirit Christology*. Eugene, OR: Pickwick, 2010.

Halleux, André de. *Patrologie et oecuménisme: Recueil d'études*. Leuven: Peeters, 1990.

———. "Toward an Ecumenical Agreement on the Procession of the Holy Spirit and the Addition of the Filioque to the Creed." In Vischer, *Spirit of God, Spirit of Christ*, 69–84.

Hanson, A. T. *Studies in the Pastoral Epistles*. London: SPCK, 1968.

Harrison, Nonna Verna. "The Trinity and Feminism." In Emery and Levering, *The Oxford Handbook of the Trinity*, 519–28.

Hart, David Bentley. *Atheist Delusions: The Christian Revolution and Its Fashionable Enemies*. New Haven: Yale University Press, 2009.

———. *The Beauty of the Infinite: The Aesthetics of Christian Truth*. Grand Rapids: Eerdmans, 2003.

———. "The Destiny of Christian Metaphysics: Reflections on the *Analogia Entis*." In *The Analogy of Being: Invention of the Antichrist or the Wisdom of God?*, edited by Thomas Joseph White, OP, 395–410. Grand Rapids: Eerdmans, 2011.

———. *The Experience of God: Being, Consciousness, Bliss*. New Haven: Yale University Press, 2013.

———. "The Hidden and the Manifest: Metaphysics after Nicaea." In *Orthodox Readings of Augustine*, edited by George E. Demacopoulos and Aristotle Papanikolaou, 191–226. Crestwood, NY: St. Vladimir's Seminary Press, 2008.

———. "The Mirror of the Infinite: Gregory of Nyssa on the *Vestigia Trinitatis*." In *Rethinking Gregory of Nyssa*, edited by Sarah Coakley, 111–31. Oxford: Blackwell, 2003.

Hasker, William. *Metaphysics and the Tri-Personal God*. Oxford: Oxford University Press, 2013.

Haugh, Richard. *Photius and the Carolingians: The Trinitarian Controversy*. Belmont, MA: Nordland, 1975.

Healy, Nicholas M. *Church, World and the Christian Life: Practical-Prophetic Ecclesiology*. Cambridge: Cambridge University Press, 2000.

———. "Practices and the New Ecclesiology: Misplaced Concreteness?" *International Journal of Systematic Theology* 5 (2003): 287–308.

Hendry, George S. *The Holy Spirit in Christian Theology*. Rev. ed. Philadelphia: Westminster, 1956.

Hengel, Martin. *Acts and the History of Earliest Christianity*. Translated by John Bowden. Philadelphia: Fortress, 1979.

Heron, Alasdair I. C. *The Holy Spirit*. Philadelphia: Westminster, 1983.

Hilary of Poitiers. *De Trinitate*. Translated by E. W. Watson, E. N. Bennett, and S. C. Gayford. In *Nicene and Post-Nicene Fathers*, vol. 9, *St. Hilary of Poitiers*, edited by W. Sanday, 40–233. Peabody, MA: Hendrickson, 1995.

Hilberath, Bernd Jochen. "Identity through Self-Transcendence: The Holy Spirit and the Fellowship of Free Persons." In Hinze and Dabney, *Advents of the Spirit*, 265–94.

Hildebrand, Stephen M. *Basil of Caesarea*. Grand Rapids: Baker Academic, 2014.

———. *The Trinitarian Theology of Basil of Caesarea: A Synthesis of Greek Thought and Biblical Faith*. Washington, DC: Catholic University of America Press, 2007.

Hill, Wesley. *Paul and the Trinity: Persons, Relations, and the Pauline Letters*. Grand Rapids: Eerdmans, 2015.

Hill, William J., OP. *The Three-Personed God: The Trinity as a Mystery of Salvation*. Washington, DC: Catholic University of America Press, 1982.

Hinze, Bradford E. "Ecclesial Repentance and the Demands of Dialogue." *Theological Studies* 61 (2000): 207–38.

———. "The Holy Spirit and the Catholic Tradition: The Legacy of Johann Adam Möhler." In *The Legacy of the Tübingen School: The Relevance of Nineteenth Century Theology for the Twentieth Century*, edited by Donald J. Dietrich and Michael J. Himes, 75–94. New York: Crossroad, 1997.

———. "Releasing the Power of the Spirit in a Trinitarian Ecclesiology." In Hinze and Dabney, *Advents of the Spirit*, 347–81.

Hinze, Bradford E., and D. Lyle Dabney, eds. *Advents of the Spirit: An Introduction to the Current Study of Pneumatology*. Milwaukee: Marquette University Press, 2001.

Hochschild, Joshua M. "Proportionality and Divine Naming: Did St. Thomas Change His Mind about Analogy?" *The Thomist* 77 (2013): 531–58.

Hofer, Andrew, OP. "Dionysian Elements in Thomas Aquinas's Christology: A Case of the Authority and Ambiguity of Pseudo-Dionysius." *The Thomist* 72 (2008): 409–42.

Horn, Friedrich Wilhelm. *Das Angeld des Geistes: Studien zur paulinischen Pneumatologie*. Göttingen: Vandenhoeck & Ruprecht, 1992.

Hoskins, Paul M. *Jesus as the Fulfillment of the Temple in the Gospel of John*. Milton Keynes: Paternoster, 2006.

Hubbard, Robert L., Jr. "The Spirit and Creation." In Firth and Wegner, *Presence, Power and Promise*, 71–91.

Humphrey, Edith M. *Ecstasy and Intimacy: When the Holy Spirit Meets the Human Spirit*. Grand Rapids: Eerdmans, 2006.

Humphries, Thomas L., Jr. *Ascetic Pneumatology from John Cassian to Gregory the Great*. Oxford: Oxford University Press, 2013.

Hunt, Anne. "Trinity, Christology, and Pneumatology." In Phan, *The Cambridge Companion to the Trinity*, 365–80.

———. "The Trinity through Paschal Eyes." In Maspero and Woźniak, *Rethinking Trinitarian Theology*, 472–89.

Hur, Ju. *A Dynamic Reading of the Holy Spirit in Luke-Acts*. London: T&T Clark, 2004.

Hurtado, Larry W. *Lord Jesus Christ: Devotion to Jesus Christ in Earliest Christianity*. Grand Rapids: Eerdmans, 2003.

Hütter, Reinhard. "The Church: The Knowledge of the Triune God: Practices, Doctrine, Theology." In *Knowing the Triune God: The Work of the Spirit in the Practices of the Church*, edited by James J. Buckley and David S. Yeago, 23–47. Grand Rapids: Eerdmans, 2001.

———. *Dust Bound for Heaven: Explorations in the Theology of Thomas Aquinas*. Grand Rapids: Eerdmans, 2012.

———. *Suffering Divine Things: Theology as Church Practice*. Translated by Doug Stott. Grand Rapids: Eerdmans, 2000.

Hütter, Reinhard, and Matthew Levering, eds. *Ressourcement Thomism: Sacred Doctrine, the Sacraments, and the Moral Life*. Washington, DC: Catholic University of America Press, 2010.

Huysmans, Ruud G. W. "The Inquisition for Which the Pope Did Not Ask Forgiveness." *The Jurist* 66 (2006): 469–82.

Ide, Pascal. *Une théologie du don. Le don dans la 'Trilogie' de Hans Urs von Balthasar*. Leuven: Peeters, 2013.

International Theological Commission. "Memory and Reconciliation: The Church and Faults of the Past." *Origins* 29, no. 39 (March 16, 2000): 625–44.

Jenson, Robert W. *Systematic Theology*. Vol. 1, *The Triune God*. Oxford: Oxford University Press, 1997.

———. *The Triune Identity: God according to the Gospel*. Philadelphia: Fortress, 1982.

———. "You Wonder Where the Spirit Went." *Pro Ecclesia* 2 (1993): 296–303.

John of Avila. *The Holy Ghost*. Translated by Ena Dargan. Chicago: Scepter, 1959.

John of Damascus. *An Exact Exposition of the Orthodox Faith*. In John of Damascus, *Writings*, translated by Frederic H. Chase Jr. Washington, DC: Catholic University of America Press, 1958.

John Paul II, Pope. *Dominum et Vivificantem*. In *The Encyclicals of John Paul II*, edited by J. Michael Miller, CSB, 244–302. Huntington, IN: Our Sunday Visitor, 2001.

———. *Ecclesia de Eucharistia*. Vatican translation. Boston: Pauline Books and Media, 2003.

———. *The Purification of Memory*. www.Vatican.va.

———. *Ut Unum Sint*. In *The Encyclicals of John Paul II*, edited by J. Michael Miller, CSB, 782–831. Huntington, IN: Our Sunday Visitor, 2001.

Johnson, Elizabeth A., CSJ. *She Who Is: The Mystery of God in Feminist Theological Discourse*. New York: Crossroad, 1992.

———. *Women, Earth and Creator Spirit*. New York: Paulist Press, 1993.

Johnson, Luke Timothy. *The Acts of the Apostles*. Collegeville, MN: Liturgical Press, 1992.

———. *Among the Gentiles: Greco-Roman Religion and Christianity*. New Haven: Yale University Press, 2009.

———. *The First and Second Letters to Timothy: A New Translation with Introduction and Commentary*. New York: Doubleday, 2001.

———. *Prophetic Jesus, Prophetic Church: The Challenge of Luke-Acts to Contemporary Christians*. Grand Rapids: Eerdmans, 2011.

———. *Religious Experience in Earliest Christianity: A Missing Dimension in New Testament Studies*. Minneapolis: Fortress, 1998.

Journet, Charles. *L'Église du Verbe incarné: Essai de théologie spéculative*. 2 vols. Paris: Desclée de Brouwer, 1951.

———. *Théologie de l'Église*. Paris: Desclée de Brouwer, 1958.

Kaczor, Christopher. "Thomas Aquinas on the Development of Doctrine." *Theological Studies* 62 (2001): 283–302.

Kany, Roland. *Augustins Trinitätsdenken*. Tübingen: Mohr, 2007.

Kärkkäinen, Veli-Matti. "'How to Speak of the Spirit among the Religions': Trinitarian Prolegomena for a Pneumatological Theology of Religions." In *The Work of the Spirit: Pneumatology and Pentecostalism*, edited by Michael Welker, 47–70. Grand Rapids: Eerdmans, 2006.

—————. *Pneumatology: The Holy Spirit in Ecumenical, International, and Contextual Perspective*. Grand Rapids: Baker Academic, 2002.

—————. *Trinity and Religious Pluralism: The Doctrine of the Trinity in Christian Theology of Religions*. Burlington, VT: Ashgate, 2004.

Kasper, Walter. *The God of Jesus Christ*. Translated by Matthew J. O'Connell. New York: Crossroad, 1997.

—————. *Mercy: The Essence of the Gospel and the Key to Christian Life*. Translated by William Madges. New York: Paulist Press, 2014.

Keating, Daniel A. "Aquinas on 1 and 2 Corinthians: The Sacraments and Their Ministers." In Weinandy, Keating, and Yocum, *Aquinas on Scripture*, 127–48.

Keating, James F., and Thomas Joseph White, OP, eds. *Divine Impassibility and the Mystery of Human Suffering*. Grand Rapids: Eerdmans, 2009.

Keaty, Anthony. "The Holy Spirit Proceeding as Mutual Love: An Interpretation of Aquinas' *Summa Theologiae* I.37." *Angelicum* 77 (2000): 533–57.

Keener, Craig S. *The Spirit in the Gospels and Acts: Divine Purity and Power*. Peabody, MA: Hendrickson, 1997.

Keith, Chris, and Anthony Le Donne, eds. *Jesus, Criteria, and the Demise of Authenticity*. London: T&T Clark, 2012.

Kereszty, Roch, OCist. *Christianity among Other Religions: Apologetics in a Contemporary Context*. New York: Alba House, 2006.

—————. "'*Sacrosancta Ecclesia*': The Holy Church of Sinners." *Communio* 40 (2013): 663–79.

Kilby, Karen. "Hans Urs von Balthasar on the Trinity." In Phan, *The Cambridge Companion to the Trinity*, 208–22.

King, Martin Luther, Jr. *Where Do We Go from Here: Chaos or Community?* Boston: Beacon, 1967.

Klingenthal Memorandum. "The Filioque Clause in Ecumenical Perspective." In Vischer, *Spirit of God, Spirit of Christ*, 3–18.

Koenig, John. *The Feast of the World's Redemption: Eucharistic Origins and Christian Mission*. Harrisburg, PA: Trinity Press International, 2000.

Komonchak, Joseph A. "Preparing for the New Millennium." *Logos* 1 (1997): 34–55.

Köstenberger, Andreas J., and Michael J. Kruger. *The Heresy of Orthodoxy: How Contemporary Culture's Fascination with Diversity Has Reshaped Our Understanding of Early Christianity*. Wheaton: Crossway, 2010.

Krauthauser, Carl. "The Council of Florence Revisited: The Union Decree in Light of the Clarification." *Diakonia* 29 (1996): 95–107.

Kristeva, Julia. *Desire in Language: A Semiotic Approach to Literature and Art.* Translated by Thomas Gora. Edited by Leon S. Roudiez. New York: Columbia University Press, 1980.

Ku, John Baptist, OP. *God the Father in the Theology of St. Thomas Aquinas.* New York: Peter Lang, 2012.

Kühn, Ulrich. *Via caritatis: Theologie des Gesetzes bei Thomas von Aquinas.* Göttingen: Vandenhoeck & Ruprecht, 1965.

Küng, Hans, and Jürgen Moltmann, eds. *Conflicts about the Holy Spirit.* New York: Seabury, 1979.

Kyne, Michael, SJ. "The Holy Spirit and Prayer." In Butterworth, *The Spirit in Action,* 143–49.

Ladaria, Luis F. *La Trinità, mistero di comunione.* Translated by Marco Zapella. Milan: Paoline, 2004.

Lamb, Matthew L. *Eternity, Time, and the Life of Wisdom.* Naples, FL: Sapientia Press of Ave Maria University, 2007.

Larchet, Jean-Claude. "À propos de la récente Clarification du Conseil Pontifical pour la Promotion de l'Unité des Chrétiens." *Le Messager orthodoxe* 129 (1997): 3–58.

La Soujeole, Benoît-Dominique de, OP. "The Economy of Salvation: Entitative Sacramentality and Operative Sacramentality." *The Thomist* 75 (2011): 537–54.

———. "The Importance of the Definition of Sacraments as Signs." In Hütter and Levering, *Ressourcement Thomism,* 127–35.

———. *Introduction to the Mystery of the Church.* Translated by Michael J. Miller. Washington, DC: Catholic University of America Press, 2014.

Laszlo, Stephen. "Sin in the Holy Church of God." In *Council Speeches of Vatican I,* edited by Hans Küng, Yves Congar, and Daniel O'Hanlon. Glen Rock, NJ: Paulist Press, 1964.

La Taille, Maurice de, SJ. "Actuation créée par Acte incréé." *Recherches de science religieuse* 18 (1928): 253–68.

Le Donne, Anthony. *Historical Jesus: What Can We Know and How Can We Know It?* Grand Rapids: Eerdmans, 2011.

———. *The Historiographical Jesus: Memory, Typology, and the Son of David.* Waco: Baylor University Press, 2009.

Leo XIII, Pope. *Divinum Illud Munus.* 1897. www.Vatican.va.

Léon-Dufour, Xavier, SJ. *Sharing the Eucharistic Bread: The Witness of the New Testament*. Translated by Matthew J. O'Connell. New York: Paulist Press, 1987.

Le Pivain, Denis-Dominique, FSSP. *L'action du saint-Esprit dans le Commentaire de l'Évangile de saint Jean par saint Thomas d'Aquin*. Paris: Téqui, 2006.

Levenson, Jon D. *Resurrection and the Restoration of Israel: The Ultimate Victory of the God of Life*. New Haven: Yale University Press, 2006.

Levering, Matthew. *The Betrayal of Charity: The Sins That Sabotage Divine Love*. Waco: Baylor University Press, 2011.

———. *Christ and the Catholic Priesthood: Ecclesial Hierarchy and the Pattern of the Trinity*. Chicago: Hillenbrand, 2010.

———. "Christ, the Trinity, and Predestination: McCormack and Aquinas." In *Trinity and Election in Contemporary Theology*, edited by Michael T. Dempsey, 244–73. Grand Rapids: Eerdmans, 2011.

———. *Christ's Fulfillment of Torah and Temple: Salvation according to Thomas Aquinas*. Notre Dame, IN: University of Notre Dame Press, 2002.

———. *Engaging the Doctrine of Creation: The Wise and Good Creator and His Theophanic, Fallen, and Redeemed Creatures*. Grand Rapids: Baker Academic, forthcoming.

———. *Engaging the Doctrine of Revelation: The Mediation of the Gospel through Church and Scripture*. Grand Rapids: Baker Academic, 2014.

———. *The Feminine Genius of Catholic Theology*. London: T&T Clark, 2012.

———. "The Holy Spirit in the Trinitarian Communion: 'Love' and 'Gift'?" *International Journal of Systematic Theology* 16 (2014): 126–42.

———. *Jesus and the Demise of Death: Resurrection, the Afterlife, and the Fate of Christians*. Waco: Baylor University Press, 2012.

———. *Mary's Bodily Assumption*. Notre Dame, IN: University of Notre Dame Press, 2014.

———. *Participatory Biblical Exegesis: A Theology of Biblical Interpretation*. Notre Dame, IN: University of Notre Dame Press, 2008.

———. *Paul in the* Summa Theologiae. Washington, DC: Catholic University of America Press, 2014.

———. *Proofs of God: Classical Arguments from Tertullian to Barth*. Grand Rapids: Baker Academic, 2016.

———. "Rationalism or Revelation? St. Thomas Aquinas and the *Filioque*." In *Spirit of God: Christian Renewal in the Community of Faith*, edited by Jeffrey W. Barbeau and Beth Felker Jones, 59–73. Downers Grove, IL: IVP Academic, 2015.

————. *Sacrifice and Community: Jewish Offering and Christian Eucharist.* Oxford: Blackwell, 2005.

————. *Scripture and Metaphysics: Aquinas and the Renewal of Trinitarian Theology.* Oxford: Blackwell, 2004.

Levering, Matthew, and Michael Dauphinais, eds. *Rediscovering Aquinas and the Sacraments: Studies in Sacramental Theology.* Chicago: Hillenbrand, 2009.

Levison, John R. *Filled with the Spirit.* Grand Rapids: Eerdmans, 2009.

————. *Inspired: The Holy Spirit and the Mind of Faith.* Grand Rapids: Eerdmans, 2013.

Lienhard, Joseph T., SJ. "Augustine and the *Filioque.*" In *Tolle Lege: Essays on Augustine and on Medieval Philosophy in Honor of Roland J. Teske, SJ,* edited by Richard C. Taylor, David Twetten, and Michael Wreen, 137–54. Milwaukee: Marquette University Press, 2011.

————. "The Baptismal Command (Matthew 28:19–20) and the Doctrine of the Trinity." In Anatolios, *The Holy Trinity in the Life of the Church,* 3–14.

Lincicum, David. "Sacraments in the Pauline Epistles." In *The Oxford Handbook of Sacramental Theology,* edited by Hans Boersma and Matthew Levering, 97–108. Oxford: Oxford University Press, 2015.

Lincoln, Andrew T. *The Gospel according to Saint John.* London: Continuum, 2005.

Link, Christian. "The Unity Movement: Christian Fellowship in the Oecumene." In Vischer, Luz, and Link, *Unity of the Church in the New Testament and Today,* 163–248.

Lison, Jacques. "L'Esprit comme amour selon Grégoire Palamas: Une influence augustinienne?" *Studia Patristica* 32 (1997): 325–32.

————. *L'Esprit répandu: La pneumatologie de Grégoire Palamas.* Paris: Cerf, 1994.

Lonergan, Bernard, SJ. *Grace and Freedom.* Edited by F. E. Crowe, SJ, and R. M. Doran, SJ. Toronto: University of Toronto Press, 2000.

————. *Verbum: Word and Idea in Aquinas.* Edited by Frederick Crowe, SJ, and Robert M. Doran, SJ. Toronto: University of Toronto Press, 1997.

Long, Steven A. *Analogia Entis: On the Analogy of Being, Metaphysics, and the Act of Faith.* Notre Dame, IN: University of Notre Dame Press, 2011.

Longenecker, Bruce W. "Rome's Victory and God's Honour: The Jerusalem Temple and the Spirit of God in Lukan Theodicy." In Stanton, Longenecker, and Barton, *The Holy Spirit and Christian Origins,* 90–102.

López, Antonio. "Eternal Happening: God as an Event of Love." *Communio* 32 (2005): 214–45.

———. *Gift and the Unity of Being*. Eugene, OR: Cascade, 2014.

Lossky, Vladimir. "Les elements de 'théologie negative' dans la pensée de saint Augustin." In Congrès International Augustinien, *Augustinus Magister*, 1:575–81. Paris: Études Augustiniennes, 1954.

———. *The Mystical Theology of the Eastern Church*. Translated by the members of the Fellowship of St. Alban and St. Sergius. Crestwood, NY: St. Vladimir's Seminary Press, 1976.

———. "The Procession of the Holy Spirit in Orthodox Trinitarian Doctrine." In *In the Image and Likeness of God*, translated by Edward Every, edited by John H. Erickson and Thomas E. Bird, 71–96. Crestwood, NY: St. Vladimir's Seminary Press, 1974.

Lössl, Joseph, SJ. "Augustine in Byzantium." *Journal of Ecclesiastical History* 51 (2000): 267–95.

———. "Augustine's 'On the Trinity' in Gregory Palamas' 'One Hundred and Fifty Chapters.'" *Augustinian Studies* 30 (1999): 69–81.

Louth, Andrew. "Late Patristic Developments on the Trinity in the East." In Emery and Levering, *The Oxford Handbook of the Trinity*, 138–49.

———. "Love and the Trinity: Saint Augustine and the Greek Fathers." *Augustinian Studies* 33 (2002): 1–16.

———. "Photios as a Theologian." In *Byzantine Style, Religion, and Civilization*, edited by Elizabeth M. Jeffreys, 206–23. Cambridge: Cambridge University Press, 2006.

———. *St. John Damascene: Tradition and Originality in Byzantine Theology*. Oxford: Oxford University Press, 2002.

Loyer, Kenneth M. *God's Love through the Spirit: The Holy Spirit in Thomas Aquinas and John Wesley*. Washington, DC: Catholic University of America Press, 2014.

Lubac, Henri de, SJ. *La postérité spirituelle de Joachim de Flore*. Vol. 1, *De Joachim à Schelling*. Paris: Éditions Lethielleux, 1979.

Lull, D. J. *The Spirit in Galatia: Paul's Interpretation of Pneuma as Divine Power*. Chico, CA: Scholars Press, 1980.

Lumen Gentium. In Flannery, *Vatican Council II*. Vol. 1, *The Conciliar and Post Conciliar Documents*, 350–426.

Macaskill, Grant. *Union with Christ in the New Testament*. Oxford: Oxford University Press, 2013.

Macchia, Frank D. *Baptized in the Spirit: A Global Pentecostal Theology.* Grand Rapids: Zondervan, 2006.

————. *Justified in the Spirit: Creation, Redemption, and the Triune God.* Grand Rapids: Eerdmans, 2010.

————. "Justified in the Spirit: Implications on the Border of Theology and Science." In *The Spirit in Creation and New Creation: Science and Theology in Western and Orthodox Realms,* edited by Michael Welker, 179–91. Grand Rapids: Eerdmans, 2012.

MacDonald, Margaret Y. *Colossians and Ephesians.* Collegeville, MN: Liturgical Press, 2008.

Mahoney, John, SJ. "'The Church of the Holy Spirit' in Aquinas." *Heythrop Journal* 15 (1974): 18–36.

————. "The Holy Spirit and Married Life." In Butterworth, *The Spirit in Action,* 102–14.

Malet, André. *Personne et amour dans la théologie trinitaire de saint Thomas d'Aquin.* Paris: Vrin, 1956.

Manselli, Raoul. *La "Lectura super apocalipsim" di Pietro di Giovanni Olivi: Ricerche sull' escatologismo medioevale.* Rome: Istituto Storico Italiano per il Medioevo, 1955.

Mansini, Guy, OSB. "Aristotle and Aquinas's Theology of Charity in the *Summa Theologiae.*" In *Aristotle in Aquinas's Theology,* edited by Gilles Emery, OP and Matthew Levering, 121–38. Oxford: Oxford University Press, 2015.

————. "Balthasar and the Theodramatic Enrichment of the Trinity." *The Thomist* 64 (2000): 499–519.

————. "Ecclesial Mediation of Grace and Truth." *The Thomist* 75 (2011): 555–83.

————. "Mercy 'Twice Blest.'" In *John Paul II and St. Thomas Aquinas,* edited by Michael Dauphinais and Matthew Levering, 75–100. Naples, FL: Sapientia Press of Ave Maria University, 2006.

Margerie, Bertrand de, SJ. *La Trinité chrétienne dans l'histoire.* Paris: Beauchesne, 1975.

Marion, Jean-Luc. *Being Given: Toward a Phenomenology of Givenness.* Translated by Jeffrey L. Kosky. Stanford, CA: Stanford University Press, 2002.

————. *In Excess: Studies of Saturated Phenomena.* Translated by Robyn Horner and Vincent Berraud. New York: Fordham University Press, 2002.

Maritain, Jacques. *On the Grace and Humanity of Jesus.* Translated by Joseph W. Evans. New York: Herder and Herder, 1969.

Marmion, Columba, OSB. *Christ, the Life of the Soul.* Translated by Alan Bancroft. Bethesda, MD: Zaccheus, 2005.

Marmion, Declan, and Rik Van Nieuwenhove. *An Introduction to the Trinity.* Cambridge: Cambridge University Press, 2011.

Marrus, Michael R. "Papal Apologies of Pope John Paul II." In *The Age of Apology: Facing Up to the Past,* edited by Mark Gibney et al., 259–70. Philadelphia: University of Pennsylvania Press, 2008.

Marshall, Bruce D. "The Absolute and the Trinity." *Pro Ecclesia* 23 (2014): 147–64.

———. "Action and Person: Do Palamas and Aquinas Agree about the Spirit?" *St. Vladimir's Theological Quarterly* 39 (1995): 379–409.

———. "Aquinas the Augustinian? On the Uses of Augustine in Aquinas's Trinitarian Theology." In Dauphinais, David, and Levering, *Aquinas the Augustinian,* 41–61.

———. "The Deep Things of God: Trinitarian Pneumatology." In Emery and Levering, *The Oxford Handbook of the Trinity,* 400–412.

———. "The Defense of the *Filioque* in Classical Lutheran Theology: An Ecumenical Appreciation." *Neue Zeitschrift für systematische Theologie und Religionsphilosophie* 44 (2002): 154–73.

———. "The Dereliction of Christ and the Impassibility of God." In Keating and White, *Divine Impassibility and the Mystery of Human Suffering,* 246–98.

———. "The Divided Church and Its Theology." *Modern Theology* 16 (2000): 377–96.

———. "*Ex Occidente Lux?* Aquinas and Eastern Orthodox Theology." In *Aquinas in Dialogue: Thomas for the Twenty-First Century,* edited by Jim Fodor and Frederick Christian Bauerschmidt, 19–46. Oxford: Blackwell, 2004.

———. "The Filioque as Theology and Doctrine: In Reply to Bernd Oberdorfer." *Kerygma und Dogma* 50 (2004): 271–88.

———. "Trinity." In *The Blackwell Companion to Modern Theology,* edited by Gareth Jones, 183–203. Oxford: Blackwell, 2004.

———. "The Unity of the Triune God: Reviving an Ancient Question." *The Thomist* 74 (2010): 1–32.

———. "What Does the Spirit Have to Do?" In *Reading John with St. Thomas Aquinas: Theological Exegesis and Speculative Theology,* edited by Michael

Dauphinais and Matthew Levering, 62–77. Washington, DC: Catholic University of America Press, 2005.

Martin, James, SJ. *Between Heaven and Mirth: Why Joy, Humor, and Laughter Are at the Heart of the Spiritual Life*. New York: HarperCollins, 2011.

Martin, Ralph. *Will Many Be Saved? What Vatican II Actually Teaches and Its Implications for the New Evangelization*. Grand Rapids: Eerdmans, 2012.

Martineau, James. *The Seat of Authority in Religion*. 4th ed. London: Longmans, Green, 1898.

Maspero, Giulio, and Robert J. Woźniak, eds. *Rethinking Trinitarian Theology: Disputed Questions and Contemporary Issues in Trinitarian Theology*. London: T&T Clark, 2012.

Mateo-Seco, Lucas Francisco. "The Paternity of the Father and the Procession of the Holy Spirit: Some Historical Remarks on the Ecumenical Problem." In Maspero and Woźniak, *Rethinking Trinitarian Theology*, 69–102.

———. *Teología Trinitaria: Dios Espíritu Santo*. Madrid: Rialp, 2005.

Matera, Frank J. *II Corinthians: A Commentary*. Louisville: Westminster John Knox, 2003.

McCall, Thomas, and Michael C. Rea, eds. *Philosophical and Theological Essays on the Trinity*. Oxford: Oxford University Press, 2009.

McCormack, Bruce. "The Lord and Giver of Life: A 'Barthian' Defence of the *Filioque*." In Maspero and Woźniak, *Rethinking Trinitarian Theology*, 230–53.

———. "Processions and Missions: A Point of Convergence between Thomas Aquinas and Karl Barth." In McCormack and White, *Thomas Aquinas and Karl Barth*, 99–126.

McCormack, Bruce L., and Thomas Joseph White, OP, eds. *Thomas Aquinas and Karl Barth: An Unofficial Catholic-Protestant Dialogue*. Grand Rapids: Eerdmans, 2013.

McDonnell, Kilian, OSB. *John Calvin, the Church, and the Eucharist*. Princeton, NJ: Princeton University Press, 1967.

———. *The Other Hand of God: The Holy Spirit as the Universal Touch and Goal*. Collegeville, MN: Liturgical Press, 2003.

McDonough, Sean M. *Christ as Creator: Origins of a New Testament Doctrine*. Oxford: Oxford University Press, 2009.

McFarland, Ian A. "Spirit and Incarnation: Toward a Pneumatic Chalcedonianism." *International Journal of Systematic Theology* 16 (2014): 143–58.

McGrath, Alister. "The Doctrine of the Trinity: An Evangelical Reflection." In George, *God the Holy Trinity*, 17–35.

McGuckin, John Anthony. "The Holy Trinity as the Dynamic of the World's Salvation in the Greek Fathers." In Anatolios, *The Holy Trinity in the Life of the Church*, 65–77.

———. "The Trinity in the Greek Fathers." In Phan, *The Cambridge Companion to the Trinity*, 49–68.

McIntyre, John. *The Shape of Pneumatology: Studies in the Doctrine of the Holy Spirit*. Edinburgh: T&T Clark, 1997.

McKnight, Scot. "Covenant and Spirit: The Origins of the New Covenant Hermeneutic." In Stanton, Longenecker, and Barton, *The Holy Spirit and Christian Origins*, 41–54.

———. *Kingdom Conspiracy: Returning to the Radical Mission of the Local Church*. Grand Rapids: Brazos, 2014.

McPartlan, Paul. *The Eucharist Makes the Church: Henri de Lubac and John Zizioulas in Dialogue*. Edinburgh: T&T Clark, 1993.

Menzies, W. W., and R. P. Menzies. *Spirit and Power: Foundations of Penetcostal Experience; A Call to Evangelical Dialogue*. Grand Rapids: Zondervan, 2000.

Meruzzi, Mauro. "Lo Spirito Santo nel Vangelo di Giovanni. E alcune note sul verbo ἐκπορεύομαι in Gv 15, 26." In *Il Filioque. A mille anni dal suo inserimento nel Credo a Roma (1014–2014)*, edited by Mauro Gagliardi, 167–98. Vatican City: Libreria Editrice Vaticana, 2015.

Meyendorff, John. *Byzantine Theology: Historical Trends and Doctrinal Themes*. New York: Fordham University Press, 1974.

Meyer, Harding. *That All May Be One: Perceptions and Models of Ecumenicity*. Translated by William G. Rusch. Grand Rapids: Eerdmans, 1999.

Milbank, John. "Can a Gift Be Given? Prolegomena to a Future Trinitarian Metaphysic." *Modern Theology* 11 (1995): 119–61.

———. "The Second Difference." In *The Word Made Strange: Theology, Language, Culture*, 171–93. Oxford: Blackwell, 1997.

Min, Anselm Kyongsuk. "God as the Mystery of Sharing and Shared Love: Thomas Aquinas on the Trinity." In Phan, *The Cambridge Companion to the Trinity*, 87–106.

———. *Paths to the Triune God: An Encounter between Aquinas and Recent Theologies*. Notre Dame, IN: University of Notre Dame Press, 2005.

———. "Solidarity of Others in the Power of the Holy Spirit: Pneumatology in a Divided World." In Hinze and Dabney, *Advents of the Spirit*, 416–43.

Miner, Robert C. "Aquinas on the Sacrament of Confirmation." In Levering and Dauphinais, *Rediscovering Aquinas and the Sacraments*, 28–38.

Moberly, R. W. L. *The Bible, Theology, and Faith: A Study of Abraham and Jesus*. Cambridge: Cambridge University Press, 2000.

———. *Prophecy and Discernment*. Cambridge: Cambridge University Press, 2006.

———. "'Test the Spirits': God, Love, and Critical Discernment in 1 John 4." In Stanton, Longenecker, and Barton, *The Holy Spirit and Christian Origins*, 296–307.

Mohelník, Benedikt Tomáš, OP. *'Gratia augmenti': Contribution au débat contemporain sur la confirmation*. Fribourg: Academic Press Fribourg, 2005.

Möhler, Johann Adam. *Unity of the Church or the Principle of Catholicism: Presented in the Spirit of the Church Fathers of the First Three Centuries*. Translated by Peter C. Erb. Washington, DC: Catholic University of America Press, 1995.

Moloney, Francis J., SDB. *Belief in the Word: Reading John 1–4*. Minneapolis: Fortress, 1992.

———. *The Gospel of John*. Collegeville, MN: Liturgical Press, 1998.

Moltmann, Jürgen. "Christliche Hoffnung: Messianisch oder transzendent? Ein theologisches Gespräch mit Joachim von Fiore und Thomas von Aquin." *Münchener Theologische Zeitschrift* 33 (1982): 241–60.

———. *The Church in the Power of the Spirit: A Contribution to Messianic Ecclesiology*. Translated by Margaret Kohl. Minneapolis: Fortress, 1993.

———. *The Source of Life: The Holy Spirit and the Theology of Life*. Translated by Margaret Kohl. Minneapolis: Fortress, 1997.

———. *The Spirit of Life: A Universal Affirmation*. Translated by Margaret Kohl. Minneapolis: Fortress, 1992.

———. "Theological Proposals towards the Resolution of the *Filioque* Controversy." In Vischer, *Spirit of God, Spirit of Christ*, 164–73.

———. *The Trinity and the Kingdom*. San Francisco: Harper & Row, 1981.

Montague, George T., SM. *The Holy Spirit: Growth of a Biblical Tradition; A Commentary on the Principal Texts of the Old and New Testaments*. New York: Paulist Press, 1976.

Montcheuil, Yves de, SJ. "La liberté et la diversité dans l'Unité." In *L'Église est une: Hommage à Moehler*, edited by Pierre Chaillet, 234–54. Paris: Bloud & Gay, 1939.

Monti, James. *A Sense of the Sacred: Roman Catholic Worship in the Middle Ages*. San Francisco: Ignatius, 2012.

Moore, Erika. "Joel's Promise of the Spirit." In Firth and Wegner, *Presence, Power and Promise*, 245–56.

Morales, Rodrigo J. *The Spirit and the Restoration of Israel: New Exodus and New Creation Motifs in Galatians*. Tübingen: Mohr Siebeck, 2010.

Mosser, Carl. "Fully Social Trinitarianism." In McCall and Rea, *Philosophical and Theological Essays on the Trinity*, 131–50.

Mühlen, Heribert. *A Charismatic Theology: Initiation in the Spirit*. Translated by Edward Quinn and Thomas Linton. New York: Paulist Press, 1978.

———. *Der Heilige Geist als Person: In der Trinität, bei der Inkarnation, und im Gnadenbund: Ich—Du—Wir*. Münster: Aschendorff, 1963.

———. *Una Mystica Persona: Die Kirche als das Mysterium der heilsgeschichtlichen Identität des heiligen Geistes, eine Person in vielen Personen*. Munich: Schöningh, 1968.

Murphy, Francesca Aran. *God Is Not a Story: Realism Revisited*. Oxford: Oxford University Press, 2007.

Neusner, Jacob. *Israel's Love Affair with God: Song of Songs*. Valley Forge, PA: Trinity Press International, 1993.

Newman, John Henry. *An Essay on the Development of Christian Doctrine*. 6th ed. Notre Dame, IN: University of Notre Dame Press, 1989.

Ngien, Dennis. *Apologetic for* Filioque *in Medieval Theology*. Milton Keynes: Paternoster, 2005.

Nichols, Aidan, OP. *Discovering Aquinas: An Introduction to His Life, Work and Influence*. London: Darton, Longman & Todd, 2002.

———. *Figuring Out the Church: Her Marks, and Her Masters*. San Francisco: Ignatius, 2013.

Nicolas, Jean-Hervé, OP. *Synthèse dogmatique: De la Trinité à la Trinité*. Fribourg: Éditions universitaires, 1985.

Nielsen, Lauge O. "Trinitarian Theology from Alcuin to Anselm." In Emery and Levering, *The Oxford Handbook of the Trinity*, 155–66.

Noonan, John T., Jr. *A Church That Can and Cannot Change: The Development of Catholic Moral Teaching*. Notre Dame, IN: University of Notre Dame Press, 2005.

North American Orthodox-Catholic Theological Consultation. "The *Filioque*: A Church-Dividing Issue?" *St. Vladimir's Theological Quarterly* 48 (2004): 93–123.

Northcott, Michael S. "Holy Spirit." In *Systematic Theology and Climate Change: Ecumenical Perspectives*, edited by Michael S. Northcott and Peter M. Scott, 51–68. London: Routledge, 2014.

Oakes, Edward T., SJ. *Infinity Dwindled to Infancy: A Catholic and Evangelical Christology*. Grand Rapids: Eerdmans, 2011.

Oberdorfer, Bernd. "Brauchen wir das Filioque? Aspekte des Filioque-Problems in der heutigen Diskussion." *Kerygma und Dogma* 49 (2003): 278–92.

———. *Filioque: Geschichte und Theologie eines ökumenischen Problems*. Göttingen: Vandenhoeck & Ruprecht, 2001.

O'Collins, Gerald, SJ. *The Second Vatican Council on Other Religions*. Oxford: Oxford University Press, 2013.

O'Regan, Cyril. *The Anatomy of Misremembering: Von Balthasar's Response to Philosophical Modernity*. Vol. 1, *Hegel*. New York: Crossroad, 2014.

———. *Gnostic Apocalypse: Jacob Boehme's Haunted Narrative*. New York: State University of New York Press, 2002.

Osborne, Catherine. "The *nexus amoris* in Augustine's Trinity." *Studia Patristica* 22 (1987): 309–14.

Owen, John. *Pneumatologia, or, A discourse concerning the Holy Spirit*. London: Nathaniel Ponder, 1674.

Pacini, Andrea. "La processione dello Spirito Santo nella teologia ortodossa contemporanea: alcune prospettive." In *Il Filioque. A mille anni dal suo inserimento nel Credo a Roma (1014–2014)*, edited by Mauro Gagliardi, 287–308. Vatican City: Libreria Editrice Vaticana, 2015.

———. *Lo Spirito Santo nella Trinità. Il Filioque nella prospettiva teologica di S. Bulgakov*. Rome: Città Nuova, 2004.

Paddison, Angus. *Scripture: A Very Theological Proposal*. London: T&T Clark, 2009.

Palamas, Gregory. *Saint Gregory Palamas: The One Hundred and Fifty Chapters; A Critical Edition, Translation, and Study*, edited by Robert E. Sinkewicz. Toronto: Pontifical Institute of Medieval Studies, 1988.

Pannenberg, Wolfhart. *Systematic Theology*. Vol. 1. Translated by Geoffrey W. Bromiley. Grand Rapids: Eerdmans, 1991.

———. *Systematische Theologie*. Vol. 1. Göttingen: Vandenhoeck & Ruprecht, 1988.

Pao, David W. *Acts and the Isaianic New Exodus*. Grand Rapids: Baker Academic, 2002.

Papanikolaou, Aristotle. *Being with God: Trinity, Apophaticism, and Divine-Human Communion*. Notre Dame, IN: University of Notre Dame Press, 2006.

———. "Contemporary Orthodox Currents on the Trinity." In Emery and Levering, *The Oxford Handbook of the Trinity*, 328–37.

———. "Sophia, Apophasis, and Communion: The Trinity in Contemporary Orthodox Theology." In Phan, *The Cambridge Companion to the Trinity*, 243–57.

Pauw, Amy Plantinga. "The Holy Spirit and Scripture." In *The Lord and Giver of Life: Perspectives on Constructive Pneumatology*, edited by David H. Jensen, 25–39. Louisville: Westminster John Knox, 2008.

Pelikan, Jaroslav. *The Christian Tradition: A History of the Development of Doctrine*. 5 vols. Chicago: University of Chicago Press, 1971–1989.

———. "The Doctrine of Filioque in Thomas Aquinas and Its Patristic Antecedents: An Analysis of *Summa Theologiae*, Part I, Question 36." In *St. Thomas Aquinas (1274–1974): Commemorative Studies*, edited by Armand Maurer, CSB, 1:315–36. Toronto: Pontifical Institute of Mediaeval Studies, 1974.

Pérez, Ángel Cordovilla. "The Trinitarian Concept of Person." In Maspero and Woźniak, *Rethinking Trinitarian Theology*, 105–45.

Perrier, Emmanuel, OP. *La fécondité en Dieu*. Paris: Parole et Silence, 2009.

Perrin, Bertrand-Marie. *L'Institution des sacrements*. Paris: Parole et Silence, 2008.

Perrin, Nicholas. *Jesus the Temple*. Grand Rapids: Baker Academic, 2010.

Perrin, Norman. *Jesus and the Language of the Kingdom: Symbol and Metaphor in New Testament Interpretation*. Philadelphia: Fortress, 1976.

———. *The Kingdom of God in the Teaching of Jesus*. London: SCM, 1963.

Petavius, Dionysius, SJ. *Dogmata Theologica*. Vol. 3. Paris: Vivès, 1865.

Phan, Peter C., ed. *The Cambridge Companion to the Trinity*. Cambridge: Cambridge University Press, 2011.

Photios, Saint. *The Mystagogy of the Holy Spirit*. Translated by Joseph P. Farrell. Brookline, MA: Holy Cross Orthodox Press, 1987.

Pinckaers, Servais, OP. "Morality and the Movement of the Holy Spirit: Aquinas's Doctrine of *Instinctus*." In *The Pinckaers Reader: Renewing Thomistic Moral Theology*, edited by John Berkman and Craig Steven Titus, translated by Mary Thomas Noble, OP, et al., 385–95. Washington, DC: Catholic University of America Press, 2005.

———. *The Sources of Christian Ethics*. Translated by Mary Thomas Noble, OP. Washington, DC: Catholic University of America Press, 1995.

Pitre, Brant. *Jesus and the Last Supper*. Grand Rapids: Eerdmans, 2015.

———. *Jesus, the Tribulation, and the End of the Exile: Restoration Eschatology and the Origin of the Atonement*. Grand Rapids: Baker Academic, 2005.

Plested, Marcus. *Orthodox Readings of Aquinas*. Oxford: Oxford University Press, 2012.

Poirel, Dominique. "Scholastic Reasons, Monastic Meditations and Victorine Conciliations: The Question of the Unity and Plurality of God in the Twelfth Century." In Emery and Levering, *The Oxford Handbook of the Trinity*, 168–80.

Pontifical Council for Promoting Christian Unity. *The Greek and Latin Traditions regarding the Procession of the Holy Spirit*. http://www.ewtn.com /library/curia/pccufilq.htm.

Poorthuis, Marcel, and Joshua Schwartz, eds. *A Holy People: Jewish and Christian Perspectives on Religious Communal Identity*. Leiden: Brill, 2006.

Pope, Stephen J. "Accountablity and Sexual Abuse in the United States: Lessons for the Universal Church." *Irish Theological Quarterly* 69 (2004): 73–88.

———, ed. *Common Calling: The Laity and Governance of the Catholic Church*. Washington, DC: Georgetown University Press, 2004.

Porter, Stanley E. *The Paul of Acts: Essays in Literary Criticism, Rhetoric, and Theology*. Tübingen: Mohr-Siebeck, 1999.

Prades, Javier. *"Deus specialiter est in sanctis per gratium": El misterio de la inhabitación de la Trinidad en los escritos de santo Tomás*. Rome: Gregorian University Press, 1993.

Principe, Walter H., CSB. "Odo Rogaldus: A Precursor of St. Bonaventure on the Holy Spirit as *Effectus Formalis* in the Mutual Love of the Father and Son." *Medieval Studies* 39 (1977): 498–505.

———. "St. Bonaventure's Theology of the Holy Spirit with Reference to the Expression 'Pater et Filius diligent se Spiritu Sancto.'" In *S. Bonaventura 1274–1974*, vol. 4, *Theologica*, edited by J. G. Bougerol, 243–69. Grottaferrata, Italy: Collegio S. Bonaventura, 1974.

Pronk, Neil. "Calvin's Doctrine of the Church." In *Calvin for Today*, edited by Joel R. Beeke, 139–54. Grand Rapids: Reformation Heritage, 2009.

Prusak, Bernard P. "Theological Considerations—Hermeneutical, Ecclesiological, Eschatological regarding *Memory and Reconciliation: The Church and the Faults of the Past*." *Horizons* 32 (2005): 136–51.

Pseudo-Dionysius. *The Divine Names*. In *The Complete Works*, translated by Colm Luibheid with Paul Rorem. New York: Paulist Press, 1987.

Radner, Ephraim. "Anglicanism on Its Knees." *First Things* 243 (May 2014): 45–50.

———. *A Brutal Unity: The Spiritual Politics of the Christian Church*. Waco: Baylor University Press, 2012.

———. *The End of the Church: A Pneumatology of Christian Division in the West*. Grand Rapids: Eerdmans, 1998.

———. "The Holy Spirit and Unity: Getting Out of the Way of Christ." *International Journal of Systematic Theology* 16 (2014): 207–20.

Rahner, Karl, SJ. "The Church of Sinners." In *Theological Investigations*. Vol. 6, *Concerning Vatican Council II*, translated by K. H. Kruger and B. Kruger, 253–69. London: Darton, Longman & Todd, 1969.

———. "The Sinful Church in the Decrees of Vatican II." In *Theological Investigations*. Vol. 6, *Concerning Vatican Council II*, translated by K. H. Kruger and B. Kruger, 270–94. London: Darton, Longman & Todd, 1969.

———. "Some Implications of the Scholastic Concept of Uncreated Grace." In *God, Christ, Mary and Grace*, translated by Cornelius Ernst, OP, 319–46. Baltimore: Helicon, 1961.

———. *The Spirit in the Church*. Translated by John Griffiths et al. New York: Seabury, 1979.

Raith, Charles, II. *Aquinas and Calvin on Romans: God's Justification and Our Participation*. Oxford: Oxford University Press, 2014.

Ratzinger, Joseph. *Called to Communion: Understanding the Church Today*. Translated by Adrian Walker. San Francisco: Ignatius, 1996.

———. *Church, Ecumenism and Politics: New Essays in Ecclesiology*. Translated by Robert Nowell. New York: Crossroad, 1988.

———. "The Ecclesiology of the Constitution *Lumen Gentium*." In *Pilgrim Fellowship of Faith: The Church as Communion*, edited by Stephan Otto Horn and Vinzenz Pfnür, translated by Henry Taylor, 123–52. San Francisco: Ignatius, 2005.

———. "The Holy Spirit as Communio: Concerning the Relationship of Pneumatology and Spirituality in Augustine." Translated by Peter Casarella. *Communio* 25 (1998): 324–37.

———. *Jesus of Nazareth: From the Baptism in the Jordan to the Transfiguration*. Translated by Adrian Walker. New York: Doubleday, 2007.

Rausch, Thomas P., SJ. *Towards a Truly Catholic Church: An Ecclesiology for the Third Millennium*. Collegeville, MN: Liturgical Press, 2003.

Reeves, Michael. *Delighting in the Trinity: An Introduction to the Christian Faith*. Downers Grove, IL: IVP Academic, 2012.

Reid, Duncan. *Energies of the Spirit: Trinitarian Models in Eastern Orthodox and Western Theology*. Atlanta: Scholars Press, 1997.

Renczes, Philipp Gabriel. "The Scope of Rahner's Fundamental Axiom in the Patristic Perspective: A Dialogue of Systematic and Historical Theology." In Maspero and Woźniak, *Rethinking Trinitarian Theology*, 254–88.

Richard of St. Victor. *On the Trinity*. Translated by Christopher P. Evans. In *Trinity and Creation: A Selection of Works of Hugh, Richard and Adam of St. Victor*, edited by Boyd Taylor Coolman and Dale M. Coulter, 209–382. Hyde Park, NY: New City Press, 2011.

Rikhof, Herwi. "The Holiness of the Church." In Poorthuis and Schwartz, *A Holy People*, 321–35.

———. "Thomas on the Church: Reflections on a Sermon." In Weinandy, Keating, and Yocum, *Aquinas on Doctrine*, 199–223.

Robson, James. *Word and Spirit in Ezekiel*. London: T&T Clark, 2006.

Rogers, Eugene F., Jr. *After the Spirit: A Constructive Pneumatology from Resources outside the Modern West*. Grand Rapids: Eerdmans, 2005.

Roman Catholic/Lutheran Joint Commission. *Facing Unity: Models, Forms and Phases of Catholic-Lutheran Church Fellowship*. Geneva: Lutheran World Federation, 1985.

Rosato, Philip J. *The Spirit as Lord: The Pneumatology of Karl Barth*. Edinburgh: T&T Clark, 1981.

Rosemann, Philipp W. "*Fraterna dilectio est Deus*: Peter Lombard's Thesis on Charity as the Holy Spirit." In *Amor amicitiae: On the Love That Is Friendship: Essays in Medieval Thought and Beyond in Honor of the Rev. Professor James McEvoy*, edited by Thomas A. F. Kelly and Philipp W. Rosemann, 409–36. Leuven: Peeters, 2004.

Routledge, Robin. "The Spirit and the Future in the Old Testament: Restoration and Renewal." In Firth and Wegner, *Presence, Power and Promise*, 346–67.

Rowe, C. Kavin. *Early Narrative Christology: The Lord in the Gospel of Luke*. Berlin: de Gruyter, 2006.

———. "The Trinity in the Letters of St. Paul and Hebrews." In Emery and Levering, *The Oxford Handbook of the Trinity*, 41–53.

Rowland, Christopher. *The Open Heaven: A Study of Apocalyptic in Judaism and Early Christianity*. London: SPCK, 1982.

Rowland, Christopher, and Christopher Tuckett, eds. *The Nature of New Testament Theology: Essays in Honour of Robert Morgan*. Oxford: Blackwell, 2006

Ruddy, Christopher. "Ecclesiological Issues behind the Sexual Abuse Crisis." *Origins* 37 (July 5, 2007): 119–26.

Sabathé, Martin. *La Trinité rédemptrice dans la* Commentaire de l'Évangile de saint Jean *par Thomas d'Aquin*. Paris: Vrin, 2011.

Sabra, George. *Thomas Aquinas' Vision of the Church*. Mainz: Matthias Grünewald Verlag, 1987.

Sagovsky, Nicholas. *Ecumenism, Christian Origins and the Practice of Communion*. Cambridge: Cambridge University Press, 2000.

Sales, Francis de. *Treatise on the Love of God*. Translated by Henry Benedict Mackey, OSB. Rockford, IL: Tan Books, 1997.

Saward, John. "*L'Église a ravi son coeur*: Charles Journet and the Theologians of *Ressourcement* on the Personality of the Church." In *Ressourcement: A Movement for Renewal in Twentieth-Century Catholic Theology*, edited by Gabriel Flynn and Paul D. Murray, 125–37. Oxford: Oxford University Press, 2012.

Scheeben, Matthias Joseph. *Gesammelte Aufsätze*. Freiburg: Herder, 1967.

Scheffczyk, Leo. "Die Trinitätslehre des Thomas von Aquin im Spiegel gegenwärtiger Kritik." *Studi Tomistici* 59 (1995): 163–90.

Schindler, D. C. "Does Love Trump Reason? Toward a Non-Possessive Concept of Knowledge." In *The Catholicity of Reason*, 85–115. Grand Rapids: Eerdmans, 2013.

Schindler, David L. "The Religious Sense and American Culture." In *A Generative Thought: An Introduction to the Works of Luigi Giussani*, edited by Elisa Buzzi, 84–102. Montreal: McGill-Queen's University Press, 2003.

Schlabach, Gerald W. *For the Joy Set before Us: Augustine and Self-Denying Love*. Notre Dame, IN: University of Notre Dame Press, 2001.

Schlier, Heinrich. *Besinnung auf das Neue Testament*. 2nd ed. Freiburg: Herder, 1967.

Schmemann, Alexander. *For the Life of the World: Sacraments and Orthodoxy*. Crestwood, NY: St. Vladimir's Seminary Press, 2002.

Schmidbaur, Hans Christian. *Personarum Trinitas: Die trinitarische Gotteslehre des heiligen Thomas von Aquin*. St. Ottilien: EOS Verlag, 1995.

Schmitz, Kenneth L. *The Gift: Creation*. Milwaukee: Marquette University Press, 1982.

Schnackenburg, Rudolf. *The Church in the New Testament.* Translated by W. J. O'Hara. New York: Seabury, 1965.

———. *The Johannine Epistles: Introduction and Commentary.* Translated by Reginald and Ilse Fuller. New York: Crossroad, 1992.

Schnelle, Udo. *Das Evangelium nach Johannes.* Leipzig: Evangelische Verlagsanstalt, 1998.

Schoon, Simon. "'Holy People': Some Protestant Views." In Poorthuis and Schwartz, *A Holy People*, 279–306.

Schulz, Michael. "The Trinitarian Concept of Essence and Substance." In Maspero and Woźniak, *Rethinking Trinitarian Theology*, 146–76.

Schumacher, Michele M. *A Trinitarian Anthropology: Adrienne von Speyr and Hans Urs von Balthasar in Dialogue with Thomas Aquinas.* Washington, DC: Catholic University of America Press, 2014.

Schwartz, Daniel. *Aquinas on Friendship.* Cambridge: Cambridge University Press, 2007.

Schweitzer, Albert. *The Quest of the Historical Jesus: A Critical Study of Its Progress from Reimarus to Wrede.* Translated by W. Montgomery. Minneapolis: Fortress, 2001.

Segal, Alan F. *Paul the Convert: The Apostolate and Apostasy of Saul the Pharisee.* New Haven: Yale University Press, 1990.

Seitz, Christopher. "The Trinity in the Old Testament." In Emery and Levering, *The Oxford Handbook of the Trinity*, 28–39.

Servais, Jacques, SJ. "The Confession of the *Casta Meretrix*." *Communio* 40 (2013): 642–62.

Sesboüé, Bernard, SJ. *Saint Basile et la Trinité: Un acte théologique au IVe siècle.* Paris: Desclée, 1998.

Sheehan, Thomas. *The First Coming: How the Kingdom of God Became Christianity.* New York: Random House, 1986.

Sherwin, Michael S., OP. *By Knowledge and by Love: Charity and Knowledge in the Moral Theology of St. Thomas Aquinas.* Washington, DC: Catholic University of America Press, 2005.

Shults, F. LeRon, and Andrea Hollingsworth. *The Holy Spirit.* Grand Rapids: Eerdmans, 2008.

Siecienski, A. Edward. *The Filioque: History of a Doctrinal Controversy.* Oxford: Oxford University Press, 2010.

Silverman, Hugh J., ed. *Philosophy and Desire.* London: Routledge, 2000.

Sinkewicz, Robert E. *Saint Gregory Palamas: The One Hundred and Fifty Chapters; A Critical Edition, Translation, and Study.* Toronto: Pontifical Institute of Medieval Studies, 1988.

———. *La théologie byzantine et sa tradition.* Vol. 2. Brussels: Brepols, 2002.

Sirks, G. J. "The Cinderella of Theology: The Doctrine of the Holy Spirit." *Harvard Theological Review* 50 (1957): 77–89.

Sokolowski, Robert. "The Revelation of the Holy Trinity: A Study in Personal Pronouns." In *Christian Faith and Human Understanding: Studies on the Eucharist, Trinity, and the Human Person,* 131–48. Washington, DC: Catholic University of America Press, 2006.

Somme, Luc-Thomas, OP. *Fils adoptifs de Dieu par Jésus Christ: La filiation divine par adoption dans la théologie de saint Thomas d'Aquin.* Paris: Vrin, 1997.

———. "La rôle du Saint-Esprit dans la vie chrétienne, selon saint Thomas d'Aquin." *Sedes Sapientiae* 26 (1988): 11–29.

Soulen, R. Kendall. *The Divine Name(s) and the Holy Trinity.* Vol. 1, *Distinguishing the Voices.* Louisville: Westminster John Knox, 2011.

Stăniloae, Dumitru. *The Experience of God.* Translated and edited by Ioan Ionita and Robert Barringer. Brookline, MA: Holy Cross Orthodox Press, 1994.

———. "The Procession of the Holy Spirit from the Father and His Relation to the Son, as the Basis of Our Deification and Adoption." In Vischer, *Spirit of God, Spirit of Christ,* 174–86.

———. *Theology and the Church.* Translated by Robert Barringer. Crestwood, NY: St. Vladimir's Seminary Press, 1980.

Stanton, Graham N., Bruce W. Longenecker, and Stephen C. Barton, eds. *The Holy Spirit and Christian Origins: Essays in Honor of James D. G. Dunn.* Grand Rapids: Eerdmans, 2004.

Studebaker, Steven M. *From Pentecost to the Triune God: A Pentecostal Trinitarian Theology.* Grand Rapids: Eerdmans, 2012.

Studer, Basil, OSB. "Spiritualità Giovannea in Agostino: Osservazioni sul commento Agostiniano alla Prima Ioannis." In *Mysterium Caritatis: Studien zur Exegese und zur Trinitätslehre in der Alten Kirche,* 143–58. Roma: Pontificio Ateneo S. Anselmo, 1999.

———. "Zur Pneumatologie des Augustinus von Hippo (*De Trinitate* 15.17.27–27.50)." In *Mysterium Caritatis: Studien zur Exegese und zur Trinitätslehre in der Alten Kirche,* 311–27. Roma: Pontificio Ateneo S. Anselmo, 1999.

Stuhlmacher, Peter. "Spiritual Remembering: John 14:26." In Stanton, Longenecker, and Barton, *The Holy Spirit and Christian Origins*, 55–68.

Stylianopoulos, Theodore. "The Filioque: Dogma, Theologoumenon or Error?" In *The Good News of Christ: Essays on the Gospel, Sacraments and Spirit*, 196–232. Brookline, MA: Holy Cross Orthodox Press, 1991.

———. "The Orthodox Position." In Küng and Moltmann, *Conflicts about the Holy Spirit*, 23–30.

Sullivan, Francis, A., SJ. "Do the Sins of Its Members Affect the Holiness of the Church?" In *In God's Hands: Essays on the Church and Ecumenism in Honour of Michael A. Fahey, SJ*, edited by Jaroslav Z. Skira and Michael S. Attridge, 247–68. Leuven: Leuven University Press, 2006.

———. *Salvation outside of the Church? Tracing the History of the Catholic Response*. Eugene, OR: Wipf & Stock, 2002.

Swain, Scott R. *The God of the Gospel: Robert Jenson's Trinitarian Theology*. Downers Grove, IL: IVP Academic, 2013.

———. "The Trinity in the Reformers." In Emery and Levering, *The Oxford Handbook of the Trinity*, 227–39.

Tanner, Kathryn. *God and Creation in Christian Theology*. Oxford: Blackwell, 1988.

———. "Social Trinitarianism and Its Critics." In Maspero and Woźniak, *Rethinking Trinitarian Theology*, 368–86.

———. "The Trinity as Christian Teaching." In Emery and Levering, *The Oxford Handbook of the Trinity*, 349–57.

Tapie, Matthew A. *Aquinas on Israel and the Church: The Question of Supersessionism in the Theology of Thomas Aquinas*. Eugene, OR: Pickwick, 2014.

Tavard, George H. "A Clarification on the 'Filioque'?" *Anglican Theological Review* 83 (2001): 507–14.

Thérèse of Lisieux. *Story of a Soul: The Autobiography of St. Thérèse of Lisieux*. Translated by John Clarke, OCD. 3rd ed. Washington, DC: ICS Publications, 1996.

Thiselton, Anthony C. *The Holy Spirit—In Biblical Teaching, through the Centuries, and Today*. Grand Rapids: Eerdmans, 2013.

Thomas Aquinas. *Commentary on the First Letter of Saint Paul to the Corinthians*. Translated by Fabian Larcher. In Thomas Aquinas, *Commentary on the Letters of Saint Paul to the Corinthians*, edited by J. Mortensen and E. Alarcón. Lander, WY: Aquinas Institute for the Study of Sacred Doctrine, 2012.

————. *Commentary on the Gospel of John: Chapters 13–21*. Translated by Fabian Larcher, OP, and James A. Weisheipl, OP. Edited by Daniel Keating and Matthew Levering. Washington, DC: Catholic University of America Press, 2010.

————. *Commentary on the Gospel of St. Matthew*. Translated by Paul M. Kimball. Camillus, NY: Dolorosa, 2012.

————. *Commentary on the Letter of Saint Paul to the Ephesians*. Translated by Matthew L. Lamb. In Thomas Aquinas, *Commentary on the Letters of Saint Paul to the Galatians and Ephesians*, edited by J. Mortensen and E. Alarcón. Lander, WY: Aquinas Institute for the Study of Sacred Doctrine, 2012.

————. *Commentary on the Letter of Saint Paul to the Romans*. Translated by Fabian Larcher, OP, et al. Lander, WY: Aquinas Institute for the Study of Sacred Doctrine, 2012.

————. *Liber contra errores Graecorum*. In *Sancti Thomae de Aquino opera omnia*, vol. 40, edited by H.-F. Dondaine. Rome: Ad Sanctae Sabinae, 1969.

————. *On the Power of God [De Potentia]*. Translated by the English Dominican Fathers. Eugene, OR: Wipf & Stock, 2004.

————. *Quaestiones disputatae de Potentia Dei, q. 10, art. 1–5*. Translated by the English Dominican Fathers. Eugene, OR: Wipf & Stock, 2004.

————. "Sermon 5: Ecce Rex Tuus." In Thomas Aquinas, *The Academic Sermons*, translated by Mark-Robin Hoogland, CP, 62–78. Washington, DC: Catholic University of America Press, 2010.

————. *The Sermon-Conferences of St. Thomas Aquinas on the Apostles' Creed*. Translated and edited by Nicholas Ayo, CSC. Notre Dame, IN: University of Notre Dame Press, 1988.

————. *Summa contra gentiles*. Book 4, *Salvation*. Translated by Charles J. O'Neil. Notre Dame, IN: University of Notre Dame Press, 1975.

————. *Summa theologiae*. Translated by the Fathers of the English Dominican Province. Westminster, MD: Christian Classics, 1981.

Thompson, Alan J. *The Acts of the Risen Lord Jesus: Luke's Account of God's Unfolding Plan*. Downers Grove, IL: InterVarsity, 2011.

Thompson, James W. *The Church according to Paul: Rediscovering the Community Conformed to Christ*. Grand Rapids: Baker Academic, 2014.

Thompson, John. *The Holy Spirit in the Theology of Karl Barth*. Allison Park, PA: Pickwick, 1991.

Thompson, Marianne Meye. "The Breath of Life: John 20:22–23 Once More." In Stanton, Longenecker, and Barton, *The Holy Spirit and Christian Origins*, 69–78.

———. *The God of the Gospel of John*. Grand Rapids: Eerdmans, 2001.

Thompson, Richard P. *Keeping the Church in Its Place: The Church as Narrative Character in Acts*. New York: T&T Clark, 2006.

Thompson, Thomas R. Review of *The Father's Spirit of Sonship*, by Thomas G. Weinandy. *Calvin Theological Journal* 32 (1997): 195–200.

Tjørhom, Ola. *Visible Church—Visible Unity: Ecumenical Ecclesiology and "The Great Tradition of the Church."* Collegeville, MN: Liturgical Press, 2004.

Tomlin, Graham. *The Prodigal Spirit: The Trinity, the Church and the Future of the World*. London: Alpha International, 2011.

Torrance, Alan J. *Persons in Communion: An Essay on Trinitarian Descriptions and Human Participation*. Edinburgh: T&T Clark, 1996.

Torrance, Thomas F. *Atonement: The Person and Work of Christ*. Edited by Robert T. Walker. Downers Grove, IL: IVP Academic, 2009.

———. "Calvin's Doctrine of the Trinity." *Calvin Theological Journal* 25 (1990): 165–93.

———. *The Christian Doctrine of God: One Being Three Persons*. Edinburgh: T&T Clark, 1996.

———. *The Trinitarian Faith: The Evangelical Theology of the Ancient Catholic Church*. Edinburgh: T&T Clark, 1988.

Torre, Michael D. "St. John Damascene and St. Thomas Aquinas on the Eternal Procession of the Holy Spirit." *St. Vladimir's Theological Quarterly* 38 (1994): 303–27.

Torrell, Jean-Pierre, OP. "La grâce du Christ." In Thomas Aquinas, *Somme théologique: Le Verbe incarné*. Vol. 2, *3a, Questions 7–15*, translated by Jean-Pierre Torrell, 395–415. Paris: Cerf, 2002.

———. "La pratique pastorale d'un théologien du XIIIe siècle: Thomas d'Aquin prédicateur." In *Recherches thomasiennes: Études revues et augmentées*, 282–314. Paris: J. Vrin, 2000.

———. *Saint Thomas Aquinas*. Vol. 2, *Spiritual Master*. Translated by Robert Royal. Washington, DC: Catholic University of America Press, 2003.

———. "Saint Thomas et l'histoire: État de la question et pistes de recherches." In *Nouvelles recherches thomasiennes*, 131–75. Paris: J. Vrin, 2008.

Towner, P. H. *The Goal of Our Instruction: The Structure of Theology and Ethics in the Pastoral Epistles*. Sheffield: JSOT Press, 1989.

Tracy, David. "Trinitarian Theology and Spirituality: Retrieving William of St. Thierry for Contemporary Theology." In Maspero and Woźniak, *Rethinking Trinitarian Theology*, 387–420.

Turek, Margaret. *Towards a Theology of God the Father: Hans Urs von Balthasar's Theodramatic Approach*. New York: Peter Lang, 2001.

Turner, Denys. *Thomas Aquinas: A Portrait*. New Haven: Yale University Press, 2013.

Turner, Max. *The Holy Spirit and Spiritual Gifts: In the New Testament Church and Today*. Rev. ed. Peabody, MA: Hendrickson, 2009.

———. *Power from on High: The Spirit in Israel's Restoration and Witness in Luke-Acts*. Sheffield: Sheffield Academic Press, 1996.

———. "The Spirit and Salvation in Luke-Acts." In Stanton, Longenecker, and Barton, *The Holy Spirit and Christian Origins*, 103–16.

Twomey, D. Vincent, SVD, and Janet E. Rutherford, eds. *The Holy Spirit in the Fathers of the Church*. Dublin: Four Courts, 2010.

Tyra, Gary. *The Holy Spirit in Mission: Prophetic Speech and Action in Christian Witness*. Downers Grove, IL: IVP Academic, 2011.

Unitatis Redintegratio. In Flannery, *Vatican Council II*. Vol. 1, *The Conciliar and Post Conciliar Documents*, 452–70.

Valliere, Paul. *Modern Russian Theology: Bukharev, Soloviev, Bulgakov; Orthodox Theology in a New Key*. Grand Rapids: Eerdmans, 2000.

Van Dusen, Henry P. Foreword to *The Holy Spirit and Modern Thought: An Inquiry into the Historical, Theological, and Psychological Aspects of the Christian Doctrine of the Holy Spirit*, by Lindsay Dewar, vii–xi. New York: Harper, 1960.

Vanhoozer, Kevin J. *The Drama of Doctrine: A Canonical-Linguistic Approach to Christian Theology*. Louisville: Westminster John Knox, 2005.

Vanier, Paul. *Théologie trinitaire chez saint Thomas d'Aquin: Evolution du concept d'action notionnelle*. Paris: Vrin, 1953.

Van Nieuwenhove, Rik, and Joseph Wawrykow, eds. *The Theology of Thomas Aquinas*. Notre Dame, IN: University of Notre Dame Press, 2005.

Vauthier, E. "Le Saint-Esprit principe d'unité de l'Église d'après Saint Thomas d'Aquin: Corps mystique et inhabitation du Saint-Esprit." *Mélanges de science religieuse* 5 (1948): 175–96; 6 (1949): 57–80.

Vischer, Lukas. "Difficulties in Looking to the New Testament for Guidance." In Vischer, Luz, and Link, *Unity of the Church in the New Testament and Today*, 7–27.

————. *Pia Conspiratio: Calvin on the Unity of Christ's Church*. Geneva: John Knox International Reformed Center, 2000.

————, ed. *Spirit of God, Spirit of Christ: Ecumenical Reflections on the* Filioque *Controversy*. London: SPCK, 1981.

Vischer, Lukas, Ulrich Luz, and Christian Link. *Unity of the Church in the New Testament and Today*. Translated by James E. Crouch. Grand Rapids: Eerdmans, 2010.

Volf, Miroslav. *Free of Charge: Giving and Forgiving in a Culture Stripped of Grace*. Grand Rapids: Zondervan, 2005.

Volf, Miroslav, and Maurice Lee. "The Spirit and the Church." In Hinze and Dabney, *Advents of the Spirit*, 382–409.

Von Speyr, Adrienne. *John: Discourses of Controversy; Meditations on John 6–12*. Translated by Brian McNeil. San Francisco: Ignatius, 1993.

————. *The World of Prayer*. San Francisco: Ignatius, 1985.

Wagner, J. Ross. *Heralds of the Good News: Isaiah and Paul in Concert in the Letter to the Romans*. Leiden: Brill, 2002.

Wainwright, Elaine M. "Like a Finger Pointing to the Moon: Exploring the Trinity and/in the New Testament." In Phan, *The Cambridge Companion to the Trinity*, 33–47.

Walsh, Liam, OP. "Sacraments." In Van Nieuwenhove and Joseph Wawrykow, *The Theology of Thomas Aquinas*, 326–64.

————. *Sacraments of Initiation: A Theology of Life, Word, and Rite*. 2nd ed. Chicago: Hillenbrand, 2011.

Watson, Francis. "The Gospel of John and New Testament Theology." In Rowland and Tuckett, *The Nature of New Testament Theology*, 248–62.

Wawrykow, Joseph P. "Franciscan and Dominican Trinitarian Theology (Thirteenth Century): Bonaventure and Aquinas." In Emery and Levering, *The Oxford Handbook of the Trinity*, 182–94.

————. *God's Grace and Human Action: "Merit" in the Theology of Thomas Aquinas*. Notre Dame, IN: University of Notre Dame Press, 1995.

————. "Grace." In Van Nieuwenhove and Wawrykow, *The Theology of Thomas Aquinas*, 192–221.

Weber, Robert, et al., eds. "Preface to the First Edition (1969)." In *Biblia Sacra: Iuxta Vulgatam Versionem*, xxix–xxxiii. Stuttgart: Deutsche Bibelgesellschaft, 1994.

Webster, John. *Holiness*. Grand Rapids: Eerdmans, 2003.

————. "On Evangelical Ecclesiology." In *Confessing God: Essays in Christian Dogmatics II*, 153–93. London: T&T Clark, 2005.

Wedderburn, Alexander J. M. "Pauline Pneumatology and Pauline Theology." In Stanton, Longenecker, and Barton, *The Holy Spirit and Christian Origins*, 144–56.

Weinandy, Thomas G., OFMCap. *Does God Change? The Word's Becoming in the Incarnation*. Still River, MA: St. Bede's Publications, 1985.

————. *Does God Suffer?* Notre Dame, IN: University of Notre Dame Press, 2000.

————. *The Father's Spirit of Sonship: Reconceiving the Trinity*. Edinburgh: T&T Clark, 1995.

————. "God and Human Suffering: His Act of Creation and His Acts in History." In Keating and White, *Divine Impassibility and the Mystery of Human Suffering*, 99–116.

————. "God *IS* Man: The Marvel of the Incarnation." In Weinandy, Keating, and Yocum, *Aquinas on Doctrine*, 67–89.

————. *Jesus: Essays in Christology*. Naples, FL: Sapientia Press of Ave Maria University, 2014.

————. "Jesus's Filial Vision of the Father." In Weinandy, *Jesus*, 279–92.

————. "Thomas Joseph White's Beatific Vision of the Incarnate Son: A Response." In Weindandy, *Jesus*, 293–301.

Weinandy, Thomas G., OFMCap, Daniel A. Keating, and John P. Yocum, eds. *Aquinas on Doctrine: A Critical Introduction*. London: T&T Clark, 2004.

————, eds. *Aquinas on Scripture: An Introduction to His Biblical Commentaries*. London: T&T Clark, 2005.

Weinandy, Thomas G., OFMCap, Paul McPartlan, and Stratford Caldecott. "Clarifying the *Filioque*: The Catholic-Orthodox Dialogue." *Communio* 23 (1996): 354–73.

Weiss, Johannes. *Jesus's Proclamation of the Kingdom of God*. Edited and translated by Richard H. Hiers and D. Larrimore Holland. Philadelphia: Fortress, 1971.

Welker, Michael. *God the Spirit*. Translated by John F. Hoffmeyer. Minneapolis: Fortress, 1994.

————, ed. *The Spirit in Creation and New Creation: Science and Theology in Western and Orthodox Realms*. Grand Rapids: Eerdmans, 2012.

Wells, Jo Bailey. *God's Holy People: A Theme in Biblical Theology*. Sheffield: Sheffield Academic Press, 2000.

White, Thomas Joseph, OP. "The Crucified Lord: Thomistic Reflections on the Communication of Idioms and the Theology of the Cross." In McCormack and White, *Thomas Aquinas and Karl Barth*, 157–92.

———. "Dyotheletism and the Instrumental Human Consciousness of Jesus." *Pro Ecclesia* 17 (2008): 396–422.

———. "The Voluntary Action of the Earthly Christ and the Necessity of the Beatific Vision." *The Thomist* 69 (2005): 497–534.

Wilken, Robert Louis. "*Fides Caritate Formata*: Faith Formed by Love." *Nova et Vetera* 9 (2011): 1089–1100.

Wilkins, Jeremy. "'The Image of This Highest Love': The Trinitarian Analogy in Gregory Palamas' *Capita 150*." *St. Vladimir's Theological Quarterly* 47 (2003): 383–412.

———. "Trinitarian Missions and the Order of Grace According to Thomas Aquinas." In *Philosophy and Theology in the Long Middle Ages: A Tribute to Stephen F. Brown*, edited by Kent Emery Jr., Russell L. Friedman, and Andreas Speer, 689–708. Leiden: Brill, 2011.

Williams, A. N. *The Ground of Union: Deification in Aquinas and Palamas.* Oxford: Oxford University Press, 1999.

Williams, Jane. *The Holy Spirit in the World Today.* London: Alpha International, 2011.

Williams, Rowan. "Balthasar and the Trinity." In *The Cambridge Companion to Hans Urs von Balthasar*, edited by Edward T. Oakes, SJ, and David Moss, 37–50. Cambridge: Cambridge University Press, 2004.

———. "The Holy Spirit in the Bible." In J. Williams, *The Holy Spirit in the World Today*, 64–71.

———. "*Sapientia* and the Trinity: Reflections on the *De trinitate*." In *Collectanea Augustiniana: Mélanges T. J. Van Bavel*, edited by B. Bruning et al., 1:317–32. Leuven: Leuven University Press, 1990.

———. "The Theology of Vladimir Nikolaievich Lossky: An Exposition and Critique." PhD diss., Oxford University, 1975.

Willis, Wendell. "The Discovery of the Eschatological Kingdom: Johannes Weiss and Albert Schweitzer." In *The Kingdom of God in 20th-Century Interpretation*, edited by Wendell Willis, 1–14. Peabody, MA: Hendrickson, 1987.

Wisse, Maarten. *Trinitarian Theology beyond Participation: Augustine's* De Trinitate *and Contemporary Theology.* London: T&T Clark, 2011.

Witherington, Ben, III. *Making a Meal of It: Rethinking the Theology of the Lord's Supper.* Waco: Baylor University Press, 2007.

Witte, John, Jr. "Moderate Religious Liberty in the Theology of John Calvin." *Calvin Theological Journal* 31 (1996): 359–403.

Wood, Susan K. "The Trinity in the Liturgy, Sacraments, and Mysticism." In Phan, *The Cambridge Companion to the Trinity*, 381–96.

Wright, Christopher J. H. *The Mission of God: Unlocking the Bible's Grand Narrative*. Downers Grove, IL: InterVarsity Press, 2006.

Wright, N. T. *Jesus and the Victory of God*. Minneapolis: Fortress, 1996.

———. *The New Testament and the People of God*. Minneapolis: Fortress, 1992.

———. *Paul and the Faithfulness of God*. Minneapolis: Fortress, 2013.

———. *The Resurrection of the Son of God*. Minneapolis: Fortress, 2003.

Yeago, David S. "*Ecclesia Sancta, Ecclesia Peccatrix*: The Holiness of the Church in Martin Luther's Theology." *Pro Ecclesia* 9 (2000): 331–54.

Yocum, John P. "Sacraments in Aquinas." In Weinandy, Keating, and Yocum, *Aquinas on Doctrine*, 159–81.

Yong, Amos. *Discerning the Spirit(s): A Pentecostal-Charismatic Contribution to Christian Theology of Religions*. Sheffield: Sheffield Academic Press, 2000.

———. *The Spirit Poured Out on All Flesh: Pentecostalism and the Possibility of Global Theology*. Grand Rapids: Baker Academic, 2005.

———. *Spirit-Word-Community: Theological Hermeneutics in Trinitarian Perspective*. Burlington, VT: Ashgate, 2002.

———. *Who Is the Holy Spirit? A Walk with the Apostles*. Brewster, MA: Paraclete, 2011.

Young, Frances. *Biblical Exegesis and the Formation of Christian Culture*. Cambridge: Cambridge University Press, 1997.

———. "The Trinity and the New Testament." In Rowland and Tuckett, *The Nature of New Testament Theology*, 286–305.

Zahl, Simeon. "The Spirit and the Cross: Engaging a Key Critique of Charismatic Pneumatology." In J. Williams, *The Holy Spirit in the World Today*, 111–29.

Zathureczky, Kornel. *The Messianic Disruption of Trinitarian Theology*. Lanham, MD: Lexington, 2009.

Zizioulas, John. "Apostolic Continuity and Orthodox Theology: Towards a Synthesis of Two Perspectives." *St. Vladimir's Theological Quarterly* 19 (1975): 75–108.

———. *Communion and Otherness: Further Studies in Personhood and the Church*. Edited by Paul McPartlan. London: T&T Clark, 2006.

———. "The Father as Cause: Personhood Generating Otherness." In Zizioulas, *Communion and Otherness*, 113–54.

————. "One Single Source: An Orthodox Response to the Clarification on the Filioque." http://agrino.org/cyberdesert/zizioulas.htm.

————. "Pneumatology and the Importance of the Person: A Commentary on the Second Ecumenical Council." In Zizioulas, *Communion and Otherness*, 178–205.

————. "Trinitarian Freedom: Is God Free in Trinitarian Life?" In Maspero and Woźniak, *Rethinking Trinitarian Theology*, 193–207.

Zuijdwegt, Geertjan. "'*Utrum caritas sit aliquid creatum in anima*': Aquinas on the Lombard's Identification of Charity with the Holy Spirit." *Recherches de théologie et philosophie médiévales* 79 (2012): 39–74.

Scripture Index

Name Index

Macaskill, Grant, 183n53, 210n2, 211n3, 237n89,
    241n108, 244n118, 245n123, 261n194,
    271n10, 282n46, 347n141, 358n184
Macchia, Frank D., 10n26, 320n35
Mahoney, John, 214nn10–11, 262n204, 340n126,
    350n155
Malet, André, 11n27, 76n21, 159n123
Mansini, Guy, 109n163, 247n133, 254n163, 367,
    368n25
Margerie, Bertrand de, 109
Margounios, Maximos, 114
Marion, Jean-uc, 35
Marius Victorinus, 109
Mark of Ephesus, 114
Marmion, Declan, 172n9, 286n57
Marshall, Bruce D., 2n4, 4n10, 6, 11n27, 21n50,
    87nn79–80, 91n92, 110n167, 116n7, 121n18,
    138n75, 143n83, 153n109, 160n124, 169,
    170n4, 190n83, 197n108, 213n8, 215n12,
    250n150, 258n179, 290, 313n7, 363n6
Mateo-Seco, Lucas Francisco, 84n61, 100n122,
    122n19, 129n39, 151n103
Maximus the Confessor, 24n57, 119, 122,
    164–66, 168, 170n3
McCormack, Bruce L., 114n3, 190n83
McDonnell, Kilian, 214–15, 328n77, 352n167
McGuckin, John Anthony, 27n69, 130n42
McIntyre, John, 270n9, 321n43
McKnight, Scot, 49n127, 236n80
McPartlan, Paul, 23n53, 122nn19–20, 125
Milbank, John, 6, 20n45, 23n54, 88n82,
    100n123, 109–11, 152n106, 153, 339n121
Min, Anselm Kyongsuk, 154n112, 158n122,
    251n150, 271, 304n131
Moberly, R. W. L., 6n16, 55n14, 68, 69n56
Möhler, Johann Adam, 4n10, 272n15
Moloney, Francis J., 60n28, 95n107, 99n115,
    241
Moltmann, Jürgen, 3, 4n8, 15, 17, 22, 110n167,
    117n8, 152n106, 169n3, 212, 236n82, 286n59
Montague, George T., 181n43, 230n65,
    243n114
Morales, Rodrigo, 44, 229n64
Mosser, Carl, 28
Mühlen, Heribert, 4n10, 10n26, 53n6, 155n115,
    213n9, 271n10

Neusner, Jacob, 49
Newman, John Henry, 147n91, 283n49
Ngien, Dennis, 152n106, 156n118
Nichols, Aidan, 341n129, 355
Nicolas, Jean-Hervé, 355

Oberdorfer, Bernd, 22n50, 81n49, 116n7, 129n42,
    152n106, 164n128
O'Collins, Gerald, 14n33, 15n37
O'Regan, Cyril, 8n20, 11n27
Origen of Alexandria, 58n21, 130, 223, 279

Pannenberg, Wolfhart, 22n50, 52n4, 169n3
Papanikolaou, Aristotle, 21n50, 124n24,
    126n29, 127n35, 135n65, 136n68, 137n73
Paul (apostle), 13, 25–27, 44, 48–49, 52, 53n6,
    59, 60–62, 65–66, 111, 157n120, 179n37,
    180, 182n53, 187n78, 200, 209n1, 215, 219,
    225, 228n62, 229, 231, 248, 259, 281n44,
    282, 300, 312, 322, 329, 332–34, 342n130,
    345, 347–48, 351
Pauw, Amy Plantinga, 70
Pelikan, Jaroslav, 124n25, 140n80, 141n82,
    147n91, 150n101, 152n107
Perrier, Emmanuel, 289
Perrin, Nicholas, 210n2, 238n91
Photius, 18n42, 129, 130n42, 138n77, 152n106
Pinckaers, Servais, 198n109, 236n81
Pitre, Brant, 230n65, 235n77, 237n91, 242n110,
    244n118, 263
Pius XI, Pope, 114, 303n128
Plantinga, Cornelius, 29
Plested, Marcus, 113
Pontifical Council for Promoting Christian
    Unity, 12, 22n53, 41, 117–20, 122, 144n83,
    165–66
Proclus, 27
Pseudo-Dionysius, 27–28, 36, 38–39, 143,
    164n128, 242, 294

Radde-Gallwitz, Andrew, 29
Radner, Ephraim, 4, 267, 268n2, 268n6, 283n49,
    291n78, 313, 316, 324n58, 326n71, 335, 364
Rahner, Karl, 4n10, 17n39, 125n26, 169, 212n6,
    250n149, 251n151, 306n140, 314, 356n177
Ratzinger, Joseph, 4n10, 13n31, 54n8, 57n17,
    60nn27–28, 71, 216n20, 306n140, 349n152,
    355
Richard of St. Victor, 12n28, 76, 90n88
Rikhof, Herwi, 340n127, 345n138, 346n139,
    357n180
Rogers, Eugene F., Jr., 16n38, 363n7
Rowe, C. Kavin, 61n32, 157n120

Sabathé, Martin, 15, 213n9, 250n149
Sabra, George, 144n85, 213n8, 214n10, 236n82,
    274n19, 283, 292n79, 298n111, 341n128
Schindler, David L., 303

Subject Index

Abraham, 45–46, 179, 235, 298, 310n2
Action Française, 303n128
Adam, 46, 81, 179
adoptionist Christology, 195
adoptive sonship, 105n140, 121n18, 194, 203, 247, 253, 293, 318–19, 326
Allison, Dale
  Jesus as eschatological prophet, 212, 220–26, 262–64
Anabaptists, 329
analogy of being, 93, 94n101
analytic philosophy, 33n88
angels, 83, 108, 237, 341n129
apophaticism, 36, 72, 123n23, 126n30, 137n73, 138, 164n129
appropriations, 65n47
Arianism, 91–92, 94, 98–99, 110, 145n86, 148, 262n205, 276
Aristotle
  category of relation, 145n86
  divine *apatheia*, 152n106
  epistemology, 18, 20, 40, 50
Augustine
  pneumatology of, 2, 4, 14n34, 51–72, 75, 85, 115n5, 121n18, 123n23, 125, 131, 192n90, 215n12
  psychological analogy, 8n20, 85, 95–96, 98–100, 103, 108, 124, 142–43, 155–56, 161, 163, 323

Babel, 46, 301
Balthasar, Hans Urs von
  account of the Spirit's freedom, 72
  the Father's *ur-kenosis*, 7n19, 8
  "trinitarian inversion," 103n131, 182

baptism
  of blood, 257–58
  Christian baptism, 61, 76n20, 192n90, 231, 242, 245, 256–60, 264–65, 281–82, 295, 307n143, 311, 328, 332, 337, 342n130, 343, 345–49, 351–53, 354n173, 355n176
  formula of, 76n20, 257, 323
  infant, 257
  Jesus's, 10, 68n54, 174, 177–78, 181, 184–85, 188, 191, 195, 201–2, 204, 209
  John's, 178
beatific vision, 201n121
bestowal model, 42n115
body of Christ. *See* church
burning bush, 203n130

Cappadocian fathers, 74n14, 75n15, 76, 118, 127, 128n35, 130–31, 132n53, 138, 145n86, 146n87, 148n93, 170n3
caritas. *See* charity
causality
  Newtonian conception, 128
charismatic movement
  Catholic, 10n26
charity, 9n24, 24n57, 38–39, 49n126, 53n7, 55, 57n18, 59, 63, 99, 172, 192, 199, 201n121, 206–7, 210, 233, 236–37, 239, 245–51, 254–55, 261–62, 265, 269n6, 271n12, 274, 280, 292, 294–300, 303–5, 328, 335–36, 338–39, 343, 356n177
Christian Platonism, 23–24, 36
christology, 13n30, 18n41
church, 10, 14, 25–26, 35, 49, 52n3, 53n6, 146, 147n89, 149, 162n125, 164, 167, 171n7,

432

Dominum et vivificantem (John Paul II), 5, 102,
    289n70
Dominus Iesus (CDF), 15n37
Donatism, 55n10, 329
Dunn, James D. G.
    Jesus as eschatological prophet, 212, 218–20,
        264, 369

ecclesiology, 10n25, 213n8–9, 336n108, 363n6
    christological grounding of, 10n25
    pneumatological grounding of, 10n25
ecology. *See* environmentalism
economy of salvation, 9, 10n25, 25, 38, 43, 49,
    66, 69, 74n14, 78n28, 79, 81, 83–84, 87n80,
    88, 104, 108, 111, 113, 114n4, 119n13,
    137–39, 157, 163, 169, 170n3, 173n13, 202,
    213n8, 262n201, 323, 359, 369
ecstatic experience of the Spirit, 26
ecumenical councils
    seven recognized by the East, 146–47
ecumenism, 270n9, 272n15, 306, 342n130
Elijah, 66, 140, 179–81, 325n59
Elisha, 140
empty tomb, 222
energies. *See* uncreated divine energies
Enoch, 179, 181
environmentalism, 300n119, 361
eros, 27, 38–40
eschatology, 45n120, 175–81, 211–12, 216–27,
    232, 235, 238n91, 263–64
    immanent end to the world, 211–12, 216–17,
        218n23, 218n25, 220–27, 238n91, 263
    realized, 223n41
essence/energies distinction, 113n1, 137n72,
    138n75, 138n77, 139
essential love verus proper love, 91, 99
Eucharist, 125n26, 212, 230n65, 237n91, 242,
    244, 256, 259n180, 260–61, 263–65, 269n6,
    295, 307, 325, 328, 334, 338–39, 344n133,
    349n154, 352–53, 354n173, 358, 360, 361n4,
    367n21, 368
Eunomianism, 81n49
Eunomius, 152n107
Eve, 46, 81
    as coming forth from Adam, 81
excommunication, 327n72
exegesis
    spiritual, 79n39
    typology, 174
exodus, 217n23, 226n55, 237n91
exorcisms, 172, 174–77, 179, 185n67, 186–87,
    198, 206, 216, 231

expiation, 56–57, 197, 245
Ezekiel (prophet), 45n120, 49n127
Ezra, 179

faith, 9n24, 59, 198, 201n121, 229, 231, 235–36,
    239n101, 243, 245–46, 249–50, 252–54, 257,
    261n194, 265, 271n13, 274n19, 295, 298,
    310n2, 311–12, 319, 324, 328, 331–32, 337,
    339, 342–43, 355, 365
    implicit, 271n13, 298, 310n2
Father, God the, 2, 3n8, 4–9, 15, 17–21, 22n50,
    23, 25–26, 28–32, 34–37, 40–44, 49–52,
    53n6, 55n11, 57, 58n22, 62–66, 68–69,
    72–75, 76n19, 77–80, 82–90, 92, 95, 97–104,
    106–11, 113n1, 114n4, 115n5, 116–17,
    119–26, 128–29, 130n42, 130n46, 131,
    132n53, 133–35, 136n68, 137–46, 149n99,
    150–51, 152n106, 153–56, 157n120, 158–68,
    170n3–4, 172n8, 178, 182, 184, 187n78,
    188–90, 191n85, 194n97, 195–96, 199–200,
    201n121, 202–3, 206–7, 211–12, 214,
    215n12, 217n20, 222, 238–41, 246, 250n149,
    251, 252n152, 255, 262, 265, 270n7, 273n18,
    274–77, 280–81, 284–91, 292n80, 293, 296,
    299, 301n122, 302n127, 307, 317n14, 323,
    325n58, 333, 346, 348, 358n184, 359–60,
    362n6, 366, 370–71
    as Abba, 172n9
    as Gift, 6–8
    image of Paternal sacrificial love, 134
    as Love, 6–9, 57
    monarchy of, 18n42, 20–21, 37n95, 115n5,
        119, 122n19, 126–27, 128n35, 130n42, 131,
        132n53, 136, 137n69, 139, 151, 155, 158–59,
        164–66, 168
    as primary principle of the Son, 17, 19n43,
        55n11
    as *principium*/principle, 9n22, 125, 129, 165
    as source/font of the Trinity, 18n42, 20, 22,
        28, 76n19, 78n28, 115n5, 116n6, 119n12,
        120, 121n17, 123, 125, 136n68, 151,
        153n109, 155n116, 158, 164, 189
    as Spirator, 125, 129, 142, 161
    as unbegotten, 55n11, 64, 78–80, 134, 290n72
    as uncaused (*anaitiatos*), 129
    as unemanated, 153n109
    as unoriginate, 22n50, 43, 56, 87n80
feminist perspective on the Spirit, 23, 36
filioque, 5, 10, 12, 18n42, 28, 72, 73n9, 85,
    87n80, 100, 113–24, 126, 127n33, 129,
    131, 133–35, 136n69, 137, 138n77, 139,
    141n82, 142–43, 144n83, 144n85, 146n88,